### 단어암기MP3 다운로드 방법

**방법**  해커스인강(HackersIngang.com) 접속 ▶
상단 메뉴 [토플 → MP3/자료 → 무료 MP3/자료] 클릭하여 다운받기

\* QR코드로 [MP3/자료] 이용하러 가기

# HACKERS SUPER VOCABULARY

www.goHackers.com

# PREFACE

**Higher education**을 위한 학문적인 이유나, 영어 서적과 저널 등을 통한 폭넓은 지식의 성취를 위하여 고급 어휘의 습득이 필요합니다. 또한 GRE, GMAT, SAT, TOEFL, 편입, 고시 혹은 취업을 준비하는 목적으로도 고급 어휘의 습득이 요구됩니다. 개개인의 꿈과 도전을 위해 선행되어야 하는 어휘 학습을 보다 효율적으로 하기 위해서는 엄선된 단어들을 정확한 의미로 쉽게 기억하는 것이 무엇보다 중요합니다.

이러한 의도로 기획된 Hackers Super Vocabulary는 다음과 같은 특성을 담고 있습니다. 먼저 통계를 통해 각종 시험에 가장 많이 등장하는 어휘들을 엄선하였으며, 어휘의 정확한 의미 전달을 위해 표제어에 대한 영문정의를 제공하였습니다. 또한 관련 단어를 표제어와 비교하는 구성을 통하여 어휘간의 미세한 의미 차이를 파악하도록 하였고, 이렇게 배열된 어휘들의 암기를 돕기 위하여 Game이라는 연상기법을 도입하였습니다. 즉, 표제어와 관련된 연상단어와의 관계를 이야기 형식으로 구성하여 단어들이 쉽게, 오랫동안 기억되도록 한 것입니다. 더불어 본문에 수록된 3,200여개의 단어들을 어근으로 재분류하여 입체적으로 복습할 수 있도록 SuperVoca Words Roots를 추가하였습니다.

고전으로서의 Hackers Super Vocabulary가 태어나기까지 기나긴 여정동안 해커스 가족들을 비롯한 여러분들의 큰 수고가 있었습니다. 표지 디자인을 예쁘게 해준 이혜정님과 디자인 진행을 맡아 새로운 시각에서 의견을 제공해준 진홍&내원부부, 그리고 연구소의 신연, 은지, 은혜(김)의 책에 대한 관심어린 조언이 도움이 되었습니다. 또한 책의 전반에 걸친 Heather, Larry, 기환의 손길과 함께 지연(11기), 정은(16기), 재형(16기), 미승, 윤아, John, 최 현, 신상갑 선생님, 유경희 선생님이 요소요소에 도움을 주었습니다. 이 책의 초석이 되는 통계 작업을 해 준 Brian(16기)에게도 깊은 감사를 드립니다. 마지막으로 늦은 밤과 주말의 휴식도 없이 책에 생명을 불어 넣어준 경원(9기), 민정, 은혜(엄), 연구팀장의 공헌에 대한 감사의 글을 남기고자 합니다.

해커스 가족들의 또 하나의 아름다운 결정체인 이 책이 인생의 올바른 길을 찾아가는 여러분들에게 작은 빛이 되기를 기원합니다.

*David Cho*

# CONTENTS

- 구성 6
- 특징 8
- 학습 방법 10
- 게임 관계 설명 12

**1**st DAY ..................... 14
**2**nd DAY ..................... 28
**3**rd DAY ..................... 44
   ● Take a Break | 격언/속담

**4**th DAY ..................... 60
**5**th DAY ..................... 74
**6**th DAY ..................... 90
   ● Take a Break | 세계 명소

**7**th DAY ..................... 108
**8**th DAY ..................... 122
**9**th DAY ..................... 138
   ● Take a Break | 미국 역사

**10**th DAY ..................... 154
**11**th DAY ..................... 170
**12**th DAY ..................... 184
   ● Take a Break | 민들레 by 하니

# SUPER VOCABULARY

**13**th DAY ............ 202
**14**th DAY ............ 216
**15**th DAY ............ 232
- Take a Break | 미국 역사

**16**th DAY ............ 248
**17**th DAY ............ 262
**18**th DAY ............ 276
- Take a Break | 영시감상

**19**th DAY ............ 292
**20**th DAY ............ 306
**21**st DAY ............ 322
- Take a Break | 재미로 보는 심리학

**22**nd DAY ............ 338
**23**rd DAY ............ 352
**24**th DAY ............ 368
- Take a Break | 명심보감

**25**th DAY ............ 384
**26**th DAY ............ 400
**27**th DAY ............ 414
- Take a Break | 영시감상

**28**th DAY ............ 430
**29**th DAY ............ 444
**30**th DAY ............ 458
- Take a Break | Self-Interview by 아슈

- Crossword Puzzle 168 / 320 / 472
- SuperVoca Words Pack 477
- SuperVoca Words Roots 507
- SuperVoca Index 543

## ORGANIZATION 구성

01 표제어

02 영문 정의

03 한글 정의

04 예문

05 예문해석

06 Game

07 Daily Check-up

08 Crossword Puzzle

09 SuperVoca Words Pack

10 SuperVoca Words Roots

11 학습방법

12 Index

13 쉬어가는 페이지

왼쪽에 가장 큰 글씨로 쓰여진 단어이며 총 1,800개에 이른다. 여러분이 30일 동안 함께 해야 할 기본 단어군이다.

표제어의 영문 Definition으로 우측 상단에 자리하고 있다. 오히려 국문보다 정확하게 단어의 의미를 설명해 줄 것이다.

영문 정의의 끝·부분에 위치하고 있다. 모국어의 빠른 의미 전달력을 이용하고, 단어를 단시간 내에 볼 경우를 위해 한글 정의를 실었다.

Definition의 아래에 해당 단어를 포함하는 문장이 있다. 단어의 뉘앙스와 정확한 용법을 파악하기에는 이 예문을 숙지하는 것이 최상이다. 예문 해석을 미리 보지 않고 스스로 예문을 해석해 보는 것도 학습에 도움이 될 것이다.

각 페이지의 하단에는 예문들의 한글 해석이 적혀 있다. 위에 나온 문장들을 해석하는 데 참고하면 도움이 될 것이다.

표제어마다 분류 표제어 : 비교어 의 형식으로 제시되는 Game이 존재한다. 이 Game들은 단어 사이의 관계(Relationship)를 이 책에서 정해 놓은 13개의 범주로 분류하여 그 단어가 갖는 정확한 뉘앙스를 익히는데 도움을 주도록 구성한 것이다.

이 책의 1일이 끝날 때마다 항상 그 끝에서 만날 수 있는 항목이다. 1일 동안 학습한 60개의 단어를 복습하고, 스스로 암기 상태를 진단할 수 있도록 구성했다. 절대, 피해 가지 말라! 복습을 게을리하는 자, 결코 단어의 왕도에 오를 수 없다!

10일치가 끝날 때마다 가볍게 퍼즐을 즐길 수 있는 부분이다. 여러분의 단어학습을 더욱 재미있게 해 줄 것이다.

1800개의 표제어에는 포함되지 않았으나, 그 중요도에 있어서 결코 표제어에 뒤지지 않는 500개의 추가 단어군이다. 본문을 숙지한 후 시간여유가 있다면, 반드시 한번쯤 학습할 수 있도록 한다.

본문에 수록된 단어들 3,200여개를 200여개의 어근으로 재분류하여 입체적으로 복습할 수 있도록 하였다. 이미 본 친숙한 단어들을 의미(어근)로 분류하여 반복함으로써 확실한 단어암기가 마무리 될 것이다.

GRE, GMAT, SAT, TOEFL 등 각종 시험을 준비하는 학습자 및 일반 학습자의 각 상황에 맞는 SuperVoca 학습법을 제시한 것이다. Hackers만의 Know-how를 십분 활용할 수 있는 기회가 될 것이다.

SuperVoca는 현재 사용되는 고급 영어 단어군을 엄격한 기준에 의해 선별한 것이다. 일상생활 중에 사전으로도 활용하고, 단어 학습 중에 빠른 단어 검색을 위한 것으로써 책 후반부에 실려 있다.

수고를 아끼지 않는 학습자들을 위해 쉬어가는 페이지가 매 3일마다 자리하고 있다. 잠시의 여유를 학습자에게 부여하기 위한 Hackers의 좋은 글모음이다.

## CHARACTER | 특징

### 01 GRE/GMAT/SAT/고급토플/편입/고시 빈출 단어 수록
이 책은 현재 시행되는 각종 영어 시험에 공통적으로 빈출되는 단어군을 중심으로 하여 필수적인 어휘를 체계적으로 습득하도록 구성한 것이다. 특히 SuperVoca의 엄격한 단어 선별 기준은 타 시험에 비해 고난이도의 어휘를 요구하는 GRE, GMAT, SAT 수험생들에게 큰 도움을 줄 수 있을 것이다.

### 02 상황별 입체학습법 제시
시험을 앞둔 학습자와 장기적인 목표 아래에 있는 학습자의 학습법이 같을 수 없다. SuperVoca에서는 축적된 Hackers의 Know-how를 통해 각 상황에 맞는 학습법을 구체적으로 제시하여, 처음 이 책을 접하는 학습자도 보다 쉽게 시작할 수 있다.

### 03 효율적인 확인 학습의 장 "Daily Check-up"
1일 학습 후 스스로 점검해 볼 수 있는 효율적인 문제 체계를 마련하여 표제어뿐만 아니라 Game의 표제어 관련 단어까지 단시간에 재확인 할 수 있도록 하였다.

### 04 표제어의 영문/한글정의 동시 표기
영단어를 파악하는 최상의 도구는 한글이 아니라 바로 영단어 그 자체이다. 단어의 의미나 단어 사이에 존재하는 뉘앙스(nuance)에 정확하게 접근할 수 있도록 쉽고 정확한 영문 정의를 수록했다. 또한, 영문 정의와 함께 모국어인 한글 정의를 이용하여 학습자가 단어의 의미를 쉽고 빨리 파악할 수 있도록 구성했다.

### 05 일상 생활에 활용 가능한 예문과 정확한 해석
단어를 설명하기 위해 어렵고 복잡한 예문을 많이 실었던 기존의 책과 달리 쉬우면서도 실생활에서 바로 사용할 수 있는 예문을 사용했다. 뿐만 아니라 각 페이지의 하단에 정확한 예문 해석을 실어 습득한 단어를 예문에 적용하는 과정에서 시간을 절약할 수 있도록 하였다.

# CHARACTER

## 06 학습정보공유와 연습문제 제공 – goHackers.com

Hackers의 다른 책들과 마찬가지로 SuperVoca 역시 Hackers 홈페이지에 마련된 게시판을 통해 이 책의 학습자들이 자유롭게 의견을 교환하고 문제 해결을 도모할 수 있도록 했으며, Hackers에서 자체 제공하는 연습 문제를 통해 책 안팎에서의 동시 학습이 이루어지도록 했다.

## 07 표제어간 유기적인 관계를 이용한 단어 연상 암기법 제시

이 책의 주요 구성 요소 중의 하나인 Game은 모든 표제어마다 그와 관련된 비교어를 미리 정의된 13개 단어관계와 함께 제시한 것이다. 이것은 표제어를 암기하는 동안 주어진 비교어와의 관계를 살펴보게 함으로써 단순암기에 의존하지 않고, 연상 작용에 의해 연쇄적으로 기억해 낼 수 있도록 구성한 것이다. 학습자들은 이 간단한 Game을 수행하는 동안 기대 이상의 표제어와 관련 단어 그리고 그 단어들간 뉘앙스를 익히게 될 것이다.

## 08 고급 영어를 위한 고급 어휘 수록

Supervoca에 수록된 1,800개의 주옥 같은 단어들은 시험에만 출제되는 이른바 '시험 전용 단어'가 아니라, 현재의 실용적 고급 영어를 위한 필수 고급 어휘들이다. 비단, 시험을 준비하기 위해서가 아니라 하더라도, 이 책의 어휘들을 익힘으로써 이미 사회적으로 요구되고 있는 원서강독, 영자신문, 각종 에세이에 걸쳐 영어 어휘력의 전반적인 수준 향상을 꾀할 수 있도록 하였다.

## 09 본문 단어들을 의미별 어근(Words Roots)으로 재 분류한 반복 학습 제시

본문의 표제어와 Game에 등장한 3,200여개의 단어들을 의미별 어근으로 재 분류하여, 이미 학습하여 친숙해진 단어들을 의미별로 반복하여 학습하도록 하였다. 단어암기법을 다각적으로 제시하여 자칫하면 지루해지거나 쉽게 잊어버리게 되는 것을 최소화 할 수 있는 장치이다.

## 10 단어암기MP3 다운로드 제공 – HackersIngang.com

HACKERS SUPER VOCABULARY 단어암기MP3는 교재에 있는 단어와 영문 정의를 정확한 Native Speakers의 발음으로 수록하고 있어 효율적인 단어 학습을 가능하게 한다. 함께 수록된 예문 청취를 통해 단어의 정확한 의미 파악과 Listening 학습 효과까지 얻을 수 있다.

## 개인학습 vs. 스터디학습

### 개별 학습방법

단어시험, 본문(표제어, 영문정의, 예문, 게임)정독, 스스로 예문 해석한 후 맞추어보기, 정독 중에 특히 안 외워지는 단어 암기, Daily Check-up, 마무리 소리내어 읽기로 하루 공부를 진행하는 것이 좋다.

### 스터디 학습방법

#### 스터디 모집

대학생의 경우 과나 동아리 위주의 팀을 결성하고, 직장인의 경우 같은 직장 내에서 스터디를 결성하는 것이 한자리에 모여 학습하는 스터디를 용이하게 한다. 적절한 인원수는 대개 4~6명이며, 해커스 스터디 모집 게시판(www.goHackers.com)을 통하는 것도 좋은 모집방법이다.

#### 학습팁

정해진 시간 동안 일정량의 단어를 학습하도록 하며, 예습은 각자 따로 하도록 하고, 모이는 시간에는 팀원이 각자 범위 내에서 출제해온 문제로 학습 정도를 진단하고 철저하게 복습할 수 있도록 해야한다.

#### 매일매일 함께 시험보기

스터디 단어학습의 최장점은 '함께 외우기가 아닌 함께 시험보기'에 있다. 즉, 시험을 통하여 단어학습을 서로 확인해 주는 것이다. 하루마다 있는 Daily Check-up을 함께 모여 시험으로 보거나, 팀원들이 교대로 문제를 내와도 좋고, 해커스 자료실에서 퀴즈 자료들을 다운받는 방법을 이용한다. 벌금 등의 기타 Penalty를 도입하는 것은 단어스터디 학습에 빠질 수 없는 좋은 방법이 된다.

#### 책임감과 결석벌금

모임 시간은 되도록 고정시켜 만나는 데 쓸데없는 시간이 낭비되는 일이 없도록 해야 한다. 이때, 팀원들 간의 책임감은 절대적인 것이며, 어느 한 사람이 학습에 태만하여 전체의 시간을 낭비하는 일이 없도록 특히 주의해야 한다. 결석하는 사람에게는 탈퇴하지는 않을 정도의 조금 과한 벌금을 부과하는 방법이 좋다.

# 상황별 학습법

## 01 영자신문, 원서를 읽거나 어휘를 향상시키고자 하는 학습자의 '어휘향상 두달 완성 학습방법'

하루 1일분씩 30일 완성 → (반복) → 하루 2일분씩 15일 완성 → (반복) → 하루 3일분씩 10일 완성

- 예문을 스스로 해석하면서 실제 문장 내에서의 정확한 용법을 익힌다.
- 예문에의 적용과 그 뉘앙스의 파악에 주력한다.
- 개별학습을 통한 실력배양과 영어를 좋아하는 분들은 단어학습을 취미로 활용해도 좋다.

## 02 편입이나 고시 등의 각종 시험 대비 학습자의 '파도타기 한달 완성 학습방법'

하루 3일분씩 10일 완성 (1일에서 시작) → (반복) → 하루 3일분씩 10일 완성 (30일에서 시작) → (반복) → 하루 3일분씩 10일 완성 (1일에서 시작)

- 가장 중요한 표제어를 완전히 암기하는데, 이때는 반드시 영문 정의 위주로 단어의 정확한 뉘앙스(nuance)를 파악하는 데 주력한다.
- 예문을 통해 실제 문장 내에서의 정확한 용법을 익힌다.
- Game(단어 두개의 관계가 있는 것)단어는 거의 대부분이 다시 표제어로 등장하므로, 완벽암기보다는 눈으로 확인을 하는 정도로 익히고 10일이 끝나면 Words Roots를 통해 반복 학습을 한다.
- 스터디를 통한 학습이 하루하루의 많은 분량 소화에 자극이 될 것이다.

## 03 GRE, GMAT, SAT, Verbal Section을 위한 학습자의 '버벌잡기 한달 완성 학습방법'

하루 3일분씩 10일 완성 + 워즈팩 3일 → (반복) → 하루 4일분씩 8일 완성 + 워즈팩 2일 → (반복) → 하루 5일분씩 6일 완성 + 워즈팩 1일

- 고난이도 어휘를 요구하는 GRE, GMAT, SAT 시험 대비를 위해서는 워즈팩의 어휘들까지 외우는 것이 좋다.
- Daily Check-up을 통해 시험에 충분히 대비할 수 있도록 하고, 잊기 쉬운 단어들을 Words Roots를 이용해 다시 기억해 낸다.
- 스터디 학습을 적극 권장한다.

## Game Relationship Table | 게임 관계설명

Hackers Super Vocabulary에서 Game이라고 명한 이 부분은 표제어와 병렬로 놓인 단어 사이의 관계를 정해진 13가지 pattern을 사용하여 독자로 하여금 단어의 뉘앙스를 익히고 Word Power를 키우도록 도와준다.

**adulterate** [ədʌ́ltərèit]
v. to make impure by adding or mixing with foreign or inferior substances | 순도를 떨어뜨리다, 불순하게 하다
Though the jeweler claimed it was pure, the gold had been ***adulterated***.

대상 — adulterate : purity [pjúərəti]
adulterate는 purity(순도)를 떨어뜨리다라는 의미이다.

[본문중]

**SYN** 동의어 관계 (Synonym) 의미도 유사하고 품사도 같은 두 단어 관계.

    **SYN** vaunt : boast
        vaunt: 자랑하다, 뽐내다    boast: 자랑하다, 뽐내다

**POS** 긍정적 관계 (Positive) 의미는 유사하나 품사가 다른 두 단어 관계.

    **POS** lamentable : pity
        lamentable: 유감스러운    pity: 유감

**ANT** 반의어 관계 (Antonym) 의미가 서로 반대이고 품사는 같은 두 단어 관계.

    **ANT** spurious : genuine
        spurious: 가짜의    genuine: 진짜의

**WO** 결여 · 부족관계 (Without) "~(한 것)에는 ~가 없다/부족하다"로 해석.

    **WO** poseur : sincerity
        poseur(허식가)에게는 sincerity(진실, 성실)가 없다.

**CN** 불가능 · 부정관계 (Cannot) "~(한 것)은 ~할 수 없다/하지 않는다"로 해석.

    **CN** infinite : exhaust
        infinite(무한한)것은 exhaust(다 써버리다, 고갈시키다)할 수 없다.

**DE** 정도관계 (Degree) 유사한 의미지만 정도의 강약, 대소, 과잉, 강제 등의 의미 차이가 있는 단어관계.

> **DE** catastrophe : mishap
> catastrophe(대참사)는 mishap(재난)보다 더 큰 불상사를 말한다.

**KIN** 종류 관계 (Kind) 일반적인 범주를 나타내는 단어와 그 범주에 속하는 다른 단어와의 관계.

> **KIN** ode : poem
> ode(송시)는 poem(시)의 일종이다.

**PAR** 부분 관계 (Part) 부분과 전체의 관계, 한 집단과 그것의 구성원, 어떤 것과 그것의 조각·껍질이나 주변, 사람·동물과 그것의 신체 일부 등을 나타내는 관계.

> **PAR** coven : witch
> witch(마녀)들은 coven(마녀단)의 구성원이다.

**CH** 특성 관계 (Character) 특정 사람·사물과 그것이 갖는 특성으로 이루어지는 관계. 동작·상태와 그것의 속성도 포함.

> **CH** miser : stingy
> miser(구두쇠)는 stingy(인색한)하다.

**PUR** 목적·수단 관계 (Purpose) 한 단어가 다른 단어의 목적이나 수단을 기술하는 관계. "~하기 위해서 ~하다" "~하기 위해서 ~을 사용한다"로 해석.

> **PUR** syllogism : disprove
> syllogism(삼단 논법)은 상대방의 의견을 논리적으로 disprove(논박하다)하는 수단으로 사용된다.

**FUN** 기능관계 (Function) 물질·도구·장소와 그것의 기능으로 이루어진 관계. 제거하는 기능도 포함.

> **FUN** awl : pierce
> awl(송곳)은 pierce(구멍을 뚫다)하기 위한 도구이다.

**인과** 인과관계 원인과 그것으로 인해 생긴 결과로 이루어진 관계. "~하면 ~이다/하게 된다" "~의 결과 ~가 발생한다"로 해석.

> **인과** downpour : flooding
> downpour(폭풍우)가 쏟아지면 flooding(홍수)이 발생한다.

**대상** 대상관계 행위, 서술과 그것의 대상 또는 주체와 그것이 추구하는 대상으로 이루어진 관계. "~(한 것)을 ~하다" "~는 ~을 한다"로 해석.

> **대상** disseminate : information
> information(정보, 지식)을 disseminate(널리 알리다)하다.

# SUPER VOCA
## FIRST DAY

자! 심호흡을 가다듬고
30일간의 상쾌한 보카여행을 떠나볼까요.

**abscond**
[æbskánd]

v. **to leave secretly and hide oneself** | 도망하다, 자취를 감추다

Though the CEO *absconded* to another country, he was extradited and forced to stand trial for the company's disastrous bankruptcy.

**KIN** abscond : depart [dipá:rt]

몰래 depart(떠나다)하는 것이 abscond이다.

**adulate**
[ǽdʒulèit]

v. **to flatter in a servile way** | 비굴하게 아첨하다

In order to get a raise, the employee *adulated* the boss.

**DE** adulate : flatter [flǽtər]

adulate는 flatter(아첨하다)보다 그 아첨의 정도가 훨씬 더 심하다.

**adulterate**
[ədʌ́ltərèit]

v. **to make impure by adding or mixing with foreign or inferior substances** | 순도를 떨어뜨리다, 불순하게 하다

Though the jeweler claimed it was pure, the gold had been *adulterated*.

**대상** adulterate : purity [pjúərəti]

adulterate는 purity(순도)를 떨어뜨리다 라는 의미이다.

**altruist**
[ǽltru:ist]

n. **one who is unselfishly devoted to improving the welfare of others** | 다른 이들의 복지 개선을 위해 헌신하는 사람, 이타주의자

Perry was a great *altruist* that touched the lives of people from all over the world.

**ANT** altruist : vulture [vʌ́ltʃər]

vulture: 다른 사람을 이용하여 탐욕을 채우는 사람

---

**TRANSLATION | 예문해석**

| | |
|---|---|
| **abscond** | 그 최고 경영자는 다른 나라로 도망갔지만 본국으로 송환되어 그 회사의 불행한 파산과 관련하여 재판을 받도록 요구되었다. |
| **adulate** | 임금인상을 얻어내기 위해, 그 직원은 상사에게 아첨을 했다. |
| **adulterate** | 보석상은 그 금이 순금이라고 주장했지만, 그것은 순도가 떨어져 있었다. |
| **altruist** | Perry는 전 세계 사람들의 삶에 영향을 준 위대한 이타주의자였다. |

## anachronism
[ənǽkrənìzm]

**n.** a chronological error | 연대기적인 오류, 시대 착오

It is an *anachronism* to attempt a life without technology in the modern world.

**WO** anachronism : chronology [krənάlədʒi]

chronology(연대)적 이해가 부족할 때 anachronism이 초래된다.

## awry
[ərái]

**adj.** turned or twisted out of place; not in proper position | 구부러지거나 비틀려 있는, 제자리에 있지 않은

Anne rushed into the meeting late with her hair unbrushed and her clothes *awry*.

**ANT** awry : orderly [ɔ́ːrdərli]

orderly: 정돈된

## blunt
[blʌnt]

**v.** to make dull | 무디게 하다

**adj.** not sharp; direct or frank in speech or manner | 무딘, (말이나 태도가) 직설적인

Amy *blunted* the corners of the coffee table in order to ensure her toddler's safety.

I would rather have people be *blunt* with me than waste time beating around the bush.

**ANT** blunt : whet [hwet]

whet: 갈아서 날카롭게 하다

## browbeat
[bráubìːt]

**v.** to intimidate or discourage by being overbearing or domineering | 횡포하고 거만하게 굴면서 위협하다, 겁주다

Lawyers are not allowed to *browbeat* witnesses that are on the stand.

**CH** browbeat : bully [búli]

bully(깡패)는 자기보다 약한 사람을 browbeat한다.

---

### TRANSLATION | 예 문 해 석

**anachronisim** 현대사회에서 기술 없이 살려는 것은 시대착오이다.
**awry** Anne은 머리와 옷이 엉망인 채로 그 모임에 늦게 뛰어들어왔다.
**blunt** Amy는 자신의 어린 아기의 안전을 위해 티 테이블의 모서리를 뭉툭하게 만들었다.
나는 사람들이 빙빙 둘러 말하며 시간을 낭비하느니 차라리 나에게 직설적인 편이 낫다.
**browbeat** 변호사는 증언대에 선 증인들을 위협할 수 없도록 되어 있다.

## canopy
[kǽnəpi]

**n. a covering usually made of cloth held on poles** | 기둥에 천을 두른 덮개(천개), 건축 차양

A *canopy* was added to the restaurant so that patrons could dine outdoors.

**FUN** canopy : cover [kʌ́vər]

canopy는 cover(덮다)의 기능을 가진다.

## clumsy
[klʌ́mzi]

**adj. awkward or lacking grace** | 어색한, 서투른

My sister is said to have *clumsy* feet because she is always tripping.

**WO** clumsy : knack [næk]

clumsy한 사람에게는 knack(기교, 요령)이 없다.

## crucial
[krúːʃəl]

**adj. critical or extremely important** | 결정적인, 중대한

It is *crucial* that you get the package to the post office on time.

**ANT** crucial : inconsequential [ìnkɑnsikwénʃəl]

inconsequential: 하찮은, 중요하지 않은

## crumble
[krʌ́mbl]

**v. to fall to pieces or collapse** | 부서지다, 무너지다

The tall building *crumbled* from the earthquake.

**CH** crumble : friable [fráiəbl]

friable(버슬버슬한)한 것은 crumble하기 쉽다.

## curt
[kəːrt]

**adj. rudely short in speech or manner** | (언행이) 무뚝뚝한, 퉁명스러운

The man at the counter was very *curt* when replying to my request.

**ANT** curt : wordy [wə́ːrdi]

wordy: 장황한, 말많은

---

### TRANSLATION | 예 문 해 석

**canopy** 고객들이 옥외에서 식사할 수 있도록 하기 위해 그 식당에 차양을 쳤다.
**clumsy** 내 여동생은 항상 넘어져서 서투른 발을 가지고 있다고 사람들이 말한다.
**crucial** 당신이 소포를 제시간에 우체국에 가져가는 것이 중요하다.
**crumble** 그 높은 건물이 지진으로 무너졌다.
**curt** 카운터의 남자가 내 요청에 퉁명스럽게 답했다.

## curtail
[kərtéil]

v. **to shorten or make less by cutting off some part** | 줄이다, 생략하다, 삭감하다

The executives *curtailed* negotiations after making no headway with the labor union.

> **ANT** curtail : protract [proutrǽkt]
> protract : 연장하다, 길게 하다

## daunt
[dɔːnt]

v. **to intimidate or lessen the courage of** | 겁주다, 기를 죽이다

Being attacked in Russia was a *daunting* experience.

> **WO** dauntless : trepidation [trèpidéiʃən]
> dauntless(겁 없는)한 사람은 trepidation(공포, 불안)을 별로 느끼지 않는다.

## diocesan
[daiɑ́səsən]

adj. **related to the area or churches under a bishop's jurisdiction** | 주교의 관할권 내의 지역이나 교회에 관련된, 교구의

The *diocesan* council overlooked the matter while the bishop was absent.

> **ANT** diocesan : ecumenical [èkjuménikəl]
> ecumenical: 전 크리스트 교회의, 보편적인

## disaffected
[dìsəféktid]

adj. **discontented and resentful, especially against authority** | (정부 등에) 불만을 품은, 분개한

Many of the Vietnam War Veterans have become *disaffected* to their country.

> **WO** disaffected : contentment [kənténtmənt]
> disaffected한 사람은 contentment(만족)를 느끼지 못한다.

## disavow
[dìsəváu]

v. **to disclaim knowledge of, responsibility for, or association with** | (알고 있음·책임·관계 등을) 부인하다, 부정하다

Jeff *disavowed* any knowledge of the robbery.

> **SYN** disavow : deny [dinái]
> deny: 부인하다, 부정하다

---

**TRANSLATION | 예문 해석**

| | |
|---|---|
| curtail | 노조와의 협상이 어떤 진도도 보이지 않자 그 중역들은 협상 일정을 축소했다. |
| daunt | 러시아에서 공격을 받은 것은 위협적인 경험이었다. |
| diocesan | 그 교구의 의회는 주교가 없는 동안에 그 문제를 대충 보고 넘겼다. |
| disaffected | 베트남 전쟁의 참전병들 상당수가 조국에 반감을 품게 되었다. |
| disavow | Jeff는 그 강도사건에 대해 아는 바가 없다며 부인했다. |

### discern
[disə́:rn]

**v. to see or understand as different; to recognize as distinct or separate** | 분별하다, 차이점을 알다

It is hard, at times, to *discern* between right and wrong.

**ANT** discerning : myopic [maiápik]

discerning: 통찰력 있는, 분별있는
myopic: 통찰력이 없는, 근시안적인

### discomfit
[diskʌ́mfit]

**v. to disconcert; to upset or make uneasy** | 쩔쩔매게 하다

The president was *discomfited* by the terrorist threats.

**ANT** discomfit : pacify [pǽsəfài]

pacify: 진정시키다, 달래다

### discommode
[dìskəmóud]

**v. to trouble or cause inconvenience** | 폐를 끼치다, 불편하게 하다

The driver was *discommoded* by the flat tire.

**ANT** discommode : assist [əsíst]

assist: 도와주다

### discompose
[dìskəmpóuz]

**v. to disturb the self-composure of** | 마음의 평정을 잃게 하다

The laughs of the other schoolchildren on the playground *discomposed* the young girl.

**CN** discompose : pacific [pəsífik]

pacific(온순한, 평화로운)한 사람은 쉽게 discompose되지 않는다.

### discontent
[dìskəntént]

**adj. unhappy or dissatisfied** | 불만이 있는
**n. dissatisfaction** | 불만

It was a point in my life when I was *discontent* and needed a change.
The people had *discontent* against the newly launched policy.

**SYN** discontent : gripe [graip]

gripe: 불만, 움켜 잡다

---

**TRANSLATION | 예 문 해 석**

| | |
|---|---|
| discern | 옳은 것과 그른 것을 분별하기는 때때로 어렵다. |
| discomfit | 대통령은 테러리스트들의 위협에 쩔쩔매게 되었다. |
| discommode | 그 운전자는 타이어가 펑크나서 불편하게 되었다. |
| discompose | 운동장에 있는 다른 학생들의 웃음소리가 어린 소녀를 괴롭게 했다. |
| discontent | 그 때는 내가 불만족을 느끼고 변화를 필요로 하던 삶의 순간이었다. |
| | 국민들은 새로 시작된 정책에 대해 불만을 가지고 있었다. |

## drudgery
[drʌ́dʒəri]

**n. uninspiring and fatiguing work** | 지루하고 힘든 일

Unskilled labor workers spend their entire lives in *drudgery*.

**ANT** drudgery : rewarding work [riwɔ́ːrdiŋ wəːrk]

rewarding work: 보람 있고 가치 있는 일

## earsplitting
[íərsplìtiŋ]

**adj. excessively loud** | 귀청이 터질 듯한

Clubs are only good for people who enjoy dancing and *earsplitting* music.

**DE** earsplitting : loud [laud]

loud(시끄러운) 보다 훨씬 더 시끄러울 때 earsplitting하다고 한다.

## ecumenical
[èkjuménikəl]

**adj. universal; promoting worldwide Christian cooperation** | 보편적인, 전 기독교 연합을 추구하는

Saving the environment is of *ecumenical* importance.

**SYN** ecumenical : general [dʒénərəl]

general: 보편적인

## elucidate
[ilúːsədèit]

**v. to make clear by explanation; to render more intelligible** | 명료하게 하다

Mary *elucidated* her actions by explaining her perspective and intentions.

**ANT** elucidate : garble [gáːrbl]

garble: 왜곡하다

## emulate
[émjulèit]

**v. to imitate or strive to equal** | 모방하다, 필적하기 위해 겨루다

Carrie *emulated* her older sister in appearance and personality.

**PUR** emulate : exemplary [igzémpləri]

exemplary(모범적인, 본보기의)한 것을 추구하여 emulate하다.

---

### TRANSLATION | 예문해석

| | |
|---|---|
| **drudgery** | 기술이 부족한 노동자들은 지루하고 힘든 일을 하며 그들의 일생을 보낸다. |
| **earsplitting** | 클럽은 춤과 귀청이 터질 듯한 음악을 즐기는 사람들에게만 좋다. |
| **ecumenical** | 환경보존은 보편적인 중요성을 가진다. |
| **elucidate** | Mary는 자신의 전망과 의도를 설명함으로써 그녀의 활동을 명확하게 했다. |
| **emulate** | Carrie는 외모와 성격에 있어서 언니를 모방하려고 애썼다. |

## equipoise
[ékwəpɔ̀iz]

**n. a state of equilibrium** | 평형상태, 균형

Will the world ever reach an *equipoise*?

**CN** equipoise : vacillate [væsəlèit]

equipoise 상태에 있는 것은 vacillate(흔들리다, 동요하다)하지 않는다.

## fervid
[fə́:rvid]

**adj. impassioned or having intense feelings** | 열정적인, 강렬한 감정을 가진

The missionary is absolutely *fervid* about her faith.

**ANT** fervid : impassive [impǽsiv]

impassive: 무감각한, 감정이 없는

## forthright
[fɔ́:rθràit]

**adj. frank or direct** | 솔직한, 직설적인

The father was *forthright* with his son about the dangers of drinking.

**CN** forthright : circumlocution [sə̀:rkəmloukjú:ʃən]

forthright하지 않고 빙빙 둘러서 말하는 것이 circumlocution(완곡한 표현)이다.

## fortify
[fɔ́:rtəfài]

**v. to strengthen physically, emotionally, or mentally** | (물리적·감정적·정신적으로) 강하게 하다

The Venetians *fortified* their Cretan castle with huge defensive walls.

**ANT** fortify : enervate [énərvèit]

enervate: 약화시키다

## furtive
[fə́:rtiv]

**adj. deceptively secret or sly** | 은밀한, 교활한

The politician's *furtive* behavior was attacked by journalists in the newspaper.

**ANT** furtive : overt [ouvə́:rt]

overt: 공공연한, 명백한

---

### TRANSLATION | 예문해석

| | |
|---|---|
| **equipoise** | 세계가 과연 평형상태에 도달할 것인가? |
| **fervid** | 그 선교사는 자신의 신념에 굉장히 열정적이다. |
| **forthright** | 아버지는 음주의 위험성에 대해 아들에게 직설적으로 말했다. |
| **fortify** | 베네치아 인들이 그들의 크레타 성을 거대한 방어벽으로 강화했다. |
| **furtive** | 그 정치인의 교활한 행동이 신문 기자들에게 비난을 받았다. |

## husband
[hʌ́zbənd]

**v.** to use sparingly or economically | 절약하다

Billy *husbanded* his monthly allowance in order to save for a new bicycle.

**ANT**   husbandry : prodigality [prɑ̀dəgǽləti]

husbandry: 절약, 농업

prodigality: 낭비

## martinet
[mɑ̀:rtənét]

**n.** a person who is strictly disciplined and adherent to forms | 엄격한 사람, 규율가

It takes a *martinet* to run a military operation.

**WO**   martinet : leniency [líːniənsi]

martinet에게서 leniency(관대함)를 찾아보기는 어렵다.

## mirth
[məːrθ]

**n.** happiness or gaiety expressed with laughter | 환희, 즐거움

Elizabeth responded with *mirth* when her boyfriend proposed to her.

**PUR**   mirth : laughter [lǽftər]

laughter(웃음)으로 mirth를 표현한다.

## misanthrope
[mísənθròup]

**n.** one who dislikes or distrusts mankind | 인간을 싫어하거나 불신하는 사람, 염세가

Polly Whitney once pointed out the irony of a *misanthrope* needing people to hate.

**CN**   misanthrope : humane [hjuːméin]

misanthrope는 humane(인도적인, 자비로운)하지 않다.

## misbehave
[mìsbihéiv]

**v.** to behave improperly | 못된 짓을 하다, 품행이 좋지 못하다

It is typical for children to *misbehave*.

**CH**   misbehave : reprobate [réprəbèit]

reprobate(방탕아, 타락한 사람)는 misbehave하는 경향이 있다.

---

### TRANSLATION | 예문해석

**husband**     Billy는 새 자전거를 사기 위해 매달 받는 용돈을 절약했다.
**martinet**    군사작전 수행은 규율에 엄격한 사람을 필요로 한다.
**mirth**       Elizabeth는 남자친구에게 청혼을 받았을 때 환희에 차서 응답했다.
**misanthrope** Polly Whitney는 미워할 사람을 필요로 하는 염세가의 아이러니를 지적한 적이 있었다.
**misbehave**   못되게 행동하는 것은 아이들의 전형적인 모습이다.

## mischievous
[místʃivəs]

**adj. tending to cause trouble; harmful** | 짓궂은, 해로운

The mother could not control her *mischievous* teen.

**CH** mischievous : brat [bræt]
brat(장난 꾸러기)는 mischievous한 특성을 지닌다.

## partial
[páːrʃəl]

**adj. having prejudice; being favorably disposed** | 편파적인, 선호하는

The manager was *partial* to his hirees and tended to promote them above others.

**ANT** partial : dispassionate [dispǽʃənət]
dispassionate: 공평무사한

**POS** partial : bias [báiəs]
bias: 편견

## partisan
[páːrtizən]

**n. one who strongly adheres to a cause, party or faction** | (대의·당·당파 등을) 강하게 신봉하는 사람, 열성적인 지지자

Lee is a *partisan* for anti-globalization.

**CH** partisan : allegiance [əlíːdʒəns]
partisan은 강한 allegiance(충성, 충직)를 가지고 있다.

## persuade
[pərswéid]

**v. to convince or urge someone by argument or entreaty** | 설득하다

You can try to *persuade* him, but I guarantee he won't be moved.

**CN** persuade : obstinate [ábstənət]
obstinate(고집 센, 완고한)한 사람을 persuade하기는 정말 어렵다.

## pertinacity
[pə̀ːrtənǽsəti]

**n. an obstinate adherence to a cause, position, or purpose** | (주장·지위·목적 등에 대한) 완고한 집착, 완고함

Darcy could not believe Elizabeth's *pertinacity* to the conspiracy theory.

**POS** pertinacity : refractory [rifrǽktəri]
refractory: 고집 센, 다루기 힘든

---

### TRANSLATION | 예문 해석

| | |
|---|---|
| mischievous | 그 어머니는 짓궂은 10대 자녀를 통제할 수 없었다. |
| partial | 그 지배인은 자신이 고용한 사람들만 선호해서 다른 직원들 보다 빨리 승진시켰다. |
| partisan | Lee는 반세계화 신봉자이다. |
| persuade | 당신이 그를 설득하려 할 수는 있겠지만, 나는 그가 설득당하지 않을 것이라고 장담한다. |
| pertinacity | Darcy는 그 음모론에 대한 Elizabeth의 완고한 집착을 믿을 수 없었다. |

## pertinent
[pə́ːrtənənt]

adj. **relevant** | 적절한, 관련있는

The judge ruled the evidence *pertinent* to the case.

**ANT** pertinent : immaterial [ìmətíəriəl]
immaterial: 관련없는, 실체 없는, 중요하지 않은

## perturb
[pərtə́ːrb]

v. **to disturb or cause confusion to someone's peace of mind** | 마음의 평화를 어지럽히다, 동요시키다

The new employee *perturbed* the manager with his lazy work habits.

**CN** perturb : stoic [stóuik]
stoic(금욕적인)한 사람은 쉽게 perturb되지 않는다.

## pervade
[pərvéid]

v. **to permeate through every part** | 널리 퍼지다, 스며들다

The scent of flowers from the garden *pervaded* the cottage.

**CN** pervasive : avoid [əvɔ́id]
pervasive(널리 미치는)한 것을 avoid(회피하다)하기는 힘들다.

## portentous
[pɔːrténtəs]

adj. **arousing amazement; being an important or serious matter; ominous** | 놀라운, 중대한, 불길한

His *portentous* words left the crowd in amazement and fear.

**ANT** portentous : auspicious [ɔːspíʃəs]
auspicious: 길조의

## portrait
[pɔ́ːrtrit]

n. **a picture or portrayal in words of a person** | 초상화, 언어에 의한 인물 묘사

There is a *portrait* of Mona Lisa hanging in the Louvre in Paris.

**대상** portrait : person [pə́ːrsn]
person을 그린 그림이 portrait(초상화)이다.

---

TRANSLATION | 예 문 해 석

| | |
|---|---|
| **pertinent** | 판사는 그 증거가 그 사건과 관련 있다고 판결을 내렸다. |
| **perturb** | 새로 온 직원은 나태한 근무 태도로 매니저의 마음을 괴롭게 했다. |
| **pervade** | 정원의 꽃 향기가 작은 시골 집에 널리 퍼져 있었다. |
| **portentous** | 그의 불길한 말이 군중을 놀라움과 두려움에 빠뜨렸다. |
| **portrait** | 파리의 루브르 박물관에 모나리자의 초상화가 걸려있다. |

## purvey
[pərvéi]

**v. to supply provisions or materials** | (식료품이나 재료를) 공급하다, 조달하다

The committee *purveyed* food and other supplies for the conference.

**CH** purvey : vendor [véndər]
vendor(파는 사람, 매각인)는 물건을 purvey하는 역할을 한다.
cf) vendee: 매수인, 물건을 사는 사람

## ribald
[ríbəld]

**adj. offensive; containing indecent humor** | 무례한, 음란한

Politicians must be careful not to make *ribald* comments during speeches.

**ANT** ribald : seemly [síːmli]
seemly: 예의 바른

## rescind
[risínd]

**v. to remove, take back, or revoke** | 폐지하다, 무효로 하다, 철회하다

The judgement was *rescinded* by the committee due to new evidence.

**대상** rescind : law [lɔː]
law(법)를 rescind하다.

## sanguine
[sǽŋgwin]

**adj. being of the color of blood; of a cheerful and confident disposition** | 핏빛의, 쾌활하고 자신감 있는

Derek had a *sanguine* temperament and always had a smile on his face.

**ANT** sanguine : despondent [dispándənt]
despondent: 풀이 죽은

## servile
[sə́ːrvil]

**adj. subservient or submissive** | 비굴한, 복종적인

Debbie is a quiet and *servile* young student who never raises her voice.

**ANT** servile : imperious [impíəriəs]
imperious: 거만한

---

**TRANSLATION | 예문 해석**

| | |
|---|---|
| purvey | 그 위원회는 회의를 위해 음식과 다른 필수품들을 공급했다. |
| ribald | 정치인들은 연설 중에 무례한 발언을 하지 않도록 주의해야 한다. |
| rescind | 새로운 증거가 나오자 그 판결은 위원회에 의해 철회되었다. |
| sanguine | Derek은 자신감 있는 기질을 가졌고 언제나 얼굴에 미소를 띠었다. |
| servile | Debbie는 결코 목소리를 높이지 않는 조용하고 순종적인 어린 학생이다. |

## squander
[skwándər]

v. **to spend foolishly; to scatter** | 헛되이 쓰다, 흩뿌리다

Michael *squandered* his entire first paycheck at the casino.

- **ANT** squander : conserve [kənsə́:rv]
  conserve: 보존하다, 유지하다

## steadfast
[stédfæ̀st]

adj. **immovable; loyal and unchanging** | 요지부동의, 충실하고 변치않는

There is nothing more valuable than a *steadfast* friendship.

- **ANT** steadfast : capricious [kəprí∫əs]
  capricious: 변덕스러운

## strut
[strʌt]

v. **to walk in a proud or arrogant way** | 거만하게 걷다

Kathy *strutted* down the hallways of her corporation, flaunting her attractiveness.

- **KIN** strut : walk [wɔ:k]
  거만하게 walk(걷다)하는 것을 strut한다고 표현한다.

## verve
[və:rv]

n. **energy or vitality; the spirit of enthusiasm** | 활기, 활력, 열의

The surfer goes at life just as he does a wave, with *verve* and confidence.

- **ANT** verve : listlessness [lístlisnis]
  listlessness: 활기 없음

## virtuous
[və́:rt∫uəs]

adj. **exhibiting excellent moral virtue** | 덕이 높은

The princess was not only kind but *virtuous*.

- **ANT** virtuous : base [beis]
  base: 천한, 상스러운

---

### TRANSLATION | 예문 해석

| | |
|---|---|
| **squander** | Michael은 그의 첫 번째 급료 전부를 카지노에서 헛되이 써버렸다. |
| **steadfast** | 확고한 우정보다 가치 있는 것은 없다. |
| **strut** | Kathy는 자신의 매력을 뽐내면서 회사의 복도를 거만하게 걸었다. |
| **verve** | 그 서퍼는 파도를 탈 때처럼 열의와 자신감을 가지고 삶을 살아나간다. |
| **virtuous** | 그 공주는 친절할 뿐만 아니라 덕이 높았다. |

## virulent
[vírjulənt]

**adj.** **being able to cause disease by breaking down bodily defense mechanisms; malignant**
| 신체의 방어체계를 무너뜨림으로써 질병을 유발할 수 있는, 유독한, 악성의

Without proper treatment, the *virulent* disease will spread throughout his body quickly and debilitate him.

**ANT** virulent : salubrious [səlú:briəs]
salubrious: 건강에 좋은

## wary
[wɛ́əri]

**adj.** **cautious or watchful of danger** | 위험에 대해 주의하고 경계하는

When walking alone at night, one should be *wary* of strangers.

**CN** wary : gulled [gʌld]
주의 깊게 **wary**하는 사람은 **gulled**(쉽게 속는)되지 않는다.

---

| TRANSLATION | 예 문 해 석 |
|---|---|
| virulent | 적절한 치료가 취해지지 않으면 그 악성 질병이 그의 몸에 급속도로 퍼져 그를 쇠약하게 만들 것이다. |
| wary | 밤에 혼자서 걸을 때는 낯선 이를 경계해야만 한다. |

# 1st Day Daily Check-up

■ Fill in the blanks with the correct letter that matches the word with its definition.

1. virulent _____
2. curt _____
3. drudgery _____
4. furtive _____
5. purvey _____
6. emulate _____
7. misanthrope _____
8. disaffected _____
9. portentous _____
10. husband _____

a. to imitate or strive to equal
b. one who dislikes or distrusts mankind
c. being able to cause disease by breaking down bodily defense mechanisms; malignant
d. rudely short in speech or manner
e. to supply provisions or materials
f. deceptively secret or sly
g. arousing amazement or being an important or serious matter; ominous
h. to use sparingly or economically
i. discontented and resentful especially against authority
j. uninspiring and fatiguing work

■ Put the correct word in each blank from the list of words below.

11. adulate는 _____보다 아첨의 정도가 훨씬 더 심하다.
12. 거만하게 walk하는 것을 _____한다고 표현한다.
13. _____들은 misbehave하는 경향이 있다.
14. _____의 동의어는 discontent(불만)이다.
15. loud보다 훨씬 더 시끄러울 때 _____하다고 한다.
16. _____하지 않고 빙빙 둘러서 말하는 것이 circumlocution이다.
17. _____의 반의어는 impassive(열정 없는)이다.
18. _____한 사람은 쉽게 discompose 되지 않는다.
19. 주의 깊게 wary하는 사람은 _____되지 않는다.
20. _____에게서 leniency를 찾아보기는 어렵다.

a. reprobate   b. gripe   c. earsplitting   d. forthright   e. pacific   f. gulled
g. flatter   h. martinet   i. fervid   j. bale   k. prodigality   l. strut

**Answer key**

1. c   2. d   3. j   4. f   5. e   6. a   7. b   8. i   9. g   10. h
11. g   12. l   13. a   14. b   15. c   16. d   17. i   18. e   19. f   20. h

# SUPER VOCA

S . E . C . O . N . D   D . A . Y

하루하루를 3.333...%라고 생각하고
단어를 외워, 30일 후 100%를 만들고 말겠다.

---

### assent
[əsént]

**v. to agree to or approve of** | 찬성하다

Max *assented* to the conditions and terms of the job.

**ANT** assent : object [əbdʒékt]
object: 반대하다

---

### assert
[əsə́ːrt]

**v. to forcefully state or declare an opinion or position; to defend one's rights** | 강하게 주장하다, 단언하다, 옹호하다

Tom *asserts* relentlessly that the judge is corrupt.

**DE** assertive : bumptious [bʌ́mpʃəs]
assertive(단언적인)한 태도가 지나치면 bumptious(오만한)하게 보인다.

---

### assiduity
[æ̀sidjúːəti]

**n. the quality of being extremely hard working and diligent** | 근면

It is *assiduity*, not necessarily intelligence, that will take you far in the world.

**WO** assiduity : slothful [slɔ́ːθfəl]
slothful(나태한, 게으른)한 사람에게는 assiduity가 없다.

---

### badger
[bǽdʒər]

**v. to tease or annoy persistently** | 조르다, 끈덕지게 괴롭히다

The boy *badgered* his sister until she started to cry.

**DE** badger : bother [báðər]
badger는 심하게 bother(귀찮게 하다)하는 것을 의미한다.

---

### TRANSLATION | 예문 해석

| | |
|---|---|
| assent | Max는 그 직업의 제반 조건에 동의했다. |
| assert | Tom은 그 판사가 부도덕하다고 가차없이 주장한다. |
| assiduity | 지적인 능력이 아니라 근면함이 이 세상에서 당신을 멀리까지 나아가게 해 줄 것이다. |
| badger | 그 소년은 여동생이 울음을 터뜨릴 때까지 끈질기게 괴롭혔다. |

## banish
[bǽniʃ]

v. **to expel or exile from a country** | 나라에서 추방하다, 망명하다

Nick was *banished* from his country for treason.

**대상** banish : country [kʌ́ntri]

banish는 country(나라)로부터 추방하는 것이다.

## carouse
[kəráuz]

v. **to drink excessively and be boisterous** | 술을 많이 마시다, 흥청거리다

Some businessmen work diligently all day and let out their stress by *carousing* until the wee hours of the morning.

**CH** carouse : roisterer [rɔ́istərər]

carouse는 roisterer(술 마시고 떠드는 사람)의 속성이다.

## desecrate
[désikrèit]

v. **to damage or defile the sanctity or sacredness of** | 신성 모독하다

The church was *desecrated* by the graffiti spray-painted on its front doors.

**ANT** desecrate : sanctify [sǽŋktəfài]

sanctify: 신성하게 하다

## desiccate
[désikèit]

v. **to dehydrate or absorb moisture** | 건조시키다

Due to the drought, the land was barren and *desiccated*.

**대상** desiccate : moisture [mɔ́istʃər]

desiccate는 moisture(습기)를 없애는 것이다.

## discredit
[diskrédit]

v. **to question the accuracy or authority of; to damage a reputation** | ~의 정확도나 권위를 의심하다, 명성을 해치다

The attorney *discredited* the witness's character by revealing his criminal history.

**PUR** discredit : invective [invéktiv]

discredit할 목적으로 invective(비난, 독설)를 퍼 붓는다.

---

TRANSLATION | 예문해석

| | |
|---|---|
| banish | Nick은 반역의 대가로 국외로 추방되었다. |
| carouse | 어떤 사업가들은 하루 종일 열심히 일하고 이른 아침까지 흥청거리며 술을 마시면서 스트레스를 풀어 낸다. |
| desecrate | 정문에 스프레이로 써 놓은 낙서들은 그 교회를 신성 모독했다. |
| desiccate | 가뭄 때문에 땅은 황폐하고 건조해졌다. |
| discredit | 그 변호사는 그 증인의 전과를 폭로함으로써 그의 인격을 손상시켰다. |

## discrete
[diskríːt]

**adj. having a separate or distinct identity** | 별개의, 분리된

Only in recent years have homosexual couples been recognized as *discrete* under the law in some countries.

**CN** discrete : overlap [òuvərlǽp]

discrete한 것들은 overlap(중복되다)되지 않는다.

## discriminate
[diskrímənèit]

**v. to perceive differences or distinctions between; to treat unfairly due to race, religion, age, or other features** | 구별하다, 차별하다

Avid watchers can *discriminate* between the various species of birds.

**대상** discriminate : difference [dífərəns]

discriminate는 difference(차이점)를 찾아내는 것이다.

## discursive
[diskə́ːrsiv]

**adj. changing topics without order; covering a wide range of subjects** | 산만한, 광범위한

The *discursive* lecture left the students informed, but a little confused.

**SYN** discursive : digressive [daigrésiv]

digressive: 본론에서 벗어난, 산만한

## disdain
[disdéin]

**v. to treat with haughty contempt** | 경멸하다
**n. a feeling of contempt** | 경멸

The Hispanic population charges that the U.S. *disdains* their people and heritage.

Young prince David Ⅲ, looked at the common people in *disdain*.

**SYN** disdain : snub [snʌb]

snub: 무시, 냉대

---

### TRANSLATION | 예문 해석

**discrete** 최근에야 동성애 커플들이 법률상 별개의 집단으로 몇몇 나라에서 인식되었다.
**discriminate** 열성적인 관찰자들은 다양한 종의 새들을 구별해낼 수 있다.
**discursive** 그 산만한 강의로 학생들은 지식을 얻었지만 약간 혼란스러웠다.
**disdain** 히스패닉계 사람들은 미국이 자신들 민족과 문화유산을 경멸한다고 비난한다.
젊은 왕자, 데이빗 3세는 평민들을 경멸하며 바라 보았다.

## disembody
[dìsembádi]

v. to free from corporeal existence | (영혼을) 육체로부터 분리하다

It is said that through meditation people have *disembodied* themselves and elevated to a purely spiritual existence.

**ANT** disembodied : corporeal [kɔːrpɔ́ːriəl]

disembodied: 육체가 없는, 실체 없는

corporeal: 육체적인, 물질적인

## disgruntle
[disgrʌ́ntl]

v. to make discontented or dissatisfied | 불만족스럽게 하다

The *disgruntled* postal workers eventually went on strike.

**ANT** disgruntled : contented [kənténtid]

disgruntled: 불만스러운

contented: 만족스러운

## disguise
[disgáiz]

v. to change the appearance of; to conceal | 변장하다, 감추다

n. a costume or change of appearance used to hide one's identity or imitate another's identity | 위장복, 변장

The thief could not be identified because he *disguised* himself with a used military uniform.

What *disguise* will you wear for Halloween?

**FUN** disguise : camouflage [kǽməflàːʒ]

disguise(위장복)는 camouflage(위장하다)하는데 사용된다.

## disgust
[disgʌ́st]

v. to offend with distastefulness | 혐오스럽게 하다

n. a strong aversion or dislike | 강한 반감이나 혐오

Melanie was *disgusted* by the rude behavior of the people sitting at the next table.

Ellie sat in *disgust* as the bitter smell of smoke filled the air.

**인과** disgust : odious [óudiəs]

odious(불쾌한)한 것은 disgust를 유발시킨다.

cf) odious는 서술대상 자체의 느낌을 표현할 때 사용되고, disgust는 관찰자의 느낌을 반영한다.

---

### TRANSLATION | 예문 해석

**disembody** 명상을 통해 사람들은 육체로부터 분리되어 순수한 영적 존재에 이르게 된다고 말한다.

**disgruntle** 불만족한 우편 직원들이 마침내 파업을 일으켰다.

**disguise** 도둑이 중고 군복으로 위장했기 때문에 발각되지 않았다.

당신은 할로윈에 어떤 변장을 할 것입니까?

**disgust** Melanie는 옆 테이블에 앉은 사람들의 무례한 행동에 혐오감을 느꼈다.

지독한 담배 냄새가 공기를 채웠기 때문에 Ellie는 혐오감을 느끼며 앉아 있었다.

## disingenuous
[dìsindʒénjuəs]

**adj. insincere or lacking in candor** | 불성실한, 솔직하지 않은

The poem criticized *disingenuous* expressions of love.

**WO** disingenuous : sincerity [sinsérəti]

disingenuous한 것에는 sincerity(성실, 진실)가 없다.

## equivocate
[ikwívəkèit]

**v. to use uncertain or ambiguous language to avoid committing to a perspective or statement** | (확실한 대답을 피하기 위해) 얼버무리다

John intentionally *equivocated* his position on abortion to avoid controversy in the office.

**WO** equivocation : clarity [klǽrəti]

equivocation(얼버무림)에는 clarity(명료, 명쾌함)가 없다.

## erudite
[érjudàit]

**adj. learned or scholarly** | 학식이 있는, 박학한

The *erudite* graduate student finished his Ph.D. in 4 years.

**CH** erudite : fathom [fǽðəm]

erudite한 사람은 fathom(통찰하다, 헤아리다) 한다.

## eschew
[istʃúː]

**v. to avoid deliberately; to shun** | 고의로 피하다, 삼가다

Phil found it difficult to *eschew* Paul because they had the same circle of friends.

**ANT** eschew : welcome [wélkəm]

welcome: 환영하다

## exultant
[igzʌ́ltənt]

**adj. filled with great joy or triumph** | 크게 기뻐하는, 의기 양양한

The newly engaged man is *exultant* because his girlfriend said yes to his proposal.

**ANT** exultant : crestfallen [kréstfɔ̀ːlən]

crestfallen: 의기 소침한, 풀이 죽은

---

**TRANSLATION | 예문해석**

| | |
|---|---|
| **disingenuous** | 그 시는 솔직하지 않은 사랑의 표현들을 비판했다. |
| **equivocate** | John은 그 사무실에서 논쟁을 피하기 위해 낙태에 관한 자신의 입장을 의도적으로 얼버무렸다. |
| **erudite** | 그 박학한 대학원생은 그의 박사학위를 4년 만에 끝냈다. |
| **eschew** | Phil은 그와 Paul이 같은 무리의 친구들을 두고 있기 때문에 Paul을 고의로 피하는 것이 어려움을 깨달았다. |
| **exultant** | 그 새로 약혼한 남자는 여자 친구가 그의 청혼을 승낙했기 때문에 환호했다. |

## fluent
[flúːənt]

**adj. facile in language; capable of flowing with ease**
| 언어에 있어서 유창한, 쉽게 술술 할 수 있는

To make it in the career world today, one must be *fluent* in at least two languages.

**DE** fluent : glib [glib]
glib(겉발림으로 유창하게 말하는)은 fluent에 비해 말만 잘하는 이라는 의미를 나타낸다.

## frugal
[frúːgəl]

**adj. sparing or thrifty**
| 검소한, 절약하는

The *frugal* man lived in a relatively modest home despite his substantial wealth.

**DE** frugal : parsimonious [pàːrsəmóuniəs]
frugal함이 지나치면 parsimonious(인색한)하다는 말을 듣는다.

**ANT** frugal : profligate [práfligət]
profligate: 낭비가 심한, 방탕한

## gouge
[gaudʒ]

**v. to cut or scoop out**
| 파내다

The archeologist began to delicately *gouge* the sedimentary rock surrounding the fossil.

**DE** gouge : engrave [ingréiv]
gouge는 engrave(조각하다)보다 더 깊고 움푹하게 파내는 것이다.

## gush
[gʌʃ]

**v. to emit in a large flow or rush**
| 세차게 흘러나오다

Water *gushed* out of the broken hose.

**DE** gush : trickle [tríkl]
trickle(똑똑 떨어지다)보다 세차게 흘러나오는 것을 gush로 묘사한다.

## hash
[hæʃ]

**v. to mince or chop finely**
| 저미다, 잘게 썰다, 다지다

After seeing the dentist, all of his food had to be *hashed* before he could eat it.

**FUN** hash : pestle [péstl]
pestle(절구 공이)은 hash 할 때 쓰인다.

---

TRANSLATION | 예 문 해 석

| | |
|---|---|
| fluent | 오늘날 직업 세계에서 성공하기 위해서는, 적어도 두 가지 언어를 유창하게 구사해야만 한다. |
| frugal | 그 검소한 남자는 자신이 가진 부에 비해 수수한 집에서 살았다. |
| gouge | 그 고고학자는 화석 주위의 퇴적암을 조심스럽게 파내기 시작했다. |
| gush | 찢어진 호스에서 물이 세차게 흘러나왔다. |
| hash | 치과의사의 진찰을 받은 후 그는 먹기 전에 모든 음식을 잘게 다져야 했다. |

www.goHackers.com

## haunt
[hɔːnt]

**v.** to frequent or continually visit; to troublingly reappear continually | 자주 들르다, 괴롭게 계속적으로 다시 나타나다

**n.** a well-frequented place | 자주 들르는 장소

Larry and his friends *haunted* the local bar and were well acquainted with the owner.

The library is the *haunt* of diligent students.

**CH** haunt : familiar [fəmíljər]

haunt(자주 방문하는 장소)는 familiar(익숙한)하다.

## insensible
[insénsəbl]

**adj.** apathetic; incapable of feeling sensation | 무감동의, 냉담한, 감각을 잃은

Ryan's *insensible* demeanor was often mistaken for arrogance and afforded him few friends.

**CN** insensible : affect [əfékt]

insensible한 사람을 affect(감동시키다, 영향을 주다)시키기는 어렵다.

## insight
[ínsàit]

**n.** the ability or act of understanding the true nature of things | 통찰력, 통찰

The wise person has *insight* into every situation.

**POS** insight : discerning [disə́ːrniŋ]

discerning: 통찰력 있는

## laud
[lɔːd]

**v.** to praise | 칭찬하다

The young woman was *lauded* for her efforts in the match, despite the fact that she lost.

**ANT** laud : berate [biréit]

berate: 크게 꾸짖다

---

### TRANSLATION | 예문해석

**haunt** Larry와 그의 친구들은 그 바에 자주 들렀고, 그 주인과 친해졌다.
도서관은 부지런한 학생들이 자주 가는 곳이다.

**insensible** Ryan의 냉담한 태도는 종종 거만함으로 오인 받아 주위에 친구들이 별로 없었다.

**insight** 현명한 사람은 모든 상황에 대한 통찰력을 가지고 있다.

**laud** 그 젊은 여성은 졌음에도 불구하고, 시합에서의 그녀의 노력에 대해 칭찬을 받았다.

## lint
[lint]

n. scraped linen used for dressing wounds
| 상처의 처치에 쓰이는 리넨 천 조각, 붕대용 천

Rick looked through the first aid kit, but could not find the *lint* to cover Anne's wound.

**FUN** lint : bleeding [blíːdiŋ]
lint는 bleeding(출혈)을 막기 위해 쓰인다.

## lush
[lʌʃ]

adj. growing thick and healthily; fertile or plentiful
| 무성하게 자라는, 다산의, 풍부한

The *lush* garden would soon provide an abundance of vegetables.

**ANT** lush : sere [siər]
sere: 시든, 마른

## maudlin
[mɔ́ːdlin]

adj. extremely sentimental or emotionally weak
| 지나치게 감상적인, 감정적으로 약한

Kelly always cries at *maudlin* movies.

**DE** maudlin : sentimental [sèntəméntl]
지나치게 sentimental(감상적인)하면 maudlin하다고 한다.

## miscreant
[mískriənt]

n. a villain; a heretic
| 악한, 이단자

The *miscreant* was exiled out of Greece.

**ANT** miscreant : saint [séint]
saint: 성인, 성자

## misdemeanor
[mìsdimíːnər]

n. a minor legal offense less serious than a felony
| 중죄보다 덜 심각한 사소한 위법 행위, 경범죄

The *misdemeanor* cost Frank a $100 fine.

**DE** misdemeanor : crime [kraim]
misdemeanor는 crime(범죄) 보다 그 정도가 가벼운 위법 행위이다.

---

### TRANSLATION | 예문 해석

**lint**    Rick은 응급 처치 상자를 뒤져 봤지만 Anne의 상처에 덮어 줄 리넨 천을 찾을 수 없었다.
**lush**    그 무성한 정원은 곧 채소를 풍부하게 공급할 것이다.
**maudlin**    Kelly는 감상적인 영화를 보면 항상 운다.
**miscreant**    그 이단자는 그리스로부터 추방되었다.
**misdemeanor**    Frank는 경범죄를 지어 100달러의 벌금을 물어야 했다.

## miser
[máizər]

**n. a person who is cruel and stingy with money** | 구두쇠

The *miser* refused to tip his waiter more than 5% of the bill.

**CH** miser : hoard [hɔːrd]

miser들은 hoard(재물 등을 몰래 축적하다)하는 특징을 가지고 있다.

## mishap
[míshæp]

**n. an unfortunate accident or occurrence** | 불운한 일

The airport lost her luggage in a *mishap*.

**DE** mishap : catastrophe [kətǽstrəfi]

catastrophe(큰 재앙)은 mishap보다 더 큰 불상사를 말한다.

## obscure
[əbskjúər]

**adj. unclear or hidden; not easily understood** | 불분명한

The professor's explanation was full of *obscure* jargon and beyond my scope of comprehension.

**CN** obscure : comprehend [kàmprihénd]

obscure한 것은 쉽게 comprehend(이해하다)할 수 없다.

## obsequious
[əbsíːkwiəs]

**adj. over attentive and obedient** | 지나치게 정중하고 순종적인, 아부하는

The student's *obsequious* behavior toward his teacher was a source of ridicule for the other kids.

**DE** obsequious : deferential [dèfərénʃəl]

deferential(공손한)의 도가 지나치면 obsequious하게 된다.

## obsess
[əbsés]

**v. to have something haunt and control one's mind and actions** | 정신을 사로잡다, 푹 빠지게 하다

Jack was so *obsessed* with Jill that he moved to another country just to be near her.

**DE** obsessed : attracted [ətrǽktid]

attracted(매혹된)의 단계를 넘어 사로 잡혀 있는 것을 obsessed되었다고 한다.

---

**TRANSLATION | 예문 해석**

| | |
|---|---|
| miser | 그 구두쇠는 웨이터에게 계산서의 5% 이상의 팁을 주는 것을 거절했다. |
| mishap | 불운하게도 공항 측이 그녀의 짐을 잃어버렸다. |
| obscure | 그 교수의 모호한 전문 용어들로 가득한 설명은 내가 이해할 수 있는 수준 이상이었다. |
| obsequious | 그 학생의 교사에 대한 아첨하는 행동은 다른 아이들에게 조롱거리가 되었다. |
| obsess | Jack은 Jill에게 푹 빠져서 단지 그녀 곁에 있기 위해 다른 나라로 이사를 갔다. |

## opulent
[ápjulənt]

**adj. wealthy** | 부유한

The *opulent* business man tipped the waiter almost 50% of the bill.

> **ANT** opulent : indigent [índidʒənt]
> indigent: 빈곤한

## ossify
[ásəfài]

**v. to change into bone; to become inflexible or rigid** | 골화되다, 보수적으로 되다, 경직화 되다

After the September 11th attacks, many Americans who were democratic and liberal *ossified*.

> **CN** ossification : flexible [fléksəbl]
> ossification(골화, 경직화)된 것은 flexible(유연한)하지 않다.

## paunchy
[pɔ́ːntʃi]

**adj. having a potbelly** | 배가 불룩 나온

Soren's *paunchy* father had obviously drunk too many beers in his day.

> **ANT** paunchy : svelte [svelt]
> svelte: 날씬한

## pluck
[plʌk]

**n. nerve** | 용기, 담력

**v. to pick or pull quickly; to remove or separate forcibly; to play by sounding the strings with the fingers** | 뽑다, 강제로 제거하다, (현악기를) 뜯다

The new reporter was known for his *pluck* when investigating a story.
Patrick *plucked* a few stray hairs around his eyebrows.

> **ANT** pluck : cowardice [káuərdis]
> cowardice: 겁

> **대상** pluck : harp [hɑːrp]
> harp(하프)를 pluck하다.

---

**TRANSLATION | 예 문 해 석**

| | |
|---|---|
| **opulent** | 그 부유한 사업가는 계산서의 거의 50%를 웨이터에게 팁으로 지불했다. |
| **ossify** | 9월 11일의 테러사건 이후, 민주적이고 자유주의자인 많은 미국인들이 보수적으로 변했다. |
| **paunchy** | 배가 불룩 나온 Soren의 아버지는, 한창 때에 맥주를 너무 많이 마셨음에 틀림없다. |
| **pluck** | 그 새로운 리포터는 사건 취재 시의 대담함으로 유명하다.<br>Patrick은 눈썹 주위에 난 털 몇 가닥을 뽑았다. |

www.goHackers.com

## plumb
[plʌm]

n. a lead weight strung at the bottom of a line to determine a true vertical
| 수직을 표시하기 위해 사용되는 줄의 끝에 달린 납으로 된 추, 연추

v. to measure depth　　| 깊이를 재다

The carpenter measured the angle of the wall with a *plumb*.

The oceanographers had to *plumb* the site to see where they could release the new scientific equipment.

**대상** plumb : depth [depθ]

plumb는 depth(깊이)를 재다 라는 의미이다.

## plummet
[plʌ́mit]

v. to fall or drop rapidly　　| 곤두박질치다

Diving to catch its prey, the inexperienced hawk accidently *plummeted* into the ground.

**DE** plummet : descend [disénd]

곧장 수직으로 빠르게 descend(내려가다)하는 것이 plummet이다.

## poseur
[pouzə́:r]

n. one who habitually pretends to be what he/she is; an insincere person
| 허식가, 위선적인 사람

Everyone could see she was just a *poseur* not a real artist.

**WO** poseur : sincerity [sinsérəti]

poseur에게는 sincerity(진실, 성실)가 없다.

## prudence
[prú:dns]

n. the ability and good judgment to govern oneself with the use of reason
| 신중함, 현명함

The King used *prudence* in making decisions about his kingdom.

**WO** prudence : daredevil [déərdèvəl]

daredevil(저돌적인 사람)에게서 prudence를 찾아보기는 어렵다.

---

TRANSLATION | 예 문 해 석

| | |
|---|---|
| plumb | 그 목수는 연추를 가지고 벽의 각도를 쟀다. |
| | 그 해양학자들은 과학 장비들을 내려놓을 곳을 찾기 위해 그 지점의 수심을 재야만 했다. |
| plummet | 그 미숙한 매는 먹이를 잡으려고 급강하하다가 그만 땅으로 곤두박질치고 말았다. |
| poseur | 누구나 그녀가 진짜 예술가가 아니라 그저 허식가라는 것을 알 수 있었다. |
| prudence | 그 왕은 왕국에 대해 결정을 내리는 데 있어서 신중했다. |

**pusillanimous**
[pjùːsəlǽnəməs]

adj. afraid, timid, or lacking courage | 소심한

The onlooker was too *pusillanimous* to help the man being robbed.

- ANT pusillanimous : stouthearted [stáuthɑ́ːrtid]
  stouthearted: 대담한

**rash**
[ræʃ]

adj. reckless or hasty and done without thinking | 분별없는, 경솔한

n. a red spot which appears on skin as a biological reaction | 뾰루지(발진)

Her decision to quit school was *rash* and she later regretted it.
The *rashes* around my neck are very sore.

- DE rash : adventurous [ædvéntʃərəs]
  무분별하게 adventurous(대담한)한 경우는 rash하다고 한다.

**reserved**
[rizə́ːrvd]

adj. characterized by reticence and self-restraint; set aside | 삼가는, 수줍은, 내성적인; 따로 남겨둔

Darcy is a rather *reserved* man, keeping to himself most of the time.

- ANT reserved : expansive [ikspǽnsiv]
  expansive: 개방적인, 활달한

**resilience**
[rizíljəns]

n. the capability to recover one's original form or health | 탄성, 회복력

The gymnast's *resilience* allowed him to recover quickly from a sprained ankle.

- ANT resilience : inability to recover [inəbíləti tə rikʌ́vər]
  inability to recover: 회복 할 수 없음

**sculpt**
[skʌlpt]

v. to carve or make a sculpture | 조각하다

The artist *sculpted* an image of the beautiful woman he fell in love with in his youth.

- KIN sculpture : cameo [kǽmiòu]
  cameo(카메오)는 보석이나 조가비를 도드라지게 새긴 sculpture(조각물)의 일종이다.

---

TRANSLATION | 예 문 해 석

| | |
|---|---|
| pusillanimous | 그 구경꾼은 너무나 소심해서 강도 당하는 그 남자를 도와주지 못했다. |
| rash | 학교를 그만 두겠다는 그녀의 결정은 성급했고, 그녀는 나중에 그것을 후회했다. |
| | 내 목 주변의 발진이 무척 쓰라리다. |
| reserved | Darcy는 대부분의 시간을 혼자서 지내는 다소 내성적인 사람이다. |
| resilience | 그 체조선수는 회복력이 좋아 삔 발목이 빨리 나았다. |
| sculpt | 그 예술가는 젊은 시절 자신이 사랑에 빠졌던 아름다운 여성의 모습을 조각했다. |

www.goHackers.com

## scrupulous
[skrúːpjuləs]

**adj. having moral integrity; attentive to detail and exactness** | 양심적인, 세심한

The congregation couldn't have asked for a more *scrupulous* pastor.

- **ANT** unscrupulousness : probity [próubəti]
  - **unscrupulousness**: 부도덕함, 파렴치함
  - **probity**: 성실, 청렴결백

## sluggard
[slʌ́gərd]

**n. a person who is continually lazy** | 게으른 사람

The *sluggard* showed up to work late every day and slept most of the time.

- **CH** sluggard : lazy [léizi]
  - sluggard는 lazy한 특성을 지니고 있다.

## smug
[smʌg]

**adj. self-satisfied; offensively arrogant** | 자기만족의, 잘난체하는

Chloe didn't like the *smug* attitude of the professional wrestlers when she asked for their autographs.

- **CH** smugness : smirk [sməːrk]
  - smirk(거만하고 자기만족적인 웃음)에는 smugness(젠체함)가 들어있다.

## smuggle
[smʌ́gl]

**v. to illegally import or export things** | 밀수하다

Five people were arrested yesterday for *smuggling* drugs into England.

- **KIN** smuggle : convey [kənvéi]
  - smuggle은 불법적인 방법으로 convey(운송하다)하는 것을 말한다.

---

### TRANSLATION | 예문해석

| | |
|---|---|
| scrupulous | 그 목사는 신도들이 더 이상 바랄 수 없을 정도로 양심적이었다. |
| sluggard | 그 게으른 사람은 매일 늦게 일하러 나타났고 대부분의 시간에 잠을 잤다. |
| smug | Chloe는 프로레슬러들에게 사인을 부탁했을 때 그들이 보여준 거만한 태도가 싫었다. |
| smuggle | 다섯 사람이 마약을 영국으로 밀수하다가 어제 체포되었다. |

## snub
[snʌb]

v. **to treat with neglect or impoliteness** | 무시하다, 무례하게 대하다

The arrogant actress *snubbed* the man offering her his coat.

**WO** snub : politeness [pəláitnis]

snub하는 사람은 politeness(공손함)의 태도를 취하지 않는다.

## stultify
[stʌ́ltəfài]

v. **to render useless or ineffectual; to cause to appear stupid** | 망쳐놓다, 무효화하다, 어리석어 보이게 하다

Johnson's previous prison record *stultified* any chances of him getting into medical school.

**ANT** stultifying : stirring [stə́:riŋ]

stultifying: 무효화하는, 못쓰게 하는

stirring: 고무하는, 활동적인

---

TRANSLATION | 예 문 해 석

**snub** 그 거만한 여배우는 코트를 내미는 남자를 무시하였다.

**stultify** Johnson은 전과기록 때문에 의과대학에 들어갈 수 있는 기회가 완전히 사라지게 되었다.

## 2nd Day Daily Check-up

■ Fill in the blanks with the correct letter that matches the word with its definition.

1. assiduity      _____    a. to change into bone; to become conventional
2. desiccate     _____    b. the quality of being extremely hard working and diligent
3. gush          _____    c. to dehydrate or absorb moisture
4. maudlin       _____    d. growing thick and healthily; fertile or plentiful
5. obsequious    _____    e. to emit in a large flow or rush
6. disgruntle    _____    f. extremely sentimental or emotionally weak
7. ossify        _____    g. changing topics without order; covering a wide range of subjects
8. lush          _____    h. to fall or drop rapidly
9. discursive    _____    i. to make discontented or dissatisfied
10. plummet      _____    j. over attentive and obedient

■ Put the correct word in each blank from the list of words below.

11. _____한 태도가 지나치면 bumptious하게 보인다.
12. 무분별하게 adventurous한 경우는 _____하다고 한다.
13. snub(무시, 냉대)의 동의어는 _____이다.
14. _____함이 지나치면 parsimonious하다는 말을 듣는다.
15. _____는 engrave보다 더 깊고 움푹하게 파내는 것이다.
16. crestfallen(낙담한)의 반의어는 _____이다.
17. welcome(환영하다)의 반의어는 _____이다.
18. _____는 camouflage(위장하다)하는데 사용된다.
19. _____는 difference(차이점)를 찾아내는 것이다.
20. _____한 것에는 sincerity(성실, 진실)가 없다.

| a. assertive | b. eschew | c. poseur | d. rash | e. disguise | f. disdain |
| g. exultant | h. disingenuous | i. frugal | j. gouge | k. discriminate | l. resilience |

**Answer key**

1. b  2. c  3. e  4. f  5. j  6. i  7. a  8. d  9. g  10. h
11. a  12. d  13. f  14. i  15. j  16. g  17. b  18. e  19. k  20. h

www.goHackers.com

해커스 어학연구소

# SUPER VOCA
## THIRD DAY

수퍼보카를 통해 당신의 능력을 보여 주세요!

---

### aboveboard
[əbʌvbɔ̀ːrd]

**adj. honest and open; being without deception**
| 공명 정대한, 기만하지 않는

In the antique business, it is absolutely imperative that one have an *aboveboard* reputation.

**ANT** aboveboard action : chicanery [ʃikéinəri]
aboveboard action: 공명 정대한 행동
chicanery: 책략, 속임수

---

### absorb
[æbsɔ́ːrb]

**v. to take up or acquire**
| 흡수하다, 습득하다

Most flowers take in nutrients by *absorbing* water and minerals from the soil.

**ANT** absorb : secrete [sikríːt]
secrete: 분비하다, 비밀로 하다

---

### advertent
[ædvə́ːrtnt]

**adj. heedful**
| 주의 깊은

David makes a good husband because he is *advertent* to the needs of others.

**ANT** advertent : inattentive [ìnəténtiv]
inattentive: 부주의한

---

### assist
[əsíst]

**v. to aid or help**
| 돕다, 거들다

Jess *assisted* her friends with their move to their new home.

**ANT** assist : discommode [dìskəmóud]
discommode: 폐를 끼치다, 불편하게 하다

---

### TRANSLATION | 예문 해석

| | |
|---|---|
| **aboveboard** | 골동품 사업에서는 공명 정대하다는 명성을 얻는 것이 절대적으로 필요하다. |
| **absorb** | 대부분의 꽃들이 흙에서 물과 무기물을 흡수함으로써 영양분을 받아들인다. |
| **advertent** | David은 타인의 요구에 주의 깊기 때문에 좋은 남편이 된다. |
| **assist** | Jess는 새 집으로 이사하는 그녀의 친구들을 도왔다. |

## associate
[əsóuʃièit]

v. **to work or socialize with; to become partners with**
| 어울리다, 제휴하다

Kids are taught not to *associate* with people who use drugs.

**CN** associate : aloof [əlúːf]

aloof(무관심한, 냉담한)한 사람들은 서로 **associate**하지 않는다.

## auspicious
[ɔːspíʃəs]

adj. **favorable or prosperous; having signs or omens of a positive nature**
| 유리한, 운이 좋은, 길조의

New Year's is an *auspicious* time to set goals for one's personal well-being.

**ANT** auspicious : unfavorable [ʌnféivərəbl]

unfavorable: 불리한

## besmirch
[bismə́ːrtʃ]

v. **to make dirty or soil; to sully**
| 더럽히다, (명예 등을) 훼손하다

President Clinton *besmirched* his reputation by having an affair.

**ANT** besmirch : honor [ánər]

honor: 명예를 주다

## blurb
[bləːrb]

n. **a brief, written publicity notice**
| 짧은 추천문

There was a *blurb* in the paper about the upcoming convention.

**KIN** blurb : notice [nóutis]

blurb은 짧은 추천문으로 notice(소개, 단평)의 일종이다.

## blurt
[bləːrt]

v. **to speak abruptly and impulsively**
| 불쑥 말하다

Daniel *blurted* out his love for her in a moment of overwhelming emotion.

**KIN** blurt : speak [spiːk]

blurt는 갑작스레 speak(말하다)하는 것이다.

---

TRANSLATION | 예 문 해 석

**associate** 아이들은 마약을 사용하는 사람들과 어울리지 않도록 가르침을 받는다.
**auspicious** 새해 첫날은 개인의 행복을 위한 목표를 정하기에 좋은 때이다.
**besmirch** 클린턴 대통령은 추문으로 그의 명성에 오점을 남겼다.
**blurb** 곧 다가오는 집회에 대해 신문에 짧은 광고가 있었다.
**blurt** Daniel은 감정이 북받치는 순간에 그녀에게 사랑한다고 불쑥 말했다.

## bluster
[blʌ́stər]

**v. to utter or act with noisy threats** | 호통치다

Samuel came home drunk and *blustered* at the cat.

> **KIN** bluster : speak [spiːk]
> bluster는 호통치듯이 speak(말하다)하는 것이다.

## caustic
[kɔ́ːstik]

**adj. corrosive or capable of destroying through chemical reaction; sarcastic** | 부식성의; 신랄한

Henry was not enjoying the *caustic* jokes that Daniel was saying about his old car.

> **CH** caustic : barb [baːrb]
> barb(날카로운 비판)는 caustic한 특징을 지니고 있다.

## cavern
[kǽvərn]

**n. a large cave** | 큰 동굴

The *caverns* of the west coast are a humbling sight.

> **대상** cavern : spelunker [spilʌ́ŋkər]
> cavern은 spelunker(동굴 탐험가)의 탐험 대상이다.

## cessation
[seséiʃən]

**n. a stopping of an action; discontinuance** | 중지, 정지

The treaty put a *cessation* to the war.

> **ANT** cessation : commencement [kəménsmənt]
> commencement: 개시, 시작

## cosmopolitan
[kàzməpálətn]

**adj. pertinent to the whole world; found in all parts of the world; having worldwide scope** | 전세계적인, 전세계에 분포한, 시야가 넓은

Most professors today are *cosmopolitan* and reside in multiple countries.

> **ANT** cosmopolitan : insular [ínsələr]
> insular: 섬의, 편협한

---

### TRANSLATION | 예문해석

**bluster** Samuel은 술에 취해 집에 도착해서 고양이에게 호통을 쳤다.
**caustic** Henry는 자기의 낡은 차를 두고 Daniel이 비꼬듯 내뱉는 농담을 별로 좋아하지 않았다.
**cavern** 서해안의 큰 동굴들은 우리를 겸허하게 만드는 광경이다.
**cessation** 그 조약으로 전쟁이 중지되었다.
**cosmopolitan** 오늘날 대부분의 교수들은 세계주의적이고 여러 나라에 거주한다.

## cosset
[kάsit]

v. **to pamper** | 귀여워하다, 응석받이로 키우다
n. **a pet** | 애완동물

If you *cosset* your child, he or she will never learn self-responsibility. Nobody wants to be treated like a *cosset*.

**ANT** cosset : slight [slait]
slight: 냉대하다, 무시하다

## court
[kɔːrt]

v. **to seek the affections or good will of** | 애정이나 호의를 구하다

It is customary in certain cultures for a young couple to *court* each other before getting married.

**ANT** court : snub [snʌb]
snub: 무시하다, 야박하게 퇴짜 놓다

## coven
[kʌ́vən]

n. **a collection of people with similarities; a group of about 13 witches** | 집회, 13인의 마녀단

The *coven* of Dutch students met every week to socialize and practice speaking.

**PAR** coven : witch [witʃ]
witch(마녀)들은 coven의 구성원이다.

## despicable
[déspikəbl]

adj. **contemptible or arousing moral indignation** | 경멸할 만한, 도덕적 분개를 유발시키는

The capture and torture of civilians in Argentina was a *despicable* act.

**ANT** despise : venerate [vénərèit]
despise: 경멸하다
venerate: 존경하다

## despondent
[dispάndənt]

adj. **depressed or discouraged** | 우울한, 낙담한

Soren has been *despondent* for almost two weeks now.

**ANT** despondent : sanguine [sǽŋgwin]
sanguine: 쾌활하고 자신감 있는

---

| TRANSLATION | 예문해석 |
|---|---|
| cosset | 아이를 응석받이로 키우면, 아이가 결코 자신에 대한 책임감을 배우지 못할 것이다. 아무도 애완동물 취급 받고 싶어하지 않는다. |
| court | 결혼하기 전에 젊은 한 쌍이 서로 구애하는 것은 몇몇 문화에서는 관습적이다. |
| coven | 네덜란드 학생들의 집회는 매주 만나서 말하기를 연습했다. |
| despicable | 아르헨티나에서 시민들을 체포하고 고문한 것은 경멸할 만한 행위였다. |
| despondent | Soren은 지금까지 거의 2주동안 침울해하고 있다. |

## disintegrate
[disíntəgrèit]

**v. to break into parts or components** | 분해시키다, 붕괴하다

The dominant political party *disintegrated* into belligerent factions under the pressure of corruption investigations.

**ANT** disintegrate : amalgamate [əmǽlgəmèit]
amalgamate: 합병하다, 혼합하다

## disinterest
[disíntərist]

**n. an impartiality; a lack of interest** | 공평무사, 사심 없음, 무관심

Her *disinterest* in the outcome of the trial makes her a reliable witness.

**ANT** disinterested : prejudiced [prédʒədist]
disinterested: 공평한
prejudiced: 편파적인

## dismantle
[dismǽntl]

**v. to take apart; to destroy the integrity of** | 분해하다, 해체하다

The technician *dismantled* the computer in order to identify the hardware problem.

**대상** dismantle : unity [júːnəti]
하나의 unity(단일체, 개체)를 dismantle하다.

## disparage
[dispǽridʒ]

**v. to degrade or belittle through speech** | 격하하다, 비하하다

The tennis player *disparaged* her opponents' abilities publicly prior to the match.

**DE** disparage : ignore [ignɔ́ːr]
disparage는 ignore(무시하다) 보다 그 정도가 더 심하다.

## disparate
[díspərət]

**adj. distinctly marked in quality or character; totally different** | 확연히 구별되는, 완전히 다른

Globalization allows people of *disparate* backgrounds to interact and conduct business.

**ANT** disparate : similar [símələr]
similar: 유사한

---

**TRANSLATION | 예 문 해 석**

| | |
|---|---|
| disintegrate | 다수당은 부패 조사의 압력속에서 서로 대립하는 소수그룹들로 분해되었다. |
| disinterest | 그녀는 재판 결과에 대해 사심을 가지고 있지 않기 때문에 믿을 만한 증인이 될 수 있다. |
| dismantle | 그 기술자는 하드웨어 문제를 찾아 내기 위해 컴퓨터를 분해했다. |
| disparage | 그 테니스 선수는 시합 전에 공개석상에서 상대선수의 실력을 비방했다. |
| disparate | 세계화가 되면서 서로 다른 배경의 사람들이 교류하며 업무를 수행할 수 있게 되었다. |

## dispassionate
[dispǽʃənət]

**adj. unaffected by passion, emotion, or prejudice; calm; impartial** | 침착한, 공평한

It is very difficult to take a *dispassionate* position on major issues such as abortion and capital punishment.

**ANT** dispassionate : partial [páːrʃəl]
partial: 불공평한, 편파적인

## disprove
[disprúːv]

**v. to prove untrue or wrong** | 그릇됨을 증명하다, 논박하다

In order to *disprove* his guilt, the accused prisoner took a lie detector test.

**PUR** disprove : syllogism [sílədʒìzm]
syllogism(삼단 논법)은 상대방의 의견을 disprove하기 위한 수단으로 사용된다.

## dispute
[dispjúːt]

**v. to oppose or debate with** | 논쟁하다
**n. an argument or verbal controversy** | 논쟁

The two companies *disputed* over the rights to produce a new flavor of coffee.
The *dispute* over child support took five hours of court time to settle.

**CN** dispute : incontrovertible [ìnkàntrəvə́ːrtəbl]
incontrovertible(논쟁의 여지가 없는)은 dispute할 필요가 없다는 의미이다.

## disregard
[dìsrigáːrd]

**v. to ignore or pay no attention to** | 무시하다

Please *disregard* that last statement.

**DE** disregard : flout [flaut]
flout(모욕하다)는 disregard보다 더 강한 어감을 가진다.

---

TRANSLATION | 예 문 해 석

**dispassionate** 낙태와 사형과 같은 주요 안건들에 대해 공평한 입장을 취하는 것은 어렵다.
**disprove** 그의 유죄를 논박하기 위해, 혐의를 받는 죄수가 거짓말 감지 테스트를 받았다.
**dispute** 두 회사는 새로운 맛의 커피 생산권을 둘러싸고 논쟁했다.
자녀양육에 관한 논쟁이 법정에서 해결되는 데 5시간이나 걸렸다.
**disregard** 그 마지막 진술을 무시하십시오.

## disrespect
[dìsrispékt]

v. **to show a lack of respect for** | 경시하다

n. **a lack of respect** | 경시

The defendant was careful not to *disrespect* the judge during her trial.

The explorer's *disrespect* for local customs was less due to his ignorance than his arrogance.

> **ANT** disrespect : homage [hámidʒ]
>
> homage: 존경, 경의

## disrupt
[disrʌ́pt]

v. **to throw into confusion; to interrupt or cause a break in the normal flow of; to rupture or break**
| 혼란시키다; 중단시키다; 붕괴시키다

The appearance of the bride's ex-boyfriend *disrupted* the wedding.

> **CH** disrupt : saboteur [sæbətə́ːr]
>
> saboteur(파괴 활동자)는 disrupt하는 사람이다.

## dissemble
[disémbl]

v. **to pretend; to put on the appearance of** | 꾸미다, 속이다, 가장하다

On her job application Jackie *dissembled* the fact that she was a college graduate even though she hadn't even finished high school.

> **WO** dissemble : honesty [ɑ́nisti]
>
> dissemble하는 사람에게서 honesty(정직, 솔직)를 찾아보기는 어렵다.

## disseminate
[disémənèit]

v. **to make known or disperse throughout; to throw about** | 널리 알리다, 흩뿌리다

The news of the attack was *disseminated* rapidly throughout the world.

> **대상** disseminate : information [ìnfərméiʃən]
>
> information(정보)을 disseminate하다

---

### TRANSLATION | 예문해석

**disrespect** 피고는 재판이 진행되는 동안 판사에게 무례하게 굴지 않기 위해 조심했다.
그 탐험가가 지역 관습을 경시하는 것은 무지 보다는 오만함에서 기인한 것이었다.

**disrupt** 신부의 전 남자친구가 나타남으로써 그 결혼식은 엉망이 되어버렸다.

**dissemble** Jackie는 실제로는 고등학교도 졸업하지 않았으면서 입사 지원서에 대학을 졸업했다고 꾸며 냈다.

**disseminate** 그 공격 소식이 빠르게 전 세계로 알려졌다.

### dissent
[disént]

**n.** a disagreement | 이의

**v.** to differ in opinion | 의견을 달리하다, 이의를 제기하다

The protesters illustrated their *dissent* against the government's position.
The group of students *dissented* with the principal's new dress code.

> **ANT** dissent : concur [kənkə́:r]
> concur: 동의하다

### dyspeptic
[dispéptik]

**adj.** having indigestion; being of ill humor | 소화불량인; 우울하고 화를 잘 내는

John couldn't help but notice Niki's *dyspeptic* appearance when he mentioned he had set her up on a blind date.

> **ANT** dyspeptic : genial [dʒí:njəl]
> genial: 온화한, 상냥한

### eavesdrop
[í:vzdrɑ̀p]

**v.** to listen to other people's conversation without them knowing | 다른 사람의 대화를 몰래 듣다

Helen discovered a horrible secret while *eavesdropping* on her sister's phone conversation.

> **KIN** eavesdrop : listen [lísn]
> eavesdrop은 listen(듣다)하는 방법 중 하나이다.

### edifice
[édəfis]

**n.** a large building of imposing appearance | 큰 건물

Many of the *edifices* found on the university campus have been standing there for over a hundred years.

> **FUN** edifice : buttress [bʌ́tris]
> buttress(버팀목)은 edifice를 지지하기 위해 사용된다.

---

| TRANSLATION | 예 문 해 석 |
|---|---|
| dissent | 시위자들은 정부의 입장에 대한 그들의 반대의사를 보여주었다. |
| | 그 학생들은 교장선생님의 새로운 복장 규제에 이의를 제기했다. |
| dyspeptic | John이 Niki에게 미팅을 주선해 놓았다고 말했을 때 그녀의 우울한 표정을 눈치채지 않을 수 없었다. |
| eavesdrop | Helen은 여동생의 전화 통화 내용을 몰래 엿듣는 도중에 끔찍한 비밀을 알게 되었다. |
| edifice | 대학 캠퍼스에서 볼 수 있는 많은 큰 건물들은 그 자리에 백 년 이상을 서 있었다. |

## elated
[iléitid]

**adj. full of high spirited pride and joy** | 의기양양한

The young man was *elated* after his girlfriend's father consented to their marriage.

**ANT** elated : hangdog [hǽŋdɔ̀(:)g]
hangdog: 풀이 죽은

## enslave
[insléiv]

**v. to subjugate or put into slavery** | 정복하다, 노예로 만들다

The African people have been kidnapped and *enslaved* by many different countries and peoples.

**ANT** enslave : manumit [mǽnjəmít]
manumit: 노예나 농노를 해방하다

## filly
[fíli]

**n. a young female horse; a lively young woman** | 암망아지, 발랄한 젊은 여자, 말괄량이

The farmers had a hard time bringing the excited *filly* in from the field.

**KIN** filly : horse [hɔːrs]
filly는 어린 암컷 horse(말)이다.

## finesse
[finés]

**n. skillful and tactful handling of a situation** | 솜씨 있고 재치 있게 상황을 다룸, 수완

John's *finesse* with cars made him the most sought after car mechanic in town.

**WO** finesse : gauche [gouʃ]
gauche(요령없는, 서투른)한 사람에게는 finesse가 없다.

## fuss
[fʌs]

**v. to take care with excessive concern; to complain** | 몸달아 설치다, 야단법석하다, 불평하다

The mother *fussed* incessantly over the newborn's slight fever.

**DE** fuss : tend [tend]
fuss는 지나치게 걱정하여 tend(돌보다)하는 것이다.

---

### TRANSLATION | 예 문 해 석

| | |
|---|---|
| **elated** | 그 젊은 남자는 여자친구의 아버지로부터 결혼 승낙을 얻고 의기양양해졌다. |
| **enslave** | 아프리카 사람들은 많은 다른 나라와 민족들에 의해 유괴되어 노예가 되었다. |
| **filly** | 그 농부들은 흥분한 암망아지를 들판에서부터 끌고 들어오는 데 어려움을 겪었다. |
| **finesse** | John의 차를 다루는 솜씨있는 수완은 그를 지역에서 가장 수요가 많은 자동차 정비공으로 만들었다. |
| **fuss** | 어머니는 그 신생아에게 약간의 열만 있어도 끊임없이 안절부절 못했다. |

### gossamer
[gásəmər]

**n.** thin and soft threads produced by spiders | 거미줄
**adj.** very light or thin | 가볍고 섬세한

The old abandoned house was covered in dust and *gossamers*.
Daniel had to work carefully with the *gossamer* material to keep from tearing it accidentally.

**ANT** gossamer : ponderous [pándərəs]
ponderous: 육중한

### hesitance
[hézətəns]

**n.** reluctance or delay | 주저, 망설임

I have some *hesitance* about buying such an expensive house right now.

**WO** hesitance : impetuous [impétʃuəs]
impetuous(충동적인)한 사람은 아무런 hesitance없이 행동한다.

### insipid
[insípid]

**adj.** tasteless or lacking interesting qualities | 맛없는, 재미 없는

Plain popcorn has a rather *insipid* flavor.

**ANT** insipid : piquant [pí:kənt]
piquant: 입맛을 돋우는

### insolent
[ínsələnt]

**adj.** rude, arrogant, or disrespectful in speech or conduct | 건방진, 무례한

Most teenagers are *insolent* when it comes to authority figures.

**WO** insolent : veneration [vènəréiʃən]
insolent한 사람은 veneration(존경, 숭배)을 가지고 있지 않다.

### insouciant
[insú:siənt]

**adj.** being lightheartedly unconcerned | 태평한

An *insouciant* attitude about life will guarantee peace, but may lead to unproductiveness.

**CN** insouciant : worry [wə́:ri]
insouciant한 사람은 worry(걱정하다)하지 않는다.

---

TRANSLATION | 예문해석

| | |
|---|---|
| gossamer | 그 오래된 폐가는 먼지와 거미줄로 덮여 있었다. |
| | Daniel은 가볍고 가는 그 재료를 실수로 찢지 않도록 조심스럽게 작업해야만 했다. |
| hesitance | 나는 지금 그렇게 비싼 집을 사는 것에 대해 약간 주저하고 있다. |
| insipid | 플레인 팝콘은 다소 맛이 심심하다. |
| insolent | 대부분의 십대들은 권위 있는 인물들에 대해 이야기 할 때 무례하다. |
| insouciant | 삶에 대한 태평스런 태도는 평화를 보장하지만, 비생산성을 가져올 지 모른다. |

### inspire
[inspáiər]

**v. to motivate or stimulate to work hard or be creative; to affect by divine influence** | 고무하다, 영감을 주다

Encouragement and praise always *inspire* my dreams and goals.

**DE** inspire : infuse [infjúːz]

inspire는 infuse(불어넣다)보다 좀 더 강한 어감을 가지고 있다.

### mislead
[mislíːd]

**v. to lead astray or down the wrong path** | 잘못 이끌다, 오해하게 하다

His e-mail *misled* me to believe that he was coming to visit.

**CH** misleading : equivocation [ikwìvəkéiʃən]

equivocation(모호한 말)은 misleading(오해하기 쉬운)하다.

### resist
[rizíst]

**v. to withstand or fend off; to oppose; to keep from enjoying** | 저항하다, 대항하다, 삼가다

The German forces *resisted* the American assault for two months.

**ANT** resist : capitulate [kəpítʃulèit]

capitulate: 항복하다, 저항을 그만두다

### resolute
[rézəlùːt]

**adj. steady or firm in purpose or dedication** | (결심이나 헌신이) 확고한

Bill made a *resolute* decision to quit smoking.

**CN** resolute : dissuade [diswéid]

resolute한 사람을 dissuade(단념시키다)하는 것은 어렵다.

### respite
[réspit]

**n. a short interval of rest; a pause or period of temporary delay** | 짧은 휴식, 중지, 일시적인 유예 기간

The Memorial Union is a place for students to go for a *respite* from their studying.

**WO** respite : labor [léibər]

respite는 labor(노동)를 안하고 쉬는 상태이다.

---

**TRANSLATION | 예문 해석**

| | |
|---|---|
| inspire | 격려와 칭찬은 항상 나의 꿈과 목표를 고취시킨다. |
| mislead | 그의 이메일을 보고 나서 그가 올거라고 잘못 판단하게 되었다. |
| resist | 독일군은 2개월간 미국의 공격에 대항했다. |
| resolute | Bill은 담배를 끊기로 확고히 결심했다. |
| respite | 그 기념회관은 학생들이 공부하다가 쉬기 위해 가는 장소이다. |

## resplendent
[rispléndənt]

**adj. brilliant or shiny; splendid** | 빛나는, 찬란한

Our kids love to walk through the department stores and see the many Christmas trees with all their *resplendent* decorations on display.

**대상** resplendent : appearance [əpíərəns]

resplendent는 appearance(외관, 외양)를 수식하는 말이다.

## taunt
[tɔːnt]

**v. to ridicule or challenge by mocking** | 비아냥거리다, 조롱함으로써 자극하다

The football player *taunted* the scholarly boy until he ran home crying.

**DE** taunt : provoke [prəvóuk]

provoke(화나게 하다)는 taunt에 비해 타인에 대한 공격성의 강도가 높다.

## truculent
[trʌ́kjulənt]

**adj. savage or destructive, sometimes belligerent** | 야만의, 파괴적인, 호전적인

Brett's moment of *truculent* behavior won him a night in prison.

**WO** truculent : gentleness [dʒéntlnis]

truculent한 사람은 gentleness(온화함, 상냥함)을 지니고 있지 않다.

## trudge
[trʌdʒ]

**v. to walk or march with difficulty** | 힘겹게 터벅터벅 걷다

The soldiers *trudged* through the jungle, weary and afraid.

**KIN** trudge : walk [wɔːk]

trudge는 힘겹게 터벅터벅 walk(걷다)하는 것이다.

## truncate
[trʌ́ŋkeit]

**v. to shorten or cut in length** | 길이를 자르다, 줄이다

The presentation was *truncated* by about 15 minutes to make it fit the schedule.

**ANT** truncate : prolong [prəlɔ́ːŋ]

prolong: 늘이다, 연장하다

---

TRANSLATION | 예 문 해 석

**resplendent** 우리 아이들은 백화점을 거닐면서 반짝반짝 빛나는 장식을 단 채 진열되어 있는 크리스마스 트리를 보는 것을 좋아한다.
**taunt** 그 미식 축구 선수가 학구적인 소년을 조롱해서 울면서 집으로 달려가게 했다.
**truculent** Brett은 한 순간의 야만적인 행동으로 감옥에서 밤을 보내게 되었다.
**trudge** 그 군인들은 지치고 공포에 질린 채 정글을 힘겹게 터벅터벅 걸었다.
**truncate** 그 발표는 일정을 맞추기 위해 15분 가량 줄여졌다.

## vault
[vɔːlt]

**n. a storage compartment or room used for the safekeeping of valuables** | 저장실, 금고실

The items in our *vault* included a diamond necklace, our wills, and $3000.

**FUN** vault : valuables [vǽljuːəblz]

vault에 valuables(귀중품)를 보관한다.

## vaunt
[vɔːnt]

**v. to brag of one's own worth** | 뽐내다, 자랑하다

*Vaunting* and gloating, the winner of the contest left the ceremony to celebrate.

**SYN** vaunt : boast [boust]

boast: 뽐내다, 자랑하다

## unsound
[ʌnsáund]

**adj. not true or logically valid; not healthy or whole** | 논리적으로 타당하지 않은, 건강하지 못한, 건전하지 못한

In a rage of anger, Kevin made an *unsound* and fatal decision to drink and drive.

**ANT** unsound : tenable [ténəbl]

tenable: 조리있는, 지지할 수 있는

## visionary
[víʒənèri]

**adj. illusory; imaginary; incapable of being realized** | 환영의, 상상의, 공상적인

**n. a daydreamer; a seer** | 몽상가, 예언가

Dave was entirely haunted by the *visionary* scene.

It takes a *visionary* to spark a revolution.

**POS** visionary : delusion [dilúːʒən]

delusion: 망상

---

### TRANSLATION | 예문해석

**vault** 우리 금고실에는 다이아몬드 목걸이, 유언장, 3000달러가 들어있다.
**vaunt** 뽐내고 잘난체 하며, 그 콘테스트의 승자는 그 축하연을 떠났다.
**unsound** 화가 치솟아서, Kevin은 술을 마시고 운전하는 불합리하고 치명적인 결정을 내렸다.
**visionary** 그 환영이 Dave의 머리에서 떠나지 않았다.
혁명을 일으키는 데에는 몽상가가 요구된다.

## 3rd Day Daily Check-up

■ Fill in the blanks with the correct letter that matches the word with its definition.

1. besmirch _____
2. insipid _____
3. truculent _____
4. unsound _____
5. truncate _____
6. aboveboard _____
7. despondent _____
8. resplendent _____
9. dyspeptic _____
10. cosset _____

a. honest and open; being without deception
b. tasteless or lacking interesting qualities
c. to pamper; a pet
d. to make dirty or to soil; to sully
e. brilliant or shiny; splendid
f. savage or destructive, sometimes belligerent
g. not healthy or whole; not true or logically valid
h. to shorten or cut in length
i. depression or discouragement
j. having indigestion; being of ill humor

■ Put the correct word in each blank from the list of words below.

11. aloof한 사람들은 서로 _____ 하지 않는다.
12. _____ 은 짧은 추천문으로 notice의 일종이다.
13. _____ 한 사람은 worry하지 않는다.
14. equivocation은 _____ 하다.
15. delusion의 의미를 가진 형용사는 _____ 이다.
16. _____ 에 valuables를 보관한다.
17. syllogism은 상대방의 의견을 논리적으로 _____ 하는 수단으로 사용된다.
18. secrete(분비하다)의 반의어는 _____ 이다.
19. _____ 는 ignore보다 그 정도가 더 심하다.
20. _____ 은 spelunker의 탐험 대상이다.

| a. misleading | b. disparage | c. cavern | d. resist | e. insouciant | f. associate |
| g. blurb | h. disprove | i. vault | j. prolong | k. visionary | l. absorb |

### Answer key

1. d  2. b  3. f  4. g  5. h  6. a  7. i  8. e  9. j  10. c
11. f  12. g  13. e  14. a  15. k  16. i  17. h  18. l  19. b  20. c

# TAKE A BREAK  쉬•어•가•는 페•이•지

## 격언/속담

* A best friend is someone who loves you when you forget to love yourself.
최고의 친구는 당신이 자신에 대한 사랑을 잊고 있을 때, 당신을 사랑해 주는 사람이다.

* A burden of one's own choice is not felt.
스스로가 선택한 짐은 무겁게 느껴지지 않는다.

* Be content with your lot; one can not be first in everything.
어느 누구도 이 세상에서 최고의 존재가 된다는 것은 불가능하다.
그렇기 때문에 사람은 어느 정도 운명에 대한 체념이 있어야 하는 것이다.

* Be wise, soar not too high to fall, but stoop to rise.
현명하라. 너무 높게 솟아올라서 떨어지기보다는, 솟아나기 위하여 굽히고 있으라.

* Do what you can with what you have and where you are.
그대가 서 있는 곳에서 그대가 가진 것으로 그대가 할 수 있는 최선의 일을 하라.

* Do not pray for easy lives. Pray to be stronger men.
편한 삶을 살 수 있기를 기도해서는 안 된다. 강한 사람이 되도록 기도해야 한다.

* Do not sorrow about making a mistake that you cannot change.
바꿀 수 없는 실수를 한 것에 대해 슬퍼하지 말라.

* Freedom is the will to be responsible to ourselves.
자유란 자신을 책임지는 의지이다.

* Passion is like genius; a miracle.
정열은 천재와 같다. 정열에 의해 기적이 생기기 때문이다.

* The man who makes no mistakes does not usually make anything.
어떠한 실수도 하지 않는 사람은 대개 아무 일도 하지 않는다.

www.goHackers.com

해커스 어학연구소

# SUPER VOCA
## FOURTH DAY

중요한 것은 출발선이 아니라 도달 지점이다.

# 4th DAY

## abstemious
[æbstíːmiəs]

**adj.** characterized by restraint in indulgences such as food and drink | 절제하는, 음식이나 술 등의 탐닉을 억제하는

The aspiring athlete was *abstemious* because of her desire to lose weight.

**CN** abstemious : indulge [indʎ́ldʒ]
abstemious한 사람은 indulge(탐닉하다)하지 않는다.

## abstract
adj. [æbstrǽkt]
n. [ǽbstrækt]

**adj.** relating to that which is not concrete; expressing a quality apart from an object | 추상적인, 관념적인

**n.** a statement summarizing the important points of a text | 요약, 개요

Philosophy studies the world of *abstract* objects while biology that of the real.
The editor demanded that the author write an *abstract* for the new textbook.

**CH** abstract : condensed [kəndénst]
abstract(개요)는 condensed(요약한, 간결한)한 특징을 가지고 있다.

## aesthete
[ésθiːt]

**n.** one having sensitivity to beauty, mostly in art | 심미가

The *aesthete's* entire home was devoted to the collection and display of scenic paintings.

**대상** aesthete : art [ɑːrt]
aesthete는 art(예술)에 관해 뛰어난 감각이 있는 사람이다.

## assuage
[əswéidʒ]

**v.** to calm; to ease pain, grief, or burden | 달래다, 고통이나 슬픔을 누그러뜨리다

My fears were *assuaged* by the presence of my best friend.

**대상** assuage : sorrow [sɑ́rou]
assuage는 sorrow(슬픔)를 달래다는 의미이다.

---

### TRANSLATION | 예문 해석

| | |
|---|---|
| **abstemious** | 그 야심 있는 운동선수는 체중을 줄이려는 마음에 음식을 절제했다. |
| **abstract** | 철학은 추상의 세계를 연구하는 반면에, 생물학은 실제 세계를 연구한다. |
| | 그 편집자는 그 작가에게 새 교과서를 위해 개요를 쓸 것을 요구했다. |
| **aesthete** | 그 심미가의 집 전체가 풍경화 수집과 전시용으로 사용되었다. |
| **assuage** | 내가 느낀 두려움은 가장 친한 친구의 존재 덕분에 진정되었다. |

## austere
[ɔːstíər]

**adj. cold and grave in appearance or manner; morally self-disciplined; having no adornment** | 엄한, 금욕적인, 꾸미지 않은

The dean appeared at the banquet with an *austere* demeanor.

The poor woman's apartment was *austere* and empty, reflecting her cold and uninviting personality.

- **SYN** austere : Spartan [spáːrtn]
  Spartan: 엄격한
- **CN** austere : decorate [dékərèit]
  austere는 decorate(꾸미다)하지 않은 상태를 의미한다.

## barefaced
[bɛ́ərfèist]

**adj. open and shameless** | 노골적인, 파렴치한

Hogan couldn't believe that his brother told a *barefaced* lie to his parents.

- **ANT** barefaced : surreptitious [sə̀rəptíʃəs]
  surreptitious: 은밀한

## bathetic
[bəθétik]

**adj. marked by banality and triviality; insincerely emotional** | 진부한, (거짓)감상적인

The *bathetic* course of his life frustrated Tom because he had dreamed of great things in his youth.

- **ANT** bathetic : offbeat [ɔːfbíːt]
  offbeat: 별난, 엉뚱한

## castigate
[kǽstəgèit]

**v. to rebuke or subject to severe criticism** | 징계하다, 혹평하다

The traveler was *castigated* harshly by the immigration officer for overstaying his visa.

- **DE** castigation : admonishment [ædmániʃmənt]
  castigation(징계)은 admonishment(훈계, 충고)에 비해 그 정도가 강하다.

---

### TRANSLATION | 예문 해석

**austere**
그 학장은 엄숙한 태도로 연회에 나타났다.
그 가난한 여성의 아파트는 단순하고 텅 비어 있었는데, 그것은 그녀의 쌀쌀맞고 호감가지 않는 성격을 반영한다.

**barefaced** Hogan은 그의 형이 부모님께 파렴치한 거짓말을 했다는 것을 믿을 수 없었다.

**bathetic** Tom은 어렸을 때 원대한 꿈을 가졌었기 때문에 그의 진부한 삶의 과정은 그를 좌절시켰다.

**castigate** 그 여행자는 비자기간이 만료된 상태로 체류한 것에 대해 이민국 직원으로부터 심한 징계를 받았다.

## cistern
[sístərn]

**n. a reservoir used to store water** | 물탱크

A *cistern* was added to the village during war time as a precaution.

**FUN** cistern : liquids [líkwidz]
cistern은 liquids(액체)를 저장하는 곳이다.

## crutch
[krʌtʃ]

**n. a support put under the arm and used to assist people to walk** | 목발

The football player was given *crutches* to use while his sprained foot was healing.

**FUN** crutch : walk [wɔːk]
crutch는 walk(걷다)하는 데 사용된다.

## crux
[krʌks]

**n. the essential point or main feature** | 핵심

The *crux* of the negotiations dealt with the equitable distribution of the corporation's stock.

**SYN** crux : gist [dʒist]
gist: 요점, 근본

## dissolute
[dísəlùːt]

**adj. lacking restraint in the indulgence of vices** | 무절제한, 방탕한

The hedonistic and *dissolute* man's vices included drinking and gambling.

**CH** dissolute : libertine [líbərtìːn]
libertine(방탕자)은 dissolute한 사람을 일컫는다.

## dissolve
[dizálv]

**v. to disappear or disperse; to liquefy** | 사라지다, 해체하다, 용해하다

The cold tablets *dissolve* in hot water or cold water.

**FUN** dissolve : solvent [sálvənt]
solvent(용제, 용매)는 물질을 dissolve시키는 데 사용된다.

**CN** dissolve : insoluble [insáljubl]
insoluble(비용해성의)한 물질은 dissolve되지 않는다.

---

**TRANSLATION | 예문해석**

| | |
|---|---|
| cistern | 물탱크 하나가 예방조치의 하나로 전시동안 그 마을에 추가되었다. |
| crutch | 그 축구 선수는 그의 삔 발이 치유되는 동안 사용할 목발을 받았다. |
| crux | 그 협상의 핵심은 그 기업의 주식을 공평하게 분배하는 것에 관한 것이었다. |
| dissolute | 쾌락주의자이고 무절제한 그 남자는 술 마시고 도박하는 등의 방탕한 생활을 했다. |
| dissolve | 그 감기 알약은 뜨거운 물이나 찬물에서 녹는다. |

## dissuade
[diswéid]

**v. to persuade someone against something** | 못하게 설득하다, 말리다

I tried hard to *dissuade* my friend from quitting his job.

> **CH** dissuade : remonstrator [rimánstreitər]
> remonstrator(항의자, 충고자)는 다른 사람을 dissuade하려고 한다.

## distort
[distɔ́:rt]

**v. to twist out of true meaning or shape** | 뒤틀다, 사실을 왜곡하다

Some people will *distort* the truth to get what they want.

> **CH** distortion : caricature [kǽrikətʃər]
> distortion(왜곡)은 caricature(풍자만화)의 특성이라고 할 수 있다.

## distract
[distrǽkt]

**v. to divert or turn one's attention away** | (마음, 주의 등) 다른 데로 돌리다, 산만하게 하다

The loud music was *distracting* me from my studies.

> **CN** distract : rapt [ræpt]
> rapt(몰두한, 열중해 있는)한 사람을 distract하기는 어렵다.

## dour
[duər]

**adj. gloomy or unhappy; stern or obstinate** | 우울한, 엄하고 완고한

It would be very nice if that *dour* man would smile for once.

> **WO** dour : geniality [dʒì:niǽləti]
> dour한 사람은 geniality(친절함, 온화함)를 지니고 있지 않다.

## excursive
[ikskə́:rsiv]

**adj. tending to digress** | 벗어나는 경향이 있는, 산만한

The professor's *excursive* lecture lacked focus and confused the students.

> **CH** excursive : digress [daigrés]
> excursive한 것은 digress(주제에서 벗어나다)하는 속성을 지닌다.

---

| TRANSLATION | 예문해석 |
|---|---|
| dissuade | 나는 친구가 직장을 그만두지 않도록 설득하려고 열심히 노력했다. |
| distort | 어떤 사람들은 자신이 원하는 것을 얻기 위해 진실을 왜곡한다. |
| distract | 그 시끄러운 음악 때문에 나는 공부에 집중할 수 없었다. |
| dour | 그 엄한 남자가 한 번이라도 미소를 짓는다면 매우 멋질 텐데. |
| excursive | 그 교수의 산만한 강의는 핵심이 없었고 학생들을 혼란시켰다. |

www.goHackers.com

## exempt
[igzémpt]

**v. to free or release from obligation or duty** | 의무로부터 면제하다

Due to diplomatic immunity, Luke was *exempted* from all the criminal charges filed against him.

> 대상  exempt : liability [làiəbíləti]
> liability(책임, 의무)로부터 exempt하다.

## fast
[fæst]

**v. to abstain from eating** | 금식하다
**adj. stuck or firmly fixed; rapidly moving** | 단단히 고정된, 빠른

The whole family *fasts* one day a month to cleanse their bodies.
The door is bolted *fast*.

> ANT  fast : eat [iːt]
> eat: 먹다

> ANT  fast : loosely attached [lúːsli ətǽtʃt]
> loosely attached: 느슨하게 붙어있는, 헐거운

## fastidious
[fæstídiəs]

**adj. extremely careful or concerned with details** | 까다로운, 꼼꼼한

Paul is so *fastidious* about cleanliness that he will do any dishes left in the sink for 10 minutes.

> DE  fastidious : careful [kɛ́ərfəl]
> 지나치게 careful(꼼꼼한)한 경우를 fastidious하다고 한다.

## fervor
[fə́ːrvər]

**n. the passion or intensity of feeling or expression** | 열정

The painter worked on his art piece with incredible *fervor*.

> CH  fervor : zealot [zélət]
> fervor가 대단히 많은 사람을 zealot(열정가)이라고 한다.

---

TRANSLATION | 예 문 해 석

| | |
|---|---|
| exempt | 외교상의 면책 때문에 Luke는 그에게 기소된 모든 범죄 혐의로부터 면제되었다. |
| fast | 모든 식구가 그들의 몸을 깨끗이 하기 위해 한 달에 한번 금식을 한다. |
| | 그 문은 볼트로 단단히 고정되어 있다. |
| fastidious | Paul은 너무 깔끔을 떨어 싱크대에 10분간 담겨 있는 접시들은 모두 설거지를 해버린다. |
| fervor | 그 화가는 놀라운 열정으로 그의 예술작품을 작업했다. |

## foster
[fɔ́:stər]

**v. to encourage and support in development or growth** | 발달이나 성장을 촉진하다, 육성하다

By reading to your children at an early age, you *foster* their educational development.

**ANT** foster : stifle [stáifl]

stifle: 억누르다

## glut
[glʌt]

**n. an excess** | 초과, 과다

**v. to overfill or overeat, especially regarding food** | 지나치게 먹다

There was a *glut* of spare parts that had to be stockpiled in the storage room.

Look at the girl! She is *glutting* with every sweet in sight!

**CH** glutton : overindulge [òuvərindʌ́ldʒ]

glutton(대식가)은 음식에 overindulge(지나치게 탐닉하다)한다.

## gourmet
[guərméi]

**n. a connoisseur of food and drink** | 미식가

The *gourmet* ordered a succulent five course meal and an expensive bottle of wine for his dinner guests.

**대상** gourmet : cuisine [kwizí:n]

gourmet는 cuisine(요리)에 대해 정통한 사람이다.

## hasten
[héisn]

**v. to act or move quickly; to accelerate** | 빠르게 하다, 가속하다

Already ten minutes late, Becky *hastened* to class.

**ANT** hasten : retard [ritá:rd]

retard: 속력을 늦추다

---

TRANSLATION | 예문해석

**foster** 아이들에게 어린 나이에 책을 읽어줌으로써, 당신은 아이들의 교육적인 발달을 촉진시킬 수 있다.
**glut** 창고에는 초과된 예비 부품이 쌓여 있었다.
저 여자 애를 봐! 눈에 띄는 모든 달콤한 것들을 먹어치우고 있어.
**gourmet** 그 미식가는 자신의 저녁 손님을 위해 맛있는 5코스 식사와 값비싼 와인 한 병을 주문했다.
**hasten** 이미 십분이 늦어서, Becky는 서둘러 수업을 받으러 갔다.

## histrionic
[hìstriánik]

**adj. dramatic or excessively emotional** | 연극조의, 극도로 감정적인

Stan's *histrionic* reaction to the announcement made everyone laugh.

> **CH** histrionic : actor [ǽktər]
> actor(배우)는 histrionic하게 행동한다.

## inure
[injúər]

**v. to make used to tolerating something undesirable** | 안 좋은 것에 익숙하게 하다, 단련시키다

The captain forced the new recruits to run three miles daily *inuring* them to the strict physical regime of military life.

> **인과** inured : tolerance [tálərəns]
> 어떠한 것에 inured(익숙해진, 단련된)해지면 tolerance(참을성, 내성)를 갖게 된다.

## instigate
[ínstəgèit]

**v. to incite or provoke** | 자극하다, 선동하다

The school board *instigated* a protest advocating equal rights for students of color.

> **ANT** instigate : quell [kwel]
> quell: 억누르다, 진압하다

## instill
[instíl]

**v. to infuse slowly; to give gradually by example or teaching** | 서서히 주입시키다, 조금씩 가르치다

Traveling *instills* an appreciation and tolerance for other cultures.

> **SYN** instill : implant [implǽnt]
> implant: 주입하다, 불어넣다

## instruct
[instrʌ́kt]

**v. to teach or direct** | 가르치다, 지시하다

The chef *instructed* his class on how to make a cheese cake.

> **PUR** instruction : apothegm [ǽpəθèm]
> apothegm(격언)은 instruction(가르침)을 위한 것이다.

---

### TRANSLATION | 예 문 해 석

| | |
|---|---|
| histrionic | 그 공지에 대한 Stan의 연극조의 반응은 모든 사람들을 웃게 만들었다. |
| inure | 그 지휘관은 신병들에게 그들이 군대 생활의 엄격한 신체적 규칙에 익숙하게 되도록 매일 3마일을 달리라고 강요했다. |
| instigate | 그 학교 위원회는 유색인종 학생들에 대한 평등권을 주창하는 항의를 선동했다. |
| instill | 여행은 다른 문화에 대한 이해와 관용을 가르쳐준다. |
| instruct | 그 주방장이 치즈 케익 만드는 법을 반 아이들에게 가르쳤다. |

## invective
[invéktiv]

**n.** insulting or abusive language or speech | 비난, 독설
**adj.** marked by abusive language | 독설의, 비난의

The angry woman yelled *invectives* at her son, but immediately regretted it.
In court, the separated couple shouted *invective* remarks to each other from across the room.

**ANT** invective : accolade [ǽkəlèid]
accolade: 칭찬

## investigate
[invéstəgèit]

**v.** to observe or examine closely and systematically | 조사하다

It is the detective's job to *investigate* crimes.

**SYN** investigate : probe [proub]
probe: 조사하다

## inveterate
[invétərət]

**adj.** habitual or firmly established | 습관적인, 뿌리깊은

The German tendency to close doors at all times is an *inveterate* character of the culture.

**ANT** inveterate : casual [kǽʒuəl]
casual: 일시적인, 임시의

## jest
[dʒest]

**n.** a joke or humorous remark; a gay and playful mood or manner | 농담, 상난

Larry's *jests* often offended those around him though it was never intended.

**ANT** jest : solemn utterance [sάləm ʌ́tərəns]
solemn utterance: 진지한 말

## jovial
[dʒóuviəl]

**adj.** good humored and cheerful | 즐거운, 쾌활한

John was attracted to her *jovial* nature.

**ANT** jovial : morose [məróus]
morose: 시무룩한, 침울한

---

**TRANSLATION | 예문 해석**

**invective** 그 화가 난 여인은 자신의 아들에게 욕설을 퍼부었지만 이내 그것을 후회했다.
법정에서 그 별거 중인 부부는 반대편에서 서로에게 비난하는 말을 해댔다.
**investigate** 범죄를 조사하는 것은 형사의 일이다.
**inveterate** 항상 문을 닫는 독일인의 경향은 그 문화의 뿌리깊은 특성이다.
**jest** Larry의 농담은 의도한 것은 아니었다 하더라도 주위 사람들을 불쾌하게 하곤 했다.
**jovial** John은 그녀의 쾌활한 성격에 매력을 느꼈다.

## listless
[lístlis]

**adj. lacking interest or energy** | 무관심한, 생기없는

Anne usually comes home from work tired and *listless*.

**ANT** listlessness : verve [vəːrv]

listlessness: 생기 없음

verve: 열정, 활기

## massive
[mǽsiv]

**adj. bulky or heavy; serious** | 부피가 큰, 육중한; 심각한

Grandfather died after a *massive* heart attack.

**ANT** massive : trivial [tríviəl]

trivial: 사소한

## maven
[méivən]

**n. an expert** | 전문가

The government called him in because he is a negotiation *maven*.

**CH** maven : experience [ikspíəriəns]

maven은 특정 방면에 대한 experience(경험)를 많이 가지고 있다.

## maverick
[mǽvərik]

**n. an independent person who resists adherence to a group; a dissenter** | 독불장군, 비동조자

William had earned the reputation of *maverick* because he never did what was expected and always did things on his own.

**ANT** maverick : follower [fάlouər]

follower: 신봉자, 추종자

## obstinate
[άbstənət]

**adj. stubbornly adhering to an opinion or purpose** | 완고한

Grandma is *obstinate* about not getting on planes because of her great fear of flying.

**DE** obstinate : firm [fəːrm]

firm(확고한, 결연한)한 태도가 지나치면 obstinate하게 된다.

---

### TRANSLATION | 예문 해석

| | |
|---|---|
| listless | Anne은 보통 지치고 생기 없는 채로 직장에서 집에 돌아온다. |
| massive | 할아버지는 심각한 심장 마비가 온 후에 돌아가셨다. |
| maven | 정부는 그가 협상 전문가이기 때문에 그를 불러들였다. |
| maverick | William은 규정대로 하지 않고, 제멋대로 행동하기 때문에 독불장군으로 평판이 나 있었다. |
| obstinate | 할머니는 나는 것에 대한 두려움 때문에 비행기를 타지 않겠다는 것에 있어서 완고하다. |

## obstruct
[əbstrʌ́kt]

**v. to block with obstacles; to impede or hinder** | 막다, 방해하다

The enforcement of the ruling was *obstructed* by a large group of protesters.

- 대상 obstruct : progress [prάgrəs]
  progress(진행)를 obstruct하다.

## obviate
[ɑ́bvièit]

**v. to do away with; to anticipate; to make unnecessary** | 제거하다, 미리 막다

Fail-safe precautions built into the design of nuclear reactors do not *obviate* the need for vigilance against accidents and catastrophe.

- PUR obviate : unnecessary [ʌnnésəsèri]
  어떤 행위를 unnecessary(무용의, 쓸데없는)한 것으로 만들기 위해 obviate한다.

## pastiche
[pæstíːʃ]

**n. a work of art that imitates the style of some previous work** | 모방작품

Modern Greek architecture is a *pastiche* of Turkish, Venetian, and Western architecture.

- ANT pastiche : original work [ərídʒənl wəːrk]
  original work: 원작

## pantechnicon
[pæntéknikàn]

**n. a van used for moving furniture** | 가구 운반차

The Watsons had to order two *pantechnicons* to move all the furniture to their new house.

- FUN pantechnicon : furniture [fə́ːrnitʃər]
  pantechnicon은 furniture(가구)를 운반하는 용도의 차이다.

## paroxysm
[pǽrəksìzm]

**n. a sudden outburst or attack of emotion; convulsion** | 갑작스러운 감정의 폭발, 발작

The patient took a turn for the better after his *paroxysm* of laughing at the antics of Dr. Adams.

- CH paroxysm : sudden [sʌ́dn]
  paroxysm은 sudden(갑자기 일어난)의 특성이 있다.

---

### TRANSLATION | 예문 해석

| | |
|---|---|
| **obstruct** | 대규모 항의자 집단에 의해 그 판정의 집행이 저지되었다. |
| **obviate** | 핵원자로 설계에 포함된 이중 안전 장치가 사고와 재앙에 대한 경계의 필요성을 없애는 것은 아니다. |
| **pastiche** | 현대 그리스 건축은 터키, 베니스, 서양 건축의 모방 작품이다. |
| **pantechnicon** | Watson 일가는 모든 가구들을 새 집으로 옮기기 위해서 2대의 가구 운반차를 불러야 했다. |
| **paroxysm** | 그 환자는 Dr. Adams의 익살에 폭소를 터뜨리고 나서 상태가 더 좋아지는 것 같았다. |

## parrot
[pǽrət]

**v. to mindlessly repeat or imitate words or actions of another** | 생각 없이 되풀이하거나 다른 사람의 말이나 행동을 흉내내다

**n. a tropical bird with a curved beak and vividly colored feathers** | 앵무새

Children often *parrot* the adults around them as the most efficient way to learn language or other new skills.

A *parrot*'s plumage and verbal potential make it a target of tropical poachers.

**WO** parrot : originality [ərìdʒənǽləti]

parrot은 originality(독창성)없이 남을 흉내내다 라는 의미이다.

## restive
[réstiv]

**adj. fidgety or agitated; unable to rest** | 안절부절 못하는, 흥분한

The children were *restive* and grouchy from riding in the back of the car for 5 hours.

**WO** restive : calmness [kɑ́ːmnis]

restive한 것에는 calmness(평온, 침착)가 없다.

## restrain
[ristréin]

**v. to hold back or control; to prevent from doing something** | 억제하다, 제지하다

John had to *restrain* himself from killing the man who had kidnapped his son.

**CN** restrain : irrepressible [ìriprésəbl]

irrepressible(억제할 수 없는)은 restrain할 수 없다는 의미이다.

## revere
[rivíər]

**v. to admire fondly and show devoted honor to** | 경외하다

The teacher is *revered* highly by all her students.

**DE** revere : respect [rispékt]

revere는 respect(존경하다)보다 존경의 정도가 더 큰 것이다.

---

TRANSLATION | 예문해석

**parrot** 아이들은 종종 언어나 다른 기술을 배우는 가장 효과적인 방법으로 그들 주변의 성인들을 흉내낸다.
앵무새는 화려한 깃털과 언어적 잠재력 때문에 열대 밀렵꾼들의 표적이 된다.

**restive** 5시간 동안 차 뒷좌석에 타고 있던 아이들은 안절 부절 못하고 심술이 나 있었다.

**restrain** John은 자신의 아들을 유괴한 그 남자를 죽이고 싶은 충동을 억제해야만 했다.

**revere** 그 교사는 모든 학생들에게 매우 존경을 받는다.

## roster
[rástər]

**n. a list of names** | 명부, 등록부

The coach posted the *roster* of the starting players for the new season.

**FUN** roster : personnel [pə́ːrsənél]
roster에는 personnel(직원) 명단이 적혀있다.

## rustic
[rʌ́stik]

**adj. relating to the countryside or old buildings; rough or coarse** | 시골의, 조야한

In Wyoming there are *rustic* cabins for rent everywhere.

**ANT** rustic : polished [páliʃt]
polished: 세련된

## scurrilous
[skə́ːrələs]

**adj. using or containing vulgar or abusive language** | 상스러운

The student was suspended for using *scurrilous* language in class.

**WO** scurrilous : propriety [prəpráiəti]
scurrilous한 것에는 propriety(예의 바름, 교양)가 없다.

## sentinel
[séntənl]

**v. to guard or watch over** | 지키다, 파수보다
**n. one who keeps guard** | 파수꾼, 감시자

John was to *sentinel* the grounds and report anything out of the ordinary.
The *sentinels* decided to go to sleep when they realized they had been sent to guard a dog house.

**CH** sentinel : watchful [wátʃfəl]
sentinel은 watchful(경계하는, 주의 깊은)하다.

## spurious
[spjúəriəs]

**adj. marked by absence of authenticity or validity** | 가짜의, 위조의

The antique the traveler purchased turned out to be *spurious*.

**ANT** spurious : genuine [dʒénjuin]
genuine: 진짜의, 진품의

---

TRANSLATION | 예문해석

**roster** 그 감독은 새로운 시즌에서 뛸 선발선수 명단을 게시했다.
**rustic** Wyoming에는 여기저기에 빌릴 수 있는 조야한 오두막들이 널려 있다.
**scurrilous** 그 학생은 수업시간 중에 상스러운 언어를 사용해서 정학을 당했다.
**sentinel** John은 구내를 지키며 평범하지 않은 것들은 모두 보고해야 했다.
그 파수꾼들은 자신들이 개집을 지키기 위해 파견되었다는 사실을 깨닫고는 잠을 자기로 결심했다.
**spurious** 여행자가 구입한 그 골동품은 가짜로 밝혀졌다.

## spurn
[spəːrn]

**v.** **to reject or treat in a contemptible or scornful way**
| 일축하다, 퇴짜놓다, 경멸하다

The company *spurned* the proposal to merge with the weak competitor.

**ANT** spurn : embrace [imbréis]
embrace: 기꺼이 받아들이다

## systematic
[sìstəmǽtik]

**adj.** **based on a system; methodical or orderly in procedure or plan**
| 조직적인, 질서 잡힌

The school was run *systematically*.

**ANT** systematic : haphazard [hæphǽzərd]
haphazard: 되는대로의, 계획성 없는

## testimony
[téstəmóuni]

**n.** **a solemn declaration made under oath; evidence**
| 선서, 선언, 증언

The witness gave his *testimony* in tears.

**ANT** testimony : perjury [pə́ːrdʒəri]
perjury: 위증

## testy
[tésti]

**adj.** **irritable or easily angered**
| 성미 급한, 쉽게 화를 내는

In the mornings, Kelly is *testy* and sluggish.

**SYN** testy : irascible [irǽsəbl]
irascible: 성미 급한, 화를 잘 내는

## unsteady
[ʌnstédi]

**adj.** **changeable or unstable**
| 변하기 쉬운, 불안정한, 비틀거리는

The vase fell off the *unsteady* book shelf.

**CH** unsteady : dodder [dádər]
dodder(휘청거리다)에는 unsteady한 속성이 포함되어 있다.

---

### TRANSLATION | 예 문 해 석

| | |
|---|---|
| **spurn** | 그 회사는 약한 경쟁사와 합병하자는 제안을 쌀쌀 맞게 거절했다. |
| **systematic** | 그 학교는 조직적으로 운영되었다. |
| **testimony** | 그 목격자는 울면서 증언을 했다. |
| **testy** | 아침마다, Kelly는 쉽게 화를 내고 느릿느릿 행동한다. |
| **unsteady** | 그 화병은 그 불안정한 선반에서 떨어졌다. |

# 4th Day Daily Check-up

**Fill in the blanks with the correct letter that matches the word with its definition.**

1. cistern _____
2. fastidious _____
3. aesthete _____
4. histrionic _____
5. listless _____
6. invective _____
7. pastiche _____
8. obviate _____
9. instigate _____
10. foster _____

a. a reservoir used to store water
b. extremely careful or concerned with details
c. one having sensitivity to beauty, mostly in art
d. dramatic or excessively emotional
e. a work of art that imitates the style of some previous works
f. to do away with; to anticipate; to make unnecessary
g. to incite or provoke
h. lacking interest or energy
i. insulting or abusive language or speech
j. to encourage and support in development or growth

**Put the correct word in each blank from the list of words below.**

11. _____ 한 사람은 indulging(탐식하다)하지 않는다.
12. _____ 은 admonishment에 비해 그 정도가 강하다.
13. casual(일시적인)의 반의어는 _____ 이다.
14. _____ 는 respect보다 존경의 정도가 더 큰 것이다.
15. _____ 한 것에는 calmness가 없다.
16. gist(요점)의 동의어는 _____ 이다.
17. _____ 은 음식에 overindulge하는 사람이다.
18. _____ 가 대단히 많은 사람을 zealot이라고 한다.
19. _____ 한 사람은 geniality를 지니고 있지 않다.
20. insoluble한 물질은 _____ 되지 않는다.

| a. dour | b. dissolve | c. crutch | d. revere | e. roster | f. abstemious |
| g. castigation | h. restive | i. crux | j. inveterate | k. glutton | l. fervor |

**Answer key**

1. a  2. b  3. c  4. d  5. h  6. i  7. e  8. f  9. g  10. j
11. f  12. g  13. j  14. d  15. h  16. i  17. k  18. l  19. a  20. b

# SUPER VOCA

FIFTH DAY

우리 그냥 외우게 해주세요~! ㅜ.ㅜ

---

## advocate
v. [ǽdvəkèit]
n. [ǽdvəkət]

v. to speak, plead, or argue in favor of  | 옹호하다, 주장하다
n. a worker or supporter of a cause  | 옹호자

Cesar Chavez was the founder of the United Farm Workers and strongly *advocated* the reform of labor laws in America.

The president had to be an *advocate* of disarmament for his political stability.

**CH** advocate : exponent [ikspóunənt]

exponent(주창자, 옹호자)는 자신의 신념을 advocate한다.

## antagonize
[æntǽgənàiz]

v. to counteract or provoke the anger of; to offend  | 대항하다, 성나게 하다

Presidents usually try to avoid *antagonizing* senators with long recess appointments.

**ANT** antagonize : propitiate [prəpíʃièit]

propitiate: 달래다, 비위를 맞추다

## attenuate
[əténjuèit]

v. to make thin; to lessen the force, magnitude, or value of  | 가늘게 하다, 약하게 하다

A long-distance relationship will *attenuate* any love.

**대상** attenuate : thickness [θíknis]

attenuate는 어떤 것의 thickness(두꺼움, 굵음, 짙음)를 줄이다 라는 의미이다.

---

### TRANSLATION | 예문 해석

**advocate**  농민연합회의 창설자였던 Cesar Chavez는 미국 노동법의 개정을 강하게 주장했다.
대통령은 자신의 정치적 안정을 위해 군비 축소 옹호자가 되어야 했다.

**antagonize**  대통령들은 보통 긴 휴회 기간 동안 지명을 함으로써 상원 의원들을 화나게 하는 것을 피하려고 애쓴다.

**attenuate**  멀리 떨어져 지내면 어떤 사랑도 약하게 될 것이다.

## busybody
[bízibàdi]

**n.** an inquisitive person, often too interested in the lives of others | 참견 잘 하는 사람

Every society has its *busybodies* who spend half their life gossiping.

**CH** busybody : intrusive [intrú:siv]

busybody는 남의 일에 intrusive(참견하는)하는 사람이다.

## caprice
[kəprí:s]

**n.** a sudden change in feeling, action, or opinion | 변덕

Most people did not trust Tom because he was known for his many *caprices*.

**POS** caprice : whimsical [hwímzikəl]

whimsical: 변덕스러운

## catalyst
[kǽtəlist]

**n.** a substance that speeds up a chemical reaction; an agent that provokes change | 촉매, 촉진제

The bombing of Pearl Harbor was America's *catalyst* into World War II.

**KIN** catalyst : enzyme [énzaim]

enzyme(효소)은 catalyst의 일종이다.

## categorical
[kætəgɔ́:rikəl]

**adj.** having no exceptions or conditions; absolute or unequivocal | 무조건적인, 절대적인, 단정적인

Robert made a *categorical* denial of any wrongdoing in his statement to the press.

**ANT** categorical : qualified [kwɑ́ləfàid]

qualified: 조건부의, 제한된

---

TRANSLATION | 예 문 해 석

**busybody** 모든 사회에는 삶의 절반을 타인의 사적인 일에 대해 떠들며 보내는 참견을 잘하는 사람들이 있다.
**caprice** Tom은 변덕이 심하기로 유명했기 때문에 대부분의 사람들은 그를 신뢰하지 않았다.
**catalyst** 진주만 폭격은 미국을 2차 세계대전으로 이끈 촉매제였다.
**categorical** Robert는 언론에 낸 성명에서 모든 범죄에 대해서 단정적으로 부인했다.

## cavil
[kǽvəl]

**v. to raise trivial objections or criticisms** | 트집잡다

Bobby loves to *cavil* at his mother just to annoy her.

**CH** cavil : quibbler [kwíblər]
quibbler(트집쟁이)는 늘 cavil하려고만 한다.

## cavort
[kəvɔ́ːrt]

**v. to bound about in a sprightly manner; to have lively fun** | 뛰어다니다, 신나게 뛰놀다

The leprechauns *cavorted* around their pot of gold.

**CH** cavort : sprightly [spráitli]
cavort에는 sprightly(기운찬, 쾌활한)한 속성이 포함되어 있다.

## civilize
[sívəlàiz]

**v. to bring out of a primitive state; to refine or socialize** | 문명화하다, 세련되게 하다

Missionaries *civilized* the tribes of New Guinea, teaching many members how to read and write.

**ANT** civilize : barbarize [báːrbəràiz]
barbarize: 야만화하다, 조잡하게 하다

## cowardice
[káuərdis]

**n. lack of courage** | 비겁, 소심

Failing to stand up for his girlfriend exhibited *cowardice* on Ron's part.

**ANT** cowardice : pluck [plʌk]
pluck: 용기, 담력

## cryptic
[kríptik]

**adj. secret or with hidden meaning** | 비밀의, 숨은, 신비스러운

The *cryptic* message puzzled the CIA.

**CH** cryptic : cipher [sáifər]
cipher(암호)는 cryptic한 특성을 가지고 있다.

---

### TRANSLATION | 예문해석

| | |
|---|---|
| cavil | Bobby는 엄마를 짜증스럽게 하기 위해 엄마에게 트집잡는 것을 좋아한다. |
| cavort | 장난을 좋아하는 작은 요정들이 자신들의 금 항아리 주변에서 신나게 뛰어 놀았다. |
| civilize | 선교사들이 뉴기니아 종족들에게 읽고 쓰는 법을 가르쳐 문명화시켰다. |
| cowardice | Ron은 여자 친구를 방어하지 못함으로써 비겁함을 드러냈다. |
| cryptic | 그 비밀스런 메시지는 CIA를 당혹스럽게 했다. |

## desultory
[désəltɔ̀:ri]

**adj. lacking in plan or purpose; lacking rational sequence or connection** | 막연한, 산만한

Chuck's parents began to worry when he turned 35 and showed no signs of changing his *desultory* ways.

**WO** desultory : plan [plæn]

desultory한 것에서 plan(계획)을 찾아보기는 어렵다.

## detach
[ditǽtʃ]

**v. to separate or disengage** | 분리하다

Once he became a teenager, Jim gradually *detached* himself emotionally from his family.

**ANT** detach : tether [téðər]

tether: 잡아매다, 밧줄

## devout
[diváut]

**adj. religiously devoted; serious about a belief or cause** | 독실한, 진지한

The *devout* Christian went to church every Sunday.

**DE** devout : sanctimonious [sæ̀ŋktəmóuniəs]

sanctimonious(독실한 척하는)하는 것은 겉으로만 devout한 체 하는 것이다.

## dexterous
[dékstərəs]

**adj. skillful or clever; artful** | 솜씨 좋은, 교묘한

The *dexterous* pitch at the end of the game brought victory to the East Coast team.

**CH** dexterous : manipulate [mənípjulèit]

manipulate(교묘하게 다루다)하는 것에는 dexterous한 속성이 들어있다.

## ditch
[ditʃ]

**n. a long narrow hole dug in the earth, usually used for water drainage or containment** | 도랑

The car went into the *ditch* because it spun out of control.

**DE** ditch : canyon [kǽnjən]

ditch는 canyon(협곡)보다 좁고 얕은 도랑을 의미한다.

---

TRANSLATION | 예 문 해 석

**desultory**    Chuck의 부모는 그가 35세가 되었는데도 일관성 없는 생활방식을 바꾸려는 기색이 보이지 않는 것을 염려하기 시작했다.
**detach**    십대가 되자 곧 Jim은 점차 가족으로부터 감정적으로 자신을 분리했다.
**devout**    그 독실한 기독교인은 매주 일요일 교회에 갔다.
**dexterous**    그 경기 마지막의 솜씨 좋은 투구가 East Coast 팀에 승리를 가져왔다.
**ditch**    그 차는 통제불능의 상태로 회전했기 때문에 도랑에 빠졌다.

www.goHackers.com

**downpour**
[dáunpɔ̀ːr]

n. **a heavy rain** | 폭우

Just as we were walking out of the park, a *downpour* came and ruined our evening.

인과 downpour : flooding [flʌ́diŋ]
downpour의 결과 flooding(홍수)이 발생한다.

**doyen**
[dɔién]

n. **an experienced and senior member of a body or group** | 대가, 고참

The *doyen* of the company suggested that it make the deal with Intel.

CN doyen : uninitiated [ʌniníʃièitid]
doyen은 uninitiated(충분한 경험이 없는)하지 않다.

**drawl**
[drɔːl]

v. **to talk using lengthened vowel sounds** | 모음을 길게 늘여서 말하다
n. **a manner of speaking slowly** | 느린 말투

Erica *drawled* her speech when she first began to study English.
It is difficult to understand people who speak with a Southern *drawl*.

CH drawl : slow [slou]
drawl은 slow(느린)하다.

**envious**
[énviəs]

adj. **feeling or showing jealousy or envy** | 부러운

Jinny became increasingly *envious* of Trisha after hearing that her boyfriend had bought her a new coat.

DE envious : greedy [gríːdi]
greedy(탐욕스러운, 갈망하는)는 envious하는 것보다 그 갈망의 정도가 강하다.

---

TRANSLATION | 예문해석

**downpour** 우리가 공원을 나와서 막 걸어가는데, 폭우가 쏟아져서 우리의 저녁을 망쳐버렸다.
**doyen** 그 회사의 고참이 인텔과 거래할 것을 제안했다.
**drawl** Erica는 처음 영어를 배우기 시작했을때 말을 길게 늘여서 했다.
모음을 길게 늘여 남부식으로 발음하는 사람들의 말은 알아듣기가 힘들다.
**envious** Jinny는 Trisha의 남자 친구가 그녀에게 새 코트를 사줬다는 얘기를 듣고 난 후 그녀를 점점 더 부러워하게 되었다.

**esteem**
[istíːm]

v. to regard with respect or reverence; to consider | 존경하다; ~로 간주하다

n. the high regard in which a person is held | 존경

The president had met many great men during his career, but he *esteemed* his father above them all.

Colin Powell is a man who has earned the *esteem* of the American people.

DE  esteem : idolize [áidəlàiz]
esteem하는 것의 정도가 지나치면 idolize(우상화하다)하게 된다.

**extant**
[ékstənt]

adj. currently or still existing | 현존하는

The largest *extant* reptile found in Asia is the Komodo dragon.

ANT  extant : extinct [ikstíŋkt]
extinct: 멸종한, 사멸한

**favorable**
[féivərəbl]

adj. expressing or facilitating approval or favor; advantageous | 호의적인, 찬성하는, 유리한

The weather on our trip was *favorable* to our outdoor plans.

ANT  unfavorable : propitious [prəpíʃəs]
unfavorable: 형편이 나쁜, 불리한
propitious: 순조로운, 좋은

**fawn**
[fɔːn]

v. to seek favor by groveling or flattery | 아첨하다

The nobles *fawned* over the King as they asked for more titles and land grants.

WO  fawning : hauteur [houtə́ːr]
fawning(아첨하는)한 사람들은 hauteur(거만, 오만)한 태도를 취하지 않는다.

---

TRANSLATION | 예 문 해 석

**esteem**  그 대통령은 자신의 생애에서 위대한 사람들을 많이 만났지만, 그 누구보다도 자신의 아버지를 존경했다.
Colin Powell은 미국인들의 존경을 받는 인물이다.

**extant**  아시아에서 발견된 현존하는 가장 큰 파충류는 코모도 왕도마뱀이다.

**favorable**  여행 중 날씨는 우리의 야외 활동 계획에 알맞았다.

**fawn**  그 귀족들은 보다 많은 직위와 토지를 요청하며 왕에게 아첨을 했다.

## faze
[feiz]

**v. to disturb or disconcert** | 마음을 혼란시키다, 당황하게 하다

The accident didn't *faze* him a bit for some reason.

**ANT** fazed : undisturbed [ʌ̀ndistə́ːrbd]

fazed: 혼란스러운
undisturbed: 마음이 편안한

## indict
[indáit]

**v. to formally accuse of a crime** | 범죄를 정식으로 기소하다

People continued to treat Mr. Johnson with suspicion though he was never *indicted* for the murder.

**대상** indict : accused [əkjúːzd]

accused(피의자)를 indict하다.

## insubordinate
[ìnsəbɔ́ːrdənit]

**adj. disobedient; refusing to adhere to authority** | 불복종하는, 반항하는

The officer announced that he would not tolerate *insubordinate* behavior.

**ANT** insubordinate : submissive [səbmísiv]

submissive: 복종적인

## intangible
[intǽndʒəbl]

**adj. not tangible; incapable of being defined or realized** | 감지할 수 없는, 실체가 없는, 파악할 수 없는

The *intangible* aura of the old man made me weak in his presence.

**CN** intangible : perceive [pərsíːv]

intangible한 것은 perceive(감지하다, 이해하다)할 수 없다.

## integral
[íntigrəl]

**adj. consisting of essential parts; entire** | 필수적인, 완전한

Happiness is an *integral* ingredient for a long life.

**ANT** integral : peripheral [pərífərəl]

peripheral: 주변적인, 중요하지 않은

---

### TRANSLATION | 예문해석

**faze** 그 사고는 어떤 이유에서인지 그를 조금도 당황하게 하지 않았다.
**indict** Mr. Johnson은 살인으로 정식 기소된 적이 전혀 없었지만 사람들은 계속해서 의심을 품고 그를 대했다.
**insubordinate** 그 장교는 어떤 불복종 행위도 그냥 넘기지 않겠다고 공표했다.
**intangible** 그 나이든 사람에게서 오는 파악할 수 없는 분위기가 그의 앞에서 나를 약하게 만들었다.
**integral** 행복은 장수를 위해 필수적이다.

## intensify
[inténsəfài]

**v.** to strengthen or increase in density or intenseness | 강하게 하다, 격렬해지다

The noise of the crowd *intensified* as the final minutes of the game wore down.

> **ANT** intensify : wane [wein]
> wane: 약해지다, 감소하다

## intent
[intént]

**n.** the purpose or plan | 의도

It was my *intent* to exercise every night, but I didn't do it.

> **ANT** intentional : accidental [æ̀ksidéntl]
> intentional: 의도적인
> accidental: 우연한

## invigorate
[invígərèit]

**v.** to stimulate or give energy to | 고무하다, 기운 나게 하다

A cold shower in the morning *invigorates* me during the hot summer months.

> **FUN** invigorate : tonic [tánik]
> tonic(강장제)은 invigorate하는 기능을 가지고 있다.

## inviolable
[inváiələbl]

**adj.** secure from profanation, assault, or violation | (신성하여) 침범할 수 없는, 불가침의

Christians regard the Bible as an *inviolable* source for inspiration and wisdom.

> **CN** inviolable : profane [prouféin]
> inviolable하다는 것은 profane(모독하다, 신성을 더럽히다)할 수 없다는 의미이다.

---

### TRANSLATION | 예 문 해 석

| | |
|---|---|
| intensify | 그 경기의 마지막 순간들이 가까워 옴에 따라 군중이 점점 더 시끄러워졌다. |
| intent | 매일 밤 운동하는 것이 나의 의도였지만, 나는 그렇게 하지 않았다. |
| invigorate | 아침에 하는 차가운 샤워는 무더운 여름철 동안 기운이 나게 한다. |
| inviolable | 기독교인들은 성경을 성령의 감화와 지혜를 주는 신성 불가침의 출처로 여긴다. |

## invulnerable
[invʌ́lnərəbl]

**adj.** **incapable of being wounded or conquered**
| 손상되지 않는, 처부술 수 없는

The *invulnerable* Superman flew through the burning fire to save the family.

**CN** invulnerable : injure [índʒər]

invulnerable한 것은 injure(손상시키다)하기 어렵다.

## latent
[léitnt]

**adj.** **present but not currently active; dormant**
| 존재는 하나 활동하지 않은, 잠재된

Lyme Disease can stay *latent* in a body for years before it affects one's health.

**ANT** latent : manifest [mǽnəfèst]

manifest: 분명히 나타난, 상품의 적하 목록

## lavish
[lǽviʃ]

**adj.** **generous in using or spending; extravagant**
| 후한, 사치스런

The *lavish* wedding was held at a posh mansion and adorned with ice sculptures.

**ANT** lavish : penurious [pənjúəriəs]

penurious: 인색한, 빈곤한

## lax
[læks]

**adj.** **careless or slacking; negligent to details**
| 부주의한, 느슨한, 해이한

Toward the end of a semester, students tend to become *lax* with their studies.

**SYN** lax : loose [luːs]

loose: 해이한, 느슨한

---

### TRANSLATION | 예 문 해 석

**invulnerable** 무적의 수퍼맨은 그 가족을 구하기 위해 불을 통과해 날아갔다.
**latent** Lyme Disease는 건강에 영향을 미치기 전에 수 년간 인체에 잠복해 있을 수 있다.
**lavish** 그 사치스런 결혼식은 대호화 저택에서 열렸고 얼음 조각들로 장식되었다.
**lax** 학기가 끝날 때쯤, 학생들은 공부에 해이해지는 경향이 있다.

## lethal
[líːθəl]

**adj.** devastatingly harmful to the point of causing death | 죽일 정도로 해로운, 치명적인

Juliet woke up a moment after Romeo had drunk the *lethal* poison.

**DE** lethal : harmful [háːrmfəl]

lethal은 죽음에 이를 만큼 극도로 harmful(유해한)하다는 의미이다.

## loyalty
[lɔ́iəlti]

**n.** faithfulness or allegiance | 충성, 충실

His *loyalty* makes him a good solider.

**WO** loyalty : perfidious [pərfídiəs]

쉽게 남을 perfidious(배반하는)하는 사람에게는 loyalty가 없다.

## luxuriant
[lʌgʒúəriənt]

**adj.** abundant or rich; marked by luxury | 풍부한, 사치스러운

My family took a *luxuriant* vacation to the tropics.

**ANT** luxuriant : Spartan [spáːrtn]

Spartan: 간소한, 엄격한

## meteoric
[miːtiɔ́ːrik]

**adj.** of or relating to meteors; relating to the speed of meteors | 유성의, 유성처럼 순식간에 일어나는

For her role in the movie *Basic Instinct*, Sharon Stone experienced a *meteoric* rise to fame.

**WO** meteoric : constancy [kánstənsi]

meteoric한 것에는 constancy(불변, 항구성)가 없다.

---

### TRANSLATION | 예문해석

**lethal** Juliet은 Romeo가 그 치명적인 독약을 마신 직후에 깨어났다.
**loyalty** 그의 충성심은 그를 좋은 군인으로 만든다.
**luxuriant** 우리 가족은 열대지방으로 사치스러운 휴가를 떠났다.
**meteoric** "원초적 본능"이라는 영화로, Sharon Stone은 순식간에 명성을 얻게 되었다.

## patent
[pǽtnt]

**n.** the written rights given to an inventor by the government to exclusively make, use, or sell an invention for a set number of years | 특허

**adj.** obvious | 명백한

A *patent* was given to Alexander Graham Bell for the invention of the telephone.

Rick spends five hours each day in front of the computer and is a *patent* addict to computer games.

**ANT** patent : occult [əkʌ́lt]

occult: 숨겨진, 불가사의한

## potable
[póutəbl]

**adj.** drinkable | 마실 수 있는

Contrary to popular belief, the tap water in New York City is *potable* and of good quality.

**CH** potable : beverage [bévəridʒ]

beverage(음료)는 potable하다.

## potentate
[póutntèit]

**n.** ruler or one who holds great power | 권세가, 유력자

In a democracy, there is no true *potentate*, only popular icons called politicians.

**CH** potentate : power [páuər]

potentate는 power(힘, 권력)를 가진 사람이다.

## resurgence
[risə́ːrdʒəns]

**n.** the coming again into activity and prominence | 재기, 부활

After the wild tech stock speculations of the 1990's, there was a *resurgence* of investment in traditionally stable companies.

**ANT** resurgent : moribund [mɔ́(ː)rəbʌ̀nd]

resurgent: 소생하는, 부활하는
moribund: 죽어가는, 소멸해가는

---

### TRANSLATION | 예문해석

**patent**  전화기의 발명으로 Alexander Graham Bell에게 특허가 주어졌다.
Rick은 컴퓨터 앞에서 매일 5시간을 보내는 명백한 컴퓨터 게임 중독자이다.

**potable**  일반적인 믿음과 반대로, 뉴욕의 수돗물은 마실 수 있고 수질도 좋다.

**potentate**  민주주의에서, 진정한 지배자는 없고, 정치가로 불리는 대중적 우상들만이 있을 뿐이다.

**resurgence**  1990년대 기술주에 대한 투기가 있은 후 다시 전통적으로 안정적인 회사에 대한 투자를 하게 되었다.

## retain
[ritéin]

v. **to keep in possession; to maintain in a certain place, condition, or position** | 보유하다, 유지하다

Bob *retains* most of his income and stores it in savings accounts.

**ANT** retain : proffer [práfər]

proffer: 제공하다

## retaliate
[ritǽlièit]

v. **to repay an injury in kind; to return like for like** | 복수하다, 앙갚음을 하다

The French *retaliated* against the Spanish for invading Cotignac.

**ANT** retaliate : forgive [fərgív]

forgive: 용서하다

## retard
[ritáːrd]

v. **to slow up or delay** | 늦추다, 지체하게 하다

Caffeine is thought to *retard* growth in children.

**ANT** retard : hasten [héisn]

hasten: 빠르게 하다, 가속하다

## shackle
[ʃǽkl]

v. **to restrain or confine to prevent from action** | 어떤 행동을 하지 못하도록 속박하다, 감금하다

David felt *shackled* by his wife, children, job, and financial obligations.

**ANT** shackle : emancipate [imǽnsəpèit]

emancipate: 해방하다

## suture
[súːtʃər]

n. **the act of surgically closing a wound** | 상처를 닫기 위한 외과적 봉합

If the *sutures* left an unsightly scar, Kara's hopes to be a model would be lost.

**ANT** suture : incision [insíʒən]

incision: 절개

---

TRANSLATION | 예문 해석

| | |
|---|---|
| retain | Bob은 그의 수입 대부분을 쓰지 않고, 저축 통장에 보유하고 있다. |
| retaliate | 프랑스는 스페인이 Cotignac을 침략한 것에 대해 복수했다. |
| retard | 카페인은 어린이들에게 있어 성장을 지연하는 것으로 여겨진다. |
| shackle | David은 자신이 아내와, 아이들과, 일과 경제적인 의무들에 의해 속박당하고 있다고 느꼈다. |
| suture | 그 봉합으로 보기 흉한 흉터가 남았더라면 Kara는 모델이 되고자 했던 희망을 잃었을 것이다. |

## testimonial
[tèstəmóuniəl]

**n. something given as an expression of thanks or admiration** | 감사나 존경의 표시로 주는 물건이나 상장

The enormous statue of the mayor served as a *testimonial* to his great service to the city.

**PUR** testimonial : appreciation [əpriːʃiéiʃən]

appreciation(감사)하기 위해 testimonial을 준다.

## tinker
[tíŋkər]

**v. to fix experimentally or unskillfully** | 시험삼아 혹은 서투르게 고치다

Janet finally called the plumber after *tinkering* with the sink by herself for an hour.

**DE** tinker : adjust [ədʒʌ́st]

tinker는 adjust(조절하다)에 비해 서투른 솜씨로 물건을 다루다 라는 의미이다.

## tonic
[tánik]

**n. a medicine or agent that invigorates and refreshes** | 강장제
**adj. causing mental, physical, or emotional vigor** | (정신적·육체적·감정적) 활력을 일으키는

Balding men hope for a hair *tonic* that will re-grow lost hair.
Helen believed the secret to her youthful appearance was the daily *tonic* juice she drank.

**FUN** tonic : invigorate [invígərèit]

tonic(강장제)은 invigorate(고무하다, 기운나게 하다)하는 기능이 있다.

## unsuitable
[ʌnsúːtəbl]

**adj. not suitable or appropriate; not acceptable or wanted** | 부적당한, 받아들일 수 없는

The retinue found the hotel room to be entirely *unsuitable* for the movie star.

**ANT** unsuitable : meet [miːt]

meet: 적당한

---

### TRANSLATION | 예문해석

**testimonial** 엄청나게 큰 시장의 동상은 시에 대한 그의 기여에 대한 감사의 표시로서 주어졌다.
**tinker** Janet은 한 시간 동안 혼자 개수대를 서투르게 고쳐본 후에 결국 배관공을 불렀다.
**tonic** 머리가 벗겨지는 사람들은 머리카락을 다시 자라게 해 줄 양모제(養毛劑)를 간절히 바란다.
Helen은 그녀의 젊은 외모의 비결이 그녀가 매일 마셨던 강장 주스라고 믿었다.
**unsuitable** 수행단은 호텔 방이 그 영화 배우에게 너무 부적절하다는 것을 알았다.

## untenable
[ʌnténəbl]

**adj. unable to be defended** | 지킬 수 없는

The captain determined that their position on the field was *untenable*, so the soldiers moved back several miles.

**CN** untenable : defend [difénd]
untenable한 것은 defend(지키다, 막다)하지 못한다.

## usurp
[juːsə́ːrp]

**v. to seize in possession of rights, power, or role of another** | (권리·권력·역할 등을) 빼앗다

The commander in chief was *usurped* by the opposing general.

**대상** usurp : power [páuər]
power(권력) 등을 빼앗는 것을 usurp라고 한다.

## vital
[váitl]

**adj. essential to life; lively, full of energy or spirit** | 필수적인, 생기가 넘치는

Nutrients and clean water are *vital* to maintaining good health.

**WO** vitality : languish [lǽŋgwiʃ]
languish(생기가 없어지다)한다는 것은 vitality(활기, 정력)가 없다는 것과 같다.

## vivacious
[vivéiʃəs]

**adj. lively or sprightly** | 활발한

The boy had a *vivacious* and pleasant character.

**ANT** vivacious : lifeless [láiflis]
lifeless: 활기없는

## votary
[vóutəri]

**n. a committed follower of a religion or cult; an enthusiast or devoted admirer** | 신자, 신봉자, 숭배자

Bush's *votaries* waited three days outside the White House to see him in person.

**ANT** votary : skeptic [sképtik]
skeptic: 무신론자, 회의론자

---

### TRANSLATION | 예문 해석

**untenable** 그 지휘관은 전쟁터에서의 그들의 위치가 방어될 수 없다고 결론을 내렸고, 그래서 병사들이 몇 마일 퇴각했다.
**usurp** 그 적 장군은 최고사령관 직을 빼앗았다.
**vital** 영양소와 깨끗한 물은 건강을 유지하는 데 필수적이다.
**vivacious** 그 소년은 활발하고 유쾌한 성격을 가졌다.
**votary** Bush의 신봉자들이 그를 직접 보기 위해 백악관 밖에서 3일을 기다렸다.

# 5th Day Daily Check-up

■ Fill in the blanks with the correct letter that matches the word with its definition.

1. categorical _____
2. desultory _____
3. retain _____
4. vivacious _____
5. usurp _____
6. potentate _____
7. integral _____
8. extant _____
9. doyen _____
10. cavort _____

a. absolute or unequivocal
b. necessary or essential; consisting of essential parts
c. currently or still existing
d. lacking in plan or purpose; lacking rational sequence or connection
e. an experienced and senior member of a body or group
f. to keep in possession; to maintain in a certain place, condition, or position
g. lively or sprightly
h. to seize in possession of rights, property, or role of another
i. a ruler or one who holds great power
j. to bound about in a sprightly manner; to have lively fun

■ Put the correct word in each blank from the list of words below.

11. exponent는 자신의 신념을 _____한다.
12. pluck(용기, 담력)의 반의어는 _____이다.
13. _____의 반의어는 tether(잡아매다)이다.
14. tinker는 _____에 비해 서투른 솜씨로 물건을 다루다라는 의미이다.
15. drawl은 _____하다.
16. greedy는 _____하는 것보다 그 갈망의 정도가 강하다.
17. _____는 죽음에 이를 만큼 극도로 harmful하다는 의미이다.
18. sanctimonious하는 것은 겉으로만 _____한 체 하는 것다.
19. quibbler는 _____하려고만 한다.
20. _____ 는 남의 일에 intrusive 하는 사람이다.

| a. slow | b. adjust | c. detach | d. cowardice | e. advocate | f. envious |
| g. lethal | h. devout | i. cavil | j. drinkable | k. unsuitable | l. busybody |

**Answer key**

1. a  2. d  3. f  4. g  5. h  6. i  7. b  8. c  9. e  10. j
11. e  12. d  13. c  14. k  15. a  16. f  17. g  18. h  19. i  20. l

www.goHackers.com

해커스 어학연구소

# Super Voca

S . I . X . T . H . D . A . Y

너무 많다구?
지금 필요한 건 걱정이 아니라 실행이다.

---

**anthology**
[ǽnθáládʒi]

**n. a collection of selected literary or artistic pieces compiled into one work** | 명문집

This *anthology* is regarded as the first Korean literary work to be translated into Mongolian for publication.

**FUN** anthology : poem [póuəm]

anthology에는 엄선된 poem(시)들이 수록되어 있다.

---

**antipathy**
[æntípəθi]

**n. aversion or strong dislike** | 반감, 혐오

The president made clear his *antipathy* to the opposition by vetoing their legislation 3 times.

**ANT** antipathy : affinity [əfínəti]

affinity: 애호, 호감

---

**artless**
[ɑ́ːrtlis]

**adj. uncultured; made without skill; having or displaying no guile** | 세련되지 못한, 서투른, 꾸밈 없는

Blake enrolled in a poetry class to improve his reputation as a crass and *artless* football player.

Americans are thought to have an *artless* attitude about other peoples and cultures.

**ANT** artlessness : urbanity [əːrbǽnəti]

artlessness: 단순, 소박함

urbanity: 세련

**WO** artless : guile [gail]

artless한 사람에게는 guile(교활함)이 없다.

---

**TRANSLATION** | 예 문 해 석

**anthology** 이 명문집은 출판을 위해 몽골어로 번역되어진 첫번째 한국 문학 작품으로 간주된다.
**antipathy** 대통령은 3번이나 그들의 입법에 거부권을 행사함으로써 야당에 대한 반감을 드러냈다.
**artless** Blake는 우둔하고 세련되지 못한 미식축구 선수라는 평판에서 벗어나고자 시 수업에 등록했다.
미국인들은 다른 민족과 문화에 대해 꾸밈없는 태도를 갖는 것으로 여겨진다.

## authentic
[ɔːθéntik]

**adj. genuine or real** | 진짜의, 실제의

The painting was deemed to be *authentic* after much inspection and scrutiny.

**WO** authenticity : fabricate [fǽbrikèit]

fabricate(위조하다)하는 것에는 authenticity(신빙성, 진짜임)가 없다.

## authorize
[ɔ́ːθəràiz]

**v. to grant permission; to invest with legal authority** | 승인하다, 권한을 부여하다

John *authorized* his wife to have access to his bank accounts.

**ANT** authorize : interdict [ìntərdíkt]

interdict: 금지하다

## bequest
[bikwést]

**n. a gift left in a will** | 유증, 유산

Edward's educational trust fund was a *bequest* left to him by his rich uncle.

**대상** bequest : testator [tésteitər]

testator(유언자)는 bequest를 남긴다.

## catholic
[kǽθəlik]

**adj. broad in scope; universal** | 광범위한, 보편적인

Amy was a woman of *catholic* interests, ranging from bungee jumping to stamp collecting.

**ANT** catholic : narrow [nǽrou]

narrow: 편협한

## cement
[simént]

**v. to bind or bring together; to unite** | 함께 묶다, 다지다, 결합하다

The marriage of their children *cemented* the two families' friendship.

**ANT** cement : fracture [frǽktʃər]

fracture: 깨다

---

### TRANSLATION | 예문해석

| | |
|---|---|
| authentic | 그 그림은 많은 정밀한 조사와 검사를 거친 후에 진품으로 간주되었다. |
| authorize | John은 부인이 그의 은행 계좌를 이용할 수 있도록 허락했다. |
| bepuest | Edward의 교육 신탁자금은 그의 부자 숙부가 남긴 유산이었다. |
| catholic | Amy는 번지점프에서 우표수집에 이르기까지 광범위한 관심사를 가진 여자였다. |
| cement | 자식들의 결혼이 그 두 집안의 우정을 다졌다. |

## charade
[ʃəréid]

**n.** a pretense or mockery　　| 위장, 흉내내기, 조롱

Though they loathed each other, the couple managed the *charade* of a marriage for the sake of their children.

**POS** charade : dissimulate [disímjulèit]

dissimulate: ~인 체하다, 위장하다

## connive
[kənáiv]

**v.** to work together in a secret or illegal manner; to collude
| 비밀스럽게 혹은 불법적으로 함께 일하다, 공모하다

The bank robbers *connived* for 3 months to plan the perfect robbery.

**CH** conniver : conspiratorial [kənspìrətɔ́:riəl]

conniver(공모자, 묵인자)는 conspiratorial(음모의, 공모의)하는 사람이다.

## deter
[ditə́:r]

**v.** to inhibit or prevent from acting by means of fear or doubt　　| 겁주어 못하게 하다, 저지하다

D.A.R.E. is a drug prevention program aimed to *deter* children from taking drugs.

**CN** deter : intrepid [intrépid]

intrepid(두려움을 모르는)한 사람을 deter하기는 어렵다.

## determination
[ditə̀:rmənéiʃən]

**n.** the conclusion or the act of deciding definitely; strong will or resoluteness　　| 결정, 강한 결심

Her *determination* is what got Sally to the top of the corporate ladder.

**ANT** determination : irresolution [irèzəlú:ʃən]

irresolution: 우유부단함

---

TRANSLATION | 예 문 해 석

**charade** 그 부부는 서로 증오했지만 자식들을 위해 결혼 아닌 결혼 생활을 해 왔다.
**connive** 은행 강도들은 완벽한 강탈을 계획하면서 3개월 동안을 공모했다.
**deter** D.A.R.E.는 아이들이 마약을 사용하지 못하게 하는 것을 목표로 하는 마약 퇴치 프로그램이다.
**determination** Sally를 그 회사의 최고 자리에 오르게 한 것은 그녀의 결단력이다.

## detour
[díːtuər]

n. a deviation from the normal route or direct course; a path or road replacing a temporarily disabled one  | 우회, 우회로

v. to go or cause to go by a roundabout way  | 우회하다, 우회하게 하다

The cab driver took a *detour* down the alley in order to avoid traffic.
We had to *detour* through Minnesota because the highway was under construction.

**대상** detour : route [ruːt]

route(길, 경로)에서 detour하다.

## encumber
[inkʌ́mbər]

v. to obstruct or impede  | 가로막다, 방해하다

Drinking in moderation is fine, but it becomes a problem when it *encumbers* one's ability to make decisions.

**ANT** encumber : remove impediment [rimúːv impédəmənt]

remove impediment: 방해물을 제거하다.

## enthusiasm
[inθúːziæzm]

n. intense interest or involvement  | 열의, 열중

The teacher's *enthusiasm* kept the children attentive in class.

**DE** enthusiasm : mania [méiniə]

enthusiasm이 지나치면 mania(열광, 열중)가 된다.

## entice
[intáis]

v. to tempt or lure by arousing hope or desire  | 꾀다, 유혹하다

The brightly lit store window with its display of all the latest toys *enticed* the little boy.

**SYN** entice : allure [əlúər]

allure: 꾀다, 유혹하다

---

TRANSLATION | 예문해석

**detour** 그 택시 운전수는 교통 체증을 피하기 위해 골목길 우회도로를 택했다.
우리는 고속도로가 공사 중에 있었기 때문에, 미네소타를 가로질러 우회해야만 했다.

**encumber** 절제하며 술을 마시는 것은 괜찮지만, 그것이 결정을 내리는 능력을 방해하는 상황이라면 문제가 된다.

**enthusiasm** 그 교사의 열의 덕택에 아이들이 수업에 계속 주의를 기울였다.

**entice** 그 어린 소년은 최신의 장난감들이 진열된 밝은 조명의 상점 윈도우에 마음을 뺏겼다.

## estimable
[éstəməbl]

**adj. capable of being valuable; worthy of esteem**
| 평가할 수 있는, 존경할 만한

The king was impressed by the *estimable* young knight's heroic deeds in battle.

**ANT** estimable : contemptible [kəntémptəbl]
contemptible: 경멸할 만한

## extinguish
[ikstíŋgwiʃ]

**v. to stop from burning**
| 불을 끄다

Luckily, the firemen *extinguished* the flames before they burned down the entire house.

**ANT** extinguish : kindle [kíndl]
kindle: 불을 붙이다

## extol
[ikstóul]

**v. to praise or glorify**
| 극찬하다

The evangelist *extolled* the virtues of his religion to every person he encountered.

**ANT** extol : excoriate [ikskɔ́:rièit]
excoriate: 호되게 비난하다

## extort
[ikstɔ́:rt]

**v. to obtain by force or illegal power**
| 강탈하다

The bully *extorted* money from the boy everyday by threatening to beat him up.

**CH** extortionist : intimidation [intìmədéiʃən]
extortionist(강탈자)들은 intimidation(위협)을 그들의 무기로 삼는다.

## fathom
[fǽðəm]

**n. a measurement of water equal to six feet**
| 길(6피트)

**v. to come to understanding through probing or thinking**
| 통찰하다, 헤아리다

The nuclear submarine was cruising undetected in the *fathoms* below. Tim couldn't *fathom* why she would do that.

**CH** fathom : erudite [érjudàit]
erudite(박식한)한 사람은 fathom한다.

---

**TRANSLATION | 예문해석**

| | |
|---|---|
| estimable | 왕은 존경할 만한 젊은 기사가 전투에서 보여준 영웅적 행동에 감명을 받았다. |
| extinguish | 운 좋게도, 불이 집 전체를 태우기 전에 소방수들이 불을 껐다. |
| extol | 그 복음주의자는 자신이 만나는 모든 사람들에게 자신의 종교의 좋은 점을 극찬했다. |
| extort | 그 깡패는 매일 소년을 협박하여 돈을 뜯어냈다. |
| fathom | 핵 잠수함은 몇 길이나 되는 바다속에서 추적당하지 않고 항해 하고 있었다. Tim은 왜 그녀가 그런 일을 하려고 하는지 이해할 수 없었다. |

## fatigue
[fətíːg]

**n. exhaustion from labor or stress** | 피로

**v. to exhaust with labor or intensive stress** | 지치게 하다

After the hard fought soccer game, a few of the players collapsed on the field in *fatigue*.

After hiking in the mountains for two hours, the hunter was *fatigued* and ready to give up the chase.

**PUR** fatigue : repose [ripóuz]

repose(휴식)를 취해 fatigue를 풀다.

## futile
[fjúːtl]

**adj. useless or completely ineffective** | 쓸모없는, 효과없는

It is *futile* to argue with her when she has made up her mind like that.

**ANT** futile : efficacious [èfəkéiʃəs]

efficacious: 효능이 있는

## intercessor
[ìntərsésər]

**n. one who mediates between two parties to reconcile differences** | 중재자

To make money the marriage counselor has even served as an *intercessor* for couples she thought should be apart.

**CH** intercessor : mediate [míːdièit]

intercessor의 주된 임무는 mediate(중재하다)하는 것이다.

## interdict
[ìntərdíkt]

**v. to prohibit or forbid in a formal or authoritative manner** | 금지하다

The role of the guards is to *interdict* anyone from entering the compound.

**ANT** interdict : authorize [ɔ́ːθəràiz]

authorize: 권한을 부여하다

## interrogate
[intérəgèit]

**v. to question formally and aggressively** | 심문하다, (정식으로) 질문하다

The inspector *interrogated* the suspect for three hours, but wasn't able to extract new information.

**SYN** interrogate : examine [igzǽmin]

examine: 심문하다, 조사하다

---

TRANSLATION | 예문 해석

**fatigue** 그 격렬한 축구 경기 후, 몇몇 선수들이 운동장에 지쳐 쓰러졌다.
2시간 동안 산을 오른 후, 그 사냥꾼은 추격을 그만 두고 싶은 마음이 들었다.

**futile** 그녀가 그렇게 마음을 정했다면 그녀와 논쟁을 벌이는 것은 쓸모 없는 일이다.

**intercessor** 그 결혼상담자는 돈을 벌기위해 자신이 보기에 헤어져야 한다고 생각되는 부부들까지도 중재했다.

**interdict** 경비원들의 역할은 누구든지 그 구역에 들어가는 것을 금지하는 것이었다.

**interrogate** 그 수사관은 혐의자를 세 시간동안 심문했지만, 새로운 정보를 찾아낼 수 없었다.

## intimate
[íntəmət]

**adj.** **marked by close association in a very private and personal matter** | 친한

**n.** **a very close friend** | 친한 친구

The relationship between the co-workers grew very *intimate* after a couple of months.

Most people meet their *intimate* either in childhood, or while attending college.

**CH** intimate : clique [kli:k]

clique(도당, 파벌)의 구성원들은 서로 **intimate**한 관계를 유지한다.

## intimidate
[intímədèit]

**v.** **to make timid; to frighten** | 위협하다

You can't *intimidate* me with your childish threats!

**CH** intimidate : bully [búli]

bully(건달)들은 주로 다른 이를 **intimidate** 한다.

## latitude
[lǽtətjù:d]

**n.** **angular distance north or south of the Earth's equator measured up to 90 degrees; freedom to act** | 위도; 허용된 자유

White, middle-class Americans take for granted the *latitude* bestowed to them by their social position in today's world.

**ANT** latitude : strict limitation [strikt lìmətéiʃən]

strict limitation: 엄격한 제한

## literal
[lítərəl]

**adj.** **being in accordance with the primary or exact meaning of words; true to fact** | 문자 그대로의, 사실에 충실한

New branches of Christianity diverge from a *literal* interpretation of the bible.

**ANT** literal : figurative [fígjurətiv]

figurative: 비유적인

---

### TRANSLATION | 예문 해석

| | |
|---|---|
| **intimate** | 직장 동료들 사이의 관계가 몇 달 후에 매우 친밀하게 되었다. |
| | 대부분의 사람들은 허물없는 친구를 유년시절이나 대학시절에 만난다. |
| **intimidate** | 당신은 유치한 협박으로 나를 위협할 수 없다. |
| **latitude** | 백인 중산층 미국인들은 오늘날의 세계에서 그들의 사회적 위치에 의해 그들에게 주어진 자유를 당연시한다. |
| **literal** | 기독교의 새로운 종파들은 성서의 문자 그대로의 해석으로부터 갈라진다. |

## lithe
[laið]

**adj. flexible; easily bent or flexed** | 유연한, 나긋나긋한

Fortunately the gymnast was *lithe* enough to handle the difficult move.

**SYN** lithe : lissome [lísəm]
lissome: 유연한, 나긋나긋한

## mawkish
[mɔ́ːkiʃ]

**adj. excessively sentimental; having a bad taste** | 지나치게 감상적인, 역겨운

The critic's review of the movie seems *mawkish* and overwrought.

**SYN** mawkish : maudlin [mɔ́ːdlin]
maudlin: 지나치게 감상적인

## meticulous
[mətíkjuləs]

**adj. excessively thorough and careful with details** | 지나치게 세심한

It takes a *meticulous* person to be a good editor.

**DE** meticulous : careful [kɛ́ərfəl]
careful(꼼꼼한)에 비해 지나치게 세심한 것을 meticulous하다고 한다.

## mitigate
[mítəgèit]

**v. to reduce the severity or pain of; to mollify or alleviate** | 경감하다, 완화시키다

The camper *mitigated* the itch of his mosquito bites by applying a cream.

**대상** mitigate : severity [səvérəti]
mitigate는 severity(격렬함, 괴로움)를 감소시키는 것이다.

## motivate
[móutəvèit]

**v. to impel or provide a reason to do something** | 동기를 부여하다

The possibility of making money *motivates* people to work hard.

**PUR** motivate : exhortation [ègzɔːrtéiʃən]
exhortation(권고, 격려)의 목적은 motivate시키는 것이다.

---

### TRANSLATION | 예문 해석

| | |
|---|---|
| lithe | 운 좋게도, 그 체조선수는 그 어려운 동작을 소화하기에 충분히 유연했다. |
| mawkish | 그 비평가의 영화평은 지나치게 감상적이고 지나치게 공들인 문체를 사용한다. |
| meticulous | 좋은 편집자가 되려면 매우 세심해야 한다. |
| mitigate | 그 캠핑하는 사람은 연고를 발라 모기에 물려 생긴 가려움증을 진정시켰다. |
| motivate | 돈을 벌 가능성은 사람들이 열심히 일하도록 동기를 부여한다. |

## noxious
[nákʃəs]

**adj. poisonous or harmful to living creatures; obnoxious** | 유독한, 불쾌한

The city was evacuated to save them from the *noxious* fumes coming out of the fast food restaurants.

**CH** noxious : venom [vénəm]

venom(독액, 독)은 noxious하다.

## orthodox
[ɔ́ːrθədɑ̀ks]

**adj. conforming to generally accepted doctrine** | 정설의, 정통의

*Orthodox* Jews must follow strict dietary laws.

**ANT** orthodoxy : heresy [hérəsi]

orthodoxy: 정설, 정교
heresy: 이단, 이설

## oxymoron
[ɑ̀ksimɔ́ːrɑn]

**n. a combination of contradictory words** | 모순 어법

The phrase "just war" is an *oxymoron* that is often used by politicians to alleviate fears that innocent civilians will be killed accidently.

**CH** oxymoron : contradictory [kɑ̀ntrədíktəri]

oxymoron은 contradictory(모순된, 양립치 않는)하다.

## pith
[piθ]

**n. the core or essential part** | 핵심

The *pith* of humanity is love.

**ANT** pith : unimportant point [ʌ̀nimpɔ́ːrtənt pɔint]

unimportant point: 중요하지 않은 사항

## ratification
[rætəfikéiʃən]

**n. formal approval and confirmation** | 비준, 승인

The *ratification* of the handgun law shocked the public.

**ANT** ratify : repeal [ripíːl]

ratify: 승인하다, 인가하다
repeal: 인가를 취소하다, 폐지하다

---

TRANSLATION | 예문해석

**noxious** 시민들을 그 패스트푸드점에서 나오는 유독한 연기에서 구하기 위해 그 도시에서 피난시켰다.
**orthodox** 정통 유태교도들은 엄격한 식사 계율을 지켜야 한다.
**oxymoron** "정당한 전쟁"이라는 구절은 무고한 민간인들이 죽게 될 지도 모른다는 두려움을 완화하기 위해 정치인들이 종종 사용하는 모순 어법이다.
**pith** 인간애의 핵심은 사랑이다.
**ratification** 그 총기법의 승인은 대중에게 충격을 주었다.

## rational
[rǽʃənl]

**adj. reasonable** | 합리적인

I habitually went for advice to my grandmother because she was a *rational* and compassionate person.

**CH** rationalization : plausible [plɔ́ːzəbl]

rationalization(합리화)된 것은 plausible(그럴듯한)하다.

## reticence
[rétəsəns]

**n. the quality of being reserved or restrained** | 과묵, 자기 속을 드러내지 않음

Jim has some *reticence* about expressing emotion.

**CN** reticent : talk [tɔːk]

reticent(과묵한)한 사람은 별로 talk(말하다)하지 않는다.

## retinue
[rétənjùː]

**n. a group of retainers or followers** | 일행, 수행원단

Queen Elizabeth has a *retinue* of 30 servants that accompany her on any of her travels.

**PAR** retinue : attendant [əténdənt]

attendant(수행원)들은 retinue의 구성원이다.

## retort
[ritɔ́ːrt]

**v. to reply rapidly and sharply, sometimes in jest; to present a count argument; to return in kind** | 재빨리 응수하다, 반박하다, 보복하다

**n. a sharp reply or counterargument** | 말대꾸, 반박

The receptionist *retorted* with a sarcastic comment.
His father's stinging *retort* wounded Aaron.

**SYN** retort : repartee [rèpərtíː]

repartee: 재치 있는 응답

---

TRANSLATION | 예 문 해 석

**rational** 할머니는 합리적이고 동정적인 사람이기 때문에, 나는 습관적으로 할머니에게 충고를 구하러 갔다.
**reticence** Jim은 감정을 표현하는 것에 대해 신중하다.
**retinue** Elizabeth 여왕은 모든 여행에 그녀와 동행하는 30명의 시종으로 구성된 수행원단을 가지고 있다.
**retort** 그 접수원은 비꼬는 말로 재빨리 응답했다.
아버지의 날카로운 응답으로 Aaron은 마음에 상처를 받았다.

## revive
[riváiv]

v. to reawaken to consciousness or life; to renew something; to revitalize | 소생시키다, 다시 기운 나게 하다

I tried to *revive* her spirits, but she was hopelessly gloomy.

**ANT** revive : wither [wíðər]

wither: 시들게 하다

## satiate
[séiʃièit]

v. to fully satisfy; to sate | 한껏 만족시키다, 물리게 하다

After the feast, my stomach was *satiated*.

**인과** satiated : food [fuːd]

food(음식)를 먹으면 satiated(배부른)하게 된다.

## satisfaction
[sæ̀tisfǽkʃən]

n. fulfillment of needs or desire; contentment; reparation for a sin or payment of a debt | 만족감; 속죄, (빚의) 상환

My morning coffee brings me great *satisfaction*.

**CN** satisfy : exacting [igzǽktiŋ]

exacting(무리한 요구를 하는, 엄격한)한 사람은 쉽게 satisfy(만족시키다)할 수 없다.

## savor
[séivər]

n. the taste or smell of something | 맛, 냄새
v. to taste or enjoy an experience | 맛보다, 음미하다

Roxanne enjoyed the *savor* of the meal and left no food to waste.
While in Thailand, I *savored* every bite of their fantastic cuisine.

**SYN** savory : palatable [pǽlətəbl]

savory: 맛있는, 향긋한

palatable: 맛있는

---

**TRANSLATION | 예문해석**

**revive** 나는 그녀를 다시 기운 나게 하려고 애썼지만, 그녀는 너무나도 우울해 했다.
**satiate** 나는 그 만찬 후에 포만감을 느꼈다.
**satisfaction** 아침 커피는 나에게 대단한 만족감을 가져온다.
**savor** Roxanne은 그 음식의 맛을 즐겨 하나도 남기지 않고 먹었다.
태국에 있는 동안, 나는 그들의 특이한 요리 모두를 한 입씩 맛보았다.

## savvy
[sǽvi]

**n. knowledge of affairs; shrewdness** | 실제적인 지식, 이해, 분별, 수완

**adj. knowledgeable and perceptive** | 식견이 있는, 정통한, 통찰력이 있는

The senator's political *savvy* has won him more than 5 re-elections.

*Savvy* presidential advisors knew of the scandal well before the media broke the story.

**ANT** savvy : tactless [tǽktlis]

tactless: 재치 없는, 요령 없는

## sly
[slai]

**adj. clever, usually implying deceptiveness** | 교활한

The *sly* fox outsmarted the owl, or so the fable goes.

**ANT** sly : artless [ɑ́ːrtlis]

artless: 순진한, 꾸밈 없는

## tawdry
[tɔ́ːdri]

**adj. gaudy in brightness of appearance** | 번지르르한, 천박한

Cynthia failed to achieve an air of elegance with that *tawdry* dress she wore.

**대상** tawdry : garment [gɑ́ːrmənt]

tawdry는 주로 garment(의복)를 묘사할 때 쓰인다.

## tether
[téðər]

**v. to fasten with a rope** | 밧줄로 매다, 속박하다

**n. a chain** | 밧줄

While sailing on the boat, Micky had to *tether* the sail tighter so it wouldn't flap around.

The neighbor's dog could not reach our yard because his *tether* was only five feet long.

**ANT** tether : loose [luːs]

loose: 풀다

---

### TRANSLATION | 예 문 해 석

**savvy** 그 상원의원은 정치적인 수완이 있어 5번이상 재선될 수 있었다.
정통한 대통령 보좌관들은 언론에서 터뜨리기 전에 미리 그 스캔들에 대해 잘 알고 있었다.
**sly** 그 교활한 여우가 부엉이를 꾀어 이겼다고 우화가 이야기 한다.
**tawdry** Cynthia는 자신이 입고 있는 그 천박한 드레스로는 우아한 분위기를 연출해내지 못했다.
**tether** 배를 타고 항해하는 동안 Micky는 돛이 펄럭이지 않도록 더 세게 묶어야만 했다.
그 이웃집 개를 묶고 있는 줄이 단지 5피트 길이이기 때문에 그 개는 우리집 마당에 닿을 수 없었다.

## thwart
[θwɔːrt]

**v. to prevent occurrence, realization, or attainment of; to baffle** | 방해하다, 당황하게 하다

The nation *thwarted* the war by giving back the hostages.

**ANT** thwart : aid [eid]

aid: 돕다, 촉진하다

## toxic
[táksik]

**adj. poisonous or harmful** | 유독한

The "Mr. Yuk" stickers are put on bottles to warn children that the contents are *toxic* and dangerous.

**CH** toxic : venom [vénəm]

venom(독)에는 toxic한 성분이 함유되어 있다.

## untoward
[ʌntóuərd]

**adj. unlucky or unfavorable; improper** | 운나쁜, 불리한, 부적당한

Julian found himself in a very *untoward* situation, having no money and no place to stay for the night.

**ANT** untoward : fortunate [fɔ́ːrtʃənət]

fortunate: 운좋은

## utter
[ʌ́tər]

**v. to speak or give utterance** | 말하다
**adj. complete or total** | 완전한

The groom *uttered* a few words of thanks to each of his guests at the wedding.

The flashlight's batteries gave out, leaving the campers in *utter* darkness.

**KIN** utter : blurt [bləːrt]

blurt는 불쑥 엉겁결에 utter(말하다)하는 것이다.

---

TRANSLATION | 예 문 해 석

**thwart** 그 나라는 인질들을 돌려보냄으로써 전쟁이 일어나는 것을 막았다.
**toxic** 병에 붙어 있는 "Mr. Yuk" 스티커들은 아이들에게 그 내용물이 유독하고 위험하다는 것을 경고하기 위한 것이다.
**untoward** Julian은 돈도 없고 밤을 보낼 장소도 없는 매우 운나쁜 상황에 처해 있음을 깨달았다.
**utter** 그 신랑은 결혼식에 온 그의 하객들 하나하나에게 몇 마디 감사의 말을 했다.
손전등의 배터리가 다 되어 그 캠핑자들은 완전한 어둠 속에 있게 되었다.

## venial
[víːniəl]

**adj.** easily excused or forgiven | 용서 받을 수 있는

In Singapore, littering is not considered a *venial* offense.

**CH** venial : excuse [ikskjúːz]

venial하다는 것은 excuse(용서하다)할 수 있다는 의미이다.

## veto
[víːtou]

**n.** an authoritative prohibition | 거부권
**v.** to prohibit, especially the passage of a law | 거부하다

The plan was circumvented by the president's *veto*.

In the end, the president *vetoed* the law legalizing marijuana.

**CH** veto : prohibitive [prouhíbitiv]

veto는 prohibitive(금지하는)하고자 하는 것이다

## watershed
[wɔ́ːtərʃèd]

**n.** a divided region that drains into another (usually larger) body of water; a critical point that marks a change of course | 분기점, 전환점

The Vietnam war was an important *watershed* in modern American history marking the end of easily justified military interventions abroad.

**ANT** watershed : routine [ruːtíːn]

routine: 일상의 과정, 판에 박힌일

## wither
[wíðər]

**v.** to dry up or shrivel; to lose vitality or freshness | 마르다, 시들다

The rose *withered* in the sun and the petals fell off.

**WO** wither : vitality [vaitǽləti]

wither하는 것에는 vitality(생기, 생명력)가 없다.

---

TRANSLATION | 예문해석

**venial** 싱가포르에서는 쓰레기를 버리는 것이 경미한 위반 행위로 간주되지 않는다.
**veto** 그 계획은 대통령의 거부권에 의해 저지 되었다.
최종적으로, 대통령은 마리화나를 합법화하는 그 법을 거부했다.
**watershed** 베트남 전쟁은 쉽게 정당화되었던 해외 군사 개입의 종식을 가져온 현대 미국사의 중요한 전환점이 되었다.
**wither** 장미가 햇볕에 시들어서 꽃잎이 떨어졌다.

# 6th Day Daily Check-up

■ Fill in the blanks with the correct letter that matches the word with its definition.

1. interdict _____
2. estimable _____
3. fathom _____
4. lithe _____
5. tawdry _____
6. untoward _____
7. savvy _____
8. reticence _____
9. noxious _____
10. mawkish _____

a. knowledgeable; practical knowledge
b. to prohibit or forbid in a formal or an authoritative manner
c. valuable; worthy of esteem
d. the quality of being reserved or restrained; to be hesitant
e. to come to understanding through probing or thinking
f. flexible; easily bent or flexed
g. poisonous or harmful to living creatures; obnoxious
h. sentimental or having a bad taste
i. difficult to work with; unlucky or unfavorable
j. gaudy in brightness of appearance

■ Put the correct word in each blank from the list of words below.

11. _____에는 엄선된 poem들이 수록되어 있다.
12. kindle(불을 붙이다)의 반의어는 _____이다.
13. _____의 주된 임무는 mediate 하는 것이다.
14. intrepid한 사람을 _____하기는 어렵다.
15. venom에는 _____한 성분이 함유되어 있다.
16. bully들은 주로 다른 이를 _____한다.
17. _____를 느끼면 repose를 취한다.
18. _____은 contradictory 하다.
19. blurt은 불쑥 엉겁결에 _____하는 것이다.
20. attendant들은 _____의 구성원이다.

| a. anthology | b. fatigue | c. tawdry | d. extinguish | e. oxymoron | f. intercessor |
| g. intimidate | h. retinue | i. deter | j. toxic | k. utter | l. sly |

Answer key

1.b  2.c  3.e  4.f  5.j  6.i  7.a  8.d  9.g  10.h
11.a  12.d  13.f  14.i  15.j  16.g  17.b  18.e  19.k  20.h

www.goHackers.com

해커스 어학연구소

# TAKE A BREAK

죽기 전 한 번쯤 꼭 가봐야 할 곳

### 1. 마추픽추

마추픽추(Machu Picchu)는 페루에 있는 잉카 문명의 고대 도시로, 안데스 산맥 밀림 속 해발 2,400미터 바위산 산턱에 위치한다. '잉카의 잃어버린 도시', '공중의 누각'으로 불리기도 하는 이곳은 외부인의 눈을 피해 하늘에 지어진 신기한 마을이자 요새와 같다. 이곳을 더욱 신비롭게 하는 것은 사람들이 어떻게 20톤이나 나가는 돌을 바위산에서 잘라내 수십 km 떨어진 산 위로 날라서 신전과 집을 지을 수 있었을까에 대한 경이로움이다.

### 2. 앙코르 와트

앙코르 와트(Angkor Wat)는 캄보디아에 위치한 사원으로, 12세기 초에 강력한 왕권을 가졌던 앙코르 왕조의 수리아바르만 2세에 의해 지어졌다. 이는 세계에서 가장 크고 아름다운 종교 건축물로, 웅장함과 섬세함 모두를 가지고 있는 건축물이며, 이전 크메르 제국의 수준 높은 건축 기술이 잘 드러난 유적이다. 많은 관광객들이 캄보디아에 오는 것은 앙코르 와트를 보기 위해서라고 말할 정도로 여행객들에게 인기를 끄는 명소이다.

쉬•어•가•는 페•이•지

### 3. 콜로세움

콜로세움(Colosseum)은 고대 로마 시대의 건축물 가운데 하나로 정식 명칭은 '플라비우스 원형경기장'이다. 여러 영화들에서 검투사들이 싸우는 장면의 배경이 되어 많은 사람들에게 친숙하기도 한 이곳은 한 번에 5만 명이나 되는 관중을 수용할 수 있었고, 검투사들의 시합과 맹수 사냥 시합, 모의 해전 등이 치러졌다. 고대 로마 시민들의 어쩌면 다소 잔혹했던 오락 역사의 현장을 살펴보기 위해 매년 많은 관광객들이 이곳을 찾고 있다.

### 4. 그랜드 캐니언

그랜드 캐니언(Grand Canyon)은 미국 애리조나주 북부에 위치한 콜로라도 강에 의해 깎여진 거대협곡으로, 그 길이는 446km에 이르고 깊이도 1,600km에 달한다. 20억 년 세월의 풍화 흔적을 볼 수 있는 지상 최대의 볼거리 중 하나로 꼽히고 있는 이곳은, 매년 약 5백만 명의 관광객이 이 광경을 바라보기 위해 이곳을 찾아온다고 하니 그 인기를 어느 정도 가늠해 볼 수 있겠다.

# SUPER VOCA

S.E.V.E.N.T.H.D.A.Y

설마 난 부분 기억 상실증 환자?
아닙니다. 당신은 극히 정상적인 게으름뱅이입니다.

## abstruse
[æbstrúːs]

**adj. difficult to understand** | 난해한

The *abstruse* terminology used in the economist's presentation confused most of his audience.

**ANT** abstruse : accessible [æksésəbl]

accessible: 이해하기 쉬운, 접근하기 쉬운

## astronomy
[əstrάnəmi]

**n. the science of matter outside the Earth's atmosphere** | 천문학

For Jeff's *astronomy* course, the teacher took them outside to look at the stars.

**대상** astronomer : planet [plǽnit]

astronomer는 planet(행성)을 연구하는 학자이다.

## attractive
[ətrǽktiv]

**adj. charming; causing interest or pleasure** | 매력적인

The *attractive* billboard caught the eye of many people as they walked down the street.

**ANT** attractive : unprepossessing [ʌ̀nipriːpəzésiŋ]

unprepossessing: 호감이 안 가는

## buttress
[bʌ́tris]

**n. a structure giving stability to a wall or building** | 버팀목
**v. to sustain or support** | 지지하다

The city mandated the addition of *buttresses* to all multi-story buildings in preparation of future earthquakes.

The well-built skyscraper was *buttressed* with reinforced steel and a stable foundation.

**FUN** buttress : edifice [édəfis]

buttress는 edifice(큰 건물)를 지지하기 위해 사용된다.

---

**TRANSLATION | 예문 해석**

**abstruse** 그 경제학자의 발표에 사용된 난해한 용어들은 대부분의 청중들을 혼동스럽게 했다.
**astronomy** Jeff의 천문학 수업 시간에, 교사는 별들을 보기 위해 그들을 밖으로 데리고 나갔다.
**attractive** 그 매력적인 광고판은 많은 사람들이 거리를 걸어갈 때 그들의 시선을 끌었다.
**buttress** 그 시는 지진에 대비하기 위해 모든 고층 건물에 버팀목을 첨가하는 내용을 의무 조항으로 규정했다.
잘 지어진 그 고층건물은 강철과 안정된 토대로 지지되었다.

## carp
[kɑːrp]

**v. to find fault or complain querulously** | 허물을 들추다, 트집잡다

The old man was always *carping* at anyone who sat near him.

**DE**  carp : complain [kəmpléin]

carp는 complain(불평하다)보다 강하게 불만을 표시하며 비판한다는 의미이다.

## caulk
[kɔːk]

**v. to make something airtight or watertight** | 물이나 공기가 통하지 않게 막다

**n. a stopper** | 마개

To prevent the wind from coming in, Andrew tried to *caulk* the cracks with sealant.

The plumber used *caulk* around the elbow joint to stop the leaking water.

**SYN**  caulk : seal [siːl]

seal: 막다, 밀봉하다

## convivial
[kənvíviəl]

**adj. festive; fond of good company** | 유쾌한, 교제를 좋아하는, 붙임성 있는

The *convivial* young boy was the most popular student in his class.

**SYN**  convivial : sociable [sóuʃəbl]

sociable: 사교적인

## destruction
[distrʌ́kʃən]

**n. the act of destroying** | 파괴

The *destruction* of the ozone layer is a significant challenge for scientists to solve.

**SYN**  destruction : demolition [dèməlíʃən]

demoliton: 파괴

## disturb
[distə́ːrb]

**v. to interrupt or put into disorder** | 방해하다, 어지럽히다

The constant nightmares *disturbed* his sleep.

**대상**  disturb : serenity [sərénəti]

disturb는 serenity(고요함, 평온)를 방해하는 것이다.

---

### TRANSLATION | 예문해석

| | |
|---|---|
| carp | 그 노인은 항상 가까이에 앉아 있는 사람의 트집을 잡는다. |
| caulk | 바람이 들이오는 것을 막기 위해 Andrew는 밀봉제로 틈새를 막으려 했다. |
| | 배관공은 물이 새는 것을 막기 위해 L자형의 이음관에 마개를 사용했다. |
| convivial | 그 붙임성 있는 소년은 그의 반에서 가장 인기 있는 학생이다. |
| destruction | 오존층의 파괴는 과학자들이 풀어야 할 중요한 과제이다. |
| disturb | 계속되는 악몽이 그의 수면을 방해했다. |

## entrap
[intrǽp]

**v.** **to catch in a trap; to lure into danger** | 덫으로 잡다, 함정에 빠뜨리다

Many well-intentioned public servants are unwittingly *entrapped* by the political machinery.

**CN**  entrap : vigilant [vídʒələnt]

vigilant(방심하지 않는, 부단히 경계하는)하고 있으면 쉽게 entrap당하지 않는다.

## equable
[ékwəbl]

**adj.** **uniform or steady; even-tempered** | 한결 같은, 평온한

The new principal's *equable* demeanor was appreciated and respected by the community.

**ANT**  equable : intemperate [intémpərit]

intemperate: 난폭한, 무절제한

## extract
[ikstrǽkt]

**v.** **to pull out with force; to excerpt** | 억지로 끌어내다, 뽑다, 발췌하다

The FBI *extracted* a confession from the accused spy.

**DE**  extract : milk [milk]

milk(착취하다, 짜내다)는 심하게 extract한다 라는 의미를 가진다.

## extraneous
[ikstréiniəs]

**adj.** **irrelevant or unrelated to the topic at hand; extrinsic or coming from the outside** | 본질과 관계 없는, 외부로부터의

Harry quickly became annoyed at the *extraneous* chatter that filled the discussion group.

**WO**  extraneous : essence [ésns]

extraneous한 것에는 essence(본질)가 없다

## extraordinary
[ikstrɔ́ːrdənèri]

**adj.** **not usual; remarkable** | 보통이 아닌, 대단한

The trip to Southern Europe was an *extraordinary* experience.

**ANT**  extraordinary : mundane [mʌ́ndein]

mundane: 평범한, 흔한

---

TRANSLATION | 예 문 해 석

| | |
|---|---|
| entrap | 많은 선의의 공무원들은 알지 못하는 사이에 정치 조직의 함정에 빠지게 된다. |
| equable | 그 새 교장의 한결 같은 태도가 그 지역 사회에 의해 높이 평가되고 존경 받았다. |
| extract | FBI는 스파이로 기소된 사람에게서 강제로 자백을 받아냈다. |
| extraneous | Harry는 그 토론모임에 주제와 관련 없는 잡담만이 오고가게 되자 바로 그것에 화를 냈다. |
| extraordinary | 남유럽으로의 여행은 특별한 경험이었다. |

## extravagant [ikstrǽvəgənt]

**adj.** recklessly wasteful; excessively expensive; exceeding the limits of reason | 낭비하는, 엄청나게 비싼, 터무니없는

Sally considered her boyfriend's tastes to be too *extravagant* for her simple lifestyle.

**ANT** extravagant : parsimonious [pàːrsəmóuniəs]

parsimonious: 인색한

## extrinsic [ikstrínsik]

**adj.** external or outside of; unessential | 외부의, 비본질적인

The *extrinsic* stain on the man's teeth was caused by years of habitual coffee drinking.

**ANT** extrinsic : immanent [ímənənt]

immanent: 내재적인, 내적인

## fatuous [fǽtʃuəs]

**adj.** foolish; unreal | 어리석은, 비현실의

Kenny's dream of becoming a race car driver was considered *fatuous* by his peers.

**ANT** fatuous : scintillating [síntəlèitiŋ]

scintillating: 재치가 번뜩이는

## fetter [fétər]

**v.** to put fetters on; to confine | 족쇄를 채우다, 속박하다
**n.** a chain or shackle for the ankles | 족쇄

After graduation, Jennifer longed to move away where she wouldn't be *fettered* by family obligations.

The *fetters* of the prisoners clinked as they marched to the fields to work.

**ANT** fetter : release [rilíːs]

release: 석방하다, 해방하다

---

TRANSLATION | 예 문 해 석

**extravagant** Sally는 자신의 남자 친구의 취향이 자신의 검소한 생활에 비해 너무 사치스럽다고 생각했다.
**extrinsic** 그 남자의 치아 외부에 생긴 착색은 수년간 습관적으로 마신 커피에서 비롯된 것이다.
**fatuous** 그의 동료들은 Kenny가 카레이서가 되겠다는 것을 어리석은 꿈이라고 생각했다.
**fetter** Jennifer는 졸업 후 가족 부양 의무에 의해 속박당하지 않을 곳으로 멀리 가기를 간절히 원했다.
죄수들이 일터로 행진하는 동안 그들의 족쇄가 철렁거렸다.

## institute
[ínstətʲùːt]

**v. to initiate or establish** | 설립하다

**n. an organization usually for education and research** | 연구소

In the early 1900s, Ataturk *instituted* what is now known as Istanbul University.

The CDC is an *institute* that researches diseases and viruses.

**ANT** institute : abrogate [ǽbrəgèit]

abrogate: 폐지하다

## intractable
[intræktəbl]

**adj. not easily directed or manipulated; unruly** | 다루기 힘든

Erica soon discovered that children at day care are *intractable* and frustrating.

**CN** intractable : manage [mǽnidʒ]

intractable한 사람은 쉽게 manage(다루다, 조종하다)할 수 없다.

## intrepid
[intrépid]

**adj. fearless or courageous** | 용감한

The *intrepid* climber reached the top of Mount Everest alone.

**ANT** intrepid : timorous [tímərəs]

timorous: 겁많은, 소심한

## intricacy
[íntrikəsi]

**n. the quality or state of being complex and elaborately detailed** | 복잡함

For English speakers, the *intricacies* of the Chinese language are far too difficult.

**CH** intricacy : tapestry [tǽpəstri]

tapestry(태피스트리)는 주로 intricacy함을 지니고 있다.

---

### TRANSLATION | 예문 해석

| | |
|---|---|
| institute | 1900년대 초반에, Ataturk는 지금 이스탄불 대학으로 알려져 있는 대학을 설립했다. CDC는 질병과 바이러스를 연구하는 기관이다. |
| intractable | Erica는 보육원의 아이들이 다루기 힘들고 짜증스럽다는 사실을 곧 알아챘다. |
| intrepid | 그 용감한 등산가가 혼자서 에베레스트 산의 정상에 도달했다. |
| intricacy | 영어를 구사하는 사람들에게 중국어의 복잡함은 너무나도 어려운 것이다. |

## intrude
[intrú:d]

**v. to enter without permission or invitation; to interrupt** | 침입하다, 방해하다

Jack *intruded* on the party in order to talk to his ex-girlfriend.

> **SYN** intrude : trespass [tréspəs]
> trespass: 침입하다, 방해하다

## jittery
[dʒítəri]

**adj. suffering from irregular random movements, often caused by stress, chemical stimulants, or excitement** | 초조해 하는, 신경과민의

The three cups of coffee made her *jittery* and unable to sit still.

> **ANT** jittery : resolute [rézəlù:t]
> resolute: 의연한, 단호한

## lassitude
[lǽsətjù:d]

**n. fatigue or listlessness** | 피로, 무기력

After a night of drinking, Brian's *lassitude* was clearly apparent to his co-workers.

> **ANT** lassitude : vim [vim]
> vim: 기력, 활기

## miff
[mif]

**v. to insult or offend slightly** | 모욕하다, 발끈하게 하다

Mr. Kronkite was *miffed* by reporter's tardiness for the interview.

> **ANT** miff : appease [əpí:z]
> appease: 달래다

## mottle
[mátl]

**n. a spot or blotch** | 얼룩, 반점
**v. to mark with spots** | 얼룩지게 하다

The painting was a random arrangement of *mottles*.
The tree had *mottled* leaves indicating it was dying of disease.

> **POS** mottled : spot [spɑt]
> mottled: 얼룩진
> spot: 얼룩, 반점

---

### TRANSLATION | 예문해석

**intrude** — Jack은 그의 전 여자친구와 이야기하기 위해 허락 없이 파티장으로 들어갔다.
**jittery** — 커피 세 잔이 그녀를 초조하고 가만히 앉아있지 못하게 만들었다.
**lassitude** — 간밤에 술을 마신 후에, Brian이 피곤해 한다는 것을 그의 동료들은 쉽게 알 수 있었다.
**miff** — Kronkite씨는 기자가 인터뷰에 늦게 나타났기 때문에 발끈해 있었다.
**mottle** — 그 그림은 반점들의 무작위적 배열이었다.
그 나뭇잎에 생긴 반점으로 보아 그 나무가 병에 걸려 죽어가고 있음을 알 수 있다.

## natty
[nǽti]

**adj. stylish and tidy, usually in reference to a man**
| 깔끔한, 말쑥한

The actor looked *natty* at the Oscars in his long black tuxedo.

**ANT** natty : slovenly [slʌ́vənli]
slovenly: 단정치 못한

## nettle
[nétl]

**n. a stinging plant with needles**
| 쐐기풀
**v. to arouse irritation or annoyance**
| 짜증나게 하다

The campers avoided walking through an open field after seeing bunches of *nettles* in it.
The waiter's arrogant attitude *nettled* me.

**ANT** nettle : conciliate [kənsílièit]
conciliate: 달래다

## nitpick
[nítpìk]

**v. to criticize small and unimportant details**
| 사소한 일에 흠을 잡다

Mothers are always *nitpicking* about their children's school performance.

**CH** nitpicker : criticize [krítəsàiz]
nitpicker(트집쟁이)는 늘 criticize(흠잡다)한다.

## obstreperous
[əbstrépərəs]

**adj. characterized by unruly noise or clamor; stubbornly resistant to control**
| 시끄럽게 떠드는, 제어할 수 없는

The birthday party became *obstreperous* as soon as the parents left.

**CN** obstreperous : control [kəntróul]
obstreperous한 것을 control(제어하다, 통제하다)하기는 쉽지 않다.

## obtuse
[əbtjúːs]

**adj. slow to understand or lacking sharpness of intellect**
| 우둔한

The man was too *obtuse* to catch the humor and wit of the play.

**WO** obtuseness : keen [kiːn]
keen(명민한)한 사람에게서는 obtuseness(우둔함)를 찾아볼 수 없다.

---

**TRANSLATION | 예문해석**

| | |
|---|---|
| natty | 오스카상 시상식에 긴 블랙 턱시도를 입고 나타난 그 배우는 말쑥해 보였다. |
| nettle | 그 야영자들은 들판에 난 쐐기풀 더미들을 보고, 그 곳을 가로질러 가지 않기로 했다. |
| | 그 웨이터의 거만한 태도는 나를 짜증나게 했다. |
| nitpick | 어머니들은 항상 아이들의 학교 성적에 대해 흠을 잡는다. |
| obstreperous | 그 생일파티는 부모님들이 떠나자마자 제어할 수 없을 정도로 소란스러워졌다. |
| obtuse | 그 남자는 너무 우둔해서 그 연극의 유머와 위트를 이해할 수 없었다. |

## ostracize
[ástrəsàiz]

**v.** to exclude or exile from a group or society by popular consent | 추방하다

Themistokles, the Ancient Greek politician, was *ostracized* from Athens for three years in the 5th century BC.

**SYN** ostracize : exile [égzail]

exile: 추방하다

## parsimonious
[pɑ̀ːrsəmóuniəs]

**adj.** excessively stingy; unwilling to spend | 인색한, 소비하기 싫어하는

Frugality was a quality she admired, but Frank's *parsimonious* habits were too much for her.

**DE** parsimonious : frugal [frúːgəl]

frugal(검소한)한 것이 지나치면 parsimonious 하다는 말을 듣는다.

## patronize
[péitrənàiz]

**v.** to act condescendingly towards someone; to provide support for or be a customer of | 선심쓰는 체 하다, 후원하다

As a rule, I try to *patronize* the local community businesses rather than large national chain stores.

**CH** patron : support [səpɔ́ːrt]

patron(후원자)은 support(지원하다)를 해주는 사람이다.

## pedagogue
[pédəgɑ̀g]

**n.** one who teaches or instructs | 선생, 교육자

The greatest *pedagogues* in the world are the ones who impart both wisdom and knowledge.

**CH** pedagogue : indoctrinate [indáktrənèit]

indoctrinate(가르치다)는 pedagogue의 특성이다.

## petrography
[pitrágrəfi]

**n.** the scientific description and classification of rocks | 암석분류학

For lack of better options, Jack took a class in *petrography* to fulfill his science requirements.

**대상** petrography : rock [rɑk]

petrography는 rock(암석)을 분류하기 위한 학문이다.

---

### TRANSLATION | 예문해석

**ostracize** 고대 그리스 정치가인 Themistokles는 기원 전 5세기 아테네에서 3년 간 추방 되었다.
**parsimonious** 검소함은 그녀가 높이 사는 자질이었지만, Frank의 인색한 행동은 그녀에게도 너무 지나쳐 보였다.
**patronize** 일반적으로 나는 전국 규모의 대형 체인점들 보다는 지역 기업들을 후원하려고 애쓴다.
**pedagogue** 세상에서 가장 위대한 교육자는 지혜와 지식 모두를 나누어 주는 사람이다.
**petrography** 더 좋은 선택이 없어서, Jack은 그의 과학 필수 과목들을 이수하기 위해 암석분류학 수업을 들었다.

## petty
[péti]

**adj. having little or no significance** | 하찮은

The two friends fought over something *petty* that managed to destroy their friendship.

**CN** petty : noticeable [nóutisəbl]
petty한 것은 noticeable(눈에 잘 띄는)하지 않다.

## pittance
[pítns]

**n. a small portion or allowance** | 소량, 약간의 수당

Jackie's mother gives her a *pittance* every month for taking out the garbage.

**DE** pittance : allowance [əláuəns]
소량의 allowance(수당, 용돈)가 pittance이다.

## pity
[píti]

**n. the feeling of sympathetic sorrow for another; something to be regretted** | 연민, 유감스러운 일

It was a *pity* we didn't get to see Jill before she left for Hawaii.

**POS** pity : lamentable [læməntəbl]
lamentable: 유감스러운

## playbill
[pléibìl]

**n. printed program of a play with a listing of cast members** | 배역의 목록이 있는 연극 프로그램 전단

Harry was very upset when he found out his name was misprinted in the *playbill*.

**FUN** playbill : cast [kæst]
playbill은 cast(배역)를 소개해준다.

## polarize
[póuləràiz]

**v. to cause to concentrate about two conflicting or contrasting positions** | 양 극단으로 분열시키다, 대립시키다

The police brutality case *polarized* the community.

**ANT** polarize : make compatible [meik kəmpǽtəbl]
make compatible: 양립시키다

---

### TRANSLATION | 예문해석

**petty** 그 두 친구는 사소한 일로 다퉈서 우정에 금이 갔다.
**pittance** Jackie의 어머니는 그녀가 쓰레기를 갖고 나가는 것에 대해 매달 약간의 용돈을 준다.
**pity** Jill이 하와이로 떠나기 전에 그녀를 보지 못한 것은 참 유감스러운 일이었다.
**playbill** Harry는 자신의 이름이 프로그램 전단에 잘못 인쇄되었다는 사실을 알게 되었을 때 매우 화가났다.
**polarize** 경찰의 잔학 행위 사건이 그 지역 사회를 양 극단으로 분열시켰다.

## posture
[pástʃər]

n. the position of the body | 자세

v. to assume a pose or behave in an artificial manner to impress others | 의도적으로 어떤 자세를 취하다, 젠체하다

Her *posture* was so bad that the chiropractor recommended a back brace.
When Dave was threatening me, he was just *posturing*.

**CN** posturer : unaffected [ʌnəféktid]
posturer(척하는 사람)는 unaffected(꾸밈없는, 있는 그대로의)하지 않다.

## potter
[pátər]

n. a person who makes pottery | 도자기공

The *potter* sold some of his brightly painted vases at the craft show.

**KIN** potter : artisan [ɑ́ːrtəzən]
potter는 artisan(기술공)의 일종이다.

## retrench
[ritréntʃ]

v. to cut down or reduce | 절감하다, 줄이다

The family *retrenched* their monthly expenses to save for a big trip.

**대상** retrench : expense [ikspéns]
expense(지출)를 retrench하다.

## routine
[ruːtíːn]

n. a regular or habitual procedure | 일상적인 일

Without my morning *routine* of exercise and breakfast, I can't get through the day awake and alert.

**ANT** routine : watershed [wɔ́ːtərʃed]
watershed: 분기점, 전환점

## saturate
[sǽtʃərèit]

v. to treat with a liquid until no more can be absorbed; to fully satisfy or complete | 흠뻑 적시다, 포화시키다

The rainstorm *saturated* the football field with muddy puddles of water.

**인과** saturated : moisture [mɔ́istʃər]
moisture(수분)를 많이 함유한 결과 saturated(포화된)된 상태가 된다.

---

### TRANSLATION | 예문 해석

**posture** 그녀의 자세가 너무나 나빠서 척추 지압사가 등 버팀대를 추천했다.
Dave가 나를 위협할때, 그는 단지 그런척 하는 것 뿐이었다.
**potter** 그 도자기공은 수공업 박람회에서 밝게 채색된 꽃병 몇 개를 팔았다.
**retrench** 그 가족은 중요한 여행에 필요한 경비를 마련하기 위해 월지출을 줄였다.
**routine** 운동과 아침식사라는 아침의 일상적인 과정이 없다면, 나는 깨어서 민활하게 하루를 보낼 수 없다.
**saturate** 폭풍우로 그 축구장이 흠뻑 젖어서 진흙 웅덩이들이 생겼다.

### squabble
[skwábl]

n. **a small argument over trivial matters** | 시시한 언쟁
v. **to quarrel or argue about unimportant things** | 사소한 말다툼을 하다

All of our *squabbles* are about Jack's smoking habit.
Neighbors are always *squabbling* about parking spaces.

**DE** squabble : dispute [dispjúːt]
squabble은 dispute(논쟁)에 비해 사소한 언쟁을 일컫는다.

### squalid
[skwálid]

adj. **very dirty or filthy** | 더러운, 추잡한

The *squalid* streets of the impoverished neighborhood can be very depressing.

**ANT** squalid : immaculate [imǽkjulət]
immaculate: 청정한, 더러워지지 않은

### squall
[skwɔːl]

n. **a sudden windstorm followed by rain or snow; a short-lived commotion** | 돌풍; 소동

The *squall* came upon the countryside without warning.

**DE** squall : commotion [kəmóuʃən]
commotion(소동)에 비해 작은 소동을 squall이라고 한다.

### squalor
[skwálər]

n. **a quality or condition of filth or degradation caused by poverty or neglect** | 불결함, 천박함

Due to current political and economic problems, *squalor* is the norm in the inner cities of America.

**ANT** squalor : splendor [spléndər]
splendor: 빛남, 뛰어남

---

TRANSLATION | 예문해석

| | |
|---|---|
| squabble | 우리가 하는 시시한 언쟁은 모두 Jack의 흡연 습관에 관한 것이었다. |
| | 이웃들은 항상 주차 공간 문제로 말다툼을 한다. |
| squalid | 가난한 동네의 지저분한 거리는 매우 음울하다. |
| squall | 그 돌발적인 소동이 경고 없이 그 지방에 갑자기 발생했다. |
| squalor | 현재의 정치적, 경제적 문제들 때문에 누추함은 미국의 시 중심지에서 일반적인 것이 되었다. |

## tatty
[tǽti]

**adj. worn or shabby** | 닳아빠진, 초라한

The homeless man near my work dresses in *tatty* clothes and carries a garbage bag.

**ANT** tatty : smart [smɑːrt]

smart: 맵시 있는, 말쑥한

## taut
[tɔːt]

**adj. tight or tense** | 팽팽한, 긴장한

His nerves were *taut* during the interview.

**대상** tautness : slacken [slǽkən]

tautness(팽팽함, 긴장감)를 slacken(느슨하게 하다)하다.

## truant
[trúːənt]

**adj. absent without permission, especially from school; shirking duty** | 무단 결석하는, 게으름 피우는

*Truant* students may struggle to catch up on lessons.

**ANT** truant : dutiful [djúːtifəl]

dutiful: 본분을 다하는, 충실한

## unwonted
[ʌnwɔ́ːntid]

**adj. out of the ordinary or unusual** | 보통 아닌, 예사롭지 않은

We experienced *unwonted* freezing this past autumn.

**ANT** unwonted : usual [júːʒuəl]

usual: 보통의

## vex
[veks]

**v. to irritate or distress** | 화나게 하다, 괴롭히다

Mike could not help but be *vexed* by the troubling news.

**ANT** vex : conciliate [kənsílièit]

conciliate: 달래다

---

TRANSLATION | 예 문 해 석

| | |
|---|---|
| tatty | 내 직장 근처의 그 행려자는 초라한 옷을 입고 쓰레기 봉지를 들고 다닌다. |
| taut | 그는 그 인터뷰 내내 긴장했다. |
| truant | 무단 결석하는 학생들은 수업을 따라잡는 데 어려움을 겪을지도 모른다. |
| unwonted | 우리는 이번 가을 예사롭지 않은 추위를 경험했다. |
| vex | Mike는 그 괴로운 소식에 화가 나지 않을 수 없었다. |

## vituperate
[vait/úːpərèit]

**v. to scold or censure severely or abusively** | 심하게 비난하다

Jessie Ventura, the Minnesota governor, was harshly *vituperated* by politicians nationwide when he was first elected.

**ANT** vituperate : admire [ædmáiər]
admire: 칭찬하다, 감탄하다

## waylay
[wéilèi]

**v. to be lying in wait to ambush; to attack from a hiding place** | 습격하기 위해 숨어서 기다리다, 급습하다

Bret was *waylaid* by a mugger from the dark alley way off the main boulevard.

**CN** waylaid : vigilant [vídʒələnt]
vigilant(부단히 경계하는)한 사람은 waylaid(급습당한)되지 않는다.

## wizen
[wí(ː)zn]

**v. to become wrinkled and begin exhibiting signs of aging; to cause to wither, shrivel, or dry up** | 나이먹다, 시들게 하다

It is hard to see your own parents become *wizened* by time.

**ANT** wizen : rejuvenate [ridʒúːvənèit]
rejuvenate: 원기를 회복하다, 원기를 회복시키다

## wry
[rai]

**adj. bent out of shape or twisted; dryly humorous** | 뒤틀린, 빈정대는

The student showed an almost *wry* attitude towards his teacher.

**DE** wry : humorous [hjúːmərəs]
humorous(해학적인)의 도를 넘어 빈정대는 것을 wry하다고 한다.

---

TRANSLATION | 예 문 해 석

**vituperate** 미네소타 주지사인 Jessie Ventura는 처음 선출되었을 때 전국적으로 정치인들에게 심하게 비난을 받았다.
**waylay** Bret은 대로에서 벗어난 어두운 샛길에서 강도에게 급습당했다.
**wizen** 자신의 부모님이 나이 드는 것은 보기 괴롭다.
**wry** 그 학생은 선생님에게 거의 빈정대는 듯한 태도를 보였다.

# 7th Day Daily Check-up

■ Fill in the blanks with the correct letter that matches the word with its definition.

1. extrinsic _____
2. jittery _____
3. lassitude _____
4. mottle _____
5. squalor _____
6. squabble _____
7. ostracize _____
8. retrench _____
9. obstreperous _____
10. nettle _____

a. external or outside of
b. suffering from irregular random movements, often caused by stress, chemical stimulants, or excitement
c. fatigue or listlessness
d. to mark with spots; a spot or blotch
e. to exclude or exile from a group or society by popular consent
f. to cut down or reduce
g. characterized by unruly noise or clamor
h. a place or situation of filth or degradation caused by poverty or neglect
i. to quarrel or argue about unimportant things
j. to arouse irritation or annoyance

■ Put the correct word in each blank from the list of words below.

11. demolition(파괴)의 동의어는 _____ 이다.
12. _____ 힌 것은 noticeable하지 않다.
13. commotion에 비해 작은 소동을 _____ 이라고 한다.
14. intemperate(난폭한)의 반의어는 _____ 이다.
15. _____ 는 rock을 분류하기 위한 학문이다.
16. _____ 는 edifice를 지지하기 위해 사용된다.
17. _____ 는 playbill의 내용을 구성하는 한 부분이다.
18. scintillating(재치가 번뜩이는)의 반의어는 _____ 이다.
19. keen한 사람에게서는 _____ 를 찾아볼 수 없다.
20. parsimonious(인색한)의 반의어는 _____ 이다.

| a. obtuseness | b. extravagant | c. inherent | d. equable | e. vituperate | f. destruction |
| g. petty | h. petrography | i. buttress | j. squall | k. cast | l. fatuous |

**Answer key**

1. a  2. b  3. c  4. d  5. h  6. i  7. e  8. f  9. g  10. j
11. f  12. g  13. j  14. d  15. h  16. i  17. k  18. l  19. a  20. b

# SUPER VOCA

E · I · G · H · T · H · D · A · Y

오늘 내가 외우지 않은 단어는
어제 시험친 이가 그토록 궁금해하던 단어이다.

## abdicate
[ǽbdəkèit]

**v. to give up power or resign from high position**
| 포기하다, 퇴위하다

The Allies forced Napoleon to *abdicate* his emperorship and exiled him to the island of Elba.

대상  abdicate : throne [θroun]
abdicate는 throne(왕권)을 포기하는 것이다.

## addict
v. [ədíkt]
n. [ǽdikt]

**v. to cause to be habitually dependent on a substance**
| ~에 탐닉시키다, 중독되게 하다

**n. one who is addicted**
| 중독자, 열광적인 애호자

The teenager became *addicted* to cigarettes and soon started smoking two packs a day.

We became online *addicts* with the release of the new computer game.

인과  addicted : dependency [dipéndənsi]
술이나 마약에 addicted(중독된)되면 그것에 대한 dependency(의존)가 생긴다.

## ameliorate
[əmíːljərèit]

**v. to make better or more tolerable; to ease; to get better**
| 개선하다, 완화시키다, 좋아지다

We may be able to *ameliorate* the suffering of patients with the new drug.

SYN  ameliorate : improve [imprúːv]
improve: 개선하다, 향상시키다

---

### TRANSLATION | 예문해석

| | |
|---|---|
| **abdicate** | 연합군은 나폴레옹을 강제로 퇴위시키고 Elba섬으로 추방시켰다. |
| **addict** | 그 십대는 담배에 중독되어 곧 하루에 두 갑씩 담배를 피우게 되었다. |
|  | 그 새로운 컴퓨터 게임의 출시로 우리는 온라인 중독자가 되었다. |
| **ameliorate** | 우리는 그 신약으로 환자들의 고통을 완화시켜줄 수 있을지 모른다. |

## amend
[əménd]

**v. to make right, usually through change; to correct** | 수정하다, 바로잡다

Congress *amended* the bill to include a more comprehensive tax plan.

**CN** amend : incorrigible [inkɔ́ːridʒəbl]

incorrigible(교정할 수 없는)은 amend할 수 없다는 의미이다.

## blemish
[blémiʃ]

**n. a noticeable imperfection; a tainted reputation** | 흠, 오점
**v. to stain or spoil by a flaw** | 더럽히다, 손상하다

The Watergate scandal was a huge *blemish* for the Nixon administration.
Jason's perfect report card was *blemished* with a B in science.

**WO** blemish : impeccable [impékəbl]

impeccable(결점 없는)한 사람에게서는 blemish를 찾아보기 힘들다.

## bode
[bóud]

**v. to be an omen of; to foreshow** | 전조가 되다

The policy *bodes* ill for the future of international cooperation on environment.

**ANT** boding ill : auspicious [ɔːspíʃəs]

boding ill: 흉조의
auspicious: 길조의

## cleft
[kleft]

**n. an opening or fissure indicating division or splitting** | 갈라진 틈
**adj. divided** | 갈라진

The tremors of the earthquake created a massive *cleft* in the street.
A *cleft* lip is one of the most common facial congenital anomalies.

**DE** cleft : chasm [kǽzəm]

chasm(깊게 갈라진 틈)은 cleft보다 깊게 갈라진 틈을 가리킨다.

---

### TRANSLATION | 예문해석

**amend** 국회는 보다 포괄적인 과세 계획안을 포함하도록 그 법안을 수정하였다.
**blemish** 워터게이트 스캔들은 닉슨 정부에게 커다란 오점을 남겼다.
Jason의 완벽한 성적표는 과학에서 B학점을 받음으로써 완전함이 손상되었다.
**bode** 그 정책은 환경에 대한 국제 협력의 앞날에 그림자를 드리운다.
**cleft** 지진으로 인한 진동으로 그 거리에는 대규모로 갈라진 틈이 생겼다.
갈라진 입술은 가장 보편적인 선천성 기형 중의 하나이다.

## clement
[klémənt]

**adj. lenient or merciful** | 관대한, 자비로운

The *clement* woman took in the deserted stray and nourished it back to health.

**ANT** clement : pitiless [pítilis]

pitiless: 무자비한

## credence
[krí:dəns]

**n. a mental belief in something as true** | 믿음, 신용

Galileo disputed the *credence* that the world was flat.

**ANT** credence : doubt [daut]

doubt: 불신

## creep
[kri:p]

**v. to move slowly and quietly close to or on the ground** | 살금살금 움직이다, 기다

The boy and his mother saw the cat *creep* into the door of the bakery.

**ANT** creep : move swiftly [mu:v swiftli]

move swiftly: 재빠르게 움직이다

## dedicate
[dédikèit]

**v. to set apart for sacred purposes; to commit oneself to a goal of life; to open to the public use** | 헌납하다, 바치다, (건물 등을) 공개하다

The men and women who immigrated to the United States from Korea *dedicated* their lives to providing their children with the best possible education.

**DE** dedication : zeal [zi:l]

zeal(열성, 열의)은 dedication(헌신)보다 특정한 일에 대한 더 강한 열의나 헌신을 나타낸다.

## diehard
[dáihà:rd]

**n. one who is strongly devoted and resists any change** | 완고한 보수주의자, 완강히 저항하는 사람

Many in the firm viewed Aaron as a *diehard* who would never approve the new budget plan.

**CN** diehard : budge [bʌdʒ]

diehard들은 쉽게 budge(생각을 바꾸다)하지 않는다.

---

### TRANSLATION | 예 문 해 석

| | |
|---|---|
| clement | 그 자비로운 여인은 그 버려진 동물을 데려와 먹이를 주어 건강한 상태로 회복시켰다. |
| credence | Galileo는 지구가 평평하다는 믿음이 맞지 않다고 논박했다. |
| creep | 그 소년과 그의 엄마는 빵집의 문으로 기어들어가는 고양이를 보았다. |
| dedicate | 한국에서 미국으로 이민 온 사람들은 자신들의 삶을 자식들이 최상의 교육을 받게 하는 데 바쳤다. |
| diehard | 그 회사의 사람들 대다수는 Aaron을 그 새로운 예산을 결코 받아들이려 하지 않는 완강한 저항자로 보았다. |

## endorse
[indɔ́:rs]

**v. to sign one's name on the back of; to give approval of**
| (수표 등에) 배서하다, 승인하다

Mr. Derrick offers this only as a suggestion, and will *endorse* any decision you arrive at.

대상  endorse : approval [əprúːvəl]
endorse는 approval(승인, 인가)을 해주는 것이다.

## endure
[indjúər]

**v. to sustain; to bear or tolerate a lasting and usually suffering state; to exist through time**
| 지탱하다, 참다, 지속하다

What cannot be cured must be *endured*.

대상  endure : affliction [əflíkʃən]
affliction(고뇌)을 endure하다.

## erect
[irékt]

**adj. upright in position**
| 똑바로 선, 직립의

**v. to be or place in an upright or raised position; to build**
| 직립하다, 수직으로 세우다, 짓다

Buckingham Palace guards are renowned for their *erect* posture.
Verena Tarrant was *erected* on her little platform, dressed in white, with flowers in her bosom.

ANT  erect : prostrate [prástreit]
prostrate: 엎드린

## execrate
[éksikrèit]

**v. to denounce; to feel loathing for**
| 비난하다, 혐오하다

Conservative Christians often *execrate* cinema and television, claiming that it corrupts the youth.

ANT  execrate : exalt [igzɔ́ːlt]
exalt: 칭찬하다

---

### TRANSLATION | 예문 해석

**endorse**  Derrick씨는 이것을 단지 하나의 안으로 제시하고, 당신이 내리는 어떤 결론도 승인할 것이다.
**endure**  치유될 수 없는 것은 참는 수 밖에 없다.
**erect**  버킹엄 궁전의 근위병들은 그들의 꼿꼿한 자세로 유명하다.
　　　　　Verena Tarrant는 하얀 옷을 입고 가슴에는 꽃을 꽂은 채 그녀의 작은 연단에 서 있었다.
**execrate**  보수적인 기독교인들은 영화와 텔레비전이 젊은이들을 타락시킨다며 비난하곤 한다.

## exemplify
[igzémpləfài]

**v. to show by example; to serve as an example of**
| 예를 들어 설명하다, 예시나 전형이 되다

The mother asked her eldest son to *exemplify* good behavior to the younger children.

**CH** exemplify : archetype [á:rkitàip]
archetype(전형)은 exemplify 될 만하다.

## fleet
[fli:t]

**v. to fade away quickly** | 빠르게 사라지다
**adj. moving swiftly; evanescent** | 빠른, 덧없는

Being in the spot light for just a *fleeting* moment was enough to make the old singer smile.

The warrior had to be *fleet* of foot to escape from the pursuing enemies.

**SYN** fleeting : meteoric [mì:tiɔ́:rik]
fleeting: 빠르게 사라지는
meteoric: 유성의, 유성처럼 잠시 스쳐 지나가는

## greet
[gri:t]

**v. to welcome or address someone** | 인사말을 하며 반기다

When George Willard came to the door, he *greeted* Belle effusively.

**ANT** greeting : valediction [vælədíkʃən]
greeting: 환영의 말
valediction: 고별사

## gregarious
[grigɛ́əriəs]

**adj. sociable; preferring the company of others**
| 사교적인, 사람들과 어울려 사는

The once shy and reticent girl had become a *gregarious* young lady.

**WO** gregariousness : recluse [réklu:s]
recluse(은둔자)는 gregariousness(사교성)가 부족하다.

---

**TRANSLATION | 예문해석**

**exemplify** 어머니는 큰 아들에게 동생들의 좋은 모범이 될 것을 부탁했다.
**fleet** 짧은 순간이나마 조명을 받은 것은 그 나이든 가수를 미소 짓게 하기에 충분했다.
그 전사는 적들의 추격으로부터 도망치기 위해 발을 빨리 움직여야만 했다.
**greet** George Willard가 문 앞에 이르렀을 때, 그는 활기에 차서 Belle에게 인사말을 했다.
**gregarious** 한 때 수줍어 하고 과묵했던 소녀가 사교적인 숙녀가 되었다.

## hedge
[hedʒ]

**n.** a bush or shrub used to line an edge | 산울타리
**v.** to evade or to protect oneself from danger | (위험으로부터) 보호하다, 피하다

The *hedges* served as a boundary between the two estates.
On her way home, Jackie *hedged* hitting the deer by swerving off of the road.

**KIN** hedge : fence [fens]
hedge는 fence(울타리, 담)의 일종이다.

## hodgepodge
[hádʒpàdʒ]

**n.** a mixture of many different things | 뒤범벅

America is a *hodgepodge* of cultures from all over the world.

**CN** hodgepodge : homogeneous [hòumədʒí:niəs]
hodgepodge는 homogeneous(동질의)한 것과는 거리가 멀다.

## hovel
[hʌ́vəl]

**n.** a small poor dwelling place; a hut | 작고 허름한 집, 오두막집

Compared to the mansion we used to live in, this place is a *hovel*.

**CN** hovel : palatial [pəléiʃəl]
hovel은 palatial(호화로운, 궁궐같은)하지 않다.

## hue
[hju:]

**n.** gradation of color; color | 색조, 색

All of the rooms in the resort are painted in various *hues* of red and blue.

**WO** hue : achromatic [æ̀krəmǽtik]
achromatic(무색의)한 것에는 hue가 없다.

## indifferent
[indífərənt]

**adj.** impartial; lacking interest or concern | 공평한, 냉담한, 무관심한

Mary's *indifferent* attitude towards school frustrated her parents.

**ANT** indifferent : avid [ǽvid]
avid: 열심인, 탐욕스러운

---

TRANSLATION | 예문해석

**hedge** 그 산울타리들은 두 사유지 사이의 경계 역할을 했다.
집에 돌아오는 길에, Jackie는 도로에서 갑자기 방향을 바꿈으로써 사슴을 치는 것을 피했다.
**hodgepodge** 미국은 전 세계 문화의 뒤범벅이다.
**hovel** 우리가 예전에 살았던 저택에 비하면 이곳은 오두막이다.
**hue** 그 리조트의 모든 객실은 빨간색과 파란색의 다양한 색조로 칠해져 있다.
**indifferent** Mary의 학교생활에 대한 무관심한 태도에 그녀의 부모는 절망스러워 했다.

## indigenous
[indídʒənəs]

**adj. native to a particular region** | 토착의

The Aborigines are the *indigenous* people of Australia.

**ANT** indigenous : exotic [igzátik]

exotic: 외래의

## indolent
[índələnt]

**adj. lazy; causing no pain** | 게으른, 무통성의

Clare's *indolent* partner caused them to receive a poor grade on the project.

**ANT** indolent : sedulous [sédjuləs]

sedulous: 근면한

## indomitable
[indámətəbl]

**adj. incapable of being stopped or subdued; unconquerable** | 굴복하지 않는, 불굴의

The Greeks besieged the *indomitable* city of Troy with the gift of a wooden horse.

**CN** indomitable : subdued [səbdjú:d]

indomitable한 것은 결코 subdued(정복된) 될 수 없다는 것을 의미한다.

## indubitable
[indjú:bətəbl]

**adj. unable to be doubted** | 의심의 여지가 없는, 명백한

The *indubitable* truth of Pierre's testimony could not be argued.

**ANT** indubitable : doubtful [dáutfəl]

doubtful: 의심스러운

## indulge
[indʎldʒ]

**v. to give in to desire; to free from inhibitions or restrictions** | (욕망이나 쾌락 등에) 빠지다, 마음대로 하다

People in Las Vegas *indulge* themselves in the wildest of vices.

**CN** indulge : abstemious [æbstí:miəs]

abstemious(절제하는)한 사람은 쾌락에 indulge하지 않는다.

---

TRANSLATION | 예 문 해 석

| | |
|---|---|
| indigenous | Aborigines는 오스트레일리아 원주민들이다. |
| indolent | Clare의 게으른 파트너 때문에 그들은 그 프로젝트에서 낮은 점수를 받았다. |
| indomitable | 그리스인들은 목마를 선물로 보내 그 굴복하지 않는 도시 트로이를 포위하였다. |
| indubitable | Pierre의 증언이 명백한 사실이라는 것은 논란의 여지가 없다. |
| indulge | 라스베가스의 사람들은 가장 방탕한 타락에 빠진다. |

## ineluctable
[ìnilʌ́ktəbl]

**adj. unchangeable or inevitable** | 바꿀 수 없는, 피할 수 없는

Fate is the belief that all of life is *ineluctable*.

**SYN** ineluctable : inescapable [ìnəskéipəbl]

inescapable: 피할 수 없는

## judicious
[dʒuːdíʃəs]

**adj. having sound judgment** | 사리 분별력이 있는, 현명한

A good mediator and friend, Karen is respectable and *judicious* at all times.

**ANT** judicious : daft [dæft]

daft: 분별력이 없는, 어리석은

## lethargic
[liθáːrdʒik]

**adj. lacking vitality or energy; apathetic** | 무기력한, 무감동의

Alex was so *lethargic* from oversleeping that he didn't care that his favorite show was on.

**WO** lethargic : energy [énərdʒi]

lethargic한 사람에게는 energy(에너지, 활력)가 없다.

## ludicrous
[lúːdəkrəs]

**adj. humorous in its absurdity** | 우스꽝스러운

"It's *ludicrous* to think that a teen-ager has the freedom to make a choice," Blaine said.

**CH** ludicrous : farce [faːrs]

farce(익살극)는 ludicrous한 특징을 지니고 있다.

## mediate
[míːdièit]

**v. to act as the middle-man for two opposing parties who are trying to reach a resolution** | 중재하다

Razali *mediated* between Myanmar's military junta and the opposition in a bid to restore democracy.

**CH** mediate : intercessor [ìntərsésər]

intercessor(중재자)들은 분쟁을 mediate한다.

---

### TRANSLATION | 예문 해석

| | |
|---|---|
| **ineluctable** | 운명이란 삶의 모든 것들이 피할 수 없는 것이라고 믿는 것이다. |
| **judicious** | 좋은 중재자이자 친구인 Karen은 존경 받을 만하며 항상 판단력이 뛰어나다. |
| **lethargic** | Alex는 지나친 수면으로 인해 무기력해져 그가 좋아하는 TV쇼가 방송되어도 신경쓰지 않았다. |
| **ludicrous** | Blaine은 "십대가 선택의 자유가 있다고 생각하는 것은 우스꽝스러워"라고 말했다. |
| **mediate** | Razali는 민주주의 정부를 재건하기 위해 미얀마의 군사정부와 반대파를 중재했다. |

## mediocre
[mìːdióukər]

**adj.** of moderate or middle-ground quality | 보통의, 평범한

The poet's work was considered *mediocre* at best.

> **ANT** mediocrity : virtuosity [vəːrtʃuásəti]
> mediocrity: 평범, 범재
> virtuosity: 걸출한 기량

## moderate
[mádərət]

**v.** to lessen the intensity of; to lead a discussion | 완화하다, ~의 의장역을 맡다

**adj.** not excessive or extreme; mediocre; temperate | 적당한, 보통의, 절제력있는

Annie *moderated* her anger after realizing it would lead to further conflict with her employer.

Many tourists are attracted to Florida due to its *moderate* climate and beautiful beaches.

> **ANT** moderate : intensify [inténsəfài]
> intensify: 강화하다

## modest
[mádist]

**adj.** showing a moderate estimation of one's own talents, abilities, and value; decent in speech and demeanor; not too large or too small | 겸손한, 얌전한, 적당한

The athlete was *modest* in victory, giving full credit to his coaches and teammates.

> **ANT** modest : brazen [bréizn]
> brazen: 뻔뻔스러운

> **DE** modest : prudish [prúːdiʃ]
> modest에 비해 지나치게 고상한 체하는 것은 prudish(고상한 체하는, 몹시 얌전 빼는)하다고 한다.

## modicum
[mádikəm]

**n.** a small amount or quantity | 소량

Even a *modicum* of moisture would be greatly appreciated by farmers in the dry season.

> **ANT** modicum : large amount [láːrdʒ əmáunt]
> large amount: 다량

---

### TRANSLATION | 예문 해석

**mediocre** 그 시인의 작품은 기껏해야 평범한 것으로 여겨졌다.
**moderate** Annie는 자신이 화를 내는 것이 고용주와의 관계를 더 악화시킬 것이라는 사실을 깨달은 후 화를 누그러뜨렸다.
많은 관광객들은 플로리다의 온화한 날씨와 아름다운 해변에 이끌린다.
**modest** 그 선수는 승리에 대해 겸손해 하며 자신의 코치와 팀원들에게 그 영광을 모두 돌렸다.
**modicum** 건기에는 아주 적은 양의 수분조차도 농부들이 감사히 여길 것이다.

## meek
[miːk]

**adj. mild, soft, or submissive** | 온순한, 유순한

Daniel's *meek* personality was often taken as a sign of weakness by others.

**WO** meek : arrogance [ǽrəgəns]

meek한 사람은 arrogance(거만함)를 가지지 않는다.

## mnemonic
[nimánik]

**n. a phrase or device that helps one remember** | 기억을 돕는 말이나 장치, 기억술

Children use *mnemonics* to help them remember difficult problems.

**FUN** mnemonic : remember [rimémbər]

mnemonic은 remember(기억하다)하는 것을 돕는다.

## nudge
[nʌdʒ]

**v. to bump or push in a very gentle manner** | 살짝 밀다, 찌르다

Steve *nudged* me with his elbow when I began dozing off in the meeting.

**DE** nudge : prod [prɑd]

nudge는 살짝 prod(찌르다)하는 것이다.

## obdurate
[ábdjurət]

**adj. stubborn in perspective** | 고집이 센, 완고한

The captain was *obdurate* to their appeals.

**DE** obdurate : firm [fəːrm]

firm(확고한)한 것이 지나치면 obdurate하다.

## obedient
[oubíːdiənt]

**adj. submissive to commands** | 순종하는, 고분고분한

*Obedient* students rarely defy their teachers.

**ANT** obedient : contumacious [kɑ̀ntjuméiʃəs]

contumacious: 순종하지 않는, 반항적인

---

**TRANSLATION | 예문 해석**

**meek** Daniel의 유순한 성격은 다른 이들에 의해 나약함의 표시로 여겨지기도 했다.
**mnemonic** 아이들은 어려운 문제를 쉽게 기억하려고 기억술을 사용한다.
**nudge** 내가 회의에서 졸기 시작하자 Steve는 팔꿈치로 나를 살짝 찔렀다.
**obdurate** 그 선장은 그들의 간청에 완고했다.
**obedient** 순종적인 학생들은 그들의 선생님들에게 거의 반항하지 않는다.

## precis
[preisíː]

**n.** a brief and accurate summary | 간결하고 정밀한 요약

Karen's *precis* highlighted all the points of the arguments.

**CH** precis : concise [kənsáis]
precis는 concise(간결한)하다.

## predict
[pridíkt]

**v.** to foretell based on scientific or personal observation | 예측하다

Economists *predict* that the global economy will experience a recession early next year.

**CH** prediction : augur [ɔ́ːgər]
augur(점쟁이)는 미래를 prediction할 수 있다.

## preen
[priːn]

**v.** to excessively groom oneself; to pride oneself on | 몸치장하다, 우쭐대다

Mary *preened* herself for two hours on the night of the school dance.

**CH** preen : dandy [dǽndi]
dandy(멋쟁이)들은 preen하는 특징을 지닌다.

## quell
[kwel]

**v.** to calm or quiet down; to suppress | 가라앉히다, 진압하다

Liz *quelled* the crying baby with a pacifier.

**ANT** quell : stir [stəːr]
stir: 선동하다, 자극하다

## quench
[kwentʃ]

**v.** to put out; to satisfy a thirst or desire | (불·빛을) 끄다, 갈증이나 욕망을 풀다

The fire fighters were unable to *quench* the forest fire and it raged out of control.

**ANT** quench : ignite [ignáit]
ignite: 불을 붙이다

---

**TRANSLATION | 예문 해석**

**precis** Karen의 간명한 요약은 모든 논쟁점들을 두드러지게 했다.
**predict** 경제학자들은 세계 경제가 내년 초에 침체를 겪을 것이라고 예측한다.
**preen** Marry는 학교 댄스의 밤에 가기 위해 2시간 동안 치장했다.
**quell** Liz는 고무 젖꼭지를 물려 우는 아이를 달랬다.
**quench** 소방관들이 산불을 진압할 수 없어 산불은 걷잡을 수 없이 퍼졌다.

## seemly
[síːmli]

*adj.* **proper and agreeable** | 품위 있는, 적합한

A *seemly* gentleman entered the room and caught her attention.

> **ANT** seemly : ribald [ríbəld]
> ribald: 점잖지 못한

## sneer
[sniər]

*v.* **to speak in a scornful, contemptuous, or derisive manner** | 비웃다
*n.* **a facial expression that exhibits scorn** | 비웃음

The crowd *sneered* at the poor attempts of the magician.
A *sneer* crossed the suspect's face as the lawyer began questioning him.

> **SYN** sneer : derision [diríʒən]
> derision: 비웃음

## speculate
[spékjulèit]

*v.* **to take a guess about something; to ponder** | 추측하다, 숙고하다

Some researchers *speculate* that the dinosaurs died off because of an increase in global volcanic activity.

> **SYN** speculate : conjecture [kəndʒéktʃər]
> conjecture: 추측하다

## spendthrift
[spéndθrìft]

*n.* **a person who wastefully spends his money** | 돈을 헤프게 쓰는 사람

Kimberly was known as a *spendthrift* because of her penchant for impulse buys.

> **CH** spendthrift : improvidence [imprávədəns]
> spendthrift는 improvidence(낭비)하는 특징을 가지고 있다.

---

### TRANSLATION | 예 문 해 석

**seemly** 한 품위있는 신사가 방에 들어와 그녀의 관심을 끌었다.
**sneer** 군중이 그 마술사의 형편없는 시도를 비웃었다.
변호사가 질문을 시작하자 그 용의자의 얼굴에 비웃음이 스쳐 지나갔다.
**speculate** 일부 연구자들은 공룡이 전 세계에 걸친 화산 활동의 증가로 인해 멸종했다고 추측한다.
**spendthrift** Kimberly는 그녀의 충동구매하는 경향 때문에 돈을 헤프게 쓰는 사람으로 알려져 있다.

## steep
[stiːp]

**adj. at an excessively high angle** | 가파른
**v. to soak in a liquid** | 적시다, 담그다

The *steep* angle of the mountain made it impossible to climb without aid of a rope.

The hint to making better raisin muffins is to *steep* the raisins in sherry.

**CH** steepness : precipice [présəpis]

precipice(절벽)는 steepness(가파름)의 특징을 지니고 있다.

## stench
[stentʃ]

**n. a foul smell** | 악취

The *stench* of rotting corpses filled the air around the river.

**대상** stench : nose [nouz]

stench는 nose(코)와 관련이 있다.

## svelte
[svelt]

**adj. slender or graceful in outline** | 날씬한, 몸매좋은

James Levine was investigating why some people can gorge themselves with food and stay *svelte*.

**ANT** svelte : paunchy [pɔ́ːntʃi]

paunchy: 배가 나온

## sweltering
[swéltəriŋ]

**adj. very hot and humid; suffering from intense heat** | 찌는 듯이 더운, 더위에 지친

The *sweltering* heat in Cambodia was unbearable for the tourists.

**POS** sweltering : heat [hiːt]

heat: 더위, 열

---

TRANSLATION | 예 문 해 석

**steep** 그 산은 가팔라서 로프의 도움없이 올라가는 것은 불가능했다.
더 좋은 건포도 머핀을 만드는 요령은 건포도를 셰리주(술)에 담그는 것이다.
**stench** 썩어가는 시체의 악취가 강 주변 공기를 가득 채웠다.
**svelte** James Levine는 왜 어떤 사람들은 음식을 배부를 때까지 먹고도 날씬할 수 있는지를 조사하고 있었다.
**sweltering** 캄보디아의 찌는 듯한 더위는 여행객들에게 견디기 힘든 것이었다.

## trenchant
[tréntʃənt]

**adj. incisive; vigorous and effective; clear-cut**
| 통렬한, 강력한, 명확한

The *trenchant* facts of the case left little for the jury to deliberate on.

**ANT** trenchant : vague [veig]

vague: 불분명한, 모호한

## troupe
[tru:p]

**n. a group of traveling performers of an opera or a play**
| 순회 공연하는 오페라나 연극단

The strain of 2 months of traveling and performing was beginning to wear the *troupe* down.

**PAR** troupe : actor [ǽktər]

actor(배우)는 troupe을 구성하는 부분이다.

## wheedle
[hwí:dl]

**v. to gain or entice by flattery or guile**
| 아첨이나 속임수로 유혹하다, 감언이설로 꾀다

Developers of some projects are *wheedling* potential clients with free food and entertainment.

**POS** wheedle : cajolery [kədʒóuləri]

cajolery: 감언이설, 구슬림

---

### TRANSLATION | 예문해석

| | |
|---|---|
| trenchant | 그 사건은 분명해서 배심원단이 심의할 것이 별로 없었다. |
| troupe | 두 달 동안의 순회 공연으로 인한 과로때문에 그 연극단은 지치기 시작했다. |
| wheedle | 몇몇 프로젝트의 개발자들이 공짜 음식과 연회로 잠재적인 고객들을 유혹하고 있다. |

# 8th Day Daily Check-up

■ Fill in the blanks with the correct letter that matches the word with its definition.

1. abdicate    _____    a. to give up power or resign from high position
2. boding      _____    b. a phrase or device that helps one remember
3. hodgepodge  _____    c. stubborn in perspective
4. mediocre    _____    d. to be an omen of; to foreshow
5. stench      _____    e. a small amount or quantity
6. preen       _____    f. a mixture of many different things
7. mnemonic    _____    g. of moderate or middle-ground quality
8. obdurate    _____    h. a foul smell
9. modicum     _____    i. to excessively groom oneself; to pride oneself on
10. diehard    _____    j. one who is strongly devoted and resists any change

■ Put the correct word in each blank from the list of words below.

11. 술이나 마약에 _____ 되면 그것에 대한 dependency가 생긴다.
12. _____ 한 사람은 arrogance를 가지지 않는다.
13. hovel은 _____ 하지 않는다.
14. impeccable한 사람에게서는 _____ 를 찾아보기 힘들다.
15. farce는 _____ 한 특징을 지니고 있다.
16. recluse에게는 _____ 가 부족하다.
17. execrate(호되게 비난하다)의 반의어는 _____ 이다.
18. chasm은 _____ 보다 깊게 갈라진 틈을 가리킨다.
19. valediction(작별인사)의 반의어는 _____ 이다.
20. _____ 는 concise하다.

a. ludicrous    b. blemish    c. palatial    d. meek      e. addicted    f. gregariousness
g. exalt        h. cleft      i. greeting    j. paunchy   k. frigid      l. precis

**Answer key**

1. a   2. d   3. f   4. g   5. h   6. i   7. b   8. c   9. e   10. j
11. e  12. d  13. c  14. b  15. a  16. f  17. g  18. h  19. i  20. l

www.goHackers.com

해커스 어학연구소

# Super Voca

N . I . N . T . H . D . A . Y

어제의 사랑은 당신 곁을 떠나도,
오늘의 단어는 영원히 당신 곁에 머무를 것입니다.

## aberrant
[əbérənt]

**adj. deviating from the norm** | 정도를 벗어난

The mother began to worry when all of her son's teachers complained of his *aberrant* behavior.

> 대상  aberrant : standard [stǽndərd]
> aberrant는 standard(표준)에서 벗어난 이라는 의미이다.

## abet
[əbét]

**v. to actively encourage or support** | 적극적으로 격려하다, 원조하다

The protesters gathered to *abet* the legalization of same-sex marriages.

> POS  abet : encouragement [inkə́ːridʒmənt]
> encouragement: 격려

## acerbic
[əsə́ːrbik]

**adj. sour or bitter in taste; harsh or acidic in mood** | 맛이 신, 떫은, 신랄한, 엄한

The medicine's *acerbic* flavor caused the child to flinch.

> ANT  acerbic : saccharine [sǽkərin]
> saccharine: 아주 달콤한

## alert
[ələ́ːrt]

**adj. watchful and aware** | 경계하는, 주의하는
**v. to notify of approaching danger or action** | 경계시키다

An *alert* security guard triggered the silent alarm during the bank robbery.

Health officials *alerted* the public about the possible outbreak of mad cow disease.

> WO  alert : somnolence [sámnələns]
> alert한 사람은 somnolence(졸린 상태)에 빠지지 않는다.

---

### TRANSLATION | 예 문 해 석

**aberrant**  그 어머니는 아들의 선생님들이 그의 행동이 이상하다고 불평을 하자 걱정이 되기 시작했다.
**abet**  그 시위자들은 동성 결혼의 법제화를 지지하기 위해 모였다.
**acerbic**  그 약의 떫은 맛 때문에 그 아이는 움찔했다.
**alert**  방심하지 않는 경비원이 은행에 강도 사건이 발생했을 때 무성 경보기를 눌렀다.
보건 관리자들은 사람들에게 광우병의 발발 가능성에 대해 경계하도록 했다.

## amenity
[əménəti]

**n.** the quality of being pleasant or agreeable; something that is conducive to convenience and pleasure　　| 쾌적함, 쾌적한 시설

Proponents say specialty hospitals offer hotel-like *amenities* to patients.

**CH**　amenity : comfortable [kʌ́mfərtəbl]
　　amenity는 이용하기에 comfortable(편안한)한 시설이다.

## anesthetic
[æ̀nəsθétik]

**n.** a drug used by doctors to prevent a patient from feeling pain　　| 마취제

**adj.** causing anesthesia; insensitive　　| 마취의, 감각이 없는

Operations on the battlefield are often performed without *anesthetics*.
Ms. Park was under the influence of *anesthetic* medications.

**FUN**　anesthetic : pain [pein]
　　anesthetic은 pain(통증)을 없애주는 기능을 한다.

## aversion
[əvə́ːrʒən]

**n.** a feeling of strong dislike　　| 매우 싫어함

A young man naturally conceives an *aversion* to labor when he receives no benefit from it.

**DE**　aversion : disinclination [dìsìnklənéiʃən]
　　aversion은 disinclination(싫음, 마음이 안 내킴)보다 싫어함의 정도가 더 크다.

## brevity
[brévəti]

**n.** shortness of speech or writing　　| 간결함

For the sake of *brevity*, you can call me Bill.

**CH**　brevity : aphorism [ǽfərìzm]
　　aphorism(격언)은 brevity한 특징을 가지고 있다.
　　cf) epigram: 풍자적인 경구

## caveat
[kǽviàːt]

**n.** a warning, caution, or protest　　| 경고, 주의, 항의

Samantha did not heed the *caveat* given by her father.

**POS**　caveat : cautionary [kɔ́ːʃənèri]
　　cautionary: 경고적인, 경계의

---

**TRANSLATION | 예문해석**

| | |
|---|---|
| amenity | 지지자들은 특별 병원들이 환자들에게 호텔과 같은 쾌적한 시설을 제공한다고 말한다. |
| anesthetic | 전쟁터에서의 수술은 종종 마취제 없이 행해진다. |
| | 박 여사는 마취가 풀리지 않은 상태였다. |
| aversion | 젊은 사람은 어떤 이익도 얻지 못할 때 자연스럽게 노동에 대한 혐오감을 품게 된다. |
| brevity | 간단하게 나를 Bill이라고 부르세요. |
| caveat | Samantha는 아버지의 경고에 주의하지 않았다. |

## charlatan
[ʃáːrlətn]

**n. one who deceivingly claims to know much**
| 많이 안다고 거짓 주장하는 사람, 허풍선이

*Charlatans* use their deceptive abilities to con wealthy people of their money.

**CH** charlatan : deceive [disíːv]

charlatan은 deceive(속이다)하는 경향이 있다.

## crest
[krest]

**n. a showy tuft on the head of a bird; the top of a hill or wave; the peak**
| 볏, 언덕이나 파도의 정상, 최고조

During the hurricane, the *crest* of the waves would reach incredible heights.

**PAR** crest : wave [weiv]

crest는 wave(파도)의 꼭대기 부분이다.

## crestfallen
[kréstfɔ̀ːlən]

**adj. having a drooping crest; depressed or dejected**
| 볏이 처진, 풀이 죽은, 의기 소침한

The employee to whom the manager had been talking went away quite *crestfallen*.

**ANT** crestfallen : exultant [igzʌ́ltənt]

exultant: 의기 양양한, 크게 기뻐하는

## deterrent
[dité:rənt]

**n. something that discourages or prevents**
| 방해하는 것, 방해

The claim that corporal punishment is an effective *deterrent* against future crimes is false.

**ANT** deterrent : inducement [indjúːsmənt]

inducement: 유도, 유도하는 것

## devastate
[dévəstèit]

**v. to bring to destruction by violent action; to overwhelm or confound**
| 황폐시키다, 압도하다, 망연자실케 하다

Rob was *devastated* when he didn't get the toy truck he wanted from Santa.

**ANT** devastated : spry [sprai]

devastated: 망연자실한

spry: 활기찬

---

TRANSLATION | 예 문 해 석

| | |
|---|---|
| charlatan | 허풍선이들은 남을 속이는 능력을 부자로부터 돈을 뜯어내는 데 쓴다. |
| crest | 폭풍이 몰아치는 동안, 파도의 물마루가 아주 높이 올라갔었다. |
| crestfallen | 매니저와 이야기를 나눈 그 직원은 상당히 낙담한 채로 떠났다. |
| deterrent | 신체적인 형벌이 미래의 범죄를 효과적으로 저하시킨다는 주장은 잘못되었다. |
| devastate | Rob은 산타 할아버지로부터 그가 원하던 장난감 트럭을 받지 못했을 때 망연자실했다. |

**dilapidate**
[dilǽpədèit]

v. **to bring into a state of decay or partial ruin; to squander**
| 황폐시키다, 낭비하다

The riots left the streets *dilapidated*.

ANT　dilapidate : restored [ristɔ́:rd]
　　　dilapidated: 황폐해진
　　　restored: 복구된

**earshot**
[íərʃàt]

n. **the distance over which a sound can be heard**
| 소리가 들리는 거리

Tom made sure we were out of *earshot* before he began telling me the latest rumors.

대상　earshot : hear [hiər]
　　　earshot은 hear(듣다)할 수 있는 범위를 말한다.

**enervate**
[énərvèit]

v. **to drain of physical or mental energy** | 약화시키다

The long work day and lack of sleep *enervated* Marie.

대상　enervate : vigor [vígər]
　　　vigor(힘)를 enervate하다.

**frenetic**
[frənétik]

adj. **frantic and nervously excited** | 열광적인

The children were *frenetic* on the last day of school.

DE　frenetic : energetic [ènərdʒétik]
　　frenetic은 energetic(정력적인)보다 그 정도가 더 세다.

**frenzy**
[frénzi]

n. **a temporary state of chaos and panic** | 광란, 격분

The scuba divers witnessed feeding *frenzy* as the sharks devoured the bait.

DE　frenzy : emotion [imóuʃən]
　　frenzy는 격정적인 emotion(감격, 흥분)의 상태이다.

---

TRANSLATION | 예문 해석

| | |
|---|---|
| **dilapidate** | 폭동은 그 거리를 폐허로 만들었다. |
| **earshot** | 내게 최근의 소문들을 말해주기 전에 Tom은 우리가 (다른 사람들이) 들을 수 있는 거리 밖에 있는 지를 확인했다. |
| **enervate** | 장시간의 업무와 수면 부족으로 Marie는 기운이 빠졌다. |
| **frenetic** | 아이들은 수업 마지막 날에 열광적이었다. |
| **frenzy** | 스쿠버 다이버들은 상어들이 그 미끼를 게걸스레 먹는 광란의 탐식을 지켜보았다. |

## gorge
[gɔːrdʒ]

**v. to eat excessively and greedily** | 마구 먹다, 탐식하다

After 3 days of fasting, Amy *gorged* herself on anything she could get her hands on.

**CN** gorge : abstemious [æbstíːmiəs]

abstemious(절제있는, 금욕적인)한 사람은 gorge하지 않는다.

## grimace
[grímǝs]

**n. a facial contortion in reaction to pain or disgust** | 고통이나 혐오에 대한 반응으로 얼굴이 일그러짐, 찡그림

Francis *grimaced* whenever she was reminded of her painful past.

**인과** grimace : pain [pein]

pain(고통)으로 인해 표정이 grimace되다.

## inept
[inépt]

**adj. not apt; not skilled in; lacking in reason or sense** | 부적당한, 서투른, 어리석은

The boy's *inept* sense of direction led us to the wrong side of the state.

**WO** inept : adroitness [ədrɔ́itnis]

inept한 사람은 adroitness(솜씨)가 없다.

## inert
[inə́ːrt]

**adj. unable to move or resist motion** | 움직이거나 저항할 수 없는, 둔한

The ropes bound the *inert* hostage to the chair.

**CN** inert : react [riːǽkt]

inert한 것은 쉽게 react(반응하다)하지 못한다.

## inevitable
[inévətəbl]

**adj. unavoidable** | 피할 수 없는

Historians regarded the war as an *inevitable* conclusion to the enmity between the two countries.

**CN** inevitable : avoid [əvɔ́id]

inevitable(피할 수 없는)한 것은 avoid 할 수 없다는 것을 의미한다.

---

**TRANSLATION | 예문해석**

| | |
|---|---|
| gorge | 3일간의 단식 후에 Amy는 손에 잡히는 것은 무엇이든 마구 먹어댔다. |
| grimace | Francis는 그녀의 고통스러운 과거가 생각날 때마다 얼굴이 일그러졌다. |
| inept | 그 소년의 서투른 방향감각이 우리를 그 주의 잘못된 쪽으로 이끌었다. |
| inert | 그 움직일 수 없는 인질은 밧줄로 의자에 묶여있었다. |
| inevitable | 역사가들은 그 전쟁을 두 국가간의 적대감에서 야기된 피할 수 없는 결론이었다고들 한다. |

## ode
[oud]

**n.** **a lyrical poem written in praise of a particular person, thing, or event** | 송시(특정 인물, 사물, 사건을 기리는 서정시)

The young poet sang an *ode* to Odysseus, the clever and courageous hero.

> **KIN** ode : poem [póuəm]
> ode는 poem(시)의 한 종류이다.

## overbearing
[òuvərbɛ́əriŋ]

**adj.** **marked by the ability to force into submission; arrogant** | 위압적인, 거만한

The *overbearing* commander shouted at and threatened his troops.

> **ANT** overbearing : meek [miːk]
> meek: 굴종적인, 순한

## overexpose
[òuvərikspóuz]

**v.** **to expose too much or too long; to expose film to excessive light** | 과다 노출시키다, (필름 등을) 빛에 과다하게 노출하다

It is well known that today's youth are *overexposed* to sex and violence because of television and the internet.

> **인과** overexposure : jaded [dʒéidid]
> overexposure(과다 등장)한 결과 jaded(진저리가 난)하게 된다.

## overindulge
[òuvərindʌ́ldʒ]

**v.** **to indulge excessively in some action** | 지나치게 탐닉하다

It is hard to not *overindulge* during the holidays and vacations.

> **CH** overindulge : glutton [glʌ́tn]
> glutton(대식가)은 음식에 대해 overindulge하는 특징이 있다.

---

### TRANSLATION | 예문해석

| | |
|---|---|
| **ode** | 젊은 시인이 영리하고 용감한 영웅인 Odysseus에 대한 송시를 노래했다. |
| **overbearing** | 위압적인 사령관이 그의 군대에게 소리를 치고 위협을 했다. |
| **overexpose** | 오늘날의 젊은이들이 텔레비전과 인터넷 때문에 섹스와 폭력에 지나치게 노출되어 있다는 것은 잘 알려진 사실이다 |
| **overindulge** | 휴일이나 휴가 기간 동안 어떤 일에 지나치게 탐닉하지 않는 것은 어렵다. |

## overture
[óuvərtʃùər]

**n.** **an introductory musical piece; a proposal** | 음악의 서곡; 제안

The composer's *overture* to the opera was enthusiastically received by the crowd.

- **ANT** overture : coda [kóudə]
  - coda: 음악의 종결부

## pedestrian
[pədéstriən]

**adj.** **ordinary; lacking wit or imagination** | 평범한, 단조로운
**n.** **a person who is walking** | 보행자

The company's *pedestrian* advertisements failed to generate sales.
There were so many *pedestrians* on the street on Sunday.

- **ANT** pedestrian : imaginative [imǽdʒənətiv]
  - imaginative: 상상력이 풍부한

## peeve
[piːv]

**v.** **to cause to be annoyed or resentful** | 화나게 하다

The housekeeper was *peeved* at his boss for leaving such a mess.

- **ANT** peeve : placate [pléikeit]
  - placate: 달래다

## pierce
[piərs]

**v.** **to cut or pass through; to make a hole in** | 꿰뚫다, 구멍을 뚫다

Lily's father would not allow her to *pierce* her ears until she turned 16.

- **FUN** pierce : awl [ɔːl]
  - awl(송곳)은 pierce하기 위한 도구이다.

## precarious
[prikɛ́əriəs]

**adj.** **unstable or insecure** | 불안정한, 위험한

You don't seem to realize that we are in a *precarious* condition.

- **WO** precarious : stability [stəbíləti]
  - precarious한 것에는 stability(안정성)가 없다.

---

### TRANSLATION | 예문 해석

**overture** 그 작곡가의 오페라 서곡을 청중들은 열심히 들었다.
**pedestrian** 그 회사의 단조로운 광고들로는 판매를 유발시키지 못했다.
일요일 거리에는 정말 많은 사람들이 걸어다니고 있었다.
**peeve** 그 관리인은 엉망진창을 만들어 놓은 것에 대해 그의 상사에게 화가 났다.
**pierce** Lily의 아버지는 Lily에게 그녀가 16살이 될 때까지는 귀 뚫는 것을 허락하려고 하지 않았다.
**precarious** 당신은 우리가 불안정한 상황에 있다는 것을 인식하고 있지 않은 것 같다.

**precede** [prisíːd]
v. to occur before in time; to come before in order or rank | ~보다 먼저 일어나다, 우선하다

Mr. Roberts made it very clear that his opinion *precedes* any of his employees'.

**WO** precedent : unique [juːník]
precedent(전례)가 없는 것은 unique(독특한)한 것이다.

**precipitate** [prisípətèit]
v. to cause to occur suddenly or abruptly | 갑작스레 발생하게 하다

The accident was *precipitated* by the younger driver not paying attention to the road.

**WO** precipitate : symptom [símptəm]
precipitate하는 것은 어떠한 symptom(징조)도 없이 갑자기 발생하는 것이다.

**preponderance** [pripándərəns]
n. superiority in weight, power, or importance | (무게, 힘, 영향력 등에 있어서의) 우위

A *preponderance* of evidence against the defendant made the prosecution's job easy.

**대상** preponderance : weight [weit]
preponderance는 weight(무게) 등에 있어서 우위에 있는 것을 말한다.

**preposterous** [pripástərəs]
adj. inverted in order; contrary to reason, nature, or commom sense | 앞뒤가 뒤바뀐, 터무니없는, (상식,도리를) 벗어난

No one paid any attention to Bill because everything he said was *preposterous*.

**ANT** preposterous : commonsensical [kámənsénsikəl]
commonsensical: 상식적인

---

TRANSLATION | 예 문 해 석

**precede** Roberts씨는 그의 의견이 어떤 사원의 의견보다도 우선한다는 것을 확실히 했다.
**precipitate** 그 사고는 젊은 운전자가 길에 주의를 기울이지 않음으로써 갑작스럽게 발생했다.
**preponderance** 피고인에게 불리한 증거가 우세해서 검사의 일이 쉬워졌다.
**preposterous** Bill이 말한 것들은 모두 터무니 없어서 어느 누구도 경청하지 않았다.

## preserve
[prizə́ːrv]

**v. to guard from destruction or injury and to maintain good condition** | 보존하다

National parks *preserve* endangered animals and the habitats they live in.

**FUN** preservative : spoilage [spɔ́ilidʒ]
preservative(방부제)는 spoilage(부패)를 막기 위한 것이다.

## prestige
[prestíːdʒ]

**n. qualities that are regarded highly in the general opinion** | 명성, 위신

Despite the *prestige* that accompanied his occupation, Larry was discontented with the long hours.

**대상** prestige : eclipse [iklíps]
eclipse(실추시키다)는 prestige 등을 실추시킨다는 의미이다.

## prevail
[privéil]

**v. to triumph over in strength or influence; to be common or frequent** | 우세하다, 널리 퍼지다

In the Civil War, the North *prevailed* over the South.

**SYN** prevalent : predominant [pridɑ́mənənt]
prevalent: 널리 퍼진, 우세한

## prevaricate
[privǽrəkèit]

**v. to cover up the truth; to misrepresent** | 진실을 숨기다, 둘러대다

The guilty child *prevaricated* to his mother when she asked who broke the vase.

**WO** prevarication : truth [truːθ]
prevarication(얼버무림, 핑계)에는 truth(진실)가 없다.

## querulous
[kwérjuləs]

**adj. continually whining or complaining** | 불평하는, 투덜거리는

The traveler could not stand taking trips with *querulous* people.

**CH** querulous : grouch [grautʃ]
grouch(불평꾼)들은 늘 querulous하다.

---

**TRANSLATION | 예문해석**

| | |
|---|---|
| preserve | 국립 공원들은 멸종 위기에 처한 동물들과 그들의 서식지들을 보존한다. |
| prestige | Larry는 그의 직업으로 인해 명성을 얻었음에도 불구하고 긴 근무시간에는 불만족스러워 했다. |
| prevail | 남북 전쟁에서 북군이 남군을 이겼다. |
| prevaricate | 엄마가 누가 화병을 깨뜨렸냐고 물었을 때, 양심의 가책을 느낀 아이가 엄마에게 둘러댔다. |
| querulous | 그 여행자는 계속해서 불평하는 사람들과 여행하는 것을 견딜 수 없었다. |

## redolent
[rédələnt]

**adj.** giving off an odor or fragrance | 향기로운

Sara's hair was *redolent* of sweet perfume.

**SYN** redolent : fragrant [fréigrənt]

fragrant: 향기로운

## redoubtable
[riːdáutəbl]

**adj.** deserving of respect; causing a scare | 존경할 만한, 무서운

The counselor was a *redoubtable* member of the faculty who many students turned to for advice.

**POS** redoubtable : regard [rigáːrd]

regard: 존경

## rudiment
[rúːdəmənt]

**n.** a basic and essential element or principle | 기초, 기본 원리

Primary school educates youth in the *rudiments* of human knowledge.

**SYN** rudiment : fundament [fʌ́ndəmənt]

fundament: 기본 원리

## rue
[ruː]

**n.** a regret about something | 후회
**v.** to regret; to grieve for | 후회하다, 슬퍼하다

The old man has *rue* regarding his failed first marriage.
Mike *rued* that he asked his wife to divorce.

**SYN** rue : remorse [rimɔ́ːrs]

remorse: 후회

## scent
[sent]

**n.** a smell or perfumed fragrance | 냄새, 향기

The faint sharp *scent* of the geraniums mingled with the odor of Ethan's smoke.

**KIN** scent : malodor [mælóudər]

malodor은 scent(냄새) 중에서도 악취를 의미한다.

---

### TRANSLATION | 예문해석

**redolent** Sara의 머리카락에서는 달콤한 향수향기가 났다.
**redoubtable** 그 카운슬러는 많은 학생들이 조언을 구하기 위해 찾아갔던 존경할 만한 교직원이었다.
**rudiment** 초등학교에서는 아이들에게 인간 지식의 기본 원리에 대해 가르친다.
**rue** 그 나이 든 남자는 그의 실패한 첫번째 결혼에 대해 유감스러워 한다.
Mike는 아내에게 이혼하자고 요구했던 것을 후회했다.
**scent** 제라늄의 희미하고 독한 향기가 Ethan의 담배 연기 냄새와 섞였다.

## sedulous
[sédʒuləs]

**adj. steadily industrious; assiduous** | 근면한

The *sedulous* student was on the honor roll every semester.

**ANT** sedulous : indolent [índələnt]

indolent: 게으른

## sidereal
[saidíəriəl]

**adj. of or related to constellations or stars** | 별자리와 관련된, 항성의

The *sidereal* bodies in our solar system show the magnificence of God's creativity.

**POS** sidereal : star [staːr]

star: 별

## skeptic
[sképtik]

**n. one who doesn't easily believe or is prone to disbelieving; one inclined to skepticism regarding religion** | 회의론자, 무신론자

The Wright Brothers proved their *skeptics* wrong by building the first working airplane.

**CN** skeptic : credulous [krédʒələs]

skeptic들은 credulous(잘 믿는) 하지 않다.

## specious
[spíːʃəs]

**adj. appearing true although it is false** | 겉 보기만 그럴싸한

The man's *specious* reasoning nearly convinced the couple to sign the contract.

**ANT** specious : valid [vǽlid]

valid: 근거가 확실한

## stentorian
[stentɔ́ːriən]

**adj. very loud** | 아주 시끄러운, 소리가 큰

The *stentorian* speeches of the artillery continued in some distant encounter, but the crashes of the musketry had almost ceased.

**DE** stentorian : audible [ɔ́ːdəbl]

stentorian한 상태는 audible(들리는)한 것보다 훨씬 시끄러운 것을 말한다.

---

### TRANSLATION | 예문 해석

| | |
|---|---|
| **sedulous** | 그 근면한 학생은 매 학기 우등생 명단에 올랐다. |
| **sidereal** | 태양계 내의 항성체들은 신의 창조성의 웅장함을 보여준다. |
| **skeptic** | 라이트 형제는 최초의 비행기를 만들어 그들을 비웃던 회의론자들이 틀렸음을 증명해 냈다. |
| **specious** | 그 남자의 겉보기만 그럴싸한 논법에 설득되어 그 커플은 계약서에 서명할 뻔 했다. |
| **stentorian** | 포병대의 큰 소리의 연설이 먼 거리에서 계속되었지만, 장총의 충돌 소리들은 거의 멈췄다. |

## sterile
[stéril]

**adj. absolutely clean; unable to reproduce** | 살균된, 불모의

It is very important that a doctor's instruments are *sterile* before use to ensure that germs are not spread.

**WO** sterile : germ [dʒəːrm]

germ(세균)이 없는 무균질 상태를 **sterile**된 상태라고 한다.

## tedious
[tíːdiəs]

**adj. boring or tiresomely elongated** | 지루한, 장황한

Editing papers is a long and *tedious* process.

**ANT** tedious : absorbing [əbsɔ́ːrbiŋ]

absorbing: 흥미 진진한

## teeter
[tíːtər]

**v. to waver or move unsteadily** | 흔들거리다, 비틀거리다

A Chinaman went by, *teetering* under the weight of the market baskets slung on a pole across his shoulders.

**SYN** teeter : totter [tátər]

totter: 비틀거리다, 흔들거리다

## theatrical
[θiǽtrikəl]

**adj. relating to the theater; unnaturally extravagant in behavior and expression** | 연극의, 과장된

The *theatrical* performance by the thespian enhanced the play greatly.

**ANT** theatrical : sober [sóubər]

sober: 과장되지 않은

## torrid
[tɔ́ːrid]

**adj. intensely hot or scorching** | 몹시 더운, 타는 듯한

In South America, siestas are taken in the middle of the day to hide from the *torrid* sun.

**ANT** torrid : arctic [áːrktik]

arctic: 극도로 추운, 혹한의

---

### TRANSLATION | 예문 해석

**sterile** 의사가 사용하는 기구들은 세균이 퍼지지 않도록 하기위해 사용 전에 살균되어야 한다.
**tedious** 문서를 교정하는 일은 길고 지루한 과정이다.
**teeter** 한 중국인 남자가 어깨 위에 걸쳐져 있는 장대에 느슨하게 걸려 있는 시장 바구니들의 무게로 비틀거리며 지나갔다.
**theatrical** 그 비극 배우의 과장된 연기로 그 연극의 가치가 훨씬 올라갔다.
**torrid** 남미에서는 타는 듯한 태양을 피하기 위해 한낮에 siesta(낮잠)를 잔다.

## trepidation
[trèpədéiʃən]

**n. anxiety or fear** | 불안, 공포

The dog's enormous size caused the little boy to approach it with *trepidation*.

**WO** trepidation : dauntless [dɔ́:ntlis]

dauntless(겁 없는)한 사람은 trepidation을 느끼지 않는다.

## trespass
[tréspəs]

**v. to enter unlawfully onto another's property or land; to commit an offense or sin** | 침입하다, 죄를 저지르다

The hunter was arrested for *trespassing* on private property.

**KIN** trespass : enter [éntər]

trespass는 불법으로 enter(들어가다)하는 것이다.

## upset
[ʌpsét]

**v. to cause emotional or physical distress to** | (정신적·신체적으로) 괴롭게 하다

Axel was *upset* that his parents wouldn't let him go to the concert.

**CN** upset : unflappable [ʌnflǽpəbl]

unflappable(쉽게 동요되지 않는, 침착한)한 사람은 쉽게 upset되지 않는다.

---

### TRANSLATION | 예문 해석

| | |
|---|---|
| **trepidation** | 어린 소년은 그 개에게 다가갈 때 그것의 엄청난 크기에 공포를 느꼈다. |
| **trespass** | 사냥꾼은 사유지를 침범하여 체포되었다. |
| **upset** | Axel은 부모님이 콘서트에 가지 못하게 해서 화가 났다. |

# 9th Day Daily Check-up

■ Fill in the blanks with the correct letter that matches the word with its definition.

1. abet _____
2. dilapidate _____
3. teeter _____
4. gorge _____
5. peeve _____
6. redolent _____
7. prevaricate _____
8. amenity _____
9. frenetic _____
10. crest _____

a. giving off an odor or fragrance
b. to cover up the truth; to misrepresent
c. to actively encourage or support
d. to squander or bring into ruin
e. to cause to be annoyed or resentful
f. to eat excessively and greedily
g. frantic and nervously excited
h. the top of a hill or wave; the peak
i. the quality of being pleasant or agreeable; something that is conducive to convenience and pleasure
j. to waver or move unsteadily

■ Put the correct word in each blank from the list of words below.

11. saccharine(아주 달콤한)의 반의어는 _____이다.
12. dauntless한 사람은 _____을 느끼지 않는다.
13. valid(근거가 확실한)의 반의어는 _____이다.
14. grouch들은 늘 _____한다.
15. malodor는 _____ 중에서도 악취를 의미한다.
16. imaginative(상상력이 풍부한)의 반의어는 _____이다.
17. _____하는 것은 어떠한 symptom도 없이 갑자기 발생하는 것이다.
18. _____한 상태는 audible한 것 보다 훨씬 시끄러운 것을 말한다.
19. earshot은 _____할 수 있는 범위를 말한다.
20. _____은 pain을 없애주는 기능을 한다.

| a. specious | b. querulous | c. scent | d. pedestrian | e. stentorian | f. hear |
| g. acerbic | h. anesthetic | i. precipitate | j. tidy | k. theatrical | l. trepidation |

**Answer key**

1. c  2. d  3. j  4. f  5. e  6. a  7. b  8. i  9. g  10. h
11. g  12. l  13. a  14. b  15. c  16. d  17. i  18. e  19. f  20. h

# TAKE A BREAK  쉬·어·가·는 페·이·지

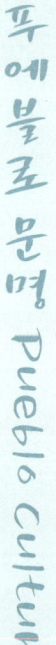

푸에블로 문명 Pueblo Culture

푸에블로는 북아메리카 남서부에 사는 인디언들로서 지금의 뉴멕시코주·애리조나주에 해당하는 지역에 살았다. 그들은 농경민으로서 백인이 들어오기 전부터 이미 관개를 하고 있었다. 예전부터 점토를 굳혀 만든 아파트식 취락을 하였으며 지금도 뉴멕시코주의 타오스에 있는 푸에블로족 마을에서 이 종류의 취락을 볼 수 있다. 이전의 바스켓 메이커(Basket Maker)문화와 푸에블로 문화를 합쳐 아나사지(Anasazi)문화라고 하는데, 기하학적 무늬를 넣은 토기와 수백 개의 방이 있는 집합주택이 특징이다. 이후 1700년대부터 에스파냐의 영향이 본격화되었지만 이들은 지금까지도 토착문화를 유지해오고 있다.

바스켓 메이커 인디언(100~500)은 수렵 및 채취생활을 하며 동굴이나 석조기둥과 아도비 벽돌로 된 곳에서 살았다. 변형 바스켓 메이커 시기(500~700)에는 농경이 주를 이루면서, 동굴 반지하 가옥이었으며 직선이나 초승달 모양으로 운집해 있었다. 발달 푸에블로 시기(700~1050) 또한 직선형·초승달형 가옥이 운집해 있었으며 이 시기에는 목화 재배가 이루어졌다. 도기 역시 다양한 모양으로 제작되어 바구니의 사용이 점차 줄었다. 고전 푸에블로 시기(1050~1300)에는 협곡과 벼랑을 따라 아파트식 가옥이 형성된 시기이다.

가옥은 벼랑 기슭에 지어졌으나 다른 지역의 가옥과 별반 다르지 않았다. 도기 기술은 고도로 발전했으며 면화나 유카실로 정교하게 직물을 짜는 기술도 있었다. 퇴행 푸에블로 시기(1300~1700)는 남쪽과 동쪽에 거주하던 인디언들이 리오그란데 계곡이나 애리조나의 화이트 산맥 지역으로 이동한 시기에 해당한다. 이전 시기보다 더 크게 지어진 가옥은 그 모양이나 건축에 있어서 열악했다. 도기 기술은 여전히 발달했으나 그 모양이 변화되었고, 직물은 그대로 유지되었다. 근대 푸에블로 시기(1700~현재)에는 에스파냐의 영향이 본격화되었다. 에스파냐는 새로운 문화를 강요하여 적대감을 야기했으며, 1600년대에 반란을 일으켰으나 곧 진압되었다. 그 이후 인디언 부족의 수와 마을은 크게 줄었으나 문화와 기술은 현재까지 보존되고 있다.

www.goHackers.com

해커스 어학연구소

# SUPER VOCA
## TENTH DAY

Out of sight, out of mind!
안보면 잊어버립니다.
매일 수퍼보카와 함께 ^-^

# 10th DAY

## affability
[æ̀fəbíləti]

**n.** the quality of being pleasant and easy to talk to
| 상냥함, 붙임성 있음

His *affability*, even to those whom he disliked, was unfailing.

**ANT** affability : surliness [sə́ːrlinis]
surliness: 무뚝뚝함

## affiliate
[əfílièit]

**v.** to accept as a member or branch; to become closely connected or associated | 회원이나 지부로 하다, 교제하다, 제휴하나

Lawrence only *affiliated* with such seedy characters under the most dire of circumstances.

**ANT** affiliate : dissociate [disóuʃièit]
dissociate: 분리하다, 관계를 끊다

## affinity
[əfínəti]

**n.** an interest or attraction to, often based on similarity
| 친밀함, 호감

The two young lovers felt an *affinity* for each other at first sight.

**ANT** affinity : antipathy [æntípəθi]
antipathy: 반감, 혐오

---

### TRANSLATION | 예문해석

| | |
|---|---|
| affability | 그의 상냥함은 그가 싫어하는 사람들에게 조차도 변치 않았다. |
| affiliate | Lawrence는 아주 긴박한 상황 하에서 불량배들과 제휴했다. |
| affinity | 그 두 젊은 연인은 첫눈에 서로에게 호감을 느꼈다. |

Hackers Super Vocabulary

## affirm
[əfə́ːrm]

**v. to maintain to be true; to confirm or ratify** | (사실이라고) 단언하다, 승인하다

Today, we *affirm* a new commitment to live out our nation's promise through civility, courage, compassion, and character.

**ANT** affirm : gainsay [gèinséi]

gainsay: (거짓이라고) 부인하다, 반박하다

## affluent
[ǽfluənt]

**adj. abundant or wealthy** | 풍부한, 부유한

Hank had grown up in an *affluent* family and always had his material needs met.

**ANT** affluent : impecunious [ìmpikjúːniəs]

impecunious: 가난한

## buffoon
[bəfúːn]

**n. a clown; a foolish and uneducated person** | 어릿광대, 어리석은 사람

The man acted like a *buffoon* in front of the kids to amuse them.

**CH** buffoon : ludicrous [lúːdəkrəs]

buffoon은 ludicrous(익살스러운)한 점을 지니고 있다.

## coward
[káuərd]

**n. a person disgracefully exhibiting lack of courage** | 비겁자

The *coward* was ostracized by his community for his lack of bravery.

**SYN** coward : dastard [dǽstərd]

dastard: 비겁자

## daft
[dæft]

**adj. foolish or insane** | 매우 어리석은, 미친

Brian's parents labeled his plans to forgo college as a *daft* decision.

**ANT** daft : judicious [dʒuːdíʃəs]

judicious: 현명한

---

### TRANSLATION | 예문 해석

**affirm** 오늘날, 우리는 공손함, 용기, 동정심, 덕성을 통해 우리나라의 비전에 따라 살아 나가겠다는 새로운 공약을 단언한다.
**affluent** Hank는 유복한 가정에서 자라 그의 물질적인 욕구가 항상 충족되었다.
**buffoon** 그 남자는 아이들을 즐겁게 해주기 위해 그들 앞에서 어릿광대처럼 행동했다.
**coward** 그 비겁자는 용기 부족 때문에 공동체에서 추방되었다.
**daft** Brian의 부모는 대학을 그만두겠다는 그의 계획이 아주 어리석은 결정이라고 했다.

## defend
[difénd]

**v.** **to protect from danger; to keep safe; to argue sympathetically for** | 방어하다, 옹호하다

Children depend upon adults to *defend* and protest their rights.

**CH** defend : apologist [əpɑ́lədʒist]

apologist(옹호자)는 어떤 정책이나 제도를 defend하는 사람이다.

## defer
[difə́:r]

**v.** **to postpone or move to a later time; to submit to another's wishes or opinions through respect** | 연기하다; 존경심에서 다른 사람의 의견을 따르다

It was impossible to *defer* the journey to Moscow any longer.

Lieberman has said he would *defer* to Gore if the former vice president decides to seek the presidency.

**ANT** deferrable : exigent [éksədʒənt]

deferrable: 연기할 수 있는

exigent: 급박한

**대상** defer : leader [líːdər]

leader(지도자)의 의견을 defer하다.

## defile
[difáil]

**n.** **a narrow valley** | 좁은 협곡

**v.** **to make impure or despicably unclean; to desecrate** | 더럽히다, 부정하게 하다, 신성모독하다

Many wild dogs lurk in the shadows of the *defile*, looking for prey.

The church had been broken into and *defiled* by vandals.

**CH** defile : narrowness [nǽrounis]

defile의 특징은 narrowness(좁음)이다.

**SYN** defile : taint [teint]

taint: 더럽히다

---

### TRANSLATION | 예문 해석

**defend** 어린이들은 그들의 권리를 옹호하고 보호하는데 있어 어른들에게 의존적이다.
**defer** 모스크바로의 여행을 더 이상 연기하는 것은 불가능했다.
Lieberman은 전 부통령이 대통령직에 입후보하기로 결정한다면 Gore의 의견을 따르겠다고 말했다.
**defile** 많은 야생 개들이 먹이를 찾으려고 좁은 협곡의 그늘에서 몰래 기다린다.
그 교회는 파괴자들에게 침범당하고 더럽혀졌다.

## definitive
[difínətiv]

**adj. supplying a final decision; precisely explicit**
| 결정적인, 명확한

The judgement of the case was *definitive* with no hope of appeal.

**ANT** definitive : provisional [prəvíʒənl]
provisional: 임시의, 잠정적인

## deft
[deft]

**adj. quick and skillful; adroit**
| 솜씨 좋은

The magician baffled the young child with his *deft* sleight of hand.

**ANT** deft : maladroit [mæ̀lədrɔ́it]
maladroit: 서투른

## defuse
[difjúːz]

**v. to remove the fuse from a bomb; to make less dangerous, tense, or hostile**
| (폭탄의) 신관을 제거하다, 진정시키다

The police *defused* the situation and coaxed the kidnappers into releasing the hostages.

**ANT** defuse : foment [foumént]
foment: 촉진하다, 선동하다

## diffidence
[dífədəns]

**n. the state of lacking self-confidence; shyness**
| 자신감이 없는 상태, 수줍음

His *diffidence* became evident in his speech and mannerisms.

**ANT** diffidence : brazenness [bréiznnis]
brazenness: 뻔뻔함

## dissonance
[dísənəns]

**n. a combination of discordant sounds; an inconsistency or lack of agreement**
| 불협화음, 불일치

The *dissonance* in their relationship grew until they finally broke up.

**ANT** dissonance : concord [kánkərd]
concord: 일치

---

### TRANSLATION | 예문 해석

| | |
|---|---|
| **definitive** | 그 사건에 대한 판결은 항소의 여지가 없는 결정적인 것이었다. |
| **deft** | 그 마술사는 솜씨 좋은 손놀림으로 그 어린 아이를 어리둥절하게 했다. |
| **defuse** | 경찰은 그 상황을 진정시켰고 그 유괴범을 구슬려 인질을 풀어주도록 했다. |
| **diffidence** | 그의 수줍음이 그의 연설과 제스처에서 명백하게 드러났다. |
| **dissonance** | 그들 관계의 불협화음이 점점 커져서 마침내 헤어지게 되었다. |

## distillate
[dístəlɪt]

**n. the condensed liquid product resulting from distillation; an essence**  | 증류된 농축액, 정수

Whiskey is a *distillate* of grain.

- CH  distillate : purity [pjúərəti]
  distillate는 purity(순도, 깨끗함)의 특성이 있다.

## divergent
[divə́ːrdʒənt]

**adj. moving apart from a common point; differing from a standard**  | 분기하는, (표준에서) 벗어난, 일탈하는

The salesman eventually convinced his boss of the financial benefits of following his unorthodox and *divergent* strategies.

- CH  divergent : aside [əsáid]
  aside(여담)는 divergent하다.

## dissipate
[dísəpèit]

**v. to disperse; to disappear by dispersion; to spend or use up carelessly**  | 흩뜨리다, 흩어져 없어지다, 탕진하다

The heavy clouds *dissipated* and the sun shone through.

In one week, Michael had *dissipated* his entire paycheck.

- DE  dissipate : diminish [dimíniʃ]
  dissipate는 diminish(감소하다)하여 결국 사라져 버리는 것이다.
- WO  dissipate : husbandry [hʌ́zbəndri]
  dissipate하는 사람에게는 husbandry(절약)가 없다.

## efface
[iféis]

**v. to obliterate or make indistinct; to make inconspicuous**  | 지우다, 희미하게 하다, 눈에 띄지 않게 하다

Michelle often *effaced* herself in an attempt to avoid being the object of attention.

- ANT  efface : bring to prominence [briŋ tə prámənəns]
  bring to prominence: 눈에 띄게 드러내다

---

TRANSLATION | 예문해석

**distillate** 위스키는 곡물의 증류액이다.
**divergent** 그 영업사원은 마침내 인습과 다르고 일탈적인 자신의 전략을 따름으로써 얻을 수 있는 재정적인 이점에 대해 그의 상사를 납득시켰다.
**dissipate** 무거운 구름이 흩어졌고 태양이 그 사이로 비쳤다.
일주일 후에, Michael은 그의 급료 전부를 탕진했다.
**efface** Michelle은 주목받는 것을 피하기 위해 종종 표면에 나서지 않았다.

## effervesce
[èfərvés]

**v.** to emit small bubbles of gas; to be high spirited or excited | 거품이 일다, 활기를 띠다, 흥분하다

Jane *effervesced* with joy upon hearing the news of her husband's successful surgery.

**ANT** effervesce : droop [druːp]
droop: 시들다, 의기소침하다

## effete
[ifíːt]

**adj.** depleted of vitality; weak; infertile | 활력을 잃은, 쇠약해진, 생산력이 없는

The *effete* senior citizen walked feebly and only with aid of a cane.

**ANT** effete : hale [heil]
hale: 정정한, 강건한

## efficacious
[èfəkéiʃəs]

**adj.** effective or able to produce an intended effect | 효능이 있는, 의도된 효과가 있는

The old woman wore the pained expression that she had long since found to be much more *efficacious* than anger.

**ANT** efficacious : futile [fjúːtl]
futile: 효과없는, 쓸모없는

## effulgent
[ifʌ́ldʒənt]

**adj.** shining brilliantly; splendid | 찬란하게 빛나는

The stars in the sky produced an *effulgent* sight.

**POS** effulgent : resplendence [rispléndəns]
resplendence: 번쩍임, 광휘

## enfeeble
[infíːbl]

**v.** to deprive of strength; to make weak or feeble | 쇠약하게 만들다

The reliance on funding has gradually *enfeebled* every state which has adopted it.

**대상** enfeeble : strength [streŋkθ]
strength(힘)를 enfeeble하다.

---

### TRANSLATION | 예문해석

| | |
|---|---|
| effervesce | Jane은 남편의 수술이 성공적이라는 소식을 듣자 기쁨으로 활기를 띠었다. |
| effete | 그 쇠약해진 노인은 지팡이가 있어야 걸을 수 있었다. |
| efficacious | 그 나이 든 여자가 오래 전부터 화내는 것보다 훨씬 더 효과가 있는 것으로 판단한 고통스런 표정을 지었다. |
| effulgent | 하늘의 별들이 눈부시게 빛나는 광경을 만들어냈다. |
| enfeeble | 기금에 의존하는 것은 그것을 채택한 모든 주를 점차적으로 쇠약하게 만든다. |

## enfranchise
[infræntʃaiz]

**v.** **to confer a franchise on; to admit a right; to set free**
| 참정권을 주다, 자치권을 주다, 자유롭게 하다

The Emancipation Proclamation *enfranchised* American slaves.

**ANT** enfranchise : enfetter [infétər]
enfetter: 족쇄를 채우다, 속박하다

## fanatic
[fənǽtik]

**n.** **a person who is marked by excessive enthusiasm**
| 열광자, 광신자

My father is a cheese cake *fanatic*.

**CH** fanatic : devoted [divóutid]
fanatic은 무언가에 devoted(몰두하고 있는, 헌신하는)되어 있는 상태의 사람이다.

## gloat
[glout]

**v.** **to think about something with victorious and malicious gratification**
| 흡족한 듯이 바라보다, 고소한 듯이 바라보다

The victor of the election *gloated* at his opponent.

**CH** gloat : smug [smʌg]
gloat하는 행위에는 smug(잘난체 하는)라는 속성이 포함되어 있다.

## impartial
[impɑ́ːrʃəl]

**adj.** **treating all sides equally; not partial**
| 공정한, 공평한

The coach couldn't find an *impartial* referee to work the game.

**CH** impartiality : arbitrator [ɑ́ːrbitrèitər]
arbitrator(중재인, 심판관)에게는 impartiality(공정함)가 있어야 한다.

## impassion
[impǽʃən]

**v.** **to arouse the passions or feelings of**
| 감동시키다, 마음을 강하게 움직이다

The president's rousing speech *impassioned* the nation to fight illiteracy.

**CN** impassion : callous [kǽləs]
callous(냉담한)한 사람은 쉽게 impassion(감동시키다)하기 어렵다.

---

TRANSLATION | 예 문 해 석

| | |
|---|---|
| enfranchise | 노예 해방령에 의해 미국의 노예들이 해방되었다. |
| fanatic | 나의 아버지는 치즈 케익광이다. |
| gloat | 그 선거의 승자는 그의 상대를 고소한 듯이 바라보았다. |
| impartial | 그 코치는 경기를 공정하게 봐줄 심판을 찾을 수가 없었다. |
| impassion | 그 대통령의 감동적인 연설은 국민들의 마음을 움직여 문맹을 퇴치하겠다는 생각을 갖게 했다. |

## imperative
[impérətiv]

**adj.** should not be avoided; mandatory or orderly | 피해서는 안될, 의무적인, 명령적인

It is *imperative* that the doctor's instructions be carried out precisely.

- **POS** imperative : order [ɔ́:rdər]
  order: 명령

## infinite
[ínfənət]

**adj.** extending indefinitely | 무한한

There is an almost *infinite* variety of people in American society.

- **CN** infinite : exhaust [igzɔ́:st]
  infinite(무한한)한 것은 exhaust(고갈시키다)해 버릴 수가 없다.

## inflame
[infléim]

**v.** to set on fire; to arouse to excessive action or feeling; to make more violent | 불을 붙이다, 자극하다, 부채질하다

The students further *inflamed* the heated situation by insulting the intelligence of the teacher.

- **ANT** inflame : assuage [əswéidʒ]
  assuage: 누그러 뜨리다

## jaundice
[dʒɔ́:ndis]

**v.** to affect adversely | 불리하게 영향을 주다

Diane's previous marriage had *jaundiced* her opinion of men until she met Josh.

- **ANT** jaundice : dispose favorably [dispóuz féivərəbli]
  dispose favorably: 유리하게 영향을 주다

## lofty
[lɔ́:fti]

**adj.** having great height; exalted or noble | 높은, 고위의, 고귀한

The prosecutor pleaded with the *lofty* judge to make a just decision.

- **ANT** lofty : ignoble [ignóubl]
  ignoble: 비천한

---

TRANSLATION | 예 문 해 석

| | |
|---|---|
| imperative | 의사의 지시에 정확히 따라야 한다. |
| infinite | 미국 사회에는 무한히 다양한 사람들이 있다. |
| inflame | 그 학생은 교사의 지성을 모욕함으로써 그 악화된 상황에 부채질을 했다. |
| jaundice | Diane이 Josh를 만나기 전까지는, 이전의 결혼 경험이 남자에 대한 그녀의 의견을 왜곡시켰다. |
| lofty | 검사가 그 고위직 판사에게 공정한 판결을 내려줄 것을 간청했다. |

## metaphor
[métəfɔ̀ːr]

**n. a figure of speech where something is used in place of another to suggest a likeness or analogy between them**
| 은유

Homeric epic is famous for its extended *metaphors*.

**CN** metaphor : literal [lítərəl]
metaphor는 literal(글자대로의, 있는 그대로의)하지 않다.

## morbid
[mɔ́ːrbid]

**adj. characterized by excessively gloomy or unwholesome thoughts and feelings; relating to disease**
| 병적인, 병의

His *morbid* thoughts nearly led him to commit suicide.

**ANT** morbid : wholesome [hóulsəm]
wholesome: 건강한

## muffle
[mʌ́fl]

**v. to wrap up or cover, in order to deaden sound**
| 소리가 나가지 않게 감싸다

A *muffled* sound was coming from the child, but his father couldn't understand it.

**ANT** muffled : plangent [plǽndʒənt]
muffled: 소리를 죽인
plangent: 소리가 울려 퍼지는

## nefarious
[nifɛ́əriəs]

**adj. wicked or evil**
| 사악한

Al Capone was the *nefarious* mastermind behind the St. Valentine's day massacre.

**POS** nefarious : wickedness [wíkidnis]
wickedness: 사악

## obey
[oubéi]

**v. to follow orders or comply with commands**
| 복종하다

The troops *obeyed* every command the officer made.

**CN** obey : recalcitrant [rikǽlsitrənt]
recalcitrant(반항하는, 말을 잘 안 듣는)한 사람은 다른 사람에게 obey하지 않는다.

---

TRANSLATION | 예 문 해 석

| | |
|---|---|
| **metaphor** | Homeric식의 서사시는 폭넓은 은유로 유명하다. |
| **morbid** | 그의 병적으로 우울한 생각들은 그를 거의 자살로 이끌었다. |
| **muffle** | 숨 죽인 소리가 아이에게서 나고 있었지만, 아버지는 그것을 이해할 수 없었다. |
| **nefarious** | Al Capone는 성 발렌타인데이 대학살의 사악한 배후 조종자였다. |
| **obey** | 그 군대는 장교가 내리는 모든 명령에 복종했다. |

## obfuscate
[ábfʌskeit]

v. **to make obscure or unclear; to confuse or baffle**　| 애매하게 하다, 당황하게 하다

The president's staff *obfuscated* the story concerning the president's alleged affair.

**ANT** obfuscate : clarify [klǽrəfài]

clarify: 분명하게 하다

## offbeat
[ɔ́ːfbìt]

adj. **unexpected or unusual**　| 색다른

The new student was too *offbeat* to fit in with the other students.

**ANT** offbeat : bathetic [bəθétik]

bathetic: 진부한, 평범한

## offend
[əfénd]

v. **to cause hurt feelings or resentment**　| 화나게 하다

*Offended* by the students' harsh criticism, the teacher left the room.

**WO** offense : euphemism [júːfəmìzm]

euphemism(완곡 어법)에는 offense(감정을 해침)를 줄만한 소지가 없다.

## officious
[əfíʃəs]

adj. **meddlesome; unofficial**　| 참견하는; 비공식의

The *officious* neighbor was known for giving unwanted advice and being noisy.

**DE** officious : attentive [əténtiv]

attentive(주의 깊은, 친절한)한 행위가 지나치면 officious한 행동이 된다.

## offish
[ɔ́(ː)fiʃ]

adj. **prone to be reserved and aloof**　| 새침하고 쌀쌀 맞은

I asked my sister why she was being so *offish*, but she gave no reply.

**ANT** offish : sociable [sóuʃəbl]

sociable: 사교적인

---

TRANSLATION | 예 문 해 석

| | |
|---|---|
| obfuscate | 그 대통령의 참모들은 대통령의 추정되는 정사에 관해 애매모호하게 말했다. |
| offbeat | 그 새로운 학생은 너무 색달라서 다른 학생들과 맞지 않았다. |
| offend | 학생들의 거친 비난에 화가 나서, 그 교사는 방을 떠났다. |
| officious | 그 참견 잘하는 이웃은 원치 않는 충고를 하며 시끄러운 것으로 알려져 있다. |
| offish | 나는 여동생에게 왜 그렇게 쌀쌀맞게 구는지를 물었지만, 그녀는 대답하지 않았다. |

## parry
[pǽri]

**v. to deflect or evade** | 모면하다, 피해 가다

Smith had been a politician for 10 years and could *parry* any reporter's question.

대상 　parry : question [kwéstʃən]
　　　question(질문)을 parry하다.

## parse
[pɑːrs]

**v. to take a sentence and analyze each component grammatically** | 문장의 각 요소를 문법적으로 분석하다

Angela *parsed* over the letter and found no mistakes.

대상 　parse : sentence [séntəns]
　　　sentence(문장)을 parse하다.

## penitent
[pénətənt]

**adj. feeling sorrow and shame over acts of sin committed** | 죄를 지은 것에 대해 슬퍼하고 뉘우치는, 참회하는

A truly *penitent* person makes amends to the people he has hurt.

SYN 　penitence : remorse [rimɔ́ːrs]
　　　penitence: 뉘우침, 참회
　　　remorse: 뉘우침

## perforate
[pə́ːrfərèit]

**v. to punch a row of holes in order to allow for easy separation** | 쉽게 분리하기 위해 열을 지어 구멍을 내다

Enid preferred the notebook with the *perforated* pages so she could tear them out.

대상 　perforate : hole [houl]
　　　perforate은 hole(구멍)을 만든다는 의미이다.

## raffish
[rǽfiʃ]

**adj. cheaply or showily vulgar; characterized by a carefree unconventionality** | 저속한, 방탕한

Amy's father worried about her becoming friendly with the *raffish* bunch of hoodlums.

WO 　raffish : decorum [dikɔ́ːrəm]
　　　raffish한 것에는 decorum(단정, 예의바름)이 없다.

---

TRANSLATION | 예 문 해 석

**parry** 　Smith는 정치인 생활을 10년 동안이나 해서 어떤 기자의 질문이라도 잘 피해 갈 수 있었다.
**parse** 　Angela가 그 편지를 문법적으로 분석했고 틀린 부분은 찾아 내지 못했다.
**penitent** 　진실로 자신의 죄를 뉘우치는 사람은 그가 상처를 준 사람들에게 보상을 한다.
**perforate** 　Enid는 구멍이 뚫려 있어서 페이지들을 찢어내기 편한 공책을 더 좋아했다.
**raffish** 　Amy의 아버지는 그녀가 평판이 나쁜 깡패들과 친하게 지내는 것을 걱정했다.

## refined
[riːfáind]

**adj. free from vulgarity; purified** | 세련된, 정제한

Tom had always lived among *refined* and cultivated people.

**ANT** refined : uncouth [ʌnkúːθ]
uncouth: 세련되지 않은

## refractory
[rifræktəri]

**adj. resistant to authority, control, pressure, or heat** | 순종하지 않는, 다루기 힘든, 내열성의

The frustrated teacher quickly sent her *refractory* student to the principal's office.

**대상** refractory : authority [əθɔ́ːrəti]
refractory는 authority(권위) 등에 저항하는 것을 일컫는다.

## safeguard
[séifgàːrd]

**v. to ensure the safety of; to protect** | 보호하다

My aim is simply to *safeguard* my reputation.

**대상** safeguard : accident [æksədənt]
safeguard는 accident(사고)로부터 보호하다는 의미이다.

## snobbish
[snábiʃ]

**adj. being a snob, one who thinks himself/herself too good for others; vulgarly pretentious** | 속물의, 거드름 피우는

A *snobbish* attitude will bring you nothing but loneliness.

**DE** snobbish : refined [rifáind]
refined(세련된)가 지나치면 snobbish한 행동이 된다.

## suffuse
[səfjúːz]

**v. to fill or spread over with fluid, color, or light** | (액체·색·빛 등으로) 채우다, 뒤덮다

The room was *suffused* with sunlight when she opened the window shades.

**DE** suffuse : tint [tint]
tint(엷게 색을 칠하다)에 비해 전체를 완전히 물들이는 것을 suffuse하다고 한다.

---

### TRANSLATION | 예문해석

**refined** — Tom은 항상 세련되고 교양 있는 사람들 사이에서 살았다.
**refractory** — 답답해진 그 교사는 그녀의 다루기 힘든 학생을 바로 교장실로 보냈다.
**safeguard** — 내 목표는 단지 내 명성을 보호하는 것이다.
**snobbish** — 속물적인 태도는 너에게 외로움만 가져다 줄뿐이다.
**suffuse** — 그 방은 그녀가 커튼을 열었을 때 햇빛으로 가득 채워졌다.

### surrender
[səréndər]

**v. to resign or give up** | 양도하다, 포기하다

James *surrendered* his job in New York to return home and care for his ailing mother.

**ANT** surrender : appropriate [əpróuprièit]

appropriate: 사취하다, 착복하다

### unfit
[ʌnfít]

**adj. unsuitable; unqualified** | 부적당한, 적임이 아닌

It was obvious that the man was *unfit* to be a soldier.

**ANT** unfit : meet [miːt]

meet: 적당한

### unflappable
[ʌnflǽpəbl]

**adj. not easily perturbed; persistently calm** | 쉽게 동요되지 않는, 침착한

One sign of a true leader is an *unflappable* reaction to crisis.

**CN** unflappable : upset [ʌpsét]

unflappable한 사람은 쉽게 upset(정신적, 신체적으로 괴롭게 하다)되지 않는다.

### vagrant
[véigrənt]

**adj. moving around without direction; wandering and unsettled** | 정처 없이 떠도는, 헤매는, 불안정한

During the depression, the streets were filled with *vagrant* children who had nowhere to go.

**ANT** vagrant : fixed [fikst]

fixed: 고정된

### veer
[viər]

**v. to shift direction sharply** | 갑자기 방향을 바꾸다

The driver *veered* off the road to avoid oncoming traffic.

**대상** veer : course [kɔːrs]

course(방향)를 veer하다.

---

**TRANSLATION | 예문해석**

| | |
|---|---|
| **surrender** | James는 고향으로 돌아가 병든 어머니를 돌보기 위해 New York에서의 일자리를 포기했다. |
| **unfit** | 그 남자가 군인이 되기에 부적당하다는 것은 명백했다. |
| **unflappable** | 진정한 지도자의 한가지 특징은 위기에 대한 침착한 반응이다. |
| **vagrant** | 거리는 불경기동안 갈 곳이 없어 정처없이 헤매는 아이들로 가득 찼다. |
| **veer** | 그 운전자는 다가오는 차량들을 피하기 위해 도로에서 갑자기 방향을 바꿨다. |

# 10th Day Daily Check-up

■ Fill in the blanks with the correct letter that matches the word with its definition.

1. affability _____
2. daft _____
3. effete _____
4. defer _____
5. morbid _____
6. refined _____
7. obfuscate _____
8. defuse _____
9. snobbish _____
10. effulgent _____

a. free from vulgarity; purified
b. foolish or insane
c. shining brilliantly; splendid
d. the quality of being pleasant and easy to talk to
e. characterized by excessively gloomy or unwholesome thoughts and feelings; relating to disease
f. weak; infertile; depleted of vitality
g. to submit to another's wishes or opinions through respect
h. to lessen the danger; to remove the fuse from a bomb
i. to make obscure or unclear
j. being a snob, one who thinks himself/herself too good for others

■ Put the correct word in each blank from the list of words below.

11. _____한 사람은 쉽게 upset되지 않는다.
12. _____의 동의어는 dastard(비겁자)이다.
13. _____하는 행위에는 smug라는 속성이 포함되어 있다.
14. _____은 ludicrous한 점을 지니고 있다.
15. narrowness는 _____의 특징이다.
16. _____는 authority 등에 저항하는 것을 말한다.
17. impecunious(가난한)의 반의어는 _____이다.
18. _____하는 사람에게는 husbandry(절약)가 없다.
19. _____은 무언가에 devoted(몰두하고 있는)된 사람이다.
20. _____는 purity의 특징이 있다.

a. buffoon   b. fanatic   c. distillate   d. suffuse   e. gloat   f. unflappable
g. coward    h. affluent  i. refractory   j. meet      k. defile  l. dissipate

**Answer key**

11. f  12. g  13. e  14. a  15. k  16. i  17. h  18. l  19. b  20. c
1. d  2. b  3. f  4. g  5. e  6. a  7. i  8. h  9. j  10. c

# 1st day~10th Day Crossword Puzzle

Answer Page 476

# Questions

### across

2. the ability and good judgment to govern oneself with the use of reason
4. to speak abruptly and impulsively
5. lacking interest or energy
8. a chronological error
10. cold and grave in appearance or manner; morally self-disciplined; having no adornment
16. growing thick and healthily; fertile or plentiful
17. skillful or clever; artful
18. to ridicule or challenge by mocking
19. to interrupt or put into disorder
20. to oppose or obstruct; to baffle

### down

1. to shorten or make less by cutting off some part
3. to subjugate or put into slavery
6. to obtain by force or illegal power
7. a substance that speeds up a chemical reaction; an agent that provokes change
9. awkward or lacking grace
11. to show by example; to serve as an example of
12. to offend with distastefulness; a strong aversion or dislike
13. learned or scholarly
14. to disturb or cause confusion to someone's peace of mind
15. drinkable

# Super Voca

## 11th DAY

영단어가 70만개래요.
그나마 우린 얼마나 다행입니까?

---

### alacrity
[əlǽkrəti]

**n. eagerness; speed or quickness** | 열의, 민첩

Bryan carried on his mission with great *alacrity*.

**WO** alacrity : apathetic [æ̀pəθétik]

apathetic(무감각한)한 사람은 alacrity가 없다.

---

### albino
[ælbáinou]

**n. abnormal pigmentation causing such characteristics as milky skin or white hair; a person or animal lacking normal pigmentation** | 피부 색소 결핍증, 백색종에 걸린 사람이나 동물

A U.S.-based Korean researcher has succeeded in changing white *albino* mice hairs to black by correcting their genetic mutation.

**WO** albinism : pigment [pígmənt]

albinism(백색종)은 pigment(색소)가 없는 증상을 뜻한다.

---

### ambivalent
[æmbívələnt]

**adj. characterized by a mixture of opposite attitudes or feelings; fluctuating in opinion** | 양면가치의, 의견을 계속 바꾸는

Even though Malcolm played a role in the company's technological revolution, he is *ambivalent* about the changes.

**WO** ambivalent : commitment [kəmítmənt]

ambivalent한 태도를 가진 사람은 확실한 commitment(공약, 언질)를 하지 않는다.

---

### TRANSLATION | 예문해석

| | |
|---|---|
| **alacrity** | Bryan은 대단히 민첩하게 임무를 수행했다. |
| **albino** | 미국에서 활동하고 있는 한 한국인 연구원이 피부 색소 결핍증에 걸린 생쥐의 유전자 변종을 바로잡아 줌으로써 이 쥐의 흰 털을 검게 만드는 데 성공했다. |
| **ambivalent** | Malcolm은 비록 그 회사의 기술 혁신에 기여했음에도 불구하고 그런 변화에는 양면적인 태도를 취했다. |

## ancillary
[ǽnsəlèri]

**adj.** **not of primary importance** | 보조적인, 부수적인

After the pressing matters are discussed, the *ancillary* topics will be covered if there is leftover time.

**ANT** ancillary : paramount [pǽrəmàunt]
paramount: 가장 중요한, 최고의

## artifact
[ɑ́ːrtəfæ̀kt]

**n.** **a manmade object of historical or archaeological interest** | 역사적, 고고학적으로 흥미로운 인공의 유물

The *artifacts* that were discovered in Italy have provided valuable information about how people lived thousands of years ago.

**FUN** artifacts : museum [mjuːzíːəm]
museum(박물관)은 artifacts를 전시하기 위한 곳이다.

## aseptic
[əséptik]

**adj.** **clear of pathogenic microorganisms** | 발병성의 미세균이 없는, 무균의

Doctors have to use *aseptic* instruments when treating patients to prevent infections.

**FUN** aseptic : disinfection [dìsinfékʃən]
disinfection(소독약, 멸균제)는 aseptic하게 만드는 기능이 있다.

## atrocious
[ətróuʃəs]

**adj.** **appallingly inhumane; wicked** | 지독히 잔혹한, 사악한

Surviving *atrocious* living conditions, the family was finally able to move out of the slums.

**DE** atrocious : bad [bæd]
atrocious는 bad(나쁜)보다 더 강한 표현이다.

## babble
[bǽbl]

**v.** **to utter meaningless sounds** | 분명치 않은 소리를 내다, 불분명하게 주절거리다

The stranger *babbled* endlessly about the reasons why I should buy his product.

**ANT** babble : express succinctly [iksprés sʌksíŋktli]
express succinctly: 명료하게 말하다

---

### TRANSLATION | 예문해석

**ancillary** 긴급한 문제들을 논의한 후에 시간이 남으면 부수적인 주제들이 다루어 질것이다.
**artifact** Italy에서 발견된 인공 유물들은 수천 년 전의 사람들이 어떻게 살았는지에 대한 중요한 정보를 제공해 주고 있다.
**aseptic** 의사들은 환자를 치료할 때 감염을 방지하기 위해 무균의 기구들을 사용해야 한다.
**atrocious** 잔혹한 상황에서 살아남기 위해, 마침내 그 가족들은 빈민굴에서 벗어나 이사할 수 있었다.
**babble** 그 낯선 이는 내가 이 물건을 사야 되는 이유를 끊임없이 주절댔다.

## beacon
[bíːkən]

**n. a signaling device, such as a lighthouse; a signal fire** | 등대, 봉화

The *beacon* gave the lost sailors hope.

**FUN** beacon : light [lait]
beacon은 light(빛)을 내는 기능을 지닌다.

## blazon
[bléizn]

**n. a coat of arms** | 문장

**v. to adorn or embellish with** | 문장으로 장식하다

A dove was added to the country's *blazon* following the ratification of the peace treaty.

The knight, *blazoned* with armor, charged the gates of the castle.

**FUN** blazon : adorn [ədɔ́ːrn]
blazon(문장)은 adorn하는 데 사용된다.

## brattish
[brǽtiʃ]

**adj. often used in reference to a spoiled child** | 무례하고 버릇없는

The *brattish* child was scolded by his mother for his rude behavior in front of the guests.

**SYN** brattish : mischievous [místʃivəs]
mischievous: 짓궂은

## chagrin
[ʃəgrín]

**n. a feeling of frustration or embarrassment caused by failure or disappointment** | (실패나 실망에서 야기된) 분함이나 난처함

Much to his *chagrin*, Phillip didn't receive the promotion his boss promised.

**ANT** chagrin : elation [iléiʃən]
elation: 의기양양

## coagulate
[kouǽgjuleit]

**v. to transform from a liquid into a mass** | 응고 시키다

There was *coagulated* blood at the corners of Hector's mouth.

**FUN** coagulant : clot [klɑt]
coagulant(응고제)는 액체를 clot(응고시키다)시킨다.

---

**TRANSLATION | 예문 해석**

| | |
|---|---|
| beacon | 그 등대 불빛은 표류하던 선원들에게 희망을 주었다. |
| blazon | 평화 조약 승인에 따라 국가의 문장에 비둘기가 들어갔다. |
| | 문장이 새겨진 갑옷을 입은 그 기사는 성문들을 공격했다. |
| brattish | 그 버르장머리 없는 어린이는 손님들 앞에서 예의없이 행동해서 어머니로부터 꾸중을 들었다. |
| chagrin | 몹시 분하게도 Phillip은 그의 상사가 약속했던 진급을 하지 못했다. |
| coagulate | Hector의 입의 양쪽 가장자리에는 응고된 피가 묻어 있었다. |

## craven
[kréivən]

**adj. lacking courage; cowardly** | 용기가 없는, 겁쟁이의

The *craven* soldiers were the first to die on the battlefield.

**CH** craven : dastard [dǽstərd]

dastard(겁쟁이, 비겁한 사람)는 craven하다.

## dabble
[dǽbl]

**v. to engage in or do something superficially; to splash and play in water** | 큰 관심 없이 피상적으로 어떤 일을 해보다, 물장구 치다

Although Tyrone *dabbled* in learning many languages, he was fluent in none.

**ANT** dabbler : specialist [spéʃəlist]

dabbler: 장난삼아 하는 사람
specialist: 전문가

## deadpan
[dédpæ̀n]

**adj. marked by a void of expression** | 무표정한

His face remained *deadpan* throughout the poker game.

**SYN** deadpan : impassive [impǽsiv]

impassive: 무표정한, 무감각한

## debase
[dibéis]

**v. to lower in value or quality** | 가치나 질을 저하시키다

The euro has dramatically *debased* the value of the Turkish lira.

**대상** debase : value [vǽljuː]

value를 debase(떨어뜨리다)하다.

## debate
[dibéit]

**v. to engage in a formal discussion** | 논쟁하다
**n. a formal argument or a discussion with opposing points** | 논쟁, 토론

The two presidential candidates *debated* on public television.
Both the participants brought up points during the *debate*.

**SYN** debate : issue [íʃuː]

issue: 논쟁, 토론

---

TRANSLATION | 예문해석

**craven** 싸움터에서 제일 먼저 죽은 자들은 겁쟁이 병사들이었다.
**dabble** 비록 Tyrone은 여러가지 언어를 조금씩 배웠지만, 유창하게 말하는 것은 없다.
**deadpan** 포커 게임을 하는 동안 줄곧 그의 얼굴은 무표정했다.
**debase** 유로화로 인해 터키의 리라화 가치가 급격히 떨어졌다.
**debate** 2명의 대통령 후보들은 공영 텔레비전 방송에 나와서 논쟁을 벌였다.
양 참가자들은 논쟁중에 중요한 사항들을 부각시켰다.

### debilitate
[dibílətèit]

**v. to weaken the strength of** | 약하게 만들다

Throwing for nine innings *debilitated* the pitcher's arm.

대상 debilitate : strength [streŋkθ]

debilitate는 strength(힘, 세기)를 약하게 만드는 것이다.

### draconian
[dreikóuniən]

**adj. very severe or harsh** | (법 등이) 매우 엄격한, 매우 가혹한

Many people believe that modern immigration laws are *draconian*.

POS draconian : severity [səvérəti]

severity: 엄격, 혹독

### drain
[drein]

**v. to cause liquid to go out from** | 배수시키다, 물을 빼내다

When the lake was *drained*, the lost boat was found.

FUN drain : colander [kʌ́ləndər]

colander(여과기)는 물을 drain하는 기능이 있다.

### dubious
[djúːbiəs]

**adj. having or showing doubt; creating uncertainty** | 의심하는, 모호한

Coach Nelson was *dubious* about his team's chances of winning after they failed to score.

WO dubious : conviction [kənvíkʃən]

dubious한 사람은 conviction(확신)을 갖고 있지 않다.

### embarrass
[imbǽrəs]

**v. to place in doubt, perplexity, or difficulties** | 당황하게 하다

The young lady was *embarrassed* by the man's attention.

DE embarrassment : humiliation [hjuːmìliéiʃən]

humiliation(굴욕)은 embarrassment(난처, 당황)보다 더욱 심하게 창피하고 무안한 감정을 나타낸다.

---

TRANSLATION | 예문해석

| | |
|---|---|
| **debilitate** | 9이닝 동안의 투구는 그 투수의 팔을 약하게 만들었다. |
| **draconian** | 많은 사람들은 새로운 이민법이 매우 엄격하다고 믿고 있다. |
| **drain** | 호수의 물이 빠지자 실종된 배가 모습을 드러냈다. |
| **dubious** | Nelson 감독은 자신의 팀이 득점에 실패하자 승리의 가능성을 의심했다. |
| **embarrass** | 그 젊은 숙녀는 그 남자의 배려에 당황했다. |

## exacerbate
[igzǽsərbèit]

**v. to increase the severity of** | 악화시키다, 더하게 하다

Pollution *exacerbates* the depletion of the ozone layer.

**SYN** exacerbate : deprave [dipréiv]

deprave: 악화시키다

## exaggerate
[igzǽdʒərèit]

**v. to overstate the truth** | 과장해서 말하다

We couldn't trust what she said because she always *exaggerates*.

**CH** exaggerated : hyperbole [haipə́ːrbəli]

hyperbole(과장법)은 exaggerated(과장된)된 수사법이다.

## fidget
[fídʒit]

**v. to move uneasily due to anxiety or restlessness** | 걱정 때문에 불안하게 행동하다, 안절부절 못하다

During a job interview, one must remember to appear calm and confident by not *fidgeting*.

**인과** fidget : nervousness [nə́ːrvəsnis]

fidget은 nervousness(초조함)의 결과로 나타나는 행동이다.

## flaccid
[flǽksid]

**adj. lacking normal firmness** | 맥없이 축 늘어진, 무기력한

Many months of not exercising made Andrew's body *flaccid*.

**WO** flaccid : firmness [fə́ːrmnis]

flaccid한 것에는 firmness(견고함)가 없다.

## flatter
[flǽtər]

**v. to excessively compliment with self-directed intentions** | 의도를 가지고 치켜 세우다, 아첨하다

A person who knows how to *flatter* also knows how to slander.

**DE** flatter : adulate [ǽdʒəlèit]

adulate(비굴하게 아첨하다)는 flatter보다 아첨의 정도가 더 심하다.

---

### TRANSLATION | 예문해석

| | |
|---|---|
| exacerbate | 공해는 오존층 감소 현상을 악화시킨다. |
| exaggerate | 우리는 그녀의 과장하는 버릇 때문에 그녀의 말을 믿을 수 없었다. |
| fidget | 취업 면접을 할 때는 불안하게 행동하지 않음으로써 침착하고 자신감 있게 보여야 함을 명심해야 한다. |
| flaccid | 여러 달 동안 운동을 하지 않아서 Andrew의 몸은 축 늘어졌다. |
| flatter | 아첨에 능한 자는 비방에도 능하다. |

## flaw
[flɔː]

**n. a fault or imperfection that devalues the whole**
| 전체의 가치를 깎아내리는 결점, 약점

Anne's lack of experience was the only *flaw* on her resume.

**DE** flaw : glitch [glitʃ]
glitch은 사소한 flaw이다.

## fragile
[frǽdʒəl]

**adj. weak and easily broken**
| 약한, 깨지기 쉬운

All the *fragile* china broke when the mover dropped the box.

**SYN** fragile : frail [freil]
frail: 허약한, 깨지기 쉬운

## frailty
[fréilti]

**n. physical weakness; a fault, especially a moral weakness**
| 약함, 약점, 결점

You should be very careful when you are handling babies because of their *frailty*.

**POS** frailty : spindly [spíndli]
spindly: 가냘픈, 허약한

## fraud
[frɔːd]

**n. an intentional deception of the truth committed for personal gain at the expense of another**
| 남을 속임으로써 이득을 취하는 것, 사기

Force and *fraud* are the two cardinal virtues in war.

**CH** fraudulent : hoax [houks]
hoax(속임수)는 fraudulent(사기의, 부정 행위의)한 특징을 지닌다.

## gibberish
[dʒíbəriʃ]

**n. unintelligible or nonsensical talk or writing**
| 아무 의미 없는 말이나 글, 횡설수설

Mrs. Earnshaw repeated over and over again some *gibberish* that nobody could understand.

**CN** gibberish : intelligible [intélədʒəbl]
gibberish은 intelligible(알기 쉬운)하지 않다.

---

TRANSLATION | 예 문 해 석

flaw　　　　Anne의 경험 부족은 그녀의 이력서 상의 유일한 결점이었다.
fragile　　　그 운반원이 상자를 떨어뜨렸을 때, 깨지기 쉬운 자기제품들이 모두 깨져버렸다.
frailty　　　아기들은 무척 약하기 때문에 다룰때 매우 조심해야 한다.
fraud　　　전쟁 때는 힘과 속임수가 두 가지의 기본적인 덕목 구실을 한다.
gibberish　 Earnshaw 여사는 아무도 이해할 수 없는 몇 마디 말을 되풀이했다.

## gibe
[dʒaib]

**n.** a mocking or derisive comment | 조롱
**v.** to tease with taunting remarks | 조롱하는 말로 괴롭히다

The crowd gave a *gibe* to the old king as he marched in the town.
The young maid *gibed* the young shepherd.

**SYN** gibe : derision [diríʒən]
derision: 조롱, 조소

## glaze
[gleiz]

**v.** to apply a smooth, glossy surface to | 유약을 발라 광택을 내다

The chef *glazed* the pastries with a thin layer of strawberry syrup.

**대상** glaze : porcelain [pɔ́ːrsəlin]
porcelain(도자기류)을 glaze하다.

## gratify
[grǽtəfài]

**v.** to give pleasure or satisfaction to | 기쁘게 하다, 만족시키다

It would *gratify* grandmother if you would stop cursing.

**대상** gratify : desire [dizaiər]
gratify는 desire(욕구, 희망)을 만족시키다 라는 뜻이다.

## gratuitous
[grətjúːətəs]

**adj.** unwarranted; free | 근거없는, 무료의, 무보수의

The doctor claimed that the charges of malpractice were *gratuitous* but the prosecutor insisted he had evidence to back up the charge.

**ANT** gratuitous : warranted [wɔ́(ː)rəntid]
warranted: 근거있는

## gravity
[grǽvəti]

**n.** the severe importance and seriousness of a person or situation | 중대함, 진지함, 엄숙함

The *gravity* of the situation hit the group like a ton of bricks.

**WO** gravity : frivolous [frívələs]
frivolous(경솔한)한 사람에겐 gravity가 없다.

---

| TRANSLATION | 예 문 해 석 |
|---|---|
| gibe | 그 무리들은 마을을 행진하는 늙은 왕을 조롱했다. |
| | 그 처녀는 그 젊은 양치기를 조롱했다. |
| glaze | 그 요리사는 페스트리에 딸기 시럽을 얇게 발라서 윤을 냈다. |
| gratify | 만일 네가 저주하기를 그만둔다면 할머니는 만족해 하실 텐데. |
| gratuitous | 그 의사는 자신의 의료과오 혐의를 근거 없는 것이라고 주장했지만, 검찰은 그의 혐의를 뒷받침하는 증거를 가지고 있다고 강변했다. |
| gravity | 그 무리는 그 장면의 엄숙함에 엄청난 충격을 받았다. |

## green [griːn]

**adj. marked by lack of experience or sophistication**
| 경험이나 세련됨이 없어서 서투른

The veteran could see that though the young man was *green* he had a great deal of potential.

**WO** green : experience [ikspíəriəns]
green한 사람은 experience(경험)가 없다.

## headlong [hédlɔ̀ːŋ]

**adj. marked by impulse and little or no forethought**
| 무분별한, 성급한

Tom always fell *headlong* in love with beautiful women before he really got to know them.

**ANT** headlong : deliberate [dilíbərət]
deliberate: 신중한, 계획적인

## inaugurate [inɔ́ːgjurèit]

**v. to bring into office with a ceremony; to begin with a ceremony**
| 취임식을 통해 취임하다, 개시하다

The president was *inaugurated* with the biggest celebration ever seen in Washington D.C.

**CH** inauguration : official [əfíʃəl]
inauguration(취임식, 준공식)은 official(공식적인)한 시작이다.

## leaden [lédn]

**adj. heavy and inert; downcast and depressed**
| 무거운, 무기력한, 우울한

The woman's heart was *leaden* upon hearing the news of her friend's passing

**ANT** leaden : vivacious [vivéiʃəs]
vivacious: 쾌활한, 활발한

---

**TRANSLATION | 예 문 해 석**

**green** 그 노련한 사람은 그 젊은이가 경험이 없어서 서투르지만 엄청난 잠재력을 가졌음을 알 수 있었다.
**headlong** Tom은 항상 잘 알기도 전에 아름다운 여자들과 성급하게 사랑에 빠졌다.
**inaugurate** 미국 대통령은 워싱턴 D.C.에서 미국 역사상 최대의 축하를 받으며 취임했다.
**leaden** 친구의 사망 소식을 듣고 그 여자의 마음은 무거워졌다.

## lien
[liːn]

**n. a legal claim to take over another's property if an obligation is not met or debt repaid** | 의무 이행을 하지 않았거나 채무가 있는 다른 사람의 재산을 차지할 수 있는 법적 청구, 선취권, 유치권

The *lien* gave the bank possession of the house unless a deposit was made within the next 24 hours.

**CH** lien : claim [kleim]

lien은 claim(청구, 요구)의 속성을 갖는다.

## matriculation
[mətrìkjuléiʃən]

**n. admission of students into a college or group** | 입학이나 입단 허가

*Matriculation* at Harvard is considered to be a great accomplishment.

**대상** matriculation : student [stjúːdnt]

matriculation은 student(학생)을 대상으로 허가하는 것이다.

## meager
[míːgər]

**adj. lacking in quality or quantity** | 질이 떨어지는, 양이 부족한

Dan's monthly salary was too *meager* for him to afford a new car.

**ANT** meagerness : amplitude [ǽmplətjùːd]

meagerness: 결핍, 불충분
amplitude: 풍부함, 충분함

## nucleate
[njúːklièit]

**v. to gather together into a nucleus** | 중심으로 모여들다

The students had already *nucleated* around the campfire.

**ANT** nucleate : scatter [skǽtər]

scatter: 흩어지다, 사라지다

## opacity
[oupǽsəti]

**n. the quality of not being transparent; the state of mental dullness** | 불투명함, 우둔함

The curtain's *opacity* was just perfect for my room.

**WO** opacity : translucent [trænsljúːsnt]

translucent(반투명한) 것은 opacity를 지니고 있지 않다.

---

TRANSLATION | 예 문 해 석

| | |
|---|---|
| lien | 24시간 내에 입금이 되지 않으면 선취권에 의해 은행이 그 집을 소유하게 될 것이었다. |
| matriculation | Harvard 대학으로부터의 입학 허가는 굉장한 성취로 인정된다. |
| meager | Dan은 월급이 너무 적어 새 차를 살 여유가 없었다. |
| nucleate | 학생들은 이미 캠프파이어 주변을 중심으로 모여들었다. |
| opacity | 그 커튼의 불투명함은 내방에 꼭 맞았다. |

### placate
[pléikeit]

**v. to appease by making concessions** | 양보로서 달래다, 진정시키다

William *placated* his girlfriend's anger by sending her flowers.

- **CN** placate : irascible [irǽsəbl]
  irascible(화를 잘 내는)한 사람을 placate하기는 쉽지 않다.

### placebo
[pləsí:bou]

**n. a medication prescribed more for the mental relief of the patient than for its actual effect on a disorder** | 플라시보, 환자를 안심시키기 위해 주는 약

The doctor gave the paranoid patient a *placebo*.

- **CN** placebo : noxious [nákʃəs]
  placebo는 noxious(유해한)하지 않다.

### prairie
[prέəri]

**n. a large area of treeless grassland** | 초원, 평원

*Prairies* are good grazing lands for cattle.

- **WO** prairie : tree [tri:]
  prairie는 tree가 없는 초원이다.

### praise
[preiz]

**n. expression of approval or admiration; the exaltation of a deity or ruler** | 칭찬, 찬양, 찬미

The ancient Egyptians' *praise* for the sun god Ra was an integral part of their religion.

- **CH** praise : hymn [him]
  hymn(찬송가, 찬가)은 praise의 노래이다.

### slacken
[slǽkən]

**v. to slow down; to make less tense** | 늦추다, 완화시키다

The prisoner's handcuffs were *slackened* after complaining they were too tight.

- **대상** slacken : tension [ténʃən]
  tension(긴장감)을 slacken하다.

---

TRANSLATION | 예문해석

| | |
|---|---|
| placate | William은 여자 친구에게 꽃을 보내서 화를 풀게 했다. |
| placebo | 그 의사는 편집증 환자에게 플라시보를 처방했다. |
| prairie | 초원은 가축에게는 적합한 방목지이다. |
| praise | 고대 이집트인들의 태양신 Ra에 대한 찬양은 그들 종교의 가장 중요한 부분이었다. |
| slacken | 그 죄수가 수갑이 너무 조인다고 불평하자 헐겁게 해주었다. |

## slake
[sleik]

**v. to satisfy a craving** | 갈망을 충족시키다

Tarzan went to the brook first and *slaked* his thirst.

**대상** slake : thirst [θəːrst]

slake는 thirst(갈증)를 해소하다 라는 뜻이다.

## soak
[souk]

**v. to make saturated by placing in liquid** | 푹 젖게 하다

The following Monday morning a heavy rain *soaked* the yard around Barbara's house.

**DE** soak : damp [dæmp]

damp(축축하게 하다)보다 더 푹 젖게 하는 것이 soak이다.

## stability
[stəbíləti]

**n. resistance to change of position or condition** | 안정, 안정성

The *stability* of a nation depends on its people.

**FUN** stability : ballast [bǽləst]

ballast(배를 안정시키기 위해 싣는 바닥짐)를 이용해 stability를 유지한다.

## staff
[stæf]

**n. a long stick used for support of the body during walking; the persons assigned to assist a commander or director** | 지팡이; 직원

The man carried his *staff* and bundle in hand.

The director announced that there would be a *staff* meeting at 8 a.m. the next morning.

**FUN** staff : walk [wɔːk]

staff는 walk(걷기)를 도와주는 보조 수단이다.

**FUN** staff : roster [rɑ́stər]

roster(명부, 등록부)에는 staff의 이름이 적혀 있다.

---

### TRANSLATION | 예문 해석

**slake**     Tarzan은 먼저 시냇가로 가서 갈증을 풀었다.
**soak**     그 다음 월요일 아침에 폭우가 내려 Barbara의 집 주변 땅이 푹 젖었다.
**stability**     한 나라의 안정성은 그 국민들에게 딜렸다.
**staff**     그 남자는 지팡이를 짚고 손에 꾸러미를 들고 있었다.
            그 국장은 다음 날 아침 8시에 직원 회의가 열린다고 발표했다.

## staid
[steid]

**adj. having a state of permanence or sedateness** | 불변의, 차분한

Darcy is typically a *staid* and unanimated person.

**ANT** staid : jaunty [dʒɔ́ːnti]
jaunty: 쾌활한, 의기 양양한

## swagger
[swǽgər]

**v. to walk with an air of arrogance** | 뽐내며 거만하게 걷다

The prince has a tendency to *swagger* as he walks through the palace.

**SYN** swagger : strut [strʌt]
strut: 거만하게 걷다

## tractable
[trǽktəbl]

**adj. easily handled or controlled** | 다루기 쉬운

Parents are happy with their children so long as they are *tractable* and obedient.

**ANT** tractable : balky [bɔ́ːki]
balky: 고집 센

## zeal
[ziːl]

**n. passionate devotion and eager pursuit of something** | 열성, 열의

Bryan contributed much *zeal* and enthusiasm to the project.

**DE** zeal : dedication [dèdikéiʃən]
zeal은 dedication(헌신)보다 특정한 일에 대한 더 강한 열의나 열성을 뜻한다.

---

### TRANSLATION | 예 문 해 석

| | |
|---|---|
| **staid** | Darcy는 대체로 차분한 편이나 활기가 부족한 사람이다. |
| **swagger** | 그 왕자는 궁전 안을 걸을 때 거만하게 걷는 버릇이 있다. |
| **tractable** | 부모는 자신의 아이들이 다루기 쉽고 순종적인 한 행복해 한다. |
| **zeal** | Bryan은 그 프로젝트에 엄청난 열정과 의욕을 쏟았다. |

# 11th Day Daily Check-up

■ Fill in the blanks with the correct letter that matches the word with its definition.

1. tractable _____
2. brattish _____
3. exacerbate _____
4. gratuitous _____
5. chagrin _____
6. deadpan _____
7. ambivalent _____
8. meager _____
9. staid _____
10. debilitate _____

a. a feeling of frustration or embarrassment caused by failure or disappointment
b. easily handled or controlled
c. characterized by a mixture of opposite attitudes or feelings; fluctuating in opinion
d. often used in reference to a spoiled child
e. to increase the severity of
f. unwarranted; free
g. to weaken the strength of
h. having a state of permanence or sedateness
i. lacking in quality or quantity
j. marked by a void of expression

■ Put the correct word in each blank from the list of words below.

11. humiliation은 _____ 보다 더욱 심하게 창피하고 무안한 감정을 나타낸다.
12. irascible한 사람을 _____ 하기는 쉽지 않다.
13. hoax는 _____ 한 특징을 지닌다.
14. _____ 는 bad(나쁜)보다 더 강한 표현이다.
15. damp보다 더 푹 젖게 하는 것이 _____ 이다.
16. _____ 은 adorn 하기 위해 사용된다.
17. roster에는 _____ 의 이름이 적혀있다.
18. _____ 는 jaunty(쾌활한, 의기 양양한)의 반의어이다.
19. _____ 은 respiration 없이도 살아갈 수 있다.
20. _____ 는 액체를 clot시킨다.

| a. soak | b. atrocious | c. staid | d. placate | e. staff | f. blazon |
| g. fraudulent | h. embarrassment | i. slake | j. coagulant | k. craven | l. anaerobe |

**Answer key**

1. b  2. d  3. e  4. f  5. a  6. j  7. c  8. i  9. h  10. g
11. h  12. d  13. g  14. b  15. a  16. f  17. e  18. k  19. l  20. j

# SUPER VOCA

## 12th DAY

결정적인 순간은 언제 올지 모릅니다.
미리미리 외워둡시다.

---

### abandon
[əbǽndən]

**v.** **to give up a person, objects, or responsibility with the intention of never returning to it** | (사람이나 물건, 책임을) 포기하다

As time passed, some rituals were *abandoned*.

**ANT** abandon : retain [ritéin]
retain: 보유하다, 유지하다

---

### adamant
[ǽdəmənt]

**adj.** **stubbornly unyielding; inflexible** | 불굴의, 확고한
**n.** **a very hard substance** | 매우 단단하고 견고한 것

The boy's *adamant* refusal to do his chores angered his mother.
The knights made their hearts hard as *adamant*.

**WO** adamant : flexibility [flèksəbíləti]
adamant한 것에는 flexibility(융통성, 유연성)가 없다.

---

### alienable
[éiljənəbl]

**adj.** **transferable to another person's ownership** | 양도할 수 있는

Grandfather Jefferson arranged the inheritance to be legally *alienable*, in case his son made poor decisions with the money.

**ANT** inalienable : surrendered [səréndərd]
inalienable: 양도 불가능한
surrendered: 포기된, 양도된

---

### amalgamate
[əmǽlgəmèit]

**v.** **to combine into a single unit or whole** | 합병하다, 융합시키다

The two companies, both fearing bankruptcy, *amalgamated* into one corporation to minimize expenses.

**ANT** amalgamate : disintegrate [disíntigrèit]
disintegrate: 붕괴시키다, 분해시키다

---

### TRANSLATION | 예문 해석

**abandon** 시간이 흐름에 따라 몇몇 관례들이 일부 폐기됐다.
**adamant** 그 소년은 자신이 맡은 허드렛일 하기를 단호하게 거부함으로써 엄마를 화나게 했다.
그 기사들은 각오를 단단히 했다.
**alienable** 할아버지인 Jefferson은 아들이 돈 관리를 서투르게 할 경우 자신이 물려준 유산을 합법적으로 다른 사람에게 양도할 수 있도록 조치했다.
**amalgamate** 그 두 회사는 공히 파산을 우려한 나머지 비용을 최소화 하기 위해서 합병했다.

## analgesia
[ænəldʒíːziə]

**n.** **the inability to feel pain but without a loss of consciousness** | 무통, 진통

The patient asked the doctor to put her into a state of *analgesia* before the operation.

**FUN** analgesic : ache [eik]

analgesic(진통제, 마취약)은 ache(고통)를 없애준다.

## antidote
[æntidòut]

**n.** **an agent used to counteract a poisonous or noxious substance** | 해독제

This is a deadly poison because there is no known *antidote* in existence.

**FUN** antidote : poisoning [pɔ́izəniŋ]

antidote는 poisoning(독)을 제거한다.

## aqueduct
[ǽkwədʌ̀kt]

**n.** **a pipe or channel that usually supplies large cities with its water supply** | 대도시에 물을 공급하는 수로, 송수관

A malfunction in the city's main *aqueduct* would inconvenience thousands of households.

**FUN** aqueduct : water [wɔ́ːtər]

aqueduct는 water(물)을 공급하는 기능을 가진다.

## barb
[bɑːrb]

**n.** **a cutting comment** | 날카로운 발언

Jim was hurt by the sarcastic *barb* made by his boss at his expense.

**CH** barb : caustic [kɔ́ːstik]

barb는 caustic(신랄한)한 특징이 있는 말이다.

## blanch
[blæntʃ]

**v.** **to take the color out of; to cause to become pale** | 표백하다, 창백하게 하다

The dry cleaner *blanched* Steve's favorite white shirt for his upcoming job interview.

**ANT** blanch : mottle [mátl]

mottle: 얼룩지게 하다

---

TRANSLATION | 예 문 해 석

| | |
|---|---|
| analgesia | 그 환자는 수술하기 전에 자신을 무통 상태로 유도해 달라고 의사에게 부탁했다. |
| antidote | 알려진 해독제가 없으므로 이것은 치명적인 독이다. |
| aqueduct | 도시의 주 송수관에 기능 장애가 생기면 수많은 가정에 불편을 끼치게 된다. |
| barb | Jim은 그가 끼친 손실에 대한 상사의 비꼬는 듯한 날카로운 발언에 상처를 받았다. |
| blanch | Steve는 곧 있을 면접에 입고 가려고 자신이 가장 좋아하는 흰 셔츠를 세탁소에 맡겨 표백했다. |

## bland
[blænd]

**adj. gentle in manner; lacking distinctive flavor; not stimulating** | 온화한, 독특한 맛이 없는, 자극성이 적은

Although fresh, the food was rather *bland*.

**ANT** bland : tangy [tǽŋi]

tangy: 맛이 톡 쏘는

## blandish
[blǽndiʃ]

**v. to persuade in a flattering manner** | 듣기 좋은 말로 아첨하다

The employee *blandished* his boss into giving him a promotion.

**PUR** blandishment : coax [kouks]

blandishment는 다른 사람을 coax(구슬리다, 부추기다)하기 위해 사용하는 감언이다.

## chameleon
[kəmíːliən]

**n. a lizard with the ability to change color of the skin; a changeable or inconstant person** | 카멜레온; 지조 없이 변덕이 심한 사람

My boyfriend changes hairstyles like a *chameleon*.

**대상** chameleon : herpetologist [hə̀ːrpətálədʒist]

herpetologist(파충류 학자)는 chameleon과 같은 파충류를 연구한다.

## coalesce
[kòuəlés]

**v. to come together** | 하나로 합쳐지다

Two stars *coalesced* and shone brightly as one.

**ANT** coalesce : disaggregate [disǽgrigèit]

disaggregate: 분해되다

---

TRANSLATION | 예문해석

**bland**    그 음식은 신선했지만 별다른 특징은 없었다.
**blandish**    그 종업원은 상사에게 아첨한 끝에 승진했다.
**chameleon**    나의 남자 친구는 카멜레온처럼 헤어스타일을 바꾼다.
**coalesce**    별 두 개가 하나로 합쳐지면서 마치 하나의 별처럼 환히 반짝였다.

## cramp
[kræmp]

**n.** a sharp pain caused by a sudden contraction of a muscle; something that restrains freedom of function
| 갑작스럽게 근육이 수축되는 고통, 속박하는 것

**v.** to restrict the freedom of by closely confining
| 속박하다, 제한하다

Mrs. Hooven found herself assailed by sharp pains and *cramps* in her stomach.

The passengers complained about the *cramped* spaces in the dining lounge.

**ANT** cramped : commodious [kəmóudiəs]

cramped: 비좁은, 갑갑한

commodious: 넓은

## deploy
[diplói]

**v.** to spread out men in battle systematically or strategically | (체계적으로 혹은 전략적으로 군대를) 전개시키다

U.S. troops were *deployed* in order to cover the border area.

**ANT** deploy : concentrate [kánsəntrèit]

concentrate: 한 곳에 집결시키다

## depose
[dipóuz]

**v.** to make a statement under oath | 증언하다

Irene was brought to the stand and she *deposed* that she had seen the murder.

**ANT** depose : perjure [pə́ːrdʒər]

perjure: 위증하다

## desiccant
[désikənt]

**n.** a substance that absorbs moisture or water; a drying agent | 습기나 물을 흡수하는 물질, 건조제

*Desiccants* are used in packages to keep the products from getting wet.

**FUN** desiccant : dry [drai]

desiccant는 dry(건조시키다)의 기능이 있다.

---

TRANSLATION | 예 문 해 석

| | |
|---|---|
| cramp | Hooven 여사는 위가 찌를 듯이 아프고 수축되는 고통이 엄습해 오는 것을 느꼈다. |
| | 그 승객들은 식당의 비좁은 공간에 대해 불평했다. |
| deploy | 국경지대를 엄호하기 위해 미군대가 전략적으로 넓게 배치되었다. |
| depose | Irene은 증언대로 가서 자신이 살인을 목격했노라고 증언했다. |
| desiccant | 건조제는 상품들이 축축해지지 않도록 하기 위해 포장에 쓰인다. |

## disentangle
[dìsentǽŋgl]

**v. to free from entanglement or difficulty** | 얽힘이나 어려움으로 부터 해방하다

In order to *disentangle* himself from the whole mess, he would have to go to the police and turn himself in.

**ANT** disentangle : snarl [snɑːrl]
snarl: 얽히게 하다

## emancipate
[imǽnsəpèit]

**v. to free from oppression or bondage** | (억압이나 노예 상태에서) 해방시키다

Abraham Lincoln helped to *emancipate* the slaves of North America.

**ANT** emancipate : shackle [ʃǽkl]
shackle: 구속하다, 감금하다

## evanescent
[èvənésnt]

**adj. vanishing like vapor** | 순간의, 덧없는

The change was subtle, *evanescent*, and hard to define, but unmistakable.

**WO** evanescent : permanency [pə́ːrmənənsi]
evanescent한 것은 permanency(영속성)가 없다.

## exalt
[igzɔ́ːlt]

**v. to intensify; to elevate in rank, power, or character; to extol** | 강화하다, (지위·권력·신분 등을) 높이다, 칭찬하다

The people *exalted* the newly elected prime minister for his charisma and insight.

**ANT** exalt : execrate [éksəkrèit]
execrate: 비난하다

## ford
[fɔːrd]

**n. a shallow area in a body of water where it is possible to cross** | 강이나 물의 건너갈 수 있을 정도로 얕은 부분, 여울

The boys could not cross the river because it was still a mile away to the next *ford*.

**PAR** ford : river [rívər]
ford는 river(강)의 얕은 부분을 일컫는다.

---

### TRANSLATION | 예문 해석

**disentangle** 그 모든 혼란에서 자신을 해방시키기 위해 그는 경찰서로 가서 자수해야만 했을 것이다.
**emancipate** Abraham Lincoln은 북미의 노예들을 해방시키기 위해 힘썼다.
**evanescent** 그 변화는 포착하기 힘들고, 순간적이고, 정의를 내리기가 어려웠지만, 그럼에도 불구하고 명백한 것이었다.
**exalt** 사람들은 새로 선출된 수상의 카리스마와 통찰력을 극구 칭찬했다.
**ford** 다음 여울은 1 마일이나 남아 있었기 때문에 소년들은 강을 건널 수 없었다.

## fungi
[fʌ́ndʒai]

n. **a subdivision of plants which include molds, mushrooms, and mildews** | 곰팡이, 버섯 등을 포함하는 식물의 일종, 균류

Diane was a botanist who specialized in the study of *fungi*.

- 대상 fungi : ecologist [iːkάlədʒist]
  fungi는 ecologist(생태학자)의 연구 대상이 될 수 있다.

## fury
[fjúəri]

n. **intense anger or rage** | 강한 분노

The father hid his *fury* in front of the guests.

- DE fury : anger [ǽŋgər]
  fury는 anger(화)의 더욱 격한 상태이다.

## grandeur
[grǽndʒər]

n. **the quality of being grand or magnificent** | 위대함, 장엄함

The *grandeur* of the pyramids in Egypt is a breathtaking site to see.

- ANT grandeur : frivolousness [frívələsnis]
  frivolousness: 사소함, 천박함

## grandiloquent
[grændíləkwənt]

adj. **extravagant in language or manner** | (말이나 행동이) 과장된

The winner's *grandiloquent* speech was too much for the audience.

- 대상 grandiloquent : language [lǽŋgwidʒ]
  grandiloquent는 주로 과장된 language를 표현할 때 쓰인다.

## inane
[inéin]

adj. **lacking substance or meaning; void of sense or intelligence** | 공허한, 알맹이 없는, 어리석은

Jack suddenly came to the realization that his life thus far had been *inane* and purposeless.

- ANT inane : meaningful [míːniŋfəl]
  meaningful: 의미있는, 중요한

---

### TRANSLATION | 예문 해석

**fungi**    Diane은 균류 연구에 정통한 식물학자였다.
**fury**    아버지는 손님들 앞에서 분노를 감추었다.
**grandeur**    이집트 피라미드의 장엄함은 굉장히 볼 만하다.
**grandiloquent**    그 수상자의 과장된 연설은 청중이 받아들이기엔 너무 거북했다.
**inane**    Jack은 지금까지의 자신의 삶이 공허하고 무의미했음을 깨달았다.

## liberal
[líbərəl]

**adj. marked by generosity; not limited to established attitudes or views** | 관대한, (성향이) 자유스런

Monet's *liberal* use of color in his paintings became a trademark for his later works.

**POS** liberality : generous [dʒénərəs]

liberality: 관대함, 관용, 후함
generous: 관대한, 후한

## libertine
[líbərtìːn]

**n. a person free of moral restrictions usually in reference to men** | 방탕하게 사는 사람(주로 남자), 방탕자, 난봉꾼

The *libertine* was known as a Casanova who sought the company of women.

**CH** libertine : dissolute [dísəlùːt]

libertine은 dissolute(방탕한)한 사람을 일컫는다.

## nibble
[níbl]

**v. to eat in small bites** | 조금씩 먹다

Tom divided the cake, and Becky *nibbled* at her piece.

**DE** nibble : gobble [gábl]

gobble(게걸스럽게 먹다)는 nibble에 비해 한꺼번에 많이 먹는 것을 의미한다.

## nuance
[njúːɑːns]

**n. a subtle distinction or variation** | 뉘앙스, 미묘한 차이, 변화

There were *nuances* in the artist's paintings that only the trained eye could catch.

**DE** nuance : distinction [distíŋkʃən]

nuance는 distinction(구별, 특징)에 비해 아주 미묘한 차이를 의미한다.

## plangent
[plǽndʒənt]

**adj. having a loud and resounding sound** | 소리가 크고 울려 퍼지는

From across the street I could hear the demonstrators' *plangent* cries.

**ANT** plangent : muffled [mʌ́fld]

muffled: 소리가 죽은

---

| TRANSLATION | 예 문 해 석 |
|---|---|
| liberal | Monet는 작품에 색을 풍부하게 사용하는데 이는 그의 후기 작품들의 특징이 되었다. |
| libertine | 그 난봉꾼은 여자 친구를 찾는 카사노바로 알려져 있다. |
| nibble | Tom이 케이크를 나눠주자 Becky는 자기 몫을 조금씩 먹었다. |
| nuance | 그 화가의 그림들에는 전문가만이 알아챌 수 있는 색채의 미묘한 차이가 있었다. |
| plangent | 길 건너편에서 시위대의 함성소리가 들려왔다. |

## plausible
[plɔ́:zəbl]

**adj. logically possible or seemingly true** | 그럴싸한

It is *plausible* that two people could fall in love at first sight, but it doesn't happen often.

**CH** plausible : rationalization [ræ̀ʃənəlizéiʃən]

rationalizaion(합리화)된 것은 plausible하다.

## primp
[primp]

**v. to take excessive care in dressing; to groom oneself** | 옷차림에 지나치게 신경 쓰다, 몸치장하다

All the girls met at Becky's house to *primp* themselves before the prom.

**SYN** primp : preen [pri:n]

preen: 모양내다, 몸치장하다

## qualify
[kwάləfài]

**v. to make eligible for a job; to modify or restrict by giving exceptions** | 적임으로 하다, 수정하다, 제한하다

Edgar was asked to *qualify* his remark about the president's inadequacy.

**ANT** qualified : categorical [kæ̀təgɔ́:rikəl]

qualified: 제한된, 조건부의

categorical: 무조건적인, 분류의

## rabble
[rǽbl]

**n. a confused or complicated crowd that lacks control; a tumultuous crowd of vulgar, noisy people** | 흔란스런 군중, 폭도

The police soon lost all control as the *rabble* swarmed the barricades.

**SYN** rabble : mob [mɑb]

mob: 폭도

## rabid
[rǽbid]

**adj. crazy or extreme in actions and thought** | 미쳐 날뛰는, (언행이) 격렬한

The *rabid* protestors took the streets of Milan with a fury.

**WO** rabid : composure [kəmpóuʒər]

rabid한 사람에게는 composure(침착)가 없다.

---

### TRANSLATION | 예 문 해 석

| | |
|---|---|
| plausible | 두 사람이 첫눈에 반할 수도 있겠지만, 그런 일은 자주 일어나지 않는다. |
| primp | 졸업 파티 전에 모든 여학생들은 옷을 차려 입고 치장하기 위해서 Becky네 집에 모였다. |
| qualify | Edgar는 의장의 자격미달에 대한 발언을 제한해 달라는 요청을 받았다. |
| rabble | 폭도들이 바리케이트로 몰려들자 경찰들은 통제력을 잃었다. |
| rabid | 그 광적인 시위대는 격분한 상태로 밀라노 거리를 점거했다. |

## rebel
v. [ribél]
n. [rébəl]

**v. to fight against an established government** | 반란을 일으키다
**n. a person who rebels** | 반란자, 반역자

The people *rebelled* against the socialist regime due to famine and poor living conditions.
The northern *rebels* were in hiding after defying the laws of the new regime.

**CH** rebel : anarchist [ǽnərkist]

anarchist(무정부주의자, 반역자)는 정부에 rebel하는 사람이다.

## rubicund
[rúːbikʌ̀nd]

**adj. having a healthy reddish color** | 혈색 좋은, 붉은 얼굴의

The typical images of Santa Clause depict a *rubicund* old man.

**ANT** rubicund : wan [wɑn]

wan: 핏기 없는, 힘 없는

## scan
[skæn]

**v. to examine quickly and systematically; to analyze into metrical patterns** | 자세히 조사하다, (시의) 운율을 살피다

The literature major *scanned* the poem in search of iambic pentameter.

**대상** scan : metrical [métrikəl]

scan은 metrical(운율적인)한 면을 분석하다 라는 의미로 쓰인다.

## scant
[skænt]

**adj. having an inadequate or insufficient supply** | 불충분한, 부족한

Society has made *scant* progress in its efforts to curb environmental pollution.

**ANT** scant : profuse [prəfjúːs]

profuse: 풍부한

---

### TRANSLATION | 예문 해석

**rebel** 사람들은 기아와 궁핍한 생활환경에 시달리다 사회주의 정부에 반란을 일으켰다.
북측 반란군들은 새 정부의 법에 반항한 후 숨었다.
**rubicund** 산타클로스의 전형적인 이미지는 혈색좋은 붉은 얼굴의 노인이다.
**scan** 그 문학 전공 학생은 시의 약강 5보격 운율을 분석했다.
**scant** 사회는 환경오염을 억제하려는 노력에 있어서 별다른 진전을 이루지 못했다.

## sham
[ʃæm]

**adj.** not genuine; fake | 가짜의
**n.** a deceptive act of imitation; a counterfeit | 속임수, 모조품
**v.** to pretend to be something; to feign | ~인 척하다, 가장하다

The *sham* diamonds were sold at an exorbitant price to unsuspecting customers.
She tried to be calm and indifferent, but it was a *sham*.
He *shamed* being ill to get out of the date.

**ANT** sham : genuine [dʒénjuin]
  genuine: 진짜의, 진품의

## sinew
[sínjuː]

**n.** a cord or band that connects muscle and bone | 근육과 뼈를 연결하는 건

Having strong *sinews* means having muscular power.

**SYN** sinewy : tendinous [téndənəs]
  sinewy: 건의
  tendinous: 건의, 건질의

## spelunker
[spilʌ́ŋkər]

**n.** one whose hobby is to explore caves | 동굴 탐험가

*Spelunkers* are daring people who like to discover new things and explore the unknown.

**대상** spelunker : cavern [kǽvərn]
  spelunker에게 cavern(동굴)은 탐험의 대상이다.

## stalemate
[stéilmèit]

**n.** the state of being deadlocked | 막다른 궁지에 몰린 상황

The industrial dispute at Waikato University remains at a *stalemate*.

**WO** stalemate : negotiations [nigòuʃiéiʃənz]
  더 이상 negotiations(협상)가 진전되지 않는 상태에 도달했을 때 stalemate에 도달했다고 한다.

---

### TRANSLATION | 예문해석

**sham**
가짜 다이아몬드가 믿고 안심한 손님들에게 터무니없이 비싼 값으로 팔렸다.
그녀는 침착하고 무관심한 척 하려고 했지만 그것은 속임수였다.
그는 데이트에서 벗어나기 위해서 아픈척 했다.

**sinew** 강한 건을 가졌다는 말은 근력이 있다는 말과 같다.
**spelunker** 동굴 탐험가들은 새로운 것들을 발견하고 알려지지 않은 것을 탐험하는 대담한 사람들이다.
**stalemate** Waikato대학의 산업분규는 해결난망이다.

## stalwart
[stɔ́:lwərt]

**adj.** characterized by outstanding strength of the body, mind, or spirit
| 육체적, 정신적으로 매우 강한

**n.** one who is strong and sturdy in body; an unwavering supporter of an organization or cause
| 신체가 건장한 사람, 신념이 굳은 사람, 확고 부동한 당원

The Secret Service is the *stalwart* security of the White House.
Without its usual band of *stalwarts*, the fundraising committee fell short of the target goal.

**CH** stalwart : constancy [kánstənsi]
stalwart는 constancy(지조가 굳음, 불변)를 지닌다.

## stammer
[stǽmər]

**v.** to speak with involuntary repetitions or stops
| 그럴 의도 없이 더듬더듬 말하다

Alexei was speaking so quickly that he began to *stammer*, unable to articulate the word "suffering."

**KIN** stammer : speak [spi:k]
stammer는 더듬거리며 speak(말하다)하는 것이다.

## stifle
[stáifl]

**v.** to smother or suffocate by confinement
| (감금이나 억제함으로써) 숨막히게 하다, 억압하다

Joanne's dreams of becoming an artist were *stifled* by her oppressive parents who wanted her to be a doctor.

**ANT** stifle : foster [fɔ́(:)stər]
foster: 촉진하다

## subdue
[səbdjú:]

**v.** to defeat; to reduce or tone down the intensity of
| 정복하다, 세력을 완화시키다

Virtuous people have the ability to *subdue* the desire for power.

**CN** subdued : indomitable [indámətəbl]
indomitable(불굴의)한 것은 결코 subdued될 수 없다는 것을 의미한다.

---

### TRANSLATION | 예문해석

**stalwart**
Secret Service는 백악관의 안보를 맡고 있는 강력한 경비체계이다.
일단의 충직한 당원들이 아니었다면, 자금 기부를 담당하는 위원회는 목표한 액수를 채울 수 없었을 것이다.

**stammer**
Alexei는 너무 급히 말하는 바람에 "고통"이란 낱말을 제대로 발음하지 못하고 말을 더듬기 시작했다.

**stifle**
예술가가 되고 싶었던 Joanne의 꿈은 그녀가 의사가 되기를 바랬던 강압적인 부모님에 의해 억압당했다.

**subdue**
고결한 사람들은 권력에 대한 욕망을 억누를 수 있다.

## subjugate
[sʌ́bdʒugèit]

**v.** **to bring under authority or control** | 정복하여 통치 하에 두다

The fascist dictator *subjugated* the people of the country with his strong military force.

- **ANT** subjugate : manumit [mǽnjumít]
  manumit: 해방하다

## sway
[swei]

**v.** **to move back and forth; to cause to change a decision or opinion** | 앞뒤로 움직이다, 동요하다

The lobbyist *swayed* many politicians to repeal the latest income tax on small business.

- **CN** sway : resolute [rézəlùːt]
  resolute(단호한)한 결심을 한 사람을 sway시키기는 어렵다.

## sybarite
[síbəràit]

**n.** **one who is luxurious or extremely sensual** | 향락을 일삼는 사람

*Sybarites* are practitioners of hedonism.

- **ANT** sybarite : ascetic [əsétik]
  ascetic: 금욕주의자

## tranquil
[trǽŋkwil]

**adj.** **free from anxiety or disturbance** | 근심 걱정 없는, 고요한

The youth developed a *tranquil* philosophy for these moments of irritation.

- **ANT** tranquil : topsy-turvy [tápsitə́ːrvi]
  topsy-turvy: 뒤죽박죽의, 혼란한

## transgress
[trænsgrés]

**v.** **to exceed or go beyond set limits; to break a law** | 제한된 한계를 넘다, 법률을 위반하다

The felon *transgressed* a recent city ordinance, which was in direct violation of his parole.

- **WO** transgress : rectitude [réktətjùːd]
  transgress한다는 것은 rectitude(공정, 올바름)가 결여되었음을 의미한다.

---

### TRANSLATION | 예 문 해 석

| | |
|---|---|
| subjugate | 그 독재자는 자신의 강력한 군대로 국민을 복종시켰다. |
| sway | 그 로비스트는 많은 정치인들을 움직여 최근에 중소기업에 부과된 세금을 무효로 만들게 했다. |
| sybarite | 향락주의자들은 쾌락주의를 실천하는 사람이다. |
| tranquil | 젊은이들은 이처럼 초조한 순간을 위해 명상 철학을 계발했다. |
| transgress | 그 중죄인은 최근의 시조례를 어겼는데, 이는 가석방 서약에 직접적으로 저촉되는 것이었다. |

## transient
[trǽnʃənt]

**adj.** **passing through with only a brief stay**
| 일시적인, 시간이 지남에 따라 변화하는

Outer beauty is *transient*, but inner beauty lasts forever.

**ANT** transient : lasting [lǽstiŋ]

lasting: 영구적인, 영속하는

## translate
[trænsléit]

**v.** **to convert written or spoken words into another language**
| 번역하다, 통역하다

The interpreter *translated* the coach's words, trying hard not to lose the meaning and humor of the original language.

**CH** translate : interpreter [intə́ːrpritər]

interpreter(통역자)는 translate 하는 사람이다.

## translucent
[trænslúːsnt]

**adj.** **transmitting but diffusing light so that objects beyond cannot be seen clearly; lucid**
| 반투명의, 명료한

The brand new car has four *translucent* windows.

**ANT** translucent : impervious to light [impə́ːrviəs tə lait]

impervious to light: 빛을 통과시키지 않는

## transparent
[trænspɛ́ərənt]

**adj.** **permitting the passage of light and a clear view of object on the other side; free from guile; clear**
| 투명한, 솔직한, 명백한

The *transparent* look on his face convinced the store owner of the boy's veracity.

**ANT** transparent : deceitful [disíːtfəl]

deceitful: 속이려 하는

---

### TRANSLATION | 예문해석

| | |
|---|---|
| transient | 외적인 아름다움은 일시적인 것이지만 내적인 아름다움은 영원히 지속된다. |
| translate | 그 통역자는 감독의 말을 통역하면서 그 속에 있는 진의와 유머를 놓치지 않으려고 애썼다. |
| translucent | 그 신형차는 4개의 반투명 플라스틱 창을 가지고 있다. |
| transparent | 그 소년의 솔직한 표정을 보고 가게 주인은 소년의 말이 진실임을 확신했다. |

## urbane
[ə:rbéin]

**adj. notably well-mannered and worldly** | 세련된, 세속적인

Although *urbane* in appearance, Jerry displayed his lack of etiquette when refusing to greet his guests.

**ANT** urbane : rustic [rʌ́stik]

rustic: 조야한

## vanish
[vǽniʃ]

**v. to disappear from sight** | 시야에서 사라지다

David Copperfield was a great magician who could make elephants *vanish* in the blink of an eye.

**CH** vanish : evanescent [èvənésnt]

evanescent(순간의, 덧없는)한 것은 곧 vanish한다는 속성을 지닌다.

---

### TRANSLATION | 예문해석

**urbane**  Jerry는 세련된 외모를 가졌지만, 손님들에게 인사하기를 거부함으로써 예의 없는 모습을 드러냈다.

**vanish**  David Copperfield는 코끼리를 눈 깜짝할 사이에 시야에서 사라지게 만들 수 있었던 위대한 마술사였다.

## 12th Day Daily Check-up

■ Fill in the blanks with the correct letter that matches the word with its definition.

1. rubicund  _____
2. alienable  _____
3. stalemate  _____
4. plangent  _____
5. evanescent  _____
6. blanch  _____
7. tranquil  _____
8. cramp  _____
9. transient  _____
10. inane  _____

a. having a loud and resounding sound
b. a sharp pain caused by a sudden contraction of a muscle; something that restrains freedom of function
c. lacking substance or meaning; void of sense or intelligence
d. to take the color out of; to cause to become pale
e. vanishing like vapor
f. free from anxiety or disturbance
g. transferable to another person's ownership
h. passing through with only a brief stay
i. having a healthy reddish color
j. the state of being deadlocked

■ Put the correct word in each blank from the list of words below.

11. mob(폭도)의 동의어는 _____ 이다.
12. _____는 다른 사람을 coax하기 위해 사용하는 감언이다.
13. _____은 dissolute한 사람을 일컫는다.
14. execrate(비난하다)의 반의어는 _____이다.
15. _____한 것 에는 flexibility가 없다.
16. deceitful(속이려 하는)의 반의어는 _____이다.
17. _____는 constancy를 지닌다.
18. _____는 disintegrate(붕괴시키다, 분해시키다)의 반의어이다.
19. resolute한 결심을 한 사람을 _____시키기는 어렵다.
20. shackle(구속하다)의 반의어는 _____이다.

a. exalt  b. emancipate  c. amalgamate  d. sway  e. transparent  f. libertine
g. blandishment  h. rabble  i. adamant  j. transgress  k. stalwart  l. sham

Answer key

1. i  2. g  3. j  4. a  5. e  6. d  7. f  8. b  9. h  10. c
11. h  12. g  13. f  14. a  15. i  16. e  17. k  18. c  19. d  20. b

www.goHackers.com

해커스 어학연구소

# TAKE A BREAK

## 민들레
*by hani*

잘 익은 벼는 고개를 숙인다 하였습니다
난 잘 익지도 않았는데 고개가 숙여집니다

누가 꺾었는지 목이 살짝 꺾인 채,아마도
내가 꺾은 것 같습니다,
장미와 백합 튤립사이에서 예뻐 보이려고 고개를
들고 싶어하는 마음만 가득한 민들레가 되어
화려함들과 나를 비교하며 행복하지 않은 순간들이
규칙적으로 찾아 듭니다

나도 꽃이 없는 풀들 사이에선 가장 아름다움이었는데

그래도 난 뛰어야 합니다
난 이미 출발선에 섰던 기억이 있고 총소리와
함께 신나게 출발했던 기억이 어렴풋하게 납니다
꼭 일등을 하고 돌아오겠다는 식의 거만함을
향기로 쏘아대며
시작했던 기억이납니다

지금와 생각해보니 그때 난
눈을 감고 있었던 것 같습니다
눈을 너무 꼬옥 감아 앞에 장애물이 있는 것을
볼 수가 없어 난 그냥 달렸나 봅니다
넘어지고 긁히고 다치고 피가 나고 멍이 들어도
뭣에 신이 났었는지
아픈 줄도 모르고 그냥 달렸나 봅니다

한참을 뛰다보니 너무 힘이 들어
나는 눈을 떴고 이제 내 앞에 있는 장애물들이
너무나 잘 보입니다 다시 눈을 감고
지금까지처럼 그냥 장애물을 모른척 밀쳐가며
달리고 싶은 마음도 가득입니다

쉬·어·가·는 페·이·지

그렇게 눈을 뜨지 않으면
더 많이 아파야 하고, 어쩌면 하얀줄을 허리로
살짝 끊으며 만세부르듯 손을 올리며
행복해 하는 그 순간이 오기전에
쓰러져버릴지도 모른다는 것을 누구보다 잘 알고
있는 나이기에 이젠 눈을 뜨고 뛰어보기로 했습니다

장애물을 넘는 일이란 쉽지 않습니다 내가 장애물을
넘는 방법을 알아가며 천천히 가는 동안 모두가 나를
앞질러 나갑니다

그렇게 고개가 꺾여버린 채 당당해지는 일이란
유쾌한 일이 아닌 것만은 확실한 것 같습니다
그래도 뛰어야함이 명백해 지는 날에는
이렇게 글을 씁니다

동네방네 알려놓고 제대로 안하면 창피하니깐
저지르는 수작이라 해둡시다
나쁘지 않은 수작이죠?

운동회때 엄마가 알려준 것처럼 오줌^^;;이
마렵다고 생각하고 열심히 뛰다보면
손목에 도장을 꽉 찍고
공책 다섯 권은 아니어도 한 권 정도는 가슴에
안고 다시 예쁜 미소를 지으며
행복한 내가 되어 있겠죠?

참가상 말구요 ^^;;

- www.goHackers.com의 유학생생일기에서 발췌했습니다.

# SUPER VOCA

T.H.I.R.T.E.E.N.T.H D.A.Y

## 13th DAY

당신은 강합니다.
오늘도 어제처럼 할 수 있다는 희망을 가지세요.

---

**abase**
[əbéis]

v. **to lower in office or esteem** | 지위를 떨어뜨리다, 품위를 깎아내리다

The *abased* executive was embarrassed by his recent demotion.

대상   abase : prestige [prestíːdʒ]

abase는 prestige(명성, 위신) 등을 떨어뜨리다 라는 의미이다.

---

**abash**
[əbǽʃ]

v. **to embarrass or make ashamed** | 당황하게 하다, 부끄럽게 하다

*Abashed* glances of wonder were exchanged by the sailors.

ANT   abash : embolden [imbóuldən]

embolden: 용기를 주다

---

**abate**
[əbéit]

v. **to lessen in amount, degree, or intensity** | 감소시키다, 완화시키다

The installation of insect light traps did little to *abate* the problem.

대상   abate : degree [digríː]

abate는 degree(정도) 등을 약화시키다 라는 의미이다.

---

**amuse**
[əmjúːz]

v. **to please or appeal to one's sense of humor** | 즐겁게 하다

The comic performer was able to *amuse* the crowd for hours.

CH   amusement : anecdote [ǽnikdòut]

anecdote(일화)는 amusement(즐거움)을 주는 짧은 이야기이다.

---

**TRANSLATION | 예 문 해 석**

| | |
|---|---|
| abase | 위신이 실추된 그 간부는 최근 강등된 사실 때문에 당황했다. |
| abash | 그 선원들은 당황스럽고 놀라운 눈빛으로 서로를 흘깃 쳐다보았다. |
| abate | 유아등(誘蛾燈)을 설치했지만 해충 퇴치 문제를 해결하는 데는 별로 도움이 되지 않았다. |
| amuse | 그 희극배우는 관객들을 몇 시간 동안 웃길 수 있었다. |

## apathetic
[æpəθétik]

**adj.** having or exhibiting a lack of feeling or concern | 무감각한, 냉담한

Alfred stood motionless, in what seemed to be an *apathetic* attitude.

**WO** apathetic : fervor [fə́ːrvər]
apathetic한 사람에게는 fervor(열정)가 없다.

## avarice
[ǽvəris]

**n.** an excessive desire for wealth | (주로 금전에 대한) 탐욕

The *avarice* of the man caused his neighbors and friends to spite him.

**ANT** avarice : generosity [dʒènərɑ́səti]
generosity: 관대, 아낌없이 주는 마음

## blast
[blæst]

**n.** a violent outburst of air or sound; an explosion | 매우 강한 바람이나 큰 소리, 폭발

The space shuttle headed for the moon with a *blast* from the main engine.

**DE** blast : whiff [hwif]
blast은 whiff(휙 부는 바람)보다 더욱 더 강한 바람이다.

## blatant
[bléitənt]

**adj.** completely obvious or vulgarly conspicuous; unpleasantly loud especially in a vulgar or offensive manner | 노골적인, 뻔뻔스런, 떠들썩한

The oil tycoon's *blatant* show of wealth was epitomized by his gold encrusted belt buckle.

**CN** blatant : ignore [ignɔ́ːr]
blatant한 것은 ignore(무시하다, 못본체 하다)하기 어렵다.

## blush
[blʌʃ]

**v.** to become red in the face from shame or nervousness | 얼굴을 붉히다

Surprised and a little embarrassed by his flattery, Tonya *blushed*.

**인과** blush : embarrassment [imbǽrəsmənt]
embarrassment(당황, 무안함)를 느껴서 blush하게 된다.

---

TRANSLATION | 예문해석

| | |
|---|---|
| **apathetic** | Alfred는 냉담한 듯한 태도를 보이며 꼼짝않고 서 있었다. |
| **avarice** | 그 남자의 탐욕은 이웃들과 친구들의 원한을 샀다. |
| **blast** | 그 우주 왕복선은 주 엔진의 폭발과 함께 달로 향했다. |
| **blatant** | 그 거대 석유회사 사장의 노골적인 부의 과시는 그의 금으로 겉치장된 벨트 죔쇠로 축약되어 보여진다. |
| **blush** | Tonya는 그의 칭찬에 놀라고 좀 당황해서 얼굴을 붉혔다. |

## brash
[bræʃ]

**adj. hasty and lacking in regard for consequences** | 성급한, 무모한

Tony's *brash* manner has gotten him in a lot of trouble.

> **ANT** brash : deliberate [dilíbərət]
> deliberate: 신중한, 계획적인

## charitable
[tʃǽrətəbl]

**adj. liberal in benediction to the needy** | 자비로운, 관대한

Tom has a *charitable* heart because he makes donations to various needy organizations on an annual basis.

> **ANT** charitableness : rancor [rǽŋkər]
> charitableness: 자비, 관용
> rancor: 원한, 증오

## chary
[tʃέəri]

**adj. very cautious; slow to give** | 매우 주의 깊은, 아까워하는

Clara knew that Mr. Gryce was *chary*, not prone to rash or impulsive decisions.

> **ANT** chary : bold [bould]
> bold: 대범한, 과감한

## chasm
[kǽzm]

**n. a deep opening in the surface of the Earth; a marked difference** | 깊게 벌어진 틈, (의견 등의) 큰 차이

The rock climbers looked down into the *chasm*.

> **DE** chasm : cleft [kleft]
> chasm은 cleft(갈라진 틈) 보다 더욱 깊게 갈라진 틈을 뜻한다.

## clarify
[klǽrəfài]

**v. to make clear or understandable** | 이해하기 쉽거나 명백하게 하다

Could you please *clarify* that statement for me?

> **대상** clarify : misunderstood [mìsʌndərstúd]
> misunderstood(오해된)된 것을 clarify하다.

---

**TRANSLATION | 예문 해석**

**brash** Tony는 무모한 태도 때문에 상당한 곤경에 처했다.
**charitable** Tom은 매번 여러 어려운 기관에 기부하는 걸로 보아 자비로운 마음을 가진 사람이다.
**chary** Clara는 Gryce씨가 경솔하거나 충동적인 결정을 내리지 않는 신중한 사람인 것을 알았다.
**chasm** 그 암벽 등반대는 깊게 벌어진 바위틈을 내려다보았다.
**clarify** 그 진술에 대해 좀 더 상세히 설명해주시겠어요?

## concede
[kənsíːd]

v. **to accept that something is true; to yield** | (사실임을) 인정하다, 시인하다, 양보하다

It is generally *conceded* that humans are social beings.

> **ANT** concede : disavow [dìsəváu]
> disavow: 부인하다

## consent
[kənsént]

v. **to give approval of; to agree to** | 승인하다, 동의하다
n. **an agreement** | 동의

Dirk *consented* to the drug test because he had no other options.
I asked my mother's *consent* to marry Shannon.

> **ANT** consent : dissent [disént]
> dissent: 의견을 달리하다

## cursory
[kə́ːrsəri]

adj. **superficial; hasty; careless** | 피상적인, 서두르는, 소홀한

The editor's *cursory* review of the document failed to reveal its structural flaws.

> **ANT** cursory : fastidious [fæstídiəs]
> fastidious: 세심한, 까다로운

## dearth
[dəːrθ]

n. **a lack or shortage of supply, especially of food** | (주로 식량의) 부족, 기근

The drought in Bengal a few years ago caused a great *dearth* of food supplies.

> **ANT** dearth : plethora [pléθərə]
> plethora: 과잉, 과다

## diaphanous
[daiǽfənəs]

adj. **characterized by such fineness of texture as to permit seeing through** | (천이) 투명한, 내비치는

In the gloom the girls' wraps glowed pallid and *diaphanous*.

> **ANT** diaphanous : opaque [oupéik]
> opaque: 불투명한

---

### TRANSLATION | 예문해석

| | |
|---|---|
| **concede** | 인간은 사회적 존재라고 일반적으로 인정된다. |
| **consent** | Dirk는 다른 선택의 여지가 없었기 때문에 그 약물 실험에 동의했다. |
| | 나는 Shannon과 결혼하기 위해 어머니의 동의를 구했다. |
| **cursory** | 그 편집자는 문서를 대충 훑어 보았기 때문에 구조적인 문제점을 발견하지 못했다. |
| **dearth** | 수년 전 벵골 지방의 가뭄으로 매우 심각한 식량부족 현상이 발생했다. |
| **diaphanous** | 어둠 속에서 그 소녀들의 숄은 색이 엷고 속이 비칠 만큼 얇고 섬세하게 빛났다. |

## discharge
[distʃáːrdʒ]

**v. to release from an obligation or from employment; to dismiss; to send out or shoot**
| (의무·근무 등에서) 해방하다, 방출하다, 쏘다

The captain was *discharged* from the army after 30 years of loyal service.

> **ANT** discharge : induct [indʌ́kt]
> induct: 취임시키다, 임명하다

## disclosure
[disklóuʒər]

**n. the exposure or revelation of something that was hidden or secret**
| 폭로, 발각

The *disclosure* of FBI reports has raised many doubts as to the actions of President Bush prior to Sept. 11th.

> **ANT** disclosure : stealth [stelθ]
> stealth: 몰래하기

## discord
[dískɔːrd]

**n. conflict or a lack of agreement**
| 불화

Wars arise from *discord* between political bodies.

> **ANT** discord : rapport [ræpɔ́ːr]
> rapport: 조화로운 관계

## drab
[dræb]

**adj. dull in appearance; cheerless**
| 칙칙한, 단조로운

The man's entire wardrobe is rather *drab*.

> **WO** drab : resplendence [rispléndəns]
> drap한 것에는 resplendence(화려함, 눈부심)가 없다.

## elate
[iléit]

**v. to make full of pride or joy**
| 자신감 차게 하다, 기분을 북돋우다

Patrick was *elated* when he was accepted into the Naval Academy.

> **ANT** elation : sullenness [sʌ́lənnis]
> elation: 의기양양
> sullenness: 침울

---

### TRANSLATION | 예문해석

**discharge** 그 지휘관은 30년간의 복무를 충실히 마치고 제대했다.
**disclosure** FBI 보고서의 내용이 밝혀짐으로써 9. 11 대참사 발생 이전의 부시 대통령의 행동에 대해 여러 가지 의문이 제기됐다.
**discord** 전쟁은 정치적 집단 간의 불화로 발발하는 것이다.
**drab** 그 남자가 갖고 있는 의상은 하나같이 좀 칙칙한 빛깔이다.
**elate** Patrick은 해군 사관학교에 합격했을 때 의기양양 했다.

## enact
[inǽkt]

v. **to make or pass a law; to act out**
| 법규화하다, (연극 등을) 상연하다

Congress *enacted* a new law that prohibits college students from drinking during the school year.

**ANT** enact : rescind [risínd]

rescind: (법률, 조약 등을) 폐지하다

## ensconce
[inskáns]

v. **to settle in a comfortable and secure place; to conceal in a secure place**
| 안전하고 편한 곳에 두다, 앉히다, 감추다

Norma deals with stress by *ensconcing* herself in her apartment and reading.

**ANT** ensconce : unsettle [ʌnsétl]

unsettle: 불안정한 상태에 처하게 하다

## extrovert
[ékstrəvə̀ːrt]

n. **an gregarious and social person**
| 외향적인 사람, 사교적인 사람

Typically the *extroverts* are the popular people in high school.

**CH** extrovert : outgoing [áutgòuiŋ]

extrovert는 outgoing(외향적인)하다.

## flirt
[fləːrt]

v. **to show light amorous interest in someone; to treat something not seriously**
| 장난 삼아 연애하다, 장난 삼아 해보다

It's unprofessional to *flirt* with colleagues at the office.

**CH** flirtatious : coquette [koukét]

coquette(바람둥이 여자)는 flirtatious(바람난, 시시덕거리는)하다.

## forbear
[fɔːrbɛ́ər]

v. **to refrain from; to hold back from; to be patient**
| 삼가다, 보류하다, 참다

Although Kelly could hardly wait to give her Mom the present, she *forbore* the urge until Christmas Day.

**SYN** forbear : forgo [fɔːrgóu]

forgo: 삼가다, 보류하다

---

TRANSLATION | 예문해석

| | |
|---|---|
| enact | 의회는 대학생들에게 재학 중에 음주를 금하도록 하는 새로운 법률을 제정했다. |
| ensconce | Norma는 자신의 아파트에서 편안한 자세로 독서를 하면서 스트레스를 푼다. |
| extrovert | 일반적으로 외향적인 사람들은 고등학교에서 인기가 있다. |
| flirt | 사무실에서 동료들과 시시덕거리는 것은 전문적이지 못하다. |
| forbear | Kelly는 어머니에게 선물을 드리고 싶은 충동을 크리스마스까지 참았다. |

## fulsome
[fúlsəm]

**adj. excessively complimentary or flattering; offensive**
| (지나치거나 역겨울 정도로) 아첨하는, 불쾌한

The bartender's *fulsome* compliments did not impress the lady server.

**DE** fulsome : complimentary [kàmpləméntəri]

fulsome은 지나치게 complimentary(칭찬하는)하는 것이다.

## graceful
[gréisfəl]

**adj. beautiful or attractive in motion or style**
| 행동이나 말씨가 우아하고 세련된

The ballerina's dancing was *graceful*, a true pleasure to watch.

**ANT** graceful and light : ponderous [pándərəs]

graceful and light: 우아하고 가벼운
ponderous: 지루한, 장황한, 육중한

## gobble
[gábl]

**v. to eat greedily and quickly**
| 게걸스레 먹다

As children, my siblings and I would make fun of our dad for always *gobbling* his dinner.

**DE** gobble : nibble [níbl]

gobble은 nibble(조금씩 먹다)하는 행위에 비하면 그야말로 게걸스럽게 먹는 것을 의미한다.

## harsh
[haːrʃ]

**adj. causing pain or irritation; severe or crude**
| 고통이나 화를 야기시키는, 혹독한

The father's *harsh* words deeply wounded his son.

**CH** harsh : pan [pæn]

pan(혹독한 비평)은 harsh하다.

## hearten
[háːrtn]

**v. to give courage or spirit to**
| 용기를 북돋우다, 격려하다

Malcolm *heartened* the brave volunteers before flying to their posts in Africa.

**대상** hearten : dejection [didʒékʃən]

hearten은 dejection(낙담, 실의)을 없애고 격려하다라는 의미이다.

---

### TRANSLATION | 예문해석

| | |
|---|---|
| fulsome | 그 바텐더가 역겨울 정도로 알랑거렸지만 그 여종업원의 마음을 사로잡지는 못했다. |
| graceful | 그 발레리나의 무용은 우아했으며 정말로 보기에 좋았다. |
| gobble | 어린 시절 나의 형제들과 나는 언제나 저녁을 게걸스럽게 드시는 아빠를 놀리곤 했다. |
| harsh | 아버지의 혹독한 말에 아들은 깊이 상처 받았다. |
| hearten | Malcolm은 용감한 의용병들이 비행기를 타고 아프리카의 기지로 가기 전에 그들을 격려했다. |

## irascible
[irǽsəbl]

**adj. characterized by a tendency toward anger and a hot temper** | 쉽게 화내는, 다혈질의

All the tenants tried to avoid the *irascible* landowner whenever possible.

**CN** irascible : placate [pléikeit]

irascible한 사람을 placate(달래다, 진정시키다)하기는 쉽지 않다.

## liability
[làiəbíləti]

**n. a legal or pecuniary obligation; a drawback or disadvantage** | 법적인 책임, 채무; 장애나 불리한 점

The company went out of business because their *liabilities* far outweighed their assets.

**대상** liability : exempt [igzémpt]

liability를 exempt(면제해 주다)하다.

**ANT** liability : asset [ǽset]

asset: 재산, 장점, 이점

## loathe
[louð]

**v. to feel extreme aversion for** | 혐오하다

Commuters often *loathe* the drive to work because of perpetual traffic and hazardous road conditions.

**DE** loathe : dislike [disláik]

loathe는 매우 강하게 dislike(싫어하다)하다 라는 뜻이다.

## measly
[mízli]

**adj. despicably small; meager** | 빈약한, 불충분한

The *measly* salary of the factory workers gave them reason to strike.

**ANT** measly : grand [grænd]

grand: 웅대한, 웅장한

---

TRANSLATION | 예 문 해 석

| | |
|---|---|
| irascible | 모든 소작인들은 다혈질인 지주를 가능한 한 피하려고 한다. |
| liability | 그 회사는 자산보다 부채가 훨씬 많았기 때문에 폐업했다. |
| loathe | 끝없는 교통체증과 위험한 도로 사정때문에 사람들은 차를 가지고 직장에 가는 것을 종종 매우 싫어한다. |
| measly | 그 공장 근로자들은 쥐꼬리만한 급료 때문에 파업에 돌입했다. |

## mince [mins]

**v. to chop or cut into little pieces; to walk with very short steps or with exaggerated primness**
| 잘게 썰다, 점잔빼며 잔 걸음으로 걷다

The princess had *minced* her way across the ballroom to attract attention to her new gown.

**KIN** mince : walk [wɔːk]

mince는 점잔빼며 잔 걸음으로 walk하는 것이다.

## opaque [oupéik]

**adj. impenetrable by light**
| 빛이 통과할 수 없는, 불투명한

The *opaque* curtains covered the room in darkness.

**ANT** opaque : diaphanous [daiǽfənəs]

diaphanous: 투명한, 내비치는

## orate [ɔːréit]

**v. to speak in an elevated and arrogant manner**
| 거만한 투의 연설조로 말하다

Pericles *orated* to the Athenians, persuading them to go to war.

**WO** oratory : modesty [mɑ́dəsti]

oratory(과장된 미사 여구)에는 modesty(알맞음, 적당함)가 없다.

## oust [aust]

**v. to kick out or force out of a position**
| 지위에서 내쫓다

The mayor was *ousted* from office after a huge scandal broke loose.

**대상** oust : incumbent [inkʌ́mbənt]

incumbent(재직자)를 oust하다.

## outgoing [áutgòuiŋ]

**adj. friendly and sociable**
| 우호적인, 사교적인, 외향성의

Although they were twins, Edward was shy and Edwin was *outgoing*.

**CH** outgoing : extrovert [ékstrəvə̀ːrt]

extrovert(외향적인 사람, 사교적인 사람)는 outgoing하다.

---

### TRANSLATION | 예문해석

| | |
|---|---|
| mince | 공주는 새 가운으로 사람들의 이목을 끌면서 파티장을 가로질러 점잔빼며 걸어갔다. |
| opaque | 그 불투명한 커튼은 방을 어둠으로 덮었다. |
| orate | Pericles는 아테네 사람들에게 전쟁에 참가하라고 연설조로 설득했다. |
| oust | 그 시장은 엄청난 추문이 알려진 후에 자리에서 쫓겨났다. |
| outgoing | 비록 둘은 쌍둥이었지만, Edward는 수줍음을 탔고 Edwin은 외향적이었다. |

## palmy
[pá:mi]

**adj. prosperous and profitable** | 번영하는, 유익한

The 1990's was a *palmy* time for technology companies.

> **POS** palmy : prosperity [prɑspérəti]
> prosperity: 번영

## penchant
[péntʃənt]

**n. a special fondness or continued inclination** | (좋아하는) 경향, 강한 기호

Lee has a *penchant* for percussion instruments.

> **ANT** penchant : aversion [əvə́ːrʒən]
> aversion: 매우 싫어함

## placid
[plǽsid]

**adj. calm or serene** | 조용한, 평온한

Jeremy was a *placid* man who rarely got angry.

> **ANT** placid : truculent [trʌ́kjulənt]
> truculent: 호전적인, 거친

## prescience
[préʃiəns]

**n. knowledge of the future or foresight** | 선견지명, 예지력

The ancient wise men claimed to have a *prescience* which all the citizens listened to and followed.

> **ANT** prescience : myopia [maióupiə]
> myopia: 근시안, 앞을 내다보지 못함, 단견

## quarrel
[kwɔ́ːrəl]

**n. a dispute or verbal conflict** | 논쟁, 말다툼

The shouting from their *quarrel* attracted a crowd.

> **DE** quarrel : spat [spæt]
> spat(승강이)은 사소한 quarrel이다.

---

TRANSLATION | 예문해석

| | |
|---|---|
| palmy | 1990년대는 과학기술 기업들이 번영하던 시기였다. |
| penchant | Lee는 타악기에 취미가 있다. |
| placid | Jeremy는 거의 화내지 않는 평온한 사람이었다. |
| prescience | 고대의 현인들은 자신들에게는 모든 시민들이 경청하고 순종해야 하는 예지력이 있다고 주장했다. |
| quarrel | 그들이 소리를 지르며 말다툼을 해서 주위 사람들의 관심이 쏠렸다. |

## quarry
[kwɔ́:ri]

**v.** **to extract by long, careful searching** | 애써 탐구해서 얻어내다

**n.** **an open pit from which building stone, limestone, or slate are acquired; a productive source** | 채석장; 풍부한 원천

The police *quarried* the location of the fugitive through an exhaustive manhunt.

We paved our driveway with stone purchased from the local *quarry*.

**FUN** quarry : marble [má:rbl]
quarry(채석장)에서는 marble을 채취한다.

## quash
[kwɑʃ]

**v.** **to extinguish forcibly and completely** | 진압하다

Modred was slain in his attempt to *quash* the revolt.

**ANT** quash : engender [indʒéndər]
engender: 발생하게 하다

## reassure
[ri:əʃúər]

**v.** **to relieve; to restore confidence** | 안심시키다, 다시 자신감을 갖게 하다

Bryan *reassured* Amelia with his friendly chuckle.

**대상** reassure : uneasiness [ʌní:zinis]
reassure는 uneasiness(불안, 걱정)를 없애주는 것이다.

## reluctant
[rilʌ́ktənt]

**adj.** **hesitant or unwilling** | 망설이는, 마지못해 하는

Elizabeth was *reluctant* to give up her weekends for work.

**ANT** reluctance : alacrity [əlǽkrəti]
reluctance: 싫음, 마지못해 함
alacrity: 열의, 민첩

## scarce
[skɛərs]

**adj.** **insufficient in quantity or inadequate to meet a demand** | 양이 부족한, 필요한 요구에 충족시키지 못하는

Truly gifted mechanics are *scarce*.

**ANT** scarce : superfluous [su:pə́:rfluəs]
superfluous: 과잉의, 넘치는

---

### TRANSLATION | 예문해석

**quarry** 경찰은 철저한 범인 수사를 통해 탈주범의 위치를 알아냈다.
우리는 그 지역 채석장에서 구입한 석채로 도로를 포장했다.
**quash** Mordred는 반란을 진압하는 과정에서 살해되었다.
**reassure** Bryan은 다정하게 미소지으며 Amelia를 안심시켰다.
**reluctant** Elizabeth는 마지못해 주말을 포기하고 일하기로 했다.
**scarce** 정말로 재능있는 기계공은 드물다.

## shard
[ʃɑːrd]

**n. a piece of broken pottery, glass, or metal** | (도자기·유리·금속의) 파편

There were *shards* everywhere on the floor from the broken mirror.

**PAR** shard : pottery [pátəri]
shard는 pottery(도자기)등의 깨진 조각이다.
cf) cake의 조각은 crumb이다.

## snarl
[snɑːrl]

**v. to make tangle and intertwined** | 뒤엉키게 하다

The fly was *snarled* in the black widow's spider web with no prospects of escaping.

**ANT** snarl : disentangle [dìsentǽŋgl]
disentangle: 엉킨 것을 풀다

## Spartan
[spáːrtn]

**n. a person with self-discipline and courage** | 자제력과 용기를 갖춘 사람

**adj. austere or simple** | 엄격한, 간소한

Mike is such a *Spartan* who rarely strays from his beliefs.

Janet's dedication to giving up worldly goods could be observed in her *Spartan* apartment.

**ANT** Spartan : luxurious [lʌgʒúəriəs]
luxurious: 사치스런, 호화로운

## spate
[speit]

**n. a sudden outburst or flood; a large amount or number** | 갑작스런 분출, 홍수, 대량, 다수

Alice was a popular columnist and received a *spate* of letters everyday.

**ANT** spate : dearth [dəːrθ]
dearth: 부족

---

### TRANSLATION | 예문 해석

**shard** 거울이 깨지면서 조각들이 마루 사방에 널려 있었다.
**snarl** 그 파리는 독거미의 거미줄에 걸려 빠져나갈 수도 없이 뒤엉켜버렸다.
**Spartan** Mike는 자신의 종교적 기준을 거의 어기지 않는 놀라도록 엄격한 사람이다.
Janet의 세속적인 물건들을 포기하려는 의지는 그녀의 간소한 아파트를 보면 알 수 있다.
**spate** Alice는 유명한 칼럼니스트라서 매일 많은 편지를 받았다.

## startle
[stá:rtl]

**v.** to cause to move involuntarily; to surprise suddenly | 펄쩍 뛰게 하다, 깜짝 놀라게 하다

**n.** a sudden start | 깜짝 놀람

Dad *startled* me yesterday while I was brushing my teeth.
The *startle* of his wife falling out of bed woke Bradley up.

**ANT** startle : lull [lʌl]

lull: 달래다, 진정시키다

## stasis
[stéisis]

**n.** a state of balance or motionlessness | 움직임이 없는 균형 상태

The Russia-U.S. relationship appears to have reached a *stasis*.

**WO** stasis : motility [moutíləti]

stasis는 motility(운동성)가 없는 균형 상태이다.

## weary
[wíəri]

**adj.** fatigued or exhausted in strength; having little patience or tolerance | 지친, 싫증난

Grandma is *weary* from the trip and must take a nap.

**ANT** weary : vivid [vívid]

vivid: 생기 있는, 빛나는

---

### TRANSLATION | 예문해석

| | |
|---|---|
| startle | 어제 이를 닦고 있을 때 아빠가 나를 깜짝 놀라게 했다. |
| | Bradley는 아내가 침대에서 떨어져 깜짝 놀라는 바람에 잠에서 깼다. |
| stasis | 러시아와 미국의 관계는 평형 상태에 도달한 듯 하다 |
| weary | 할머니는 여행때문에 지쳐서 낮잠을 주무셔야만 한다. |

# 13th Day Daily Check-up

■ Fill in the blanks with the correct letter that matches the word with its definition.

1. liability _____
2. cursory _____
3. abase _____
4. shard _____
5. ensconce _____
6. blatant _____
7. chary _____
8. penchant _____
9. apathetic _____
10. drab _____

a. very cautious; slow to give
b. to settle in a comfortable and secure place
c. having or exhibiting a lack of feeling or concern
d. a special fondness or continued inclination
e. dull in appearance; cheerless
f. unpleasantly loud in a vulgar or offensive manner
g. a piece of broken pottery, glass, or metal
h. to lower in office or esteem
i. a legal or pecuniary obligation; a drawback or disadvantage
j. superficial; hasty; careless

■ Put the correct word in each blank from the list of words below.

11. _____는 whiff보다 더욱 더 강한 바람이다.
12. compliment가 지나치면 불쾌감을 줄 수 있는 _____가 된다.
13. _____는 engender(발생하게 하다)의 반의어이다.
14. plethora(과잉)의 반의어는 _____이다.
15. _____는 motility가 없는 균형 상태이다.
16. _____은 sullenness(침울)의 반의어이다.
17. spat은 사소한 _____이다.
18. _____는 generosity(관대)의 반의어이다.
19. disentangle(엉킨 것을 풀다)의 반의어는 _____이다.
20. _____에는 modesty가 없다.

a. fulsomeness   b. quarrel   c. blast   d. quarry   e. oratory   f. dearth
g. gobble        h. elation   i. snarl   j. stasis   k. quash    l. avarice

Answer key

1. i   2. j   3. h   4. g   5. b   6. f   7. a   8. d   9. c   10. e
11. c   12. a   13. k   14. f   15. j   16. h   17. b   18. l   19. i   20. e

# SUPER VOCA

F.O.U.R.T.E.E.N.T.H D.A.Y

## 14th DAY

아들아! 나는 퀴즈를 낼 테니 너는 단어를 외거라.

---

**abbreviate**
[əbríːvièit]

v. **to shorten by contraction, especially of words** | (단어를) 줄여쓰다

The word 'Mister' has come to be *abbreviated* as 'Mr.'

**대상** abbreviate : word [wəːrd]

word(단어)의 길이를 abbreviate하다.

---

**abhor**
[æbhɔ́ːr]

v. **to regard with intense loathing or horror** | 몹시 싫어하다

Carrie *abhorred* the condescending manner in which her classmate spoke.

**DE** abhor : dislike [disláik]

abhor는 강도 면에서 dislike(싫어하다)의 어감 보다 더욱 싫어하다는 의미이다.

---

**abide**
[əbáid]

v. **to endure; to remain fixed in a state or condition** | 지속하다, 머물다

The composer's passion for writing music *abided* until his untimely death.

**ANT** abiding : evanescent [èvənésnt]

abiding: 영구적으로 지속되는
evanescent: 순간적인

---

**accessible**
[æksésəbl]

adj. **able to be influenced; approachable; easily understandable** | ~의 영향을 받기 쉬운, 접근하기 쉬운, 이해하기 쉬운

The university lecture was not *accessible* to the high school students.

**CN** accessible : abstruse [æbstrúːs]

abstruse(난해한)한 사상은 accessible하지 않다.

---

**TRANSLATION | 예문 해석**

**abbreviate** 'Mister' 라는 단어는 'Mr.' 로 축약되게 되었다.
**abhor** Carrie는 그녀의 반 친구의 생색내는 듯이 말하는 태도를 너무 싫어했다.
**abide** 그 작곡가의 음악에 대한 열정은 그가 때이르게 사망할 때까지 지속되었다.
**accessible** 그 대학강의는 고등학생들에게는 이해되지 않았다.

## achromatic
[ækrəmǽtik]

**adj. having no hue; consisting of black, gray, or white** | 무색의

The *achromatic* door caused many visitors to miss the entrance completely.

**WO** achromatic : hue [hju:]

achromatic은 hue(색상)가 없는 이라는 의미이다.

## adhere
[ædhíər]

**v. to hold on to or stick to something** | 고수하다, 들러붙다

The glue will *adhere* with remarkable tenacity.

**CN** adhere : slippery [slípəri]

slippery(매끌매끌한)한 표면에는 다른 물체가 adhere할 수 없다.

## alibi
[ǽləbài]

**n. the verifiable claim to have been in a place other than where and when a crime occurred** | 현장 부재 증명, 알리바이

He fabricated an incongruous *alibi*.

**PUR** alibi : exculpate [ékskʌlpèit]

exculpate(무죄로 하다)하게 하는데 있어서 alibi가 수단으로 사용된다.

## amble
[ǽmbl]

**v. to walk slowly** | 느릿느릿 걷다

The couple *ambled* lazily through their garden after dinner.

**KIN** amble : walk [wɔːk]

amble은 천천히 walk(걷다)하는 것이다.

## ambrosial
[æmbróuziəl]

**adj. pleasing to the taste or smell** | 맛이 아주 좋은, 향긋한

The *ambrosial* drink was heralded by many as the nectar of the gods.

**대상** ambrosial : food [fuːd]

ambrosial(맛이 좋은)은 food(음식)를 서술하는 말이다.

---

### TRANSLATION | 예 문 해 석

| | |
|---|---|
| achromatic | 그 무색의 문은 많은 방문객들이 입구를 전혀 찾지 못하게 했다. |
| adhere | 그 접착제는 강력한 접착력으로 들러붙으려 한다. |
| alibi | 그는 앞뒤도 안 맞는 알리바이를 꾸며냈다. |
| amble | 그 부부는 저녁식사 후에 자신들의 정원을 천천히 걸었다. |
| ambrosial | 그 맛좋은 음료는 많은 사람들에 의해 신의 음료라고 전해졌다. |

## amicable
[ǽmikəbl]

**adj. friendly and peaceful** | 우호적인, 평화적인

The *amicable* men came to a settlement quickly.

**ANT** amicable : inimical [inímikəl]
inimical: 적대적인, 반목하는

## ancestor
[ǽnsestər]

**n. a family member from whom one is descended** | 조상

Our family tree traces our *ancestors* back to the 14th century.

**대상** ancestor : heirloom [ɛ́ərlùːm]
ancestor가 남긴 것을 heirloom(상속물)이라고 한다.
cf) testator(유언자)가 남긴 것은 bequest(유산, 유물)라고 한다.

## aphorism
[ǽfərìzəm]

**n. a short saying containing a principle** | 짧은 격언, 경구

People who practice Confucianism use *aphorisms* to guide their lives.

**CH** aphorism : brevity [brévəti]
aphorism은 brevity(간략함)를 지닌다.

## archaic
[aːrkéiik]

**adj. referring to the time up to the Classical period in Ancient Greece; old fashioned or antiquated** | 고대 그리스의, 예스러운

The factory's *archaic* methods of production slowed the growth of the company.

**ANT** archaism : neologism [niːálədʒìzm]
archaism: 고어
neologism: 신조어

## arid
[ǽrid]

**adj. extremely dry; lacking rain or water supply** | 매우 건조한, 습기가 없는

The *arid* acres of his farm scarcely yielded enough to keep his household fed through the winter.

**CH** arid : desert [dézərt]
desert(사막)는 arid하다.

---

**TRANSLATION | 예문해석**

| | |
|---|---|
| amicable | 그 우호적인 남자는 금방 타협에 도달했다. |
| ancestor | 우리 족보는 14세기까지 거슬러 올라간다. |
| aphorism | 유교를 실천하는 사람들은 경구를 삶의 지침으로 삼는다. |
| archaic | 공장의 낡은 생산 설비는 회사의 성장을 늦췄다. |
| arid | 건조한 그의 농장 지대에서는 겨우 내내 그의 가족들이 먹기에는 너무 부족한 작물이 수확됐다. |

## ascetic
[əsétik]

**adj.** strict self-discipline for religious reasons | 종교적 이유로 금욕적인

**n.** one who lives a severe and disciplined life for the purpose of religious devotion | 금욕주의자

John had lived an *ascetic* life until he came to the very liberal and adventurous lifestyle of the city.

After his accident, Peter gave up his material possessions and moved to India where he lived as an *ascetic*.

**CH** ascetic : self-denial [sélfdináiəl]
ascetic은 self-denial(자제력)이 강하다.

## aside
[əsáid]

**n.** deviation; a message that strays from the main theme | 일탈, 여담

**adv.** away from other people | 옆에 떨어져서

The lecturer's *asides* were becoming increasingly divergent from the subject matter.

Matt stood *aside* while he waited for the speaker to introduce him.

**CH** aside : divergent [divə́ːrdʒənt]
aside(여담)는 divergent(벗어난, 일탈하는)하다.

## augur
[ɔ́ːgər]

**n.** one who foretells using omens | 예언자

Louis went to the *augur* to discover his fate.

**CH** augur : prediction [pridíkʃən]
augur는 prediction(예측)할 수 있는 능력이 있다.

## avid
[ǽvid]

**adj.** enthusiastically dedicated; desirous to the point of greed | 열심인, 탐욕스런

So *avid* was Jamie in his pursuit of affluence that he soon forgot the friends who aided him in his quest.

**ANT** avid : indifferent [indífərənt]
indifferent: 냉담한, 무관심한

---

### TRANSLATION | 예문해석

**ascetic**  John은 매우 자유롭고 모험에 찬 삶의 방식을 지닌 그 도시에 오기 전까지는 금욕주의적 삶을 살았다.
Peter는 사고를 겪은 후에 자신의 소유물을 모두 포기하고 인도로 가서 금욕주의자로 살았다.

**aside**  강사의 여담은 점점 더 주제에서 멀어졌다.
Matt은 연사가 자신을 소개하기를 기다리는 동안 옆에 서 있었다.

**augur**  Louis는 자신의 운명을 알기 위해 예언자를 찾아갔다.

**avid**  Jamie의 부에 대한 추구는 너무나 강해서 자신의 부탁으로 자기를 도와줬던 친구들도 곧 잊어버렸다.

## bribe
[braib]

**n.** money or favors given to a person in a position of judgment or authority for personal gain or relief from legal trouble | 뇌물

**v.** to offer a bribe | 뇌물로 매수하다

The mobster offered the judge a *bribe* to rule in his favor.

The senator was sued for having *bribed* the prime minister.

**CN** bribe : incorruptible [ìnkərʌ́ptəbl]

incorruptible(청렴한, 매수할 수 없는)한 사람은 **bribe**할 수 없다.

## chiaroscuro
[kià:rəskjúərou]

**n.** an artistic method or design that employs light and dark shades without concern for color | 명암대조법

*Chiaroscuro* was employed by the artist to create a perception of shadows in the sketch.

**CH** chiaroscuro : contrast [kántræst]

**chiaroscuro**는 명암의 **contrast**(대조)를 그 특징으로 갖는 예술 기법이다.

## chicanery
[ʃikéinəri]

**n.** illegal deception or trickery | 속임수, 책략

Many Americans think that President Bush used *chicanery* to win the last election.

**ANT** chicanery : aboveboard action [əbʌ́vbɔ̀:rd ǽkʃən]

**aboveboard action**: 공정한 행동

## cliche
[kli(:)ʃéi]

**n.** an overly familiar phrase | 진부한 상투어

A typical American *cliche* is "Cat got your tongue?"

**CH** cliche : hackneyed [hǽknid]

**cliche**는 말 그대로 **hackneyed**(진부한)한 표현이다.

---

### TRANSLATION | 예문해석

**bribe**
그 폭력배는 유리한 판결을 받기위해 판사에게 뇌물을 제공했다.
그 의원은 국무총리에게 뇌물을 주어서 고소당했다.

**chiaroscuro**
명암대조법은 스케치에 그림자 개념을 생각해낸 예술가들에 의해 도입되었다.

**chicanery**
많은 미국인들은 부시 대통령이 지난 선거에서 승리하기 위해 속임수를 썼다고 생각한다.

**cliche**
미국의 전형적인 상투적 문장 중의 하나는 "Cat got your tongue?(할 말을 잊었냐?)"이다.

**deception** [disépʃən]

n. **something that tricks or makes something untrue seem true** | 속임수

The master criminal was skilled at the art of *deception*.

> **CH** deceptive : ruse [ruːz]
> ruse(책략, 계략)는 deceptive(속이는, 현혹시키는)하다.

**dehydrate** [diːháidreit]

v. **to remove water from** | 탈수하다, 건조시키다

Mummification involves *dehydrating* the corpse for longer preservation.

> **대상** dehydrate : water [wɔ́ːtər]
> water(물)을 없애서 dehydrate하다.

**eccentric** [ikséntrik]

adj. **deviating far from the norm; odd** | 전형에서 벗어난, 기묘한

Carrington was the most *eccentric* person Gore had ever met.

> **SYN** eccentric : offbeat [ɔːfbíːt]
> offbeat: 엉뚱한, 기이한

**embolden** [imbóuldən]

v. **to make bold; to encourage** | 용기를 주다, 대담하게 하다

Sybil was *emboldened* by her sister's words and confronted her boss about the problem.

> **ANT** embolden : appall [əpɔ́ːl]
> appall: 오싹하게 하다, 질겁하게 하다

**embrace** [imbréis]

v. **to hold close with the arms; to take up willingly or eagerly** | 끌어 안다, 기꺼이 받아들이다

Roger quickly *embraced* the idea of expanding his business.

> **ANT** embrace : spurn [spəːrn]
> spurn: 일축하다, 퇴짜놓다, 경멸하다

---

**TRANSLATION | 예문 해석**

| | |
|---|---|
| **deception** | 그 악당두목은 속임수에 능했다. |
| **dehydrate** | 미이라화(化)에는 시체를 장기 보관하기 위한 탈수 작업이 포함된다. |
| **eccentric** | Carrington은 Gore가 이제껏 만나본 중에서 가장 기묘한 사람이었다. |
| **embolden** | Sybil은 여동생의 말에 용기를 얻어 그 문제에 대해 상사에게 항의했다. |
| **embrace** | Roger는 자신의 사업을 확장하자는 견해를 바로 받아들였다. |

## excerpt
[éksəːrpt]

**n. a part or quote taken from a larger work; an abstract**
| 긴 지문에서 얻은 발췌, 개요

Heather keeps a book with all her favorite *excerpts* that she reads for inspiration.

**SYN** excerpt : summary [sʌ́məri]
summary: 개요, 요약

## fabric
[fǽbrik]

**n. the underlying structure or matrix; cloth material**
| 기초가 되는 구조; 천

The *fabric* of the dress is not exactly what she wants.

**KIN** fabric : linen [línin]
linen(아마포)은 fabric의 한 종류이다.

## fabricate
[fǽbrikèit]

**v. to create or make, often with the purpose of lying**
| (주로 속일 목적으로) 꾸며내다, 위조하다

The student *fabricated* a story to tell his teacher that explained why his homework was late.

**WO** fabricate : authenticity [ɔ̀ːθentísəti]
fabricate하는 것에는 authenticity(신빙성, 진짜임)가 없다.

## facetious
[fəsíːʃəs]

**adj. merry or jocular**
| 쾌활한, 익살스런

Victor's *facetious* comment was met with great amusement by his co-workers.

**대상** facetious : speech [spiːtʃ]
facetious는 speech(말)을 묘사하는데 쓰인다.

## gash
[gæʃ]

**n. a deeply cut flesh wound**
| 깊게 베인 상처

The paramedics found a large *gash* in the stabbing victim's right side.

**DE** gash : cut [kʌt]
gash는 cut(베인 상처)보다 더 깊은 상처이다.

---

TRANSLATION | 예 문 해 석

| | |
|---|---|
| excerpt | Heather는 읽으면 영감이 얻어지는 자신이 선호하는 모든 인용문이 들어있는 책을 가지고 있다. |
| fabric | 그 드레스의 천은 정말로 그녀가 원하는 것이 아니다. |
| fabricate | 그 학생은 자신의 숙제가 늦은 이유를 선생님께 설명할 이야기를 꾸며냈다. |
| facetious | Victor의 익살스런 발언은 직장 동료들에게 커다란 즐거움을 주었다. |
| gash | 그 의료보조원은 칼에 찔린 희생자의 오른쪽 옆구리에서 깊이 베인 큰 상처를 발견해냈다. |

## genteel
[dʒentíːl]

**adj. elegant and refined in manner; polite** | 우아한, 고상한, 정중한

Brad's *genteel* demeanor belied his true maliciousness.

**ANT** genteel : churlish [tʃə́ːrliʃ]
churlish: 거친, 무례하고 천박한

## incendiary
[inséndièri]

**n. a person who intentionally sets fires; an agitator** | 방화범, 반란을 선동하는 사람

Charlie was hired as an *incendiary* to stir up anger among the workers.

**CH** incendiary : agitate [ǽdʒitèit]
incendiary은 agitate(선동하다)하는 사람이다.

## incense
[ínsens]

**v. to make very angry** | 몹시 화나게 하다

The recollection of Alexei's last act *incensed* his wife.

**ANT** incense : propitiate [prəpíʃièit]
propitiate: 달래다

## labor
[léibər]

**n. physical or mental exertion; work** | 노동, 노력

The crop pickers *labored* under the hot sun, stopping only for a drink of water.

**WO** labor : respite [réspit]
respite(휴식)는 labor하지 않는 상태를 말한다.

## labyrinth
[lǽbərìnθ]

**n. a complicated maze where someone is easily lost** | 길을 잃기 쉬운 복잡한 미로

McDougal's cave was a vast *labyrinth* of crooked walkways.

**CH** labyrinth : tortuous [tɔ́ːrtʃuəs]
labyrinth는 tortuous(비비꼬인)한 특징이 있다.

---

### TRANSLATION | 예문 해석

**genteel** Brad의 우아한 품행은 그의 본래의 악의를 숨긴 것이다.
**incendiary** Charlie는 노동자들 사이에서 분노를 불러 일으켜서 반란을 선동할 사람으로 고용되었다.
**incense** Alexei의 마지막 행동을 떠올리며 그의 부인은 격분했다.
**labor** 수확하는 사람들은 뜨거운 태양 아래서 일하며, 물을 마실 때만 일을 멈췄다.
**labyrinth** McDougal의 동굴은 꼬부라진 통로가 있는 광대한 미로였다.

## lacerate
[lǽsərèit]

**v. to cut or tear open; to cause deep mental or emotional pain to** | 찢다, 마음을 상하게 하다

His colleague's tragic death *lacerated* the fireman, and his guilty conscience drove him to see a therapist.

> **SYN** lacerate : distress [distrés]
>
> distress: 마음을 상하게 하다, 괴롭히다

## licentious
[laisénʃəs]

**adj. not having moral restraints, especially sexual restraints** | 방탕한

The man went to the cathedral and confessed of his *licentious* behavior.

> **ANT** licentiousness : moral restraint [mɔ́ːrəl ristréint]
>
> licentiousness: 방탕함
>
> moral restraint: 도덕적 절제

## nebulous
[nébjuləs]

**adj. lacking distinct form; unclear** | 불분명한, 막연한

Banks and investors prefer the structure of a corporation to the often more *nebulous* organization of a sole proprietorship.

> **ANT** nebulous : unambiguous [ʌ̀næmbígjuəs]
>
> unambiguous: 분명한, 명백한

## nicety
[náisəti]

**n. delicacy or exactness of perception; a subtle distinction** | 정확, 정밀; 미묘한 차이

The consultant's *nicety* of the situation allowed her to immediately think of an alternative remedy.

> **SYN** nicety : precision [prisíʒən]
>
> precision: 정확, 정밀

---

### TRANSLATION | 예문 해석

| | |
|---|---|
| **lacerate** | 그 소방관의 동료의 비극적인 죽음은 죄책감을 느끼는 그의 마음을 괴롭혔고, 그는 치료를 받으러 갔다. |
| **licentious** | 그 남자는 성당으로 가서 자신의 방탕한 행동을 고백했다. |
| **nebulous** | 은행들과 투자자들은 대개 단독 소유주의 다소 불분명한 조직보다는 법인을 더 선호한다. |
| **nicety** | 그 상담가의 상황 인식은 매우 정확해서 곧바로 대안 요법을 제시했다. |

## noble
[nóubl]

**adj.** having or showing high qualities; being of high birth

| 기품 있는, 고상한, 신분이 높은

The actions of virtue are *noble* and require no other reward.

> **SYN**  noble : lofty [lɔ́:fti]
>
> lofty : 고상한, 고귀한

## peccadillo
[pèkədílou]

**n.** a slight sin or fault

| 가벼운 죄, 사소한 잘못

The conquistador committed a *peccadillo* to the priest but quickly made amends for it.

> **DE**  peccadillo : sin [sin]
>
> peccadillo는 사소한 sin(죄)이다.

## recalcitrant
[rikǽlsitrənt]

**adj.** opposing or defiant of authority

| 권위에 대해 저항하는, 복종하지 않는

In general, the people of France have been historically *recalcitrant*.

> **CN**  recalcitrant : obey [oubéi]
>
> recalcitrant하는 사람은 쉽게 obey(복종하다)하지 않는다.

## recant
[rikǽnt]

**v.** to renounce a previous belief or statement

| 기존의 신념이나 주장을 포기하나, 철회하나

Helen's refusal to *recant* her Christian faith led to her imprisonment for more than a year.

> **대상**  recant : belief [bilí:f]
>
> recant는 기존의 belief(신념)를 철회하는 것이다.

---

### TRANSLATION | 예 문 해 석

| | |
|---|---|
| **noble** | 덕스러운 행동은 그 자체로 고상하며 다른 어떤 보상도 추구하지 않는다. |
| **peccadillo** | 그 정복자는 성직자에게 가벼운 죄를 범했지만 즉시 이를 시정했다. |
| **recalcitrant** | 일반적으로 프랑스인들은 역사적으로 권위에 저항해온 사람들이었다. |
| **recant** | Helen은 기독교 신앙을 포기하기를 거부함으로써 1년 이상 감옥살이를 해야 했다. |

### saboteur
[sǽbətə́ːr]

**n. one who sabotages** | 파괴 행위를 하는 사람

The *saboteurs*' underhanded tactics led to the demise of the agency.

**CH** saboteur : disrupt [disrʎpt]

saboteur는 사회를 disrupt(붕괴하다)시킬 목적으로 파괴 행위를 일삼는 사람이다.

### sobriety
[səbráiəti]

**n. seriousness in manner; self-restraint** | 진지함, 절제

*Sobriety* is one of the most important tenets of Buddism.

**WO** sobriety : sumptuous [sʎmptʃuəs]

sumptuous(사치스러운)한 생활에는 sobriety가 없다.

### sublime
[səbláim]

**adj. majestic; lofty and eminent; impressive and noble** | 장엄한, 고귀한

There is but one step from the *sublime* to the ridiculous.

**ANT** sublime : base [beis]

base: 미천한

### submerge
[səbmə́ːrdʒ]

**v. to put completely under water** | 물속에 잠기게 하다

When the submarine was completely *submerged*, the sailors on shore let out a great cheer.

**CN** submerge : buoyant [bɔ́iənt]

buoyant(부력이 있는)한 것은 submerge할 수 없다.

### subside
[səbsáid]

**v. to fall downward; to become less active** | 가라앉다, 잠잠해지다

The storm eventually *subsided*.

**ANT** subside : intensify [inténsəfài]

intensify: 격렬해지다

---

**TRANSLATION | 예문해석**

| | |
|---|---|
| **saboteur** | 그 파괴주의자들의 비밀스런 작전 행동들은 그 정부기관의 소멸을 가져왔다. |
| **sobriety** | 절제는 불교의 가장 중요한 교리 중 하나이다. |
| **sublime** | 고귀함과 우스꽝스러움은 한 걸음 차이이다. |
| **submerge** | 그 잠수함이 완전히 물에 잠기자 해안의 수병들은 큰 환호성을 내질렀다. |
| **subside** | 폭풍은 마침내 잠잠해졌다. |

## subsidiary
[səbsídièri]

**adj. of the second importance; furnishing support**
| 부차적인, 보조하는

Truancy was a *subsidiary* reason for why Dan was let go.

**CH** subsidy : supportive [səpɔ́ːrtiv]

subsidy(보조금)는 supportive(부양하는, 보조적인)하는 기능이 있는 돈이다.

## substantial
[səbstǽnʃəl]

**adj. material; considerable in importance or amount**
| 물질의, 중요한

The bank would not finance Kelly's loan without *substantial* personal property.

**SYN** substantial : corporeal [kɔːrpɔ́ːriəl]

corporeal: 물질적인, 실체적인

## subterfuge
[sʌ́btərfjùːdʒ]

**n. a deceptive artifice that conceals the truth**
| 진실을 가리기 위한 속임수

Roberta's apparent happiness with her domestic life was nothing more than *subterfuge* that masked a lonely and empty existence.

**WO** subterfuge : candor [kǽndər]

subterfuge에는 candor(솔직, 정직)가 없다.

## subvert
[səbvə́ːrt]

**v. to overturn from the foundation** | 파괴하다, 전복시키다

The rebels *subverted* the existing regime and replaced it with a democratic system of government.

**SYN** subvert : sabotage [sǽbətàːʒ]

sabotage: (계획, 정책 등을) 고의로 파괴하다

---

### TRANSLATION | 예문해석

**subsidiary** 무단 결석은 Dan이 해고당한 부차적인 원인이었다.
**substantial** 그 은행은 Kelly에게 유형 자산이 없이는 대출을 해주려하지 않았다.
**subterfuge** Roberta가 가정 생활에 행복을 느끼는 것처럼 보이는 것은 외롭고 허무한 실존을 가리기 위한 위장에 불과했다.
**subvert** 반란군들은 기존 정권을 전복시키고 민주주의 체제를 구축했다.

## succinct
[sʌksíŋkt]

**adj. precise and clear expression in writing and speaking** | 말이나 글이 간결하고 명확한

Mrs. Fisher summed it up to her friend in a *succinct* remark: "You must marry as soon as you can."

**ANT** express succinctly : babble [bǽbl]
　　express succinctly: 명료하게 말하다
　　babble: 불분명하게 주절거리다

## succor
[sʌ́kər]

**n. help when in trouble or need** | 원조, 구조

The homeless woman found *succor* at the local shelter.

**SYN** succor : relief [rilíːf]
　　relief: 구조, 구원

## taciturn
[tǽsətə̀ːrn]

**adj. not talkative; uncommunicative** | 과묵한, 터놓지 않는

Alex enjoyed Beth's company even though she was *taciturn* by nature.

**ANT** taciturn : loquacious [loukwéiʃəs]
　　loquacious: 말하기 좋아하는, 수다스러운

## vaccinate
[vǽksənèit]

**v. to prevent disease by giving an injection of dead virus** | 예방 접종하다

Children must be *vaccinated* for the flu in the winter months.

**PUR** vaccination : immunity [imjúːnəti]
　　vaccination(예방 접종)의 목적은 immunity(면역)를 가지게 하는데 있다.

## vibrant
[váibrənt]

**adj. full of life** | 생동적인, 약동하는

A *vibrant* complexion can signal younger, healthier individuals.

**ANT** vibrant : flagging [flǽgiŋ]
　　flagging: 축 늘어지는, 쇠퇴하는

---

### TRANSLATION | 예문 해석

| | |
|---|---|
| succint | Mrs. Fisher는 친구에게 간단히 요약해서 말했다. "넌 가능한 빨리 결혼해야 해." |
| succor | 그 집없는 여자는 지역 보호 시설에서 원조를 받았다. |
| taciturn | Alex는 Beth가 말수가 적었음에도 불구하고 그녀와 어울리는 것을 좋아했다. |
| vaccinate | 겨울철에 아이들은 독감 예방접종을 받아야 한다. |
| vibrant | 생동적인 얼굴빛은 좀 더 젊고 건강한 사람들의 특징이다. |

## waver
[wéivər]

**v.** to be indecisive or vacillate | 우유부단하다, 동요하다

Alex finally made a decision after two weeks of *wavering* back and forth.

**POS** waver : irresoluteness [irézəlù:tnis]
irresoluteness: 결단력 없음

---

TRANSLATION | 예 문 해 석

**waver**　　Alex는 2주간 갈팡질팡하다 결국 결정을 내렸다.

# 14th Day Daily Check-up

■ Fill in the blanks with the correct letter that matches the word with its definition.

1. recalcitrant  _____
2. facetious  _____
3. aphorism  _____
4. recant  _____
5. excerpt  _____
6. succor  _____
7. chicanery  _____
8. nebulous  _____
9. incense  _____
10. subterfuge  _____

a. to make very angry
b. to renounce a previous belief or statement
c. illegal deception or trickery
d. help when in trouble or need
e. a part or quote taken from a larger work; an abstract
f. a deceptive artifice that conceals the truth
g. lacking distinct form; unclear
h. a short saying containing a principle
i. opposing or defiant of authority
j. merry or jocular

■ Put the correct word in each blank from the list of words below.

11. spurn(쫓아내다)의 반의어는 _____이다.
12. desert는 _____ 하다.
13. _____는 사소한 sin이다.
14. exculpate하게 하는데 있어서 _____가 수단으로 사용된다.
15. _____는 supportive하는 기능이 있는 돈이다.
16. _____하는 것에는 authenticity가 없다.
17. evanescent(순간적인)의 반의어는 _____이다.
18. _____는 사회를 disrupt시킬 목적으로 파괴 행위를 일삼는 사람이다.
19. _____는 tortuous한 특징이 있다.
20. _____는 prediction할 수 있는 능력이 있다.

| a. fabricate | b. sublime | c. arid | d. alibi | e. abiding | f. licentious |
| g. subsidy | h. embrace | i. augur | j. saboteur | k. peccadillo | l. labyrinth |

**Answer key**

1. i  2. j  3. h  4. b  5. e  6. d  7. c  8. g  9. a  10. f
11. h  12. c  13. k  14. d  15. g  16. a  17. e  18. j  19. l  20. i

www.goHackers.com

해커스 어학연구소

# 15th DAY

FIFTEENTH DAY

SUPER VOCA

벌써 수퍼보카의 반을 끝내셨군요. 화이팅!

---

**accolade**
[ǽkəlèid]

n. **praise or honor** | 칭찬, 영예, 상

In 1967 Michael won *accolades* for his role as a mass murderer in "In Cold Blood."

**ANT** accolade : invective [invéktiv]
invective: 비난, 독설

---

**anchor**
[ǽŋkər]

v. **to fasten by an anchor** | (배를) 닻으로 고정시키다
n. **a heavy object that holds a ship in place** | 닻

Bryan *anchored* the ship as far off shore as possible.
Nautilus used the air brake instead of an *anchor* to stop moving.

**FUN** anchor : shift [ʃift]
anchor는 배를 shift(움직이다)하지 않도록 하는 기능이 있다.

---

**archetype**
[ɑ́ːrkitàip]

n. **a prototype; an ideal example of a type** | 원형, 전형

The *archetype* of an Ancient Greek woman was Aphrodite.

**CH** archetype : exemplify [igzémpləfài]
archetype은 exemplify(예시가 되다) 될 만한 가치를 지니고 있다.

---

**TRANSLATION | 예문해석**

| | |
|---|---|
| accolade | 1967년에 Michael은 "In Cold Blood"란 영화에서 대학살자 역으로 수상했다. |
| anchor | Bryan은 가급적 해안에서 멀리 배를 정박시켰다. |
| | 노틸러스 호는 닻 대신 공기 제동장치를 사용해서 움직임을 멈추었다. |
| archetype | 고대 희랍 여인의 전형은 Aphrodite였다. |

## archive [áːrkaiv]

**n. the place where historical documents and records are kept** | 문서 보관소

According to the suit, the National *Archives* and Records Administration first learned that Zimet was trying to sell the documents in late February and early March.

**FUN** archive : manuscript [mǽnjuskrìpt]
archive는 manuscript(원고)를 보관하는 기능을 한다.

## bucolic [bjuːkálik]

**adj. referring to the rural life of the herdsman** | 목부의, 전원 생활의

I don't love the hectic urban lifestyle, but I prefer it to a *bucolic* life here.

**ANT** bucolic : urban [əːrbən]
urban: 도시의

## constellation [kànstəléiʃən]

**n. the formation of stars that make a shape or design** | 어떤 모양이나 구조를 형성하는 별들의 진형, 별자리

Mary and John stared at the sky identifying as many *constellations* as they could.

**PAR** constellation : star [staːr]
star(별)은 constellation을 이루는 부분이다.

## constitute [kánstətʃùːt]

**v. to lay the foundation for or set up; to appoint one to a high office or place of dignity** | 기초를 세우다, 설립하다, 임명하다

Henderson was *constituted* as the new ambassador in July.

**ANT** constitute : abdicate [ǽbdikèit]
abdicate: 사임하다

## cower [káuər]

**v. to shrink in fear** | (두려움에) 움츠리다

Every time the owner raised his voice, the dog *cowered* in the corner.

**인과** cower : fear [fiər]
fear(두려움)으로 인해 cower하다.

---

| TRANSLATION | 예문 해석 |
|---|---|
| archives | 그 소장에 따르면 국립 공문서 보관청은 Zimet이 그 문서들을 팔려고 했다는 것을 2월 하순과 3월 초에 처음 알았다. |
| bucolic | 나는 소모적인 도시의 생활 방식을 좋아하는 것은 아니지만 이곳의 전원생활보다는 그쪽이 더 좋다. |
| constellation | Mary와 John은 가능한 한 많은 별자리를 찾아내기 위해 하늘을 유심히 쳐다보았다. |
| constitute | Henderson은 7월에 새 대사로 임명되었다. |
| cower | 주인이 목소리를 높일 때마다 그 개는 두려움에 구석에서 움츠렸다. |

## delirium
[dilíəriəm]

**n.** a state of mental confusion and disorientation | 혼란과 방향 상실의 정신 상태

The force of the blow put Liz into a temporary *delirium*.

**CH** delirium : confusion [kənfjúːʒən]

delirium은 confusion(혼란, 혼동)의 상태이다.

## exhaust
[igzɔ́ːst]

**v.** to use up completely | 다 써버리다

The small clinic's resources were *exhausted* while treating patients from the bus accident.

**CN** exhaust : infinite [ínfənət]

infinite(무한한)한 것은 exhaust할 수 없다.

## exhort
[igzɔ́ːrt]

**v.** to urge strongly with argument | 강력히 권고하다

Mr. Smith *exhorted* the company's administrative committee to cut down on expenditures.

**CH** exhortative : urge [əːrdʒ]

exhortative(권고하는)하는 것에는 urge(권고하다)하는 속성이 포함되어 있다.

## facile
[fǽsil]

**adj.** easily accomplished; superficial | 쉽게 이룬, 피상적인

The bachelor's *facile* reasons for marriage turned off any woman he dated.

**WO** facile : profundity [prəfʌ́ndəti]

facile한 것에는 profundity(심오함)가 없다.

## facilitate
[fəsílətèit]

**v.** to help make easier; to help in progress | 용이하게 하다, 촉진하다

Technology has unarguably *facilitated* communication.

**ANT** facilitate : impede [impíːd]

impede: 방해하다

---

### TRANSLATION | 예문 해석

| | |
|---|---|
| delirium | 거센 바람은 Liz를 일시적인 혼란 상태에 빠뜨렸다. |
| exhaust | 버스 사고의 환자들을 치료하는 동안 그 작은 병원의 물자들이 바닥났다. |
| exhort | Smith씨는 회사의 운영 위원회에게 지출을 줄이라고 강력하게 권고했다. |
| facile | 그 총각의 결혼에 대한 피상적인 생각들은 그가 데이트 하는 여자들에게 별로 흥미를 주지 못했다. |
| facilitate | 기술 발달로 의사소통이 쉬워진 것은 이론의 여지가 없다. |

## feckless
[féklis]

**adj. irresponsible or feeble** | 무책임한, 무기력한

The father was upset at his daughter's *feckless* behavior at school.

**ANT** feckless : responsible [rispánsəbl]

responsible: 책임 있는

## foible
[fɔ́ibl]

**n. a minor fault in someone's character** | 성격상의 사소한 결점

The father's *foibles* did not prevent his son from admiring him.

**DE** foible : failing [féiliŋ]

foible은 사소한 failing(결점)이다.

## friable
[fráiəbl]

**adj. easily breakable; easily reduced to powder** | 부서지기 쉬운, 버슬버슬한

The water filtered into underlying, particularly *friable* soil.

**CH** friable : crumble [krʌ́mbl]

friable한 것은 crumble(부스러지다)하기 쉽다.

## glib
[glib]

**adj. able to speak smoothly and easily without hesitation stemming from superficiality** | 겉발림으로 유창하게 말하는

The *glib* speaker told his life story to an entraptured audience.

**DE** glib : fluent [flúːənt]

glib는 fluent(유창한)에 비해 말만 잘하는 이라는 의미를 내포한다.

## grieve
[griːv]

**v. to feel sorrow and grief over something** | 슬퍼하다

We were shocked and *grieved* at the wanton murder he had committed.

**POS** grieve : sorrow [sárou]

sorrow: 슬픔

---

### TRANSLATION | 예문 해석

| | |
|---|---|
| feckless | 아버지는 자기 딸이 학교에서 저지른 무책임한 행동에 화가 났다. |
| foible | 아버지에게 성격상의 결점이 있었음에도 불구하고 아들은 여전히 그를 존경했다. |
| friable | 물은 지하의, 특히 버슬버슬한 흙 속으로 스며들었다. |
| glib | 그 달변의 강사는 도취된 관중들에게 자신의 인생이야기를 했다. |
| grieve | 우리는 그가 무자비한 살인을 저지른 데 대해 충격을 받고 슬퍼했다. |

## guidance
[gáidns]

**n. direction as to a decision; counselling** | 안내, 지도

His uncle's *guidance* helped Patrick through adolescence.

**CH** guidance : mentor [méntər]

mentor(믿을 만한 조언자, 교사)는 guidance를 해주는 사람이다.

## hackneyed
[hǽknid]

**adj. common or dull** | 상투적인, 진부한

The *hackneyed* sentiments of the play caused people to audibly groan at its triteness.

**CH** hackneyed : cliche [kli(ː)ʃéi]

cliche(진부한 상투어)는 말 그대로 hackneyed한 표현이다.

## ichthyologist
[ìkθiáləd ʒist]

**n. one who studies fish** | 어류학자

The number of fish in Long Lake was determined by the *ichthyologist*.

**대상** ichthyologist : salmon [sǽmən]

ichthyologist는 salmon(연어)과 같은 어류를 연구하는 학자이다.

## incipient
[insípiənt]

**adj. beginning to exist** | 이제 막 시작하는, 초기의

The work is still in the *incipient* stage.

**CN** incipient : realized [ríːəlàizd]

incipient한 것은 realized(달성된, 실현된)되지 않은 것이다.

## incite
[insáit]

**v. to move to action; to provoke or stir up** | 격려하다, 자극하다, 선동하다

William *incited* a physical altercation with the police officer by resisting arrest.

**PUR** incite : persiflage [pə́ːrsəflàːʒ]

incite하기 위해 persiflage(야유)를 보낸다.

---

**TRANSLATION | 예 문 해 석**

| | |
|---|---|
| guidance | Patrick은 삼촌의 지도로 무사히 사춘기를 보낼 수 있었다. |
| hackneyed | 그 연극의 진부한 정서는 관객들의 불만섞인 웅성거림을 자아냈다. |
| ichthyologist | Long Lake에 서식하는 물고기의 수는 그 어류학자에 의해 측정되었다. |
| incipient | 그 작업은 아직도 초기 단계에 있다. |
| incite | William은 연행을 거부함으로써 경찰관과 몸싸움을 벌였다. |

## inclement
[inklémənt]

**adj. severe or merciless** | 냉혹한, 무자비한

The *inclement* man's heart was not touched by the starving children.

**ANT** inclement : balmy [bɑ́ːmi]
balmy: 온화한, 위안이 되는

## incogitant
[inkɑ́dʒətənt]

**adj. inconsiderate or thoughtless** | 무분별한, 경솔한

I found my brother's teasing of my boyfriend to be extremely *incogitant*.

**WO** incogitant : thought [θɔːt]
incogitant한 행동은 thought(생각)없이 하는 것이다.

## inherent
[inhíərənt]

**adj. existing as an essential constituent or characteristic; intrinsic** | 고유의, 타고난

Religious freedom was the *inherent* reason why the Pilgrims settled in America.

**ANT** inherent : extrinsic [ikstrínsik]
extrinsic: 외부로부터의

## inhibit
[inhíbit]

**v. to discourage or restrain from doing something** | 제지하다, 금지하다

Most parents *inhibit* their children from staying up late at night.

**ANT** inhibit : foment [foumént]
foment: 조장하다

## laconic
[ləkɑ́nik]

**adj. using few words; brief to the point** | 말수 적은, 간결한

Chris didn't enjoy trying to make conversation with the *laconic* guest.

**WO** laconic : volubility [vɑ̀ljəbíləti]
laconic한 사람에게서는 volubility(수다스러움)을 찾아볼 수 없다.

---

TRANSLATION | 예 문 해 석

| | |
|---|---|
| inclement | 그 냉혹한 남자는 굶어 죽어가는 아이들을 보고도 전혀 동정의 마음이 일지 않았다. |
| incogitant | 나는 동생이 내 남자 친구를 괴롭히는 것을 매우 경솔한 행동이라고 생각했다. |
| inherent | 종교의 자유는 최초의 이주자들이 미국에 정착한 고유의 이유였다. |
| inhibit | 대부분의 부모들은 자녀들이 밤늦게까지 자지 않고 있는 것을 금한다. |
| laconic | Chris는 과묵한 손님하고 말상대하기를 좋아하지 않았다. |

## lucid
[lúːsid]

**adj. easily understood; clear** | 쉽게 이해되는, 명료한

The student wrote a *lucid* explanation of his behavior, expressing regret.

**CN** lucid : obfuscate [ábfʌskeit]

lucid한 것은 obfuscate(판단 등을 흐리게 하다)하지 않는다.

## mockery
[mákəri]

**n. derision; a subject of ridicule** | 조롱, 놀림감

Lily's *mockery* of his singing voice hurt his feelings.

**CH** mockery : burlesque [bərlésk]

burlesque(풍자적 희극)는 mockery하는 내용을 담고 있는 풍자적 희극이다.

## outmaneuver
[àutmənjúːvər]

**v. to defeat or overcome by skillful maneuvering** | (노련한 책략으로) ~을 이기다, 극복하다

In martial arts, speed and precision are important in *outmaneuvering* your opponent.

**ANT** outmaneuver : yield [jiːld]

yield: 굴복하다

## pacific
[pəsífik]

**adj. peaceful; appeasing** | 평온한, 융화적인

The *pacific* demeanor of the kindergarten teacher was unappreciated by her students.

**CN** pacific : discompose [dìskəmpóuz]

pacific한 사람을 discompose(마음의 평정을 잃게 하다)시키기는 어렵다.

## palatable
[pǽlətəbl]

**adj. satisfactory or acceptable to the taste** | 맛있는, 입에 맞는

Hunger makes any fare *palatable*.

**SYN** palatable : savory [séivəri]

savory: 맛있는, 향긋한

---

**TRANSLATION | 예문해석**

| | |
|---|---|
| lucid | 그 학생은 후회하며 자신의 행동에 대해 명확한 설명을 했다. |
| mockery | Lily는 그의 노래하는 목소리를 조롱해서 그의 마음을 상하게 했다. |
| outmaneuver | 무술에서의 속도와 정확함이 적을 이기는 데 있어서 중요하다. |
| pacific | 그 유치원 교사의 평온한 행동은 아이들에게는 별 의미가 없었다. |
| palatable | 배가 고프면 어떤 음식도 맛이 있기 마련이다. |

### paucity
[pɔ́ːsəti]

**n.** smallness in number or quantity | 소수, 소량

The *paucity* of the group allowed them to travel together.

**ANT** paucity : slew [sluː]
slew: 다량

### pliant
[pláiənt]

**adj.** easily flexed; compliant | 유연한, 유순한

The wire coat hanger was *pliant* enough to bend into different shapes.

**SYN** pliant : lithe [laið]
lithe: 유연한

### preclude
[priklúːd]

**v.** to make impossible or prevent for the future; to exclude | 불가능하게 하다, 방해하다, 배제하다

His choice not to go to college has *precluded* any possibility for a good career.

**ANT** preclude : enclose [inklóuz]
enclose: 에워싸다, 집어넣다

### pristine
[prístiːn]

**adj.** belonging to the earliest period; pure or unspoiled | 원시의, 더럽혀지지 않은

The *pristine* beauty of the lake caused everyone to stare in awe.

**CN** pristine : taint [teint]
pristine한 것은 taint(더럽히다, 타락시키다)되지 않은 것이다.

### pliable
[pláiəbl]

**adj.** flexible and easily bent; yielding readily to others | 유연한, 유순한

The *pliable* gymnast was able to do the splits with the greatest of ease.

**SYN** pliable : supple [sʌ́pl]
supple: 유연한, 유순한

---

TRANSLATION | 예 문 해 석

**paucity** 그 단체에 속한 사람들 중 몇명만이 그들이 여행에 합류하는 것을 허락했다.
**pliant** 그 철사로 된 코트 걸이는 유연해서 다양한 모양으로 구부러졌다.
**preclude** 대학에 진학하지 않기로 함으로써 그의 출세 가능성은 완전히 사라졌다.
**pristine** 그 호수의 더럽혀지지 않은 아름다움은 모든 사람들이 경외심을 가지고 바라보게 했다.
**pliable** 그 유연한 체조선수는 두 다리를 직선으로 벌리고 앉는 동작을 아주 쉽게 해낼 수 있었다.

## pucker
[pʌ́kər]

**v. to contract into wrinkles** | 주름잡다, 오므리다

Her lips were *puckered* in anticipation of a kiss.

> 대상  pucker : mouth [mauθ]
>
> mouth(입)를 pucker(오므리다)하다.

## puckish
[pʌ́kiʃ]

**adj. mischievous or impish** | 장난을 좋아하는, 장난꾸러기의

With a *puckish* gleam in her eye, Sarah ate the cake that was meant for the dinner guests.

> ANT  puckish : sober [sóubər]
>
> sober: 진지한, 술 취하지 않은

## quibble
[kwíbl]

**v. to find fault for trivial reasons** | 트집잡다

The heirs *quibbled* over the equitable distribution of the inheritance.

> CH  quibbler : cavil [kǽvəl]
>
> quibbler(트집쟁이)는 늘 cavil(트집 잡다)하려고만 한다.

## quiescence
[kwaiésns]

**n. inactivity or silence** | 활동 없음, 정적

The night's *quiescence* lulled Sarah to sleep.

> ANT  quiescence : tumult [tjú:mʌlt]
>
> tumult: 소란, 소요

## recidivism
[risídəvìzm]

**n. continual return to bad habits, especially criminal relapse** | 상습적 범행

The drug user's *recidivism* made any attempts at rehabilitaion useless.

> CH  recidivism : relapse [rilǽps]
>
> recidivism는 relapse(재발하다)하는 범죄를 의미한다.

---

| TRANSLATION | 예문 해석 |
|---|---|
| pucker | 그녀는 키스를 기대하며 입술을 오므렸다. |
| puckish | Sarah는 장난기어린 눈빛을 반짝거리며, 저녁 손님들을 위해 준비된 케이크를 먹었다. |
| quibble | 그 상속인들은 유산의 공평한 분배를 놓고 서로 트집을 잡았다. |
| quiescence | 밤의 정적에 마음이 평온해진 Sarah는 잠에 빠졌다. |
| recidivism | 그 마약중독자의 상습적 범행 앞에서는 그를 정상으로 복귀시키려는 어떤 노력도 소용없었다. |

## reciprocate
[risíprəkèit]

**v. to move backward and forward; to give things or feelings in return** | 왕복 운동을 하다, 주고 받다

The pendulum of the clock *reciprocated* slowly once every hour.

**ANT** reciprocate : move unidirectionally [muːv jùːnidirékʃənəli]

move unidirecitonally: 한 방향으로 움직이다

## reckless
[réklis]

**adj. disregardful of consequences; heedless** | 앞뒤를 가리지 않고 무모한, 부주의한

Many wars have been avoided by patience but have also been precipitated by *reckless* haste.

**ANT** reckless : circumspect [sə́ːrkəmspèkt]

circumspect: 신중한

## recluse
[rékluːs]

**n. one who lives in solitude** | 속세를 떠나 홀로 사는 은둔자

For two years John wandered through Arizona, living as a *recluse* in the desert.

**WO** recluse : gregariousness [grigɛ́əriəsnis]

recluse에게는 gregariousness(사교성)가 없다.

## recondite
[rékəndàit]

**adj. abstruse or obscure** | 난해한, 모호한

Quantum physics is a *recondite* subject for the average layman.

**ANT** recondite : widely understood [wáidli ʌ̀ndərstúd]

widely understood: 널리 이해된

## reconnoiter
[rìːkənɔ́itər]

**v. to conduct a preliminary survey, especially in order to gather military information** | 사전 조사를 하다, 정찰하다

A scout was sent ahead to *reconnoiter* the position of the enemy.

**PUR** reconnoiter : information [ìnfərméiʃən]

information(정보)을 얻기 위해 reconnoiter하다.

---

| TRANSLATION | 예 문 해 석 |
|---|---|
| reciprocate | 그 시계의 추는 한 시간에 한 번만 느리게 왕복 운동한다. |
| reckless | 많은 전쟁이 인내의 힘으로 억제되는가 하면 무모한 조급증 때문에 촉발되기도 한다. |
| recluse | John은 2년간 애리조나의 각지를 떠돌아다니며, 사막에서 은둔자로 살았다. |
| recondite | 양자 물리학은 보통의 평범한 사람들에게는 난해한 분야이다. |
| reconnoiter | 정찰병이 적의 위치를 파악하기 위해 미리 보내졌다. |

## rehabilitate
[rìːhəbílətèit]

**v. to fix or restore to proper condition; to restore to a healthy condition** | 재건하다, 건강한 상태로 회복하다

After the accident, James had to *rehabilitate* his broken leg.

**POS** rehabilitation : convalesce [kànvəlés]

rehabilitation: 회복, 재건

convalesce: 병에서 회복하다

## rickety
[ríkiti]

**adj. being in an unstable condition; weak or inclined to break** | 불안정한, 약한, 곧 부서질 것 같은

The *rickety* floor of the old house creaked as Michelle walked across it.

**대상** rickety : furniture [fə́ːrnitʃər]

furniture(가구) 등이 오래되면 rickety한 상태가 된다.

## schism
[sízm]

**n. a division or disharmonic situation** | 분열, 불화

A *schism* arose between Turkey and Greece after a group of illegal immigrants were found living in Athens.

**ANT** schism : unanimity [jùːnəníməti]

unanimity: 만장일치

## secondary
[sékəndèri]

**adj. of second importance** | 부차적인, 그다지 중요하지 않는

My primary responsibility is to my family; my *secondary* responsibility to my job.

**ANT** secondary : preponderant [pripándərənt]

preponderant: 우세한, 압도적인

## sociable
[sóuʃəbl]

**adj. naturally enjoying the companionship of others** | 사교적인

Kelly is a gay and *sociable* girl who loves parties.

**SYN** sociable : convivial [kənvíviəl]

convivial: 사교적인, 연회를 즐기는

---

### TRANSLATION | 예문 해석

**rehabilitate** 사고를 당한 후, James는 부러진 다리를 낫게 해야 했다.
**rickety** Michelle이 그 낡은 가옥의 약한 마루 위를 걷자 삐걱거리는 소리가 났다.
**schism** 일단의 불법 이주자들이 아테네에 살고 있음이 알려진 후 터키와 그리스 사이에 불화가 발생했다.
**secondary** 나의 우선적인 책임은 가족에 대한 것이고, 부차적인 책임은 직업에 대한 것이다.
**sociable** Kelly는 파티를 좋아하는 명랑하고 사교적인 소녀이다.

## stickler
[stíklər]

**n. one who insists on exactness or completeness in the observance of something** | 꼼꼼하고 까다로운 사람

My grammar teacher is a *stickler* for correcting grammar errors.

**CH** stickler : exacting [igzǽktiŋ]

stickler는 exacting(무리한 요구를 하는)하다.

## synopsis
[sinápsis]

**n. a summary capturing the main points** | 주제를 파악할 줄거리, 적요

The busy professor asked his assistant to give him a *synopsis* of the article.

**CH** synopsis : conciseness [kənsáisnis]

synopsis는 conciseness(간결함)를 그 특성으로 가지고 있다.

## tacit
[tǽsit]

**adj. implied without being spoken** | 암묵적인

The face she made at that moment was a *tacit* cue for me to leave.

**대상** tacit : infer [infə́ːr]

tacit한 것을 infer(추측하다)해서 알아내다.

## ticklish
[tíkliʃ]

**adj. sensitive to tickling; easily offended or upset** | 간지럼 잘 타는, 화를 잘내는

Jane's *ticklish* disposition made her sensitive to criticism.

**ANT** ticklish : imperturbable [ìmpərtə́ːrbəbl]

imperturbable: 쉽사리 흥분하지 않는, 차분한

## vacillate
[vǽsəlèit]

**v. to sway from one side to the other; to fluctuate in mind or opinion** | 흔들리다, 망설이다

The dancer's body rhythmically *vacillated* to the beat of the music.

**WO** vacillate : equipoise [ékwəpɔ̀iz]

vacillate하는 것에는 equipoise(평형, 균형)가 없다.

---

TRANSLATION | 예 문 해 석

| | |
|---|---|
| stickler | 우리 문법 선생님은 문법적 오류를 까다롭게 고쳐주신다. |
| synopsis | 그 바쁜 교수는 조수에게 그 기사의 줄거리를 가져오라고 요구했다. |
| tacit | 그 순간에 그녀가 지은 표정은 나보고 떠나라는 무언의 신호였다. |
| ticklish | Jane의 신경질적인 성격은 그녀를 비판에 민감하게 반응하도록 만들었다. |
| vacillate | 그 댄서는 음악의 박자에 맞춰 율동적으로 몸을 움직였다. |

## vociferous
[vousífərəs]

adj. **offensively loud; given to vehement outcry** | 떠들썩한, 큰 소리로 외치는

The fans' *vociferous* voices attempted to distract opposing teams.

**ANT** vociferous : serene [sərí:n]

serene: 고요한, 평온한

## wicked
[wíkid]

adj. **vicious or evil** | 사악한

The truly *wicked* people of the world live alone.

**POS** wickedness : nefarious [nifέəriəs]

wickedness: 사악, 악의

nefarious: 사악한

---

### TRANSLATION | 예 문 해 석

**vociferous** 팬들은 상대팀의 주의를 흩뜨리기 위해 떠들썩하게 굴었다.
**wicked** 세상에서 정말로 사악한 사람들은 고립되어 살아간다.

# 15th Day Daily Check-up

■ Fill in the blanks with the correct letter that matches the word with its definition.

1. inclement _____
2. pliant _____
3. quiescence _____
4. laconic _____
5. bucolic _____
6. hackneyed _____
7. feckless _____
8. tacit _____
9. exhort _____
10. palatable _____

a. common or dull
b. satisfactory or acceptable to the taste
c. to urge strongly with argument
d. implied without being spoken
e. inactivity or silence
f. severe or merciless
g. using few words; brief to the point
h. referring to the rural life of the herdsman
i. easily flexed; compliant
j. irresponsible or feeble

■ Put the correct word in each blank from the list of words below.

11. extrinsic (외부의, 고유의 것이 아닌)의 반의어는 _____ 이다.
12. _____ 은 사소한 failing이다.
13. _____ 은 sordid(더러운)의 반의어이다
14. _____ 는 fluent에 비해 말만 잘하는 이란 의미를 내포한다.
15. _____ 는 manuscript를 보관하는 기능을 한다.
16. supple (유연한, 고분고분한)은 _____ 의 동의어이다.
17. _____ 는 relapse하는 범죄를 의미한다.
18. infinite한 것은 _____ 할 수 없다.
19. _____ 은 exemplify될 만한 가치를 지니고 있다.
20. _____ 는 impede(방해하다)의 반의어이다.

| a. vacillate | b. archetype | c. pristine | d. exhaust | e. archive | f. glib |
| g. foible | h. inherent | i. pliable | j. facilitate | k. incogitant | l. recidivism |

Answer key

1. f  2. i  3. e  4. g  5. h  6. a  7. j  8. d  9. c  10. b
11. h  12. g  13. c  14. f  15. e  16. i  17. l  18. d  19. b  20. j

## TAKE A BREAK 쉬·어·가·는 페·이·지

### 멕시코 전쟁 Mexican war

1845년 대통령 J.K. 포크는 목화재배 확대를 바라는 대농장주(大農場主)들의 요구에 따라 멕시코와 텍사스 매수교섭을 벌였으나 실패하였다. 양국 군대 간의 충돌은 계속되었고, 미국의회는 1846년 5월 11일 멕시코에 대하여 정식으로 전쟁을 선포하였다. 이 전쟁은 노예 문제를 둘러싼 대립격화를 두려워한 대서양 연안의 각 주(州)의 반대에도 불구하고 미국군의 승리로 끝났다. 1848년 2월 양국은 과달루페-이달고 조약을 체결, 미국은 희망하는 서부의 영토확장을 달성하였지만, 정치적으로 남부의 발언권이 증대되고, 노예제를 둘러싼 논쟁이 더욱 격화되는 결과를 가져왔다.

원래 인디언들의 땅이었던 텍사스에 백인이 나타난 것은 1591년 에스파냐의 피네다가 최초였다. 17세기 후반부터 에스파냐인이 텍사스에 정착하기 시작하여 1691년에는 에스파냐령이 되었다. 점점 늘어나던 미국인 이주자들이 1835년 반란을 일으켰지만 알라모 요새의 싸움에서 패배하였다. 하지만 센해싱트 싸움에서는 멕시코군을 격파하고 이듬해에는 독립을 이룩하여 텍사스 공화국을 세웠다. 1845년 미국에 병합되어 그해 12월 29일 텍사스 주(州)가 되었다. 이러한 발전과정 때문에 텍사스 주에는 멕시칸이라고 부르는 메스티소의 비율이 높다.

www.goHackers.com

해커스 어학연구소

# 16th DAY

시작이 반이랬는데,
설마 지금이 시작이라구요?

---

**accrete**
[əkríːt]

**v. to increase gradually by addition**
| 서서히 부착 증대 시키다, 부착해서 자라다

The money that Fred had invested 14 years ago had *accreted* to a large amount.

- **KIN** accrete : grow [grou]

  accrete는 서서히 부착되어 grow(증가하다, 자라다)하는 것이다.

**align**
[əláin]

**v. to put or fall into line**
| 일렬로 정렬시키다

The interior decorators *aligned* the coffee table with the couches.

- **ANT** aligned : askew [əskjúː]

  aligned: 일렬로 정렬된
  askew: 비스듬한

**animate**
[ǽnəmèit]

**v. to enliven or fill with life**
| 활기 있게 하다, 생명을 불어넣다

Seth was a smart and *animated* boy with enthusiasm and expression.

- **ANT** animation : lassitude [lǽsətjùːd]

  animation: 생기, 활기
  lassitude: 무기력, 피로

**ardent**
[áːrdənt]

**adj. passionate and torrent; displaying strong enthusiasm**
| 열정적인, 열광적인

The *ardent* opponents to the death penalty lined up to protest outside the prison walls.

- **ANT** ardent : tepid [tépid]

  tepid: 미지근한, 열의가 없는

---

### TRANSLATION | 예문 해석

| | |
|---|---|
| accrete | Fred가 14년 전에 투자했던 돈이 점점 불어나서 큰 액수가 되었다. |
| align | 그 실내 장식가는 커피 테이블을 쇼파와 일렬로 정렬시켰다. |
| animate | Seth는 열정과 풍부한 표정을 지닌 영리하고 활달한 소년이었다. |
| ardent | 강력한 사형 반대론자들이 감옥 담장 밖에 줄지어 서서 시위를 벌였다. |

## audacious
[ɔːdéiʃəs]

**adj. recklessly adventurous or brave** | 대담한, 호기로운

The *audacious* tricks of the stuntman awed the audience.

**WO** audacious : trepidation [trèpədéiʃən]
audacious한 사람에게는 trepidation(공포)이 없다.

## blight
[blait]

**n. a disease which destroys or ruins plants** | 식물을 죽게 하는 병, 마름병

**v. to wither up; to frustrate or destroy** | 시들게 하다, 망치다

The pine tree was dying of *blight*.
Tom hoped that Mary wouldn't forget his shoes, but the hope was *blighted*.

**SYN** blight : ruin [rúːin]
ruin: 망치다

## cacophony
[kəkɑ́fəni]

**n. dissonant sounds** | 불협화음

The Sirens tortured their victims with a *cacophony* of singing and wailing.

**ANT** cacophony : melody [mélədi]
melody: 아름다운 선율

## coda
[kóudə]

**n. an independent concluding part of an artistic work** | (음악이나 이야기의) 종결부

Finally in the *coda*, the book moves forward to 1999 for its embracing, reflective conclusion.

**ANT** coda : prelude [préljuːd]
prelude: 서곡

## decorous
[dékərəs]

**adj. being decent or proper** | 단정한, 예의바른

The *decorous* young man never lost his temper or said anything out of line.

**ANT** decorous : mangy [méindʒi]
mangy: 지저분한

---

### TRANSLATION | 예문 해석

| | |
|---|---|
| audacious | 그 스턴트맨의 대담한 묘기는 관중들을 놀라게 했다. |
| blight | 그 소나무는 마름병으로 죽어가고 있었다. |
| | Tom은 Mary가 자신의 신발을 잊어버리지 않기를 바랐지만 그 희망은 꺾였다. |
| cacophony | Siren들은 노래와 울부짖는 소리의 불협화음으로 희생자들을 괴롭게 했다. |
| coda | 마침내 종결부에서 그 책은 포괄적이고 깊이있는 결론을 위해 다시 1999년으로 옮겨간다. |
| decorous | 그 점잖은 청년은 결코 화를 내거나 경우에 어긋나는 말을 하지 않았다. |

### decrepit
[dikrépit]

**adj. weakened, worn out, or impaired by old age or much use** | 쇠약한, (오래되어서) 낡은

The *decrepit* old man spent the last ten years of his life in bed.

**ANT** decrepit : vigorous [vígərəs]

vigorous: 활력 있는

### didactic
[daidǽktik]

**adj. tending to teach or moralize** | 가르치려고 하는, 설교적인

Although he was an extremely intelligent man, his *didactic* attitude was not liked by anyone.

**CH** didactic : teach [tiːtʃ]

didactic한 사람은 teach(가르치다)하려는 속성을 지닌다.

### dodder
[dάdər]

**v. to shake from age or overall weakness of the body; to totter** | (노령이나 쇠약함으로 인해) 몸을 떨다, 비틀거리다

Grandmother Betty *doddered* on her way from the house to the car.

**CH** dodder : unsteady [ʌnstédi]

dodder에는 unsteady(불안정한)한 속성이 포함되어 있다.

### emigrate
[émigrèit]

**v. to leave one's country to live in another** | 이민 가다

Andy's parents *emigrated* to Canada in search of a better future for their family.

**ANT** emigrate: repatriate [riːpéitrièit]

repatriate: 본국으로 송환하다

### eminent
[émənənt]

**adj. highly ranked or prominent** | 지위가 높은, 저명한

Dressed in full attire, the *eminent* General led the parade through the town's main street.

**CH** eminence : luminary [lúːmənèri]

luminary(특정 분야에서의 권위자)는 eminence(저명함)를 가지고 있다.

---

**TRANSLATION | 예문 해석**

**decrepit** 그 쇠약한 노인은 그의 말년의 10년을 병상에서 보냈다.
**didactic** 그는 매우 지적인 사람이었으나, 그의 설교적인 태도는 누구에게도 환영받지 못했다.
**dodder** Betty할머니는 집에서 자동차까지 가는 도중에 휘청거렸다.
**emigrate** Andy의 부모는 가족의 보다 나은 미래를 추구하여 캐나다로 이민갔다.
**eminent** 그 유명한 장군은 정장을 잘 차려입고 마을의 중심가를 통과하는 퍼레이드를 이끌었다.

## encourage
[enkə́ːridʒ]

**v. to inspire or give hope to someone** | 기운을 북돋우다, 희망을 주다

Criticism of the government should not only be tolerated, but *encouraged*.

**CH** encourage : hortatory [hɔ́ːrtətɔ̀ːri]

hortatory(용기를 주는, 권고하는)한 것은 encourage하는 속성을 지닌다.

## enigma
[ənígmə]

**n. something puzzling or hard to explain and understand** | 수수께끼, 불가사의한 것

Kay's recent behavior was an *enigma* to those who knew her.

**CH** enigma : impenetrable [impénətrəbl]

enigma는 impenetrable(불가해의)한 것이다.

## epigram
[épəgræ̀m]

**n. a wise saying, often in poetic form** | 경구, 풍자시

Sometimes the doctor made philosophic *epigrams* which he used as encouragement through the hardships in his life.

**CH** epigram : wise [waiz]

epigram은 wise(사려 깊은)한 내용을 담고 있다.

## epilogue
[épəlɔ̀ːg]

**n. the conclusion to a literary work or play; afterword** | (문학작품이나 연극의) 맺음말, 발문

The *epilogue* of Don Quixote's first book foretells the coming of a second adventure for the valiant knight.

**ANT** epilogue : preface [préfis]

preface: 서문

## excoriate
[ikskɔ́ːrièit]

**v. to censure harshly** | 호되게 비난하다

Mr. Arafat has been *excoriated* harshly by President Bush because of the many Palestinian suicide bombings.

**ANT** excoriate : extol [ikstóul]

extol: 극찬하다

---

### TRANSLATION | 예문해석

| | |
|---|---|
| encourage | 정부에 대한 비판은 허용되어야 할 뿐만 아니라 장려되어야 한다. |
| enigma | Kay의 최근의 행동은 그녀를 아는 사람들에게는 수수께끼였다. |
| epigram | 때때로 그 의사는 인생의 고난을 헤쳐나갈 때 용기를 얻기 위해 철학적인 경구를 지어냈다. |
| epilogue | 돈키호테 첫 권의 발문은 이 용감한 기사의 두 번째 모험을 예고한다. |
| excoriate | 아라파트 의장은 수많은 팔레스타인 사람의 자폭 공격 때문에 부시 대통령으로부터 강력히 비난받았다. |

## exculpate [ékskʌlpèit]

**v. to forgive or excuse of a criminal charge** | 무죄로 하다, 면해주다

The defendant argues that the new evidence should *exculpate* him.

**PUR** exculpate : alibi [ǽləbài]
exculpate하게 하는데 있어서 alibi(알리바이)가 수단으로 사용된다.

## faction [fǽkʃən]

**n. a select group within a larger group** | (당 내부의) 소수 그룹, 파벌

Only the most outstanding *faction* of students was selected to represent the school at the ceremony.

**SYN** faction : clique [kli:k]
clique: 도당, 파벌

## fade [feid]

**v. to slowly disappear; to lose freshness** | 천천히 사라지다, 바래다

Old soldiers never die; they just *fade* away.

**대상** fade : loudness [láudnis], brightness [bráitnis]
fade는 소리의 loudness(크기)나 빛의 brightness(밝기)가 점점 줄어드는 것이다.

## faint [feint]

**adj. weak or dizzy; lacking courage or strength; lacking clarity or loudness** | 힘없는, 어지러운, 무기력한, (소리 등이) 약한

The *faint* voices began to grow louder as Mary got closer to the door.

**ANT** faint : stentorian [stentɔ́:riən]
stentorian: 소리가 큰

## fecundity [fikʌ́ndəti]

**n. the productiveness of a person, thing, or animal** | 다산성, 비옥함

Research shows that high *fecundity* is often balanced by high mortality.

**ANT** fecundity : barrenness [bǽrənnis]
barrenness: 불모, 불임

---

### TRANSLATION | 예 문 해 석

| | |
|---|---|
| exculpate | 그 피고인은 새로운 증거가 자신의 무죄를 입증해줄 것이라고 주장한다. |
| faction | 학생들 중 가장 우수한 집단만이 선발되어 그 기념식에서 학교를 대표했다. |
| fade | 노병들은 결코 죽지 않는다. 단지 사라질 뿐이다. |
| faint | Mary가 문쪽으로 다가갈수록 그 희미한 소리는 점점 커졌다. |
| fecundity | 연구에 의하면 높은 다산성은 종종 높은 사망률에 의해 균형이 유지된다고 한다. |

## frigid
[frídʒid]

**adj. extremely cold** | 매우 추운

Mars has *frigid* weather conditions.

**DE** frigid : cool [kuːl]

frigid는 cool(시원한)한 정도를 넘어 훨씬 추운 상태를 의미한다.

## gainsay
[gèinséi]

**v. to oppose or state as untrue** | 반박하다, (거짓이라고) 부인하다

I *gainsaid* my sister's claim that I had stolen Mom's money.

**ANT** gainsay : affirm [əfə́ːrm]

affirm: (사실이라고) 단언하다, 승인하다

## grind
[graind]

**v. to reduce to powder by friction; to wear down or polish by friction** | 빻다, 갈다

Flour is made by *grinding* wheat.

**FUN** grind : pestle [péstl]

pestle은 grind하기 위해 사용하는 막자나 절구 공이를 말한다.

cf) mortar(막자 사발)은 pestle과 함께 grind하는데 쓰인다.

## guile
[gail]

**n. deceit or trickery** | 교활함, 간사함

Looking into her large clear eyes, Bruce could see nothing that would indicate *guile*.

**WO** guile : naive [nɑːíːv]

naive(순진한)한 사람에게는 guile이 없다.

## hamstring
[hǽmstrìŋ]

**v. to cripple or incapacitate** | 절름발이로 만들다, 무력화하다

The relief efforts were *hamstrung* by the unexpected storm.

**대상** hamstring : effectiveness [iféktivnis]

어떤 것의 effectiveness(효과, 효험)을 hamstring하다.

---

TRANSLATION | 예 문 해 석

| | |
|---|---|
| **frigid** | 화성은 매우 추운 기상조건을 지닌다. |
| **gainsay** | 내가 엄마의 돈을 훔쳤다는 누나의 주장을 나는 부인했다. |
| **grind** | 밀가루는 밀을 갈아 만든다. |
| **guile** | Bruce에게는 그 소녀의 크고 맑은 눈에 교활함이 전혀 보이지 않았다. |
| **hamstring** | 구호의 노력은 예기치 못한 폭풍으로 무력화 되었다. |

## heinous
[héinəs]

**adj. hatefully wicked** | 극악한

Many consider Hitler's extermination of the Jews to be the most *heinous* act in history.

**ANT** heinous : venial [víːniəl]

venial: (죄가) 가벼운, 용서받을 수 있는

## hidebound
[háidbàund]

**adj. stubbornly conservative; having dry skin adhering closely to underlying flesh** | 고루한, (가죽이) 뼈만 남은

Some critics say that present-day Korean society is much less hierarchical and *hidebound* than it was during the country's long pre-modern period.

**DE** hidebound : conservative [kənsɔ́ːrvətiv]

hidebound는 conservative(보수적인)보다 더 보수적인 이라는 뜻이다.

## hideous
[hídiəs]

**adj. ugly to the point of being offensive** | 생김새가 극히 혐오스런, 아주 불쾌한

The Medusa was a mythological *hideous* creature whose face would turn any men to stone.

**WO** hideous : pulchritude [pʌ́lkrətjùːd]

hideous한 사람이나 물건에는 pulchritude(아름다움)가 결여 되어 있다.

## incontrovertible
[inkɑ̀ntrəvə́ːrtəbl]

**adj. not open to argument; unquestionable** | 논쟁의 여지가 없는, 명백한

Despite *incontrovertible* evidence, the jury found the defendant innocent.

**CN** incontrovertible : dispute [dispjúːt]

incontrovertible한 것은 dispute(논쟁하다)할 필요가 없다.

## incorrigible
[inkɔ́ːridʒəbl]

**adj. unruly; unable to reform** | 제멋대로 구는, 교정할 수 없는

The *incorrigible* young man could not be controlled by anyone, not even his parents.

**CN** incorrigible : amend [əménd]

incorrigible한 것은 amend(바로잡다)할 수 없다.

---

**TRANSLATION | 예 문 해 석**

**heinous** 많은 사람들이 히틀러의 유태인 학살이 역사상 가장 사악한 행위라고 생각한다.
**hidebound** 일부 비평가들은 현재의 한국 사회가 장기간에 걸친 전근대기보다도 훨씬 덜 계급적이고 덜 보수적이라고 주장한다.
**hideous** Medusa는 어떤 사람이라도 돌로 만들어버린 신화에 등장하는 혐오스런 괴물이다.
**incontrovertible** 명백한 증거에도 불구하고, 그 배심원들은 피고가 무죄라고 판결했다.
**incorrigible** 막돼먹은 그 청년은 누구도, 심지어 그의 부모조차도 어쩔 도리가 없었다.

## inculpate
[inkʌ́lpeit]

**v.** to blame or convict of a wrongful act with the use of evidence or proof  | 증거를 이용해 죄를 씌우다

Pierre was *inculpated* by the new evidence brought forth by the prosecution.

**ANT** inculpate : exonerate [igzánərèit]

exonerate: 무죄임을 입증하다

## indefensible
[ìndifénsəbl]

**adj.** incapable of being defended or excused  | 방어할 수 없는, 변호의 여지가 없는

The company's decision not to recall the defective laptop is *indefensible*.

**ANT** indefensible : tenable [ténəbl]

tenable: 공격에 견딜 수 있는, 지지할 수 있는, 조리 있는

## inimical
[inímikəl]

**adj.** being hostile or opposed to someone or something  | 적대적인, 반목하는

Peter's cold, *inimical* voice towards Michael indicated the bad blood between the two.

**ANT** inimical : amicable [ǽmikəbl]

amicable: 우호적인

## inimitable
[inímətəbl]

**adj.** not able to be mimicked  | 흉내낼 수 없는

The actor's stellar performance was *inimitable*.

**CN** inimitable : copy [kápi]

inimitable한 것은 copy(모방하다, 흉내내다)할 수 없다.

## jaded
[dʒéidid]

**adj.** being worn out and tired  | 지친, 진저리가 난

Jack seemed *jaded*, but he interrupted his comrade with a voice of calm confidence.

**인과** jaded : overexposure [òuvəriskpóuʒər]

overexposure(과다 등장)한 결과 jaded하게 된다.

---

### TRANSLATION | 예문해석

**inculpate** — Pierre는 검찰이 제시한 새로운 증거로 인해 범죄에 연루되었다.
**indefensible** — 결함이 있는 노트북을 회수하지 않기로 한 그 회사의 결정은 변호의 여지가 없다.
**inimical** — Peter의 Machael을 향한 차갑고 적대적인 목소리는 둘 사이의 적의를 드러냈다.
**inimitable** — 그 남자배우의 빼어난 연기는 흉내내기 힘들었다.
**jaded** — Jack은 염증이 난 듯 했지만, 차분히 확신에 찬 목소리로 동료의 말을 제지했다.

## jocund
[dʒákənd]

**adj. being in high spirits** | 유쾌한, 즐거운

After the football victory, the fans were *jocund* and celebrated all night.

**ANT** jocund : morose [məróus]

morose: 시무룩한, 침울한

## occult
[əkʌ́lt]

**adj. hidden from general view or knowledge** | 숨겨진, 불가사의한

The *occult* entrance to the club was only accessible with a special key.

**ANT** occult : patent [pǽtnt]

patent: 명백한

## orderly
[ɔ́:rdərli]

**adj. neatly organized** | 정돈된, 체계적인

The secretary's desk had been arranged in a neat and *orderly* fashion.

**ANT** orderly : awry [ərái]

awry: 제자리에 있지 않은, 구부러지거나 비틀려 있는

## pedantic
[pədǽntik]

**adj. being a pedant; ostentatious of learning** | 현학적인, 아는 체하는

The three Spanish professors laughed heartily at the *pedantic* Classics student who spent his entire time studying one Ancient Greek book.

**DE** pedantic : scholarly [skálərli]

pedantic은 scholarly(학자의, 학자적인)한 척하는 것이다.

## persiflage
[pə́:rsəflɑ̀:ʒ]

**n. light teasing or banter** | 가벼운 장난이나 놀림, 야유

The *persiflage* between the old friends belied the actual tension that strained their relationship.

**PUR** persiflage : incite [insáit]

incite(자극하다)하기 위해 persiflage를 하다.

---

### TRANSLATION | 예문 해석

**jocund** 축구에서 승리한 후에 팬들은 매우 즐거워했고 밤새 축제를 벌였다.
**occult** 그 클럽의 숨겨진 문은 특별한 열쇠를 가져야 들어갈 수 있었다.
**orderly** 그 비서는 책상을 깨끗하고 정돈된 방식으로 정리했다.
**pedantic** 그 세 명의 스페인 교수들은 모든 시간을 고대 그리스의 책 한 권에 쏟는 학자인 척 하는 그 고전주의파 학생을 맘껏 비웃었다.
**persiflage** 그 옛 친구들 사이의 가벼운 장난은 그들의 관계를 조이고 있던 실제의 긴장 상태를 숨겼다.

## philistine
[fíləstìːn]

**n. one who is uncultured and ignorant** | 교양 없고 무식한 사람

The world is full of *philistines* who care only for money and nothing for culture and the arts.

**CN** philistine : cultivated [kʌ́ltəvèitid]

philistine은 cultivated(교양 있는, 세련된)하지 않다.

## plagiarism
[pléidʒərìzm]

**n. the use of another's words and ideas as one's own** | 다른 사람의 말이나 사상을 도용함, 표절

*Plagiarism* is practiced by students now more than ever as the internet has made it easier to copy others' works.

**대상** plagiarism : ideas [aidíːəz]

ideas(사상)은 plagiarism의 대상이 된다.

## rectify
[réktəfài]

**v. to make right; to correct** | 수정하다, 개정하다

The businessman tried to *rectify* his mistakes of being an absentee father by spending more time with his children.

**대상** rectify : treaty [tríːti]

treaty(계약, 협정)를 rectify하다.

## rectitude
[réktətjùːd]

**n. the state of right and good morals; the quality of being correct in judgment** | 정직, 청렴, 공정함

The moral *rectitude* of humanity is of the utmost concern, especially for world religious leaders.

**WO** rectitude : corruptionist [kərʌ́pʃənist]

corruptionist(부패한 관리)에게는 rectitude가 없다.

---

| TRANSLATION | 예문해석 |
|---|---|
| philistine | 이 세상은 돈만 생각하고 문화나 예술에 대해서는 전혀 관심이 없는 교양 없는 사람들로 가득 차 있다. |
| plagiarism | 인터넷이 다른 사람의 작업을 쉽게 복사할 수 있도록 해주는 요즘 다른 어느 때보다도 많은 표절이 학생들에 의해 행해지고 있다. |
| rectify | 그 사업가는 더 많은 시간을 아이들과 함께 보냄으로써 아버지 노릇을 제대로 못했던 잘못을 고치려고 했다. |
| rectitude | 인류의 도덕적 청렴성은 최대의 관심거리이며 전세계의 종교 지도자들에게는 특히 그렇다. |

## secure
[sikjúər]

**v. to protect from risk of loss and danger; to guarantee** | 안전하게 하다, 보장하다

**adj. free from danger** | 안전한

Laws alone cannot *secure* freedom of expression; in order that every man present his views without penalty there must be a spirit of tolerance in the entire population.

The commander had his entire unit make a *secure* temporary defensive site.

**ANT** secure : precarious [prikɛ́əriəs]
precarious: 위험한, 불안정한

## sedate
[sidéit]

**v. to make calm** | 진정시키다

**adj. keeping a serious and quiet manner** | 차분한, 조용한

The lawyer had to *sedate* his client from yelling against the judge to avoid the maximum sentence.

Jane looked a little more pale than usual, but more *sedate* than Elizabeth had expected.

**ANT** sedate : roil [rɔil]
roil: 휘젓다, 화나게 하다

## sycophant
[síkəfənt]

**n. one who flatters those in power to get what he/she wants** | 아첨하는 사람

Hollywood stars often complain that true friends are hard to find among the plethora of *sycophants*.

**CH** sycophant : fawn [fɔːn]
sycophant는 fawn(아첨하다)한다.

## stiff
[stif]

**adj. firm and difficult to bend** | 단단해서 구부리기 어려운, 굳은

Thomas woke up with a *stiff* neck after sleeping in an awkward position.

**WO** stiff : suppleness [sʌ́plnis]
stiff한 물질은 suppleness(유연함)가 없다.

---

**TRANSLATION | 예문해석**

**secure** 법만으로는 표현의 자유를 보장할 수 없다. 다시 말해서, 누구나 자신의 의견을 처벌받지 않고 제시할 수 있으려면 전체 국민의 관용정신이 필요하다.
그 지휘관은 휘하의 전 장병으로 하여금 안전한 임시 방어 지역을 구축하도록 했다.

**sedate** 변호사는 의뢰인이 최고형을 받지 않도록 하기 위해 판사에게 소리지르지 못하도록 진정시켜야만 했다.
Jane은 평상시보다 좀더 창백해 보였지만 Elizabeth가 생각했던 것보다 더 차분해 보였다.

**sycophant** 할리우드 스타들은 너무나 많은 아첨꾼들 속에서 참된 친구를 찾기가 힘들다고 종종 불평한다.

**stiff** Thomas는 잘못된 자세로 잤기 때문에 일어날 때 목이 뻣뻣했다.

## tact
[tækt]

**n. the capability to act so as not to offend people**
| 타인의 기분을 상하지 않게 행동하는 재치, 요령

Tom was completely lacking *tact* and was of no romantic interest to Sue.

**CH** tactless : offend [əfénd]
tactless(재치 없는, 요령 없는)한 것은 offend하는 속성을 갖는다.

## thicken
[θíkən]

**v. to make more thick; to increase the density of**
| 두껍게 만들다, 짙게 하다, 진하게 하다

Coagulants *thicken* blood which aid in the clotting of injured vessels.

**FUN** thicken : coagulant [kouǽgjulənt]
coagulant(응고제)는 액체를 thicken하는 기능이 있다.

## trickle
[tríkl]

**v. to drip or fall as drops** | 똑똑 떨어지다

Pierre felt the tears *trickle* under his spectacles and hoped they would not be noticed.

**DE** trickle : gush [gʌʃ]
trickle보다 세차게 흘러나오는 것을 gush(세차게 흘러나오다)로 묘사한다.

## uncouth
[ʌnkú:θ]

**adj. lacking in tact and grace** | 투박한, 세련되지 않은

Mattie remembered the shyness he had felt at approaching her in his *uncouth* clothes.

**CH** uncouth : churl [tʃə́rl]
churl(시골뜨기, 상스러운 사람)은 uncouth하다.

---

**TRANSLATION | 예문 해석**

| | |
|---|---|
| tact | Tom은 재치가 전혀 없어서 Sue에게 낭만적인 매력을 불러일으키지 못했다. |
| thicken | 응고제는 피를 짙게 함으로써 상처난 혈관이 응고되는 것을 돕는다. |
| trickle | Pierre는 안경 밑으로 눈물이 떨어지는 것을 느끼며 이를 알아채지 못하기를 바랐다. |
| uncouth | Mattie는 촌스러운 옷을 입고 그녀에게 가까이 갔을 때 느꼈던 부끄러움을 떠올렸다. |

## unctuous
[ʌ́ŋktʃuəs]

**adj. characterized by insincere kindness; having the quality of oil** | 겉으로만 상냥하게 하는; 기름기가 많은

Many products, such as candles and oil, are made from the body parts of *unctuous* animals, such as whales.

**CH** unctuous : salve [sæv]
salve(연고)는 보통 unctuous하다.

## uphold
[ʌphóuld]

**v. to support or sustain something to ensure its proper use** | 지키다, 유지하다

It is the job of every citizen to *uphold* the law.

**ANT** uphold : abrogate [ǽbrəgèit]
abrogate: 폐지하다

## vague
[veig]

**adj. unclear or inexplicit** | 불분명한, 모호한

Nicholas had formed a *vague* mental picture from the sparse description he had been given.

**ANT** vague : trenchant [tréntʃənt]
trenchant: 뚜렷한, 날카로운

## vehement
[víːəmənt]

**adj. intensely emotional; marked by forceful energy** | 열렬한, 열정적인, 강렬한

In a rage of anger she shouted *vehement* words at the group of onlookers.

**ANT** vehement : apathetic [æ̀pəθétik]
apathetic: 무감각한, 냉담한

---

**TRANSLATION | 예 문 해 석**

| | |
|---|---|
| **unctuous** | 양초나 기름 같은 제품들은 고래처럼 기름기 많은 동물의 몸의 일부로 만들어진다. |
| **uphold** | 법을 지키는 것은 모든 시민의 의무이다. |
| **vague** | Nicholas는 주어진 몇 마디 말에서 희미한 형상을 생각해냈다. |
| **vehement** | 그녀는 너무도 화가 나서 구경꾼들에게 심한 말을 퍼부었다. |

# 16th Day Daily Check-up

■ Fill in the blanks with the correct letter that matches the word with its definition.

1. enigma          _____
2. audacious       _____
3. rectitude       _____
4. dodder          _____
5. fecundity       _____
6. inculpate       _____
7. decorous        _____
8. uncouth         _____
9. excoriate       _____
10. jocund         _____

a. to censure harshly
b. to shake from age or overall weakness of the body
c. lacking in tact and grace
d. to blame or convict of a wrongful act with the use of evidence or proof
e. the state of right and good morals; the quality of being correct in judgement
f. being decent or proper
g. something puzzling or hard to explain and understand
h. the productiveness of a person, thing, or animal
i. being in high spirits
j. recklessly adventurous or brave

■ Put the correct word in each blank from the list of words below.

11. _____한 것은 amend 할 수 없다.
12. _____은 wise한 내용을 담고 있다.
13. patent(명백한)은 _____의 반의어이다.
14. amicable(우호적인)의 반의어는 _____이다.
15. luminary는 _____를 가지고 있다.
16. _____는 fawn한다.
17. _____는 impenetrable 한 성격을 갖는다.
18. salve는 보통 _____하다.
19. _____는 ruin(망치다)의 동의어이다.
20. _____는 cool한 정도를 넘어 훨씬 추운 상태를 의미한다.

| a. enigma | b. decrepit | c. occult | d. eminence | e. sedate | f. epigram |
| g. frigid | h. blight | i. unctuous | j. incorrigible | k. inimical | l. sycophant |

**Answer key**

1. g  2. j  3. e  4. b  5. h  6. d  7. f  8. c  9. a  10. i
11. j  12. f  13. c  14. k  15. d  16. l  17. a  18. i  19. h  20. g

# SUPER VOCA

S . E . V . E . N . T . E . E . N . T . H . D . A . Y

# 17th DAY

되돌아갈 수 없는 길이라면 차라리 끝까지 가라.

---

### abstain
[æbstéin]

**v. to prevent oneself from; to avoid doing something deliberately** | 회피하다, 삼가다

It is a common social practice to *abstain* from gossiping publicly.

**대상** abstain : forbidden [fərbídn]

forbidden(금지된)것을 abstain하다.

---

### acute
[əkjúːt]

**adj. sharp or severe; characterized by penetrating intellectual perception** | 예리한, 모진, 통찰력이 날카로운

The professor is brilliant because she is an *acute* thinker.

**CH** acute : discerner [disə́ːrnər]

discerner(감별사, 판단자)는 acute한 식별력을 지닌다.

---

### aggrandize
[əgrǽndaiz]

**v. to increase in strength or importance** | (힘이나 중요성을) 증가시키다

Over the past decade China has *aggrandized* its influence in world affairs.

**대상** aggrandize : strength [streŋkθ]

aggrandize는 strength(강도, 힘)를 증가시키는 것이다.

---

### aggravate
[ǽgrəvèit]

**v. to irritate or make worse** | 화나게 하다, 악화시키다

The loud construction *aggravated* many nearby residents.

**SYN** aggravate : exacerbate [igzǽsərbèit]

exacerbate: 악화시키다

---

### TRANSLATION | 예문 해석

**abstain**  공개적으로 험담하기를 삼가는 것이 일반적인 사회적 관행이다.
**acute**  그 여교수는 예리한 사고력을 지닌 사람이라서 재기가 넘친다.
**aggrandize**  지난 수십년간 중국은 국제 문제에서의 자신들의 영향력을 증가시켜 왔다.
**aggravate**  건축 현장의 소음 때문에 많은 이웃 주민들이 화가 났다.

## aggrieve
[əgríːv]

v. **to distress or bring trouble to** | 괴롭히다, 고통을 주다

Eva looked downcast and *aggrieved* after her father's surgery.

**ANT** aggrieve : gratify [grǽtəfài]
gratify: 기쁘게 하다

## argot
[áːrgou]

n. **a secret language or idiom specific to the context** | 은어

The two uttered an *argot* so as not to be understood by the others.

**SYN** argot : jargon [dʒáːrgən]
jargon: 은어, 전문용어

## augment
[ɔːgmént]

v. **to make larger, greater, or more intense** | 증가시키다, 증대시키다

Chad *augmented* his income by working an extra part time job.

**ANT** augment : abate [əbéit]
abate: 줄이다, 완화시키다

## bedlam
[bédləm]

n. **a state of extreme confusion or noisy uproar** | 극도로 혼란하거나 시끄러운 상태, 대소동

Weddings are such a *bedlam* of activities that the bridal party is always exhausted afterwards.

**ANT** bedlam : serenity [sərénəti]
serenity: 고요함, 평온

## bigot
[bígət]

n. **one who holds strong to their own prejudices and opinions about other's race or religion** | 인종이나 종교 등에 대해 편협한 견해를 지닌 사람, 고집쟁이

In the rural areas of the country there are more *bigots* because they have less exposure to different kinds of people.

**WO** bigot : tolerance [tálərəns]
bigot에게는 tolerance(관용, 포용력)가 없다.

---

**TRANSLATION | 예문해석**

**aggrieve** Eva는 아버지가 수술을 받은 후 풀이 죽고 괴로워 보였다.
**argot** 그 두 사람은 다른 사람들이 알아듣지 못하도록 은어를 사용했다.
**augment** Chad는 파트타임으로 일을 더 해서 수입을 증가시켰다.
**bedlam** 결혼식은 여러 활동들의 큰 소동이어서 그 후 피로연 때는 항상 지치게 된다.
**bigot** 시골에서는 다른 종류의 사람들을 접할 기회가 적기 때문에 시골 사람 중에는 고집쟁이가 많다.

### cantankerous
[kæntǽŋkərəs]

**adj. difficult to deal with; ill-tempered** | 다루기 힘든, 성미 고약한

If Ron doesn't have his espresso in the morning, he becomes *cantankerous* for the whole day.

**ANT** cantankerous : genial [dʒíːnjəl]
genial: 상냥한, 온화한

### circumference
[sərkʌ́mfərəns]

**n. the distance around a closed circle** | 원의 둘레

The *circumference* of the watermelon is triple that of the pear.

**PAR** circumference : circle [sə́rkl]
circumference는 circle(원)에 포함되는 부분이다.

### cogent
[kóudʒənt]

**adj. very compelling; appealing to the mind or reason** | 강력한, 설득력 있는

A missionary's job is to be *cogent* in delivering the message of God.

**CH** cogent : convince [kənvíns]
cogent하는 것은 convince(확신시키다, 납득시키다)하려는 속성을 지닌다.

### cognizant
[kágnəzənt]

**adj. having an awareness or knowledge** | 인식하고 있는, 알고 있는

It is said that the oracles of Ancient Greece were *cognizant* of the ways of the gods.

**ANT** cognizant : unaware [ʌ̀nəwɛ́ər]
unaware: 모르는

---

**TRANSLATION | 예 문 해 석**

| | |
|---|---|
| cantankerous | 만약 아침에 에스프레소를 마시지 못하면 Ron은 하루 종일 성미가 고약해진다. |
| circumference | 그 수박의 둘레 길이는 배의 세 배이다. |
| cogent | 선교사의 역할은 하나님의 말씀을 설득력 있게 전달하는 것이다. |
| cognizant | 고대 그리스 제사장들은 신의 뜻을 알고 있었다고 전해진다. |

## consummate
v. [kánsəmèit]
adj. [kənsʌ́mət]

**v. to complete or finish** | 완성하다, 달성하다
**a. skilled or perfect** | 유능한, 완벽한

The two corporate leaders *consummated* their merger with a glass of wine.
Hiller was the *consummate* politician with his brilliant smile and excellent speaking skills.

**ANT** consummate : amateurish [æ̀mətʃúəri∫]
amateurish: 아마추어 같은, 완벽하지 못한

## digress
[daigrés]

**v. to move away from the main subject** | 주제에서 벗어나다

Our conversation *digressed* from academia to our plans for Friday night.

**대상** digress : subject [sʌ́bdʒikt]
subject(주제)에서 digress하다.

## dogged
[dɔ́(:)gid]

**adj. stubbornly unyielding** | 완고한, 끈질긴

Sherlock Holmes was *dogged* in his pursuit to solve a mystery.

**ANT** dogged : yielding [jíːldiŋ]
yielding: 순종적인, 고분고분한

## doggerel
[dɔ́ːgərəl]

**n. irregular and awkward poetry, usually used in a comic sense** | 우스꽝스러운 엉터리 시

As the soldier marched he sang a bit of a *doggerel* in a high and quavering voice.

**KIN** doggerel : verse [vəːrs]
doggerel은 verse(시)의 일종이다.

## effusive
[ifjúːsiv]

**adj. excessively demonstrative; gushy** | 심정을 토로하는, 감정을 쏟아내는

Mrs. Lee's *effusive* personality began to grate on her dinner guests.

**ANT** effusive : reticent [rétəsənt]
reticent: (표현 등을) 억제한, 과묵한, 말을 삼가는

---

TRANSLATION | 예문해석

**consummate** 그 두 회사의 대표들은 포도주 건배를 끝으로 합병 절차를 마쳤다.
Hiller는 눈부신 미소와 훌륭한 말솜씨를 지닌 완벽한 정치가 였다.
**digress** 우리의 대화는 학문적인 것에서 금요일 밤 계획에 관한 것으로 벗어났다.
**dogged** 셜록 홈즈는 미스테리를 해결하기 위해 끈질기게 매달린다.
**doggerel** 그 군인은 행진하면서 높고 떨리는 목소리로 엉터리 시 한 구절을 읊었다.
**effusive** Mrs. Lee의 감정을 쏟아내는 성격은 저녁 식사에 초대된 사람들의 신경을 거슬리게 했다.

### engender
[indʒéndər]

**v. to produce or bring into being** | 발생하게 하다, 생기게 하다

There had been so much enthusiasm *engendered* that Carrie believed herself deeply in love.

**ANT** engender : quash [kwɑʃ]
quash: 없애버리다, 진압하다

### engross
[engróus]

**v. to take all the attention of; to occupy completely** | 집중시키다, 몰두시키다

The book *engrossed* readers with an intense and imaginative plot.

**SYN** engrossed : absorbed [əbsɔ́ːrbd]
engrossed: 몰두한, 사로잡힌
absorbed: 몰두한

### fiasco
[fiǽskou]

**n. a complete and utter failure** | 대실패

Terry's friends had procrastinated too long in planning his birthday party and as a result it was a *fiasco*.

**ANT** fiasco : notable success [nóutəbl səksés]
notable success: 대성공

### frustrate
[frʌ́streit]

**v. to make discouraged; to block or prevent someone from doing something** | 좌절 시키다, 낙담시키다, 망치다, 헛되게 하다

I was *frustrated* that he didn't show up on time.

**ANT** frustrate : abet [əbét]
abet: 선동하다, 부추기다

### infuse
[infjúːz]

**v. to introduce or put into by pouring; to fill with something** | 주입하다, 불어 넣다

The newly wed wife *infused* her husband's bachelor pad with a homely atmosphere.

**DE** infuse : inspire [inspáiər]
inspire(고무하다, 영감을 주다)는 infuse보다 좀 더 강한 어감을 가지고 있다.

---

### TRANSLATION | 예문해석

**engender** Carrie는 정신을 차릴 수 없을 만큼 상대방에게 열중했으므로 자신이 사랑에 깊이 빠져 있다고 생각했다.
**engross** 그 책은 강렬하고 상상력 넘치는 플롯으로 독자들을 사로잡았다.
**fiasco** Terry의 생일 파티를 계획하는 데 그의 친구들이 너무 지체해 버렸고 그 결과로 파티는 완전히 실패작이었다.
**frustrate** 나는 그가 약속 시간에 맞춰 나타나지 않아서 매우 실망했다.
**infuse** 신혼의 아내는 남편이 총각시절 살던 그 집에 가정적인 분위기를 불어넣었다.

## ingenious
[indʒíːnjəs]

**adj. having or showing cleverness or creativity, especially in designing or in solving problems** | 아주 영리한, 독창적인

Cornell's *ingenious* orchestral score was lauded as a masterpiece.

**ANT** ingenious : prosaic [prouzéiik]

prosaic: 상상력 없는, 무미 건조한

## ingenue
[ǽndʒənjúː]

**n. a naive young lady** | 순진한 소녀

The actress played the role of the *ingenue* who the lead male fell in love with.

**WO** ingenue : sophistication [səfìstəkéiʃən]

ingenue에게서는 sophistication(세상 물정에 익숙하여 닳고 닳음)의 모습을 볼 수 없다.

## negligent
[néglidʒənt]

**adj. tending to neglect; careless or casual** | 태만한, 부주의한

The doctor's *negligent* actions resulted in a permanent impairment for the patient.

**ANT** negligent : vigilant [vídʒələnt]

vigilant: 방심하지 않는, 부단히 경계하는

## odious
[óudiəs]

**adj. very unpleasant; causing disgust** | 불쾌한, 혐오스러운

The *odious* smell in the kitchen emanated from the spoiled food.

**인과** odious : disgust [disgʌ́st]

odious한 것을 본 결과 disgust(매스꺼움, 혐오감)를 느끼게 된다.

## ominous
[ɑ́mənəs]

**adj. of a bad omen; threatening** | 불길한, 험악한

The *ominous* occurrence of events this week foretells of a greater disaster.

**ANT** ominous : auspicious [ɔːspíʃəs]

auspicious: 길조의

---

TRANSLATION | 예 문 해 석

| | |
|---|---|
| ingenious | Cornell의 독창적인 교향 악곡은 걸작이라는 칭송을 받았다. |
| ingenue | 그 여배우는 남자주인공을 사랑에 빠지게 하는 순진한 소녀 역을 맡았다. |
| negligent | 그 의사의 부주의한 행동때문에 그 환자는 영구적인 손상을 입게 되었다. |
| odious | 부엌의 불쾌한 냄새는 썩은 음식에서 나는 것이었다. |
| ominous | 금주에 발생한 그 불길한 사건들은 더 큰 재난의 발생을 예고하는 것이다. |

## opine
[oupáin]

**v.** to state as one's own opinion; to express an opinion | 의견을 말하다, 의견을 나타내다

The doctor *opined* that the indisposition arose from fatigue and he prescribed rest.

**CH** opine : pundit [pʌ́ndit]

pundit(석학)는 늘 opine하는 경향이 있다.

## ostentation
[ὰstentéiʃən]

**n.** a showy display to impress others | 겉치레, 허식

The wealthy are not disliked for their riches, but rather for their *ostentatious* behavior.

**ANT** ostentation : artlessness [ɑ́ːrtlisnis]

artlessness: 꾸밈없음

## persevere
[pə̀ːrsəvíər]

**v.** to persist in an undertaking despite difficulties or obstacles | (어려움이나 장애에) 굴하지 않고 버티어 내다

Those who keep their goals in mind shall *persevere*.

**ANT** persevere : give up [giv ʌp]

persevere: 인내하다

give up: 포기하다

## philanthropist
[filǽnθrəpist]

**n.** one who acts in goodwill towards others | 박애주의자, 자선가

The noted *philanthropist* was known for his generous donations and benevolent spirit.

**CH** philanthropist : eleemosynary [èlimásənèri]

philanthropist는 eleemosynary(자선적인)하다.

## pigment
[pígmənt]

**n.** a color created for decoration (i.e., makeup); a coloring matter in a cell of animals and plants | 안료, 색소

The *pigment* in her lips and cheeks were red from the cold.

**WO** pigment : albinism [ǽlbənìzm]

albinism(색소 결핍증, 백색종)은 pigment가 부족한 증상이다.

---

### TRANSLATION | 예 문 해 석

**opine** 그 의사는 환자의 가벼운 질병이 피로 때문에 생겼다고 진단하고 휴식을 취하라는 처방을 써줬다.

**ostentation** 부자들은 그들의 부유함 때문에 아니라 허세를 부리를 행동 때문에 미움을 받는다.

**persevere** 가슴에 목표를 품고 있는 사람들은 끝까지 인내해낼 것이다.

**philanthropist** 그 유명한 박애주의자는 후한 기부와 자비로운 성품으로 잘 알려져 있다.

**pigment** 날씨가 추워서 그녀의 입술과 볼이 붉은 색조를 띠었다.

## rage
[reidʒ]

**n. uncontrolled anger** | 격분

Aaron's bouts of *rage* when drinking scared his family members.

> **DE** rage : anger [ǽŋgər]
> rage는 억제되지 않는 강한 anger(화)를 뜻한다.

## rant
[rænt]

**v. to speak or write in a violent or angry manner** | 폭언하다, 화난 투로 말하거나 적다

The townspeople had grown accustomed to the crazy man *ranting* about his life.

> **인과** rant : anger [ǽŋgər]
> anger(화, 분노)때문에 rant(폭언하다)하게 된다.

## rapprochement
[ræprouʃmáːŋ]

**n. the establishment or renewal of good relations, especially between two nations; the state of reconciliation** | (특히 국가간의) 친선 관계의 확립, 친교 회복, 화해

The *rapprochement* of the two nations is necessary for trade negotiations to take place.

> **ANT** rapprochement : estrangement [istréindʒmənt]
> estrangement: 불화

## refuse
n. [réfjuːs]
v. [rifjúːz]

**n. waste or garbage** | 쓰레기
**v. to turn down or express a desire to not comply** | 거절하다, 마다하다

The city's *refuse* was dumped at a nearby landfill.
I wouldn't *refuse* any invitation to a free meal.

> **FUN** refuse : landfill [lǽndfìl]
> landfill(쓰레기 매립지)은 refuse를 매립하는 곳이다.

---

### TRANSLATION | 예문 해석

**rage**     Aaron이 술을 마시면 격분하는 증상때문에 그의 가족들은 겁에 질렸다.
**rant**     마을사람들은 자신의 인생에 대해 폭언을 하는 그 미친 남자에 점차 익숙해졌다.
**rapprochement**     두 나라의 지도자간에 친선 재수립은 무역 협상이 이루어지게 하는 데 필수적이다.
**refuse**     시에서 발생하는 쓰레기는 근처의 쓰레기 매립장에 버려졌다.
             나는 공짜로 식사를 주는 초대는 어떤 것이라도 거절하지 않았다.

## regimen
[rédʒəmən]

**n. a plan or system for daily life usually intended to improve health** | 음식과 운동을 통해 건강을 증진시키는 양생법

Soldiers in any army follow a strict *regimen* of diet, exercise, and discipline.

**PUR** regimen : health [helθ]

regimen는 health(건강)를 증진시키기 위해 행해지는 처방법이다.

## reign
[rein]

**n. rule by a monarch; the period during which a royalty has power; pervasive dominance** | 통치, 치세, 지배

The *reign* of King Louis XIII brought much prosperity to France.

**PUR** reign : coronation [kɔ̀:rənéiʃən]

coronation(대관식)은 reign을 양도하기 위한 것이다.

## righteous
[ráitʃəs]

**adj. upright according to moral law** | 도덕적으로 올바른

Hector prides himself on his *righteous* and proper character.

**ANT** righteous : reprobate [réprəbèit]

reprobate: 타락한

## roil
[rɔil]

**v. to stir up or cause to move quickly** | 휘젓다, 혼란케 하다

Throwing rocks into a pond always *roils* the fish.

**ANT** roil : sedate [sidéit]

sedate: 진정시키다

## sagacious
[səgéiʃəs]

**adj. keen; having the ability to discern judgment** | 기민한, 현명한

It is said the most *sagacious* are the slowest to speak.

**WO** sagacity : simpleton [símpltən]

simpleton(바보, 얼간이)에게는 sagacity(현명함)가 없다.

---

TRANSLATION | 예문 해석

| | |
|---|---|
| **regimen** | 어떤 부대에 배치된 군인들은 규정식과 운동 및 훈련으로 짜여진 엄격한 양생법을 준수한다. |
| **reign** | 루이 13세 왕의 치세에 프랑스는 크게 융성했다. |
| **righteous** | Hector는 의롭고 고매한 자신의 성품에 자부심을 갖고 있다. |
| **roil** | 연못에 돌을 던지면 언제나 물고기가 놀라 도망가곤 한다. |
| **sagacious** | 가장 현명한 사람들이 말을 아낀다고 한다. |

## sage
[seidʒ]

**n. a wise man** | 현인

The *sage* was often sought by the people of the village for advice.

- **CH** sage : judicious [dʒuːdíʃəs]
  
  sage는 judicious(현명한)한 사람이다.

## scintillate
[síntəlèit]

**v. to give off sparks; to be brilliant** | 불꽃을 내다, 재치가 번뜩이다

The *scintillating* story kept Anne up all night.

- **ANT** scintillating : fatuous [fætʃuəs]
  
  scintillating: 불꽃을 튀기는, 재치가 번뜩이는
  
  fatuous: 어리석은, 우둔한

## shift
[ʃift]

**v. to move slightly; to change ideas or position** | 움직이다, 신념이나 입장 등을 바꾸다

Eugene *shifted* on the couch to make room for his friend.

- **FUN** shift : anchor [æŋkər]
  
  anchor(닻)는 배를 shift하지 않도록 하는 기능이 있다.

## significant
[signífikənt]

**adj. having consequence or meaning; fairly large in amount or quantity** | 중요한, 의미있는, 상당한

William Shakespeare is ranked as a *significant* literary figure.

- **ANT** significant : paltry [pɔ́ːltri]
  
  paltry: 가치 없는, 하찮은

## skimp
[skimp]

**v. to put forth minimal attention, money, or effort** | 인색하게 굴다, 대충하다

The employer was in the habit of *skimping* his workers.

- **POS** skimp : parsimony [páːrsəmòuni]
  
  parsimony: 인색함

---

**TRANSLATION | 예 문 해 석**

| | |
|---|---|
| sage | 마을 사람들은 종종 조언을 구하러 그 현인을 찾아왔다. |
| scintillate | Anne은 그 재치가 빛나는 이야기를 밤새 읽었다. |
| shift | Eugene은 친구에게 소파의 자리를 내주기 위해 옆으로 옮겨 앉았다. |
| significant | William Shakespeare는 중요한 문인이란 평가를 받는다. |
| skimp | 그 고용주는 직원들에게 인색하게 구는 경향이 있다. |

## slight
[slait]

**v. to treat as small or unimportant** | 무시하다, 냉대하다

The *slighted* worker continued to keep his discontent hidden under a cheerful smile.

**ANT** slight : cosset [kásit]

cosset: 귀여워 하다, 응석받이로 키우다

## stimulant
[stímjulənt]

**n. that which creates a temporary increase of energy or activity** | 흥분제, 자극제

As coffee contains a *stimulant*, drinking it can result in increased alertness.

**ANT** stimulant : soporific [sɑ̀pərífik]

soporific: 최면제, 수면제

## swift
[swift]

**adj. able to move rapidly** | 재빠른

The danger of capsizing increases when rafting in *swift* currents.

**ANT** move swiftly : creep [kriːp]

creep: 살금살금 기다

## swill
[swil]

**v. to drink rapidly or greedily** | 벌컥벌컥 마시다

For an hour I ate tacos and *swilled* glasses of tequila that were filled again by the time they'd been put back on the bar.

**DE** swill : sip [sip]

swill은 sip(홀짝거리며 마시다)에 비해 빠른 속도로 벌컥벌컥 마시는 것을 의미한다.

## taint
[teint]

**v. to corrupt or spoil** | 타락시키다, 더럽히다

Tracy's fall off the bike *tainted* her image of motorcycling.

**CN** taint : pristine [prístiːn]

pristine(원시의, 더럽혀지지 않은)한 것은 taint되지 않은 것이다.

---

### TRANSLATION | 예문 해석

| | |
|---|---|
| slight | 무시받던 노동자는 자신의 불만을 밝은 웃음 속에 계속 감추고 있었다. |
| stimulant | 커피에는 자극제가 포함되어 있기 때문에, 커피를 마시면 각성도가 증가할 수 있다. |
| swift | 래프팅할 때 물살이 빨라지면 배가 뒤집힐 위험이 커진다. |
| swill | 한 시간 동안 나는 타코스를 먹으며, 바에 내려 놓을 때쯤이면 다시 채워지는 테킬라 몇 잔을 벌컥벌컥 들이켰다. |
| taint | Tracy는 자전거에서 떨어져서 자전거 선수라는 이미지를 구겼다. |

## tease
[tiːz]

**v.** to annoy by provoking or pestering; to mock playfully
| 괴롭히다, 놀리다

The other kids *teased* Bill everyday because he wore glasses.

- **CH** tease : ruffian [rʌ́fiən]
  ruffian(깡패, 악한)은 타인을 tease하는 사람이다.

## ungainly
[ʌngéinli]

**adj.** lacking grace or ease of movement or form; clumsy
| 외모나 움직임이 볼품 없는, 어설픈

Alex's *ungainly* gait concealed his natural athletic prowess.

- **ANT** ungainly : lissome [lísəm]
  lissome: 민첩한, 날렵한, 유연한

## urge
[əːrdʒ]

**v.** to advise someone strongly; to impel; to present a forceful argument
| 권고하다, 몰아대다, 강한 주장을 펼치다

City officials *urged* the public to use water sparingly until the drought passed.

- **CH** urge : exhortative [igzɔ́ːrtətiv]
  exhortative(권고하는)것에는 urge하는 속성이 포함되어 있다.

## vagary
[véigəri]

**n.** an unpredictable happening; an erratic action
| 예측 불허의 상황, 엉뚱한 행동

The *vagary* of the horse races is the very excitement of them.

- **CN** vagary : predict [pridíkt]
  vagary는 predict(예측하다)할 수 없다.

## vigilant
[vídʒələnt]

**adj.** keenly alert; watchful for danger
| 방심하지 않는, 부단히 경계하는

The *vigilant* guards kept watch over the town as everyone slept.

- **CN** vigilant : entrap [intrǽp]
  vigilant하고 있으면 쉽게 entrap(덫에 걸다, 함정에 빠뜨리다)당하지 않는다.

---

### TRANSLATION | 예문 해석

| | |
|---|---|
| tease | 다른 아이들은 Bill이 안경을 쓴다고 매일 괴롭혔다 |
| ungainly | Alex의 어설픈 걸음걸이는 그의 타고난 강건한 용맹함을 가렸다. |
| urge | 시의 공무원들은 시민들에게 가뭄이 끝날 때까지 물을 아껴쓸 것을 권고했다. |
| vagary | 예측불허라는 상황이 바로 경마를 흥미롭게 만드는 특성이다. |
| vigilant | 그 경계를 늦추지 않는 파수꾼은 모든 사람들이 자는 동안 마을을 지켰다. |

**vignette**
[vinjét]

n. **a brief scene in a play or movie** | (연극이나 영화의) 짤막한 장면

Thankfully the movie's pedestrian love *vignette* was brief.

**KIN** vignette : scene [siːn]
vignette은 scene(장면)의 일종이다.

**vigor**
[vígər]

n. **active force of the body or mind** | 힘, 활력

They rowed with *vigor* using quick strokes.

**대상** vigor : enervate [énərvèit]
vigor를 enervate(약화시키다)하다.

**whim**
[hwim]

n. **a sudden and unreasonable change of mind** | 변덕

Tracy skipped work and went to Atlantic City on a *whim*.

**POS** whimsical : caprice [kəpríːs]
whimsical: 변덕스러운
caprice: 변덕

---

TRANSLATION | 예 문 해 석

| | |
|---|---|
| vignette | 다행히 그 영화의 지루한 사랑의 장면은 짧았다. |
| vigor | 그들은 신속한 상하 주법으로 힘차게 물살을 헤쳐나갔다. |
| whim | Tracy는 변덕이 생겨 결근하고 Atlantic City에 갔다. |

# 17th Day Daily Check-up

**Fill in the blanks with the correct letter that matches the word with its definition.**

1. philanthropist _____
2. skimp _____
3. aggrieve _____
4. swill _____
5. regimen _____
6. dogged _____
7. vagary _____
8. cognizant _____
9. roil _____
10. engross _____

a. to take all the attention of; to occupy completely
b. an unpredictable happening; an erratic action
c. a plan or system for daily life usually intended to improve health
d. to put forth minimal attention, money, or effort
e. to stir up or cause to move quickly
f. having an awareness or knowledge
g. to drink a large amount of something
h. stubbornly unyielding
i. one who acts in goodwill towards others
j. to distress or bring trouble to

**Put the correct word in each blank from the list of words below.**

11. subject에서 _____하다.
12. _____하고 있으면 쉽게 entrap당하지 않는다.
13. _____에게는 tolerance가 없다.
14. abet(부추기다)의 반의어는 _____이다.
15. _____는 cosset(귀여워하다)의 반의어이다.
16. forbidden된 것을 _____하다.
17. _____는 strength를 증가시키는 것이다
18. _____한 것을 본 결과 disgust를 느끼게 된다.
19. _____는 amateurish(완벽하지 못한)의 반의어이다.
20. _____은 scene의 일종이다.

| a. slight | b. consummate | c. opine | d. aggrandize | e. vigilant | f. bigot |
| g. abstain | h. vignette | i. ungainly | j. frustrate | k. digress | l. odious |

**Answer key**

1. i  2. d  3. j  4. g  5. c  6. h  7. b  8. f  9. e  10. a
11. k  12. e  13. f  14. d  15. a  16. g  17. b  18. l  19. b  20. h

# SUPER VOCA

E.I.G.H.T.E.E.N.T.H D.A.Y

# 18th DAY

'이 단어를 외우는 것은 불가능해'는 '다시 한번 이 단어를 외우도록 시도해야 해'와 같은 말이다.

## abject
[ǽbdʒekt]

adj. **in a miserable or low condition; lacking in pride or spirit** | 비참한, 천한, 비굴한

The *abject* neighborhood was often the scene of violent crimes.

**ANT** abject : spirited [spíritid]

spirited: 힘찬, 활발한

## abjure
[æbdʒúər]

v. **to reject or renounce something under oath** | (주의·신앙 등을) 공공연하게 버리다

Mr. Linton *abjured* his involvement with the cult.

**ANT** abjure : espouse [ispáuz]

espouse: 지지하다

## adjust
[ədʒʌ́st]

v. **to bring to a more satisfactory state; to adapt or conform** | 조절하다, 바로잡다, 순응하다

Laura settled herself comfortably far back in her corner, *adjusting* her skirt and murmuring.

**DE** adjust : tinker [tíŋkər]

tinker(시험삼아 혹은 서투르게 고치다)는 adjust에 비해 서투른 솜씨로 물건을 다루다라는 의미이다.

## agitate
[ǽdʒətèit]

v. **to disturb or irritate the mind or emotions** | 휘젓다, 선동하다

The revolution leader *agitated* the frenzied crowd into storming the city hall.

**CH** agitate : incendiary [inséndièri]

incendiary(선동자)는 agitate하는 사람이다.

---

| TRANSLATION | 예 문 해 석 |

| | |
|---|---|
| **abject** | 그 비참한 지역은 종종 난폭한 범죄의 현장이었다. |
| **abjure** | Linton씨는 그 사교종파와의 관계를 완전히 끊었다. |
| **adjust** | Laura는 스커트를 바로하고 혼잣말을 중얼거리면서 모서리 깊숙한 곳에 편히 앉았다. |
| **agitate** | 그 혁명 지도자는 격분한 군중들을 선동해서 시청으로 쳐들어가도록 만들었다. |

## askew [əskjúː]

**adj. not straight; awry** | 비스듬한, 비뚤어진

The artist complained that one of his paintings in the gallery was *askew*.

**ANT** askew : aligned [əláind]
aligned: 일렬로 정렬된

## awkward [ɔ́ːkwərd]

**adj. lack of ease or skill** | 서투른

Lewis' *awkward* social skills were a hinderance of his job.

**ANT** awkward : dexterous [dékstərəs]
dexterous: 솜씨 좋은

## bait [beit]

**v. to lure; to tease** | (미끼로) 꾀다, 괴롭히다

The terrorists *baited* their hostages with the tips of their rifles.

**ANT** bait : mollify [máləfài]
mollify: 달래다

## banal [bənǽl]

**adj. uninteresting or trite** | 시시한, 진부한

Brian did poorly on his creative writing assignment because the professor thought it was a *banal* piece of writing.

**CH** banal : platitude [plǽtətjùːd]
platitude(진부한 이야기)는 banal한 특징을 가지고 있다.

## belabor [biléibər]

**v. to attack verbally; to explain or insist on excessively; to hit vigorously** | 말로 공격하다, 집요하게 논하다, 세게 치다

Strangers came to my house and *belabored* me with their strange beliefs.

**DE** belabor : assert [əsə́ːrt]
belabor는 assert(주장하다)에 비해 집요하게 논하다 라는 의미이다.

---

TRANSLATION | 예 문 해 석

**askew** 작가는 갤러리에 있는 자신의 그림 중 하나가 비뚤어졌다고 불평했다.
**awkward** Lewis의 서투른 사교력은 직장에서 걸림돌이 되었다.
**bait** 테러리스트들이 총 끝으로 인질들을 괴롭혔다.
**banal** Brian의 창작 글쓰기 과제는 교수가 진부하다고 생각했기 때문에 매우 좋은 점수를 받지 못했다.
**belabor** 낯선 사람들이 우리집에 와서 나에게 집요하게 자신들의 이상한 신앙을 논했다.

## bristle
[brísl]

**v.** to stand stiffly on end like bristles in anger; to show anger | (화나서 털 등이) 곤두서다, 화를 내다

The hair on Peter's head *bristled* even after many brushings with a comb.

인과 bristle : anger [ǽŋgər]

anger(화)가 나서 털 등이 bristle하게 된다.

## cajole
[kədʒóul]

**v.** to coax or persuade with charm | 감언이설로 꾀다, 설득하다

The salesman *cajoled* the woman into buying a new car.

POS cajolery : wheedle [hwíːdl]

cajolery: 감언이설
wheedle: 감언이설로 꾀다

## candid
[kǽndid]

**adj.** honest and straightforward | 정직한, 솔직한

Charles' *candid* story did not leave out his own role in the crime.

ANT candid : furtive [fə́ːrtiv]

furtive: 은밀한

## candor
[kǽndər]

**n.** the quality of honesty and straightforwardness in expression; impartiality | 솔직, 정직, 공평

The political candidate's *candor* won over many voters who were impressed by his frankness.

WO candor : palter [pɔ́ːltər]

palter(속이기 위하여 얼버무리다)하는 사람에게는 candor가 없다.

## clique
[klíːk]

**n.** an exclusive group of people | 도당, 파벌

The jock's *clique* was comprised of fellow football players and their cheerleader girlfriends.

SYN clique : faction [fǽkʃən]

faction: 파벌

---

### TRANSLATION | 예문해석

| | |
|---|---|
| bristle | Peter의 머리카락은 여러 번의 빗질 후에도 계속 곤두섰다. |
| cajole | 그 외판원은 그 여자가 차를 구입하도록 감언이설로 설득했다. |
| candid | Charles는 그 범죄에서의 자신의 역할도 빠뜨리지 않고 다 이야기 했다. |
| candor | 그 입후보자는 그의 정직함에 감명받은 많은 유권자들을 자기편으로 만들었다. |
| clique | 그 운동선수의 일당들은 동료 미식축구 선수들과 그들의 치어리더 여자친구들로 이루어져있다. |

## conceal
[kənsíːl]

**v. to hide or keep secret** | 숨기다, 비밀로 하다

The widow could not *conceal* her tears at her late husband's funeral.

**ANT** conceal : divulge [diváldʒ]

divulge: 폭로하다

## concentrate
[kánsəntrèit]

**v. to bring or direct toward a common center; to make less dilute** | 집중하다, 한 곳에 집결시키다, 농축하다

The endangered species were found in a highly *concentrated* area, allowing the conservationists to locate them easily.

**ANT** concentrate : deploy [diplói]

deploy: 전개시키다

## conciliate
[kənsílièit]

**v. to gain or win back the good feelings of** | 호의를 얻다, 화해하다

The new president tried to *conciliate* the press after the sordid scandal.

**CH** conciliatory : sop [sɑp]

sop(뇌물)은 conciliatory(회유적인, 달래는)하다.

## concise
[kənsáis]

**adj. brief and exact** | 간결한, 간명한

The style of the letter was decidedly terse and *concise*.

**ANT** concise : verbose [vərbóus]

verbose: 말이 많은, 장황하게 말하는

## concord
[kánkɔːrd]

**n. an agreement** | 의견 일치

The sisters finally reached a *concord* about the layout of their bedroom.

**WO** concord : inconsonant [inkánsənənt]

inconsonant(일치하지 않는)한 것에는 concord가 없다.

---

### TRANSLATION | 예문 해석

| | |
|---|---|
| conceal | 그 미망인은 죽은 남편의 장례식에서 눈물을 감출 수 없었다. |
| concentrate | 멸종위기에 빠진 종(種)들은 한 곳에 모여 있기 때문에 자연보호자들의 눈에 쉽게 띈다. |
| conciliate | 신임 대통령은 그 추잡한 스캔들 이후에 기자들의 환심을 사기 위해 애썼다. |
| concise | 그 편지의 형식은 아주 짤막하고 간결했다. |
| concord | 그 자매들은 마침내 자신들의 침실의 구조에 대해 합의에 도달했다. |

**concur**
[kənkə́ːr]

v. **to approve or agree** | 동의하다, 의견이 일치하다

Representatives of the two countries *concur* that the trade agreement will be highly beneficial.

**ANT** concur : dissent [disént]

dissent: 의견을 달리하다, 이의를 제기하다

**condemn**
[kəndém]

v. **to find guilty by law; to express extreme disapproval of** | 유죄판결을 내리다, 강하게 비난하다

Paul *condemned* nothing hastily, or without taking account of circumstances.

**ANT** condemn : countenance [káuntənəns]

countenance: 찬성하다, 허용하다

**condense**
[kəndéns]

v. **to thicken or make more dense; to abridge or make more concise** | 응축하다, 요약하다

Cliff's notes are *condensed* versions of books that can be read instead of the actual novel.

**CH** condensed : abstract [ǽbstrækt]

abstract(개요)는 condensed(요약한, 간결한)한 특징을 가지고 있다.

**condescend**
[kàndəsénd]

v. **to talk at someone in an arrogant manner; to descend to a less formal or dignified level** | 우월감을 가지고 생색내며 말하다, 자신을 낮추다

The magazine article was *condescending* in its sympathy for the plight of the impoverished nation.

**CH** condescending : patronize [péitrənàiz]

patronize(선심 쓰는 체 하다) 하는 행위에는 condescending(생색을 내는 듯한)한 속성이 포함되어 있다.

---

TRANSLATION | 예 문 해 석

**concur** 양국 대표들은 그 무역 협정이 매우 유익할 것이라는 데 동의한다.
**condemn** Paul은 어떤 것도 상황 판단 없이 성급히 비난하지는 않았다.
**condense** Cliff의 노트는 요약본이라서 실제 소설대신 읽어도 된다.
**condescend** 그 잡지 기사는 생색내는 듯한 동정심으로 가난한 나라의 처지를 다루었다.

## condone
[kəndóun]

**v. to pardon, disregard, or overlook voluntarily; to accept but not completely agree with** | 용서하다, 눈감아 주다

The mother didn't *condone* the outlandish behavior of her daughter.

**ANT** condone : denounce [dináuns]

denounce: 비난하다

## dappled
[dǽpld]

**adj. marked with spots; spotted** | 얼룩진

Virginia preferred her *dappled* horse to all the other plain horses.

**POS** dappled : spot [spɑt]

spot: 얼룩

## deject
[didʒékt]

**v. to make sad or tired** | 낙담시키다

Though Jane generally had a positive attitude, there were periods when she was *dejected*.

**대상** dejection : hearten [háːrtn]

hearten(용기를 북돋우다, 격려하다)은 dejection(낙담, 실의)을 없애고 격려하다는 의미이다.

## drivel
[drívəl]

**v. to speak carelessly and senselessly** | 허튼 소리를 하다

The actor *driveled* all over the media looking for any kind of publicity.

**CH** drivel : nonsensical [nɑnsénsikəl]

drivel하는 것에는 nonsensical(터무니 없는, 부조리한)한 속성이 포함되어 있다.

## eleemosynary
[èlimásənèri]

**adj. relating to charity; benevolent** | 자선의, 자선적인

The unexpected outpouring of *eleemosynary* gifts touched the missionaries deeply.

**CH** eleemosynary : philanthropist [filǽnθrəpist]

philanthropist(박애주의자, 자선가)는 eleemosynary하다.

---

### TRANSLATION | 예문 해석

**condone** 어머니는 자기 딸의 기이한 행동을 그냥 넘어가지 않았다.
**dappled** Virginia는 모든 다른 평범한 말보다 그녀의 얼룩말을 더 좋아했다.
**deject** Jane은 보통 긍정적인 태도를 보이지만 낙담할 때가 있었다.
**drivel** 그 배우는 어떤 종류의 명성이라도 얻고 싶어서 이곳 저곳의 대중매체에 허튼 소리를 늘어놓았다.
**eleemosynary** 기대하지 못했던 자선품들이 쏟아져 나오자 선교사들은 깊이 감동을 받았다.

## enlarge
[inláːrdʒ]

**v. to expand or make larger** | 확장하다, 넓히다

In 1697 the bank was allowed to *enlarge* its capital stock.

**ANT** enlarge : retrench [ritréntʃ]

retrench: 줄이다, (비용을) 절감하다

## fetid
[fétid]

**adj. stinky; horribly malodorous** | 악취를 풍기는

The *fetid* odor made the girls nauseous.

**대상** fetid : smell [smel]

fetid는 smell(냄새)에 관한 형용사이다.

## flit
[flit]

**v. to dart across or move quickly** | 휙 지나가다, 빠르게 이동하다

Tracy's role as the angel in the school play was to *flit* across the stage gracefully.

**KIN** flit : move [muːv]

flit는 빠르게 move(움직이다)하는 것이다.

## frivolity
[frivάləti]

**n. the act of being light-hearted** | 경솔한 행동

He did not like to combine *frivolity* with the serious business of hunting.

**WO** frivolous : gravity [grǽvəti]

frivolous(경솔한)한 사람에게는 gravity(진지함)가 없다.

## gait
[geit]

**n. the way a person walks or moves** | 걸음걸이

Diana walked into the meeting with a confident *gait*.

**대상** gait : walk [wɔːk]

gait는 어떤 사람의 walk(걷다)하는 모양을 묘사하는 것이다.

---

### TRANSLATION | 예 문 해 석

| | |
|---|---|
| enlarge | 1697년에 그 은행은 증자가 허용되었다. |
| fetid | 그 악취는 여자들을 구역질나게 했다. |
| flit | Tracy는 학교 연주에서 우아하게 무대를 휙 가로질러 지나가는 천사 역할을 맡았다. |
| frivolity | 그는 사냥이라는 위험한 일을 경솔하게 다루는 것을 좋아하지 않았다. |
| gait | Diana는 자신감에 찬 걸음걸이로 모임에 걸어 들어갔다. |

## grouch
[grautʃ]

n. a habitually complaining person; a sulky or peevish mood | 불평꾼, 시무룩함

The children were all afraid of the *grouch* who sat in front of the corner store.

**CH** grouch : querulous [kwérjuləs]

grouch는 querulous(불평하는, 투덜거리는)하다.

## hike
[haik]

n. a long walk for leisure; an abrupt increase | 하이킹, 기습인상

v. to increase; to rise upward | 인상하다, 올라가다

The government's tax *hike* caused a sudden increase in product price.

The Federal Reserve Chairman *hiked* the interest rate in hopes of slowing inflation.

**ANT** hike : backset [bǽksèt]

backset: 역행

## idolater
[aidálətər]

n. one who worships idols; one who blindly adores another | 우상 숭배자, (맹목적인) 숭배자

In today's society, most people are *idolaters* of money.

**CH** idolater : reverent [révərənt]

idolater는 reverent(숭배하는, 공경하는)하는 특성이 있다.

## iniquitous
[iníkwətəs]

adj. unjust; wicked or sinful | 부당한, 사악한

The *iniquitous* freight rates had been implanted due to a lack of competition in the shipping industry.

**ANT** iniquity : rectitude [réktətjùːd]

iniquity: 부당, 불법

rectitude: 공정, 올바름

---

TRANSLATION | 예 문 해 석

| | |
|---|---|
| grouch | 아이들은 모퉁이 가게 앞에 앉아 있는 심술 궂은 사람을 모두 무서워했다. |
| hike | 정부의 갑작스런 세금 인상은 상품가격의 급격한 증가를 초래했다. |
| | 연방 준비 은행장은 인플레이션을 늦추려고 이자율을 높였다. |
| idolater | 오늘날 사회에서, 대부분의 사람들은 돈을 숭배한다. |
| iniquitous | 선박 산업에서의 경쟁력 부족 때문에 부당한 화물 운임률이 고착되었다. |

## irk
[əːrk]

**v. to make irritated or annoyed** | 짜증나게 하다, 화나게 하다

It *irked* Helen that Matt forgot her birthday.

**DE** irk : enrage [inréidʒ]

enrage(격노시키다)는 몹시 irk하는 것이다.

## jejune
[dʒidʒúːn]

**adj. lacking in interest; dull and boring** | 재미가 부족한, 지루한

The *jejune* novel put me to sleep after the first page.

**WO** jejune : interest [íntərəst]

jejune한 것은 interest(흥미, 재미)가 없다.

## lugubrious
[lugjúːbriəs]

**adj. sad or mournful** | 슬퍼하는, 우울한

A dog let out a long, *lugubrious* howl outside.

**ANT** lugubrious : jovial [dʒóuviəl]

jovial: 즐거운, 쾌활한

## maladroit
[mæ̀lədrɔ́it]

**adj. inept; lacking in skill or grace** | 서투른, 솜씨없는, 요령없는

The *maladroit* young lady is not fit to be a dancer.

**ANT** maladroit : deft [deft]

deft: 솜씨 좋은

## morose
[məróus]

**adj. sullen and glum** | 시무룩한, 침울한

Janet guessed from Jason's *morose* mood that the test did not go very well.

**ANT** morose : jocund [dʒɑ́kənd]

jocund: 유쾌한, 즐거운

---

TRANSLATION | 예 문 해 석

| | |
|---|---|
| irk | Matt가 자기 생일을 잊어버린데 대해 Helen은 화가 났다. |
| jejune | 그 지루한 소설은 첫 장을 넘긴 후 나를 잠들게 했다. |
| lugubrious | 개 한 마리가 밖에서 길고 슬프게 짖어댔다. |
| maladroit | 서투른 그 아가씨는 무용수가 될 만한 소질이 없다. |
| morose | Janet은 Jason의 침울한 기분에서 그가 시험을 잘 보지 못했다는 것을 추측했다. |

## naive
[nɑːíːv]

**adj.** **marked by unaffected simplicity; childlike** | 고지식한, 순진한

The *naive* young lawyers were still full of ideal hopes as they entered the work force.

**ANT** naive : worldly [wə́ːrldli]
worldly: 세속적인

## nonentity
[nɑnéntəti]

**n.** **a person of no significance, importance, or influence** | 중요성이나 영향력이 없는 사람

Having been considered a *nonentity* his whole life, Albert aspired to be a world renowned author one day.

**WO** nonentity : consequence [kɑ́nsəkwèns]
nonentity는 consequence(중요성)이 없는 사람이다.

## pontificate
[pɑntífəkèit]

**v.** **to speak in an arrogant and dogmatic manner** | 오만하고 독단적인 태도로 말하다

The brilliant professor was disliked because he had a tendency to *pontificate* during his lectures.

**KIN** pontificate : speak [spiːk]
pontificate는 speak(말하다)의 한 형태이다.

## procrastinate
[proukrǽstənèit]

**v.** **to delay or put off doing something** | 미루다, 늑장부리다

The jury *procrastinated* their decision, asking the judge for more time to deliberate.

**WO** procrastinate : alacrity [əlǽkrəti]
alacrity(열의, 민첩)가 없는 사람은 매사 procrastinate한다.

## reject
[ridʒékt]

**v.** **to refuse or decline** | 거절하다, 사절하다

Union leaders *rejected* the latest counteroffer by the steel industry due to an insufficient health plan.

**DE** reject : scorn [skɔːrn]
scorn(경멸조로 거절하다)은 경멸과 조소의 감정을 가지고 reject하는 것이다.

---

**TRANSLATION** | 예문 해석

**naive** 그 순진한 변호사들은 일을 시작할 때 까지도 희망으로 가득 차 있었다.
**nonentity** Albert는 그의 평생 동안 보잘것 없는 사람으로 여겨졌기 때문에, 언젠가는 세계적으로 유명한 작가가 되기를 열망했다.
**pontificate** 그 유능한 교수는 강의 시간에 오만하게 말하는 경향이 있어서 사람들이 싫어했다.
**procrastinate** 배심원단은 더 고려할 시간을 판사에게 요청하여 결정을 미루었다.
**reject** 노조 위원장들은 그 철강 회사의 불충분한 보건정책때문에 최근에 제기된 제안을 거절했다.

## shirk
[ʃəːrk]

**v. to avoid responsibility or duty; to neglect** | (책임이나 의무를) 회피하다, 게으름 피우다

John has tried to *shirk* the responsibility.

**CH** shirk : malingerer [məlíŋɡərər]

malingerer는 자신의 일이나 의무를 shirk하려고 꾀병 부리는 사람이다.

## skirt
[skəːrt]

**v. to avoid** | 회피하다

Tom *skirted* the issue of his family by changing the subject.

**SYN** skirt : evade [ivéid]

evade: 회피하다

## skit
[skit]

**n. a short and comic or dramatic performance** | 익살극

Our *skit* at summer camp had the children in stitches.

**KIN** skit : drama [drάːmə]

skit은 drama(극) 중에서 짧고 익살스런 연극이다.

## slipshod
[slípʃὰd]

**adj. carelessly wearing loose shoes; carelessly done; looking shabby** | 신발을 질질 끌며 걷는, 아무렇게나 하는, 단정치 못한

A *slipshod* man passed me on the street, wearing a ragged coat and torn pants.

**SYN** slipshod : slovenly [slʌ́vənli]

slovenly: 단정치 못한, 더러운

## smirk
[sməːrk]

**n. an arrogant and self-satisfied smile** | 거만하고 자기만족적인 웃음

Emily's *smirk* upon hearing the news of her rival company's demise indicated she knew of it beforehand.

**CH** smirk : smugness [smʌ́gnis]

smirk에는 smugness(자기만족, 젠체함)가 들어있다.

---

**TRANSLATION** | 예 문 해 석

| | |
|---|---|
| shirk | John은 책임을 지지 않으려고 애썼다. |
| skirt | Tom은 이야기의 주제를 바꿈으로 자신의 가족에 대해 말하는 것을 회피했다. |
| skit | 여름 캠프에서의 우리의 익살극은 아이들이 배꼽을 쥐고 웃도록 만들었다. |
| slipshod | 해진 외투와 찢어진 바지를 입은 단정치 못한 남자가 거리에서 나를 스쳐 지나갔다. |
| smirk | Emily가 경쟁사의 폐업 소식을 듣고 거만한 미소를 지은 것을 보니 그 소식을 미리 알고 있었던 것 같다. |

## spiritual
[spírit∫uəl]

**adj. regarding the spirit; incorporeal** | 정신적인

Religion addresses purely *spiritual* concerns.

> **ANT** spiritual : carnal [ká:rnl]
>
> carnal: 물질적인, 육체의

## stir
[stə:r]

**v. to mix together; to cause movement; to provoke deliberately** | 섞다, 흔들다, 자극하다

The news writer *stirred* controversy when she wrote an editorial on the legislation of gun control.

> **ANT** stir : quell [kwel]
>
> quell: 진압하다, 억누르다

## thirsty
[θə́:rsti]

**adj. desiring to drink; strongly craving something** | 목마른, 강렬히 희망하는

The *thirsty* man greedily drank from the water fountain.

> **인과** thirsty : imbibe [imbáib]
>
> thirsty하게 되면 imbibe(마시다)한다.

## trite
[trait]

**adj. commonplace or stale** | 진부한

The maxim is so old that it is *trite* -- it is laughable.

> **SYN** trite : hackneyed [hǽknid]
>
> hackneyed: 진부한

## turncoat
[tə́:rnkòut]

**n. a traitor; one who switches allegiances** | 반역자, 변절자

One of the greatest crimes is to be a *turncoat* against your country.

> **WO** turncoat : constancy [kánstənsi]
>
> turncoat에게는 constancy(지조가 굳음, 불변)가 없다.

---

### TRANSLATION | 예문 해석

| | |
|---|---|
| spiritual | 종교는 순수하게 정신적인 데에 관심을 갖는다. |
| stir | 그 신문기자는 총기류 제한 입법에 관한 사설을 써서 논쟁을 불러 일으켰다. |
| thirsty | 그 목마른 사람은 (분수식의) 음료대에서 나오는 물을 마구 들이켰다. |
| trite | 그 속담은 너무 낡아서 진부하다. 즉, 웃음거리이다. |
| turncoat | 가장 큰 범죄 중에 하나는 조국을 배반하는 것이다. |

## unique [juːníːk]

**adj. being the one of its kind; very unusual** | 유일한, 별난

This *unique* individual was an ex-soldier turned religionist.

**WO** unique : precedent [présədnt]

precedent(전례)가 없는 것은 unique한 것이다.

## unjustifiable [ʌ̀ndʒʌ́stəfàiəbl]

**adj. impossible to justify or excuse** | 이치에 맞지 않는, 변명할 수 없는

Harry could not explain his *unjustifiable* absence to his teacher.

**ANT** unjustifiable : tenable [ténəbl]

tenable: 조리있는, 지지할 수 있는

## unkempt [ʌnkémpt]

**adj. messy or not clean** | 흐트러진, 깔끔하지 못한

The garden appeared *unkempt*, with overgrown weeds.

**ANT** unkempt : dapper [dǽpər]

dapper: 깔끔한, 말쑥한

---

### TRANSLATION | 예문 해석

| | |
|---|---|
| unique | 이 별난 사람이 바로 광신자가 된 퇴역군인이었다. |
| unjustifiable | Harry는 선생님께 무단결석에 대해 변명할 수 없었다. |
| unkempt | 정원은 잡초가 무성하게 자라 깔끔하지 않아 보였다. |

# 18th Day  Daily Check-up

■ Fill in the blanks with the correct letter that matches the word with its definition.

1. deject _____
2. flit _____
3. slipshod _____
4. bristle _____
5. iniquitous _____
6. condone _____
7. abject _____
8. procrastinate _____
9. clique _____
10. shirk _____

a. an exclusive group of people
b. unjust; wicked or sinful
c. to dart across or move quickly
d. to avoid responsibility or duty; to neglect
e. to stand stiffly on end like bristles; to show anger
f. to accept but not completely agree with
g. to delay or put off doing something
h. in a miserable or low condition; lacking in pride or spirit
i. carelessly wearing loose shoes; looking shabby
j. to make sad or tired

■ Put the correct word in each blank from the list of words below.

11. _____는 assert에 비해 집요하게 논하다라는 의미이다.
12. tenable(조리있는, 지지할 수 있는)의 반의어는 _____이다.
13. _____는 hackneyed(진부한)의 동의어이다.
14. dexterous(솜씨가 좋은)은 _____의 반의어이다.
15. _____에는 smugness(자기만족, 젠체함)가 들어있다.
16. scorn은 경멸과 조소의 감정을 가지고 _____하는 것이다.
17. _____의 반의어는 rectitude(공정, 올바름)이다.
18. _____하는 것에는 nonsensical(터무니 없는, 부조리한)한 속성이 포함되어 있다.
19. tinker는 _____에 비해 서투른 솜씨로 물건을 다루다 라는 의미이다.
20. _____은 countenance(찬성하다, 허용하다)의 반의어이다.

a. reject   b. iniquity   c. unjustifiable   d. belabor   e. awkward   f. condemn
g. cajole   h. adjust     i. maladroit       j. drivel    k. trite      l. smirk

Answer key

1. j   2. c   3. i   4. e   5. b   6. f   7. h   8. g   9. a   10. d
11. d  12. c  13. k  14. e  15. l  16. a  17. b  18. j  19. h  20. f

# TAKE A BREAK

쉬·어·가·는 페·이·지

**영시 감상** *by Emily Dickinson*

### I like a look of Agony

I like a look of Agony,
Because I know it's true—
Men do not sham convulsion,
Nor simulate, a Throe—
The Eyes glaze once— and that is Death—
Impossible to feign
The Beads upon the Forehead
By homely Anguish strung.

### 나는 고뇌의 표정이 좋다

나는 고뇌의 표정이 좋아.
그것이 진실임을 알기에—
사람은 경련을 피하거나
고통을 흉내낼 수 없다.
눈빛이 일단 흐려지면—그것이 죽음이다.
꾸밈없는 고뇌가
이마 위에 구슬땀을
꿰는 척할 수는 없는 법이다.

www.goHackers.com

해커스 어학연구소

# SUPER VOCA

## 19th DAY

단어 정복! 수퍼보카하기 나름이에요~

---

**allay**
[əléi]

v. **to relieve; to calm** | 완화시키다, 가라앉히다
The travel agent *allayed* the man's concerns about airsafety.

- **ANT** allay : aggravate [ǽgrəvèit]
  aggravate: 악화시키다

---

**alleviate**
[əlíːvièit]

v. **to lessen; to make pain more bearable** | 완화하다, (고통 등을) 견디기 쉽게 하다
By putting forth a new reform bill, the president took measures to *alleviate* poverty.

- **대상** alleviate : stress [stres]
  stress(정신적 압박감)를 alleviate하다.

---

**anterior**
[æntíəriər]

adj. **occurring before or earlier** | 먼저 일어난, 선행한
*Anterior* events have led investors to believe that the technology sector is extremely volatile.

- **ANT** anterior : ensuing [insúːiŋ]
  ensuing: 뒤따라 일어나는

---

**antic**
[ǽntik]

n. **ludicrous or funny actions** | 익살스런 동작
adj. **odd or fanciful** | 별난, 괴상한
The comedy show was full of *antics* that had us bursting with laughter.
A clown's *antic* foolery entertains young and old audience members.

- **대상** antic : behavior [bihéivjər]
  antic은 behavior(행동)를 묘사하는데 쓰인다.
- cf) facetious(익살맞은, 쾌활한)는 speech를 묘사하는데 쓰인다.

---

### TRANSLATION | 예문 해석

**allay** 그 여행사 직원은 비행기의 안전성에 관한 그 남자의 우려를 가라앉혔다.
**alleviate** 새로운 개혁법안을 제안함으로써 대통령은 빈곤을 완화시킬 조치를 취했다.
**anterior** 먼저 일어난 사건은 투자자들로 하여금 기술 부문이 지극히 변화하기 쉽다고 믿도록 만들었다.
**antic** 그 코미디쇼는 익살스런 동작들로 가득 차 있어 우리를 배꼽을 잡고 웃게 만들었다.
광대의 괴상하고 어리석은 행동이 노소의 관중들을 즐겁게 해준다.

## bale
[beil]

**n. great evil; anguish; large and closely pressed bundles of goods** | 불행, 괴로움; 짐꾸러미

The news of great *bale* in the neighboring town caused immense chaos.

- **ANT** bale : mirth [məːrθ]
  - mirth: 환희, 즐거움

## beleaguer
[bilíːgər]

**v. to annoy persistently; to besiege** | 끊임없이 괴롭히다, 포위하다

The children *beleaguered* their parents for a vacation to Disney World.

- **ANT** beleaguer : mollify [málǝfài]
  - mollify: 달래다

## belie
[bilái]

**v. to give a wrong impression; to contradict; to show to be wrong** | 실제 모습을 속이다, ~와 모순되다, 그릇된 것임을 나타내 보이다

The generally cold first impression I often give people *belies* my soft and caring heart.

- **ANT** belie : confirm [kǝnfǝ́ːrm]
  - confirm: 확증하다

## braggart
[brǽgǝrt]

**n. one who boasts about oneself loudly** | 제 자랑을 크게 하는 사람

Brandon's accomplishments were numerous, but he could never be accused of being a *braggart*.

- **SYN** braggart : braggadocio [brægǝdóuʃìòu]
  - braggadocio: 제 자랑하는 사람, 허풍선이

## calibrate
[kǽlǝbrèit]

**v. to determine by comparison with a standard** | (눈금을) 표준에 맞추다, 조정하다

Thermometers should be *calibrated* daily to ensure accurate readings.

- **ANT** calibrated : unstandardized [ʌnstǽndǝrdàizd]
  - calibrated: 표준에 맞춰진
  - unstandardized: 표준에 맞춰지지 않은

---

TRANSLATION | 예문 해석

**bale** 이웃 마을에 닥친 불행에 관한 소식은 큰 혼란을 불러일으켰다.
**beleaguer** 아이들은 디즈니 월드로 놀러 가자고 부모를 자꾸 졸랐다.
**belie** 사람들이 종종 받는 내 첫인상이 대체로 차갑지만 사실 나는 부드럽고 남을 배려하는 따뜻한 마음을 갖고 있다.
**braggart** Brandon의 업적은 셀 수 없이 많지만, 그는 제 자랑을 하는 사람이라고 비난 받은 적이 한 번도 없다.
**calibrate** 정확한 온도를 알기 위해서는 매일 온도계의 눈금을 맞춰야 한다.

## cipher
[sáifər]

**n. a message created using a cryptographic system** | 암호 체계를 사용해서 만든 메시지, 암호문

The intelligence agency is reading through thousands of e-mails and trying to figure out which are *ciphers*.

**CH** cipher : cryptic [kríptik]

cipher는 cryptic(비밀의, 숨은)하다.

## dandy
[dǽndi]

**n. a man with extravagant outer appearance** | 멋쟁이

What a *dandy* you are today, dressed in your Sunday best!

**CH** dandy : preen [príːn]

dandy는 preen(몸치장하다)한다.

## debrief
[diːbríːf]

**v. to interrogate for the purpose of finding out information that was discovered during a military operation** | 군 임무에서 알아낸 정보를 보고하게 하다

The men were given one day to rest before having to present a *debriefing* to their superiors.

**대상** debrief : information [ìnfərméiʃən]

information(정보)를 debrief하게 하다.

## deleterious
[dèlitíəriəs]

**adj. harmful or noxious** | 해로운, 유독한

George's indigestion was caused by the *deleterious* ingredients in his soup.

**ANT** deleterious : salutary [sǽljutèri]

salutary: 건강에 좋은

---

### TRANSLATION | 예 문 해 석

**cipher** 정보국에서는 수천 통의 이메일을 정독하여 어떤 것이 암호문인지를 알아내려고 한다.
**dandy** 오늘 나들이옷을 차려 입은 당신은 정말 멋쟁이군요!
**debrief** 그 남자들은 알아낸 정보를 그들의 상관에게 보고하기 전 하루의 휴식을 얻었다.
**deleterious** George의 소화불량은 그의 스프 속에 들어있던 해로운 성분들 때문에 생겼다.

## deliberate
v. [dilíbərèit]
adj. [dilíbərət]

**v.** to consider carefully | 신중하게 생각하다

**adj.** intended; resulting from careful and thorough consideration | 계획적인, 신중한

The jury *deliberated* the case for five long hours before reaching a verdict.

The *deliberate* nature of the interview process allowed the company to selectively screen all the candidates.

**ANT** deliberate : impetuous [impétʃuəs]

impetuous: 충동적인, 성급한

## delicate
[délikət]

**adj.** very fine or subtle; easy to break | 섬세한; 쉽게 깨지는

Despite her *delicate* physical appearance, Nancy enjoyed outdoor activities and camping.

**ANT** delicate : husky [hʌ́ski]

husky: 거친

## dilate
[dailéit]

**v.** to discourse at length; to swell or widen | 장황하게 말하다, 팽창시키다, 넓히다

The heavy torrents of rain *dilated* the river causing it to flood.

**ANT** dilate : contract [kɑ́ntrækt]

contract: 수축시키다, 좁히다

## dilettante
[dílitɑ̀ːnt]

**n.** an admirer of the arts; a person having a superficial interest in an art | (예술 등의) 애호가, 아마추어 예술가

Matt had never studied art formally, but he was a *dilettante* who appreciated artistic works on his own.

**CH** dilettante : superficial [sùːpərfíʃəl]

dilettante는 전문적인 지식 없이 그저 취미 삼아 superficial(피상적인)하게 예술을 대하는 사람이다.

---

TRANSLATION | 예문 해석

**deliberate** 배심원들은 무려 다섯 시간이나 그 사건을 심의한 후 평결을 내렸다.
그 신중한 인터뷰 과정은 회사가 지원자들을 선별해서 가려낼 수 있게 했다.
**delicate** Nancy는 섬세한 외양을 지녔음에도 불구하고, 야외 활동과 캠핑을 즐겼다.
**dilate** 폭풍우가 쏟아져 강물이 불어났고 결국 홍수가 났다.
**dilettante** Matt는 예술을 정식으로 공부한 적은 없었지만, 스스로 예술작품을 찾아 감상하는 애호가였다.

## eclipse
[iklíps]

**v.** to make obscure or darker; to cause to decline in importance, fame, or reputation
| ~의 빛을 가리다, (중요성·명성 등을) 실추시키다

**n.** the complete or partial blocking out of one celestial body over another
| 식(蝕)

Modern technology has *eclipsed* the innovations of early American inventors such as Benjamin Franklin.

To witness a total *eclipse* of the sun is a once in a lifetime opportunity.

> 대상  eclipse : prestige [prestí:dʒ]
> eclipse는 prestige(명성) 등을 실추시키다는 의미이다.

## elliptical
[ilíptikəl]

**adj.** shaped like an ellipse; marked by economy of expression; relating to deliberate obscurity
| 타원의, (표현이) 생략된, 애매한

No one knew exactly what inspired Anna's *elliptical* comments.

> ANT  elliptical : palpable [pǽlpəbl]
> palpable: 명백한

## enlighten
[enláitn]

**v.** to give knowledge to; to provide with previously lacking insight or information
| 가르치다, 교화하다, 계몽하다

The teacher *enlightened* his students about the dangers of smoking.

> PUR  enlighten : explanation [èksplənéiʃən]
> enlighten하기 위해 explanation(설명)한다.

## filibuster
[fíləbʌstər]

**n.** the use or an instance of delaying or preventing legislative action by making long speeches
| 의사 진행 방해

The senator attempted to use a *filibuster* in hopes of staving off a vote on the floor.

> CH  filibuster : delay [diléi]
> filibuster는 의사진행을 delay(지연시키다)하는 것이다.

---

TRANSLATION | 예문해석

| | |
|---|---|
| eclipse | 현대 기술의 발전으로 벤자민 프랭클린과 같은 미국의 초기 발명가들의 기술 혁신이 빛을 잃게 됐다. <br> 개기 일식을 보는 것은 일생에 한번 뿐인 기회이다. |
| elliptical | Anna가 무슨 이유로 그 같이 애매한 발언을 했는지 아무도 정확히 알지 못했다. |
| enlighten | 그 선생님은 학생들에게 담배의 위험성을 가르쳤다. |
| filibuster | 그 상원의원은 의원석에서 행해질 투표를 저지하려는 의도로 의사진행 방해 행위를 시도했다. |

## filigree
[fíləgrìː]

**n.** **detailed ornamentation of fine gold or silver wire**
| 금이나 은선의 섬세하고 복잡한 세공

Alice took from one of the drawers a black leather card-case lined with silver *filigree*.

**CH** filigree : delicacy [délikəsi]
filigree는 delicacy(섬세함)의 특징이 있는 금이나 은의 선세공이다.

## flannel
[flǽnl]

**n.** **a blend of wool and cotton used for clothing**
| 의류에 쓰이는 양모와 면의 혼합물, 플란넬 천

*Flannel* pajamas are the warmest thing to wear to sleep in the winter.

**KIN** flannel : cloth [klɔ(ː)θ]
flannel은 cloth(직물)의 일종이다.

## fondness
[fándnis]

**n.** **a warm affection; a strong liking or inclination** | 애정, 기호

Maggie had a particular *fondness* for plants.

**DE** fondness : adoration [ædəréiʃən]
신에 대한 숭배를 의미하거나 종종 열렬한 사랑을 의미하는 adoration은 fondness 보다 정도면에서 더 강하다.

## hale
[heil]

**adj.** **healthy or sound; retaining exceptional health and vigor**
| 건강한, 정정한

At the age of eighty my grandfather was strong and *hale*.

**ANT** hale : effete [ifíːt]
effete: 쇠약해진, 활력을 잃은

## ken
[ken]

**n.** **range of sight; abstract range of perception**
| 시야, 이해의 범위

The poor ship sank in *ken* of the shore.

**대상** ken : see [siː]
ken은 see(보다)할 수 있는 범위를 뜻한다.

---

TRANSLATION | 예 문 해 석

| | |
|---|---|
| filigree | Alice는 서랍에서 섬세하게 세공한 은선으로 모서리를 두른, 검은 가죽으로 만든 명함 케이스를 하나 꺼냈다. |
| flannel | 플란넬 파자마는 가장 따뜻한 겨울 잠옷이다. |
| fondness | Maggie는 식물들을 특히 좋아했다. |
| hale | 우리 할아버지는 80세에도 힘있고 정정하셨다. |
| ken | 그 불운한 선박은 해안이 보이는 곳에서 침몰했다. |

## landfill
[lǽndfil]

**n. an area of land used to dump refuse in and continuously cover with land** | 쓰레기 매립지

The city of New York puts its trash in a *landfill* on Staten Island.

> **FUN** landfill : refuse [réfju:s]
>
> landfill은 refuse(쓰레기)를 매립하는 곳이다.

## malicious
[məlíʃəs]

**adj. arising from the desire to cause pain or stress to someone** | 악의 있는, 심술궂은

Barry's vindictiveness towards his rival was often viewed in a *malicious* light.

> **ANT** malicious : benevolent [bənévələnt]
>
> benevolent: 선의의, 호의적인

## malign
[məláin]

**v. to speak or write evil about someone** | 헐뜯다
**adj. evil** | 해로운

The food critic *maligned* the restaurant in his weekly column for poor service and barely edible food.

The press made a *malign* comment about the governor for accepting campaign funds from a major crime syndicate.

> **ANT** malign : eulogize [júːlədʒàiz]
>
> eulogize: 칭송하다, 찬사를 보내다

## malinger
[məlíŋgər]

**v. to pretend to be sick or incapable in order to avoid work or duty** | 일을 안하려고 꾀병 부리다

After a long night at the party, I *malingered* to stay home and sleep.

> **CH** malingerer : shirk [ʃəːrk]
>
> malingerer는 자신의 일이나 의무를 shirk(회피하다)하기 위해 꾀병 부리는 사람이다.

---

### TRANSLATION | 예문해석

| | |
|---|---|
| **landfill** | 뉴욕시는 Staten Island에 있는 쓰레기 매립지에 쓰레기를 버린다. |
| **malicious** | Barry의 경쟁 상대에 대한 보복적인 행위는 종종 악의적으로 보여진다. |
| **malign** | 그 음식 비평가는 자신의 주간 칼럼에서 그 식당의 불친절한 서비스와 거의 먹을 수 없는 음식을 헐뜯었다. |
| | 언론은 거대 범죄 조직으로부터 선거자금을 받았다는 이유로 주지사를 비난했다. |
| **malinger** | 파티에서 밤을 지새운 뒤, 나는 집에서 잠을 자기 위해 꾀병을 부렸다. |

## mend [mend]

**v. to repair or reform; to improve in health**
| 고치다, 수선하다, (환자 등이) 나아지다

It was not easy for Frank's mother to *mend* the tattered shirt he ruined while playing football.

**ANT** mend : rend [rend]
rend: 찢다

## mendacious [mendéiʃəs]

**adj. dishonest; marked by deception**
| 거짓의, 허위의

The press secretary's *mendacious* statement was later discovered by the media.

**WO** mendacious : truth [truːθ]
mendacious한 것에는 truth(진실)가 없다.

## mulish [mjúːliʃ]

**adj. excessively obstinate**
| 고집 불통의

The two senators appeared equally *mulish* in their debate, neither would yield even the smallest concession.

**WO** mulish : flexibility [flèksəbíləti]
mulish한 사람에게는 flexibility(융통성, 유연성)가 없다.

## mundane [mʌ́ndein]

**adj. relating to the everyday activities of life; secular**
| 흔한, 평범한, 세속의

Even the most *mundane* jobs are appreciated by the unemployed.

**ANT** mundane : extraordinary [ikstrɔ́ːrdənèri]
extraordinary: 보통이 아닌, 대단한

## nondescript [nὰndiskrípt]

**adj. lacking any outstanding features or qualities; common or normal**
| 특징 없는, 평범한

To Betty's dismay, her blind-date was a rather *nondescript* man.

**ANT** nondescript : conspicuous [kənspíkjuəs]
conspicuous: 두드러진, 현저한

---

### TRANSLATION | 예문 해석

**mend** 축구를 하다가 누더기가 된 Frank의 셔츠를 그의 어머니가 수선하는 일은 쉽지 않았다.
**mendacious** 그 보도 담당 비서의 허위 발언은 후에 매스컴에 의해 밝혀졌다.
**mulish** 두 상원의원은 똑같이 고집불통이어서 토론 중에 작은 양보하나 조차도 하지 않으려고 했다.
**mundane** 가장 흔한 일자리 조차도 실업자들에게는 환영받는다.
**nondescript** Betty는 미팅 상대가 이렇다 할 특징이 없는 남자인 것을 알고 실망했다.

## obligate
[ábləgèit]

**v.** **to legally or morally commit** | (법률·도덕상의) 의무를 지우다

The conditions of settlement to which the railroad *obligated* itself are very explicit.

**ANT** obligatory : discretionary [diskréʃənèri]

obligatory: 의무로써 지워지는

discretionary: 자유 의사에 맡겨진

## panache
[pənǽʃ]

**n.** **a feathered plume on a helmet; flamboyance in style and action** | 투구의 깃털 장식, 허세

The singer performed the routine with plenty of *panache*.

**ANT** panache : humility [hjuːmíləti]

humility: 겸손

## phlegmatic
[flegmǽtik]

**adj.** **showing a slow and stolid temperament** | 무기력한, 냉담한

Brian's *phlegmatic* nature prevented him from succeeding in the world of day trading.

**CN** phlegmatic : arouse [əráuz]

phlegmatic한 사람을 arouse(자극하다)하기는 어렵다.

## polish
[páliʃ]

**v.** **to make glossy and smooth; to refine in manners** | 광내다, 세련되게 하다

Robert's language became more *polished* year after year.

**ANT** polished : rustic [rʌ́stik]

polished: 세련된

rustic: 조야한

## prate
[preit]

**v.** **to talk or chatter foolishly with little purpose** | 별 목적 없이 수다 떨다, 지껄이다

**n.** **foolish or idle talk** | 쓸데없는 말, 수다

Lucy *prated* about the latest gossip with Ethel.

**CH** prate : aimless [éimlis]

prate하는 것에는 aimless(목적 없는)한 속성이 포함되어 있다.

---

TRANSLATION | 예문해석

| | |
|---|---|
| obligate | 철도 당국이 책임지기로 한 해결 조건은 아주 명백했다. |
| panache | 그 가수는 허세로 가득 찬 판에 박힌 공연을 했다. |
| phlegmatic | Brian은 무기력한 천성 때문에 당일 매매의 세계에서 성공하지 못했다. |
| polish | 해를 거듭할수록 Robert의 말솜씨는 눈에 띄게 더욱 세련되어 갔다. |
| prate | Lucy는 Ethel과 최근의 소문에 대해 수다를 떨었다. |

## prospect
**v.** [prəspékt]
**n.** [práspekt]

**v. to examine and explore an area for mineral deposits** | 시굴하다

**n. something expected** | 가망, 기대

The panhandlers *prospected* the area for gold and other minerals.
Having many job prospects, the employee was free to leave her job at will.

> **대상** prospect : mineral [mínərəl]
> mineral(광물)을 찾아 prospect하다.

## prowl
[praul]

**v. to search with predatory intent** | 사냥감을 찾아 헤매다

Large cats will *prowl* stealthily in search of prey to eat.

> **대상** prowl : prey [prei]
> prey(먹이)를 찾아 prowl하다.

## pulchritude
[pʌ́lkrətjùːd]

**n. physical beauty or attractiveness** | (육체적) 아름다움, 미모

The prince was taken aback by the maiden's exquisite *pulchritude*.

> **ANT** pulchritude : homeliness [hóumlinis]
> homeliness: 못생김, (용모가) 매력없음

## relapse
[rilǽps]

**v. to worsen after getting better; to go back to bad habits** | 다시 악화되다, 재발하다, 다시 타락하다

**n. the recurrence of symptoms of a disease after a period of improvement** | 재발

Mr. Miles *relapsed* into drug use after many years of staying clean.
Don't forget to keep taking these medications to prevent a possible *relapse*.

> **CH** relapse : recidivism [risídəvìzm]
> recidivism(상습적 범행)은 relapse하는 범죄를 의미한다.

## release
[rilíːs]

**v. to set free; to open to the public** | 석방하다, 해방하다, 공개하다

The prisoner was *released* early from jail for good behavior.

> **ANT** release : constrain [kənstréin]
> constrain: 구속하다, 제약하다

---

### TRANSLATION | 예문해석

**prospect** 거지들은 금과 다른 광석들을 찾기 위해 그 지역을 시굴했다.
다른 직업을 찾을 가망은 많았기 때문에 그 직원은 의지대로 일자리를 떠날 수 있었다.
**prowl** 큰 고양이들은 사냥감을 찾아 살금살금 돌아다닌다.
**pulchritude** 왕자는 그 소녀의 눈부신 아리따움에 당황해서 어찌할 바를 몰랐다.
**relapse** Miles씨는 몇 년 동안 마약을 끊었다가 다시 손을 뗐다.
혹시 모를 재발을 막기 위해 이 약들을 잊지말고 드십시오.
**release** 그 죄수는 바르게 행동해서 빨리 석방됐다.

## relevant
[réləvənt]

**adj. having a connection; applicable** | 관련이 있는, 적절한

The judge deemed the evidence *relevant* to the case and admitted it.

**SYN** relevant : pertinent [pə́:rtənənt]
pertinent: 관련이 있는, 적절한

## relieve
[rilí:v]

**v. to ease pain or suffering; to liberate from worries or fears; to take the place of someone** | (고통 등을) 덜다, (걱정이나 공포에서) 해방하다, 교대하다

*Relieved* that her husband was safe, Elizabeth began to scold him for not calling.

**FUN** relieve : anodyne [ǽnoudàin]
anodyne(고통을 완화시키는 약, 진통제)에는 relieve하는 기능이 있다.

## relinquish
[rilíŋkwiʃ]

**v. to give up or withdraw from; to release** | 포기하다, 그만두다, (쥐고 있던 것을) 놓다

Rhea *relinquished* custody rights to her children in exchange for weekly visits and alimony.

**ANT** relinquish : procure [proukjúər]
procure: 획득하다

## reward
[riwɔ́:rd]

**v. to recompense for a worthy or evil act** | 선행이나 악행을 되갚다

Everything we do to others will one day come back to us and we will be *rewarded* for our actions.

**ANT** rewarding work : drudgery [drʌ́dʒəri]
rewarding work: 보람되고 가치 있는 일
drudgery: 지루하고 힘든 일

## rile
[rail]

**v. to agitate or enrage** | 화나게 하다

The animals were *riled* by the intruding zoo-keeper.

**CH** rile : choleric [kɑ́lərik]
choleric(화를 잘내는)한 사람은 쉽게 rile된다.

---

TRANSLATION | 예 문 해 석

relevant  그 판사는 그 증거가 사건과 관련이 있다고 생각하고 이를 채택했다.
relieve  Elizabeth는 남편이 안전하다는 사실에 안도하며 전화하지 않은 것을 나무랐다.
relinquish  Rhea는 아이들 양육권을 포기하는 대신 매주 방문할 수 있는 권리와 이혼 수당을 얻게 되었다.
reward  우리가 다른 이에게 행하는 모든 것들은 언젠가 다시 우리에게 돌아와 우리는 그 행동에 대한 보상을 받게 될 것이다
rile  그 동물들은 동물원 관리인이 들이닥친 탓에 사나워졌다.

## salient
[séiliənt]

**adj. noticeable or conspicuous; jutting out** | 두드러진, 돌출한

Bright neon lights were the most *salient* features of the building.

**ANT** salient : inconspicuous [ìnkənspíkjuəs]

inconspicuous: 눈에 띄지 않는

## sensation
[senséiʃən]

**n. a perception by means of one of the sense organs; excitement or heightened feeling** | 감각, 감동, 감흥

The heat from the sun sent a wave of *sensation* through my body.

**WO** sensation : numb [nʌ́m]

numb(감각을 잃은, 무감각한)한 사람은 sensation이 없다.

## solemn
[sáləm]

**adj. serious or sacred** | 진지한, 신성한

The cadet's *solemn* face conveyed the importance of the responsibilities bestowed upon him.

**ANT** solemn utterance : jest [dʒest]

solemn utterance: 진지한 말

jest: 농담, 장난

## solicitous
[səlísətəs]

**adj. expressing concern; eagerly desirous; extremely careful** | 걱정하는, 염원하는, 세심한

Steven's *solicitous* attention to his wife endeared him to the in-laws.

**WO** solicitous : insouciance [insúːsiəns]

solicitous한 사람에게는 insouciance(태평, 무관심)가 없다.

## tolerance
[tάlərəns]

**n. the ability of accepting beliefs or practices differing from one's own; the ability to endure pain or hardship; the capacity to become less responsive to a substance with repeated use or exposure** | 관용, 포용력, 참을성, 내성

Al gradually built up his *tolerance* to alcohol while attending college.

**인과** tolerance : inured [injúərd]

어떤 것에 inured(익숙해진, 단련된)한 상태가 되면 그것에 대한 tolerance가 생긴다.

---

### TRANSLATION | 예문 해석

| | |
|---|---|
| salient | 밝은 네온 빛은 그 빌딩의 가장 두드러진 특징이었다. |
| sensation | 태양열의 감동이 내 몸을 휩쓸고 지나갔다. |
| solemn | 그 생도의 엄숙한 표정은 그에게 부과된 책임이 얼마나 중요한지 말해준다. |
| solicitous | Steven은 아내에게 세심한 관심을 쏟기 때문에 처가의 사랑을 받는다. |
| tolerance | Al은 대학에 다니면서 서서히 술에 대한 내성을 키웠다. |

## unlimited
[ʌnlímitid]

**adj. having no restrictions; infinite** | 무제한의, 끝없는

Olive's health club membership was for *unlimited* use during the weekdays.

**ANT** unlimited : circumscribed [sə̀ːrkəmskráibd]
circumscribed: 제한된

## valiant
[væljənt]

**adj. brave or exhibiting courage** | 용감한

The *valiant* knight was welcomed home with a celebratory feast at the palace.

**WO** valiance : pusillanimous [pjùːsəlǽnəməs]
pusillanimous(소심한, 겁많은)한 사람에게는 valiance(용기)가 없다.

## vilify
[víləfài]

**v. to slander or harshly criticize** | 비방하다, 헐뜯다

Propaganda *vilified* the British government during the Revolutionary War.

**ANT** vilify : adulate [ǽdʒuləit]
adulate: 비굴하게 아첨하다

## volatile
[válətil]

**adj. evaporating rapidly without much change in temperature or pressure; tending to become violent; ever-changing** | 휘발성의, (성격 등이) 쉽게 격해지는, 심하게 변동하는

Jane had grown up with a *volatile* father who would get violent when angered.

**CN** volatile : stabilize [stéibəlàiz]
volatile한 사람은 stabilize(안정시키다)하기 어렵다.

## vulgarity
[vʌlgǽrəti]

**n. that which offends good tastes or manners** | 저속, 천박

The fan's *vulgarity* offended the spectators sitting in close proximity and he was soon escorted out of the stadium.

**WO** vulgarity : gentle [dʒéntl]
gentle(상냥한, 예의바른)한 사람에게서는 vulgarity를 찾아 볼 수 없다.

---

**TRANSLATION | 예 문 해 석**

| | |
|---|---|
| **unlimited** | Olive는 주중에는 무제한으로 헬스클럽을 이용할 수 있다. |
| **valiant** | 그 용감한 기사는 궁전에서 축하연을 베풀어 줄 정도로 열렬한 환영을 받았다. |
| **vilify** | 선전은 혁명 전쟁 중에 영국을 헐뜯었다. |
| **volatile** | Jane은 화가 나면 폭력적으로 변하는 격한 성격의 아버지 밑에서 자랐다. |
| **vulgarity** | 그 팬의 저속함은 가장 가까이에 있던 관중을 불쾌하게 만들어서 그는 곧 경기장 밖으로 끌려나갔다. |

# 19th Day Daily Check-up

■ Fill in the blanks with the correct letter that matches the word with its definition.

1. fondness   _____
2. belie      _____
3. pulchritude _____
4. ken        _____
5. filigree   _____
6. vilify     _____
7. malinger   _____
8. deleterious _____
9. rile       _____
10. obligate  _____

a. harmful or noxious
b. to slander or harshly criticize
c. to pretend to be sick or incapable in order to avoid work
d. physical beauty or attractiveness
e. detailed ornamentation of fine gold or silver wire
f. to agitate or enrage
g. to morally or legally commit
h. to give a wrong impression; to contradict; to show to be wrong
i. range of sight; abstract range of perception
j. a warm affection

■ Put the correct word in each blank from the list of words below.

11. numb한 사람은 _____이 없다.
12. _____는 의사진행을 delay하는 하는 것이다.
13. _____한 사람을 arouse하기는 어렵다.
14. _____는 전문적인 지식 없이 그저 취미 삼아 superficial하게 예술을 대하는 사람이다.
15. eulogize(칭찬하다)의 반의어 _____이다.
16. _____한 것에는 truth가 없다.
17. _____는 pertinent(관련이 있는, 적절한)의 동의어이다.
18. mollify(달래다)는 _____의 반의어이다.
19. _____한 사람은 stabilize하기 어렵다.
20. _____한 사람에게는 flexibility가 없다.

a. relevant   b. filibuster   c. mulish      d. dilettante   e. elliptic    f. malign
g. sensation  h. mendacious   i. volatile    j. beleaguer    k. phlegmatic  l. alleviate

**Answer key**

1. j   2. h   3. d   4. i   5. e   6. b   7. c   8. a   9. f   10. g
11. g  12. b  13. k  14. d  15. f  16. h  17. a  18. j  19. i  20. c

# SUPER VOCA

## T.W.E.N.T.I.E.T.H D.A.Y

## 20th DAY

이제 그만봐도 되겠다구요? 농담도 잘하십니다~

---

### aloft
[əlɔ́(ː)ft]

**adv. high above in the air** | 하늘 높이

The sight of the eagles soaring *aloft* inspired Amos to paint a picture.

**ANT** stay aloft : founder [fáundər]
stay aloft: 높이 떠 있다
founder: 침몰하다, 가라앉다

---

### amphibian
[æmfíbiən]

**n. an animal that can live in water and on land** | 수륙 양서 동물, 양서류

*Amphibians* have physical attributes which allow them to survive on land and in water.

**KIN** amphibian : frog [frɔːg]
frog(개구리)는 amphibian의 한 종류이다.

---

### arctic
[ɑ́ːrktik]

**adj. extremely cold and frigid** | 극도로 추운, 혹한의

The *arctic* tundra is home to only the fittest of wildlife.

**ANT** arctic : torrid [tɔ́rid]
torrid: 극서의

---

### balk
[bɔːk]

**v. to stop short and refuse to go on; to thwart** | 갑자기 멈추다, 방해하다

The horse *balked* and would not proceed into the dark forest.

**ANT** balk : move ahead willingly [muːv əhéd wíliŋli]
move ahead willingly: 기꺼이 앞으로 가다

---

### TRANSLATION | 예문해석

**aloft** 하늘 높이 솟아 오르는 독수리의 모습이 Amos에게 그림을 그리도록 영감을 주었다.
**amphibian** 양서류는 땅과 물에서 모두 생존할 수 있게 해주는 신체적 특질을 가진다.
**arctic** 혹한의 동토대에는 그곳에 적응한 야생 동물들만 살 수 있다.
**balk** 그 말은 갑자기 멈추었고, 어두운 숲 속으로 더 이상 들어가려고 하지 않았다.

## ballast
[bǽləst]

**n.** a heavy substance used to improve the stability of a ship | 배를 안정시키기 위하여 싣는 바닥짐

Without the *ballast*, the ship will roll too much.

> **FUN** ballast : stability [stəbíləti]
> ballast를 이용해 stability(안정성)를 유지한다.

## balm
[bɑːm]

**n.** a balsamic resin; a soothing, healing, or comforting agent | 방향성 수지, 진통제, 위안

Lip *balm* is an essential for people who live in cold winter climates.

> **FUN** balm : irritation [irətéiʃən]
> balm은 irritation(화, 자극, 염증)을 가라앉히는 기능을 한다.

## belligerent
[bəlídʒərənt]

**adj.** inclined to fight; pertaining to war | 호전적인, 전쟁의

The *belligerent* drunks were arrested by the police after harassing a group of young men.

> **ANT** belligerent : conciliatory [kənsíliətɔ̀ːri]
> conciliatory: 회유적인, 달래는

## beloved
[bilʌ́vid]

**adj.** dearly or highly loved | 아주 사랑받는

Princess Diana, *beloved* by all, was greatly mourned after the tragic car accident.

> **ANT** beloved : spurned [spəːrnd]
> spurned: 경멸조로 거절당한, 냉대받는

---

**TRANSLATION | 예문 해석**

**ballast** 바닥짐이 없다면 배는 몹시 흔들릴 것이다.
**balm** 입술크림은 추운 겨울 기후 속에서 살아가는 사람들에겐 필수적이다.
**belligerent** 그 싸우기 좋아하는 술주정꾼들은 일단의 청년들을 괴롭혔다는 이유로 경찰에 체포됐다.
**beloved** 모든 사람들의 사랑을 한 몸에 받았던 다이애나 황태자비는 그 비극적인 사건 후 대대적인 애도를 받았다.

## bolster
[bóulstər]

**n.** a long pillow or cushion | 긴 베개, 받침대

**v.** to support with a bolster; to give a boost to | 덧베개로 받쳐주다, 기운내게 하다

Most people with back problems use a *bolster* for support when sitting in a chair.

An extended rest and a good meal *bolstered* the morale of the troops.

**FUN** bolster : support [səpɔ́ːrt]
bolster는 support(받치다, 지지하다)하는 기능이 있다.

## bully
[búli]

**n.** one who repeatedly harasses and intimidates those weaker than himself | 약한 사람을 괴롭히는 사람

Poor little John has his lunch money taken away daily by the school *bully*.

**CH** bully : browbeat [bráubìːt]
bully는 자기보다 약한 사람을 browbeat(위협하다, 겁주다)한다.

## callous
[kǽləs]

**adj.** hardened and thickened; having calluses ; unfeeling | 굳어진, 못박힌, 냉담한

Greg's finger tips have become *callous* from playing guitar.

**인과** callous : friction [fríkʃən]
friction(마찰)의 결과로 피부가 callous하게 된다.

## callow
[kǽlou]

**adj.** immature and inexperienced | 미숙한, 경험이 없는

The man's *callow* ways often caused him to be shortsighted in his goals.

**ANT** callow : mature [mətʃúər]
mature: 성숙한

## cart
[kɑːrt]

**n.** a wheeled vehicle used to transport goods, often pulled by animals | 물건을 수송하기 위해 쓰는 (종종 동물이 끄는) 바퀴 달린 운반구, 짐수레

My grandfather started making money by selling watermelons from a *cart* he would pull into the city.

**KIN** cart : caisson [kéisn]
caisson(탄약차)는 cart의 일종이다.

---

**TRANSLATION | 예문해석**

**bolster** 허리에 문제가 있는 사람들은 대부분 의자에 앉을 때 지지하기 위해 받침대를 사용한다.
증가된 휴식기간과 질높은 식사는 군대의 사기를 진작시켰다.

**bully** 덩치가 작은 John은 불쌍하게도 매일 그 불량 학생한테 점심 값을 빼앗겼다.

**callous** Greg는 기타를 너무 많이 쳐서 손가락 끝에 못이 박혔다.

**callow** 그 남자의 미숙한 방식은 그가 목표를 추진할 때 종종 근시안적으로 만들었다.

**cart** 할아버지는 짐수레를 시내까지 끌고 가서 수박을 팔아 돈을 벌기 시작하셨다.

## collapse
[kəlǽps]

**v.** to lose strength; to fall or break down | 쇠약해지다, 무너지다

The poorly built building *collapsed* once the storm hit.

> **DE** collapse : implode [implóud]
> implode는 내파하다라는 뜻으로 collapse에 비해 강도가 높다.

## collude
[kəlúːd]

**v.** to conspire | 공모하다

Anarchists *collude* against the government.

> **KIN** collude : cooperate [kouápərèit]
> collude는 음모를 꾸미기 위해 여러 사람들과 cooperate(협동하다)하다 라는 의미이다.

## culpable
[kʎlpəbl]

**adj.** guilty; deserving blame | 유죄의, 비난 받을 만한

Are video games *culpable* for the recent violence in school?

> **CH** culpable : blame [bleim]
> culpable하다는 것은 blame(비난)받을 만하다는 의미이다.

## disgorge
[disgɔ́ːrdʒ]

**v.** to discharge or eject from the throat and mouth | 토하다, 목이나 입에서 쏟아내다

The dog *disgorged* its meal onto the floor.

> **SYN** disgorge : vomit [vámit]
> vomit: 토하다

## errant
[érənt]

**adj.** deviating or straying from the established course | 잘못된, 정도에서 벗어난

Tom's *errant* behavior worried his father greatly.

> **대상** errant : course [kɔːrs]
> errant는 일정한 course(흐름, 방향)으로부터 벗어나는 것이다.

---

### TRANSLATION | 예 문 해 석

| | |
|---|---|
| collapse | 부실공사를 통해 지어진 그 빌딩은 태풍이 불자 무너졌다. |
| collude | 무정부주의자들은 반정부 계획을 공모한다. |
| culpable | 비디오 게임이 최근 학교에서 발생한 폭력사건에 책임이 있는가? |
| disgorge | 그 개는 바닥에 먹이를 토했다. |
| errant | Tom의 빗나간 행동은 아버지를 매우 걱정시켰다. |

### eulogize
[júːlədʒàiz]

**v. to extol or speak highly of** | 칭송하다, 찬사를 보내다

President Bush *eulogized* the citizens of New York City for their reaction to the September 11th attacks.

**CH** eulogize : encomiast [enkóumiæst]

encomiast(찬양하는 사람, 아첨하는 사람)는 eulogize하는 특징이 있다.

### fallacious
[fəléiʃəs]

**adj. based on false information or ideas; tending to deceive** | 그릇된, 거짓의

The product's *fallacious* advertising swindled many consumers of their hard earned money.

**ANT** fallacious : veracious [vəréiʃəs]

veracious: 진실한, 정확한

### falter
[fɔ́ːltər]

**v. to move unsteadily; to speak or act hesitantly** | 비틀거리다, 머뭇거리다

Michael *faltered* for a few moments before finally speaking.

**SYN** falter : hesitate [hézətèit]

hesitate: 머뭇거리다, 망설이다

### gall
[gɔːl]

**v. to vex or become irritated** | 초조하게 하다, 화나게 하다
**n. bile in liver; rudeness** | 담즙; 뻔뻔스러움

The teacher was *galled* by Daniel's actions.

Richard Nixon had the *gall* to deny on national television any connection to Watergate.

**ANT** gall : assuage [əswéidʒ]

assuage: 진정시키다, 달래다

---

**TRANSLATION | 예 문 해 석**

| | |
|---|---|
| eulogize | 부시 대통령은 9.11 테러 사건이 발생했을 때 뉴욕시민들이 보여준 대응자세에 깊은 찬사를 보냈다. |
| fallacious | 그 제품에 대한 그릇된 광고는 소비자들이 힘들게 번 돈을 빼앗았다. |
| falter | Michael은 몇 분 동안 머뭇거리다가 결국 말을 꺼냈다. |
| gall | 선생님은 Daniel의 행동 때문에 화가 머리끝까지 났다.<br>Richard Nixon은 뻔뻔스럽게도 국영 TV방송에서 워터게이트와 연루된 것이 전혀 없다고 부인했다. |

## gull
[gʌl]

**v. to cheat or trick** | 속이다
**n. a large sea bird that has a loud call** | 갈매기

People are willing to *gull* for what they desire.
The incoming ship was followed by a flock of curious *gulls*.

> **PUR**  gull : chicanery [ʃikéinəri]
> gull하기 위해 chicanery(속임수, 책략)를 쓴다.

## illiterate
[ilítərət]

**adj. unable to read or write** | 문맹의

The *illiterate* man attempted to conceal his secret by pretending to be an erudite.

> **ANT**  illiterate : erudite [érjudàit]
> erudite: 학식이 있는

## jolt
[dʒoult]

**v. to strike suddenly and forcefully so as to cause movement; to move or disturb with a sudden, hard blow** | 세게 흔들다, 갑작스런 충격으로 움직이거나 흔들리다

Rachael was *jolted* backwards by the collision of the cars.

> **KIN**  jolt : move [muːv]
> jolt는 단순히 move하는 것이 아니라 세게 흔들다 라는 뜻이다.

## lull
[lʌl]

**v. to calm or soothe** | 달래다, 진정시키다

Every night the mother *lulls* her baby to sleep with a song.

> **ANT**  lull : gall [gɔːl]
> gall: 화나게 하다, 초조하게 하다

---

### TRANSLATION | 예문해석

| | |
|---|---|
| gull | 사람들은 자신이 원하는 바를 위해서는 기꺼이 속인다. |
| | 입항하는 선박을 호기심에 찬 갈매기들이 줄지어 따라왔다. |
| illiterate | 문맹인 그 남자는 박식한 척 함으로써 자신의 비밀을 숨기려고 했다. |
| jolt | 차의 충돌로 인해 Rachael은 뒤로 나가 떨어졌다. |
| lull | 밤마다 그 어머니는 자장가를 들려주어 아기를 재웠다. |

## malleable
[mǽliəbl]

**adj. capable of being shaped, as by hammering or rolling; tractable** | 모양을 만들기 쉬운, 가단성의, 유순한

Copper was the first *malleable* metal to be uncovered and its flexibility led to rapid innovations.

**대상** malleable : shape [ʃeip]

malleable한 것은 쉽게 shape를 바꿀 수 있는 것이다.

## malodor
[mælóudər]

**n. a horrid, offensive smell** | 악취

Oral *malodor* is often the result of irregular brushing and improper hygiene.

**KIN** malodor : scent [sent]

maodor는 scent(냄새) 중에서도 악취를 의미한다.

## mellifluous
[məlífluəs]

**adj. having a rich, sweet, and smooth flow** | 감미로운

A beautiful *mellifluous* melody floated into the room.

**대상** mellifluous : music [mjúːzik]

music(음악)이 듣기 좋은 때 mellifluous라는 단어를 쓴다.

## mollify
[máləfài]

**v. to ease or appease** | 달래다

The wife *mollified* her enraged husband.

**ANT** mollify : beleaguer [bilíːgər]

beleaguer: 끊임없이 괴롭히다

## oblige
[əbláidʒ]

**v. to constrain by physical, moral, or legal force; to render a service to** | (물리적·도덕적·법적인) 의무를 지우다; 호의를 베풀다

Kent *obliged* Mary by helping her move to a new apartment.

**ANT** oblige : discommode [dìskəmóud]

discommode: 폐를 끼치다, 불편하게 하다

---

### TRANSLATION | 예문 해석

| | |
|---|---|
| malleable | 구리는 가단성을 가진 금속 중 최초로 발견된 것이며, 그런 유연한 성질은 빠른 기술 혁신에 기여했다. |
| malodor | 입에서 나는 악취는 불규칙적인 이닦기와 부적당한 위생 때문에 생기는 것이다. |
| mellifluous | 아름답고 감미로운 음악소리가 방안에 퍼졌다. |
| mollify | 아내는 잔뜩 화가 난 남편을 달랬다. |
| oblige | Kent는 Mary가 새 아파트로 이사가는 것을 돕는 호의를 베풀었다. |

## obliterate
[əblítəréit]

**v. to destroy or remove all traces of** | 파괴하다, 흔적을 없애다

The city was *obliterated* from the war.

> **DE** obliterate : remove [rimúːv]
> obliterate는 흔적이 없도록 완전히 remove(제거하다)하는 것이다.

## oblivion
[əblíviən]

**n. the state of being forgotten; the act of forgetting** | 잊혀진 상태, 망각

The young delinquent's misdeeds were buried as an act of *oblivion* the moment he turned eighteen.

> **POS** oblivion : forget [fərgét]
> forget: 잊다

## palliate
[pǽlièit]

**v. to lessen the effect of; to make less severe** | 완화시키다

Doctors hoped the new drug would *palliate* the side effects of chemotherapy on cancer patients.

> **대상** palliate : severity [səvérəti]
> severity(격렬함, 괴로움)를 palliate(완화시키다)하다.

## pallid
[pǽlid]

**adj. looking pale; lacking liveliness** | (안색이) 창백한, 생기 없는

Watching television became a *pallid* substitute for exercise after James broke his leg.

> **SYN** pallid : wan [wɑn]
> wan: 핏기 없는, 힘 없는

## palpable
[pǽlpəbl]

**adj. obvious or capable of being felt** | 명백한, 만질 수 있는

The scar on his knee is *palpable* to the touch.

> **ANT** palpable : elliptical [ilíptikəl]
> elliptical: 애매한, 생략된

---

**TRANSLATION | 예문해석**

| | |
|---|---|
| **obliterate** | 그 도시는 전쟁으로 흔적조차 사라졌다. |
| **oblivion** | 그 어린 범죄자의 비행은 그가 18세가 되던 해 망각되어 묻혀 버렸다. |
| **palliate** | 의사들은 새로운 의약품이 암 환자들에 대한 화학치료의 부작용을 완화시키기를 바랬다. |
| **pallid** | James는 다리가 부러진 후에 TV시청을 운동 대신하는 활기없는 활동으로 삼았다. |
| **palpable** | 그의 무릎을 만져보면 흉터 자리가 분명히 있다. |

## palter
[pɔ́ːltər]

v. to act or speak in a deceitful way; to equivocate | (속이기 위하여) 얼버무리다

Phillip *paltered* in front of the principal, hoping to get his classmate in trouble.

**WO** palter : candor [kǽndər]

palter하는 사람에게는 candor(솔직, 정직)가 없다.

## pellucid
[pəlúːsid]

adj. allowing for light to pass without diffusing or distorting; easily comprehensible | 투명한, 명료한

The professor's *pellucid* method of teaching was popular among his students.

**ANT** pellucid : evasive [ivéisiv]

evasive: 이해하기 어려운, 회피하는

## pillory
[píləri]

n. a wooden device with holes for a head and hands that is used to publicly display a criminal as punishment; laughingstock | (형틀의 한 종류인) 칼; 웃음거리

The villagers threw tomatoes at the man in the *pillory*.

**FUN** pillory : punish [pʌ́niʃ]

pillory는 punish(벌주다)하는 데 쓰는 도구이다.

## pine
[pain]

n. a type of coniferous evergreen tree | 소나무
v. to fail in health because of sorrow; to desire intensely | 슬픔으로 인해 수척해 지다; 갈망하다

Throughout the world *pines* are cultivated for their use as Christmas trees.

Justin *pined* for the opportunity to paint in Italy.

**POS** pine : longing [lɔ́(ː)ŋiŋ]

longing: 갈망, 동경

---

TRANSLATION | 예 문 해 석

**palter** Phillip은 반 친구가 곤란에 처하길 바라며 교장 앞에서 얼버무렸다.
**pellucid** 그 교수의 명료한 교수법은 학생들 사이에서 인기였다.
**pillory** 마을 사람들은 칼찬 그 남자 죄수에게 토마토를 던졌다.
**pine** 전세계적으로 소나무는 크리스마스 트리로 사용되기 위해 재배된다.
Justin은 Italy에서 그림을 그릴 수 있는 기회를 갈망했다.

## pollster
[póulstər]

**n. a person who conducts a poll** | 여론조사원

The *pollsters* are busy during election time.

> **CH** pollster : canvass [kǽnvəs]
> pollster는 canvass(여론 조사하다)한다.

## ponder
[pándər]

**v. to carefully think on and reflect about** | 신중하게 생각하다

Eric *pondered* all day over the social questions that his professor raised in class.

> **WO** ponder : imprudence [imprúːdns]
> 매사에 ponder하는 사람은 imprudence(경솔함)가 없다.

## punctilious
[pʌŋktíliəs]

**adj. concerned with every detail; strictly adhering to etiquette or formalities** | 세심한, 격식을 차리는

Soren is an honest and very *punctilious* German, very much representing the general German culture.

> **ANT** punctilious : remiss [rimís]
> remiss: 부주의한, 태만한

## pundit
[pándit]

**n. a learned person** | 박식한 사람, 석학

The *pundit* gave lectures on globalization at universities across the world.

> **CH** pundit : opine [oupáin]
> pundit는 늘 opine(의견을 말하다) 하는 경향이 있다.

## rafter
[rǽftər]

**n. a sloping beam that is used to support the roof** | 지붕을 받치는 비스듬한 들보, 서까래

Once the *rafters* were put in, the house started to take shape.

> **FUN** rafter : roof [ruːf]
> rafter는 roof(지붕)을 지지한다.

---

TRANSLATION | 예 문 해 석

| | |
|---|---|
| **pollster** | 여론조사원들은 선거 때는 바쁘다. |
| **ponder** | Eric은 교수가 수업시간에 제기했던 사회 문제들을 온종일 골똘히 생각했다. |
| **punctilious** | Soren은 정직하고 매우 꼼꼼한 독일인으로서, 일반적인 독일문화의 많은 부분을 보여준다. |
| **pundit** | 그 석학은 세계 도처의 대학들에서 세계화에 관해 강연했다. |
| **rafter** | 일단 서까래가 놓이자 집은 형태를 갖추기 시작했다. |

## rancor
[ræŋkər]

**n.** long-lived and bitter hatred | (뿌리 깊은) 원한, 증오

The doctor's *rancor* towards the tobacco industry emanated from treating lung cancer patients.

**ANT** rancor : charitableness [tʃǽrətəblnis]

charitableness: 자비, 관용

## random
[rǽndəm]

**adj.** lacking a fixed goal, plan, or procedure; happening accidentally or haphazardly | 정해진 목표나 계획이 없는, 무작위의

Martin's *random* business proposal failed to attract any investors.

**WO** random : pattern [pǽtərn]

random한 것은 정해진 pattern(양식, 패턴)이 없는 것이다.

## rend
[rend]

**v.** to tear apart violently | 난폭하게 잡아 찢다

Kathy's unfaithful husband *rent* her heart.

**DE** rend : tear [tɛər]

rend는 난폭하게 tear(찢다)하다 라는 의미이다.

## sanctimonious
[sæ̀ŋktəmóuniəs]

**adj.** claiming to be more holy than one really is | 독실한 체하는

The preacher's *sanctimonious* spiel about tithing had many of the congregation shaking their heads.

**DE** sanctimonious: devout [diváut]

sanctimonious하는 것은 겉으로만 devout(독실한)한 체 하는 것이다.

## sincere
[sinsíər]

**adj.** honest and true in one's thoughts, actions, and expressions | 성실한, 진실한

Everyone trusts Lily because of *sincere* concern for others.

**WO** sincerity : poseur [pouzə́ːr]

poseur(허식가)에게는 sincerity가 없다.

---

**TRANSLATION | 예문 해석**

| | |
|---|---|
| rancor | 그 의사의 담배 산업을 향한 깊은 증오는 폐암 환자들을 치료하면서 생긴 것이었다. |
| random | Martin은 되는 대로 사업 제안을 했기 때문에 어떤 투자자의 관심도 얻지 못했다. |
| rend | Kathy는 부정(不貞)한 남편 때문에 몹시 상심했다. |
| sanctimonious | 그 목사가 독실한 체하며 십일조에 대해 한 연설은 많은 수의 신도들이 고개를 젓게 만들었다. |
| sincere | Lily의 배려는 언제나 진실하기 때문에 모두가 그녀를 신뢰한다. |

**solidify** [səlídəfài]

v. **to make hard or solid; to make strong or united**
| 굳히다, 단결시키다

Dropping temperatures *solidified* the freezing pond into ice.

ANT solidify : pulverize [pʌ́lvəràiz]
pulverize: 가루로 만들다, 분쇄하다

**sparse** [spɑːrs]

adj. **existing in small amounts; scanty; thinly scattered**
| 적은, 부족한, 희박한

Water is often *sparse* in the desert.

ANT sparse : copious [kóupiəs]
copious: 많은, 풍부한

**spleen** [spliːn]

n. **an organ of the body involved in the filter and restoration of blood; ill temper**
| 비장(脾臟); 악의, 울화

Nicholas vented his *spleen* on his wife.

SYN spleen : malice [mǽlis]
malice: 악의, 앙심

**sullen** [sʌ́lən]

adj. **resentfully irritated and silent**
| 침울한, 뚱한

The *sullen* little boy's mood was lifted with a trip to the amusement park.

ANT sullenness : elation [iléiʃən]
sullenness: 침울
elation: 의기 양양

**sunder** [sʌ́ndər]

v. **to break apart; to separate by violence**
| 가르다, 떼다, 찢다

The tree was *sundered* after the lightening strike.

DE sunder : divide [diváid]
sunder는 divide(나누다)에 비해 그 어감이 더 강하다.

---

TRANSLATION | 예 문 해 석

| | |
|---|---|
| solidify | 기온이 떨어져 몹시 추운 연못이 얼어버렸다. |
| sparse | 대개 사막에서는 물이 부족하다. |
| spleen | Nicholas는 아내에 대한 악의를 드러냈다. |
| sullen | 어린 소년의 침울한 기분은 놀이공원으로 놀러가면서 좋아졌다. |
| sunder | 그 나무는 번갯불에 맞아 산산 조각났다. |

## syllogism
[sílədʒìzm]

**n.** a deductive structure of an argument that includes a major premise, a minor premise, and a conclusion; deduction  | 삼단 논법, 연역법

Aristotle's doctrine of *syllogism* was the basis of formal logic.

**PUR** syllogism : disprove [disprúːv]

syllogism은 상대방의 의견을 논리적으로 disprove(논박하다, 반증을 들다)하는 수단으로 사용된다.

## tangy
[tǽŋi]

**adj.** having a sharp, distinctive flavor or odor  | 맛이 톡 쏘는, 냄새가 코를 찌르는

Japanese cooking often uses the kabosu to produce a *tangy* flavor.

**ANT** tangy : bland [blænd]

bland: 독특한 맛이 없는, 자극성이 적은

## tarnish
[táːrniʃ]

**v.** to dull the luster of; to discolor; to bring disgrace upon  | 흐리게 하다, 변색시키다, (명예를) 더럽히다

The once shiny trophy had become *tarnished* over time.

**대상** tarnish : silver [sílvər]

silver(은)의 광택을 tarnish하다.

## veneer
[vəníər]

**n.** a superficial or false appearance; a thin layer of wood or plastic that covers a cheap material  | 겉치장, 합판의 겉 겹, 화장판

The wooden *veneer* on the table was beautiful.

**PAR** veneer : furniture [fə́ːrnitʃər]

veneer는 furniture(가구)의 겉에 붙이는 장식용의 얇은 나무나 플라스틱을 의미한다.

## volition
[voulíʃən]

**n.** an act of free will; the power of determining  | 의지, 결단력

Voting is an act of intelligent *volition*.

**WO** volition : vacillating [vǽsəléitiŋ]

vacillating(우유부단한, 망설이는)한 사람에게는 volition이 없다.

---

TRANSLATION | 예문 해석

| | |
|---|---|
| **syllogism** | 아리스토텔레스의 삼단 논법은 형식 논리학의 기본 토대였다. |
| **tangy** | 일본 요리는 톡 쏘는 풍미를 내기 위해 kabosu를 자주 쓴다. |
| **tarnish** | 한 때는 빛났던 트로피가 시간이 지나면서 흐리게 변색되었다. |
| **veneer** | 그 테이블의 나무판은 예뻤다. |
| **volition** | 투표는 이성적인 결단력을 보여주는 행동이다. |

## 20th Day Daily Check-up

■ Fill in the blanks with the correct letter that matches the word with its definition.

1. pellucid _____
2. mellifluous _____
3. callow _____
4. spleen _____
5. balm _____
6. rend _____
7. lull _____
8. fallacious _____
9. bolster _____
10. punctilious _____

a. based on false information or ideas; tending to deceive
b. immature and inexperienced
c. to violently tear apart
d. an organ of the body involved in the filter and restoration of blood; ill temper
e. to enhance strength or give a boost to
f. allowing for light to pass without diffusing or distorting; easily comprehensible
g. concern about precise behavior according to conventions; scrupulous
h. to calm or soothe
i. having a rich, sweet and smooth flow
j. a balsamic resin; a cream that soothes when applied to the skin

■ Put the correct word in each blank from the list of words below.

11. _____는 음모를 꾸미기 위해 cooperate하다 라는 의미이다.
12. _____는 단순히 move하는 것이 아니라 흔들면서 움직이다 라는 뜻이다.
13. _____는 authoritativeness를 가지고 있다.
14. _____하기 위해 chicanery를 쓴다.
15. _____하는 사람은 candor가 없다.
16. _____는 자기보다 약한 사람을 browbeat 한다.
17. 금속 등이 _____되어 dull하게 되었다.
18. friction의 결과로 피부가 _____하게 된다.
19. discommode(불편을 끼치다)의 반의어는 _____이다.
20. _____는 배의 stability를 위해 사용하는 바닥짐이다.

| a. jolt | b. palter | c. malleable | d. collude | e. gull | f. bully |
| g. pundit | h. ballast | i. tarnish | j. culpable | k. callous | l. oblige |

Answer key

11. d  12. a  13. g  14. b  15. e  16. f  17. i  18. k  19. l  20. h
1. f  2. i  3. b  4. d  5. j  6. c  7. h  8. a  9. e  10. g

# 11th day~20th Day Crossword Puzzle

Answer Page 476

# Questions

### across

3. looking pale; dull
4. having or showing doubt; creating uncertainty
5. a stubbornly unyielding; inflexible
8. to extract by long, careful searching
9. the inability to feel pain but without a loss of consciousness
14. logically possible or seemingly true
15. to lessen; to make pain more bearable
18. to wear down into powder using friction
19. an overly familiar phrase
20. to thicken or make more dense

### down

1. to lose strength and to fall or break down
2. tending to teach or moralize
6. a large area of treeless grassland
7. messy or not clean
10. to put completely under water
11. to give courage or spirit to
12. the state of being forgotten; the act of forgetting
13. to move backward and forward
16. to introduce or put into
17. to lower in value or quality

# 21st DAY

Hey you!
어제 외웠던 **sanctimonious** 기억 나?

---

**acme**
[ǽkmi]

**n. the highest point** | 극치, 전성기

Having reached the *acme* of her political career, the woman planned to retire after the end of her second presidential term.

**ANT** acme : nadir [néidər]

nadir: 최하점

---

**admirable**
[ǽdmərəbl]

**adj. deserving admiration** | 칭찬할 만한, 훌륭한

Ms. Johnson possessed many *admirable* qualities, but it was her patience and commitment to her students' academic welfare that earned her the prestigious "Distinguished Teaching Award."

**ANT** admirable : vituperative [vaitjú:pərèitiv]

vituperative: 비난하는, 헐뜯는

---

**beneficial**
[bènəfíʃəl]

**adj. advantageous to personal or social well-being** | 이득이 되는

Volunteer work is *beneficial* to all parties involved.

**ANT** beneficial : noisome [nɔ́isəm]

noisome: 해로운, 불쾌한

---

**bombast**
[bámbæst]

**n. pretentious speech or writing; grandiloquence** | 허풍, 호언장담

The professor's article, no more than a *bombast*, was denied publication.

**CH** bombast : pompous [pámpəs]

bombast는 pompous(젠체하는, 허풍떠는)하다.

---

### TRANSLATION | 예문 해석

**acme** 그 여자는 정치 이력의 극치에 도달했기 때문에, 자신의 두번째 대통령 임기 후에 사퇴하기로 했다.
**admirable** Ms. Johnson은 많은 장점들을 지니고 있었지만, 그녀가 "Distinguished Teaching Award"라는 귀한 상을 수상하게 해 준 것은 그녀의 인내와 학생들의 학문적 복지를 향한 헌신이었다.
**beneficial** 자원봉사는 관련된 모든 이들에게 이익이 된다.
**bombast** 그 교수의 논문은 허풍으로 가득 차 있었기 때문에 출판이 거절되었다.

## bromide
[bróumaid]

**n. a commonplace or trite remark** | 흔해 빠진 말, 진부한 이야기

The *bromides* offered to the crying girl did nothing to ease her pain and sorrow.

- **CH** bromide : hackneyed [hǽknid]
  bromide는 hackneyed(진부한)한 말이다.

## calumniate
[kəlʌ́mnièit]

**v. to injure someone's reputation by making cruel false statements about him/her** | 비방하다

To divert attention from his own poor performance, Jason *calumniated* a co-worker, going so far as to accuse him of embezzlement.

- **PUR** calumniate : falsehood [fɔ́:lshùd]
  falsehood(허위, 거짓말)로 타인을 calumniate한다.

## comfort
[kʌ́mfərt]

**v. to console or make another feel at peace** | 위로하다, 편안하게 하다

There was nothing I could say to *comfort* my grieving friend over the loss of his pet rabbit.

- **ANT** comfort : aggrieve [əgríːv]
  aggrieve: 괴롭히다, 고통을 주다

## confession
[kənféʃən]

**n. the religious act of admitting guilt** | 죄의 자백, 고해

Prisoners on death row are permitted a *confession* with a priest before their execution.

- **대상** confession : guilt [gilt]
  confession은 스스로 guilt(죄)를 인정하고 털어놓는 행위를 말한다.

## confirm
[kənfə́:rm]

**v. to make certain or attest to the truth; to make valid by a legal act** | 확증하다, 승인하다

Before approving a new medical product, the country's food and drug administration must *confirm* the validity of the company's claims.

- **대상** confirm : hypothesis [haipɑ́θəsis]
  hypothesis(가설)를 confirm하다.

---

### TRANSLATION | 예문 해석

**bromide** 그 흔해 빠진 말은 울고 있는 여자아이에게 그녀의 고통과 슬픔을 달래줄 그 무엇도 되지 못했다.
**calumniate** Jason은 자신의 형편없는 업무성과로부터 관심을 흩뜨리기 위해, 직장 동료를 비방했을 뿐 아니라, 횡령죄까지 씌웠다.
**comfort** 나는 자신의 애완 토끼의 죽음을 슬퍼하는 친구에게 해줄 수 있는 말이 없었다.
**confession** 사형수 감방의 죄수들에게는 처형 전 신부님에게 고해할 수 있는 기회가 허용된다.
**confirm** 식품 의약청은 새로운 의약품을 승인하기 전에 신청 내용이 옳은 것인지를 확실히 확인 해야 한다.

## conform
[kənfɔ́ːrm]

**v. to obey or comply with; to follow the actions and manners of others** | 복종하다, 따르다

Young people have always refused to *conform* to the conventional standards of the day.

**WO** conformity : maverick [mǽvərik]

maverick(독불장군)은 관습에 conformity(복종, 따름)하지 않는다.

## confuse
[kənfjúːz]

**v. to disturb or mix up; to make unclear or incomprehensible** | 혼란하게 하다, 불분명하게 하다

Too much alcohol *confuses* the senses and slows the brain.

**CH** confusion : delirium [dilíəriəm]

delirium(정신착란)에 빠지면 confusion(혼란, 혼동)의 상태를 겪는다.

## congeal
[kəndʒíːl]

**v. to solidify or harden** | 경화시키다, 굳어지게 하다

The blood had *congealed* around the wound on his head.

**ANT** congeal : liquefy [líkwifài]

liquefy: 액화 시키다

## congenial
[kəndʒíːnjəl]

**adj. warm and friendly; of the same nature or disposition** | 온화한, 성격이 맞는

Stepan was *congenial* and kind to all his co-workers.

**ANT** congenial : draconic [dreikánik]

draconic: 엄격한

## congruent
[kəngrúːənt]

**adj. being in agreement or harmony; in geometry, exactly the same in shape and size** | 일치하는, (수학) 합동하는

The company's long-range goals are *congruent* with my own.

**대상** congruent : dimension [diménʃən]

수학에서 congruent 하는 것은 두 도형의 dimension(면적)이 같은 것을 일컫는다.

---

### TRANSLATION | 예문 해석

| | |
|---|---|
| **conform** | 젊은이들은 언제나 자신이 속한 시대의 전통적인 규범에 따르기를 거부한다. |
| **confuse** | 술을 너무 많이 마시면 감각이 혼란해지고 이해가 느려진다. |
| **congeal** | 그가 머리에 입은 상처 부근의 피가 응고되었다. |
| **congenial** | Stepan은 모든 동료들에게 온화하고 친절했다. |
| **congruent** | 이 회사의 장기 계획은 나의 그것과 일치한다. |

## convalesce
[kànvəlés]

**v. to recover or recuperate from illness** | 병에서 회복하다, 재기하다

When Samantha was *convalescing* after her surgery, the nurses insisted she get up and walk even though it was painful.

**POS** convalesce : rehabilitation [rì:həbìlətéiʃən]
rehabilitation: 회복, 재건

## cultivate
[kʌ́ltəvèit]

**v. to prepare land for growing crops; to develop an understanding or interest through study** | 경작하다, 계발하다

The Minister of Agriculture had a keen interest in *cultivating* barren land with new irrigation systems.

**ANT** cultivate : stunt [stʌnt]
stunt: 발육을 저해하다, 성장을 방해하다

## decode
[di:kóud]

**v. to convert code into an understandable language** | 이해할 수 있는 말로 변환하다, 해독하다

By *decoding* the cryptic emails, the FBI was able to uncover a huge drug trade.

**대상** decode : encoded [inkóudid]
encoded(암호화된)한 것을 decode하다.

## deluge
[déljuːdʒ]

**n. a great flow; a heavy downpour; an overwhelming amount or number** | 홍수, 폭우, 쇄도

A *deluge* hit Napier, flooding streets and property.

**DE** deluge : drizzle [drízl]
drizzle(이슬비)은 deluge보다 훨씬 적은 양의 비를 말한다.

## delusion
[dilúːʒən]

**n. an erroneous belief or opinion; an idea that is not true** | 잘못된 믿음이나 의견, 망상

Charles lived his life under the *delusion* that money brings happiness.

**POS** delusion : visionary [víʒənèri]
visionary: 상상의, 공상적인

---

### TRANSLATION | 예문 해석

**convalesce**  Samantha가 수술 후 병에서 회복될 때, 간호사들은 고통스럽더라도 일어나서 걸을 것을 권유했다.
**cultivate**  농무부 장관은 새로운 관개 시스템으로 건조지를 개발하는데 관심이 많았다.
**decode**  FBI는 암호화된 이메일을 해독함으로써 거대 마약 거래를 노출시킬 수 있었다.
**deluge**  폭우가 Napier를 덮쳐서 거리와 토지가 물에 잠겼다.
**delusion**  Charles는 돈이 행복을 가져다 준다는 망상을 가지고 살았다.

## dilute
[dilúːt]

**v. to weaken or thin by adding a liquid** | 희석하다

In Greece, wine is *diluted* with water to avoid heavy intoxication.

**ANT** dilute : concentrate [kánsəntrèit]

concentrate: 농축하다

## diminish
[dimíniʃ]

**v. to decrease in number, quality, or force** | 줄다, 감소하다

Yesterday's thunderstorm *diminished* into a slight drizzle overnight.

**ANT** diminution : augmentation [ɔ̀ːgmentéiʃən]

diminution: 감소

augmentation: 증대

## ditty
[díti]

**n. a short, simple song** | 단가, 소가곡 (짧은 노래)

Mothers usually sing a *ditty* to put their baby to sleep.

**KIN** ditty : song [sɔːŋ]

ditty는 짧은 song(노래, 시가)를 일컫는다.

## flinch
[flintʃ]

**v. to recoil or shrink in fear or pain** | (두려움이나 고통으로 인해) 움찔하다, 움츠러들다

After years of abuse, the dog *flinched* every time anyone raised their voice.

**인과** flinch : fear [fiər]

fear(두려움) 때문에 flinch하게 된다.

## foment
[foumént]

**v. to stir up trouble; to enhance the development of something; to incite** | 문제를 촉발시키다, 조장하다, 선동하다

Authorities accused opposition parties of using the media to *foment* widespread public discord.

**ANT** foment : defuse [diːfjúːz]

defuse: (위험, 긴장을) 완화시키다

---

### TRANSLATION | 예문 해석

| | |
|---|---|
| dilute | 그리스에서는 도수를 낮추기 위해 포도주에 물을 부어 희석시킨다. |
| diminish | 어제의 천둥번개가 밤새 가는 이슬비로 약해졌다. |
| ditty | 어머니는 보통 아이를 재우기 위해 짧은 노래를 부른다. |
| flinch | 수년간 학대를 받은 후에 그 개는 어떤 사람이라도 목소리를 높이기만 하면 움츠러들었다. |
| foment | 정부는 야당이 대중매체를 이용해서 널리 퍼진 국민적 불화를 조장했다고 비난했다. |

## galvanize
[gǽlvənàiz]

**v. to shock with an electric current; to arouse to action**
| 전기로 자극하다, 자극하여 ~를 하게하다

Campaigns designed to *galvanize* the public into action by appealing to reason can be sustained over those that appeal to emotions.

**DE** galvanize : stimulate [stímjulèit]

galvanize는 stimulate(자극하다)에 비해 더 큰 강도로 자극하는 것이다.

## hem
[hem]

**n. the edge of a garment** | 옷의 끝 자락

**v. to surround or confine; to fold back and stitch down the edge of** | 둘러싸다, (옷 가장자리를) 감치다

The mother helped her daughter to shorten the *hem* of her dress.

The valley was not discovered until recently because large mountains *hemmed* it in.

**PAR** hem : garment [gá:rmənt]

hem은 garment(의복)의 끝 부분이다.

## homage
[hámidʒ]

**n. expression of high regard** | 존경, 경의

Two hundred football players came to pay *homage* to the great coach who had been dear to them all.

**ANT** homage : disrespect [dìsrispékt]

disrespect: 경시

## humane
[hju:méin]

**adj. characterized by concern or compassion for human or animal life** | 자비로운, 인도적인

Harvey had the *humane* habit of rescuing and caring for stray dogs.

**CN** humane : misanthrope [mísənθròup]

misanthrope(염세가)는 humane하지 않다.

---

**TRANSLATION | 예문해석**

**galvanize** 대중의 이성에 호소함으로써 자극하여 행동하게 하는 캠페인은 감정에 호소하는 것보다 더 큰 지지를 받을 수 있다.

**hem** 어머니는 딸이 자기 드레스의 단을 감치는 것을 도와주었다.
그 계곡은 큰 산들로 둘러싸여 있었던 탓에 최근까지 발견되지 않았었다.

**homage** 200명의 축구 선수들이 그들 모두에게 소중한 존재였던 훌륭한 감독에게 경의를 표하러 왔다.

**humane** Harvey는 길잃은 개들을 데려와서 돌봐주는 인정있는 습관을 가졌다.

## humble
[hʌmbl]

**adj. not arrogant or proud; modest** | 겸손한

The Dali Lama remains a *humble* man, untouched by his fame and notoriety.

**ANT** humble : imperious [impíəriəs]

imperious: 거만한

## humility
[hju:míləti]

**n. the quality of being humble** | 겸손

*Humility* is considered a virtue, but one should really testify to one's own achievements.

**CH** humility : supplicant [sʌ́plikənt]

supplicant(애원하는 사람)는 humility를 지닌다.

## illuminate
[ilú:mənèit]

**v. to fill with light; to make clear** | 빛나게 하다, 분명하게 하다

Rather than interpreting, Terry prefers reading painting descriptions that can *illuminate* the painter's intention.

**ANT** illuminate : obfuscate [ábfʌskeit]

obfuscate: 애매하게 하다, 당황하게 하다

## immanent
[ímənənt]

**adj. existing or remaining within; inherent** | 내재적인, 내적인

Atheists believe that a spiritual being is *immanent* in people.

**ANT** immanent : extrinsic [ikstrínsik]

extrinsic: 외부로부터의

## immaterial
[ìmətíəriəl]

**adj. unimportant or irrelevant; having no substance or body** | 중요치 않거나 관련이 없는, 실체 없는

The judge declared the evidence *immaterial* and would not allow it in court.

**ANT** immaterial : pertinent [pə́:rtənənt]

pertinent: 관련이 있는, 적절한

---

### TRANSLATION | 예 문 해 석

**humble** 딜라이 라마는 자신을 향한 명성과 악평에 혼들리지 않고 겸손한 태도를 유지했다.
**humility** 겸손은 미덕으로 여겨지지만, 자신의 성과는 확실히 증명할 수 있어야 한다.
**illuminate** Terry는 그림을 해석하기 보다는 작가의 의도가 명확하게 드러나는 설명을 읽는 것을 더 좋아한다.
**immanent** 무신론자들은 신성한 존재는 사람들 속에 내재되어 있다고 믿는다.
**immaterial** 판사는 그 증거가 사건과 관련이 없어 법정에서 인정하지 않을 것이라고 선언했다.

## imminent
[ímənənt]

**adj.** ready or about to happen | 임박한

The soldier, fighting in the midst of a bloody battle, knew he was in *imminent* peril.

**SYN** imminent : forthcoming [fɔːrθkʌmiŋ]
forthcoming: 가까이 다가오는

## lament
[ləmént]

**v.** to express sadness or mourning for | 한탄하다

The entire town *lamented* the death of its popular mayor.

**SYN** lament : deplore [diplɔ́ːr]
deplore: 한탄하다

## lexicographer
[lèksəkágrəfər]

**n.** one who edits and compiles a dictionary | 사전 편집자

*Lexicographers* must be diligent and meticulous to produce an accurate dictionary.

**대상** lexicographer : dictionary [díkʃənèri]
lexicographer는 dictionary(사전)을 만드는 사람이다.

## limerick
[límərik]

**n.** a humorous poem of around five lines | 5행의 희시

The Irish are famous for their *limericks*.

**KIN** limerick : poem [póuəm]
limerick은 poem(시)의 한 종류이다.

## luminary
[lúːmənèri]

**n.** a prominent or respected person, usually in a specific field of academia; something that gives off light | 특정 분야에서의 권위자; 발광체

The *luminary* professor Richard Feynman is best known for his revision of the theory of quantum electrodynamics.

**CH** luminary : eminence [émənəns]
luminary는 eminence(저명함)를 가지고 있다.

---

### TRANSLATION | 예문 해석

**imminent** 피비린내 나는 전투 한복판에 있던 그 병사는 자신에게 위기가 닥쳐오고 있음을 깨달았다.
**lament** 그 도시 전체가 인기있던 시장의 죽음을 슬퍼했다.
**lexicographer** 사전 편집자는 정확한 사전을 만들려면 근면하고 꼼꼼해야 한다.
**limerick** 아일랜드인은 5행 희시로 유명하다.
**luminary** Richard Feynman 교수는 양자 전기 역학 이론을 수정한 것으로 잘 알려진 권위자이다.

## membrane
[mémbrein]

**n. a thin layer covering living tissue; cell membrane** | 얇은막, 세포막

Both plant and animal cells have *membranes* to protect the nucleus and to filter incoming and outgoing substances.

**PAR** membrane : cell [sel]

membrane은 cell(세포)의 한 부분이다.

## momentous
[mouméntəs]

**adj. of very great importance or significance** | 중대한

For many teenagers, the day that they graduate from high school is a *momentous* occasion.

**DE** momentous : important [impɔ́:rtənt]

momentous한 것은 important(중요한) 보다 더 중요한 것을 묘사할 때 사용된다.

## nomad
[nóumæd]

**n. a person with no fixed home who moves with his/her tribe depending on season and resources** | 유목민

As a prisoner of Ottoman Turks, the young girl was sold to an Arabic *nomad* and thus sentenced to serve the wandering man until death.

**WO** nomad : abode [əbóud]

nomad에게는 일정한 abode(주거지)가 없다.

## numb
[nʌm]

**adj. without any sensation; apathetic or indifferent** | 감각을 잃은, 무감각한

**v. to make unresponsive or insensitive** | 감각을 잃게하다, 마비시키다

The dentist used a drug to make the patient's mouth *numb* before extracting a tooth.

Alice didn't bother to *numb* her ear before she pierced it because everyone said it would not hurt.

**FUN** numb : anesthetic [æ̀nəsθétik]

anesthetic(마취제)의 기능은 수술할 부위를 numb하게 만드는 것이다.

---

### TRANSLATION | 예 문 해 석

**membrane** 식물과 동물의 세포들 속에는 세포핵을 보호하고, 드나드는 물질들을 걸러내기 위한 세포막이 있다.
**momentous** 많은 십 대들에게, 그들이 고등학교를 졸업하는 날은 중요한 날이다.
**nomad** 오스만 투르크족의 죄수였던 그 어린 소녀는 아랍 유목민에게 팔려 가서 평생 방랑자의 시중을 들게 되었다.
**numb** 그 치과 의사는 치아를 뽑기 전에 환자의 입을 무감각하게 만들기 위해 약물을 사용했다.
모든 사람들이 아프지 않을 거라고 했기 때문에, Alice는 귀를 뚫기 전에 마취하는 수고를 겪지 않았다.

## paltry
[pɔ́:ltri]

**adj. small or meager; despicable** | (금액이) 얼마 안 되는, 하찮은

The laborer received a *paltry* wage for his week's work, barely enough to feed his small family.

**ANT** paltry : significant [signífikənt]

significant: 상당한, 중요한

## premeditate
[pri:médətèit]

**v. to plan or consider in advance** | 미리 계획하거나 고려하다

Sentencing is more severe for convicted individuals who *premeditate* their crimes because the planning implies cruelty.

**ANT** premeditated : offhand [ɔ́:fhǽnd]

premeditated: 미리 계획된

offhand: 즉석에서, 사전 준비 없이

## remiss
[rimís]

**adj. negligent or careless in the performance of one's duties or responsibilities** | (직무나 책임에) 태만한, 부주의한

The employee was reprimanded for being *remiss* and forgetting to lock the office.

**SYN** remiss : indolent [índələnt]

indolent: 게으른, 나태한

## ruminate
[rú:mənèit]

**v. to think over repeatedly** | 깊이 생각하다

Tim grew restless as he *ruminated* over whether or not to accept the job offer.

**ANT** ruminative : unreflective [ʌ̀nrifléktiv]

ruminative: 깊이 생각하는

unreflective: 경솔한

## salubrious
[səlú:briəs]

**adj. promoting or favorable to health** | 건강에 좋은, 유익한

A short workout every morning is a *salubrious* daily routine.

**ANT** salubrious : baneful [béinfəl]

baneful: 해로운

---

### TRANSLATION | 예문 해석

**paltry** 그 노동자는 노동의 대가로 몇 명의 식구들을 먹이기도 힘들만큼 적은 주급을 받았다.
**premeditate** 범죄를 미리 계획한다는 것은 잔인성을 암시하기 때문에 그런 범죄자들은 더 엄한 판결을 받는다.
**remiss** 그 종업원은 근무에 태만했고, 사무실의 자물쇠를 채우는 것을 잊어버렸다는 이유로 질책을 받았다.
**ruminate** Tim은 일자리를 제의받고 이의 수락 여부를 깊이 생각할수록 점점 불안해졌다.
**salubrious** 아침마다 하는 달리기나 다른 운동은 건강에 좋은 습관이다.

## salve
[sæv]

n. **a medical ointment** | 연고

v. **to soothe or cure** | 완화하다, 치료하다

The veterinarian put a *salve* on the animal's wound to alleviate the pain.

After sitting in the sun for some time, Jimmy had to *salve* himself with aloe in order to lessen the discomfort from the sunburn.

> **CH** salve : unctuous [ʌ́ŋktʃuəs]
> salve는 unctuous(기름기 있는)한 특징이 있다.

## solvent
[sάlvənt]

adj. **able to pay all legal debts** | 지불능력이 있는

n. **a substance capable of dissolving another substance** | 용매

The gifted businessman managed to keep his company *solvent* throughout the long economic recession.

Many housewives use bleach as a *solvent* to get rid of stains around the house.

> **ANT** solvent : bankrupt [bǽŋkrʌpt]
> bankrupt: 지급 불능의, 파산자

## somber
[sάmbər]

adj. **dark colored; depressed or serious in mood or character** | 칙칙한, 우울한

Kitty's mood became *somber* when the policeman pulled her over for speeding.

> **ANT** somber : droll [droul]
> droll: 익살스러운

## symbiotic
[sìmbaiάtik]

adj. **characterized by the coexistence of two different organisms that may benefit both parties** | 공생하는

A *symbiotic* relationship between two species develops over a long period of evolution.

> **CH** symbiosis : interdependent [ìntərdipéndənt]
> symbiosis(공생)하는 유기체들은 interdependent(상호의존적인)하다.

---

### TRANSLATION | 예문해석

**salve**
그 수의사는 그 동물의 고통을 덜어 주기 위해 상처에 연고를 발랐다.
잠시 동안 햇볕에 앉아 있은 후, Jimmy는 햇볕에 탄 피부의 통증을 알로에로 완화시켜야 했다.

**solvent**
그 재능있는 사업가는 용케 긴 불경기 동안 자신의 회사가 지불 능력이 있도록 유지했다.
많은 주부들이 집안의 얼룩을 제거하기 위해 표백제를 용매로 사용한다.

**somber**
경찰이 속도위반으로 차를 세우게 했을 때 Kitty의 기분은 우울해졌다.

**symbiotic**
두 종 사이의 공생관계는 장기간에 걸친 진화에 의해 형성되었다.

## temerity
[təmérəti]

**n. foolish boldness; recklessness** | 무모함, 만용

Alicia's *temerity* led her to scream at her boss.

**WO** temerity : timorous [tímərəs]

timorous(소심한, 겁많은)한 사람은 temerity가 전혀 없다.

## vim
[vim]

**n. a large amount of energy and vitality** | 기력, 활기

The old grandmother was so full of *vim* and vigor that she tired out her grandchildren with her play.

**ANT** vim : lassitude [lǽsətjùːd]

lassitude: 무기력, 피로

## voluble
[váljubl]

**adj. marked by knowledgeable and rapid speech** | 유창한, 달변의

Laura is *voluble* in her protestations, especially when discussing environmental issues.

**ANT** voluble : reticent [rétəsənt]

reticent: 과묵한

## voluminous
[vəlúːmənəs]

**adj. having great volume, size, or number** | 부피가 큰, 대형의, 많은

Sharon's look of resignation indicated she had given up searching for her sister in the *voluminous* crowd.

**ANT** voluminous : scanty [skǽnti]

scanty: 부족한

## voluptuary
[vəlʌ́ptʃuèri]

**n. a person addicted to luxury and sensual pleasures** | 쾌락을 좇는 사람, 방탕한 사람

Bernice was a true *voluptuary* who enjoyed regular gourmet meals and weekend spa getaways.

**ANT** voluptuous : ascetic [əsétik]

voluptuous: 방탕한, 관능적인

ascetic: 금욕적인

---

TRANSLATION | 예문 해석

| | |
|---|---|
| temerity | Alicia는 얼마나 무모한지 상사를 향해 소리를 질러댔다. |
| vim | 나이든 할머니는 활기와 생기로 차 있어서, 같이 놀았던 손자 손녀들을 지치게 만들었다. |
| voluble | Laura는 이의를 제기할 때, 특히 환경 문제를 논의할 때는 유창하다. |
| voluminous | Sharon의 체념한 표정은 그녀가 수 많은 사람들 중에 자기의 동생을 찾는 것을 포기했음을 나타낸다. |
| voluptuary | Bernice는 정기적으로 미식을 즐기고 주말마다 온천 휴양지를 찾는 진정한 쾌락주의자였다. |

## wan
[wɑn]

**adj. unnaturally pale; lacking strength or vigor**
| 핏기 없는, 힘 없는

The doctor's pale and *wan* face indicated that his 36 hour shift ran too long.

**ANT** wan : rubicund [rúːbikʌnd]

rubicund: 혈색이 좋은

## wander
[wǽndər]

**v. to roam aimlessly; to go astray**
| 정처없이 돌아다니다; 탈선하다

They had permitted him to freely *wander* about the prison.

**SYN** wander : drift [drift]

drift: 방랑하다, 표류하다

## wane
[wein]

**v. to weaken or lessen in size; to diminish**
| 약해지다, 작아지다, 감소하다

The heat of the sun had begun to *wane*, but the air was filled with a pink brightness.

**ANT** wane : intensify [inténsəfài]

intensify: 격렬해지다

## windbag
[wíndbæg]

**n. a talkative person who says nothing important**
| 쓸데없는 이야기만 늘어놓는 사람, 수다쟁이

Nobody pays attention to that old *windbag* because he talks incessantly about the weather.

**CH** windbag : verbosity [vəːrbάsəti]

windbag은 verbosity(수다)를 즐겨 하는 사람이다.

---

### TRANSLATION | 예 문 해 석

| | |
|---|---|
| wan | 그 의사의 창백한 얼굴은 36시간의 교대 근무가 너무 긴 것이라는 사실을 잘 말해준다. |
| wander | 그들은 그가 자유롭게 교도소 안을 걸어다니도록 허용했었다. |
| wane | 태양의 열기가 약해지자, 대기는 밝은 핑크빛으로 가득 찼다. |
| windbag | 그 나이든 수다쟁이는 끊임없이 날씨 이야기를 했기 때문에 아무도 그에게 관심을 기울이지 않았다. |

# 21st Day Daily Check Up

■ Fill in the blanks with the correct letter that matches the word with its definition.

1. membrane _____
2. immanent _____
3. foment _____
4. solvent _____
5. congruent _____
6. paltry _____
7. deluge _____
8. remiss _____
9. confirm _____
10. temerity _____

a. to stir up trouble or enhance the development of something
b. small or meager; despicable
c. only existing in the mind
d. being negligent in one's duties or responsibilities
e. to make certain or attest to the truth; to make valid by a legal act
f. able to pay all legal debts
g. a great flow; a heavy downpour; an overwhelming amount or number
h. foolish boldness; recklessness
i. a thin layer covering living tissue; cell membrane
j. being in agreement or harmony; in geometry, exactly the same in shape and size

■ Put the correct word in each blank from the list of words below.

11. _____에게는 일정한 abode가 없다.
12. _____는 verbosity를 즐겨 하는 사람이다.
13. _____하는 유기체들은 interdependent 하다.
14. _____은 draconic(엄격한)의 반의어이다.
15. disrespect(불경)의 반의어는 _____이다.
16. _____는 eminence를 가지고 있다.
17. reticent(과묵한)의 반의어는 _____이다.
18. noisome(해로운)의 반의어는 _____이다.
19. _____는 미래에 까지 영향을 미치므로 important보다 더 중요한 것을 묘사할 때 사용된다.
20. falsehood는 타인을 _____하는 데 이용된다.

a. voluble  b. symbiosis  c. windbag  d. symbiotic  e. calumniate  f. beneficial
g. congenial  h. momentous  i. voluminous  j. luminary  k. nomad  l. homage

**Answer key**

1. i   2. c   3. a   4. f   5. j   6. b   7. g   8. d   9. e   10. h
11. k   12. c   13. b   14. g   15. l   16. j   17. a   18. f   19. h   20. e

# TAKE A BREAK

재미로 보는 심리학

**플라세보 효과**

플라세보 효과란 약효가 전혀 없는 거짓 약을 진짜 약으로 가장, 환자에게 복용토록 했을 때 환자의 병세가 호전되는 효과를 말하고, 위약 효과라고도 불린다. 이는 제2차 세계 대전 중 약이 부족할 때 많이 쓰였던 방법이다. 2007년 미국국립보건원 실험 결과, 수면제를 먹고 평소보다 쉽게 잠드는 것은 효능과 관계없이 약을 복용했다는 사실만으로 심리적 안정을 느끼는 '플라세보 효과'라는 게 밝혀졌다. 드문 경우이긴 하지만 암을 고친 사례도 있다고 한다.

플라세보 효과의 문제점은 이것이 의사들의 기만행위나, 사이비 종교로 이어지기 쉽다는 것이다. 효과를 과대 포장하고 자기 암시를 주고 이것을 종교화할 경우 위험한 상황이 만들어질 수도 있다. 플라세보 효과가 의료에서 가지는 가장 큰 문제는 재현이 불가능하다는 것이다. 현대 의학이 성립 가능한 이유는 A라는 환자에게 B라는 약을 주면 C만큼의 결과가 기대된다는 것이라고 할 수 있는데, 플라세보 효과는 C의 결과를 예측할 수 없다는 문제를 가지고 있다.

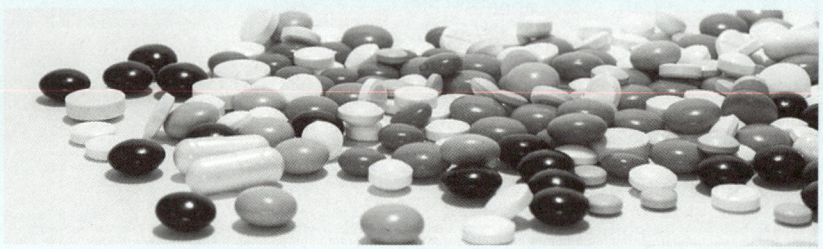

쉬•어•가•는 페•이•지

## 불면증의 원인

불면증은 수면을 이루지 못하는 수면장애 증세를 말한다. 적어도 1개월 이상 잠들기가 어렵거나, 잠이 들더라도 자주 깨는 일이 일주일 기준 3회 이상이 나타나면 불면증이라고 할 수 있다. 물론 이런 이유로 낮 시간 동안 매우 피곤함을 호소하거나 수면 부족으로 인한 장애들이 나타나야 불면증이다. 불면증이 습관성으로 나타나면 몸에 해로운 영향을 가져올 수 있는데, 만성 불면증은 뇌의 장애와 자율신경 및 내분비의 이상, 두통 등의 신체적 고통, 정신병 등을 가져올 수 있다. 가벼운 불면증은 커피나 홍차 등의 카페인을 많이 섭취한 경우나, 각성제나 비타민 등의 약제를 사용한 경우, 환경의 변화나 스트레스 등으로 인해 찾아올 수 있다.

또 다른 불면증의 원인으로는 수면에 대한 비합리적 신념을 들 수 있다. 예를 들면 '하루에 10시간 이상은 자야 한다' 는 수면에 대한 비합리적 신념을 갖고 있는 사람이 수면에 대한 결핍을 느낄 경우, 낮잠을 자거나 늦게까지 침대에 깨어 있는 채로 누워 있는 등 부적절한 대처 행동을 하게 되는 것이다. 결국 수면에 대한 비합리적 신념을 교정하지 못하고 이러한 행동으로 이어지면, 비합리적 신념이 강화되고 그로 인해 불면증이 지속되는 악순환을 가져온다.

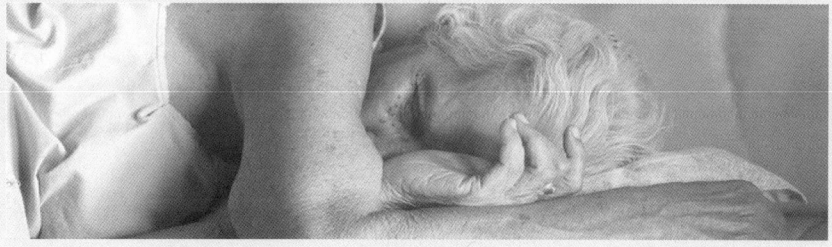

# SUPER VOCA

T.W.E.N.T.Y.S.E.C.O.N.D.D.A.Y

## 22ⁿᵈ DAY

밥숟갈을 놓느냐, 단어를 외우느냐 그것이 문제로다.

---

**admonish**
[ædmániʃ]

**v. to reprove gently but seriously** | 훈계하다, 타이르다

She softly *admonished* her husband for criticizing his brother's irresponsible lifestyle.

**DE** admonish : denounce [dináuns]

admonish는 denounce(비난하다)보다 약한 어감으로 온화하게 타이른다는 의미이다.

---

**arrhythmic**
[əríðmik]

**adj. lacking steady rhythm** | 규칙적인 리듬이 없는

Sandy brought the car to the mechanic because of an *arrhythmic* sound in the engine.

**SYN** arrhythmic : erratic [irǽtik]

erratic: 일정하지 않은, 변덕스런

---

**brat**
[bræt]

**n. a spoiled, troublesome child** | 버릇없고 말썽을 일으키는 꼬마, 장난꾸러기

Karen loved her nieces, but she had to admit that they were *brats*.

**CH** brat : mischievous [místʃivəs]

brat은 mischievous(짓궂은)하다.

---

**bumptious**
[bʌ́mpʃəs]

**adj. offensively self-assertive** | 오만한

The *bumptious* student didn't have many friends because of his aggressive attitude.

**DE** bumptious : assertive [əsə́:rtiv]

지나치게 assertive(단정적인)한 사람은 bumptious하게 보인다.

---

| TRANSLATION | 예문해석 |
|---|---|
| admonish | 그녀는 동생의 무책임한 생활태도를 비난하는 남편을 부드러운 어조로 타일렀다. |
| arrhythmic | Sandy는 엔진에서 나오는 불규칙적인 리듬의 소리때문에 차를 정비소에 가지고 갔다. |
| brat | Karen은 그녀의 조카들을 사랑했지만, 그들이 말썽꾸러기라는 것은 인정해야만 했다. |
| bumptious | 그 오만한 학생은 공격적인 태도 때문에 친구가 별로 없었다. |

## command
[kəmǽnd]

**n. an order meant to be obeyed** | 명령

The admiral sent a *command* for the fleet of ships to anchor in the bay.

> **DE** command : entreaty [intríːti]
> command는 entreaty(간청)보다 강압적인 명령이다.

## commend
[kəménd]

**v. to praise** | 칭찬하다

The brave citizen was *commended* for saving a child from drowning.

> **DE** commend : esteem [istíːm]
> esteem(존경하다)은 commend보다 사람, 가치 등을 더 높게 평가하는 것이다.

## commodious
[kəmóudiəs]

**adj. comfortably spacious** | 넓은

The room was bright and *commodious*.

> **ANT** commodious : constricted [kənstríktid]
> constricted: 비좁은

## commonplace
[kámənplèis]

**adj. ordinary** | 평범한
**n. something that is common or frequent** | 공통적이거나 흔한 것

The enlightened students had evidently lost the power of doing and saying *commonplace* things.
All over Korea, it was *commonplace* to see fans wearing Red Devil shirts.

> **WO** commonplace : originality [ərìdʒənǽləti:]
> commonplace에는 originality(독창성)가 없다.

## commonsensical
[kàmənsénsikəl]

**adj. having a practical way of thinking** | 상식적인

The philosopher is the antithesis to the *commonsensical* person.

> **ANT** commonsensical : preposterous [pripástərəs]
> preposterous: 터무니없는

---

| TRANSLATION | 예 문 해 석 |
|---|---|
| command | 그 제독은 함대에게 만에 정박하라는 명령을 전달했다. |
| commend | 그 용감한 시민은 익사 직전의 어린이를 구출해내서 칭찬을 받았다. |
| commodious | 그 방은 밝고 널찍했다. |
| commonplace | 그 똑똑한 학생들은 평범한 일들을 말하고 행하는 능력을 상실했음이 분명했다. |
| | 한국 전역에 걸쳐 붉은 악마 티셔츠를 입는 팬들을 흔히 볼 수 있었다. |
| commonsensical | 철학자는 상식적인 사람과는 대조적이다. |

### commotion
[kəmóuʃən]

**n. a condition of excitement and confusion** | 동요, 소동

Curious upon hearing the *commotion* in the boss' office, Mina decided to investigate.

> **DE** commotion : squall [skwɔːl]
> squall(소동)은 commotion에 비해 작은 소동을 의미한다.

### comparable
[kámpərəbl]

**adj. equal in value to; similar** | 필적할 만한, 유사한

The atmosphere of Saturn is *comparable* to that of Jupiter.

> **ANT** comparable : disparate [díspərət]
> disparate: 확연히 구별되는, 완전히 다른

### compendious
[kəmpéndiəs]

**adj. characterized by concise expression** | (요점을 잘 잡아) 간결한

The professor's *compendious* remarks impressed the faculty board.

> **CH** compendious : encyclopedia [ensàikləpíːdiə]
> encyclopedia(백과사전)는 설명이나 묘사가 compendious하다는 특징을 가진다.

### complacence
[kəmpléisəns]

**n. contented satisfaction with oneself** | 자기만족, 자아도취

Steve's *complacence* infuriated his ambitious girlfriend and eventually resulted in their break-up.

> **WO** complacence : anxiety [æŋzáiəti]
> complacence를 가지고 있는 사람은 anxiety(고민, 불안)가 없다.

### complain
[kəmpléin]

**v. to express dissatisfaction or grief; to formally make a charge** | 불평하다, 고발하다

It is common for students to *complain* about their teachers.

> **DE** complain : carp [kɑːrp]
> carp(트집잡다)는 complain보다 강하게 불만을 표시하며 비판한다는 의미이다.

---

**TRANSLATION | 예문 해석**

**commotion** 상사의 사무실에서 소동이 벌어졌다는 얘기를 듣고 호기심이 생겨 Mina는 그 내막을 캐보기로 결심했다.
**comparable** 토성의 대기는 목성의 대기와 유사하다.
**compendious** 그 교수의 간결한 발언은 교수 위원회를 감동시켰다.
**complacence** Steve의 자기 도취적인 태도에 야망이 있는 여자 친구는 분노했으며 결국 두 사람은 갈라섰다.
**complain** 학생들은 흔히 선생님들에 대해 불평한다.

## complexity
[kəmpléksəti]

**n. the quality of being intricate; that which is complicated** | 복잡성, 복잡한 것

The *complexity* of life and the universe baffles the human mind.

**POS** complexity : convoluted [kánvəlù:tid]

convoluted: 복잡한

## compliment
[kámpləmənt]

**n. a positive expression of admiration or praise** | 칭찬

The gentleman's *compliment* was well received by the elegant lady.

**ANT** compliment : invective [invéktiv]

invective: 비난, 독설

## compose
[kəmpóuz]

**v. to calm or tranquilize; to form** | 차분하게 하다, 구성하다

It is imperative that emergency responders remain *composed* during a crisis situation.

**ANT** composed : distraught [distrɔ́:t]

composed: 침착한, 차분한

distraught: 정신이 혼란한, 미친

## comprehend
[kàmprihénd]

**v. to understand the meaning or significance of** | 이해하다

Cossette at first did not *comprehend* what the old woman was trying to tell her.

**CN** comprehend : ambiguous [æmbígjuəs]

ambiguous(애매한)한 것은 comprehend하기 힘들다.

---

**TRANSLATION** | 예문해석

| | |
|---|---|
| complexity | 인생과 우주의 복잡성 때문에 인간은 마음이 편할 날이 없다. |
| compliment | 그 귀부인은 신사의 칭찬에 흡족해했다. |
| compose | 위기 상황에서는 비상 전화 상담자들이 차분한 마음을 유지하는 것이 필수적이다. |
| comprehend | Cossette는 그 할머니가 자기에게 무슨 말을 하려고 하는지 처음엔 이해하지 못했다. |

**compress**
[kəmprés]

v. **to press together or compact** | 누르다, 압축하다

The best way to stop a nose bleed is to lean forward and *compress* the nose.

**FUN** compression : clamp [klæmp]

clamp(꺾쇠)는 단단히 compression(압축)하는 기능을 지닌 도구이다.

**compromise**
[kámprəmàiz]

n. **an agreement or settlement reached in which all parties benefit and lose some** | 상호간에 절충해서 이루어낸 타협

The two countries reached a *compromise* that would end the fighting.

**PUR** compromise : mediation [mìːdiéiʃən]

compromise를 이루기 위해서 mediation(중재)한다.

**compunction**
[kəmpʌ́ŋkʃən]

n. **a sense of distress resulting from guilt** | 양심의 가책

Cynthia had not the least *compunction* for what she had said.

**WO** compunction : unrepentant [ʌnripéntənt]

unrepentant(뉘우치지 않는)하는 사람은 compunction이 없다.

**conjecture**
[kəndʒéktʃər]

v. **to infer without evidence** | 어림짐작하다, 추측하다

Elinor could only *conjecture* about their relationship because her husband didn't talk about it much.

**SYN** conjecture : speculate [spékjulèit]

speculate: 추측하다, 숙고하다

**damp**
[dæmp]

adj. **wet; slightly moist** | 축축한

v. **to moisten** | 축축하게 하다

The morning dew left the ground *damp*.

Mike *damped* his handkerchief and wiped up the dust.

**DE** damp : soak [souk]

soak(푹 젖게 하다)은 damp에 비해 흠뻑 젖게 하다 라는 의미이다.

---

TRANSLATION | 예 문 해 석

compress  코피를 멈추게 하는 가장 좋은 방법은 코를 누르면서 몸을 앞으로 숙이는 것이다.
compromise  그 두 나라는 전투를 종결시킬 타협에 도달했다.
compunction  Cynthia는 자기가 한 말에 대해 털끝만큼의 가책도 느끼지 않았다.
conjecture  Elinor는 남편이 그들의 관계에 대해 별로 말해주지 않았기 때문에 어림짐작할 수 밖에 없었다.
damp  아침 이슬이 뜰 촉촉히 적셨다.
   Mike는 손수건을 살짝 적셔서 먼지를 닦아 냈다.

**dank**
[dæŋk]

adj. **unpleasantly wet and cool** | 축축하고 서늘한

The air was *dank* and stale in the cargo hold of the huge freighter.

POS　dank : moisture [mɔ́istʃər]
moisture: 습기, 수분

**denigrate**
[dénigrèit]

v. **to defame; to deny the value of** | 명예를 훼손하다, 무시하다

The coach *denigrated* the capabilities of the opposing team.

ANT　denigrate : honor [ánər]
honor: 존경하다, 영예를 주다

**denounce**
[dináuns]

v. **to openly declare as reprehensible** | 비난하다

Martin *denounced* the government for its tough new welfare policy.

DE　denounce : admonish [ædmániʃ]
denounce는 admonish(훈계하다, 타이르다)보다 강하게 질책하는 것이다.

**din**
[din]

n. **a loud and persistent noise** | 연속적인 큰 소음

The *din* of the party inhibited the neighbor's sleep.

SYN　din : clamor [klǽmər]
clamor: 외침, 소란

**enmity**
[énməti]

n. **hatred or animosity** | 적의, 증오

Ratcliffe did not think Carrington's *enmity* a thing to be overlooked.

ANT　enmity : concord [kánkɔːrd]
concord: 우호, 조화, 일치

---

TRANSLATION | 예문해석

| | |
|---|---|
| dank | 거대한 화물선 안의 선적 공간의 공기는 축축하고 퀴퀴했다. |
| denigrate | 그 감독은 상대팀의 전력을 무시했다. |
| denounce | Martin은 정부의 완강한 새 복지 정책을 공공연히 비난했다. |
| din | 시끄러운 파티 때문에 이웃집 사람들은 잠을 설쳤다. |
| enmity | Ratcliffe는 Carrington의 적의를 간과해서는 안 될 것으로 생각했다. |

## footloose
[fútlùːs]

**adj. having no attachments or ties; free to go as one pleases** | 속박 없는, 어디든 마음대로 갈 수 있는

The man had been *footloose* most of his life, but now felt he wanted to settle down.

**WO** footloose : attachment [ətǽtʃmənt]

footloose하다는 것은 attachment(부착물, 부속물)이 없다는 것을 의미한다.

## gargantuan
[gɑːrgǽntʃuən]

**adj. huge or massive in size** | 거대한, 크기가 엄청난

The *gargantuan* redwood trees in California are the biggest in the world, growing over 100 meters tall.

**DE** gargantuan : large [lɑːrdʒ]

gargantuan은 엄청나게 large(큰)의 의미를 가진다.

## genial
[dʒíːnjəl]

**adj. friendly and warm** | 상냥한, 온화한

Lyman seemed to be every man's friend, because his *genial* disposition even puts strangers at ease.

**ANT** genial : mordant [mɔ́ːrdənt]

mordant: 신랄한, 독설적인

## hamper
[hǽmpər]

**v. to hinder or disrupt** | 방해하다

Last minute work at the office *hampered* Billy's plan to get an early start on the weekend.

**ANT** hamper : facilitate [fəsílətèit]

facilitate: 촉진하다, 용이하게 하다

## hangdog
[hǽŋdɔ̀(ː)g]

**adj. dejected or depressed; feeling embarrassed over a guilty conscience** | 풀이 죽은, 좌절한, 죄의식을 느끼는

The boy left the classroom with a *hangdog* expression on his face when the teacher told him to go to the principal's office.

**ANT** hangdog : elated [iléitid]

elated: 의기양양한

---

### TRANSLATION | 예문해석

**footloose** 그는 자신의 일생의 대부분을 어디든 자유로이 다니며 살았지만 이제는 어딘가에 정착하고 싶다는 생각이 들었다.

**gargantuan** California의 거대한 삼나무들은 100미터 이상 자라서 세계에서 가장 크다.

**genial** 낯선이조차도 편안하게 만드는 온화한 성품때문에 Lyman은 모든 사람의 친구처럼 보였다.

**hamper** 직장에서 마지막 일거리는 주말을 일찍 시작하려고 했던 Billy의 계획을 방해했다.

**hangdog** 그 소년은 선생님이 교장실로 가라고 했을 때 풀죽은 표정으로 교실을 떠났다.

## hankering
[hǽŋkəriŋ]

**adj.** having a strong desire or yearning | 열망하는

Barney rummaged through the fridge to satisfy his *hankering* for a midnight snack.

**ANT** hankering : odious [óudiəs]

odious: 혐오하는

## hymn
[him]

**n.** a song of praise to God; a song or poem of praise or joy | 찬송가, 찬가

The Church *hymns* filled the air on that Sunday morning.

**CH** hymn : praise [preiz]

hymn은 praise(찬양, 찬미)의 노래이다.

## ignite
[ignáit]

**v.** to set on fire | 불을 붙이다

Richard *ignited* his match across the rough sandpaper.

**ANT** ignite : quench [kwentʃ]

quench: 불을 끄다

## immune
[imjúːn]

**adj.** free from or not susceptible to disease | 면역성을 지닌

Mike seems to be *immune* from illness because he never gets sick.

**PUR** immunity : vaccination [væksənéiʃən]

vaccination(예방 접종)의 목적은 병균에 대해 immunity(면역)를 가지게 하기 위한 것이다.

## immutable
[imjúːtəbl]

**adj.** unchangeable | 불변의

Physicists like to believe that their discipline defines the *immutable* laws of nature.

**WO** immutable : vicissitude [visísətjùːd]

immutable한 것에는 vicissitude(변화, 변천)가 없다.

---

### TRANSLATION | 예문해석

**hankering**  Barney는 한밤중에 간식이 너무 먹고 싶어서 냉장고를 뒤졌다.
**hymn**  그 주일 아침에 교회의 찬송가 소리가 하늘에 울려 퍼졌다.
**ignite**  Richard는 까끌까끌한 사포에 성냥을 그어 불을 피웠다.
**immune**  Mike는 결코 아프지 않기 때문에 병에 면역성을 갖고 있는 것 같다.
**immutable**  물리학자들은 자신들의 학문분야가 불변의 자연 법칙을 규정한다고 믿는다.

## jingoism
[dʒíŋgouìzm]

**n. strong nationalism and a hate for foreign countries**
| 호전적 애국주의

After the September 11th attacks, there was an excess of *jingoism* in America.

**대상** jingoism : nation [néiʃən]

jingoism은 자신의 nation(국가)에 대한 지나친 우월감을 표출하는 것이다.
cf) chauvinism(맹목적 애국주의)이 타국에 대한 적개심으로 강화된 것이 jingoism이다.

## languid
[læŋgwid]

**adj. with minimal energy or excitement; listless**
| 열의 없는, 기운 없는, 노곤한

Barry's *languid* expression belied the excitement he felt inside.

**WO** languid : energy [énərdʒi]

languid한 사람은 energy가 없다.

## leniency
[líːniənsi]

**n. a merciful or tolerant disposition or practice**
| 관대함

On occasion, the teacher exhibited *leniency* for her students' misbehavior, but usually she was very strict and quick to punish.

**WO** leniency : martinet [màːrtənét]

martinet(엄격한 사람, 규율가)에게서는 leniency를 찾아보기 힘들다.

## link
[liŋk]

**n. a single connecting structure in a series; a relationship; connecting factor**
| 연결고리, 연관, 연결된 요소

Research has clearly established a *link* between cigarette smoking and lung cancer.

**PAR** link : chain [tʃein]

link가 모여서 chain이 된다.

## longing
[lɔ́(ː)ŋiŋ]

**n. a strong desire or emotional need; yearning**
| 갈망, 동경

Miguel was full of *longing* for his girlfriend far away.

**POS** longing : pine [pain]

pine: 갈망하다

---

**TRANSLATION | 예 문 해 석**

**jingoism** 9.11 사건 이후 미국에는 호전적 애국주의가 팽배해 있었다.
**languid** Barry의 노곤한 표정은 그가 마음속으로 느낀 흥분을 감추었다.
**leniency** 그 여선생님은 때로는 학생들의 나쁜 행동을 관대하게 넘어가지만, 보통 매우 엄격하고 주저 없이 벌을 줬다.
**link** 연구 결과가 흡연과 폐암사이의 연결고리를 분명히 확증했다.
**longing** Miguel은 먼곳에 있는 여자 친구가 몹시 그리웠다.

## mangy [méindʒi]

**adj.** having blotches or bare spots on the skin; sordid
| 옴이 오른, 지저분한

Homeless people are *mangy* looking because they lack life's necessities.

**ANT** mangy : decorous [dékərəs]
decorous: 단정한

## mania [méiniə]

**n.** an excessively intense enthusiasm, interest, or desire
| 열광, 열중

Christmas shopping *mania* turns ordinary people into frenzied, desperate customers.

**DE** mania : enthusiasm [inθúːziæzm]
enthusiasm(열의, 열중)이 지나치면 mania가 된다.

## manifest [mǽnəfèst]

**n.** a list of cargo or passengers on a ship or airplane
| (항공기나 선박의) 화물 적하 목록, 승객 명단

**adj.** obvious
| 명백한

Any freight that is not listed on the *manifest* cannot be cleared through customs.

Kindness is *manifest* in humanity at Christmas time.

**FUN** manifest : cargo [káːrgou]
manifest에는 cargo(화물)의 목록이 적혀있다.

## manipulate [mənípjulèit]

**v.** to operate or control in a skillful manner; to control or change by deceitful means for a self-serving purpose
| 교묘하게 다루다, 자신에게 유리하도록 조작하다

The tax broker *manipulated* his accounts in order to pocket some of the money.

**CH** manipulate : dexterous [dékstərəs]
manipulate하는 것에는 dexterous(솜씨 좋은, 교묘한)한 속성이 들어있다.

**ANT** manipulative : guileless [gáilis]
manipulative: 속임수의, 교묘하게 다루는
guileless: 정직한

---

TRANSLATION | 예문 해석

| | |
|---|---|
| mangy | 집없는 사람들은 생활필수품을 갖추고 있지 못해 지저분한 모습을 하고 있다. |
| mania | 크리스마스의 쇼핑 열기는 평범한 사람들을 광적이고 필사적인 소비자로 바꿔놓는다. |
| manifest | 적하 목록에 기재되어 있지 않은 화물은 세관을 통과할 수 없다. |
| | 성탄절에는 누구나 확실히 친절해진다. |
| manipulate | 그 세금 중개인은 자신의 장부를 조작해서 일부를 착복했다. |

## munificent
[mjuːnífəsnt]

**adj. very liberal or generous; lavish** | 후한, 아낌없이 주는

The chief offered me a *munificent* benefits package to stay with the company longer.

**ANT** munificent : parsimonious [pɑ̀ːrsəmóuniəs]

parsimonious: 인색한

## pompous
[pámpəs]

**adj. exhibiting self-importance or arrogance; bombastic** | 젠체하는, 허풍떠는

There is something very *pompous* in his style and mannerisms.

**CH** pompous : bombast [bámbæst]

bombast(호언장담)는 pompous한 특성이 있다.

## ramshackle
[rǽmʃæ̀kl]

**adj. poorly constructed or likely to fall down; being in disrepair** | 금방이라도 부서질 듯이 약하게 만들어진; 파손된

The *ramshackle* old vehicle sat rusting in the drive way.

**WO** ramshackle : soundness [sáundnis]

ramshackle한 차나 건물은 soundness(건실함)가 없다.

## remonstrance
[rimánstrəns]

**n. a formal statement that lists grievances; an expression of protest** | 진정서, 항의

The workers submitted a *remonstrance* listing the reasons for their dissatisfaction with management.

**CH** remonstrator : dissuade [diswéid]

remonstrator(항의자, 충고자)는 다른 사람을 dissuade(못하게 설득하다, 말리다)한다.

## remorse
[rimɔ́ːrs]

**n. a sincere, often painful sense of regret** | 후회, 뉘우침

I was full of *remorse* for having hurt my sister with my vicious criticism.

**SYN** remorse : rue [ruː]

rue: 후회

---

### TRANSLATION | 예문해석

| | |
|---|---|
| munificent | 사장님은 내가 회사에 더 오래 근무하도록 하기 위해 후한 수당을 제시했다. |
| pompous | 그의 태도와 말투 속에는 매우 거만한 구석이 있다. |
| ramshackle | 부서질 듯한 그 낡은 차량은 녹슨 채 개인 도로에 버려져 있었다. |
| remonstrance | 노동자들은 관리상의 불만족한 점들을 나열한 항의문을 제출했다. |
| remorse | 나는 누나에게 악의적인 비난을 함으로써 기분을 상하게 한 데 대해 깊이 뉘우쳤다. |

## remunerate
[rimjúːnərèit]

**v. to compensate** | 보상하다

The company will *remunerate* their traveling salesmen for any reasonable expenses incurred.

**ANT** remunerative : unrequited [ʌ̀nrikwáitid]
remunerative: 보상하는
unrequited: 보답 없는

## somnolence
[sámnələns]

**n. a state of sleepiness** | 졸림

The students were nearing *somnolence* due to the teacher's monotone voice.

**WO** somnolence : alert [ələ́ːrt]
alert(경계하는)한 사람은 쉽게 somnolence에 빠지지 않는다.

## stalk
[stɔːk]

**v. to observe and pursue someone out of derangement or obsession** | 정신 착란이나 집착으로 인해 어떤 사람을 관찰하거나 뒤쫓다

Stella suspected the man was *stalking* her because he regularly waited outside her office and walked behind her a few blocks.

**KIN** stalk : follow [fálou]
stalk는 부정적 의미의 follow(따르다)의 종류가 된다.

## summit
[sʌ́mit]

**n. the highest point or highest attainable level** | 최고점, 정점

Presley climbed to the *summit* of one of the hills.

**SYN** summit : apex [éipeks]
apex: 정점, 극치

## sumptuous
[sʌ́mptʃuəs]

**adj. luxurious or costly** | 호사스런, 고가의

The house had a very *sumptuous* appearance, so I knew I couldn't afford it.

**WO** sumptuous : sobriety [səbráiəti]
sumptuous한 생활에는 sobriety(절제)가 없다.

---

### TRANSLATION | 예 문 해 석

**remunerate** 그 회사는 순회하는 외판직원이 입은 합당한 손해액을 모두 보상할 것이다.
**somnolence** 학생들은 단조로운 선생님의 목소리로 인해 잠에 빠져들고 있었다.
**stalk** Stella는 그 남자가 정기적으로 사무실 밖에서 자신을 기다리고 몇 블록뒤에서 걸어왔기 때문에 자신을 뒤쫓는 것으로 의심했다.
**summit** Presley는 그 언덕들 중 하나의 정상에 올랐다.
**sumptuous** 그 집의 외관이 매우 호사스러웠기 때문에, 나는 그것을 살 형편이 안된다는 것을 깨달았다.

## sympathetic
[sìmpəθétik]

adj. **exhibiting compassion; being able to associate with and understand another's situation or position**
| 동정하는, 타인의 처지에 공감하는

Harry's *sympathetic* words demonstrated his understanding of his friends suffering.

**ANT** sympathetic : callous [kǽləs]

callous: 냉담한, 무감각한

## timorous
[tímərəs]

adj. **fearful or timid** | 겁많은, 소심한

Worried about the cat, the *timorous* mouse never scampered about the house for very long.

**WO** timorous : temerity [təmérəti]

timorous한 사람은 temerity(무모함, 만용)가 없다.

## tumult
[tjú:mʌlt]

n. **the disorderly noise of an excited crowd; mental or emotional agitation** | 소란, 소요, 정신적인 동요

The tiny earthquake left Paul in a *tumult* of fear and anxiety even though it hardly registered on the Richter Scale.

**ANT** tumult : serenity [sərénəti]

serenity: 고요함, 평온

---

### TRANSLATION | 예문 해석

| | |
|---|---|
| **sympathetic** | Harry는 동정어린 말을 함으로써 친구의 고통에 대한 이해를 표현했다. |
| **timorous** | 그 겁많은 쥐는 고양이가 무서워서 결코 집에서 오래 뛰어놀지 않았다. |
| **tumult** | 그 작은 지진은 라이터 지진계에도 기록되지 않을 정도였지만 Paul은 공포와 불안에 떨었다. |

# 22nd Day Daily Check-up

■ Fill in the blanks with the correct letter that matches the word with its definition.

1. jingoism _____
2. remonstrance _____
3. compendious _____
4. sympathetic _____
5. compliment _____
6. denigrate _____
7. munificent _____
8. commodious _____
9. hamper _____
10. dank _____

a. exhibiting compassion; being able to associate with and understand another's situation or position
b. strong nationalism
c. unpleasantly wet and cool
d. very liberal or generous; lavish
e. characterized by concise expression; comprehensive
f. a formal statement that lists grievances; an expression of protest
g. spacious and comfortable
h. to hinder or disrupt
i. a positive expression of admiration or praise
j. to defame; to deny the value of

■ Put the correct word in each blank from the list of words below.

11. unrepentant하는 사람은 _____ 이 없다.
12. _____ 를 이루기 위해서 mediation 한다.
13. decorous(단정한)의 반의어는 _____ 이다.
14. ambiguous한 것은 _____ 하기 힘들다.
15. rue(후회)의 동의어는 _____ 이다.
16. enthusiasm이 지나치면 _____ 가 된다.
17. _____ 은 clamor(소란)의 동의어이다.
18. 지나치게 assertive한 사람은 _____ 하게 보인다.
19. _____ 한 사람은 temerity가 없다.
20. vaccination의 목적은 병균에 대해 _____ 를 가지게 하는 것이다.

a. remorse   b. comprehend   c. hangdog   d. mania   e. timorous   f. immunity
g. compunction   h. din   i. mangy   j. bumptious   k. compromise   l. sumptuous

**Answer key**

1. b  2. f  3. e  4. a  5. i  6. j  7. d  8. g  9. h  10. c
11. g  12. k  13. j  14. b  15. a  16. d  17. h  18. j  19. e  20. f

# SUPER VOCA

## 23rd DAY

비가와도, 태풍이 몰아쳐도, 어떠한 어려움이 있어도 우리의 단어여행은 계속됩니다. 쭈욱~

---

**acrimonious**
[ækrəmóuniəs]

adj. **bitter and caustic** | 모진, 신랄한

The memory of my parents' *acrimonious* divorce made me fear marriage for a long time.

- **WO** acrimonious : goodwill [gúdwil]
  acrimonious한 것은 goodwill(호의)가 없다.

---

**apocalypse**
[əpákəlìps]

n. **a prophetic revelation, usually concerning the end of the world** | (세계 종말에 대한) 묵시, 계시

According to environmentalists, a sharp rise in global temperatures could portend an *apocalypse*.

- **SYN** apocalyptic : prophetic [prəfétik]
  apocalyptic: 묵시의, 예언적인
  prophetic: 예언의

---

**bare**
[bɛər]

adj. **nude or exposed; unadorned and simple** | 벗겨진, 노출된, 있는 그대로의

Telling the *bare* truth was easier than telling a complicated lie.

- **ANT** bare : occult [əkʌ́lt]
  occult: 숨겨진, 불가사의한

---

**berate**
[biréit]

v. **to scold or criticize severely** | 호되게 꾸짖다

The military unnecessarily *berates* its officers to instill blind obedience and devotion.

- **ANT** berate : laud [lɔːd]
  laud: 칭찬하다

---

### TRANSLATION | 예문 해석

**acrimonious** 부모님의 모진 이혼의 기억은 오랫동안 내가 결혼을 두려워하도록 만들었다.
**apocalypse** 환경 전문가들에 의하면 전 세계적인 기온의 급격한 상승은 종말의 전조일 수도 있다고 한다.
**bare** 있는 그대로를 말하는 것이 복잡한 거짓말을 하는 것보다 쉽다.
**berate** 군대는 장교들에게 맹목적인 복종과 헌신을 주입시키기 위해 불필요하게 꾸짖는다.

## canvass
[kǽnvəs]

*v.* to discuss or examine carefully with other people; to take a poll | 상세히 조사·검토하다, 여론 조사하다

The group *canvassed* the neighborhood to determine if it was a conservative or liberal area.

**CH** canvass : pollster [póulstər]

pollster(여론조사원)는 canvass한다.

## circumlocution
[sə̀ːrkəmloukjúːʃən]

*n.* the use of an excessive quantity of words to express something | 쓸데없이 많은 단어를 사용해서 완곡하게 표현하는 것, 둘러대기

*Circumlocution* is usually a sign of nervousness or anxiety.

**CN** circumlocution : forthright [fɔ́ːrθràit]

circumlocution은 forthright(솔직한)하지 않다.

## circumscribe
[sə̀ːrkəmskráib]

*v.* to mark off or surround by a circle or boundary; to restrict | 경계를 긋다, 제한하다

The new law *circumscribed* the strength of unions by prohibiting strikes that lasted longer than a week.

**ANT** circumscribed : unlimited [ʌ̀nlímitid]

circumscribed: 제한된

unlimited: 무제한의, 끝없는

## circumspect
[sə́ːrkəmspèkt]

*adj.* cautious in considering all the possible consequences; prudent | 조심성있는, 신중한

To be *circumspect* is necessary in life if one is to live wisely.

**ANT** circumspect : rash [ræʃ]

rash: 경솔한

---

| TRANSLATION | 예 문 해 석 |
|---|---|
| canvass | 그 집단은 그곳이 보수적인 지역인지 개방적인 지역인지를 알아보기 위해 주민들을 상대로 여론조사를 했다. |
| circumlocution | 완곡한 표현은 대개 초조함이나 긴장감의 표시이다. |
| circumscribe | 그 새로운 법은 일주일 이상 지속되는 파업을 금지함으로써 노동조합의 세력을 제한했다. |
| circumspect | 인생을 현명하게 살려면 신중함이 반드시 필요하다. |

## circumvent
[sə́ːrkəmvént]

**v. to avoid; to go around** | 회피하다, 우회하다

Rather than finish his assignment, the student *circumvented* it with excuses.

**ANT** circumvent : confront [kənfrʌ́nt]

confront: 직면하다

## clog
[klɑg]

**v. to block or hinder; to become overfull** | 막다, 막히게 하다

The stream was *clogged* by debris from the landslide.

**WO** clog : drainage [dréinidʒ]

clog하게 되면 drainage(배수)가 되지 않는다.

## coagulant
[kouǽgjulənt]

**n. an agent which causes a liquid to thicken into a semisolid state** | 응고제

Corn starch is a *coagulant* used to make the sauce thicker.

**FUN** coagulant : thicken [θíkən]

coagulant는 액체를 thicken(진하게 하다)하는 기능이 있다.

## contradictory
[kɑ̀ntrədíktəri]

**adj. unable to both be true at the same time; opposing** | 모순된, 양립치 않는, 정반대의

It is *contradictory* to pursue peace and plan for war at the same time.

**CH** contradictory : oxymoron [ɑ̀ksimɔ́ːrɑn]

oxymoron(모순 어법)은 contradictory하다.

## contrite
[kəntráit]

**adj. feeling regret or sadness for having done wrong or caused harm** | 뉘우치는

Catherine offered a *contrite* apology for having torn her sister's favorite sweater.

**SYN** contrite : compunctious [kəmpʌ́ŋkʃəs]

compunctious: 뉘우치는, 후회하는

---

**TRANSLATION | 예문해석**

**circumvent** 그 학생은 숙제를 끝내려고 하기보다 변명으로 피하려고 했다.
**clog** 그 개울은 산사태로 인한 잔해물들로 막혔다.
**coagulant** 옥수수 전분은 소스를 걸쭉하게 만드는 데 쓰이는 응고제이다.
**contradictory** 평화를 추구하는 동시에 전쟁을 계획하는 것은 모순이다.
**contrite** Catherine은 언니가 가장 아끼는 스웨터를 찢은 것을 뉘우치며 사과했다.

## contumacious
[kəntjuméiʃəs]

**adj.** disobedient or rebellious | 순종하지 않는, 반항적인

The *contumacious* anarchists refused to register for the draft.

**ANT** contumacious : obedient [oʊbíːdiənt]

obedient: 순종하는, 고분고분한

## convention
[kənvénʃən]

**n.** a conference or meeting where people come to listen to lecturers; a social custom or rule of behavior | 집회, 관습, 전통

As Ray walked on with Verena, he asked her about the Women's *Convention*.

Cervantes' Don Quixote is a satire that pokes fun at the romantic chivalric *conventions* of 15th century Spain.

**ANT** conventional : eccentric [ikséntrik]

conventional: 틀에 박힌

eccentric: 전형에서 벗어난, 기묘한

## convert
[kənvə́ːrt]

**v.** to change from one belief or view to another; to alter the nature of | 개종 시키다, (성격을) 변화시키다

Due to the ardency and fervor of their belief, Muslims are almost impossible to *convert*.

**CH** convert : proselytizer [prásəlitàizər]

proselytizer는 convert할 목적으로 전도하는 사람, 전도사를 뜻한다.

## conviction
[kənvíkʃən]

**v.** a strong belief or opinion; the process or act of finding someone guilty of a crime, especially in a court | 확신, 신념, 유죄 판결

Hillary Clinton is a woman of strong political *convictions*.

**WO** conviction : dubious [djúːbiəs]

dubious(의심하는)한 사람은 conviction(확신)을 갖고 있지 않다.

---

| TRANSLATION | 예문해석 |
|---|---|
| contumacious | 그 반항적인 무정부주의자들은 징병을 거부했다. |
| convention | Ray는 Verena와 함께 가면서 그녀에게 그 여성 집회에 관해 질문했다. |
| | 세르반테스의 돈키호테는 15세기 스페인의 낭만적 기사 전통을 비웃는 풍자이다. |
| convert | 이슬람교도들의 종교적 열정과 열의 때문에 그들을 개종시킨다는 것은 거의 불가능하다. |
| conviction | Hillary Clinton은 강한 정치적 신념을 가진 여성이다. |

## convince
[kənvíns]

**v. to make someone believe that something is true**
| 확신시키다, 납득시키다

Ma'am Bougon was *convinced* that Marius was an accomplice to the robbery the night before.

**CH**  convince : cogent [kóudʒənt]

cogent(설득력 있는)한 것은 convince하는 속성을 지닌다.

## convoluted
[kánvəlùːtid]

**adj. twisted or coiled; complex or hard to understand**
| 꼬인, 뒤엉킨, 복잡한

The human maze was so *convoluted* that the students couldn't find their way out.

**POS**  convoluted : complexity [kəmpléksəti]

complexity: 복잡성

## daredevil
[déərdèvəl]

**n. one who is recklessly bold or performs dangerous and potentially harmful stunts**
| 저돌적인 사람

The *daredevil* jumped off a 30 ft cliff with his bicycle into the river.

**WO**  daredevil : prudence [prúːdns]

daredevil에게는 prudence(신중함)가 없다.

## derelict
[dérəlikt]

**adj. abandoned, especially by the owner or occupant**
| 주인에게 버려져 유기된

**n. a person without a home or means of support**
| 집 없는 사람, 사회의 낙오자, 부랑자

The *derelict* warehouse was used as a playground by the neighborhood children.

The *derelict* pleaded with passing pedestrians for some spare change or a bite to eat.

**ANT**  derelict : pillar of society [pílər əv səsáiəti]

pillar of society: 사회의 중심 세력

---

**TRANSLATION | 예문해석**

| | |
|---|---|
| convince | Bougon마님은 Marius가 지난밤에 일어났던 강도사건의 공범이라고 확신했다. |
| convoluted | 그 미로는 복잡하게 꼬여 있었기 때문에 학생들이 출구를 찾을 수 없었다. |
| daredevil | 그 무모한 사람은 자전거를 타고 30피트 절벽 아래의 강으로 뛰어내렸다. |
| derelict | 그 버려진 창고는 이웃 어린이들의 놀이터로 이용되었다. |
| | 그 부랑자는 지나가는 사람들에게 동전이나 먹을 것을 구걸했다. |

## dire
[daiər]

**adj. terrible; desperately urgent** | 끔찍한, 절박한

With the economy in a *dire* situation, the unemployment rate was at its highest level since the Depression.

**ANT** dire : pleasant [plézənt]
pleasant: 유쾌한, 기분좋은

## dulcet
[dʌ́lsit]

**adj. extremely pleasant and melodious to the ear** | 듣기에 매우 즐겁고 감미로운

The *dulcet* voices of the children's choir filled the church sanctuary every Sunday.

**ANT** dulcet : cacophonous [kəkɑ́fənəs]
cacophonous: 귀에 거슬리는

## dune
[djuːn]

**n. a hill or ridge created by the wind** | 바람에 의해 만들어진 모래 언덕이나 산등성이

The sand *dunes* of the Egyptian desert appeared to go on forever.

**인과** dune : wind [wind]
dune은 wind(바람)에 의해 만들어진다.

## duration
[djuréiʃən]

**n. the time that something continues or exists; the quality of lasting** | 지속 기간, 내구성

The *duration* of the flight from Frankfurt to Seoul is eleven hours.

**대상** duration : curtail [kərtéil]
duration을 curtail(줄이다)하다.

## ennui
[ɑːnwíː]

**n. a feeling of boredom or dissatisfaction from lack of interest** | 권태, 지루함에서 비롯된 불만족

It was only to her closest friends that she acknowledged she was tortured by *ennui*.

**WO** ennui : enthusiastic [inθúːziæstik]
enthusiastic(열정적인)한 사람은 ennui를 느끼지 않는다.

---

### TRANSLATION | 예문해석

**dire** 경제가 암울한 상황에서 실업률은 대공황 이후 최고치에 달하고 있었다.
**dulcet** 감미로운 어린이 성가대의 목소리는 매주 일요일 교회를 가득 채웠다.
**dune** 이집트 사막의 모래 언덕들은 영원히 계속 존재할 것만 같다.
**duration** 프랑크푸르트에서 서울까지의 비행시간은 11시간이다.
**ennui** 그녀는 가장 친한 친구들에게만 권태로 인해 고통받는다고 고백했다.

## erode
[iróud]

**v. to wear or wash away** | 침식하다

With time, a small creek can *erode* even solid granite.

> **SYN** erode : corrode [kəróud]
> corrode: 침식하다, 부식하다

## erratic
[irǽtik]

**adj. having no fixed course or regular pattern; eccentric** | 일정하지 않은, 변덕스런, 별난

Over the past few years, the Aegean winter has become more and more *erratic*.

> **ANT** erratic : permanent [pə́:rmənənt]
> permanent: 불변의, 영속하는

## farce
[fɑ:rs]

**n. a light comic play filled with ridiculous situations** | 익살극

The entire evening was such a disastrous *farce*!

> **KIN** farce : performance [pərfɔ́:rməns]
> farce는 performance(공연)의 한 종류이다.

## forbid
[fərbíd]

**v. to hinder or prevent from** | 금지하다

The law *forbids* the sale or use of marijuana.

> **대상** forbidden : abstain [æbstéin]
> forbidden(금지된)된 것을 abstain(삼가다)하다.

## garble
[gɑ́:rbl]

**v. to distort, confuse, or mix up** | 왜곡하다, 내용을 잘못 전하다

The static *garbled* Leslies' phone conversation with her friend.

> **ANT** garble : elucidate [ilú:sədèit]
> elucidate: 명료하게 하다

---

### TRANSLATION | 예 문 해 석

| | |
|---|---|
| erode | 시간이 지나면 작은 시내가 단단한 화강암도 침식할 수 있다. |
| erratic | 지난 몇 해 동안 에게해의 겨울은 점점 변덕스러워 졌다. |
| farce | 그 저녁시간은 내내 그야말로 끔찍한 희극이었다! |
| forbid | 그 법은 마리화나의 매매 및 사용을 금지한다. |
| garble | 잡음으로 인해 Leslies는 친구와의 전화통화를 알아듣기 어려웠다. |

## genuine
[dʒénjuin]

**adj. authentic or true; honest or sincere** | 진짜의, 진품의, 진실한

The appraiser deemed the Monet to be *genuine*.

**ANT** genuine : spurious [spjúəriəs]
spurious: 가짜의, 위조의

## harebrained
[héərbrèind]

**adj. foolish and reckless** | 어리석은, 경망스러운

The *harebrained* man decided to dance in the public fountain in his underwear.

**SYN** harebrained : giddy [gídi]
giddy: 경솔한, 현기증 나는

## larder
[lá:rdər]

**n. the place where the food supply is stored** | 식료품 저장소

The *larder* for flour storage is the highest place in the house in order to keep out pests.

**FUN** larder : food [fu:d]
larder는 food(식품)를 보관하는 기능을 한다.

## manumit
[mænjumít]

**v. to free from slavery** | (노예 상태에서) 해방하다

As the Union army invaded the South, it *manumitted* all the plantation slaves it encountered.

**ANT** manumit : enslave [insléiv]
enslave: 노예로 만들다

## merchandise
[mə́:rtʃəndàiz]

**n. the items or goods sold in business** | 상품

Good *merchandise* at good prices can only be found at the markets.

**FUN** merchandise : warehouse [wéərhàus]
warehouse(창고)는 merchandise를 저장하는 저장소이다.

---

**TRANSLATION | 예문 해석**

| | |
|---|---|
| genuine | 감정가는 그 모네의 작품을 진품인 것으로 인정했다. |
| harebrained | 그 경망스런 남자는 속옷차림으로 분수대에서 춤을 추기로 결심했다. |
| larder | 밀가루를 보관하는 저장소는 해충들이 접근하지 못하도록 집에서 가장 높은 곳에 있다. |
| manumit | 연합군은 남부를 공격하면서 만나는 농장 노예들을 모두 해방시켰다. |
| merchandise | 저렴한 가격을 지닌 좋은 상품들은 시장에서만 찾아볼 수 있다. |

## minuscule
[mínəskjùːl]

**adj. very small** | 미소한

His handwriting was so *minuscule* that I could only read it with a magnifying glass.

ANT  minuscule : enormous [inɔ́ːrməs]
enormous: 거대한

## minute
adj. [mainjúːt]
n. [mínit]

**adj. very small** | 매우 작은
**n. 60 seconds** | 분

Investigators are trained to pick up on the *minutest* clues that criminals leave behind.

Minute after *minute*, her hunger gnawed at her.

ANT  minute : gargantuan [gɑːrgǽntʃuən]
gargantuan: 거대한

## moratorium
[mɔ̀ːrətɔ́ːriəm]

**n. a legally authorized delay of payment; a suspension of some activity considered to be bad** | 지불 유예, 일시적 정지

Due to unstable political conditions, the U.S. put a *moratorium* on all flights to Pakistan.

WO  moratorium : activity [æktívəti]
moratorium은 activity(활동)가 정지된 상태이다.

## mordant
[mɔ́ːrdənt]

**adj. biting or bitter in manner or style** | 신랄한, 독설적인

The movie received a *mordant* review.

ANT  mordant : genial [dʒíːnjəl]
genial: 상냥한, 온화한

## penurious
[pənjúəriəs]

**adj. very stingy; extremely poor** | 인색한, 빈곤한

The character Scrooge was the most *penurious* of men.

ANT  penurious : lavish [lǽviʃ]
lavish: 후한, 사치스런

---

TRANSLATION | 예문해석

| | |
|---|---|
| minuscule | 그의 글씨는 너무 작아서 돋보기로 봐야 읽을 수 있다. |
| minute | 수사관들은 범죄자들이 남긴 최소의 단서를 포착할 수 있도록 훈련받는다. |
| | 시간이 흐를수록 그녀는 배고픔으로 괴로워했다. |
| moratorium | 불안정한 정치상황 때문에 미국은 모든 파키스탄으로의 비행을 일시 중지시켰다. |
| mordant | 그 영화는 신랄한 비평을 받았다. |
| penurious | 스크루지란 인물은 가장 인색한 사람이었다. |

## perceive
[pərsíːv]

**v. to become aware of through the senses; to understand** | 감지하다, 이해하다

The way my friend and I *perceived* the movie was very different.

**CN** perceive : intangible [intǽndʒəbl]

intangible(감지할 수 없는, 실체가 없는)한 것은 **perceive**할 수 없다.

## plod
[plɑd]

**v. to walk heavily and slowly** | 터벅터벅 걷다

The young man *plodded* along the dark streets in silence to his house.

**KIN** plod : walk [wɔːk]

**plod**는 터벅터벅 walk(걷다)하는 라는 의미이다.

## probe
[proub]

**v. to investigate or examine** | 조사하다
**n. a penetrating inquiry or investigation** | 철저한 조사

The Senate *probed* the President about his involvement with Russian spies.

The *probe* uncovered fraud and bribery as an integral part of the company's dealings.

**SYN** probe : investigate [invéstəgèit]

investigate: 조사하다

## probity
[próubəti]

**n. integrity; honesty** | 청렴결백

The idea of *probity* in all financial dealings was deeply ingrained in him by his business class.

**ANT** probity : shiftiness [ʃíftinis]

shiftiness: 교활함, 믿을 수 없음, 부정직

---

TRANSLATION | 예 문 해 석

**perceive** 친구와 나의 영화감상법은 매우 차이가 있었다.
**plod** 그 젊은이는 어두운 거리를 조용히 터벅터벅 걸어서 자신의 집으로 갔다.
**probe** 상원에서는 대통령의 러시아 첩보원과의 연루 여부에 관해 조사했다.
회사를 임밀하게 조사한 결과 사기와 뇌물이 회사 거래상의 중요한 부분을 차지하고 있다는 것이 밝혀졌다.
**probity** 금전 거래상의 정직의 개념이 경영 수업에 의해 그의 마음속 깊이 아로새겨졌다.

## proclivity
[prouklívəti]

**n.** an inclination or tendency | 경향, 성향

Sam has a *proclivity* for drastic mood swings.

**ANT** proclivity : antipathy [æntípəθi]

antipathy: 반감, 혐오

## procure
[proukjúər]

**v.** to obtain or take possession of | 획득하다

During the will reading, Georgia *procured* many worthless personal effects of her late great aunt.

**ANT** procure : relinquish [rilíŋkwiʃ]

relinquish: 포기하다

## prod
[prɑd]

**v.** to incite into action with a pointed instrument; to urge or remind someone | 찌르다, 재촉하다

The cowboy *prodded* the cattle to get them moving.

**DE** prod : nudge [nʌdʒ]

nudge(살짝 찌르다)는 살짝 prod 하는 것이다.

## prodigal
[prɑ́digəl]

**adj.** recklessly wasteful with money | 방탕한

Larry was accused of being *prodigal* with company funds for expending a Lear jet for his daily commute.

**ANT** prodigality : husbandry [hʌ́zbəndri]

husbandry: 절약

## profane
[prəféin]

**adj.** debased; treating sacred things with contempt or disrespect | 불경스런, 신성을 더럽히는

Bildad had told them that no *profane* songs would be allowed on board the Pequod.

**ANT** profane : inviolate [inváiəlt]

inviolate: 신성한

---

### TRANSLATION | 예 문 해 석

| | |
|---|---|
| **proclivity** | Sam은 감정이 급격하게 변화하는 경향이 있다. |
| **procure** | 유서 낭독시에, Georgia는 돌아가신 이모 할머니에게서 쓸모없는 개인 물건들만 잔뜩 물려 받았다. |
| **prod** | 그 목동은 가축들이 움직이도록 막대기로 꾹꾹 찔렀다. |
| **prodigal** | Larry는 회사돈으로 개인 제트기를 타고 통근하는 방탕한 생활을 한 혐의를 받았다. |
| **profane** | Bildad는 그들에게 Pequod에 탑승한 후에는 불경스런 노래들을 불러서는 안된다고 말했다. |

## proffer
[práfər]

v. **to offer for acceptance** | 제공하다, 제출하다

The defense rejected the plea bargain *proffered* by the prosecution.

**ANT** proffer : retain [ritéin]
retain: 보유하다, 유지하다

## profligate
[prάfligət]

adj. **extravagant; dissolute** | 낭비하는, 방탕한
n. **one who is recklessly wasteful; a dissolute man** | 돈을 함부로 낭비하는 사람, 방탕아

The government officer was charged for *profligate* spending of the taxpayer's money.

The *profligate* could not control his credit spending and was mired in debt.

**대상** profligate : money [mʌ́ni]
profligate는 money(돈)을 함부로 낭비하는 이라는 의미이다.

## profuse
[prəfjúːs]

adj. **plentiful; generous** | 풍부한, 관대한

The garden had *profuse* blooms during the spring season.

**ANT** profuse : skimpy [skímpi]
skimpy: 부족한

## prohibit
[prouhíbit]

v. **to forbid by law; to prevent someone from having or doing something** | 법으로 금지하다, 방해하다

Laws *prohibiting* minors from drinking help protect their health.

**CH** prohibitive : veto [víːtou]
veto(거부권)는 prohibitive(금지하는)한 성격을 지닌다.

---

TRANSLATION | 예 문 해 석

**proffer** 피고측은 검찰이 제시한 유죄 답변 교섭을 거절했다.
**profligate** 그 정부관료는 납세자의 돈을 낭비했다는 혐의를 받았다.
그 방탕한 사람은 카드 사용을 조절하지 못해서 빚더미에 시달렸다.
**profuse** 정원에는 봄철 동안 많은 꽃이 피었다.
**prohibit** 미성년자의 음주를 금지하는 법은 그들의 건강을 보호하는 데 도움이 된다.

### puny
[pjúːni]

**adj. weak and small** | 작고 허약한

The *puny* landowner looked silly next to his tall and strong field worker.

**SYN** puny : weakly [wíːkli]

weakly: 허약한, 병약한

### riveting
[rívitiŋ]

**adj. engrossing one's attention; fascinating** | 매혹적인, 황홀하게 하는

The lecture on "The State of the Environment in East Asia" was far from *riveting*, and everyone left in the middle of it.

**ANT** riveting : vapid [væpid]

vapid: 지루한

### stodgy
[stádʒi]

**adj. boring or tedious** | 싫증나는, 지루한

Living in a small town becomes *stodgy* and predictable for most people.

**SYN** stodgy : dull [dʌl]

dull: 지루한

### stoic
[stóuik]

**adj. showing little or no feelings; dispassionated** | 금욕적인, 냉정한

**n. one apparently unaffected by pleasure or pain** | 금욕주의자

The *stoic* look on Jeanie's face masked the disappointment she felt when passed over for the promotion.

Alex's indifferent attitude towards everything caused people to refer to him as a *stoic*.

**CN** stoic : perturb [pərtə́ːrb]

stoic(금욕적인)한 사람은 쉽게 perturb(동요시키다)시킬 수 없다.

---

**TRANSLATION | 예문해석**

**puny**   그 왜소한 지주가 키가 크고 힘이 센 자기 일꾼 옆에 서자 바보처럼 보였다.
**riveting**   동 아시아의 환경 상황에 대한 강연은 매혹적인 것과는 거리가 멀었고 모든 사람들이 중간에 자리를 떴다.
**stodgy**   작은 마을에서의 삶은 대부분의 사람들에게 있어 쉽게 지루하고 뻔한 것이 된다.
**stoic**   Jeanie는 냉담한 표정을 지음으로써 승진에서 제외된 데에서 느끼는 실망감을 감췄다.
Alex는 만사에 무심한 태도를 보였기 때문에 사람들은 그를 금욕주의자라고 불렀다.

## unobtrusive
[ʌ̀nəbtrúːsiv]

**adj. not obtrusive or blatant; inconspicuous**
| 나서지 않는, 조심성 있는

Catherine was soothed and calmed by his simple and *unobtrusive* demeanor.

**ANT**  unobtrusive : blatant [bléitənt]

blatant: 뻔뻔스런, 노골적인

## variegate
[vɛ́əriəgèit]

**v. to make varied and diverse**   | 변화를 주다, 다양하게 하다

*Variegating* the menu brought in more new customers than the manager expected.

**SYN**  variegate : vary [vɛ́əri]

vary: 변화를 주다, 다양하게 하다

---

| TRANSLATION | 예 문 해 석 |
|---|---|
| unobtrusive | Catherine은 그의 단순하고 조심스런 처신에 안정을 되찾고 조용해졌다. |
| variegate | 메뉴를 다양하게 만든 것은 매니저가 기대했던 것보다 많은 손님을 끌어 들이게 했다 |

# 23rd Day Daily Check-up

■ Fill in the blanks with the correct letter that matches the word with its definition.

1. canvass _____     a. a person without a home or means of support
2. probity _____     b. to avoid; to go around
3. penurious _____   c. recklessly wasteful with money
4. convict _____     d. weak and small
5. puny _____        e. to free from slavery
6. mordant _____     f. integrity; honesty
7. circumvent _____  g. to discuss or examine carefully with other people; to take a poll
8. prodigal _____    h. extremely frugal; hating to spend money
9. derelict _____    i. to declare or prove someone guilty, especially in a court
10. manumit _____    j. biting or bitter in manner or style

■ Put the correct word in each blank from the list of words below.

11. _____는 investigate(조사하다)의 동의어이다.
12. _____는 food를 보관하는 기능을 한다.
13. _____에는 forthright가 없다.
14. _____된 것은 clarity가 없다.
15. dull(지루한)은 _____의 동의어이다.
16. unlimited(제한이 없는)의 반의어는 _____이다.
17. genial(온화한)의 반의어는 _____이다.
18. _____는 antipathy(성미에 맞지 않음)의 반의어이다.
19. _____ 상태가 되면 drainage가 되지 않는다.
20. _____에게는 prudence가 없다.

| a. proclivity | b. garbled | c. stodgy | d. mordant | e. probe | f. circumscribed |
| g. daredevil | h. larder | i. clog | j. proffer | k. circumlocution | l. unobtrusive |

Answer key

1. g   2. f   3. h   4. i   5. d   6. j   7. b   8. c   9. a   10. e
11. e  12. h  13. k  14. b  15. c  16. f  17. d  18. a  19. i  20. g

www.goHackers.com

해커스 어학연구소

# SUPER VOCA

T.W.E.N.T.Y.F.O.U.R.T.H D.A.Y

## 24th DAY

여러분, 단어와 함께 영어를 잘하겠단 꿈은 반드시 이루어집니다! Dreams come true!

---

**abridge**
[əbrídʒ]

v. **to shorten or condense, especially written works**
| (책 등을) 요약하다

The *abridged* version of Lonesome Dove is available for people who don't have the time to read it in its entirety.

대상  abridge : length [leŋkθ]
abridge는 length(길이)를 줄이는 것이다.

---

**acrid**
[ǽkrid]

adj. **having an irritatingly pungent or harsh taste or odor**
| 맛이나 향이 불쾌하도록 자극적인

The *acrid* smell of rotting garbage is revolting.

ANT  acrid : savory [séivəri]
savory: 맛있는, 향긋한

---

**agonize**
[ǽgənàiz]

v. **to suffer in agony or torture; to suffer great emotional, mental or physical pain**
| 몹시 괴로워하다, (심리적·정신적·육체적) 고통을 겪다

It is *agonizing* to see my clients remain in jail when they are innocent.

DE  agonized : distressed [distrést]
agonized(고통스러운)된 것은 distressed(괴로워하는)된 것 보다 괴로움이 더 심하다.

---

### TRANSLATION | 예 문 해 석

| | |
|---|---|
| **abridge** | Lonesome Dove의 요약판은 책 전체를 읽을 시간적 여유가 없는 사람들에게 도움이 된다. |
| **acrid** | 썩는 쓰레기에서 나는 악취는 비위를 상하게 한다. |
| **agonize** | 나의 의뢰인들이 무죄임에도 불구하고 계속 교도소에 갇혀 있음을 보는 것은 몹시 가슴 아픈 일이다. |

## aloof
[əlúːf]

**adj. reserved and remote; indifferent**
| 서먹서먹한, 무관심한, 냉담한

The man remained *aloof* and refused to participate in the party games.

**ANT** aloof : gregarious [grigέəriəs]
gregarious: 사교적인

## amorphous
[əmɔ́ːrfəs]

**adj. lacking shape or form; lacking organization**
| 형태가 없는, 조직이 없는

Gene could not appreciate the *amorphous* mass of clay as abstract art.

**WO** amorphous : conformation [kὰnfɔːrméiʃən]
amorphous한 것에는 conformation(형태, 구조)이 없다.

## anecdote
[ǽnikdòut]

**n. a short and humorous narrative about one's own experiences**
| 일화

Matthew, a journalist from Dublin, always has great *anecdotes* to share with his friends.

**CH** anecdote : amusement [əmjúːzmənt]
anecdote는 amusement(즐거움)를 주는 짧은 경험담이다.

## anomalous
[ənάmələs]

**adj. irregular or differing from the norm**
| 변칙적인, 특이한

The regulators recognized that events like the Enron bankruptcy are relatively *anomalous* in a well-functioning economy.

**ANT** anomalous : typical [típikəl]
typical: 전형적인

## apologize
[əpάlədʒàiz]

**v. to express regret for a faulty action or behavior; to make a formal defense or justification**
| 사과하다, 변명하다, 해명하다

I am sorry it happened, and now I publicly *apologize* for what I did.

**인과** apologize : contrite [kəntráit]
contrite(뉘우치는)하면 apologize한다.

---

### TRANSLATION | 예문 해석

**aloof** 그 남자는 무관심해서 파티 게임에 참여하는 것도 거절했다.
**amorphous** Gene은 형태없는 진흙덩어리를 추상 미술로서 감상할 수 없었다.
**anecdote** Dublin 출신의 언론인인 Matthew는 친구들에게 들려줄 굉장한 일화들을 많이 알고 있다.
**anomalous** 조정자들은 원활한 경제 체제에서의 Enron사의 파산과 같은 사건들을 비교적 이례적인 것으로 여긴다
**apologize** 나는 그런 일이 일어난 것을 유감으로 생각하며 이제 공개적으로 내 행동을 사과한다.

## apoplectic
[æ̀pəplέktik]

**adj. extremely and noticeably angry; furious** | 몹시 화가 난

Sheila was *apoplectic* with rage over the salesperson's comment about her waist size.

**ANT** apoplectic : calm [kɑ:m]

calm: 차분한

## arrest
[ərést]

**v. to take into custody by legal authority; to catch someone's attention; to make inactive** | 체포하다, 주의를 끌다, (진행·성장 등을) 저지하다

Three men were *arrested* for the bank robbery.

My attention was *arrested* by the mime performing on the street.

The plant's growth was *arrested* by lack of adequate sunlight and sufficient water.

**ANT** arrest : vitalize [váitəlàiz]

vitalize: 생명을 주다, 생기를 불어넣다

## bark
[bɑ:rk]

**v. to shout or snap at someone; to howl** | 소리치다, 짖다
**n. the hard outer layer of a tree** | 나무의 외피

The dog's *barking* kept the neighbors up all night.

People collect sap from a rubber tree by stripping off a piece of *bark* and placing a container under the exposed area.

**PAR** bark : tree [tri:]

bark는 tree(나무)의 겉 부분이다.

## burgeon
[bə́:rdʒən]

**v. to grow rapidly; to sprout** | 급성장하다, 싹트다

Once the rain came, new wildflowers *burgeoned* all across the field.

**ANT** burgeon : wither [wíðər]

wither: 시들다

---

TRANSLATION | 예문해석

**apoplectic**  Sheila는 그 판매원이 자신의 허리 사이즈에 대해 한 말 때문에 극도로 화가 났다.
**arrest**  세 남자가 은행을 털었다는 이유로 체포되었다.
나는 거리에서 공연되는 무언극을 정신없이 구경했다.
알맞은 햇빛과 충분한 물이 없어서 그 식물의 성장이 저지되었다.
**bark**  그 개가 짖는 소리 때문에 이웃 사람들은 온밤을 뜬눈으로 밤을 새웠다.
사람들은 고무나무 껍질의 일부를 벗긴 후, 노출된 부분 아래에 용기를 놓아 수액을 모은다.
**burgeon**  비가 내리고 나자 야생화들이 들판 전체에 싹을 틔웠다.

## burlesque
[bərlésk]

**n.** a comic literary or theatrical work that pokes fun at people or events with grotesque exaggeration
| 풍자하는 문학작품이나 연극, 풍자적 희극

*Burlesques* satirizing the president are a common feature on the Saturday Night Live show.

**CH** burlesque : mockery [mákəri]
burlesque는 mockery(조롱)하는 내용을 담고 있는 풍자적 희극이다.

## choleric
[kάlərik]

**adj.** easily irritated or upset
| 화를 잘 내는

The commander of the regiment was an elderly, *choleric* man who snapped angrily at every little thing.

**CH** choleric : rile [rail]
choleric한 사람은 rile(화나게 하다)하기 쉽다.

## chord
[kɔːrd]

**n.** three or more musical notes played together
| 화음

Sonya struck the first *chord* of the prelude.

**PAR** chord : note [nout]
여러 개의 note(음조)가 모여서 하나의 chord를 만들어 낸다.

## choreograph
[kɔ́ːriəgræf]

**v.** to arrange the dances and movements for dancers to perform
| 안무하다

Madonna's concerts are always well *choreographed* and worth the money to see.

**대상** choreography : dance [dæns]
choreography(안무)는 dance(춤)를 만들어 가는 행위이다.

## combust
[kəmbʌ́st]

**v.** to burn
| 연소되다

The pile of wood *combusted* after the camper threw gasoline and a match on it.

**ANT** combustible : nonflammable [nɑnflǽməbl]
combustible: 가연성의
nonflammable: 불연성의

---

### TRANSLATION | 예 문 해 석

**burlesque**    대통령을 풍자하는 희극은 Saturday Night Live에 자주 등장한다.
**choleric**    그 연대장은 나이가 많았고, 사소한 일에도 호되게 소리치는 화를 잘 내는 사람이었다.
**chord**    Sonya는 진주곡의 첫 번째 화음을 쳤다.
**choreograph**    Madonna의 콘서트는 항상 안무가 훌륭하고, 돈내고 볼 가치가 있다.
**combust**    그 야영객이 휘발유를 붓고 성냥을 긋자 나무더미가 불에 탔다.

## constrict
[kənstríkt]

**v. to cause something to become narrower and smaller**
| 좁고 작게 만들다, 압축시키다

The renovations opened up the kitchen, but *constricted* the living room space.

**ANT** constricted: commodious [kəmóudiəs]
- constricted: 비좁은
- commodious: 넓은

## contagion
[kəntéidʒən]

**n. a disease that can be transmitted through direct or indirect contact**
| 접촉 전염병

The *contagion* spread quickly through the community because the doctors were unsure of the correct prevention methods.

**KIN** contagion : cold [kould]
- cold(감기)는 contagion의 한 종류이다.

## cooperate
[kouápərèit]

**v. to work together towards the same goal**
| 협동하다

It was only through *cooperation* between the two companies that the project could be finished on time.

**KIN** cooperate : collude [kəlúːd]
- collude(공모하다)는 음모를 꾸미기 위해 여러 사람들과 cooperate하다 라는 의미이다.

## cronyism
[króunìzəm]

**n. the partiality to one's friends in political appointments or business contracts**
| 친한 사람 편을 들어 자리를 주는 것, 편파주의

*Cronyism* was a big problem at the firm until the new owner took over the task of hiring.

**대상** cronyism : intimate [íntəmət]
- cronyism은 intimate(친구)을 편들기 위한 것이다.

---

### TRANSLATION | 예문해석

| | |
|---|---|
| constrict | 수리로 주방은 커졌지만 거실의 공간은 좁아졌다. |
| contagion | 의사들이 마땅한 예방법을 찾지 못했기 때문에 지역사회에서 접촉 전염병이 빠르게 전파되었다. |
| cooperate | 그 프로젝트가 계획된 시간에 맞춰 완성될 수 있었던 것은 오로지 두 회사가 협력한 덕분이었다. |
| cronyism | 그 새로운 소유주가 인사 업무를 관장하기전까지는 편파주의가 그 회사의 큰 문제였다. |

## croon
[kruːn]

**v. to sing or speak softly** | 낮은 소리로 노래를 부르다, 낮게 중얼거리다

Alice was softly *crooning* to herself during class.

**KIN** croon : sing [siŋ]

croon은 조용하게 노래 부르다 라는 의미로 sing의 한 종류이다.

## curb
[kəːrb]

**v. to restrain or restrict** | 제한하다, 억제하다

Heather *curbed* her spending habit by cutting up all her credit cards.

**ANT** curb : goad [goud]

goad: 선동하다

## distraught
[distrɔ́ːt]

**adj. greatly agitated by conflict of emotions; insane** | 정신이 혼란한, 미친

The couple was deeply *distraught* over the kidnapping of their child.

**DE** distraught : troubled [trʌ́bld]

distraught는 troubled(불안한, 괴로운)의 강도가 매우 큰 감정 상태이다.

## droll
[droul]

**adj. having a funny or odd character** | 익살스러운

Adults found his *droll* comments comical.

**ANT** droll : somber [sɑ́mbər]

somber: 우울한, 칙칙한

## elongate
[ilɔ́ːŋgeit]

**v. to make longer** | 늘리다

The speechwriter *elongated* the Presidential Address by adding a piece concerning world hunger.

**ANT** elongate : shorten [ʃɔ́ːrtn]

shorten: 줄이다

---

TRANSLATION | 예 문 해 석

| | |
|---|---|
| croon | Alice는 수업 중에 나지막한 목소리로 노래를 흥얼거렸다. |
| curb | Heather는 자신의 신용카드를 모두 자름으로써 소비 습관을 억제했다. |
| distraught | 그 부부는 아이가 유괴당하자 감정이 심하게 동요되었다. |
| droll | 어른들은 그의 익살스러운 말이 우스꽝스럽다고 생각했다. |
| elongate | 그 연설문 작성자는 세계의 기근에 관한 부분을 추가함으로써 대통령 연설문을 늘렸다. |

## exonerate
[igzánərèit]

**v. to clear of guilt; to relieve of responsibility**
| 무죄임을 입증하다; 의무를 면제하다

I am relieved that I have been *exonerated* from the criminal charges.

**ANT** exonerate : inculpate [inkʌ́lpeit]

inculpate: 죄를 씌우다

## gloom
[gluːm]

**n. a feeling of despair or sadness** | 우울

A *gloom* set over the people as they heard that fighting in the Middle-East had broken out again.

**ANT** gloom : glee [gliː]

glee: 환희

## glossy
[glási]

**adj. having a smooth and shiny surface** | 광택 나는, 반들반들한

The horses in his stable with their *glossy* manes were clearly well cared for.

**FUN** glossy : varnish [váːrniʃ]

varnish(광택제)는 glossy한 상태로 만드는 기능이 있다.

## groove
[gruːv]

**n. a long narrow hole; a set routine** | 가늘고 긴 홈; 판에 박힌 일상

*Grooves* were placed onto handlebars for a better grip.

**POS** groove : striated [stráieitid]

striated: 홈이 있는

## harbinger
[háːrbindʒər]

**n. one that indicates or foreshadows what is to come**
| 선구자, 전조

In the Bible, the Book of Revelation contains several *harbingers* about the end of the world.

**CH** harbinger : presage [présidʒ]

harbinger는 presage(예고하다, 전조가 되다)한다.

---

**TRANSLATION | 예 문 해 석**

| | |
|---|---|
| exonerate | 나는 범죄 혐의를 벗은 것에 안도했다. |
| gloom | 중동에서 또다시 전쟁이 벌어졌다는 보도를 접하자 사람들은 우울해졌다. |
| glossy | 반들반들한 털을 가진 마구간에 있는 말들은 확실히 보살핌을 잘 받는다. |
| groove | 손잡이에는 좀더 손쉽게 잡을 수 있도록 하기 위해 가늘고 긴 홈이 나 있다. |
| harbinger | 성경에서 계시록편은 세상의 종말에 대한 몇가지 전조를 담고 있다. |

## myopia
[maióupiə]

**n.** a visual defect that causes short-sightedness; inability to think or plan into the future
| 근시, 미래를 생각하고 대비하지 못함, 근시안적임

Fun seekers who spurn life's responsibility are said to suffer from *myopia*.

**ANT** myopia : prescience [préʃiəns]
prescience: 선견지명

## peremptory
[pərémptəri]

**adj.** not permitting refusal; offensively self-assured
| 단호한, 거만한

The director became rather *peremptory* after the great success of his last film.

**CN** peremptory : fawn [fɔːn]
peremptory한 사람은 fawn(아첨하다)하는 일이 없다.

## porcelain
[pɔ́ːrsəlin]

**n.** a hard, white ceramic ware often highly decorated
| 자기류 제품

The girl's *porcelain* doll smashed to pieces when it fell on the floor.

**대상** porcelain : glaze [gleiz]
porcelain을 glaze(광택내다) 하다.

## pore
[pɔːr]

**n.** a minute opening in tissue | 조직의 작은 구멍
**v.** to read carefully or studiously | 주의 깊게 읽다

Sun exposure, or any kind of heat, causes skin *pores* to open.
The night before the exam, the college student *pored* over her lecture notes.

**PAR** pore : membrane [mémbrein]
membrane(세포막)에는 pore(작은 구멍)가 있다.

---

### TRANSLATION | 예문 해석

**myopia** 삶의 의무들을 외면하고 재미만을 추구하는 사람들은 그런 근시안 때문에 손해를 보게 된다.
**peremptory** 그 감독은 자신의 마지막 영화가 성공을 거둔 후 다소 거만해졌다.
**porcelain** 그 소녀의 자기인형은 마룻바닥에 떨어지자 산산조각이 났다.
**pore** 햇볕이나 다른 종류의 열에 노출되면 피부의 작은 구멍들이 열린다.
시험 전날 밤, 그 여대생은 자신의 강의 노트를 열심히 읽었다.

## proliferate
[prəlífərèit]

**v. to increase in number or multiply at a rapid rate** | 급격하게 증식하다

Vaccines have stopped a number of diseases from *proliferating*.

**ANT** proliferate : dwindle [dwíndl]
dwindle: 감소하다

## prolix
[proulíks]

**adj. drawn out too long; characterized by an excess of words** | 장황한

The *prolix* style of his speech lost the audience's attention.

**WO** prolix : terseness [tə́ːrsnis]
prolix한 글에는 terseness(간결함)가 없다.

## prominent
[prámənənt]

**adj. standing out beyond a surface; well-known or eminent; obvious** | 돌출한, 저명한, 두드러진

The maiden had large and very *prominent* blue eyes.

**ANT** prominent : inconspicuous [ìnkənspíkjuəs]
inconspicuous: 눈에 띄지 않는

## promote
[prəmóut]

**v. to advance in rank or position; to contribute to the progress of** | 승진하다, 장려하다

Having a famous athlete like Magic Johnson *promote* the fight against AIDS has helped raise awareness immeasurably.

**ANT** promote : impede [impíːd]
impede: 방해하다

## propitiate
[prəpíʃièit]

**v. to pacify or appease; to obtain the good favor of** | 달래다, 비위 맞추다

I took an orange from my pocket in order to *propitiate* the belligerent monkey.

**ANT** propitiate : incense [ínsens]
incense: 몹시 화나게 하다

---

### TRANSLATION | 예문해석

| | |
|---|---|
| proliferate | 백신은 많은 질병들이 급격하게 증식하는 것을 막았다. |
| prolix | 그의 장황한 연설은 청중의 외면을 받았다. |
| prominent | 그 처녀는 크고 매우 도드라진 푸른 눈을 갖고 있었다. |
| promote | Magic Johnson같은 유명한 운동 선수가 AIDS퇴치 운동에 앞장서도록 하는 것은 사람들의 의식을 높이는데 헤아릴 수 없이 큰 도움이 된다. |
| propitiate | 나는 그 사나운 원숭이의 비위를 맞추기 위해 호주머니에서 오렌지 한 개를 꺼내어 주었다. |

## propitious
[prəpíʃəs]

**adj. favorable or lucky** | 순조로운, 좋은, 행운의

The terrace at Bellomont on a September afternoon is *propitious* for sentimental musings.

**ANT** propitious : inauspicious [inɔːspíʃəs]

inauspicious: 형편이 나쁜, 불운한, 불길한

## propriety
[prəpráiəti]

**n. appropriateness; good manners** | 타당성, 예의 바름, 교양

Susan's outdated ideas of *propriety* are better suited for someone living in Victorian England.

**ANT** propriety : presumption [prizʌ́mpʃən]

presumption: 뻔뻔스러움, 추정, 가정

## prosaic
[prouzéiik]

**adj. ordinary or dull; lacking in imagination** | 단조로운, 지루한, 진부한

The book was derided by critics as a *prosaic* piece of fiction.

**WO** prosaic : ingenuity [indʒənjúːəti]

prosaic한 글에는 ingenuity(독창성)가 없다.

## proscribe
[prouskráib]

**v. to prohibit or banish publicly** | 금지하다, 공개적으로 추방하다

In the Johnson's household, phone calls after 9 p.m. were strictly *proscribed*.

**ANT** proscribe : sanction [sǽŋkʃən]

sanction: 인가하다, 재가하다

## proselytize
[prάsəlitàiz]

**v. to try to persuade someone to change their belief or religion** | 전도하다, 개종시키다

The missionaries *proselytized* the people of Zimbabwe.

**대상** proselytize : religion [rilídʒən]

proselytize는 누군가의 religion(종교)을 바꾸도록 하는 것이다.

---

### TRANSLATION | 예문 해석

**propitious** 9월 오후 Bellomont의 테라스는 감상적인 명상을 즐기기에 좋은 장소였다.
**propriety** Susan의 예의바름에 대한 시대에 뒤떨어진 견해는 빅토리아 시대의 영국에 살았던 사람들에게 더 잘 어울린다.
**prosaic** 그 책은 평론가들에게 진부한 소설 나부랭이로 취급되어 비웃음을 샀다.
**proscribe** Johnson집안에서는 오후 9시 이후에 전화를 거는것이 엄격히 금지되었다.
**proselytize** 그 선교사들은 짐바브웨 사람들을 개종시켰다.

## prosper
[práspər]

**v. to flourish or achieve; to grow in wealth** | 번창하다, 번영하다

Airline businesses *prosper* during the holiday seasons.

> **ANT** prosperous : impecunious [ìmpikjúːniəs]
>
> prosperous: 부유한, 번영하는
>
> impecunious: 가난한

## rarefy
[rɛ́ərəfài]

**v. to become thin or less dense; to become purer** | 희석하다, 드물게 하다, 순화하다

Mixing in some water, the chemist *rarefied* the thick solution.

> **ANT** rarefy : condense [kəndéns]
>
> condense: 응축하다

## scorn
[skɔːrn]

**v. to show disdain; to reject with extreme contempt** | 경멸하다, 경멸조로 거절하다

**n. a feeling of disrespect or contempt** | 경멸

The bigoted townspeople *scorned* the disfigured man and cast him out of the community.

Failure has unfairly become the target of *scorn* in modern society.

> **DE** scorn : reject [ridʒékt]
>
> scorn은 경멸과 조소의 감정으로 reject(거절하다)하는 것이다.

## serendipity
[sèrəndípəti]

**n. something not earned but luckily found** | 우연히 발견된 좋은 것

Peggy discovered true love by *serendipity* and not by a well-planned endeavor.

> **WO** serendipity : effort [éfərt]
>
> serendipity는 별다른 effort(노력)없이 발견되는 뜻밖의 좋은 물건을 뜻한다.

## serene
[səríːn]

**adj. calm or free of unpleasant change** | 고요한, 평온한

The *serene* waters of Long Lake are a beautiful sight.

> **ANT** serene : tumultuous [tjuːmʌ́ltʃuəs]
>
> tumultuous: 소란스러운

---

**TRANSLATION | 예문해석**

**prosper** 항공사들은 휴가철에 번창한다.
**rarefy** 그 화학자는 물을 좀 부어서 그 진한 용액을 희석했다.
**scorn** 그 편견있는 마을 사람들은 그 몰골이 보기 흉한 남자를 조소로 경멸하며 마을에서 쫓아냈다.
현대 사회에서 실패는 부당하게 경멸의 대상이 된다.
**serendipity** Peggy는 잘 계획된 노력이 아닌 우연을 통해 진정한 사랑을 발견했다.
**serene** Long Lake의 고요한 물결은 아름다운 풍경이다.

## sordid
[sɔ́ːrdid]

**adj. dirty or wretched; mean; vulgar** | 지저분한, 야비한, 저속한

Jack's reputation was forever tainted by his *sordid* extramarital affair.

**ANT** sordid : noble [nóubl]

noble: 고상한

## spontaneous
[spɑntéiniəs]

**adj. happening without outward forces or causes; done without having been planned in advance** | 자발적인, 미리 계획되지 않은

Online ticketing has been a godsend for people who make *spontaneous* travel plans.

**CH** spontaneous : extemporization [ekstèmpərizéiʃən]

extemporization(즉석 연주, 즉흥적 작품)은 spontaneous하다.

## sporadic
[spərǽdik]

**adj. happening in irregular or scattered instances** | 간헐적인, 산발적인

Greg's *sporadic* coughing disturbed the other opera patrons.

**ANT** sporadic : regular [régjulər]

regular: 규칙적인

## threadbare
[θrédbɛ̀ər]

**adj. worn and shabby, usually with thread showing; hackneyed** | 누더기의, 초라한, 진부한

Barry's *threadbare* excuses for his financial problems ran thin with his parents.

**WO** threadbare : novelty [nάvəlti]

threadbare한 것은 novelty(참신함, 신기로움)가 없다.

## unremarkable
[ʌ̀nrimάːrkəbl]

**adj. unworthy of attention or praise** | 시시한

Our trip to Cancun was rather *unremarkable*.

**ANT** unremarkable : signal [sígnəl]

signal: 훌륭한, 주목할 만한

---

| TRANSLATION | 예문해석 |

**sordid** — Jack의 명성은 그 저속한 외도사건으로 영원히 더럽혀졌다.
**spontaneous** — 온라인 티켓팅은 미리 계획되지 않은 여행계획을 세우는 사람들에게는 신의 축복과도 같은 것이다.
**sporadic** — Greg의 간헐적인 기침은 다른 오페라 관중을 방해했다.
**threadbare** — Barry의 경제적인 문제에 대한 진부한 변명은 그의 부모님께 설득력을 보여주지 못했다.
**unremarkable** — Cancun으로의 우리의 여행은 좀 시시했다.

## unrepentant
[ʌnripéntənt]

**adj.** **unwilling to ask forgiveness for a sin or wrong-doing** | 뉘우치지 않는

The killer was *unrepentant*, even at his execution.

**ANT** unrepentant : penitential [pènəténʃəl]

penitential: 회개하는

## verbose
[vəːrbóus]

**adj.** **wordy or long-winded** | 말이 많은, 장황한

St. Augustine's writings are extremely *verbose*.

**ANT** verbose : concise [kənsáis]

concise: 간결한, 간명한

## verdant
[vɔ́ːrdnt]

**adj.** **covered with green growth; green in the sense of naive or inexperienced** | 초목으로 뒤덮힌, 미숙한

The *verdant* prairies of South Dakota are ideal for grazing cattle.

**ANT** verdant : sterile [stéɾil]

sterile: 불모의

## vicarious
[vaikɛ́əriəs]

**adj.** **lived and understood through the experience of another; substitutionary** | 남의 경험을 통해 대신 접해보는, 대리의

Because she couldn't travel, Alice's grandmother lived *vicariously* through her grandchildren's experiences.

**ANT** vicarious : firsthand [fə́ːrsthǽnd]

firsthand: 직접 해보는

## wholesome
[hóulsəm]

**adj.** **promoting health of body, mind, or spirit; healthy** | 건강에 좋은, 건강한

Michael urged him to embrace the opportunity of taking *wholesome* exercise in the open air.

**ANT** wholesome : morbid [mɔ́ːrbid]

morbid: 병적인, 병의

---

**TRANSLATION | 예문해석**

| | |
|---|---|
| **unrepentant** | 그 살인범은 사형 집행장에서조차 뉘우치는 기색이 없었다. |
| **verbose** | 성 아우구스티누스의 저서들은 그 내용이 매우 장황하다. |
| **verdant** | South Dakota의 짙푸른 초원들은 가축을 방목하기에 이상적이다. |
| **vicarious** | Alice의 할머니는 여행을 할 수 없었기 때문에, 손자 손녀들의 경험을 통해 대리만족을 느끼며 살았다. |
| **wholesome** | Michael은 그가 야외에서 건강에 좋은 운동을 할 기회를 갖기를 강력히 권했다. |

# 24th Day Daily Check-up

■ Fill in the blanks with the correct letter that matches the word with its definition.

1. anecdote  _____
2. prolix  _____
3. threadbare  _____
4. burgeon  _____
5. vicarious  _____
6. propriety  _____
7. groove  _____
8. combust  _____
9. sordid  _____
10. anomalous  _____

a. dirty or wretched; mean; vulgar
b. to burn
c. lived and understood through the experience of another; substitutionary
d. drawn out too long; characterized by an excess of words
e. to grow rapidly; to sprout
f. appropriateness or good manners
g. a short and humorous narrative about one's own experiences
h. irregular or differing from the norm
i. worn and shabby, usually with thread showing
j. a long narrow hole; a set routine

■ Put the correct word in each blank from the list of words below.

11. varnish는 _____ 한 상태로 만드는 기능이 있다.
12. _____ 는 inauspicious(불운한)의 반의어이다.
13. _____ 는 dance를 만들어가는 행위이다.
14. _____는 chronic(만성적인)의 반의어이다.
15. _____ 한 것에는 conformation이 없다.
16. premeditate(미리 계획하다)의 반의어는 _____이다.
17. _____는 tree의 겉 부분이다.
18. _____ 는 별다른 effort없이 발견되는 뜻밖의 좋은 물건을 뜻한다.
19. _____한 글에는 ingenuity가 없다.
20. gregarious(사교적인)의 반의어는 _____이다.

a. apoplectic   b. choreograph   c. serendipity   d. spontaneous   e. amorphous   f. bark
g. verbose   h. prosaic   i. propitious   j. aloof   k. sporadic   l. glossy

**Answer key**

1. g  2. d  3. i  4. e  5. c  6. f  7. j  8. b  9. a  10. h  11. l  12. i  13. b  14. k  15. e  16. d  17. f  18. c  19. h  20. j

## TAKE A BREAK  쉬·어·가·는 페·이·지

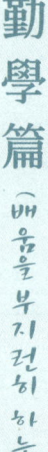

**勤學篇** (배움을 부지런히 하는 글)

\* 子夏曰 博學而篤志하고 切問而近思면 仁在其中矣니라
(자하왈 박학이독지하고 절문이근사면 인재기중의니라.)

자하(子夏)가 말하였다. 널리 배워서 뜻을 두텁게 하고,
간절하게 묻고 가까이에서 생각해 나가면 인(仁)이 그 가운데 있다.

배우기를 널리하지 않으면 잘 지켜나가지 못하고,
뜻이 독실하지 못하면 힘써 행할 수가 없으며, 간절하게 묻고
현실적인 일들을 생각하면 인(仁)이 저절로 그 안에 있다는
〈논어〉 자장편(子張篇)에 나오는 말이다.


\* 莊子曰 人之不學은 如登天而無術하고 學而智遠이면
如披祥雲而覩靑天하고 登高山而望四海니라
(장자왈 인지불학은 여등천이무술하고 학이지원이면
여피상운이도청천하고 등고산이망사해니라)

장자가 말하였다. 사람이 배우지 않으면 하늘에 오르려는데
재주가 없는 것과 같고, 배워서 지혜가 원대해지면
상서(祥瑞)로운 구름을 헤치고 푸른 하늘을 보며
산에 올라 사해를 바라보는 것과 같다.

큰 뜻을 세우고 훌륭한 장래를 설계하고서 배움에 힘쓰지 않는 것은
마치 아무 방법 없이 하늘을 오르려는 것처럼 무모하다.
배워서 지려(智慮)가 풍부해 져야만 성공을 기대하고 전도가 탁 트이게 된다.


― 공자의 [명심보감]에서 발췌했습니다.

www.goHackers.com

해커스 어학연구소

# SUPER VOCA

## 25th DAY

노병은 사라져도 단어는 사라지지 않는다.
단지 잊어버릴 뿐이다.

---

### apostate
[əpásteit]

**n. one who renounces a faith or cause** | 배교자, 변절자

The *apostate* from the Republican Party was welcomed by the Democrats.

**WO** apostasy : faith [feiθ]

apostasy(배신, 변절)는 faith(믿음, 신용)를 저버리는 행위이다.

---

### appall
[əpɔ́ːl]

**v. to cause one to be shocked or offended** | 오싹하게 하다, 질리게 하다

The social worker was *appalled* by the working conditions of the sweatshop.

**ANT** appall : embolden [imbóuldən]

embolden: 용기를 주다, 대담하게 하다

---

### appeal
[əpíːl]

**v. to attract or please; to have a case reviewed by the court** | 호감을 사다; 항소하다

Diamonds *appeal* to women more than any other precious stone.

**CH** appeal : applicant [ǽplikənt]

applicant(지원자)는 자신의 장점을 가지고 appeal함으로써 선택받으려고 한다.

---

### appease
[əpíːz]

**v. to calm or allay** | 달래다, 가라앉히다

Nothing could *appease* her fears and worries.

**ANT** appease : miff [mif]

miff: 발끈하게 하다

---

### TRANSLATION | 예문 해석

| | |
|---|---|
| apostate | 공화당의 변절자는 민주당의 환영을 받았다. |
| appall | 사회 복지사는 그 노동 착취 공장의 작업 환경을 보고 소름이 끼쳤다. |
| appeal | 다이아몬드는 다른 어떤 보석보다 여성들의 흥미를 끈다. |
| appease | 아무것도 그녀의 두려움과 근심을 가라앉힐 수 없었다. |

## arouse
[əráuz]

**v.** to excite or stimulate; to awaken from sleep
| 자극하다, 잠에서 깨어나게 하다

The girl's interest was still further *aroused* by the spectacular show at the circus.

**CN** arouse : phlegmatic [flegmǽtik]
phlegmatic(무기력한, 냉담한)한 사람을 arouse하기는 어렵다.

## arrange
[əréindʒ]

**v.** to make preparations for; to put in proper order; to settle
| 준비하다, 정돈하다, 해결하다

Julia *arranged* her new textbooks on her new desk.

**ANT** orderly arrangement : welter [wéltər]
orderly arrangement: 가지런히 정돈함
welter: 뒤죽박죽 상태

## bootless
[bú:tlis]

**adj.** unprofitable; ineffective
| 무익한, 쓸모없는

Your many *bootless* business ventures have also bankrupted you personally.

**WO** bootless : worth [wəːrθ]
bootless한 것은 worth(가치)가 없다.

## breach
[briːtʃ]

**v.** to violate
| 위반하다
**n.** a violation of a law or obligation
| 법이나 책무의 위반

The man *breached* his contract with the school and left two months early.
The guard was accused of a *breach* of protocol.

**대상** breach : covenant [kʌ́vənənt]
covenant(계약, 서약)를 breach하다.

## buoyant
[bɔ́iənt]

**adj.** cheerful or happy; floatable
| 쾌활한, 부력이 있는

A life vest is a very *buoyant* device.

**CN** buoyant : submerge [səbmə́ːrdʒ]
buoyant한 것은 submerge(물속에 잠기게 하다)할 수 없다.

---

### TRANSLATION | 예문해석

**arouse** 그 소녀의 관심은 여전히 서커스의 화려한 쇼에 쏠려 있었다.
**arrange** Julia는 새 교재들을 그녀의 새 책상위에 정리했다.
**bootless** 너의 많은 무익한 벤처 사업들은 너를 개인적으로도 파산시켰다.
**breach** 그 남자는 학교와 맺었던 계약을 위반하고 두 달 먼저 사직했다.
그 경비는 규정위반으로 기소되었다.
**buoyant** 구명조끼는 물에 잘 뜨는 기구이다.

## chef
[ʃef]

**n. a professional cook who heads a large kitchen staff** | 주방 직원들의 우두머리인 전문 요리사, 주방장

The aspiration of all students in culinary school is to be the head *chef* of their own restaurants one day.

**대상** chef : banquet [bǽŋkwit]

chef에게 banquet(진수 성찬)은 그가 요리하려는 대상이 된다.

## clout
[klaut]

**n. a heavy blow; power or influence** | 강타, 영향력

The mayor had a lot of *clout* over the police department.

**ANT** clout : impuissance [impjúːisns]

impuissance: 무능, 무기력, 허약

## colonnade
[kàlənéid]

**n. a series of columns spaced out in regular intervals** | 일정한 간격으로 늘어선 기둥의 연속, 건축 열주

*Colonnades* are used by architects to give a building a more stately and grand appearance.

**PAR** colonnade : pillar [pílər]

pillar(기둥)는 colonnade를 이루는 한 부분이다.

## contraction
[kəntrǽkʃən]

**n. the shortening and thickening of muscle; the process of becoming smaller** | 근육의 수축, 축소

A *contraction* of muscle transforms into force.

**DE** contraction : convulsion [kənvʌ́lʃən]

convulsion(경련)은 근육이 극도로 contraction된 것이다.

## coquette
[koukét]

**n. a woman who flirts to exploit men** | 남자를 이용하려 유혹하는 여자, 요부

The novel featured a *coquette* who captivated everyone with her charm.

**CH** coquette : flirtatious [fləːrtéiʃəs]

coquette는 flirtatious(바람난, 시시덕거리는)하다.

---

**TRANSLATION | 예 문 해 석**

| | |
|---|---|
| chef | 요리학교의 모든 학생들의 포부는 훗날 자신이 소유한 식당의 주방장이 되는 것이다. |
| clout | 그 시장은 경찰국에 큰 영향력을 행사했다. |
| colonnade | 열주는 건축가들이 건물에 더 웅장하고 당당한 풍채를 주고자 할 때 쓰인다. |
| contraction | 근육의 수축은 힘으로 옮겨진다. |
| coquette | 그 소설에는 자신의 매력으로 모두를 사로잡은 요부가 등장했다. |

## debacle
[deibá:kl]

**n.** a sudden destruction; a complete failure
| 파괴, 완전한 실패

The campaign was a *debacle* and a waste of money.

**ANT** debacle : landslide [lǽndslàid]
landslide: 압도적인 승리, 산사태

## decadence
[dékədəns]

**n.** a period of decay; the condition of low morals; the state of being overindulgent
| 쇠퇴기, 타락, 제멋대로인 상태

The *decadence* of April's spending habit was a constant source of contention between her and her husband.

**ANT** decadence : wholesomeness [hóulsəmnis]
wholesomeness: 건전

## dingy
[díndʒi]

**adj.** darkened or discolored with dirt
| 먼지로 거무스름해지거나 퇴색한

The *dingy* motel room was badly in need of new wallpaper and other renovations.

**CN** dingy : glisten [glísn]
dingy한 것은 glisten(반짝반짝 빛나다)하지 않는다.

## disabuse
[dìsəbjúːz]

**v.** to free somebody from a falsehood or misconception
| (그릇된 생각·관념에서) 깨게 하다

Magellan *disabused* the belief that the world was flat.

**대상** disabuse : fallacy [fǽləsi]
disabuse는 fallacy(그릇된 생각, 오류)에서 깨게 한다는 의미이다.

## dread
[dred]

**n.** extreme fear or terror
| 극도의 공포

The people in the war-torn city live in *dread* of further shelling.

**인과** dread : cringe [krindʒ]
dread를 느낀 결과 몸을 cringe(움찔하다)하게 된다.

---

| TRANSLATION | 예문 해석 |

| debacle | 그 선거운동은 완전한 실패였으며 돈만 낭비했다. |
| decadence | April의 방탕한 소비습관은 그녀와 남편 사이의 끊임없는 다툼의 원인이었다. |
| dingy | 먼지로 거무스름해진 모텔 방은 새 벽지와 수리가 질실히 필요했다. |
| disabuse | Magellan은 지구가 평평하다는 그릇된 믿음을 깼다. |
| dread | 전쟁으로 파괴된 그 도시의 사람들은 또다시 포격이 있을까 두려움에 떨며 산다. |

## dupe
[djuːp]

**v. to trick or fool** | 속이다

**v. one who is easy to trick; a fool** | 잘 속는 사람, 얼간이

That he could have chosen to *dupe* her in so ready a manner seemed a cruel thing.

Mary's naive and innocent nature often made her seem like a *dupe*.

**CH** dupe : gullible [gʌ́ləbl]

dupe(얼간이)는 gullible(잘 속는)한 특징이 있다.

## enhance
[inhǽns]

**v. to advance or improve** | 향상시키다

Tammy *enhanced* the softness of her hair by applying a heavy conditioner.

**ANT** enhance : mar [mɑːr]

mar: 망쳐놓다, 훼손하다

## exotic
[igzátik]

**adj. excitingly different; foreign or not native** | 색다른, 외래의

The *exotic* breed of panda was the most popular attraction at the zoo.

**ANT** exotic : indigenous [indídʒənəs]

indigenous: 토착의

## foot-dragging
[fútdræ̀giŋ]

**n. deliberate slowness in action** | 느림, 의도적인 지연

The employee's constant *foot-dragging* cost her job.

**WO** foot-dragging : expedite [ékspədàit]

expedite(일을 신속하게 처리하다)하는 사람에게서는 foot-dragging의 태도를 찾아볼 수 없다.

---

### TRANSLATION | 예문 해석

**dupe** 그가 그렇게 교묘히 그녀를 속일수도 있었다는 것은 잔인한 일 같았다.
Mary는 고지식하고 순진하기 때문에 종종 얼간이처럼 보이기도 한다.
**enhance** Tammy는 강력한 컨디셔너를 발라 머릿결을 더욱 부드럽게 만들었다.
**exotic** 외래종인 팬더곰은 동물원에서 가장 인기좋은 동물이었다.
**foot-dragging** 그 여종업원은 계속 의도적으로 업무 처리를 지연시켜서 해고당했다.

## grotesque
[groutésk]

**adj.** **outlandish in character or appearance; differing greatly from the acceptable norm**
| 괴상한, 일반적으로 받아들여지는 기준에서 벗어난

It is always more fun to dress as something *grotesque* on Halloween.

**DE** grotesque : fantastic [fæntǽstik]
grotesque한 것은 fantastic(환상적인, 별난)한 것을 넘어서 괴상한 것이다.

## hive
[haiv]

**n.** **a place that is busy with activity** | 활발한 움직임으로 분주한 장소

The store became a *hive* during the Christmas season.

**CH** hive : active [ǽktiv]
hive는 active(활동적인)한 곳을 말한다.

## impact
n. [ímpækt]
v. [impǽkt]

**n.** **a forceful contact or consequence; a significant impression of one thing on another** | 강한 충돌, 충격, 영향, 효과
**v.** **to forcefully strike or affect** | 강한 충격을 주다, 큰 영향을 끼치다

An *impact* with the steering wheel during the accident bruised the driver's forehead.

The experiences in science high school *impacted* Daniel's personality a lot.

**FUN** impact : buffer [bʌ́fər]
buffer(완충장치)는 impact(충격)를 막기 위한 것이다.

## impassive
[impǽsiv]

**adj.** **unsusceptible to emotional or physical pain; showing no emotion** | 무감각한, 감정이 없는, 무표정한

Fleming always sat with the same *impassive* and absent-minded air during the boss' rantings.

**SYN** impassive : deadpan [dédpæ̀n]
deadpan: 무표정한

## impeccable
[impékəbl]

**adj.** **flawless; incapable of sinning or doing wrong**
| 흠 없는, 죄를 범하지 않는

Joe was an *impeccable* hero in his younger brother's eyes.

**WO** impeccable : blemish [blémiʃ]
impeccable한 사람에겐 blemish(흠, 오점)가 없다.

---

TRANSLATION | 예 문 해 석

| | |
|---|---|
| grotesque | Halloween에 뭔가 괴상한 옷차림을 하면 언제나 더욱 재미가 있다. |
| hive | 그 상점은 크리스마스 시즌 동안에 분주한 장소가 되었다. |
| impact | 그 사고당시 충격으로 운전대와 부딪힌 운전사는 이마에 멍이 들었다. |
| | 과학고에서의 경험은 Daniel의 성격에 많은 영향을 끼쳤다. |
| impassive | Fleming은 상사가 고함치는 동안 여느때와 마찬가지로 무표정하고 얼빠진 모습으로 앉아있었다. |
| impeccable | 동생의 눈에 Joe는 나무랄 데 없는 영웅이었다. |

## menace [ménis]

**n.** something that poses a danger or threatens injury or harm　| 위협, 협박

**v.** to pose a threat or endanger against　| 위협하다

Drug dealers are a *menace* to society.
The Roman Empire was *menaced* by its barbaric neighbors.

> **인과**　menacing : fear [fiər]
> menacing(위협적인) 일을 겪은 결과 fear(두려움)를 느끼게 된다.

## notable [nóutəbl]

**adj.** impressive or worthy of notice　| 인상적인, 주목할 만한

The professor was given an award for his *notable* research.

> **ANT**　a notable success : fiasco [fiǽskou]
> notable success: 대성공
> fiasco: 대실패

## parable [pǽrəbl]

**n.** a brief fictitious story that illustrates a moral or religious value　| 우화

Children's bedtime stories are often *parables*.

> **KIN**　parable : story [stɔ́:ri]
> parable은 story(이야기)의 한 종류이다.

## paranoia [pæ̀rənɔ́iə]

**n.** a mental disorder characterized by persistent delusions of being grand, or of being persecuted by others; extreme suspicion and distrust of others　| 편집증, 망상증, (타인에 대한 근거 없는) 심한 불신

During a war there is always a general *paranoia* in society.

> **DE**　paranoia : suspicion [səspíʃən]
> suspicion(의심)이 지나치면 paranoia가 된다.

---

### TRANSLATION | 예문해석

| | |
|---|---|
| menace | 마약 거래상들은 사회에 위협적인 존재들이다.<br>로마제국은 야만적인 이웃나라들의 위협을 받았다. |
| notable | 그 교수는 주목할 만한 연구 업적으로 상을 받았다. |
| parable | 어린이들이 잠잘 때 듣는 동화들은 대개 우화이다. |
| paranoia | 전쟁 중엔 언제나 심한 불신이 사회에 만연한다. |

## platitude
[plǽtətjùːd]

n. **a dull or banal remark; the state of being boring or insipid** | 진부한 이야기, 단조로움

The preacher's sanctimonious *platitudes* wore on his congregation.

**CH** platitude : banal [bənǽl]
platitude는 banal(진부한) 이야기이다.

## plethora
[pléθərə]

n. **an excessive or overabundant amount** | 과다, 과잉

The wedding couple received a *plethora* of gifts at their wedding reception.

**ANT** plethora : dearth [dəːrθ]
dearth: 부족, 결핍

## plot
[plɑt]

n. **the main story in a fictional work; a plan made in secret** | 이야기 구성; 음모

Although the book's writing style is intriguing, the *plot* is rather dull.
They laid out their little *plot* against Madeleine and elaborated it carefully.

**KIN** plot : plan [plæn]
plot은 비밀리에 만들어진 plan(계획)이다.

## preach
[priːtʃ]

v. **to give a sermon; to advise earnestly** | 설교하다, 훈계하다

One should only *preach* what they practice.

**CH** preacher : sermon [sə́ːrmən]
preacher(설교자, 목사)는 sermon(설교)을 하는 사람이다.

---

**TRANSLATION | 예문 해석**

**platitude** 그 설교자의 독실한 척 늘어놓는 상투어구는 이제 회중들에겐 지겨운 것이 되었다.
**plethora** 결혼하는 그 커플은 피로연에서 많은 선물을 받았다.
**plot** 비록 그 책의 문장 스타일은 흥미를 자아내나, 플롯은 좀 지루하다.
그들은 Madeleine에 대한 조그만 음모를 꾸미고 이를 신중하게 다듬었다.
**preach** 사람은 자기가 실천하는 것만을 남에게 권해야 한다.

## preamble
[príːæmbl]

**n. the introductory statement or fact** | 서문

The *preamble* to the new law highlighted the government's commitment to protect forests.

**CH** preamble : introductory [ìntrədʌ́ktəri]

preamble은 introductory(소개하는)하다.

## prostrate
[prɑ́streit]

**adj. lying flat and face down; completely exhausted** | 엎드린, 기진 맥진한

**v. to lie or throw flat with the face down** | 엎드리다

After an incredibly long and strenuous day of work, Brian came home and lay down *prostrate* on his bed.

The beggar *prostrated* himself on the man's feet in hopes of some clemency.

**ANT** prostrate : upright [ʌ́pràit]

upright: 일어선, 직립의

## protract
[proutrǽkt]

**v. to continue or prolong unnecessarily** | 질질 끌다, 연장하다

Blucher's neck made a sickeningly *protracted* crackling sound.

**ANT** protract : curtail [kərtéil]

curtail: 줄이다

## protuberance
[proutjúːbərəns]

**n. the state or quality of bulging** | 돌출, 혹

Nolan had a strange *protuberance* on his cheek that he asked the doctor to examine.

**ANT** protuberance : concavity [kɑnkǽvəti]

concavity: 오목한 부분

## provident
[prɑ́vədənt]

**adj. providing money and other things you need for the future; prudent; economical** | 선견지명이 있는, 신중한, 절약하는

Lilly is a *provident* person who saves 15% of her paycheck each month.

**CH** improvidence : spendthrift [spéndθrift]

spendthrift(돈을 헤프게 쓰는 사람)는 improvidence(낭비)하다.

---

### TRANSLATION | 예문해석

**preamble** 새로운 법의 서문은 정부의 삼림보호 공약을 돋보이게 했다.

**prostrate** 믿을 수 없을 만큼 길고 고된 하루 일을 마친 후 Brian은 집에 돌아와 침대에 엎드린 채로 뻗었다.
그 거지는 온정적인 조치를 기대하며 남자의 발에 엎드렸다.

**protract** Blucher의 목에서 바삭거리는 소리가 넌더리가 날 만큼 계속 났다.

**protuberance** Nolan은 볼에 이상한 혹이 생겨서 검진을 받으러 갔다.

**provident** Lilly는 매달 월급의 15%를 저축하는 절약성있는 사람이다.

## provincial
[prəvínʃəl]

**adj. coming from a province; unsophisticated or narrow-minded** | 지방민의, 세련되지 않은, 편협한

The brilliant and sophisticated writer's *provincial* nature surprised his audience of readers.

**ANT** provincial : cosmopolitan [kàzməpálətn]
cosmopolitan: 시야가 넓은, 세계주의의

## provisions
[prəvíʒənz]

**n. preparatory measures; a stock of needed food or supplies** | 예비장치, 식량, 저장품

The travelers stopped at the nearest town to get *provisions* for their hike.

**FUN** provisions : larder [láːrdər]
larder(창고)는 provisions를 저장하는 기능을 갖고 있다.

## provoke
[prəvóuk]

**v. to cause anger; to evoke a feeling or emotional reaction** | 화나게 하다, 감정을 불러 일으키다

Elizabeth, looking to have a quarrel, *provoked* Darcy by shouting abuses at him.

**DE** provoke : taunt [tɔːnt]
provoke는 taunt(비아냥거리다)보다 타인에 대한 공격성의 강도가 높다.

## quotidian
[kwoutídiən]

**adj. occurring everyday** | 매일 일어나는, 평범한

Personal hygiene such as brushing one's teeth is a *quotidian* chore.

**ANT** quotidian : striking [stráikiŋ]
striking: 인상적인, 현저한

## rapacious
[rəpéiʃəs]

**adj. grasping or taking by force; extremely greedy** | 강탈하는, 탐욕적인

Many hoped that the *rapacious* strangers would be induced to leave the town quickly.

**DE** rapacious : covetous [kʌ́vitəs]
rapacious는 covetous(탐내는)보다 남의 것을 훨씬 더 탐내는 이라는 의미를 가지고 있다.

---

**TRANSLATION | 예문해석**

**provincial** 그 명석하고 재치있는 작가가 편협한 성격을 드러내서 독자인 청중들은 놀라게 했다.
**provisions** 그 여행자들은 가장 가까운 마을에 들러 여행용 양식을 구입했다.
**provoke** 말다툼할 기회를 노리던 Elizabeth는 Darcy에게 비난을 퍼부어 감정을 자극했다.
**quotidian** 양치와 같은 개인위생은 일상사중 하나이다.
**rapacious** 많은 사람들은 그 불한당같은 이방인들이 설득을 받아들여 빨리 마을에서 떠나기를 바랐다.

## repartee
[rèpərtí:]

**n. a quick, clever reply** | 재치 있는 응답

Our neighbor was a witty man, famous for pleasant *repartees*.

**SYN** repartee : retort [ritɔ́:rt]

retort: 말대꾸, 반박

## repatriate
[ri:péitrièit]

**v. to return to country of origin** | 본국으로 송환하다

In the mid 1900s, Greece and Turkey *repatriated* each other's citizens to their home countries.

**ANT** repatriate : emigrate [émigrèit]

emigrate: 이민가다

## riot
[ráiət]

**v. to raise a riot; to practice unrestrained revelry** | 폭동을 일으키다, 방탕한 생활을 하다

**n. public violence as a group, usually protesting power or authority** | 폭동

*Rioting* in Italy, especially Milan and Florence, is a common occurrence. Most Korean stores in L.A were known to have been robbed in the *riot*.

**CH** rioter : hodgepodge [hɑ́dʒpɑ̀dʒ]

rioter(폭도)는 거리를 hodgepodge(뒤범벅)으로 만드는 특징이 있다.

## route
[ru:t]

**n. a traveled path; a designated course of action** | 길, 경로

The *route* to the top of that mountain is long and winding.

**대상** route : detour [dí:tuər]

route에서 detour(우회하다)하다.

---

### TRANSLATION | 예문해석

| | |
|---|---|
| repartee | 우리 이웃사람은 기지있는 남자인데 유쾌하고 재치있는 답변을 하기로 유명했다. |
| repatriate | 1900년대 중반 그리스와 터키는 상대 국가 국민들을 본국으로 송환했다. |
| riot | 이탈리아, 특히 밀라노와 플로렌스에서 폭동은 흔한 일이다. |
| | 그 폭동 속에서 대부분의 L.A. 한인 상가들이 강탈당한 것으로 알려졌다. |
| route | 그 산의 정상으로 가는 길은 멀고 꾸불꾸불하다. |

## separate
[sépərèit]

**v. to set or move apart; to legally part before a divorce; to disunite** | 분리하다, 별거하다, 반목하다

The two students were *separated* after their fight in the playground.

Kate and Tom didn't quite know how to break the news to their children that they were *separated*.

- **ANT** separate : meld [meld]
  - meld: 혼합시키다, 결합시키다

## sip
[sip]

**v. to take small drinks** | 홀짝거리며 마시다

*Sipping* her coffee, Mary read the morning newspaper before heading to work.

- **DE** sip : swill [swil]
  - swill(벌컥벌컥 마시다)은 sip에 비해 빠른 속도로 벌컥벌컥 마시는 것을 의미한다.

## slouch
[slautʃ]

**v. to let one's shoulders and neck fall forward** | 어깨와 목을 구부리다, 몸을 굽히다

The young man *slouched* at his desk.

- **ANT** slouch : stand erect [stænd irékt]
  - stand erect: 똑바로 서다

## slovenly
[slʌ́vənli]

**adj. untidy or dirty** | 더러운, 단정치 못한

Harran's groping hand met that of a *slovenly* little Dutchman.

- **ANT** slovenly : natty [nǽti]
  - natty: 깔끔한, 말쑥한

## smother
[smʌ́ðər]

**v. to deprive of oxygen; to cover up and destroy** | 질식시키다, (불을) 덮어서 끄다, 은폐하다

The fireman *smothered* the flames with a wet blanket.

- **SYN** smother : choke [tʃouk]
  - choke: 질식시키다

---

### TRANSLATION | 예문해석

| | |
|---|---|
| separate | 그 두 학생은 운동장에서 싸우고 난 뒤 사이가 벌어졌다. |
| | Kate와 Tom은 자신들의 별거소식을 어떻게 아이들에게 알려야 할지 정말 난감했다. |
| sip | Mary는 커피를 홀짝이면서 일터로 가기 전에 아침신문을 읽었다. |
| slouch | 그 젊은이는 책상쪽으로 몸을 구부렸다. |
| slovenly | Harran의 더듬던 손이 꾀죄죄한 한 네덜란드인의 손에 닿았다. |
| smother | 그 소방수는 젖은 담요로 불을 껐다. |

## soothe [suːð]

**v. to comfort or ease pain; to relax or calm** | 고통을 덜다, 달래다

Alice tried unsuccessfully to *soothe* her sobbing friend.

**ANT** soothe : rankle [rǽŋkl]

rankle: 괴롭히다, 화나게 하다

## sop [sɑp]

**v. to give a conciliatory gift or bribe; to take up liquid by absorbing it** | 화친의 선물을 주다, 빨아들이다

**n. a bribe** | 뇌물

Grandpa would always *sop* up his soup with his bread.

The feuding tribes exchanged *sops* in order to maintain the accord of the two tribes.

**CH** sop : conciliatory [kənsíliətɔ̀ːri]

sop은 conciliatory(회유적인, 달래는)하다.

## treacherous [trétʃərəs]

**adj. characterized by betrayal of fidelity or trust; unreliable or dangerous** | 배반하는, 믿을 수 없는, 위험한

In the entertainment business, some people are *treacherous* and only befriend you while you're famous.

**ANT** treacherous : faithful [féiθfəl]

faithful: 충실한

## vertigo [və́ːrtigòu]

**n. dizziness or weakness; a disordered or confused state of mind** | 현기증, 혼란

Beth went to the doctor because she was repeatedly experiencing *vertigo*.

**SYN** vertigo : dizziness [dízinis]

dizziness: 어지럼증

---

### TRANSLATION | 예 문 해 석

| | |
|---|---|
| soothe | Alice가 흐느껴 우는 친구를 진정시키려고 노력했지만 실패했다. |
| sop | 할아버지는 늘 빵을 스프에 찍어 드시곤 했다. |
| | 반목 상태에 있던 부족들은 서로간의 유대를 유지하기 위해 화친의 선물을 교환했다. |
| treacherous | 연예계에서 어떤 사람들은 믿을 수 없는 존재이며, 단지 당신이 유명할때만 친구로 지내려는 속셈을 가지고 있다. |
| vertigo | Beth는 계속 현기증이 나서 병원에 갔다. |

## voracious
[vɔːréiʃəs]

**adj. having an insatiable appetite** | 식욕이 왕성한

After playing football all day Timmy was *voracious* and ready for dinner.

**CN** voracious : satisfy [sǽtisfài]
voracious한 사람은 좀처럼 satisfy(만족시키다)할 수 없다.

---

TRANSLATION | 예 문 해 석

**voracious** 온 종일 축구를 한 뒤에 Timmy는 식욕이 왕성해져서 바로 저녁을 먹을 준비가 돼있었다.

# 25th Day Daily Check-up

■ Fill in the blanks with the correct letter that matches the word with its definition.

1. debacle  _____
2. repatriate  _____
3. provident  _____
4. plethora  _____
5. quotidian  _____
6. parable  _____
7. preamble  _____
8. voracious  _____
9. breach  _____
10. slouch  _____

a. the introductory statement or fact
b. having an insatiable appetite
c. a sudden destruction; a complete failure
d. occurring everyday
e. an excessive or overabundant amount
f. a brief fictitious story that illustrates a moral or religious value
g. to return to country of origin
h. a violation of a law or obligation
i. to let one's shoulders and neck fall forward
j. providing money and other things you need for the future; prudent; economical

■ Put the correct word in each blank from the list of words below.

11. larder는 _____를 저장하는 기능을 갖고 있다.
12. dizziness(어지럼증)의 동의어는 _____이다.
13. applicant는 자신의 장점을 가지고 _____함으로써 선택받으려고 한다.
14. fallacy를 _____ 하다
15. suspicion이 지나치면 _____가 된다.
16. _____ 한 것은 worth가 없다.
17. choke(질식시키다)의 동의어는 _____이다.
18. _____는 faith를 저버리는 행위이다.
19. _____를 느낀 결과 몸을 cringe하게 되다.
20. convulsion은 근육이 극도로 _____ 된 것이다.

| a. paranoia | b. enhance | c. provisions | d. platitude | e. appeal | f. smother |
| g. bootless | h. vertigo | i. disabuse | j. apostasy | k. contraction | l. dread |

Answer key

1. c  2. g  3. j  4. e  5. d  6. f  7. a  8. b  9. h  10. i
11. c  12. h  13. e  14. i  15. a  16. g  17. f  18. j  19. l  20. k

www.goHackers.com

해커스 어학연구소

# SUPER VOCA

T.W.E.N.T.Y.S.I.X.T.H D.A.Y

## 26th DAY

보여줘, 보여줘, 보여줘!!
너의 그 집중력을!!!

---

**abundant**
[əbʌ́ndənt]

adj. **plentiful or amply supplied** | 풍부한, 충분히 공급된
The garden produced an *abundant* amount of vegetables this year.

ANT abundant : scant [skænt]
scant: 불충분한, 부족한

---

**acquisition**
[ækwəzíʃən]

n. **the attainment or purchase of something; the gaining of knowledge or information** | 물건의 획득이나 구입, 지식이나 정보의 습득
David's most recent *acquisition* was a convertible car.

ANT acquisition : divestiture [divéstətʃər]
divestiture: 박탈

---

**amenable**
[əmíːnəbəl]

adj. **responsible or answerable; readily brought to submission or obedience** | 책임이 있는, 순종하는
All citizens of the U.S. are *amenable* to the supreme law of the land -- the U.S. Constitution.

ANT amenable : querulous [kwérjuləs]
querulous: 불평하는, 투덜거리는

---

**anonymous**
[ənánəməs]

adj. **not identified or of unknown authorship** | 익명의, 저작자 미상의
Rosy received an *anonymous* bouquet of flowers at work.

CN anonymous : identify [aidéntəfài]
anonymous한 것은 누구에 의한 것인지 identify(확인하다, 증명하다)할 수 없다.

---

**TRANSLATION | 예 문 해 석**

| | |
|---|---|
| **abundant** | 그 정원은 올 해 풍성한 양의 채소들을 생산해냈다. |
| **acquisition** | David가 가장 최근에 구입한 것은 컨버터블 승용차였다. |
| **amenable** | 미국의 모든 시민들은 자신들의 최고 법인 헌법을 따른다. |
| **anonymous** | Rosy는 직장에서 누군가 익명으로 보낸 꽃다발을 받았다. |

## ascend
[əsénd]

v. to rise or move upward | 상승하다, 올라가다

Tanner *ascended* to the penthouse by helicopter because the elevator was out of order.

**ANT** ascend : descend [disénd]

descend: 내려가다

## bleed
[bliːd]

v. to lose blood; to ooze out | 출혈하다, 흘러나오다

Mark lay on the street, *bleeding* profusely.

**FUN** bleeding : tourniquet [túərnikit]

tourniquet(지혈대)는 bleeding(출혈)을 막는 물건이다.

## burnish
[bə́ːrniʃ]

v. to polish or make shiny by rubbing; to shine forth | 닦아서 광내다, 빛나다

The maid spent the entire day *burnishing* the trophies and statues.

**인과** burnish : lustrous [lʌ́strəs]

burnish하면 lustrous(빛나는)한 상태가 된다.

## candidate
[kǽndidèit]

n. a person who aspires to be elected or appointed to a certain position | 후보자, 지원자

There are only three *candidates* for the job, and all are equally qualified.

**FUN** candidate : slate [sleit]

slate(후보자 명단)는 candidate의 이름을 적어놓은 명단이다.

## celebrity
[səlébrəti]

n. a famous or widely known living person; fame | 유명인사, 명성

Audrey Hepburn's role in *Roman Holiday* transformed her from an unknown actress into a *celebrity*.

**ANT** celebrity : obscurity [əbskjúərəti]

obscurity: 알려지지 않은 사람

---

TRANSLATION | 예문해석

**ascend** Tanner는 엘리베이터가 고장나서 헬리콥터를 타고 탑옥에 올라갔다.
**bleed** Mark는 심하게 출혈을 하며 길에 누워 있었다.
**burnish** 그 하녀는 하루종일 트로피와 조각상들을 닦아 광을 냈다.
**candidate** 그 일자리에는 단지 세 명의 지원자밖에 없었으며 모두 동등한 자격을 갖추고 있었다.
**celebrity** 오드리 헵번은 '로마의 휴일'에 출연함으로써 무명 여배우에서 유명인사가 되었다.

## contravene
[kɑ̀ntrəvíːn]

**v. to violate; to oppose in argument** | 위반하다, 반대하다

In Singapore, *contravening* even minor laws can bring severe punishments.

**ANT** contravene : buttress [bʌ́tris]

buttress: 지지하다

## convulsion
[kənvʌ́lʃən]

**n. violent, involuntary muscular contractions** | 심하고 무의식적인 근육의 수축, 경련

During a seizure, people with epilepsy often experience *convulsions* that rack their whole bodies.

**DE** convulsion : contraction [kəntrǽkʃən]

근육이 극도로 contraction(수축)된 것이 convulsion이다.

## coronation
[kɔ̀ːrənéiʃən]

**n. the act or occasion of crowning a sovereign** | 대관, 대관식

The *coronation* ceremony of Queen Elizabeth II was extremely elaborate.

**PUR** coronation : reign [rein]

coronation은 reign(통치권)을 양도하기 위한 것이다.

## counterfeit
[káuntərfit]

**adj. forged or falsified** | 위조된, 가짜의

**v. to forge; to attempt to deceive by pretense** | 위조하다, 속이다

**n. a copy that is presented as the original; an act of forging** | 위조품, 위조

They had no way to differentiate the *counterfeit* product from the genuine one.

The business of *counterfeiting* luxuries seems to be expanding.

The new U.S. currency has reduced the amount of *counterfeits* circulating in the economy.

**SYN** counterfeit : forgery [fɔ́ːrdʒəri]

forgery: 위조품, 위조

---

### TRANSLATION | 예문해석

**contravene** 싱가포르에서는 중요하지 않은 법을 위반해도 무거운 처벌을 받는다.
**convulsion** 간질이 있는 사람들은 종종 몸에 심한 고통을 주는 경련을 경험한다.
**coronation** Elizabeth 2세의 대관식은 굉장히 공들인 것이었다.
**counterfeit** 그들에게는 위조품과 진품을 가려낼 방법이 없었다.
모조 사치품 산업이 확장세에 있는 것으로 보인다.
새로운 미국 통화는 유통되는 위조 지폐의 양을 줄였다.

## countermand
[kàuntərmǽnd]

v. to take back or cancel an order | 명령을 철회하다, 취소하다

The security advisor *countermanded* the operation in fear of causing too many civilian casualties.

**대상** countermand : order [ɔ́ːrdər]

countermand는 order(명령)을 취소하는 것이다.

## credulous
[krédʒuləs]

adj. overly eager to believe; naive | 지나치게 잘 믿는, 순진한

It was *credulous* of the tourist to believe the local salesman.

**CN** credulous : skeptic [sképtik]

skeptic(회의론자)은 credulous하지 않다.

## delegate
n. [déligət]
v. [déligèit]

n. a representative with the power to speak or act on behalf of others | 대표

v. to send as a representative; to entrust to another | 대표로서 파견하다, 위임하다

Each state sent a number of *delegates* to the national convention.
Minister Kim was *delegated* to represent South Korea at APEC 2000.

**CH** delegation : represented [rèprizéntid]

delegation(대표단)은 어떤 집단을 represented(대표하는)한다.

## detection
[ditékʃən]

n. the act of discovering the true character, fact, or existence of | 간파, 탐지

Early *detection* of most cancers ensures a high survival rate.

**PUR** indetection : camouflage [kǽməflàːʒ]

indetection(발각되지 않음)을 위해 camouflage(위장을 하다)한다.

## diatribe
[dáiətràib]

n. an abusive speech or writing, usually ironical or satirical | (주로 비꼬는 듯 표현한) 통렬한 비난의 말이나 글

The protestant preacher went into a *diatribe* against the Catholic Church.

**CH** diatribe : abuse [əbjúːz]

diatribe는 심한 abuse(욕설, 독설)가 사용되는 말이다.

---

TRANSLATION | 예문 해석

| | |
|---|---|
| countermand | 그 안전 고문은 막대한 민간인 사상자를 만들어낼 것을 염려하여 그 작전을 철회했다. |
| credulous | 그 관광객이 그 지역 세일즈맨을 믿은 것은 순진한 일이었다. |
| delegate | 국제 컨벤션에 각 주에서 몇 명의 대표들을 파견했다. |
| | 김 장관은 APEC 2000에 남한 대표로 파견되었다. |
| detection | 대부분의 암들은 초기에 발견되면 높은 생존률을 보인다. |
| diatribe | 그 신교 교회 목사는 카톨릭 교회에 대하여 통렬한 비난을 하기 시작했다. |

### dignify
[dígnəfài]

**v. to ennoble or give dignity to** | 위엄 있게 하다

The senator's presence *dignified* the local charity's fund raising event.

**ANT** dignify : demean [dimí:n]

demean: 품격을 떨어뜨리다

### distress
[distrés]

**n. physical or emotional pain or suffering; trouble or danger** | 고통, 궁지

**v. to upset or cause suffering** | 괴롭히다

Her husband's death caused her great *distress*.
The young boy was *distressed* by his parents' argument.

**대상** distress : alleviate [əlí:vièit]

distress를 alleviate(완화하다)하다.

### drench
[drentʃ]

**v. to saturate or soak thoroughly** | 흠뻑 적시다

On the way home I was completely *drenched* by a rain shower.

**DE** drench : douse [daus]

drench는 흠뻑 douse(물에 적시다)하다 라는 의미이다.

### dwindle
[dwíndl]

**v. to decrease or make steadily less** | 점차 감소하다, 감소시키다

As the depression hit, sales at the Evans' family store *dwindled* to less than one third of normal volume.

**ANT** dwindle : proliferate [proulífərèit]

proliferate: 급격하게 증식하다

### embed
[imbéd]

**v. to put into another substance** | 파묻다

The gardener carefully *embedded* the bulbs in the dirt.

**ANT** embed : disinter [dìsintə́:r]

disinter: 발굴하다, 드러내다

---

**TRANSLATION | 예문 해석**

| | |
|---|---|
| dignify | 상원의원의 참석은 지역 자선단체의 기금 모금 행사에 위엄을 더했다. |
| distress | 그녀의 남편의 죽음은 그녀에게 큰 고통을 주었다. |
| | 그 어린 소년은 부모님들의 언쟁때문에 괴로웠다. |
| drench | 집으로 오는 길에 소나기가 내리기 시작해서 나는 완전히 흠뻑 젖어버렸다. |
| dwindle | 불경기가 닥치면서, Evans 가족 상점의 매출은 평소의 삼분의 일로 줄었다. |
| embed | 그 정원사는 흙 속에 조심스럽게 뿌리들을 파묻었다. |

## enunciate
[inʌ́nsièit]

**v.** to express or pronounce clearly and articulately | 명확히 표현하거나 발음하다

The teacher asked the presenting student to *enunciate* clearly for the class.

**ANT** enunciate : waffle [wɑ́fl]
waffle: 모호한 말로 얼버무리다

## extenuate
[iksténjuèit]

**v.** to lessen or diminish the seriousness or magnitude | (심각성이나 중요성을) 경감하다

Mary's elaborate excuses did little to *extenuate* her mistake.

**대상** extenuate : seriousness [síəriəsnis]
extenuate는 seriousness(심각성) 등을 경감한다는 의미이다.

## fidelity
[fidéləti]

**n.** faithfulness | 충성

The *fidelity* of a subordinate is always in question.

**ANT** fidelity : apostasy [əpɑ́stəsi]
apostasy: 배신, 변절

## fortunate
[fɔ́ːrtʃənət]

**adj.** lucky or receiving unexpected good fortune | 운 좋은

Beth is *fortunate* to have won the trip to New York.

**ANT** fortunate : untoward [ʌntóuərd]
untoward: 운 나쁜, 불리한

## grove
[grouv]

**n.** a group of trees cultivated for growing fruit | 작은 과수원

The *grove* of orange trees in Oscar's backyard produced the most delicious oranges.

**PAR** grove : tree [triː]
tree(나무)는 grove를 구성한다.

---

TRANSLATION | 예 문 해 석

| | |
|---|---|
| enunciate | 그 교사는 발표를 하고 있던 학생에게 급우들을 위하여 좀 더 명확하게 발음하라고 요구했다. |
| extenuate | Mary의 면밀한 해명은 그녀가 저지른 실수의 심각성을 경감하는 데 별로 크게 작용하지 못했다. |
| fidelity | 하급자의 충성도는 늘 논쟁의 대상이 된다. |
| fortunate | Beth는 운 좋게도 뉴욕 여행 기회를 얻어낼 수 있었다. |
| grove | Oscar네 뒤뜰에 있는 오렌지 나무 과수원은 가장 맛있는 오렌지를 생산했다. |

## grudge
[grʌdʒ]

**n.** a feeling of resentment | 원한, 악의

**v.** to reluctantly give or admit | 주기를 꺼려하다

I can't believe she still holds a *grudge* against me for a mistake I made three years ago!

We should not *grudge* helping any human being in need.

**ANT** grudge : good will [gud wil]

good will: 선의

## infect
[infékt]

**v.** to contaminate with a disease or sickness; to corrupt | 감염시키다, 타락시키다

Many people became *infected* with the plague that spread throughout the country.

**FUN** infection : antibiotic [æntaibaiɑ́tik]

antibiotic(항생제)는 infection(감염)을 치료하기 위해 사용된다.

## inveigle
[invíːgl]

**v.** to lure or entice | 유인하다, 꾀다

The charmer *inveigled* the young lady.

**KIN** inveigle : interest [íntərəst]

inveigle은 속임수나 미끼를 이용해 관심을 갖게 한다 라는 의미로 interest(관심을 갖게 하다)하는 것의 일종이다.

## kindle
[kíndl]

**v.** to start a fire; to arouse or stir up | 불 붙이다, (감정을) 자극하다, 부추기다

Feelings of attraction and affection quickly *kindled* between them.

**ANT** kindle : extinguish [ikstíŋgwiʃ]

extinguish: 불을 끄다

---

TRANSLATION | 예 문 해 석

**grudge** 내가 3년 전에 저지른 실수 때문에 그녀가 아직도 나에게 악의를 품고 있다는 사실을 믿을 수 없다!
우리는 도움을 필요로 하는 모든 사람을 돕는데 주저하지 말아야 한다.
**infect** 많은 사람들이 전국을 휩쓴 역병에 감염되기 시작했다.
**inveigle** 그 매혹적인 남성이 젊은 숙녀를 유인했다.
**kindle** 서로 이끌리며 사랑하는 감정이 그들 사이에 즉시 불붙었다.

## liken
[láikən]

**v. to regard or see as similar; to compare** | 비유하다

A divorce is often *likened* to the death of a marriage

> 대상 **liken : similarity** [sìməlǽrəti]
>
> liken은 similarity(유사점)를 비교하는 것이다.
>
> cf) **discriminate**: 구별하다 (차이점을 비교하다)

## lustrous
[lʌ́strəs]

**adj. bright; radiant in character** | 빛나는, 매력적인

Brigette's *lustrous* hair shone under the afternoon sun.

> 인과 **lustrous : burnish** [bə́ːrniʃ]
>
> burnish(광내다)하면 lustrous한 상태가 된다.

## mandatory
[mǽndətɔ̀ːri]

**adj. required or obligatory** | 의무적인, 강제적인

Every new employee must take a *mandatory* drug test.

> 대상 **mandatory : comply** [kəmplái]
>
> mandatory한 것을 comply(따르다)하다.

## mentor
[méntər]

**n. a trusted tutor** | 믿을 만한 조언자, 교사

The young boy's *mentor* was his older brother.

> CH **mentor : guidance** [gáidns]
>
> mentor는 guidance(안내, 지도) 해 주는 사람이다.

## murmur
[mə́ːrmər]

**v. to speak or complain with an unclear tone** | 낮은 소리로 중얼거리다, 투덜거리다

David *murmured* foul words under his breath.

> KIN **murmur : speak** [spiːk]
>
> murmur는 speak(말하다)의 한 종류이다.

---

| TRANSLATION | 예문 해석 |
|---|---|
| liken | 이혼은 종종 결혼의 죽음으로 비유된다. |
| lustrous | Brigette의 윤기나는 머리카락은 오후 햇살 아래서 빛났다. |
| mandatory | 모든 신입 직원은 의무적으로 약물 테스트를 받아야 한다. |
| mentor | 그 어린 소년의 선생은 그의 형이었다. |
| murmur | David는 나직한 목소리로 욕을 중얼거렸다. |

### painstaking
[péinztèikiŋ]

**adj. illustrating diligent care and work** | 노고를 아끼지 않는

Pat went to *painstaking* lengths to ensure the party was a success.

**ANT** painstaking : slipshod [slípʃàd]

slipshod: 아무렇게나 하는, 단정치 못한

### permit
[pərmít]

**v. to authorize or give consent** | 허가하다

**n. an official warrant or license** | 영장, 면허

Trespassers are not *permitted* on the Rosenbach's land.

**ANT** permit : proscribe [prouskráib]

proscribe: 금지하다

### pernicious
[pərníʃəs]

**adj. highly destructive or deadly** | 매우 유해한

Cocaine is illegal because of its *pernicious* effects on a user's mind and body.

**DE** pernicious : harmful [hɑ́ːrmfəl]

pernicious는 매우 harmful(유해한)한 이라는 의미이다.

### perspicacious
[pə̀ːrspəkéiʃəs]

**adj. being of keen discernment** | 통찰력 있는

The *perspicacious* jury could clearly see all the flaws in the defense lawyer's argument.

**ANT** perspicacious : stupid [stjúːpid]

stupid: 머리가 둔한, 어리석은

### pledge
[pledʒ]

**n. a binding promise or oath** | 서약, 맹세

**v. to make a pledge or swear** | 맹세하다

Every morning the students said the *Pledge* of Allegiance to the flag.
Adam *pledged* his sword to the chieftain.

**대상** pledge : renounce [rináuns]

renounce는 이미 전에 했던 pledge를 단념하다 라는 뜻이다.

---

**TRANSLATION | 예문해석**

| | |
|---|---|
| painstaking | Pat는 파티를 확실하게 성공적인 것으로 만들기 위하여 모든 노고를 아끼지 않았다. |
| permit | Rosenbach의 영토에서는 불법 침입자들이 허용되지 않는다. |
| pernicious | 코카인은 복용자의 정신과 육체에 미치는 치명적인 영향 때문에 불법이다. |
| perspicacious | 그 통찰력 있는 배심원단은 피고측 변호사의 주장의 헛점을 명확하게 짚어낼 수 있었다. |
| pledge | 매일 아침마다 학생들은 국가에 대한 맹세를 하였다.<br>Adam은 자기의 두목에게 칼을 두고 맹세했다. |

## polemic
[pəlémik]

n. **an aggressive attack on or disputation against** | 논쟁, 반론, 반박

The freedom fighter's *polemics* have already lasted over two hours!

**ANT** polemic : agreement [əgríːmənt]
agreement: 동의, 호응

## precursor
[priːkə́ːrsər]

n. **one that indicates the arrival of another; a predecessor** | 전조, 선구자, 선임자

The compact disc player was a *precursor* to the mini-disc player.

**ANT** precursory : derivative [dirívətiv]
precursory: 선구의, 전조의
derivative: 유도된, 파생된

## prodigious
[prədídʒəs]

adj. **huge in bulk or quantity; marvelous** | 거대한, 놀라운

The project will require a *prodigious* amount of money.

**ANT** prodigious : pinpoint [pínpɔ̀int]
pinpoint: 아주 작은

## prune
[pruːn]

n. **a dried plum** | 말린 자두
v. **to reduce or cut off parts, usually of plants** | 가지를 치다

The children preferred to eat raisins over *prunes*.
The old woman *prunes* her hedges every Sunday.

**KIN** prune : plum [plʌm]
prune은 말린 plum(자두)이다.

## rude
[ruːd]

adj. **inelegant or impolite in manner or action; crude or simple** | 무례한, 조야한

It is *rude* to interrupt someone's conversation.

**CH** rude : churl [tʃə́(ː)rl]
churl(시골뜨기, 상스러운 사람)은 rude한 사람을 뜻한다.

---

TRANSLATION | 예 문 해 석

**polemic** 그 자유를 위해 싸우는 사람의 반론은 이미 두 시간 이상이나 계속되고 있다.
**precursor** CD 플레이어는 미니 디스크 플레이어의 초기모델이었다.
**prodigious** 그 프로젝트는 엄청난 액수의 돈을 필요로 할 것이다.
**prune** 아이들은 말린 자두보다 건포도를 더 좋아한다.
그 할머니는 매주 일요일마다 울타리 나무가지들을 친다.
**rude** 누군가의 대화를 방해하는 것은 무례한 일이다.

## sanction
[sǽŋkʃən]

**n.** official approval or permission | 재가, 인가
**v.** to formally approve | 인가하다

The EU's human rights *sanctions* are being ignored by Turkey.
Now, the President is ready to *sanction* the reinforcement of the local army.

**ANT** sanction : interdict [íntərdíkt]
interdict: 금지하다

## scheme
[skiːm]

**n.** a plot or secret program of action | 계획, 음모
**v.** to plot | 음모를 짜다

Soren and Heather came up with a *scheme* to make extra money.
Daniel has already noticed that the rival company is *scheming* against him.

**KIN** scheme : plan [plæn]
scheme은 plan(계획하다)의 일종이다.

## sere
[siər]

**adj.** dried and withered | 시든, 마른

The vase full of old flowers, wilted and *sere*, didn't look very cheerful on the kitchen table.

**ANT** sere : lush [lʌʃ]
lush: 무성하게 자라는, 다산의, 풍부한

## sermon
[sə́ːrmən]

**n.** a speech on conduct or duty usually given by a religious leader | 설교

The *sermon* topic this Sunday was philanthropy.

**CH** sermon : preacher [príːtʃər]
preacher(설교자, 목사)는 sermon(설교)하는 사람이다.

---

### TRANSLATION | 예문 해석

**sanction**
EU의 인권 제재조약은 터키에 의해 무시되고 있다.
이제 대통령은 지방 군대에 대한 증원을 인가할 준비가 되어 있다.

**scheme**
Soren과 Heather는 추가적으로 돈을 벌 수 있는 계획을 생각해냈다.
Daniel은 경쟁사가 자신을 상대로 음모를 꾸미고 있음을 이미 알아차리고 있었다.

**sere**
그 시들고 말라 빠진 꽃이 잔뜩 꽂힌 꽃병은 부엌의 식탁 위에서 그다지 유쾌해 보이지 않았다.

**sermon**
이번 주일 설교의 주제는 박애주의였다.

## shun
[ʃʌn]

v. **to avoid and stay away from** | 멀리하다, 기피하다

I was *shunned* by my co-workers.

**ANT** shun : haunt [hɔːnt]

haunt: 자주 들리다

## stingy
[stíndʒi]

adj. **lacking generosity; unwilling to spend money** | 관대함이 결여된, 인색한

Christmas is not the time to be *stingy*.

**CH** stingy : miser [máizər]

miser(구두쇠)는 stingy한 사람을 말한다.

## submission
[səbmíʃən]

n. **a surrender or compliance** | 복종

The sieging army starved the city into *submission*.

**WO** submission : insubordinate [ìnsəbɔ́ːrdənit]

insubordinate(불복종하는, 반항하는)하는 사람은 아무에게나 submission하지 않는다.

## summon
[sʌ́mən]

v. **to call or send for, usually officially** | 소환하다

Tom has been *summoned* to court.

**FUN** summon : citation [saitéiʃən]

citation은 증인을 법정으로 summon하기 위한 소환장이다.

## tame
[teim]

adj. **domesticated; submissive or harmless; spiritless or dull** | 길들인, 유순한, 생기없는, 따분한

The party was considered *tame* by many of the guests who were in attendance.

**ANT** tame : racy [réisi]

racy: 활기찬, 생동하는, 통쾌한

---

TRANSLATION | 예문 해석

| | |
|---|---|
| shun | 나는 동료 직원들의 기피의 대상이었다. |
| stingy | 크리스마스는 인색하게 굴 때가 아니다. |
| submission | 점령군은 음식을 바닥나게 함으로써 그 도시를 복종하도록 만들었다. |
| summon | Tom은 법정에 소환되었다. |
| tame | 파티에 참석했던 많은 사람들은 그 파티가 재미없었다고 생각했다. |

## tender
[téndər]

**adj. soft or delicate** | 부드러운, 미묘한

Nothing is more *tender* than the love of a doting grandmother.

**ANT** tender : hardy [há:rdi]

hardy: 단단한, 강건한

## terminate
[tə́:rmənèit]

**v. to close or end; to finish** | 끝내다

The factory officially *terminated* her employment.

**ANT** termination : inception [insépʃən]

termination: 종결, 종료

inception: 시초, 시작

## vindicate
[víndəkèit]

**v. to show the validity of; to defend; to free from an accusation, suspicion, or doubt with supporting proof** | 정당함을 입증하다, 옹호하다, 혐의·의혹을 풀다

The jury's not-guilty verdict *vindicated* the defendent.

**ANT** vindicate : impugn [impjú:n]

impugn: 논박하다, 비난하다

## void
[vɔid]

**v. to empty or clear; to nullify** | 비우다, 없애다, 무효화하다

**n. an empty space or absence** | 공허

**adj. empty or containing nothing** | 텅 빈

The cashier *voided* the transaction.

After their child left for college, they tried to fill the *void* in their life with arts and crafts.

*Void* of contact with other monkeys, the captured monkey became listless and lethargic.

**SYN** void : empty [émpti]

empty: 텅 빈

---

TRANSLATION | 예 문 해 석

**tender** 맹목적인 할머니의 사랑보다 더 부드러운 것은 없다.
**terminate** 그 공장은 그녀와의 고용관계를 공식적으로 끝냈다.
**vindicate** 배심원단의 무죄 평결은 피고인의 혐의를 벗겨주었다.
**void** 그 출납원은 그 거래를 무효화했다.
자식들이 대학으로 떠나고 난 후, 그들은 인생의 공허함을 미술과 공예로 채웠다.
그 잡혀온 원숭이는 다른 원숭이들과의 접촉이 없이 생기없고 무기력해졌다.

# 26th Day  Daily Check-up

■ Fill in the blanks with the correct letter that matches the word with its definition.

1. polemic  _____
2. stingy  _____
3. enunciate  _____
4. amenable  _____
5. grudge  _____
6. lustrous  _____
7. drench  _____
8. sere  _____
9. contravene  _____
10. submission  _____

a. to reluctantly give or admit
b. dried and withered
c. bright; radiant in character
d. to express or pronounce clearly and articulately
e. to violate; to oppose in argument
f. an aggressive attack on or disputation against
g. a surrender or compliance
h. responsible or answerable; readily brought to submission or obedience
i. lacking generosity; unwilling to spend money
j. to saturate or soak thoroughly

■ Put the correct word in each blank from the list of words below.

11. _____는 매우 harmful한 이라는 의미이다.
12. _____는 guidance를 해 주는 사람이다.
13. _____는 flourish(번영하다)의 반의어이다.
14. racy(활기찬, 생동하는)은 _____이 반의어이다.
15. _____은 interdict(금지하다)의 반의어이다.
16. derivative(유도된, 파생된)의 반의어는 _____이다.
17. churl은 _____한 사람을 뜻한다.
18. _____는 심한 abuse가 사용되는 말을 의미하는 것이다.
19. skeptic은 _____하지 않다.
20. disinter(발굴하다)의 반의어는 _____이다.

| a. dwindle | b. prune | c. precursory | d. pernicious | e. credulous | f. tame |
| g. mentor | h. rude | i. embed | j. diatribe | k. fidelity | l. sanction |

**Answer key**

11. d  12. g  13. a  14. e  15. l  16. c  17. h  18. j  19. e  20. i
1. f  2. i  3. d  4. h  5. a  6. c  7. j  8. b  9. e  10. g

# 27th DAY

자, 이제 거의 다 되었습니다.
3일만 참고 찐한 책걸이를 기대해보죠!

## applause
[əplɔ́ːz]

**n. the clapping of hands at a performance to express approval** | 박수갈채

The *applause* from the crowd filled the stadium.

**PUR** applause : approval [əprúːvəl]

approval(찬성, 승인)을 표현하기 위해 applause를 보낸다.

## arduous
[áːrdʒuəs]

**adj. difficult or strenuous** | 어려운, 노력이 요구되는

The *arduous* climb up the mountain took three days.

**ANT** arduous : facile [fǽsil]

facile: 별다른 노력이 필요 없을 정도로 쉬운

## asperity
[əspérəti]

**n. harshness or roughness** | 매서움, 거칠음

Todd spoke with an *asperity* during the meeting that intimidated potential detractors.

**ANT** asperity : mildness [máildnis]

mildness: 부드러움

## aspirant
[ǽspərənt]

**n. one who seeks or desires to succeed or advance** | 야망이 있는 사람, 열망자

*Aspirants* to the succession of leadership schemed for months before the dictator's death.

**CH** aspirant : quarry [kwɔ́ːri]

aspirant는 quarry(애써 탐구해서 얻어내다)하는 사람이다.

---

### TRANSLATION | 예문해석

| | |
|---|---|
| applause | 관중들의 박수갈채가 스타디움을 가득 채웠다. |
| arduous | 그 힘든 등산은 3일이나 걸렸다. |
| asperity | Todd는 회의 때 무척 매섭게 말해서 그를 감히 비판하는 사람이 없도록 만들었다. |
| aspirant | 지도자의 자리를 계승하려 열망했던 사람들은 그 독재자가 죽기 전 몇달 동안 음모를 꾸몄다. |

## capitulate
[kəpítʃulèit]

**v. to surrender or acquiesce on agreed terms** | 항복하다, 협의하다

I *capitulated* to the chief's request to work over-time.

**ANT** capitulation : resistance [rizístəns]
- capitulation: 항복
- resistance: 저항

## comity
[kάməti]

**n. a state of civility and respect between peoples or nations** | 예의바름, 겸양, 화합

The *comity* of races has been the goal of many great leaders such as Martin Luther King Jr. and Gandhi.

**ANT** comity : enmity [énməti]
- enmity: 적의, 증오

## copious
[kóupiəs]

**adj. abundant or plentiful in quantity or quality** | 풍부한

The thunderstorm brought *copious* rain to the Serengeti Plains.

**ANT** copious : sparse [spɑːrs]
- sparse: 희박한, 부족한

## curmudgeon
[kərmΛ́dʒən]

**n. an ill-tempered and hostile person** | 심술궂고 적대적인 사람

No one knew how to act around the *curmudgeon* because everything seemed to set him off.

**ANT** curmudgeon : agreeable person [əgríːəbl pə́ːrsn]
- agreeable person: 상냥한 사람

## deafening
[défəniŋ]

**adj. excessively loud** | 지나치게 시끄러운

Every time Korea scored a goal the crowd raised a *deafening* cheer.

**DE** deafening : loud [laud]
- deafening은 loud(시끄러운)보다 훨씬 더 시끄러운 정도를 말한다.

---

| TRANSLATION | 예문해석 |
|---|---|
| capitulate | 나는 초과근무를 하라는 상사의 요구에 굴복했다. |
| comity | 인종 간의 화합은 Martin Luther King Jr.나 Gandhi와 같은 많은 위대한 지도자들의 목표가 되어 왔다. |
| copious | 그 폭풍은 Serengeti 평원에 엄청난 비를 뿌렸다. |
| curmudgeon | 무엇이든 그를 폭발시켜버릴 것 같았기 때문에 그 심술궂은 사람 주위에서 어떻게 행동해야 할 지 아무도 몰랐다. |
| deafening | 한국이 득점할 때마다 사람들은 굉장히 시끄러운 환호를 보냈다. |

### demur
[dimə́ːr]

v. **to object** | 반대하다
n. **a protest or hesitation** | 반대, 망설임

It is my right to *demur* to vote.
David proposed to his girlfriend who agreed without *demur*.

- **SYN** demur : objection [əbdʒékʃən]
  objection: 반대, 이의

### deplete
[diplíːt]

v. **to use up; to lessen or reduce** | 고갈시키다, 감소시키다

The army *depleted* its food supply quickly.

- **ANT** deplete : enrich [inrítʃ]
  enrich: 풍부하게 하다

### deplore
[diplɔ́ːr]

v. **to express or feel sadness or regret; to condemn or strongly disapprove of** | 한탄하다, 비난하다

The President stated that he *deplored* the deaths of the children in Somalia.

- **ANT** deplore : rejoice [ridʒɔ́is]
  rejoice: 기뻐하다

### divulge
[divʌ́ldʒ]

v. **to proclaim or disclose; to reveal and make known** | 공언하다, 폭로하다

Fred *divulges* all his secrets to his best friend.

- **ANT** divulge : conceal [kənsíːl]
  conceal: 숨기다, 비밀로 하다

### dolt
[doult]

n. **a stupid or foolish person** | 어리석은 사람, 바보

Sean felt like a *dolt* after he answered his professor's question incorrectly.

- **CH** dolt : stupid [stjúːpid]
  dolt는 stupid(어리석은)하다.

---

| TRANSLATION | 예문 해석 |

| | |
|---|---|
| **demur** | 투표에 반대하는 것은 나의 권리이다. |
| | David은 여자친구에게 청혼했고 그녀는 망설임없이 승낙했다. |
| **deplete** | 그 군대는 식량 보급을 급속히 감소시켰다. |
| **deplore** | 대통령은 소말리아 어린이들의 죽음을 애도한다는 성명을 발표했다. |
| **divulge** | Fred는 자신의 모든 비밀을 가장 친한 친구에게 털어놓는다. |
| **dolt** | Sean은 교수의 질문에 틀린 대답을 한 후에 자신이 바보처럼 느껴졌다. |

## euphemism
[júːfəmìzm]

n. the use of a mild or inoffensive expression instead of one that is offensive or aggressive | 완곡어법

A tactful person uses *euphemisms* in their daily language.

**WO** euphemism : offense [əféns]
euphemism에는 offense(감정을 해침)를 줄만한 소지가 없다.

## euphonious
[juːfóuniəs]

adj. pleasing to the ear | 듣기 좋은

The *euphonious* music lulled the baby to sleep.

**ANT** euphonious : cacophonous [kəkǽfənəs]
cacophonous: 불협 화음의, 귀에 거슬리는

## expedite
[ékspədàit]

v. to accelerate or rush a process | 가속시키다, (일을) 신속히 처리하다

Nat had his VISA application *expedited* so that he could leave the country on time.

**WO** expedite : foot-dragging [fútdræ̀giŋ]
expedite하는 사람에게서는 foot-dragging(의도적인 지연)의 태도를 찾아볼 수 없다.

## expenditure
[ikspénditʃər]

n. the act of spending; that which is spent or used | 지출, 소비, 비용

The family maintained careful records of all its *expenditures*.

**WO** expenditure : parsimonious [pàːrsəmóuniəs]
parsimonious(인색한)한 사람의 사전에는 expenditure가 없다.

## exponent
[ikspóunənt]

n. one that exemplifies or advocates something; a mathematical symbol expressing the raising of a power | 주창자; 지수

Tracy is an *exponent* of recycling.

**CH** exponent : advocate [ǽdvəkèit]
expondent는 자신의 신념을 advocate(주장하다, 옹호하다)한다.

---

TRANSLATION | 예문해석

| | |
|---|---|
| euphemism | 재치 있는 사람은 일상 언어에서 완곡어법을 사용한다. |
| euphonious | 듣기 좋은 음악이 아이를 진정시켜 잠들게 했다. |
| expedite | Nat는 제 시간에 그 나라를 떠날 수 있도록 비자신청을 신속히 처리하였다. |
| expenditure | 그 가족은 모든 지출을 꼼꼼하게 기록하는 것을 잘 지키고 있었다. |
| exponent | Tracy는 재활용을 지지하는 사람이다. |

## figurative
[fígjurətiv]

**adj.** representing by a figure; metaphorical

| 숫자로 표시된, 비유적인

The preacher often uses *figurative* language in his sermons.

**ANT** figurative : literal [lítərəl]

literal: 문자 그대로의

## flaunt
[flɔːnt]

**v.** to display ostentatiously

| 과시하다

Sheila *flaunted* her new dress at the school dance.

**ANT** flaunt : ensconce [inskáns]

ensconce: 감추다

## flounder
[fláundər]

**v.** to move about or proceed clumsily and ineffectually

| 버둥거리다, 허둥대다

He *floundered* about the room in his drunken stupor.

**ANT** flounder : slide [slaid]

slide: 활주하다, 미끄러지다

## flourish
[flə́ːriʃ]

**v.** to thrive or prosper; to make a sweeping and showy gesture

| 번영하다, 과시하며 휘두르는 몸짓을 취하다

America *flourished* in wealth during the 1980s.

**ANT** flourish : waste away [weist əwéi]

waste away: 쇠퇴하다

## haphazard
[hæphǽzərd]

**adj.** by chance or random; without planning

| 우연한, 되는대로의 계획성 없는

Nietzsche's essays are written in a *haphazard* manner that confuses the readers.

**ANT** haphazard : methodical [məθɑ́dikəl]

methodical: 규칙적인

---

### TRANSLATION | 예문 해석

| | |
|---|---|
| **figurative** | 그 설교자는 종종 자신의 설교에 은유적인 언어를 사용한다. |
| **flaunt** | Sheila는 학교의 댄스 모임에서 새 드레스를 과시했다. |
| **flounder** | 그는 술에 취해 인사불성이 되어 방안에서 이리저리 허둥대고 다녔다. |
| **flourish** | 아메리카는 1980년대에 번영을 누렸다. |
| **haphazard** | 니체의 수필들은 너무 아무렇게나 쓰여져서 독자들을 혼란시킨다. |

## hyperbole
[haipə́ːrbəli]

n. **a dramatic exaggeration** | 과장법

The use of *hyperbole* in writing is often intended for comical relief.

**CH** hyperbole : exaggerated [igzǽdʒərèitid]
hyperbole은 exaggerated(과장된)된 수사 어법이다.

## impecunious
[ìmpikjúːniəs]

adj. **habitually poor or without money** | 가난한, 무일푼의

My billionaire friend Jeff started off as an *impecunious* inventor living off table scraps.

**ANT** impecunious : affluent [ǽflu(ː)ənt]
affluent: 부유한

## impede
[impíːd]

v. **to get in the way of or to slow the progress of** | 방해하다, 지체시키다

The construction on the bridge *impeded* the morning traffic.

**ANT** impede : facilitate [fəsílətèit]
facilitate: 촉진하다

## imperious
[impíəriəs]

adj. **having an arrogant attitude; intensely compelling** | 거만한, 긴급한

Laura silenced her subordinates with an *imperious* glare.

**WO** imperious : humility [hjuːmíləti]
imperious한 사람은 humility(겸손)가 없다.

## impermeable
[impə́ːrmiəbl]

adj. **not allowing passage through its surface or substance** | 관통할 수 없는

This new fabric is *impermeable* to wind.

**CN** impermeable : penetrate [pénətrèit]
impermeable한 것은 penetrate(관통하다)할 수 없다.

---

TRANSLATION | 예 문 해 석

**hyperbole** 글쓰기에서 과장법의 사용은 종종 희극적인 안도감을 주기 위해 의도된다.
**impecunious** 먹다남은 음식으로 생계를 이어가던 가난한 발명가인 내 친구 Jeff는 억만장자가 되었다.
**impede** 다리 위의 건설공사가 아침의 교통 소통을 방해했다.
**imperious** Laura는 거만한 눈빛으로 부하들을 침묵시켰다.
**impermeable** 이 새 직물은 바람이 통하지 않는다.

## imperturbable
[ìmpərtə́ːrbəbl]

**adj. serene or extremely calm** | 침착한, 쉽게 동요하지 않는

Gloria remained *imperturbable* before her piano concert relaxedly imagining a grand performance.

**ANT** imperturbable : restive [réstiv]

restive: 안절부절 못하는, 흥분한

## impervious
[impə́ːrviəs]

**adj. impenetrable; not capable of being disturbed or damaged** | 뚫을 수 없는, 손상되지 않는

The robbers could not open the *impervious* safe even with explosives.

**CN** impervious : damaged [dǽmidʒd]

impervious 한 것은 damaged(손상된) 하지 않는다.

## impetuous
[impétʃuəs]

**adj. impulsive; marked by violent force of action or manner** | 충동적인, 격렬한

Gabby's one vice was her habit of *impetuous* shopping.

**WO** impetuous : hesitation [hèzətéiʃən]

impetuous한 사람의 행동에는 hesitation(주저, 망설임)이 없다.

## implacable
[implǽkəbl]

**adj. incapable of being appeased or changed** | 달래거나 바꿀 수 없는

There is no use in arguing with Connor because he is *implacable*.

**CN** implacable : compromise [kάmprəmàiz]

implacable한 사람과는 compromise(타협하다)하기 어렵다.

## implode
[implóud]

**v. to violently collapse inward** | 안으로 폭발하다, 내파하다

The volcano *imploded*, saving the lives of the nearby villagers.

**DE** implode : collapse [kəlǽps]

implode는 내파하다 라는 뜻으로 collapse에 비해 강도가 높다.

---

### TRANSLATION | 예문해석

**imperturbable** Gloria는 자신의 피아노 연주회 전에 굉장한 연주를 편안히 상상하며 침착하게 있었다.
**impervious** 그 강도들은 폭약으로도 손상되지 않는 그 금고를 열 수가 없었다.
**impetuous** Gabby의 한 가지 결함은 그녀의 충동적인 쇼핑 습관이다.
**implacable** Connor는 도저히 바꿀 수 없는 사람이기 때문에 그와 논쟁을 해봤자 아무런 소용이 없다.
**implode** 그 화산이 안으로 폭발해서 마을 사람들은 목숨을 건졌다.

## induce
[indjúːs]

**v. to persuade or influence; to cause to make happen** | 설득하여 ~을 하게하다, 유발하다

Ivy was *induced* to work harder by the enticement of stock options.

**ANT** inducement : deterrent [ditə́ːrənt]

inducement: 유도, 유도하는 것

deterrent: 방해, 방해하는 것

## instrumentalist
[ìnstrəméntlist]

**n. one who plays a musical instrument** | 기악 연주자

The band was composed of one lead singer and three *instrumentalists*.

**대상** instrumentalist : symphony [símfəni]

instrumentalist은 symphony(교향곡)를 연주하는 사람이다.

## nepotism
[népətìzm]

**n. favoritism based on family relations** | 친족에 대한 편파 주의

Uncle Jim exhibited *nepotism* by hiring his irresponsible nephew to work at the store.

**대상** nepotism : relative [rélətiv]

nepotism은 relative(친인척)를 편드는 주의이다.

## nocturnal
[nɑktə́ːrnl]

**adj. related to or active during the night** | 야간의, 야행성의

Owls are *nocturnal* creatures.

**ANT** nocturnal : diurnal [daiə́ːrnl]

diurnal: 낮의

## opportune
[àpərtjúːn]

**adj. suitable or appropriate for a certain moment or purpose** | 특정한 시기나 목적에 적당한, 알맞은

David waited for the *opportune* moment to make his escape from the prison.

**POS** opportune : convenience [kənvíːnjəns]

convenience: 형편에 맞음, 편리함

---

### TRANSLATION | 예 문 해 석

**induce** Ivy는 스톡 옵션의 유혹에 의해 더 열심히 일하도록 설득되었다.

**instrumentalist** 그 밴드는 한 명의 리드 싱어와 세 명의 연주자로 구성되어 있다.

**nepotism** Jim 아저씨는 무책임한 조카를 가게에 고용함으로써 자신의 친족 편파주의를 내보였다.

**nocturnal** 올빼미는 야행성 동물이다.

**opportune** David는 탈옥하기 적절한 시간을 기다렸다.

## peck
[pek]

**n. a short light kiss** | 가벼운 키스

In Europe, people give each other a *peck* on the cheek when they greet each other.

**KIN** peck : kiss [kis]

peck은 이마나 볼에 가볍게 하는 kiss(키스)이다.

## repel
[ripél]

**v. to reject or drive away; to cause distaste** | 거절하다, 쫓아버리다, 혐오감을 주다

The taxi driver's rudeness *repelled* the customer from leaving a tip.

**CH** repel : repugnant [ripʌ́gnənt]

repugnant(불쾌한, 혐오스러운)한 것은 repel하는 속성이 있다.

## repertoire
[répərtwà:r]

**n. the list of artistic pieces (dramas, plays, dances, etc.) that an artist or group can perform** | 상연 목록, 연주 목록

Paul has a varied *repertoire* of guitar music that he performs for friends.

**FUN** repertoire : play [plei]

play(연극)의 제목을 적어 놓은 목록을 repertoire라고 한다.

## replete
[riplí:t]

**adj. full of or complete** | 가득 찬, 완전한

A traditional Greek meal is *replete* with olives and feta.

**ANT** repletion : want [wɔ(:)nt]

repletion: 가득 참

want: 부족, 결핍

## repose
[ripóuz]

**v. to lie down or take a rest** | 드러눕다, 쉬다

**n. rest** | 휴식

Tom's favorite spot to *repose* is in his hammock.

Daniel had such a peaceful face in *repose*.

**PUR** repose : fatigue [fətí:g]

repose를 취해 fatigue(피로)를 풀다.

---

| TRANSLATION | 예 문 해 석 |

**peck** 유럽에서는 사람들이 서로를 맞이할 때 서로의 볼에 가벼운 키스를 한다.

**repel** 그 택시 운전사의 무례함이 승객에게 혐오감을 주어서 그는 팁을 받지 못했다.

**repertoire** Paul은 친구들을 위해 연주할 다양한 종류의 기타 음악 연주 목록을 갖고 있다.

**replete** 전통적인 그리스의 음식에는 올리브와 페타 치즈가 가득 들어있다.

**repose** Tom이 가장 좋아하는 휴식 장소는 그의 해먹 안이다.
쉬는 동안 Daniel의 얼굴은 그렇게 평화롭게 보일 수가 없었다.

## repudiate
[ripjú:dièit]

v. **to renounce or reject as true; to disown or formally separate from; to refuse to pay a debt** | 부인하다, 의절하다, (빚 갚기를) 거절하다

The scientist *repudiated* the claim that his research was biased.

**ANT** repudiate : concede [kənsí:d]

concede: (사실임을) 인정하다, 시인하다

## scatter
[skǽtər]

v. **to disperse in all directions; to strew or divide into random portions** | 흩어지게 하다, 흩뿌리다

The wind *scattered* leaves across the yard.

**CN** scattering : overlap [òuvərlǽp]

scattering(흩어져 있는, 드문드문한)된 것은 overlap(겹쳐지다, 중복되다)하지 않는다.

## sophisticate
[səfístəkèit]

v. **to make worldly-wise or complex; to refine** | 처사에 능하게 만들다, 복잡하게 만들다, 세련되게 하다

n. **one who knows about socially important matters** | 교양인

Heather tried to *sophisticate* her friend Soren by sending him on a trip to Europe.

Jane prefers to attend social events that draw *sophisticates*.

**ANT** sophisticated : barbaric [bɑːrbǽrik]

sophisticated: 교양 있는, 세련된
barbaric: 교양 없는, 야만적인

## soporific
[sɑ̀pərífik]

n. **a drug or agent used to induce sleep** | 수면제, 최면제

adj. **tending to induce sleep** | 졸리게 하는

Norma took a *soporific* for her insomnia.

John was lulled to sleep by that *soporific* movie.

**FUN** soporific : sleep [sli:p]

soporific은 sleep(잠)을 유발하는 기능이 있다.

---

TRANSLATION | 예문해석

**repudiate** 그 과학자는 자신의 연구가 편향되었다는 주장을 부인했다.
**scatter** 바람이 불어 나뭇잎들이 마당 구석구석에 흩어졌다.
**sophisticate** Heather는 그녀의 친구인 Soren을 유럽에 여행 보내어 세련되게 만들려고 노력했다.
Jane은 교양인들이 모여드는 사교 행사에 참석하기를 더 좋아한다.
**soporific** Norma는 불면증 때문에 수면제를 복용했다.
그 졸리는 영화는 John을 잠재워 버렸다.

## splint
[splint]

**n. a device used to support and keep a joint or fractured bone from moving** | 접합 부위를 지지하거나 골절된 뼈가 움직이지 않도록 유지시키는 데 이용하는 기구, 부목

The *splint* was uncomfortable and inconvenient because all her movements were restricted by it.

**FUN** splint : mobility [moubíləti]

splint는 mobility(유동성)가 없도록 하는 것이다.

## stealth
[stelθ]

**n. the quality of being secretive and covert** | 은밀, 비밀

A leopard uses *stealth* to catch its prey.

**POS** stealth : furtive [fə́ːrtiv]

furtive: 은밀한

## supercilious
[sùːpərsíliəs]

**adj. showing an arrogant manner** | 거만한

Matthew's *supercilious* smirk angered his ex-girlfriend.

**ANT** supercilious : obsequious [əbsíːkwiəs]

obsequious: 고분고분한, 아첨하는

## superficial
[sùːpərfíʃəl]

**adj. relating to the surface; lacking depth; shallow** | 표면의, 피상적인, 천박한

America is thought to have a *superficial* and materialistic culture.

**CH** superficial : dilettante [dílitὰːnt]

dilettante(아마추어 예술가)는 전문적인 기술없이 그저 취미삼아 superficial하게 예술을 대하는 사람이다.

## superior
[səpíəriər]

**adj. upper or better; of higher rank or stature** | 우월한, 상위의, 우수한

Just because something costs more doesn't mean it has *superior* quality.

**CH** superiority : authority [əθɔ́ːrəti]

authority(권위자, 대가)는 superiority(우월, 우위)를 가지고 있다.

---

### TRANSLATION | 예문해석

**splint** 그녀의 모든 움직임이 부목에 의해 제한이 되었기 때문에 부목은 불쾌하고 불편했다.
**stealth** 표범은 먹이를 사냥하기 위해 은밀함을 이용한다.
**supercilious** Matthew의 거만하고 능글맞은 웃음이 그의 전 여자 친구를 화나게 만들었다.
**superficial** 미국은 피상적이고 물질적인 문화를 갖고 있는 것으로 여겨진다.
**superior** 가격이 비싸다는 것이 질이 더 우수함을 의미하지는 않는다.

## supine
[suːpáin]

**adj. lying on one's back with face upward; suggesting lethargy or passivity** | 드러누운, 무기력한, 활발치 못한

Travis' *supine* answer to everything was always either 'I don't know' or 'I don't care'.

**ANT** supine : vigilant [vídʒələnt]

vigilant: 방심하지 않는, 부단히 경계하는

## taper
[téipər]

**v. to progressively narrow or diminish in width** | 갈수록 폭이 좁아지다

I have never liked wearing pants with *tapered* legs.

**대상** taper : width [widθ]

taper는 width(폭)이 좁아지는 것이다.

## tepid
[tépid]

**adj. lukewarm; lacking in enthusiasm or passion** | 미지근한, 열정이 부족한

Heathcliffe's *tepid* style of speaking did little to attract people to him.

**ANT** tepid : fervid [fə́ːrvid]

fervid: 열정적인

## tortuous
[tɔ́ːrtʃuəs]

**adj. winding or crooked** | 구불구불한

The *tortuous* mountain roads are difficult to drive on.

**CH** tortuous : labyrinth [lǽbərinθ]

labyrinth(미로)는 tortuous한 특징이 있다.

## typo
[táipou]

**n. an error in typing (short for 'typographical error')** | 오타

One *typo* ruined the entire letter, which I then had to re-type.

**대상** typo : text [tekst]

text(원문, 본문)에 나타난 오류를 typo라고 한다.

---

### TRANSLATION | 예문 해석

| | |
|---|---|
| supine | Travis는 만사에 '잘 몰라' 아니면 '신경 안써' 라는 무기력한 대답으로 일관했다. |
| taper | 나는 폭이 점점 좁아지는 바지는 결코 좋아하지 않는다. |
| tepid | Heathcliffe의 열의 없이 말하는 방식은 다른 사람들의 관심을 끌지 못했다. |
| tortuous | 구불구불한 산길들을 따라 운전하는 일은 어렵다. |
| typo | 오타 하나가 편지를 다 망쳐버려서, 타이핑을 다시 해야만 했다. |

## vapid
[vǽpid]

**adj. lacking taste or flavor; lacking spirit, liveliness, or interest** | 맛없는, 무기력한, 지루한

Sue left the concert because of the *vapid* music.

> **ANT** vapid : riveting [rívitiŋ]
>
> riveting: 매혹적인, 황홀하게 하는

## vapor
[véipər]

**n. a barely visible gas; something unsubstantial** | 증기, 실체가 없는 것

There was a lot of *vapor* in the air from Michael's cooking.

> 인과 vaporization : heat [hiːt]
>
> vaporization(증발)은 heat(열)에 의해서 발생한다.

---

| TRANSLATION | 예 문 해 석 |
|---|---|
| **vapid** | Sue는 지루한 음악 때문에 콘서트장을 나왔다. |
| **vapor** | Michael이 요리를 해서 공기 중에 수증기가 많이 생겼다. |

# 27th Day  Daily Check-up

■ Fill in the blanks with the correct letter that matches the word with its definition.

1. impermeable  _____
2. supercilious  _____
3. euphonious  _____
4. tortuous  _____
5. aspirant  _____
6. taper  _____
7. induce  _____
8. flounder  _____
9. impecunious  _____
10. opportune  _____

a. suitable or appropriate for a certain moment or purpose
b. habitually poor or without money
c. winding or crooked
d. to move about or proceed clumsily and ineffectually
e. showing an arrogant manner
f. not allowing passage through its surface or substance
g. to progressively narrow or diminish in width
h. one who seeks or desires to succeed or advance
i. pleasing to the ear
j. to persuade or influence; to cause to make happen

■ Put the correct word in each blank from the list of words below.

11. restive(들떠 있는)의 반의어는 _____이다.
12. _____에는 offense를 줄 만한 소지가 없다.
13. _____한 사람은 zeal이 없다
14. _____는 object(반대하다)의 동의어이다.
15. diurnal(낮의)의 반의어는 _____이다.
16. _____은 exaggerated된 수사 어법이다.
17. _____은 resistance(저항)의 반의어이다.
18. _____은 sleep을 유발하는 기능이 있다.
19. methodical(규칙적인)의 반의어는 _____이다.
20. _____한 사람은 humility가 없다.

a. nocturnal  b. capitulation  c. imperturbable  d. imperious  e. hyperbole  f. demur
g. euphemism  h. vapid  i. soporific  j. implode  k. haphazard  l. expenditure

Answer key

1. f  2. e  3. i  4. c  5. h  6. g  7. j  8. d  9. b  10. a
11. c  12. g  13. h  14. f  15. a  16. e  17. b  18. i  19. k  20. d

# TAKE A BREAK   쉬•어•가•는 페•이•지

영시 감상

*by Henry Wadsworth Longfellow

### A Psalm of Life

Tell me not, in mournful numbers,
"Life is but an empty dream!"
For the soul is dead that slumbers,
And things are not what they seem.

Life is real! Life is earnest!
And the grave is not its goal;
"Dust thou art, to dust returnst,"
Was not spoken of the soul.

Not enjoyment, and not sorrow,
Is our destined end or way;
But to act, that each to-morrow
Find us farther than to-day.

### 인생의 찬가

슬픈 사연으로 내게 말하지 말아라.
인생은 한낱 헛된 꿈에 불과하다고!
잠자는 영혼은 죽은 것이어니
만물은 외양의 모습 그대로가 아니다.

인생은 진실이다! 인생은 진지하다!
무덤이 그 종말이 될 수는 없다.
"너는 흙이니 흙으로 돌아가라."
이 말은 영혼에 대해 한 말은 아니다.

우리가 가야 할 곳, 또한 가는 길은
향락도 아니요 슬픔도 아니다.
저마다 내일이 오늘보다 낫도록
행동하는 그것이 목적이요 길이다.

www.goHackers.com

해커스 어학연구소

# SUPER VOCA

T.W.E.N.T.Y.E.I.G.H.T.H.D.A.Y

## 28th DAY

그 때를 아십니까?
사전 씹어먹던 그 처절한 그 시절.....

---

**abrade**
[əbréid]

**v. to wear away by friction; to irritate** | 마모시키다, 신경질나게 하다

During the Ice Age, the advance of icebergs abraded the continent.

인과   abrade : friction [fríkʃən]

friction(마찰)의 결과 abraded(마모된)된다.

---

**acquiesce**
[æ̀kwiés]

**v. to yield to or comply with unwillingly or passively** | (마지못해) 동의하다

Sandra acquiesced to her parents and gave up her dream to be a dancer.

CN   acquiesce : intransigent [intrǽnsədʒənt]

intransigent(비타협적인 사람)는 acquiesce 하지 않는다.

---

**aerate**
[ɛ́əreit]

**v. to supply with oxygen or air** | 공기나 산소를 통하게 하다

It is important to aerate the water in a fish tank.

대상   aerate : oxygen [ɑ́ksidʒən]

aerate는 oxygen(산소)를 통하게 한다는 뜻이다.

---

**ambiguity**
[æ̀mbigjúːəti]

**n. the state of having more than one meaning; uncertainty in meaning** | 애매 모호함, 모호한 표현

The purpose of contracts is to remove any ambiguity regarding each party's responsibility.

WO   ambiguous : clarity [klǽrəti]

ambiguous(애매한)한 표현에는 clarity(명료, 명쾌함)가 없다.

---

### TRANSLATION | 예 문 해 석

| | |
|---|---|
| abrade | 빙하기에 빙산의 이동으로 인해 대륙이 마모되었다. |
| acquiesce | Sandra는 마지못해 부모님의 말에 동의하고 무용수가 되려던 꿈을 포기했다. |
| aerate | 어항의 물에 공기가 통하도록 하는 것은 중요하다. |
| ambiguity | 계약의 목적은 양자간의 책임에 있어 어떤 모호함이라도 없애기 위한 것이다. |

## appreciate
[əpríːʃièit]

**v. to be grateful for; to understand the value or quality of**
| 감사하다, 진가를 인정하다

More than the flowers and cards, I *appreciated* the visits by my friends when I was ill.

**PUR** appreciation : testimonial [tèstəmóuniəl]

testimonial(감사장)은 appreciation(감사)을 표현하기 위한 것이다.

## approbation
[æ̀prəbéiʃən]

**n. formal or official approval; praise**
| 승인, 찬성

The soldier's valor in combat earned him the military's highest *approbation*, the Medal of Honor.

**SYN** approbation : praise [preiz]

praise: 칭찬

## appropriate
adj. [əpróupriət]
v. [əpróuprièit]

**adj. suitable or fitting**
| 적당한

**v. to set apart for a specific use**
| 사취하다

A handshake is *appropriate* when greeting someone.

The baker *appropriated* half of the bakery's monthly flour supply to make bread for his daughter's wedding.

**CH** appropriate : embezzler [imbézlər]

embezzler(착복자, 횡령자)는 appropriate하는 사람이다.

## approve
[əprúːv]

**v. to consent or accept as favorable or satisfactory**
| 찬성하다, 승인하다

The committee *approved* the building of a new school.

**PUR** approval : applause [əplɔ́ːz]

approval(찬성, 승인)을 표현하기 위해 applause(박수갈채)를 보낸다.

---

### TRANSLATION | 예문해석

**appreciate** 나는 아플 때 꽃이나 카드보다 친구들의 방문에 더 감사했다.

**approbation** 전투에서 그 군인이 보여준 용맹함과 용기를 치하하기 위해서 군대 최고의 훈장인 명예훈장이 수여되었다.

**appropriate** 누군가에게 인사할 때 악수가 적절하다.
그 제과업자는 자신의 딸 결혼식에 쓸 빵을 만들기 위해 그 달 밀가루 공급량의 절반을 착복했다.

**approve** 그 위원회는 새로운 학교의 건립을 찬성했다.

## approximate
[əpráksəmit]

**adj.** **almost exact; quite similar** | 거의 정확한, 근접한

The contractor's *approximate* cost of the renovation was more than the purchase price of the house.

**DE** approximate : precise [prisáis]

'정확한'이라는 의미를 가지고 있는 **precise**와 '거의 정확한'이라는 의미를 가지고 있는 **approximate** 사이에는 확실한 차이가 있다.

## barbarize
[bá:rbəràiz]

**v.** **to make savage or crude** | 야만화하다, 조잡하게하다

Hedonists are usually accused of *barbarizing* human society.

**ANT** barbarize : civilize [sívəlàiz]

civilize: 문명화하다, 세련되게하다

## brazen
[bréizn]

**adj.** **made of brass; marked by unrestrained boldness** | 놋쇠로 만든, 뻔뻔스런

Sue showed no remorse in telling her professor a *brazen* lie.

**ANT** brazen : modest [mádist]

modest: 겸손한

## cabal
[kəbǽl]

**n.** **a secretive scheme or plot; a group of conspiring plotters** | 비밀 음모, 비밀 음모단

A *cabal* of rebels plotted to overthrow the government.

**KIN** cabal : association [əsòusiéiʃən]

**cabal**은 비밀리에 결성된 **association**(공동단체) 일종이다.

## capricious
[kəpríʃəs]

**adj.** **unpredictable or unexpected; changing frequently** | 예측할 수 없는, 변덕스러운

The *capricious* character of forest fires makes it dangerous for the infantry to battle.

**WO** capricious : deliberation [dilíbəréiʃən]

**capricious**한 사람은 **deliberation**(숙고, 신중함)이 없다.

---

**TRANSLATION** | 예문해석

| | |
|---|---|
| approximate | 그 청부인의 대략의 집수리 비용은 그 집의 구입 가격보다 더 높았다. |
| barbarize | 쾌락주의자들은 대개 인간 사회를 야만화한다는 비난을 받는다. |
| brazen | Sue는 교수님에게 뻔뻔스런 거짓말을 한 것에 대해 어떤 양심의 가책도 보이지 않았다. |
| cabal | 반란군 비밀 결사단은 정부를 전복시키려는 음모를 세웠다. |
| capricious | 산불의 변덕스러운 성격때문에 보병이 전투하기에 위험하다. |

## circuitous
[səːrkjúːətəs]

**adj.** having a circular or roundabout course; speaking or acting in an indirect manner | 우회로의, 돌려 말하는

The defendant's plea was *circuitous* and did no good for his case.

**WO** circuitous : directness [diréktnis]

circuitous한 말에는 directness(직접적임)를 지닌 표현이 없다.

## consolidate
[kənsάlədèit]

**v.** to join together to reduce in number | 통합하다, 합병하다

The family *consolidated* all their debts into one payment plan.

**ANT** consolidate : dissolve [dizάlv]

dissolve: 해체하다

## conspire
[kənspáiər]

**v.** to join in a plot or scheme to do a wrongful or unlawful act | 함께 나쁜 일을 꾸미다, 공모하다

The three tenants *conspired* against their landlord

**CH** conspiratorial : conniver [kənáivər]

conniver(공모자, 묵인자)는 conspiratorial(음모의, 공모의)는 사람이다.

## dapper
[dǽpər]

**adj.** stylish and neat in appearance | 말쑥한, 깔끔한

The *dapper* young man caught Jessica's eye.

**ANT** dapper : unkempt [ʌnkémpt]

unkempt: 흐트러진, 깔끔하지 못한

## debunk
[diːbʌ́ŋk]

**v.** to expose the falseness or sham of | (거짓·허위 등을) 폭로하다

The defendant's plea was *debunked* by the witness' testimony.

**ANT** debunk : shroud [ʃráud]

shroud: 숨기다, 덮다

---

TRANSLATION | 예문해석

| | |
|---|---|
| circuitous | 피고의 답변은 우회적이었으며 그의 사건에 아무런 도움이 되지 못했다. |
| consolidate | 그 가족은 그들의 모든 채무를 하나의 상환 계획안에 통합시켰다. |
| conspire | 그 세 명의 소작인은 영주에 대항하려 공모했다. |
| dapper | 말쑥한 젊은 청년이 Jessica의 시선을 끌었다. |
| debunk | 피고의 답변은 목격자의 증언에 의해 사실이 아님이 폭로되었다. |

## decant [dikǽnt]

**v. to transfer or pour from one vessel into another** | (액체를 한 병에서 다른 병으로) 따르다

Mrs. Hawes was in the kitchen, *decanting* buttermilk into a bottle.

**FUN** decanter : pour [pɔːr]
decanter(마개 달린 유리병)는 pour(따르다)하기 위한 용기이다.

## deceive [disíːv]

**v. to trick or cheat; to make something untrue seem true** | 속이다

It is more shameful to mistrust one's friends than to be *deceived* by them.

**CH** deceive : charlatan [ʃáːrlətn]
charlatan(허풍선이)는 deceive하는 경향이 있다.

## decelerate [diːsélərèit]

**v. to slow down or reduce speed** | 속도를 줄이다

When the police car appeared around the corner, Miss Bart *decelerated* quickly.

**FUN** decelerate : brake [breik]
brake(제동기)는 속력을 decelerate하는 기능을 한다.

## demagogue [déməgàg]

**n. a speaker who appeals to the audience's passions or prejudices** | 청중의 열정이나 편견에 호소하며 말하는 사람, 선동자

*Demagogues* will always exist because people will always look to charismatic people who say what they want to hear.

**SYN** demagogue : rabble-rouser [rǽbl-ràuzər]
rabble-rouser: 민중 선동가

## demolish [dimáliʃ]

**v. to tear down or destroy** | 파괴하다

The old residential district was *demolished* to make room for a stadium.

**SYN** demolition : destruction [distrʌ́kʃən]
demolition: 파괴
destruction: 파괴

---

### TRANSLATION | 예문해석

**decant** Hawes 부인은 부엌에서 버터우유를 병에다 따르고 있었다.
**deceive** 친구에 의해 속임을 당하는 것보다 친구를 불신하는 일이 더 부끄러운 일이다.
**decelerate** 경찰차가 길 모퉁이에 나타나자 Bart 양은 속도를 신속하게 줄였다.
**demagogue** 사람들은 항상 자신들이 듣고 싶어하는 이야기를 해 줄 카리스마적인 사람을 향할 것이기 때문에 선동자는 언제까지나 존재할 것이다.
**demolish** 그 오래된 주거 지역이 경기장을 위한 공간을 만들기 위해 파괴되었다.

## deprecate
[déprikèit]

**v. to belittle or express disapproval of** | 경시하다, 비난하다

It is more useful to offer solutions than to just *deprecate* others' ideas.

> **CN** self-deprecating : swagger [swǽgər]
> self-deprecating(자기 비하하는)하는 사람은 swagger(뽐내며 거만하게 걷다)하지 않는다.

## depreciate
[depríːʃièit]

**v. to lower the value of; to belittle; to decrease in value or estimation** | 가치를 감소시키다, 경시하다, 가치가 떨어지다

Japan has *depreciated* the yen in hopes of spurring exports.

> **대상** depreciation : value [vǽljuː]
> depreciation(가치 하락)는 value(가치)의 하락을 의미한다.

## deprivation
[dèprivéiʃən]

**n. the state of being in want or need; the state of being deprived; loss** | 부족, 박탈, 상실

Food *deprivation* is a problem in many areas in Africa.

> **ANT** deprivation : surfeit [sə́ːrfit]
> surfeit: 과다, 폭식

## deracinate
[diːrǽsənèit]

**v. to uproot** | 뿌리째 뽑다

The new police chief worked tirelessly to *deracinate* the last vestiges of corruption in his department.

> **ANT** deracinate : plant [plænt]
> plant: (식물을) 심다, 설립하다

## edible
[édəbl]

**adj. suitable to be eaten** | 먹을 수 있는

Bob's cooking smells bad, but it is *edible*.

> **CH** edible : meat [miːt]
> meat(고기)은 edible하다.

---

### TRANSLATION | 예 문 해 석

| | |
|---|---|
| **deprecate** | 다른 사람의 생각을 단순히 비난하는 것보다 해결책을 제시하는 것이 더 유용하다. |
| **depreciate** | 일본은 수출을 촉진하려는 희망으로 엔화가치를 떨어뜨렸다. |
| **deprivation** | 식량 부족은 아프리카의 많은 지역들에서 문제가 되고 있다. |
| **deracinate** | 새 경찰서장은 관할 내 부패의 최후의 흔적이라도 뿌리뽑기 위해 지칠 줄 모르고 일했다. |
| **edible** | Bob의 요리는 냄새가 좋지 않지만, 먹을 만하다. |

## elude
[ilúːd]

**v. to avoid or escape** | 회피하다

The fugitive *eluded* the police by hiding in the swamp.

> **SYN** elude : evade [ivéid]
> evade: 회피하다

## enclose
[inklóuz]

**v. to surround on all sides; to put inside** | 에워싸다, 집어넣다

The family dog was left *enclosed* in his cage while everyone was away.

> **FUN** enclose : envelope [énvəlòup]
> envelope(봉투)는 편지를 enclose하는 기능을 가진다.

## encomium
[enkóumiəm]

**n. enthusiastic praise; a formal expression of praise** | 극찬, 찬사

Pericles' funeral oration was an *encomium* that extolled the virtues of Athenian citizens.

> **SYN** encomium : eulogy [júːlədʒi]
> eulogy: 찬사, 찬송

## ephemeral
[ifémərəl]

**adj. lasting a very brief time** | 순간의

Whatever had happened had been so *ephemeral* that now he wondered if he had not deceived himself.

> **CN** ephemeral : endure [indjúər]
> ephemeral한 것은 endure(지속하다)하지 않는다.

## expurgate
[ékspərgèit]

**v. to remove or cleanse of something unwanted or offensive** | (바라지 않거나 불온한 것을) 삭제하다

The youth group *expurgated* the vulgar graffiti from the walls.

> **CH** expurgate : censor [sénsər]
> censor(검열관)는 expurgate하는 일을 한다.

---

### TRANSLATION | 예문해석

| | |
|---|---|
| elude | 그 도망자는 늪에 숨어서 경찰을 피했다. |
| enclose | 그 가족의 개는 모두가 외출 중일 때 자신의 집에 갇힌 채 남게 되었다. |
| encomium | Pericles의 장례식 추도사 연설은 아테네 시민들의 덕목을 칭찬하는 찬사였다. |
| ephemeral | 모든 일들이 너무나도 순간적으로 일어났기 때문에 그는 지금 혹시 자기가 잘못 생각하고 있는 것은 아닌지 궁금해졌다. |
| expurgate | 젊은 청년들이 벽들 위에 적혀있는 천박한 낙서들을 지웠다. |

**impress** [imprés]

v. **to create a vivid image of; to affect strongly, often favorably** | 깊은 인상을 주다, 감동시키다

The teacher was *impressed* with the student's study habits.

CN  impression : stickler [stíklər]

stickler(꼼꼼하고 까다로운 사람)는 타인에게 impression(감동)을 줄 수가 없다.

**impromptu** [imprámptjuː]

adj. **done on the spot without preparation** | 즉흥적인

*Impromptu* skits are usually the most fun for both the audience and actors.

SYN  impromptu : improvisatorial [imprὰvəzətɔ́ːriəl]

improvisatorial: 즉흥의

**imprudent** [imprúːdnt]

adj. **thoughtless or unwise; lacking discretion** | 경솔한, 무분별한

*Imprudent* loans to develop countries resulted in defaults in the 1980's.

WO  imprudent : discretion [diskréʃən]

imprudent한 사람은 discretion(분별)이 없다.

**impugn** [impjúːn]

v. **to discredit through criticism** | 논박하다, 비난하다

Becky *impugned* Stan's motives for enrolling in a woman's studies course.

ANT  impugn : vindicate [víndəkèit]

vindicate: 옹호하다, 정당함을 입증하다

**insular** [ínsələr]

adj. **relating to an island; having a narrow viewpoint because of isolation** | 섬의, 편협한

Joan's *insular* viewpoints come from being raised in a rural and homogenous area.

ANT  insular : cosmopolitan [kὰzməpálətn]

cosmopolitan: 전세계적인, 시야가 넓은

---

TRANSLATION | 예 문 해 석

| | |
|---|---|
| impress | 선생님은 그 학생의 학습 습관에 깊은 감명을 받았다. |
| impromptu | 즉흥적인 촌극들은 대개 관객들과 배우들 모두에게 가장 재미있다. |
| imprudent | 국가 개발을 위한 무분별한 국채로 1980년대에 채무 불이행이 초래되었다. |
| impugn | Becky는 여성학 과정에 등록하려던 Stan의 동기를 비난했다. |
| insular | Joan의 편협한 시각들은 시골에서 비슷한 성질을 지닌 사람들 사이에서 자라난 데서 기인한 것이다. |

## intuition
[ìntjuːíʃən]

**n.** quick and ready insight; immediate apprehension or cognition | 직관, 육감, 즉각적인 이해

Without enough information, Samuel chose to make a decision based on *intuition*.

**CN** intuition : reasonable [ríːzənəbl]

intuition만으로 결정을 내리는 사람은 reasonable(논리적인)하지 않다.

## lapse
[læps]

**n.** a minor failure | 사소한 실수
**v.** to gradually fall from a previous standard | 나쁜 상태로 빠지다

The judge ruled that the defendant merely had a *lapse* in judgement and did not require any disciplinary action.

The patient's heart condition *lapsed* until he finally passed away.

**DE** lapse : error [érər]

lapse는 사소한 error(잘못)이다.

## loquacious
[loukwéiʃəs]

**adj.** wordy or prone to excessive talk | 장황한, 수다스러운

Fredrick was *loquacious* in large groups but seemed to always speak out of nervousness.

**ANT** loquacious : taciturn [tǽsətəːrn]

taciturn: 과묵한

## moth
[mɔ(ː)θ]

**n.** a lepidopterous insect that eats and destroys clothes and grains | 의류와 곡물을 먹고 해를 입히는 나비과의 곤충, 옷좀나방

Mary's winter clothes had not been properly packed and were consequently full of *moth* holes.

**ANT** moth-eaten : new and fresh [njuː ən freʃ]

moth-eaten: 좀 먹은, 오래되고 낡은

new and fresh: 새롭고 신선한

---

### TRANSLATION | 예문해석

**intuition** Samuel은 충분한 정보가 없어서 직관을 바탕으로 결정을 내리기로 했다.
**lapse** 판사는 피고가 단지 판단착오를 저지른 것 뿐이라 어떠한 징계조처도 필요하지 않다고 판결을 내렸다.
그 환자의 심장 상태는 악화되어 결국 그는 세상을 떠나게 되었다.
**loquacious** Fredrick은 많은 사람들 앞에서 수다스러웠지만 항상 긴장한 채로 말하는 것 같았다.
**moth** Mary의 겨울 옷들은 제대로 포장되지 않아서 결국 좀이 많이 먹었다.

## mural
[mjúərəl]

n. **a painting done on a wall** | 벽화

The three-story high *mural* in Manhattan was designed to advocate peace.

- 대상 mural : wall [wɔːl]
  mural은 wall(벽)에 그리는 그림이다.

## paradigmatic
[pÆrədigmÆtik]

adj. **relating to an example or pattern** | 전형적인, 예증하는

The police officer gave a *paradigmatic* talk about safety precautions.

- WO paradigmatic : anomaly [ənáməli]
  paradigmatic한 것은 anomaly(예외, 변칙)와는 거리가 멀다.

## paradox
[pÆrədàks]

n. **an apparently self-contradictory statement opposed to common sense** | 역설

The term 'bittersweet' is a famous poetic *paradox*.

- CH paradox : oxymoron [àksimɔ́ːran]
  oxymoron(모순 어법)은 paradox적인 어법으로 구성된 수사학이다.

## paragon
[pÆrəgàn]

n. **an example or model of excellence** | 본보기, 전형

Cynthia was a *paragon* of health having balanced diet, exercise, work, and rest.

- 대상 paragon : imitate [ímətèit]
  paragon을 imitate(본받다, 모방하다)하다.

## paramount
[pÆrəmàunt]

adj. **supreme in rank or power; of chief concern** | 최고의, 주요한

Stopping terrorism is the *paramount* goal of world leaders this year.

- ANT paramount : ancillary [Ænsəlèri]
  ancillary: 보조의, 부수적인

---

TRANSLATION | 예 문 해 석

| | |
|---|---|
| mural | 맨하탄에 있는 3층 높이의 벽화는 평화를 지지하기 위하여 디자인된 것이다. |
| paradigmatic | 그 경찰 간부는 안전 예방책들에 관한 전형적인 발언을 했다. |
| paradox | '달콤 씁쓸한'이라는 용어는 유명한 시적 역설이다. |
| paragon | Cynthia는 균형잡힌 식사와 운동, 일, 그리고 휴식을 취하는 건강의 전형이었다. |
| paramount | 테러리즘을 중지시키는 일이 올해 세계의 지도자들의 주요 목표이다. |

## piquant
[píːkənt]

**adj. stimulating and pleasant to taste; spicy; provocative or intriguing** | 입맛을 돋우는, 얼얼한, 흥미를 자아내는

The chili served at the dinner was perfectly *piquant*.

**ANT** piquant : insipid [insípid]

insipid: 맛없는, 재미 없는

## rapt
[ræpt]

**adj. focused or wholly absorbed; carried away or enraptured** | 몰두한, 넋 나간, 황홀한

The audience watched Evil Kenivel with *rapt* attention as he attempted to jump the Grand Canyon.

**ANT** rapt : distracted [distrǽktid]

distracted: 산만한

## reprehensible
[rèprihénsəbl]

**adj. worthy of blame or criticism** | 비난받아 마땅한

Some do not consider stealing food for survival as *reprehensible*.

**CH** reprehensible : censure [sénʃər]

reprehensible하다는 것은 censure(비난)받아 마땅하다는 의미이다.

## reprobate
[réprəbèit]

**n. a morally unprincipled person** | 타락한 사람, 방탕아
**adj. condemned or damned as morally corrupt** | 타락한
**v. to disapprove** | 비난하다

The *reprobate* couldn't find a sympathetic ear anywhere.

The criminal's *reprobate* actions caused him to be sentenced to 20 years in prison.

The priest *reprobated* the young children as they were caught spraying graffiti on the church walls.

**CH** reprobate : misbehave [mìsbihéiv]

reprobate는 misbehave(못된 짓을 하다, 품행이 좋지 못하다)하는 경향이 있다.

---

TRANSLATION | 예 문 해 석

**piquant** 저녁 만찬에 나온 칠리는 무지하게 얼얼한 자극적인 맛이었다.
**rapt** 관중들은 Evil Kneivel이 그랜드 캐넌을 뛰어 넘으려 하는 것을 넋을 잃고 지켜보았다.
**reprehensible** 어떤 사람들은 살아남기 위해 음식을 훔치는 것이 비난받을 만한 일이라 생각하지 않는다.
**reprobate** 그 타락한 사람은 어디에서도 자신의 말에 공감하여 들어주는 사람을 찾을 수 없었다.
그 범죄자는 자신의 사악한 행위로 인해 20년 형을 언도 받았다.
그 사제는 교회 벽에 그래피티를 그리다가 잡힌 어린 아이들을 꾸짖었다.

## reprove
[iprúːv]

**v. to scold or express disapproval of** | 꾸짖다, 야단치다

Little John's crying was *reproved* by his grandmother.

**DE** reprove : reprimand [réprəmænd]

reprimand는 공식적으로 징계하다라는 의미를 가지고 있어 reprove보다 정도가 더 심하다.

## repugnance
[ripʌ́gnəns]

**n. a strong dislike; something offensive or contradictory** | 혐오, 적대적이거나 모순되는 것

Bats are unjustly regarded with *repugnance* by people.

**CH** repugnant : repel [ripél]

repugnant(불쾌한)한 것은 repel(혐오감을 주다)하는 속성이 있다.

## saint
[séint]

**n. a person of great virtue and piety that becomes canonized** | 위대한 덕과 신앙심을 가지고 있어 신성시 되는 사람, 성인, 성자

Mother Teresa was considered a *saint* because of her tireless work with the poor.

**ANT** saint : miscreant [mískriənt]

miscreant: 악한, 이단자

## straightforward
[strèitfɔ́ːrwərd]

**adj. clear and direct; free from obscurity or vagueness** | 솔직한, 똑바른, 명료한

The homework assignment was pretty *straightforward*.

**ANT** straightforward : circumlocutory [sə̀ːrkəmlákjutɔ̀ːri]

circumlocutory: 빙 둘러서 말하는

## supple
[sʌ́pl]

**adj. easily bent; yielding or compliant** | 유연한, 유순한

The gymnast's legs were muscular but *supple*.

**WO** supple : rigidity [ridʒídəti]

supple한 물질은 rigidity(단단함, 경직)가 없다.

---

### TRANSLATION | 예문해석

**reprove** 어린 John은 울다가 그의 할머니에게 야단맞았다.
**repugnance** 사람들은 부당하게도 박쥐를 혐오스러운 것으로 여긴다.
**saint** Teresa 수녀는 가난한 사람들에 대한 그녀의 지칠 줄 모르는 봉사 때문에 성녀로 여겨졌다.
**straightforward** 그 숙제는 매우 명료한 것이었다.
**supple** 그 체조 선수의 다리는 근육질이었지만 유연했다.

## supplicant
[sʌ́plikənt]

**n. one who asks humbly and earnestly**
| (겸손하고 진심어린 태도로) 애원하는 사람

The *supplicant* knelt before the altar and asked God for help.

**CH** supplicant : beseeching [biːsíːtʃiŋ]

supplicant는 beseeching(간청하는)하는 사람을 뜻한다.

## suppress
[səprés]

**v. to use force to subdue or put down; to conceal or keep secret**
| 진압하다, 억누르다, 사실을 감추다

The authorities *suppressed* the rioters with tear gas and water-hoses.

**SYN** suppress : quell [kwel]

quell: 진압하다

## tirade
[táireid]

**n. a long speech filled with criticism and usually vulgarity**
| (보통 무례한 언사로 이루어진) 비난조의 연설

The terminated worker went on a *tirade* before marching out of the office.

**CH** tirade : critical [krítikəl]

tirade는 critical(비판적인, 흠을 들추는)하다.

## veracious
[vəréiʃəs]

**adj. truthful or accurate**
| 진실한, 정확한

The investigative committee's report, criticized as a cover up, was *veracious* and unbiased.

**ANT** veracious : fallacious [fəléiʃəs]

fallacious: 그릇된, 거짓의

---

### TRANSLATION | 예문해석

**supplicant** 그 애원자는 제단 앞에 무릎을 꿇고 하나님에게 도움을 간청했다.
**suppress** 당국은 최루가스와 물 대포 호스를 가지고 소요자들을 진압했다.
**tirade** 해고당한 그 노동자는 사무실을 걸어나가기 전에 장광설을 계속 늘어 놓았다.
**veracious** 조사 위원회의 보고는 비록 속임수라 비난받기도 했지만 정확하고 공정한 것이었다.

# 28th Day Daily Check-up

■ Fill in the blanks with the correct letter that matches the word with its definition.

1. impromptu _____
2. rapt _____
3. depreciate _____
4. aerate _____
5. paradigmatic _____
6. circuitous _____
7. supplicant _____
8. encomium _____
9. acquiesce _____
10. dapper _____

a. energetic and lively praise
b. done on the spot without preparation
c. stylish and neat in appearance
d. one who asks humbly and earnestly
e. having a circular or roundabout course; speaking or acting in an indirect manner
f. to yield to or comply with unwillingly or passively
g. to supply with oxygen or air
h. focused or wholly absorbed; carried away or enraptured
i. to decrease in value or estimation; to belittle
j. relating to an exemplary or illustrating pattern

■ Put the correct word in each blank from the list of words below.

11. censor는 _____ 하는 일을 한다.
12. _____ 는 cosmopolitan(국제적인, 시야가 넓은)의 반의어이다.
13. envelope는 _____ 하는 기능을 가진다.
14. repugnant한 것은 _____ 하는 속성이 있다.
15. _____ 은 비밀리에 결성된 association의 일종이다.
16. _____ 한 사람은 discretion이 없다.
17. mendacious(허위의)의 반의어는 _____ 이다.
18. embezzler(착복자, 횡령자)는 _____ 하는 사람이다.
19. charlatan(허풍선이)은 _____ 하는 경향이 있다.
20. _____ 한 사람은 deliberation(숙고, 신중함)이 없다.

a. repel    b. expurgate    c. ephemeral    d. veracious    e. appropriate    f. depreciate
g. insular    h. deceive    i. imprudent    j. enclose    k. capricious    l. cabal

**Answer key**

1. b  2. h  3. i  4. g  5. j  6. e  7. d  8. a  9. f  10. c
11. b  12. g  13. j  14. a  15. l  16. i  17. d  18. e  19. h  20. k

# SUPER VOCA

T.W.E.N.T.Y.N.I.N.T.H D.A.Y

# 29th DAY

산소같은 당신에게
수퍼보카가 함께 합니다.

---

**adept**
[ədépt]

**adj. highly skilled or experienced** | 숙련된, 노련한

The new student is very *adept* at math.

**ANT** adept : clumsy [klʌ́mzi]

clumsy: 서투른

---

**adore**
[ədɔ́ːr]

**v. to worship as a deity; to regard with extreme fondness and loving admiration** | 신적 존재로 숭배하다, 지극히 흠모하다

Hindus *adore* the cow as a symbolic representative of the life-preserving aspect of their religion.

**SYN** adore : revere [rivíər]

revere: 경외하다, 숭배하다

---

**anodyne**
[ǽnədàin]

**n. a drug that relieves or allays pain** | 고통을 완화시키는 약, 진통제

The doctor prescribed a powerful *anodyne* for her backpains.

**FUN** anodyne : relieve [rilíːv]

anodyne에는 relieve(고통 등을 덜다)하는 기능이 있다.

---

**apposite**
[ǽpəzit]

**adj. highly appropriate or relevant** | 적절한

That evidence is very *apposite* to this case.

**ANT** apposite : extraneous [ikstréiniəs]

extraneous: 관계없는, 외래의

---

### TRANSLATION | 예문 해석

| | |
|---|---|
| adept | 새로 온 그 학생은 수학에 아주 능통하다. |
| adore | 힌두교 신자들은 소를 삶을 보호하는 자신들 종교의 상징적인 표상으로 여겨 숭배한다. |
| anodyne | 의사는 그녀의 요통을 완화시키기 위해 강력한 진통제를 처방하였다. |
| apposite | 그 증거는 이 사건에 매우 적절한 것이다. |

## approach
[əpróutʃ]

**v. to come closer or nearer to; to approximate** | 다가가다, 접근하다

As the hour of departure *approached*, the two lovers held each other closer.

**DE** approach : accost [əkɔ́(:)st]

accost(다가가서 말을 걸다)는 단순히 다가가는 것이 아니라 적극적으로 approach하여 말을 거는 것이다.

## aware
[əwɛ́ər]

**adj. having knowledge or understanding of; alert to** | 알고 있는, 주의 깊은

A soldier must always be *aware* of his surroundings.

**ANT** unaware : cognizant [kágnəzənt]

unaware: 모르는
cognizant: 알고 있는

## boor
[buər]

**n. a crude or insensitive person; a peasant** | 촌뜨기, 농사꾼

My ex-husband is an unpleasant *boor*!

**WO** boor : sensitivity [sènsətívəti]

boor에게는 sensitivity(감각, 눈치)가 없다.

## chaotic
[keiátik]

**adj. lacking any order** | 혼란한, 무질서한

The crowds at the World Cup games were *chaotic* and wild.

**SYN** chaotic : disordered [disɔ́:rdərd]

disordered: 혼란한, 어질러진

## churlish
[tʃə́(:)rliʃ]

**adj. rude or vulgar; lacking civil grace** | 거친, 무례하고 천박한

It was *churlish* of Cheryl to refuse our dinner invitation.

**ANT** churlish : genteel [dʒentí:l]

genteel: 우아한, 고상한, 정중한

---

TRANSLATION | 예 문 해 석

| | |
|---|---|
| approach | 출발 시간이 다가왔을 때 두 연인은 서로를 더욱 꼭 껴안았다. |
| aware | 군인은 항상 자신의 주변 상황을 의식하고 있어야 한다. |
| boor | 내 전 남편은 불쾌한 촌뜨기 녀석이다! |
| chaotic | 월드컵 대회의 관중들은 무질서하고 난폭했다. |
| churlish | Cheryl이 우리의 저녁 식사 초대를 거절한 것은 무례한 일이었다. |

## coarse
[kɔːrs]

**adj. rough or crude; of poor quality; lacking refinement or taste** | 거친, 조잡한, 질낮은, 세련되지 못한

Toby was a tough boy whose *coarse* mannerisms reflected his difficult life.

**ANT** coarse : refined [rifáind]

refined: 세련된, 정교한

## coerce
[kouə́ːrs]

**v. to bring to act by force or threat** | 강요하다

The rebels *coerced* the villagers into hiding them from the army.

**POS** coercion : extort [ikstɔ́ːrt]

coercion: 강제, 강요

extort: 무리하게 강요하다

## colander
[kʌ́ləndər]

**n. a bowl with perforations used to drain liquids and rinse foods** | 액을 걸러내거나 음식물을 헹구는 데 쓰는 체가 달린 그릇, 여과기

Washing vegetables is much easier if you have a *colander*.

**FUN** colander : drain [drein]

colander는 drain(걸러내다, 배수하다)하는 기능이 있다.

## compatible
[kəmpǽtəbl]

**adj. capable of existing together harmoniously** | 양립할 수 있는

If you could only see them in their daily life, you would see how truly *compatible* they are.

**ANT** make compatible : polarize [póuləràiz]

make compatible: 양립시키다

polarize: 양 극단으로 분열 시키다, 대립시키다

## complaisance
[kəmpléisns]

**n. the disposition to comply** | 정중, 고분고분함

Our new housekeeper came highly recommended and was lauded by her previous employers for her *complaisance* and efficiency.

**WO** complaisance : intractable [intrǽctəbl]

intractable(다루기 힘든)한 사람들에게는 complaisance가 없다.

---

| TRANSLATION | 예 문 해 석 |
|---|---|
| coarse | Toby는 그의 조잡한 버릇에서 어려웠던 생활이 내비치는 거친 소년이었다. |
| coerce | 반란군들은 마을사람들을 협박해 군대로부터 자신들을 숨겨주도록 했다. |
| colander | 야채를 씻을 때 체 달린 그릇을 가지고 하면 훨씬 쉽다. |
| compatible | 만약 당신이 일상생활을 하는 그들의 모습을 볼 수 만 있다면, 당신은 그들이 얼마나 진실로 잘 어울리는 사람인지 알 수 있을 것이다. |
| complaisance | 우리의 새 가정부는 적극적으로 추천받아 왔으며 그의 전 고용인들은 그녀의 고분고분함과 효율성을 칭찬하였다. |

## corporeal
[kɔːrpɔ́ːriəl]

**adj. bodily; tangible or material** | 육체의, 물질적인

The restless crowd wanted something more than verbal promises; they wanted *corporeal* guarantees.

**ANT** corporeal : intangible [intǽndʒəbl]

intangible: 감지할 수 없는, 실체가 없는

## correspond
[kɔ̀ːrəspánd]

**v. to communicate by letters; to be in agreement or to match** | 편지를 주고 받다, 일치하다

I *correspond* with friends in London, Seoul, and Athens nearly everyday.

**대상** correspond : letters [létərz]

correspond는 letters(편지)를 주고 받는다는 뜻이다.

## detract
[ditrǽkt]

**v. to lower the importance, quality, or value of; to divert or take away from** | (중요성·질·가치 등을) 떨어뜨리다, 주의를 딴데로 돌리다

The unfurnished basement *detracted* from the otherwise charming house.

**SYN** detract : devalue [diːvǽljuː]

devalue: (가치를) 감소시키다

## disperse
[dispə́ːrs]

**v. to cause to break up or scatter; to scatter or dissipate** | 해산시키다, 흩어지게 하다, 흩어지다

The crowd *dispersed* as the riot police made their way through the demonstration.

**ANT** disperse : flock [flɑk]

flock: 떼지어 모이다

## dispirit
[dispírit]

**v. to discourage morale or dishearten** | 사기를 꺾다, 낙담시키다

The team's first game loss *dispirited* their loyal fans.

**대상** dispirit : morale [mərǽl]

dispirit은 morale(의욕, 사기)를 꺾는다는 뜻이다.

---

### TRANSLATION | 예문 해석

| | |
|---|---|
| corporeal | 불안한 사람들은 구두적인 약속 이상의 것을 원했다. 그들은 실질적인 보증을 원했다. |
| correspond | 나는 거의 매일 런던, 서울, 아테네에 있는 친구들과 편지를 주고 받는다. |
| detract | 설비가 갖춰지지 않은 지하실이 그렇지 않았더라면 매력적이었을 집의 가치를 떨어뜨렸다. |
| disperse | 폭동진압 경찰대가 시위대를 뚫고 들어오자 군중들은 해산했다. |
| dispirit | 그 팀의 예상치 못한 첫 게임 패배는 충성스런 팬들을 낙담시켰다. |

## endow
[indáu]

**v. to grant money to for the support of; to furnish with something freely and naturally**
| (기금을) 기부하다, (신이) 천성적으로 부여하다

The millionaire *endowed* the hospital with enough money to build a new wing.

**CH**  endowment : patron [péitrən]

patron는 endowment(기증)를 하는 후원자이다.

## engrave
[ingréiv]

**v. to impress deeply or form by incision on wood or metal; to carve figures, letters, or designs**
| 새기다, 조각하다

The lovers *engraved* their names into a tree trunk.

**DE**  engrave : gouge [gaudʒ]

gouge는 engrave에 비해 둥글고 깊게 움푹 조각하다 라는 의미이다.

## enormity
[inɔ́ːrməti]

**n. great wickedness**
| 극악

Picasso captured the *enormity* of the Spanish Civil War in his painting, Guernica.

**SYN**  enormity : atrocity [ətrásəti]

atrocity: 극악, 포악

## entreat
[intríːt]

**v. to ask for or request earnestly**
| 간청하다

The peasant *entreated* the King to spare his life.

**DE**  entreaty : command [kəmǽnd]

command(명령)는 entreaty(간청)에 비해 강압적인 요구이다.

## espouse
[ispáuz]

**v. to marry; to advocate or support**
| 결혼하다, 지지하다

Luis *espouses* Marxism and teaches it to his students.

**ANT**  espouse : abjure [æbdʒúər]

abjure: (주의 · 신앙 등을) 공공연하게 버리다

---

### TRANSLATION | 예문 해석

| | |
|---|---|
| endow | 그 백만장자는 새로운 병동을 지을 수 있을 만큼의 충분한 돈을 병원에 기부했다. |
| engrave | 그 연인들은 나무 둥치에 그들의 이름을 새겨 넣었다. |
| enormity | Picasso는 그의 그림 '게르니카'에서 스페인 시민 전쟁의 극악무도함을 포착했다. |
| entreat | 농부는 국왕에게 자신의 목숨을 살려달라고 간청했다. |
| espouse | Luis는 마르크스주의를 지지하며 그것을 학생들에게 가르친다. |

## estrange
[istréindʒ]

**v.** to arouse enmity in where there had been friendliness; to remove from an accustomed environment
| 이간하다, 소원하게 하다, (평상시의 환경에서) 멀리하다

Constant quarreling over inheritance finally *estranged* the two brothers.

**ANT** estrangement : rapprochement [ræ̀prouʃmɑ́ːŋ]
estrangement: 불화, 이간
rapprochement: 친교 회복, 화해

## exorbitant
[igzɔ́ːrbətənt]

**adj.** excessive or exceeding the appropriate limits
| 과도한, 터무니없는

An *exorbitant* amount of money was paid to the actress for her latest movie.

**WO** exorbitant : moderation [mɑ̀dəréiʃən]
exorbitant한 것에는 moderation(알맞음)이 없다.

## extricate
[ékstrəkèit]

**v.** to free from an entanglement | (곤란한 상태에서) 구출하다

Kyle *extricated* himself from the situation by leaving the country.

**대상** extricate : snarl [snɑːrl]
snarl(혼란한 상태)에서 extricate하다.

## havoc
[hǽvək]

**n.** devastation or widespread destruction; disorder or chaos
| 대파괴, 대혼란, 혼잡

Even brief power outages can cause *havoc* in city life.

**ANT** havoc : serenity [sərénəti]
serenity: 고요함, 평온

## hedonist
[híːdənist]

**n.** one that lives life by the doctrine that pleasure and happiness is the sole good
| 쾌락주의자

It has always been a dream of mine to quit my day job and become a practicing *hedonist*.

**ANT** hedonist : ascetic [əsétik]
ascetic: 금욕주의자

---

**TRANSLATION | 예문 해석**

| | |
|---|---|
| estrange | 유산 상속에 대한 끊임없는 말다툼으로 결국 두 형제는 서로 멀어지고 말았다. |
| exorbitant | 최신작 영화의 대가로 터무니 없이 많은 액수의 돈이 그 여배우에게 지급되었다. |
| extricate | Kyle은 그 나라를 떠남으로써 그 상황으로부터 탈출했다. |
| havoc | 잠깐 동안의 정전이라해도 도시 생활에서는 대혼란을 일으킬 수 있다. |
| hedonist | 일상적인 직업을 그만두고 쾌락주의자 생활을 하는 것이 항상 내 꿈 중의 하나였다. |

## hypothesis
[haipάθəsis]

**n. a testable but improvable theory** | 가설, 추측

The scientist proposed his *hypothesis* before beginning experimentation.

**대상** hypothesis : confirm [kənfə́ːrm]

hypothesis를 confirm(확증하다) 하다.

## ignominious
[ìgnəmíniəs]

**adj. disgraceful or shameful** | 불명예스러운, 수치스러운

Despite the team's *ignominious* loss, the coach still praised their efforts.

**ANT** ignominious : lofty [lɔ́ːfti]

lofty: 높은, 고귀한

## incriminate
[inkrímənèit]

**v. to suggest that someone is guilty; to bring an accusation against** | 유죄를 증명하다, 고소하다, 고발하다

Mary *incriminated* the factory by claiming they hired undocumented workers.

**ANT** incriminate : exonerate [igzánərèit]

exonerate: 무죄임을 입증하다

## innovate
[ínəvèit]

**v. to create or introduce as new; to do something in a new way** | 새로운 것을 받아들이다, 혁신하다

Consultants *innovate* procedures to help companies run more efficiently.

**ANT** innovative : hidebound [háidbàund]

innovative: 혁신적인

hidebound: 고루한, 대단히 보수적인

## lubricant
[lúːbrikənt]

**n. a substance used to reduce friction or heat between two substances or surfaces** | 윤활제

If the hinges of the door get squeaky, just apply some oil *lubricant*.

**FUN** lubricant : abrasion [əbréiʒən]

lubricant는 abrasion(마모)을 방지하는 윤활제이다.

---

### TRANSLATION | 예문해석

| | |
|---|---|
| hypothesis | 그 과학자는 실험을 시작하기에 앞서 그의 가설을 제출했다. |
| ignominious | 팀의 불명예스러운 패배에도 불구하고 코치는 여전히 그들의 노고를 칭찬했다. |
| incriminate | Mary는 밀입국자들을 고용한 공장을 고발했다. |
| innovate | 컨설턴트들은 기업들이 좀 더 효과적으로 운영될 수 있도록 하기 위해서 업무처리 과정을 개선한다. |
| lubricant | 문의 경첩이 삐걱거리기 시작하면 약간의 오일 윤활제를 바르면 된다. |

## monotonous
[mənátənəs]

**adj.** unchanging or tediously uniform; unvarying in tone
| 한결같이 지루한, 어조가 변함없는, 단조로운

The despised teacher spoke in such a *monotonous* tone as to put her students to sleep.

**CH** monotonous : drone [droun]

drone은 monotonous한 저음 또는 monotonous한 말투의 사람을 가리키는 말이다.

## oracle
[ɔ́(ː)rəkl]

**n.** one who divines the future | 미래를 점치는 사람, 선지자

In ancient civilizations, people would travel for days to consult the *oracle* about their futures.

**CH** oracle : prophecy [práfəsi]

oracle은 prophecy(예언)을 할 수 있는 사람이다.

## perplex
[pərpléks]

**v.** to confuse; to make complicated | 당황하게 하다, 복잡하게 하다

Her husband's odd behavior *perplexes* Betty at times.

**SYN** perplex : nonplus [nɑnplʌ́s]

nonplus: 당황하게 하다

## presage
[présidʒ]

**v.** to foretell or predict the future; to portend
| 예고하다, 전조가 되다

People were amazed when they saw that what the man *presaged* actually came to pass.

**CH** presage : harbinger [háːrbindʒər]

harbinger(선지자)는 presage한다.

## propagate
[prɑ́pəgèit]

**v.** to publicize, spread, or disperse; to cause to breed or multiply
| 선전하다, 전파하다, 번식시키다, 증식시키다

Many companies *propagate* their products through television ads to maximize their target audience.

**ANT** propagate : check [tʃek]

check: 저지하다, 억제하다

---

TRANSLATION | 예 문 해 석

**monotonous** 혐오의 대상이었던 그 교사는 학생들을 잠들게 할 정도의 너무나 단조로운 어조로 말을 했다.
**oracle** 고대 문명 사회에서 사람들은 자신의 미래에 대해 선지자의 조언을 듣기 위해 며칠 동안 여행하곤 했다.
**perplex** Betty의 남편의 이상한 행동은 그녀를 때때로 당황하게 만든다.
**presage** 사람들은 그 남자가 예언한 일이 실제로 일어나는 것을 보고는 놀랐다.
**propagate** 많은 기업들은 대상으로 하는 고객을 최대화 하고자 TV 광고를 통해 자사의 상품들을 선전한다.

## propensity
[prəpénsəti]

**n. an intense inclination or tendency** | 강한 경향, 성향

Michael has a *propensity* to spend too much money on beer.

**ANT** propensity to dislike : predilection [prìːdəlékʃən]

propensity to dislike: 싫어하는 경향

predilection: 좋아함, 편애

## reap
[riːp]

**v. to harvest or obtain** | 수확하다, 획득하다

Local farmers expect to *reap* a rich wheat harvest this year due to very favorable conditions.

**FUN** reap : scythe [saið]

scythe는 reap할 때 사용하는 큰 낫이다.

## reconcile
[rékənsàil]

**v. to harmonize or bring back together** | 조화시키다, 화해시키다

The couple *reconciled* their differences and got back together.

**ANT** reconciliation : rift [rift]

reconciliation: 화해, 조화

rift: 균열, 불화

## regressive
[rigrésiv]

**adj. tending to move backward; decreasing in rate as the base decreases** | 후퇴하는, (세금이) 역누진하는

*Regressive* tax policies unjustly favor the rich.

**ANT** regressive : forward [fɔ́ːrwərd]

forward: 전방의, 전진하는

## rejoice
[ridʒɔ́is]

**v. to give or feel great joy** | 기쁘게 하다, 기뻐하다

The world *rejoiced* at the end of the World War.

**ANT** rejoice : deplore [diplɔ́ːr]

deplore: 몹시 한탄하다

---

TRANSLATION | 예문 해석

**propensity** Michael은 맥주 마시는 데 돈을 너무 많이 낭비하는 경향이 있다.
**reap** 지역 농민들은 유리한 조건들 때문에 올해 풍성한 밀 수확을 기대하고 있다.
**reconcile** 그 커플은 그들의 견해 차이를 조정한 후 함께 돌아왔다.
**regressive** 역누진세 정책이 부당하게도 부자들을 도와주고 있다.
**rejoice** 세계 대전의 종결에 전 세계가 기뻐했다.

## renovate
[rénəvèit]

**v. to restore or revive to a more lively and better state** | (더 활기있고 나은 상태로 만들기 위해) 쇄신하다

Tom was contracted to *renovate* six houses in the downtown area.

**SYN** renovate : renew [rinjúː]
renew: 쇄신하다, 재개하다

## reproach
[ripróutʃ]

**v. to criticize or rebuke** | 비난하다
**n. disapproval or criticism** | 비난, 질책

The superintendent *reproached* the teacher for her harsh comments during class.

The superintendent looked at the teacher with *reproach*.

**DE** reproach : upbraid [ʌpbréid]
upbraid는 신랄하게 비난하다라는 의미로 reproach보다 비난의 강도가 높다.

## resonant
[rézənənt]

**adj. having a rich and continuous sound; echoing** | 울려 퍼지는

The singer has a *resonant* voice that fills the concert hall.

**ANT** resonant : muffled [mʌfld]
muffled: 소리를 죽인

## respire
[rispáiər]

**v. to breathe** | 숨쉬다

It is refreshing to *respire* in the clean mountain air.

**FUN** respiration : lung [lʌŋ]
lung(폐)은 respiration(호흡)의 기능이 있다.

---

| TRANSLATION | 예 문 해 석 |
|---|---|
| renovate | Tom은 도심지 지역의 여섯 채의 집들을 개조하기로 계약했다. |
| reproach | 교장 선생님은 수업 시간 동안 그 여선생이 가혹한 비판을 했다고 질책했다. |
| | 교장 선생님은 비난하는 표정으로 그 선생님을 바라 보았다. |
| resonant | 그 가수는 연주회장을 가득 메우며 낭랑하게 울려 퍼지는 목소리를 가졌다. |
| respire | 깨끗한 산의 공기를 호흡하는 일은 상쾌한 일이다. |

## slur
[slə:r]

**v.** to speak unclearly or obscurely: to cast unkind remarks on
| 불분명하게 말하다, 비방하다

**n.** a slurred utterance; an insulting remark
| 분명치 않게 발음함, 모욕, 비방

The men *slurred* insults at each other.

The lecturer was difficult to understand because he spoke with a *slur*.

**KIN** slur : speech [spi:tʃ]

slur는 불분명한 speech(말)이다.

## stern
[stə:rn]

**adj.** harsh in manner; unsmiling or having a harsh or gloomy appearance
| 엄격한, (표정이) 험악한

There was a *stern* expression on Jeff's face when he came home from work that day.

**SYN** stern : austere [ɔ:stíər]

austere: 엄한, 금욕적인

## sturdy
[stə́:rdi]

**adj.** having rugged physical strength; firmly built
| 힘센, (물건이) 튼튼한

Mountain climbers require *sturdy* shoes to carry them through rough terrain.

**ANT** sturdy : decrepit [dikrépit]

decrepit: 쇠약한, (오래되서) 낡은

## subordinate
[səbɔ́:rdənət]

**adj.** lower in rank or importance
| 하위의, 중요도가 낮은

Top-ranking five-star generals are nevertheless *subordinate* to a civilian president.

**ANT** subordinate : principal [prínsəpəl]

principal: 주요한, 중요한

---

TRANSLATION | 예 문 해 석

| | |
|---|---|
| slur | 그 남자들은 서로에게 욕을 하였다. |
| | 그 강사는 불분명하게 발음했기 때문에 강의를 알아듣기 힘들었다. |
| stern | 그날 직장 일을 마치고 집에 돌아왔을 때, Jeff의 얼굴에는 단호한 표정이 서려있었다. |
| sturdy | 산악 등반가들은 그들이 거친 지형을 뚫고 지나갈 수 있게 해주는 튼튼한 신발을 필요로 한다. |
| subordinate | 최고위의 별 다섯개를 단 장군들일지라도 민간인 대통령 아래에 있다. |

## surreptitious
[sə̀ːrəptíʃəs]

**adj. doing something secretly or by stealth** | 비밀의, 몰래하는

The run-away slave made a *surreptitious* escape through the South.

- **ANT** surreptitious : barefaced [bέərfèist]
  barefaced: 노골적인, 파렴치한

## tenable
[ténəbl]

**adj. capable of being defended or supported against assault; based on sound reasoning**
| 공격에 견딜 수 있는, 지지할 수 있는, 조리있는

The Themistoclean Wall of Athens was not *tenable* for long and the city fell to the invaders.

- **ANT** tenable : indefensible [ìndifénsəbl]
  indefensible: 방어할 수 없는
- **ANT** tenable : unjustifiable [ʌndʒʌ́stəfàiəbl]
  unjustifiable: 이치에 맞지 않는

## tenacious
[tənéiʃəs]

**adj. persistent in adhering to something** | 집요한, 끈질기게 고수하는

The *tenacious* girl stubbornly clung to her version of the truth.

- **CN** tenacious : yield [jiːld]
  tenacious한 사람은 yield(포기하다, 굴복하다)하지 않는다.

## tend
[tend]

**v. to be disposed or inclined; to care for or watch over**
| ~하는 경향이 있다, 돌보다

The shepherd *tended* his sheep which were scattered about the hillside.

- **DE** tend : fuss [fʌs]
  fuss(몸달아 설치다)는 tend에 비해 지나치게 돌보거나 염려한다는 의미를 지닌다.

## torpid
[tɔ́ːrpid]

**adj. deprived of the power of motion or feeling**
| 활발치 못한, 무신경한

Jess is just getting over a cold and is a bit *torpid*.

- **ANT** torpid : ebullient [ibʌ́ljənt]
  ebullient: (원기, 열정이) 넘쳐 흐르는

---

TRANSLATION | 예 문 해 석

| | |
|---|---|
| **surreptitious** | 탈주한 그 노예는 남쪽으로 몰래 도망쳤다. |
| **tenable** | 아테네의 Themistoclean 벽은 공격을 오래 견디지 못했으며 따라서 도시는 침략자에게 패했다. |
| **tenacious** | 그 고집센 소녀는 자신의 입장에서 진실이라고 주장한 것을 고수했다. |
| **tend** | 그 목동은 언덕 주변에 흩어져 있던 양떼들을 돌보았다. |
| **torpid** | Jess는 이제 막 감기에서 회복하는 중이라 아직 좀 무기력하다. |

## unanimity
[jùːnəníməti]

**n. the state of complete agreement or unity** | 만장 일치

The committee, for once, was in *unanimity*.

**ANT** unanimity : schism [sízm]
schism: 불화, 분열

## upbraid
[ʌpbréid]

**v. to scold or criticize severely** | 심하게 꾸짖다, 신랄하게 비판하다

*Upbraided* and punished, the children walked sullenly to their rooms.

**DE** upbraid : reproach [ripróutʃ]
upbraid는 reproach(비난하다)에 비해서 비난의 강도가 높다.

## venal
[víːnl]

**adj. capable of being purchased; corrupt** | 돈으로 매수 할 수 있는, 부패한

One *venal* official does not corrupt an entire government.

**WO** venal : probity [próubəti]
venal한 사람에게는 probity(청렴결백)함이 없다.

---

TRANSLATION | 예 문 해 석

**unanimity**  위원회는 이번 만은 만장 일치였다.
**upbraid**  심하게 혼나고 벌까지 받은 아이들은 부루퉁해져서 방으로 돌아갔다.
**venal**  한 사람의 부패한 공무원이 전체 정부를 부패시키지는 않는다.

# 29th Day Daily Check-up

■ Fill in the blanks with the correct letter that matches the word with its definition.

1. espouse _____
2. sturdy _____
3. monotonous _____
4. complaisance _____
5. propagate _____
6. subordinate _____
7. chaotic _____
8. endow _____
9. coerce _____
10. venal _____

a. unchanging or tediously uniform; unvarying in tone
b. to publicize or transmit; to continue or increase through reproduction
c. the disposition to comply
d. lower in rank or importance
e. to bring to act by force or threat
f. to grant money to for the support of; to furnish with something freely and naturally
g. capable of being purchased; corrupt
h. to marry; to advocate or support
i. lacking any order
j. having rugged physical strength; firmly built

■ Put the correct word in each blank from the list of words below.

11. command는 _____ 에 비해 강압적인 명령이다.
12. _____ 한 것에는 moderation이 없다.
13. _____ 는 불분명한 speech이다
14. extraneous(관계없는)의 반의어는 _____ 이다.
15. barefaced(공공연한)의 반의어는 _____ 이다.
16. gouge는 _____ 에 비해 깊게 움푹 조각하다 라는 의미이다.
17. cognizant (알고 있는)의 동의어는 _____ 이다.
18. _____ 는 schism(분열)의 반의어이다.
19. revere(경외하다)의 동의어는 _____ 이다.
20. rift(불화)는 _____ 의 반의어이다.

a. reconciliation  b. aware  c. slur  d. exorbitant  e. apposite  f. surreptitious
g. entreaty  h. compatible  i. perplex  j. engrave  k. adore  l. unanimity

**Answer key**

1. h  2. j  3. a  4. c  5. b  6. d  7. i  8. f  9. e  10. g
11. g  12. d  13. c  14. e  15. f  16. j  17. b  18. l  19. k  20. a

# SUPER VOCA

T.H.I.R.T.I.E.T.H  D.A.Y

# 30th DAY

열심히 공부한 당신. 떠나라!
(1일부터 한번 더 보고~)

## awl
[ɔːl]

**n.** a pointed tool used to make or put holes in leather or wood | 송곳

The craftsman packed his *awl* with the rest of his equipment.

**FUN**  awl : pierce [piərs]

awl은 pierce(꿰뚫다)하는 기능이 있다.

## baneful
[béinfəl]

**adj.** destructive or harmful | 파멸시키는, 해로운

Racism is a *baneful* ill that is perpetuated by the fear of the unfamiliar.

**ANT**  baneful : salubrious [səlúːbriəs]

salubrious: 건강에 좋은, 유익한

## benevolence
[bənévələns]

**n.** an act of kindness or generosity | 관대하고 친절한 행동

The charitable organization praised the *benevolence* of the individual who made a large donation.

**ANT**  benevolent : malicious [məlíʃəs]

benevolent: 선의의, 호의적인
malicious: 악의 있는, 심술궂은

## bonhomie
[bànəmíː]

**n.** well-natured friendliness | 상냥함, 온후

The police officer was loved by the town for his continuous *bonhomie*.

**POS**  bonhomie : amicable [ǽmikəbl]

amicable: 우호적인, 온화한

---

### TRANSLATION | 예 문 해 석

| | |
|---|---|
| awl | 그 장인은 자신의 송곳을 나머지 다른 장비들과 함께 챙겼다. |
| baneful | 인종차별은 낯선 것에 대한 두려움 때문에 영속되는 해악이다. |
| benevolence | 그 자선 단체는 큰 기부를 한 개인의 관대하고 친절한 행동을 칭찬했다. |
| bonhomie | 그 경찰 간부는 친절하고 상냥한 태도 때문에 시민들 모두의 사랑을 받았다. |

## cargo
[ká:rgou]

**n. goods in large quantities that are transported via airplane, boat, or truck** | 화물

The *cargo* ships that depart the port every morning are always on time.

**FUN** cargo : manifest [mǽnəfèst]

manifest는 '명백한'이라는 의미도 있지만 선박이나 항공기에 싣는 화물의 리스트인 '적하 목록'의 의미로도 쓰인다.

## caricature
[kǽrikətʃər]

**n. an exaggerated representation that distorts features in a comical way** | 인물의 모습을 일그려 뜨려 과장되게 그린 풍자 만화

We had our *caricatures* drawn at the county fair.

**CH** caricature : distortion [distɔ́:rʃən]

caricature는 distortion(왜곡)되게 그려진 그림이다.

## coax
[kouks]

**v. to patiently persuade through flattery or gentle urging** | 구슬리다, 부추기다

Kelly tried hard to *coax* her boyfriend into attending the play.

**PUR** coax : blandishment [blǽndiʃmənt]

blandishment는 다른 사람을 coax하기 위해서 사용하는 감언이다.

## defy
[difái]

**v. to openly refuse or confront with resistance; to dare or challenge** | 거부하다, 반대하다, 도전하다

You deliberately *defied* me and now you will pay the consequences!

**ANT** defy : obey [oubéi]

obey: 복종하다

## deride
[diráid]

**v. to ridicule** | 비웃다

The Herald Tribune takes every opportunity it can to *deride* President Bush.

**POS** deride : mockery [mákəri]

mockery: 조롱

---

TRANSLATION | 예문 해석

| | |
|---|---|
| cargo | 매일 아침마다 항구를 떠나는 화물선들이 항상 제 시간을 지켰다. |
| caricature | 우리는 시골 장에서 우리의 풍자 인물화를 그렸다. |
| coax | Kelly는 그녀의 남자 친구를 구슬러서 파티에 참석하게 만들려고 열심히 노력했다. |
| defy | 너는 나에게 의도적으로 도전했으니 이제 그 대가를 치르게 될 것이다! |
| deride | The Herald Tribune지는 부시 대통령을 비웃기 위하여 가능한 한 모든 기회를 포착하고 있다. |

## derivative
[dirívətiv]

**adj.** **taken or obtained from another; unoriginal**  | 유도된, 파생된

The carmaker's latest design was criticized for being *derivative* and unoriginal.

**ANT** derivative : precursory [priːkə́ːrsəri]
precursory: 선구의, 전조의

## elevate
[éləvèit]

**v.** **to raise or lift up**  | 올리다

Michael *elevated* my spirits this morning by calling to say hello.

**ANT** elevation : debasement [dibéismənt]
elevation: 상승
debasement: 저하

## epicure
[épikjùər]

**n.** **one who takes great pleasure in sensual activities, such as eating and drinking**  | 미식가

Though he writes for the weekend food page, Jamieson does not consider himself an *epicure*.

**CH** epicure : discriminating [diskrímənèitiŋ]
epicure는 보통 사람과 달리 음식의 미묘한 맛을 까다롭게 discriminating(구별하는) 하는 경향이 있다.

## evade
[ivéid]

**v.** **to escape or avoid through stratagem, especially responsibilities, obligations, or questions**  | (책략을 이용해서 책임·의무·질문을) 회피하다

The governor *evaded* answering the question by changing the subject.

**대상** evade : answer [ǽnsər]
evade는 answer(답)를 회피하다 라는 의미이다.

## evict
[ivíkt]

**v.** **to legally force someone out of a property**  | 합법적으로 퇴거 시키다

Lori was *evicted* for not paying her rent on time.

**대상** evict : tenant [ténənt]
evict는 tenant(거주자)를 법적 절차를 거쳐 몰아낸다는 의미이다.

---

### TRANSLATION | 예문해석

| | |
|---|---|
| derivative | 그 자동차 회사의 최근 작품은 다른 것에서 유도된 비독창적인 것이라고 비난받았다. |
| elevate | 오늘 아침 Michael이 안부 전화를 걸어 내 기분을 북돋아주었다. |
| epicure | Jamieson은 비록 주말 음식란에 글을 쓰지만, 자신을 미식가라고 생각하지는 않는다. |
| evade | 그 주지사는 주제를 바꿈으로써 질문에 대한 답변을 회피했다. |
| evict | Lori는 제 시간에 집세를 내지 못해 쫓겨났다. |

## flavor
[fléivər]

**n.** a distinct taste; a characteristic or quality | 독특한 맛, 특색

The *flavor* of the pudding was quite similar to vanilla.

- 대상 flavor : gustation [gʌstéiʃən]
  gustation(미각)은 flavor를 감별해 내는 감각이다.

## garish
[gɛ́əriʃ]

**adj.** offensively or excessively flashy and showy | 지나치게 화려한

I couldn't believe the *garish* dress that woman was wearing at the dance!

- DE garish : colorful [kʌ́lərfəl]
  garish는 색채가 불쾌할 정도로 지나치게 colorful하다는 의미이다.

## halcyon
[hǽlsiən]

**adj.** peaceful; prosperous | 평화로운, 번영하는

Nostalgia distorts people's memories with false recollections of *halcyon* years past.

- ANT halcyon : tempestuous [tempéstʃuəs]
  tempestuous: 소요의, 동란의, 폭풍우의

## heed
[hi:d]

**v.** to give attention to or consider | 주의하다, 유의하다

Smokers don't *heed* the health warnings on cigarette packages.

- SYN heed : hearken [hɑ́:rkən]
  hearken: 귀를 기울이다, 경청하다

## heresy
[hérəsi]

**n.** a belief, opinion, or doctrine that goes against the church's belief or dogma | 이설, 이단

In colonial America, people were burned at the stake for *heresy* and witchery.

- ANT heresy : orthodoxy [ɔ́:rθədɑ̀ksi]
  orthodoxy: 정설, 정교

---

### TRANSLATION | 예문해석

| | |
|---|---|
| flavor | 그 푸딩의 맛은 바닐라의 맛과 매우 흡사했다. |
| garish | 나는 댄스 파티에서 그 여자가 입고 있던 지나치게 화려한 의상을 믿을 수가 없었다! |
| halcyon | 향수는 사람들의 기억을 왜곡시켜 지난 날을 평화로운 시절로 잘못 기억하게 만든다. |
| heed | 흡연자들은 담배 갑에 적힌 건강에 대한 경고에 주의를 기울이지 않는다. |
| heresy | 식민지 시대의 미국에서는 사람들이 이단과 마녀행위의 죄목으로 말뚝에 묶여 화형당했다. |

## heretic
[hérətik]

**n. one who commits heresy; one who dissents from church dogma** | 이단자, 교회의 교리를 따르지 않는 사람

The *heretics* of the 16th century were executed publicly.

**CH** heretic : unconformity [ʌ̀nkənfɔ́ːrməti]

heretic의 주장은 정설과 unconformity(불일치)한다.

## illustrate
[íləstrèit]

**v. to demonstrate or clarify with examples; to provide with pictures** | 예를 들어 설명하다, 그림과 함께 제시하다

The author hired an artist to *illustrate* the cover of his book.

**대상** illustrate : picture [píktʃər]

illustrate는 책이나 문서에 picture(그림)을 함께 제시한다는 의미이다.

## ingrain
[íngrèin]

**adj. natural; deep seated** | 타고난, 뿌리 깊은

**v. to impress or fix deeply into one's mind or nature** | (마음 속에) 심어주다

Elephants use *ingrain* senses to migrate from one feeding ground to the next.

The importance of education was *ingrained* in me since childhood.

**ANT** ingrained : extrinsic [ikstrínsik]

ingrained: 타고난, 뿌리 깊은

extrinsic: 외부로부터의

## ingratiate
[ingréiʃièit]

**v. to gain respect or acceptance deliberately with good deeds** | 일부러 좋은 일을 함으로써 환심을 사다, 알랑거리다

To show he was not trying to *ingratiate* himself with Vronsky, Sven promptly added some slightly critical remarks.

**ANT** ingratiate : discomfit [diskʌ́mfit]

discomfit: (계획 등을) 좌절시키다

---

### TRANSLATION | 예문해석

**heretic** 16세기의 이단자들은 공개적으로 처형되었다.
**illustrate** 그 저자는 자신의 책의 표지를 그려 줄 미술가를 고용했다.
**ingrain** 코끼리들은 타고난 감각을 이용하여 하나의 서식지에서 다른 곳으로 이주한다.
교육의 중요성은 어린 시절 이후부터 나의 마음속에 자리잡았다.
**ingratiate** 자신이 Vronsky의 환심을 사기 위해 노력하고 있지 않다는 사실을 보여주기 위해, Sven은 즉시 다소 비판적인 말들을 몇 마디 덧붙였다.

### iridescent
[ìrədésnt]

**adj.** giving off different colors in varying lights and angles | 다양한 빛과 각도로 다른 색깔을 내는

The *iridescent* material of her dress caught everyone's eyes.

**ANT** iridescent : monochromatic [mànəkroumǽtik]
monochromatic: 단색광의

### irrepressible
[ìriprésəbl]

**adj.** impossible to control, restrain, or hold down | 억제할 수 없는

Sometimes Pat gets the *irrepressible* urge to buy new clothes, and nothing will stop him until he does.

**CN** irrepressible : quell [kwel]
irrepressible한 것은 quell(억누르다, 진압하다)할 수 없다.

### irritate
[írətèit]

**v.** to annoy or make angry; to inflame | 화나게 하다, 염증을 일으키다

Tom *irritated* his injury by constantly scratching the injured area.

**FUN** irritation : balm [bɑːm]
balm(진통제, 위안)은 irritation(화, 자극, 염증)을 가라앉히는 기능을 한다.

### juggernaut
[dʒʌ́gərnɔ̀ːt]

**n.** an unstoppable force that crushes everything in its path | 불가항력, 도저히 막을 수 없는 거대한 힘

The tornadoes of North America are *juggernauts* that destroy hundreds of homes each year.

**CH** juggernaut : unstoppable [ʌnstʌ́pəbl]
juggernaut는 unstoppable(멈추게 할 수 없는)하다.

### landmark
[lǽndmɑ̀ːrk]

**n.** an important turning point in history; a prominent object that acts as a guide | 역사적으로 중요한 전환점, 안내 표지물

The biggest *landmark* in the small town was the local church.

**CH** landmark : conspicuous [kənspíkjuəs]
landmark는 conspicuous(두드러진, 현저한)하다.

---

TRANSLATION | 예 문 해 석

| | |
|---|---|
| **iridescent** | 그녀의 드레스의 여러 가지 빛깔을 내는 재질이 모든 사람들의 눈을 사로잡았다. |
| **irrepressible** | Pat은 가끔 새 옷을 사고 싶은 억제할 수 없는 충동을 느끼며, 실제로 옷을 구입할 때까지 그 무엇도 그를 막을 수 없다. |
| **irritate** | Tom은 상처가 난 부위를 계속 긁어서 염증이 일어나게 만들었다. |
| **juggernaut** | 북미지역의 토네이도들은 매년 수백 호의 가구를 파괴하는 불가항력적인 현상들이다. |
| **landmark** | 그 작은 마을에서 가장 큰 표지물은 마을 내 교회이다. |

## logic
[ládʒik]

**n. the science of the principles of reasoning; valid explanation or rationalization** | 논리학, 논리

The judges' decisions were sound in *logic* and in law.

**WO** logic : fallacy [fǽləsi]

fallacy(허위, 그릇된 생각)에는 logic이 없다.

## lug
[lʌg]

**v. to carry or pull with extreme effort** | 힘을 다해 질질 끌다

Sally *lugged* her baggage all the way from the airport to downtown, 20 miles away.

**KIN** lug : carry [kǽri]

lug는 질질 끌면서 carry(운반하다, 나르다)한다는 의미이다.

## lurk
[ləːrk]

**v. to lie in wait** | 잠복하다

Young children often believe that monsters *lurk* under their beds.

**KIN** lurk : wait [weit]

lurk는 몰래 기다린다는 의미로 wait의 한 종류로 볼 수 있다.

## meander
[miǽndər]

**v. to wander aimlessly and idly** | 정처 없이 방황하다

Silvia often spent her afternoons *meandering* through the forest lost in deep thought.

**ANT** meander : proceed purposefully [prəsíːd pə́ːrpəsfuli]

proceed purposefully: 목적을 갖고 나아가다

## moribund
[mɔ́(ː)rəbʌnd]

**adj. being in the final stages of death** | 죽어가는, 소멸해 가는

The *moribund* patient asked for his family to stay at his bedside.

**ANT** moribund : resurgent [riːsə́ːrdʒənt]

resurgent: 소생하는

---

TRANSLATION | 예 문 해 석

logic    그 재판관들의 결정은 논리적으로나 법률적으로 옳았다.
lug      Sally는 공항에서 20마일이나 떨어진 시내까지 그녀의 가방을 힘을 다해 끌고 갔다.
lurk     어린 아이들은 종종 자신들의 침대 밑에 괴물들이 잠복해 있다고 믿는다.
meander  Silvia는 자주 깊은 생각에 잠긴 채 저녁 시간을 숲속을 정처 없이 방황하는데 보냈다.
moribund 죽어가던 그 환자는 자신의 가족들에게 침대곁에 있어달라고 부탁했다.

## parity
[pǽrəti]

**n. the quality of being on an equal level in status, value, or amount** | 동등, 동위, 동량

There should be *parity* in educational opportunites for all students.

**POS**   parity : equivalent [ikwívələnt]

equivalent: 동등한, 같은 가치의

## parlance
[páːrləns]

**n. a particular manner of speaking** | 특유의 말투, 어법

Legal *parlance* intimidates and deters lay people from carefully reading their contracts.

**대상**   parlance : speak [spiːk]

speak(말하다)하는 것을 언급할 때 parlance(어조, 말투)란 단어를 사용한다.

## perfidious
[pərfídiəs]

**adj. faithless or disloyal; having treacherous characteristics** | 신의없는, 배반하는

The *perfidious* knight was executed by the king for treason.

**WO**   perfidious : loyalty [lɔ́iəlti]

perfidious한 사람은 loyalty(성실, 충실, 충성)가 없다.

## perfunctory
[pərfʌ́ŋktəri]

**adj. done quickly as a matter of routine; mechanical; lacking enthusiasm or interest** | 겉날림의, 기계적인, 열의 없는

Jack viewed his job as just a *perfunctory* part of his day, preferring to focus his attention on evening outings.

**WO**   perfunctory : inspiration [ìnspəréiʃən]

inspiration(영감, 고무, 고취)이 없는 사람은 항상 perfunctory하게 일을 처리한다.

## peripatetic
[pèrəpətétik]

**adj. moving or traveling around; itinerant** | 순회하는, 돌아다니는

I lead a *peripatetic* life, jumping from country to country.

**ANT**   peripatetic : sedentary [sédntèri]

sedentary: 정착해 있는, 정착성의

---

TRANSLATION | 예 문 해 석

| | |
|---|---|
| parity | 모든 학생에게 교육 기회가 동등해야 한다. |
| parlance | 법률용어는 평범한 사람들이 계약서를 세심하게 읽는 것에 겁을 먹고 단념하게 만든다. |
| perfidious | 배신한 그 기사는 대역죄로 왕에 의해 처형되었다. |
| perfunctory | Jack은 자신의 일을 단지 일상의 한 부분으로 보고, 저녁에 나가서 하는 일들에 관심을 집중하는 것을 좋아한다. |
| peripatetic | 나는 이 나라에서 저 나라로 떠돌아다니며 방랑하는 생활을 하고 있다. |

## peripheral
[pərífərəl]

**adj. constituting an outer boundary; not of central importance** | 주변의, 중요하지 않은

The driver's impaired *peripheral* vision led to his accident.

**ANT** periphery : core [kɔːr]

periphery: 주변, 주위

core: 핵심

## perjure
[pə́ːrdʒər]

**v. to lie deliberately under oath** | 위증하다

The mother of the accused *perjured* herself in order to save her son's life.

**ANT** perjure : depose [dipóuz]

depose: (선서나 공술 문서에 의하여) 증언하다

## profundity
[prəfʌ́ndəti]

**n. wisdom that is profound and obscure** | 심오하고 묻혀 있는 지혜, 지적 깊이

The *profundities* that he heard as a young boy were now beginning to make sense to him as an adult.

**WO** profundity : glib [glib]

glib(겉발림으로 유창하게 말하는)은 profundity가 없는 상태이다.

## pry
[prai]

**v. to impertinently inquire into another's life; to move or lift with a lever** | 주제넘게 타인의 일을 캐묻다; 지레로 들어 올리다

Jason was always careful not to *pry* into people's personal lives.

**DE** prying : inquisitive [inkwízətiv]

prying은 inquisitive(호기심이 강한)보다 주제넘게 참견해서 캐묻는 이라는 의미를 지니고 있다.

---

### TRANSLATION | 예 문 해 석

| | |
|---|---|
| peripheral | 그 운전자는 주변 시력이 손상되어서 사고를 당했다. |
| perjure | 피고의 어머니는 아들의 생명을 구하기 위하여 위증을 했다. |
| profundity | 그가 소년이었을 때 들었던 그 심오한 지적 깊이들은 이제 어른이 되서야 이해되기 시작했다. |
| pry | Jason은 다른 사람들의 개인적인 생활을 캐묻지 않으려고 늘 조심했다. |

## purlieu
[pə́ːrljuː]

**n.** a district lying on the bounds or outskirts; a frequently visited place | 변두리, 자주 가는 장소

After work John and his friends usually get a few drinks at a *purlieu* close to work.

**ANT** purlieu : infrequent place [infríːkwənt pleis]

infrequent place: 자주 가지 않는 장소

## purloin
[pərlɔ́in]

**v.** to steal; to take by theft | 훔치다, 절도하다

The accountant *purloined* from the petty cash box at work.

**KIN** purloin : appropriate [əpróuprièit]

purloin은 appropriate(사취하다)의 일종이다.

## redundant
[ridʌ́ndənt]

**adj.** excessive or superfluous; unnecessarily wordy or repetitive | 과잉의, 남아도는, 장황한

Lay-offs were imminent as the merger had made many positions *redundant*.

**CH** redundant : reiterate [riːítərèit]

reiterate(반복하여 말하다)하는 것에는 redundant한 속성이 포함되어 있다.

## refute
[rifjúːt]

**v.** to prove wrong; to deny and question the accuracy of | 틀렸음을 증명하다, 반박하다

The president of the company *refuted* the allegations of bribery upon him.

**ANT** refute : affirm [əfə́ːrm]

affirm: (사실이라고) 단언하다, 승인하다

## scribble
[skríbl]

**v.** to write quickly and carelessly, usually illegibly | 알아보기 힘들 정도로 갈겨 쓰다, 낙서하다

The note left on the table was *scribbled* and she couldn't read it.

**KIN** scribble : write [rait]

scribble은 write(쓰다)의 한 종류로 볼 수 있다.

---

### TRANSLATION | 예문 해석

**purlieu** John과 친구들은 일이 끝난 후 대개, 직장에서 가까운 단골 술집에서 술을 몇 잔씩 한다.
**purloin** 그 회계사는 직장의 작은 현금함에서 돈을 훔쳤다.
**redundant** 합병으로 인해 많은 자리가 불필요하게 남아 해고조치가 시급하게 되었다.
**refute** 그 회사의 회장은 자신에게 제기된 뇌물 행위 주장을 반박했다.
**scribble** 테이블 위에 남겨진 쪽지는 휘갈겨 써져 있어서 그녀는 그것을 읽을 수 없었다.

**scrutinize**
[skrú:tənàiz]

v. **to examine or look closely and carefully**
| 자세히 조사하다, 유심히 보다

Eddie *scrutinized* the phone bill that was much more expensive than he expected.

- DE  scrutinize : observe [əbzə́:rv]

  scrutinize는 보다 자세하게 observe(관찰하다)한다는 의미이다.

**sentient**
[sénʃənt]

adj. **able to perceive through sense; conscious**
| 지각력이 있는, 의식적인

Humans assume that they are only *sentient* beings in the universe.

- ANT  sentient : unconscious [ʌnkʌ́nʃəs]

  unconscious: 무의식적인

**sprightly**
[spráitli]

adj. **spirited or having a gay lightness**
| 기운찬, 쾌활한

The *sprightly* old grandmother pranced around the house.

- CH  sprightly : cavort [kəvɔ́:rt]

  cavort(신나게 뛰놀다)에는 sprightly라는 속성이 포함되어 있다.

**striate**
[stráieit]

v. **to mark with striae or striations**
| 줄무늬를 내다

The barber pole is *striated* and universally recognized.

- POS  striated : groove [gru:v]

  striated: 홈이 있는

  groove: 가늘고 긴 홈

**stridency**
[stráidnsi]

n. **the quality of being loud, harsh, and grating**
| 귀에 거슬림, 삐걱거림

The *stridency* of an emergency alerts nearby individuals to heed the urgent situation.

- KIN  stridency : sound [saund]

  stridency는 귀에 거슬리는 sound(소리)이다.

---

TRANSLATION | 예 문 해 석

scrutinize   Eddie는 그가 예상했던 것보다 훨씬 많이 나온 전화요금 청구서를 자세히 살펴 보았다.
sentient     인간은 자신들이 우주에서 유일하게 지각력있는 존재라고 생각한다.
sprightly    그 쾌활한 할머니는 집 주위를 뛰어다녔다.
striate      이발소 간판대에는 줄무늬가 있고 이는 전세계적으로 인지된다.
stridency    귀에 거슬리는 경보음은 주위 사람들에게 긴급한 상황에 주의를 기울이도록 경계시킨다.

## surfeit
[sə́ːrfit]

**n. an excessive amount; overindulgence in food or drink**
| 과다, 폭식

After the feast, the men who consumed a *surfeit* of food couldn't move for hours.

**ANT** surfeit : deprivation [dèprivéiʃən]

deprivation: 부족

## thrive
[θraiv]

**v. to flourish or grow vigorously; to prosper in success or wealth**
| 무성하게 자라다, 번영하다

It is a common trait of athletes to *thrive* on pressure and competition.

**ANT** thriving : flagging [flǽɡiŋ]

thriving: 번영하는

flagging: 쇠퇴하는, 축 늘어지는

## trivial
[tríviəl]

**adj. unimportant or ordinary**
| 하찮은, 평범한

One must not concern himself too much with *trivial* matters.

**ANT** trivial : substantial [səbstǽnʃəl]

substantial: 중요한

## turgid
[tə́ːrdʒid]

**adj. swollen or bloated; excessively embellished**
| 부푼, 지나치게 치장된, 과장된

The *turgid* whale carcass could not be removed from the beach.

**ANT** turgid : deflated [difléit]

deflated: 수축된, 오므라든

## unruly
[ʌnrúːli]

**adj. not disciplined or obedient; wild or uncontrolled**
| 제멋대로인, 난폭한

The *unruly* children ignored the teacher's commands.

**SYN** unruly : obstreperous [əbstrépərəs]

obstreperous: 제어할 수 없는, 시끄럽게 떠드는

---

### TRANSLATION | 예문해석

| | |
|---|---|
| surfeit | 잔치가 끝난 후, 폭식을 한 사람들은 몇 시간 동안 움직일 수 없었다. |
| thrive | 압박과 경쟁을 딛고 성공을 이루는 것이 운동선수들의 공통적인 특성이다. |
| trivial | 사소한 문제들을 가지고 지나치게 걱정하지 말아야 한다. |
| turgid | 부푼 고래의 시체를 해변에서 치울 수 없었다. |
| unruly | 제멋대로인 아이들은 선생님의 명령을 무시했다. |

## upright
[ʌ́pràit]

**adj. standing up or in a vertical position** | 일어선, 직립의

The doll sat *upright* on the nightstand.

**ANT** upright : prostrate [prάstreit]

prostrate: 엎드린, 굴복한

## variable
[vɛ́əriəbl]

**adj. varying or changing; inconstant** | 쉽게 변하는, 변덕스러운

The *variable* weather is rather unpredictable this time of year.

**ANT** variable : immutable [imjúːtəbl]

immutable: 불변의

## verify
[vérəfài]

**v. to establish the truth or accuracy of** | 확증하다

The man's testimony was *verified* by independent witnesses who were also at the scene of the accident.

**대상** verify : accuracy [ǽkjurəsi]

verify는 어떤 것의 accuracy(정확성) 등을 입증한다는 의미이다.

---

### TRANSLATION | 예문 해석

| | |
|---|---|
| upright | 그 인형은 침대용 스탠드 위에 똑바로 앉혀져 있었다. |
| variable | 한 해 중 이맘 때는 날씨가 변덕스러워서 예측 불가능하다. |
| verify | 그 남자의 증언은 그 사고 장소에 있었던 또 다른 증인들에 의해서 사실임이 증명되었다. |

# 30th Day Daily Check-up

■ Fill in the blanks with the correct letter that matches the word with its definition.

1. parlance _____
2. sprightly _____
3. ingratiate _____
4. purloin _____
5. coax _____
6. irritate _____
7. evict _____
8. turgid _____
9. peripatetic _____
10. heresy _____

a. moving or traveling around; itinerant
b. to steal; to take by theft
c. to annoy or make angry; to inflame
d. a belief, opinion, or doctrine that goes against the church's belief or dogma
e. a particular manner of speaking
f. to legally force someone out of a property
g. swollen or bloated; excessively embellished
h. spirited or having a gay lightness
i. to patiently persuade through flattery or gentle urging
j. to gain respect or acceptance deliberately with good deeds

■ Put the correct word in each blank from the list of words below.

11. debasement(저하)는 _____의 반의어이다.
12. _____는 질질 끌면서 carry한다는 의미이다.
13. _____는 음식의 미묘한 맛을 까다롭게 discriminating하는 경향이 있다.
14. deprivation(부족)의 반의어는 _____이다.
15. _____ 한 사람은 loyalty가 없다.
16. mockery의 의미를 지닌 동사는 _____이다.
17. resurgent(소생하는)의 반의어는 _____이다.
18. precursory(선구의)의 반의어는 _____이다.
19. landmark는 _____한 특성을 갖는다.
20. _____는 색채가 불쾌할 정도로 지나치게 colorful하다는 의미이다.

| a. derivative | b. conspicuous | c. elevation | d. moribund | e. pry | f. epicure |
| g. surfeit | h. lug | i. deride | j. perfidious | k. garish | l. trivial |

**Answer key**

1. e  2. h  3. j  4. b  5. i  6. c  7. f  8. g  9. a  10. d
11. c  12. h  13. f  14. g  15. j  16. i  17. d  18. a  19. b  20. k

# 21st day~30th Day Crossword Puzzle

Answer Page 476

# Questions

### across

3. cheerful or happy; floatable
7. having a strong desire or yearning
9. bright; radiant in character
10. to give a conciliatory gift or bribe; to take up liquid by absorbing it
12. a legally authorized delay of payment; a suspension of something
13. to patiently persuade through flattery or gentle urging
15. the use of an excessive quantity of words to express something
17. witty or clever retort
18. to weaken or thin by adding a liquid
19. a humorous poem of around five lines
20. flawless; incapable of sinning or doing wrong

### down

1. a surrender or compliance
2. not identified or of unknown authorship
4. impulsive; marked by violent force of action or manner
5. with minimal energy or excitement; listless
6. debased; marked by a vulgarity or by disrespecting something sacred
8. to infer without evidence
11. feeling regret or sadness for having done wrong or caused harm
14. to accelerate or rush a process
16. to contaminate with a disease or sickness; to corrupt

# TAKE A BREAK

## Self-Interview *by 아슈

도착한 지 1주일이 되었습니다.
사돈의 팔촌을 뒤져봐도 아는 이 하나 없는, 물설고, 말설고, 낯설고, 공기조차 생소한 이 미국에서 말 걸 사람 하나 없는 이때, 스스로와 이런 대화를 나누며 다짐해봅니다.
'잊지도 말고, 잊혀지지도 말자고...'

이제 만 1주일 째 미국생활을 맞이하고 있는 아슈입니다.

Q : 영어는 잘 됩니까?
A : 잘되면 여기 왔겠습니까? ㅠ.ㅠ

Q : 뭐 먹고 삽니까?
A : 처음에 시장 가기 전엔 계속 '굶기 신공', '수워먹기 신공' 등등을 발휘했었으나, 이제 샌드위치 도시락도 싸가지고 다니고, 밥도 해먹고, 파스타도 해먹고, 그렇습니다.

Q : 시차는 극복했습니까?
A : 남들하곤 좀 다르게 저녁 먹고 정확히 8시(우리나라 오후 1시)면 잠이 몰려오는 까닭에;;; 그리고 아침 6시(밤 11시)면 또 칼같이 일어나는.. 역시 밤 생활을 오래 한 탓이 아닐까 싶습니다.

Q : California라던데 날씨 죽입니까?
A : 추워서 죽입니다. 전기장판 안 가져왔으면 죽을 뻔했습니다.

Q : 수업은 어떻습니까?
A : 지금 '선이수과목'을 3개 듣고 있구요. 어제부터 막 시작했습니다만.. 죽음입니다.

Q : 왜 죽음입니까?
A : 그게 죽음이 아니면, 제가 한국사람이겠습니까?
전공이 전공인지라 수업의 대부분이 주변 사람과 '떠들기', '글로 적어 내기'입니다. 한시라도 입을 가만히 두면, 점수가 깎인다 이 말입니다.

Q : 잘됐네요. 특기 아닙니까.
A : 이보세요. 영어로 해야 하니까 문제죠...

Q : 예습 복습을 철저히 하면 될 거 아닙니까.
A : 각 과목당 읽어야 할 책이 세 권입니다. 한 과목당 봐야 할 기본 시험이 세 번이고, 한 과목당 내야 할 기본 페이퍼가 세 개씩입니다. 그리고 각 과목별로 매주 리포트를 내거나, 프리젠테이션을 하거나, 리서치를 해야 하죠.

쉬●어●가●는  페●이●지

Q : 조.. 조금 힘들겠군요.
A : 조금이겠습니까...?

Q : 한국인은 많습니까?
A : 미국인보다는 적습니다.

Q : 이 사람이 장난합니까.
A : 사실을 얘기한 것뿐인데요.

Q : LA에 가면 한국말만 하고도 산다던데, 한국인끼리만 몰려다니고 뭐 그러지는 않습니까?
A : 여기 와서 한국인, 딱 한 명하고 얘기해봤습니다. 그것도 길 건너다 가방 상표 보고 그냥 말 걸었죠. 한인타운도 어딘가 있겠지만, 저 같은 뚜벅이에게는 서울만큼 먼 곳입니다.

Q : 흠흠.. 영어 공부하러 갔으니 그 정도는 인내해야죠.. 그런데 서울이 그만큼 먼 곳입니까?
A : 당장은.. 갈 수 없으니.. 천국만큼 먼 곳이죠..

Q : 이만 마무리해야겠군요. 마지막으로 한마디 해보시죠.
A : 그 땅이 그리운 것이 아니라, 그리운 사람들이 그곳에 있기에 그립다고.. 그렇게 전해주세요. 그냥 일단은.. 열심히 살려 하니까, 열심히 살아달라고.. 그냥.. 그만큼. 딱.. 나 떠나오기 전 그만큼의 자리에서요. 더 가까워지지도, 더 멀어지지도.. 말구요.

- www.goHackers.com의 유학생생일기에서 발췌했습니다.

# Crossword Puzzle Answer

Page 168
1st day ~ 10th day

Page 320
11th day ~ 20th day

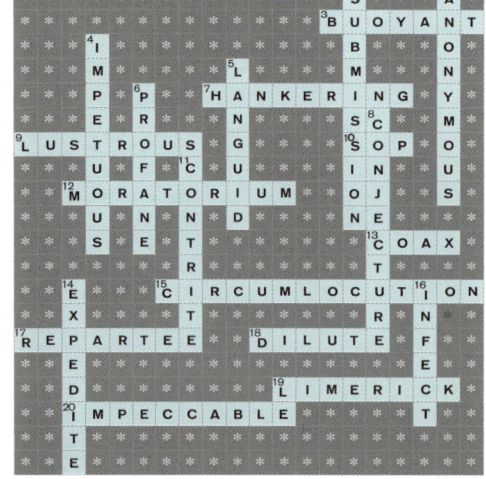

Page 472
21st day ~ 30th day

# SuperVoca
## Words Pack

**abeyance** [əbéiəns] 중지
n. a state in which something is not being operated, momentarily halted

**abnegate** [ǽbnigèit] 거절하다, 거부하다
v. to refuse or reject; to deny

**abrogate** [ǽbrəgèit] 없애다, 폐지하다
v. to get rid of or abolish

**absolve** [æbzálv] 죄를 용서하다, 의무로부터 자유롭게 하다
v. to free or pardon of guilt or obligation

**acclaim** [əkléim] 갈채하다, 환호하다
v. to passionately honor someone or something

**acclimate** [ǽkləmèit] 길들이다, 새로운 환경에 적응하다
v. to adapt to or get used to a new environment or circumstance

**accommodate** [əkámədèit] 편의를 제공하다
v. to have room for; to hold comfortably without crowding

**accord** [əkɔ́ːrd] 일치하다; 동의, 조화
v. to have no conflict; to be in an agreement
n. an arrangement between two parties where a common understanding is made

**address** [ədrés] 연설하다, 연설 [ǽdres] 주소
v. to talk to a person or group of people
n. a location for a certain area or a speech given by a person

**adumbration** [ædʌ́mbreiʃən] 부분적이고 조심스럽게 드러냄, 전조
n. a partial and guarded disclosure

**adversary** [ǽdvərsèri] 적
n. an opponent that one competes with

**agenda** [ədʒéndə] 의사 일정
n. a certain schedule or list of things that someone uses as a guide

**aggressive** [əgrésiv] 공격적인, 정력적인
adj. offensive or hostile; bold and energetic

**alacritous** [əlǽkrətəs] 쾌활한, 열망하는
adj. cheerful and eager

**alchemy** [ǽlkəmi] 기본적인 금속을 황금으로 변환시키려 했던 화학 기술, 연금술
n. a false science of chemistry that sought to convert base metals into gold

**allege** [əlédʒ] 단언하다
v. to verbally claim that something has occurred without any proof

**alliterate** [əlítərèit] 두운을 사용해서 글이나 말을 하다
v. to speak or write using the same sound at the beginning of each word

**allude** [əlúːd] 넌지시 말하다
v. to speak or imply to something not by direct means

**anaerobe** [ǽnəròub] 무기성 생물
n. an organism capable of living without oxygen

**anarchist** [ǽnərkist] 무정부주의자
n. a person who believes in, desires, and tries to obtain a society or state without government

**anemic** [əníːmik] 생기나 에너지가 없는, 결핍의
adj. having little or no vitality or energy

**anvil** [ǽnvəl] 금속을 다듬는 데 쓰이는 무거운 강철 각대, 모루
n. a heavy iron block used to hammer and shape metals

**apophasis** [əpáfəsis] 어떤 사항에 대하여 언급하지 않겠다고 함으로써 넌지시 암시하는 어법
n. the act of referring to something by denying that it will be mentioned

**apparel** [əpǽrəl] 의상
n. clothing; attire

**apprehension** [æprihénʃən] 염려, 이해, 체포
n. a sense of panic that something unfortunate will occur; understanding; arrest

**assume** [əsjúːm] 가정하다, 추정하다, 책임을 맡다
v. to conceive that something is truthful; to take on certain responsibilities

**astound** [əstáund] 매우 놀라게 하다
v. to surprise or astonish someone

**astringent** [əstríndʒənt] 수렴제
n. a liquid substance used to close openings, usually to stop blood loss or other bodily fluids

**asymmetrical** [èisəmétrikəl] 비대칭의, 균형이 맞지 않는
adj. having two sides of a certain object that are not the same; unbalanced

**athletics** [æθlétiks] 운동경기
n. a type of exercise or sport which involves physical activity

**attach** [ətǽtʃ] 붙이다, 소속시키다
v. to join or associate objects together

**avulse** [əvʌ́ls] 찢어서 분리하다
v. to tear apart forcibly

**awning** [ɔ́ːniŋ] 차일, 차양
n. a type of material used as a cover from rain or sun, erected over a door or window

**backdrop** [bǽkdrɑ̀p] 배경
n. the setting; the background

**badinage** [bæ̀dənɑ́ːʒ] 놀리다; 야유
v. to verbally taunt someone in a carefree way
n. a playful conversation that involves making fun of one another; banter

**ballot** [bǽlət] 후보의 명단이 있는 투표용지 혹은 후보자 명단
n. a ticket or piece of paper listing the candidates to be voted on during an election

**band** [bænd] 묶다; 묶는데 쓰이는 도구, 무리
v. to connect or assemble into a group
n. any type of material that is used to bind an object or hold multiple objects together; a group

**banquet** [bǽŋkwit] 진수성찬, 연회
n. an elaborate formal dinner for special occasions

**baseboard** [béisbɔ̀ːrd] 굽도리널, 밑판자
n. a border between the wall and the floor found along side the base of the wall

**baseness** [béisnis] 혐오스러움, 역겨움, 비열함
n. the quality of being vile, disgusting and contemptible

**bedeck** [bidék] 꾸미다, 장식하다
v. to adorn or decorate

**befuddle** [bifʌ́dl] 혼란에 빠뜨리다, 혼미하게 하다
v. to confuse, perplex, or stupefy

**benediction** [bènədíkʃən] 축복, 축복 기도
n. a blessing; the invocation of a blessing

**betray** [bitréi] 배신하다
v. to break one's trust or promise; to be unfaithful or unloyal

**biased** [báiəst] 치우친, 편향된
adj. having a preference that impairs impartial judgement

**bliss** [blis] 황홀하거나 극도로 행복한 상태
n. state of ecstasy or extreme happiness

**blizzard** [blízərd] 눈보라
n. a heavy snow storm with high winds

**blooming** [blúːmiŋ] 한창 젊은, 번영하는
adj. thriving with youth or health; flourishing

**blunder** [blʌ́ndər] 심각한 실수, 생각 없이 저질러진 터무니 없는 실수
n. a serious error or mistake caused by stupidity or carelessness

**boggle** [bágl] 깜짝 놀라다
v. to be overwhelmed with fright or amazement

**border** [bɔ́ːrdər] ~에 접하다, 경계짓다; 경계
v. to be along the edges or next to something
n. a boundary or a part that forms the exterior of something

**bottleneck** [bátlnèk] 속도를 늦추게 하다, 방해하다; 좁은 통로
v. to slow down or impede by obstructing
n. a narrow or obstructed passage way

**branch** [bræntʃ] 가지, 분야
n. a part or division of a larger whole

**bravado** [brəváːdou] 용감한 척 허세를 부림
n. a false show of courage

**bravura** [brəvjúərə] 연주 스타일이나 기술의 화려함
n. brilliance in performance style or technique

**breezeway** [bríːzwèi] 두 구조물을 연결하는 옆이 트이고 지붕이 있는 복도
n. a passage way with a roof and no sides that connects two structures

**bruit** [bruːt] 소문이나 소식을 퍼뜨리다
v. to spread rumors or news

**budge** [bʌdʒ] 조금 움직이다
v. to move or push slightly

**bungle** [bʌ́ŋgl] 서투르게 망쳐 놓거나 효과 없이 처리하다
v. to botch or manage ineffectively

# C

**cadge** [kædʒ] 구걸하여 억지로 얻다
v. to receive through begging

**calcify** [kǽlsəfài] 석회화하다
v. to become or transform into a hard stony object through the disposition of calcium salts forming lime

**camaraderie** [kæ̀məráːdəri] 우정
n. a sense of trust and closeness that is shared among friends

**cameo** [kǽmiòu] 카메오 출연, 카메오 세공
n. a minor role played by a prominent actor in a single scene of a movie; a type of jewelry

**capture** [kǽptʃər] 포로로 하다, 사로 잡다; 포로, 포획
v. to catch or arrest
n. someone that has been caught, or the act of catching someone

**cartographer** [kɑːrtɑ́grəfər] 지도제작자
n. someone whose profession is drawing maps

**cautious** [kɔ́ːʃəs] 조심성 있는, 신중한
adj. careful, guarded, and wary

**centrifuge** [séntrəfjùːdʒ] 원심분리기
n. a machine that uses centrifugal force to separate materials of different densities

**charge** [tʃɑːrdʒ] 고소하다, 죄 등을 뒤집어 씌우다
v. to accuse or blame someone of wrongdoing

**chisel** [tʃízl] 조각칼
n. a tool used in sculpting wood or stone

**chromatic** [kroumǽtik] 색과 관련된
adj. relating to colors

**chronological** [krànəládʒikəl] 연대순의
adj. portrayed in the same time order as they occurred

**circular** [sə́ːrkjələr] 원의, 원형의, 순환성의
adj. shaped like a circle

**clarion** [klǽriən] (옛 악기) 클라리온
n. a medieval brass wind instrument that makes a very high pitched sound

**clinch** [klintʃ] 단단히 고정시키다, 세게 쥐다
v. to hold or grip tightly

**cloture** [klóutʃər] 의회에서 토론을 종결하고 표결에 들어가는 과정
n. a procedure for closing a discussion and taking a vote in parliament

**coeval** [kouíːvəl] 동시대나 같은 기간에 존재한
adj. existing at the same age or during the same time period

**commitment** [kəmítmənt] 의무, 공약
n. loyalty to a cause or obligation; a pledge to do something in the future

**comply** [kəmplái] 응하다, 따르다
v. to conform to or obey regulations or commands

**concatenate** [kɑnkǽtənèit] 잇다, 연결하다
v. to link or connect in a series

**conclude** [kənklúːd] 결론짓다, 결정하다
v. to reach a decision through facts given as support

**concrete** [kɔ́nkriːt] 확고한, 구체적인; 콘크리트
adj. being clear and specific
n. a construction material consisting of a mixture of sand, small stones, cement, and water

**condign** [kəndáin] 적절한, 잘 맞는
adj. appropriate and fitting

**condolence** [kəndóuləns] 슬픔이나 고통에 대한 위로의 표시, 애도
n. an expression of sympathy for someone's grief, pain, or sorrow

**confine** [kənfáin] 한정하다, 가두다
v. to restrict something to a limited space

**connect** [kənékt] 잇다, 연결하다, 접속하다
v. to join or attach objects together

**connoisseur** [kɑ̀nəsə́ːr] 권위자, 감식가
n. someone who enjoys and is knowledgeable about a particualr subject matter; a person of discriminating taste

**constant** [kɑ́nstənt] 변하지 않는 것, 상수, 불변량; 불변의, 일정한
n. something that never changes; a number or a value in mathematics that is always the same
adj. continuing to occur or happen for a long time

**constrain** [kənstréin] 구속하다, 제약하다
v. to hold tightly and confine

**contain** [kəntéin] 담고있다, 포함하다
v. to include something inside or as a part

**continence** [kántənəns] 극기, 자제, 절제
n. self restraint and moderation

**continuance** [kəntínjuəns] 계속, 연속
n. condition of permanence or uninterrupted action

**contrast** [kántræst] 대조, 대비
n. the difference between two things when you compare them to one another

**converge** [kənvə́ːrdʒ] 집중하다, 수렴하다
v. to concentrate on; to meet at a certain place or point

**conversant** [kənvə́ːrsənt] 정통한, 여러 주제에 대해 이야기할 수 있는
adj. knowledgeable and able to talk about various subjects

**conversion** [kənvə́ːrʒən] 전환
n. the development or procedure of changing something into a different condition or shape

**convey** [kənvéi] 운반하다, (생각을) 전달하다; 수송
v. to deliver to another; to produce data or ideas to be acknowledged or perceived by another
n. transportation

**cornucopia** [kɔ̀ːrnjukóupiə] 풍부함, 풍요
n. an abundance, richness, or variety

**corrode** [kəróud] 부식하다, 침식하다
v. to slowly destroy through some sort of chemical reaction such as rust

**coterie** [kóutəri] 동료, 일파, 서클
n. a small, select circle of people

**countenance** [káuntənəns] 표정, 지지; 허용하다, 찬성하다
n. someone's appearance, usually their facial expressions; encouragement or support
v. to allow or approve of something

**counter** [káuntər] 계수대; 반대의
n. a table or another long flat surface where the undertaking of money, business or food takes place
adj. having to do with reversals or opposing certain acts

**courage** [kə́ːridʒ] (정신적인) 용기, 담력
n. a characteristic where one performs dangerous or difficult duties in spite of being afraid

**course** [kɔːrs] 흐름, 방향
n. a route or path that someone or something can follow

**courtroom** [kɔ́ːrtrù(ː)m] 법정
n. a room where a legal preceding takes place

**cozen** [kʌzn] 기만하다, 심하지 않은 속임수를 쓰다
v. to deceive or cheat in a small way

**crass** [kræs] 천한, 저속한
adj. inelegant and vulgar

**creek** [kriːk] 작은 만
n. a smaller version of a river or stream

**crescendo** [kriʃéndou] 점점 커지는 소리
n. a noise that gradually becomes louder

**crockery** [krάkəri] 도자기 그릇
n. plates and dishes made of clay for eating and serving food

**crouch** [krautʃ] 무릎을 굽혀 웅크리다
v. to stoop with knees bent

**crumb** [krʌm] 빵 부스러기
n. a very small portion or piece of bread that has fallen off

**cunning** [kʌ́niŋ] 교활한, 간사한
adj. having the talent to accomplish things usually through tricks and deception

**curate** [kjuərət] 보좌신부, 부목사
n. a clergyman who is an aide to the priest

## D

**dawdle** [dɔ́ːdl] (시간을) 낭비하다, 빈둥 거리다
v. to waste time while going somewhere or doing something

**decibel** [désəbèl] 데시벨(음향 측정단위)
n. the unit for measuring sound

**declamation** [dèkləméiʃən] 웅변, 열변
n. a firm and emphatic statement or speech

**deflect** [diflékt] 빗나가다
v. to make something or someone deviate off its original course

**demand** [dimǽnd] 요구하다
v. to strongly ask for something

**demotic** [dimάtik] 평범한, 대중적인
adj. common or popular; relating to the common people

**demystify** [diːmístəfài] 신비함을 없애다, 깨우쳐주다
v. to take away the mystery from; to make clear

**denial** [dináiəl] 부정, 반박
n. refusal to accept reality or truth

**denunciation** [dinʌ̀nsiéiʃən] 공공연하게 비난하는 행위
n. the act of publicly censuring

**dependence** [dipéndəns] 의뢰, 신뢰, 종속상태
n. the need for something or on someone in order to sustain oneself

**deportation** [dìːpɔːrtéiʃən] 어떤 사람을 국외로 추방시킴
n. the expulsion or banishment of a person from a country

**descendant** [diséndənt] 자손, 후예
n. biological offspring of a given ancestor or ancestors

**descent** [disént] 하강, 낙하
n. the act of descending or passing downward

**despise** [dispáiz] 혐오하다, 싫어하다
v. to hate or loathe

**detainment** [ditéinmənt] 지연, 저지, 억류
n. a condition where someone or something is forcibly confined in a particular place or area

**detrimental** [dètrəméntl] 해로운
adj. having a damaging or destructive effect

**devote** [divóut] 헌신하다
v. to spend much time and energy on something or someone

**diction** [díkʃən] 말로 표현되는 방법, 어법, 말투
n. the manner in which something is expressed in words

**diligence** [dílədʒəns] 근면, 배려
n. a steady effort on a given task

**diocese** [dáiəsis] 주교 관구
n. the area which a bishop takes controls

**dirge** [dəːrdʒ] 애도가
n. a slow sad song that is usually sung at a funeral

**disagreeable** [dìsəgríːəbl] 불유쾌한, 마음에 안드는
adj. being unpleasant

**disarm** [disáːrm] 무장해제하다, 적의를 없애다
v. to deprive of weapons or other means of hostility; to render harmless or defenseless

**discrepancy** [diskrépənsi] 사실이나 주장에서의 차이, 불일치
n. difference or divergence in facts or claims

**disengage** [dìsengéidʒ] 해방하다, 중지하다
v. to release something from connection or attachment; to discontinue

**disjoint** [disdʒɔ́int] 분리하다, 일치점을 없애버리다
v. to disconnect; to destroy the logical or chronological coherence of

**dismiss** [dismís] 해산시키다, 해고하다
v. to send away or force someone to leave a job

**disquiet** [diskwáiət] 평정을 잃음, 걱정, 불안
n. lack of peace or rest; anxiety or restlessness

**dissect** [disékt] 해부하다, 자세히 조사하다
v. to cut open and examine a body for scientific purposes

**doctrine** [dάktrin] 교리, 주의
n. a series of principles or beliefs

**doleful** [dóulfəl] 슬픔으로 가득찬, 음울한
adj. filled with sorrow and grief

**dolorous** [dάlərəs] 슬픔이나 고통을 내비치는
adj. showing sadness, grief, or pain

**donor** [dóunər] 자선 기금이나 단체에 돈이나 물품을 기증하는 사람
n. one who gives money or goods to fund

**downplay** [dáunplèi] 중요치 않게 여기다
v. to make something seem less significant

**doze** [douz] 선잠을 자다
v. to sleep lightly, for a short period of time

**drill** [dril] 송곳, 훈련
n. a pointed tool for making holes; a way of training through repetition

**dutiful** [djú:tifəl] 의무감에서 권위자에게 기꺼이 순종하는
adj. willingly obedient to superiors out of a sense of duty

# E

**eaglet** [í:glit] 독수리 새끼
n. a baby eagle

**ebullience** [ibʌ́ljəns] 넘치는 기운
n. overflowing exuberance

**ecologist** [i:kάlədʒist] 생태학자
n. a person who is studying ecology

**eddy** [édi] 주류를 거슬러 흐르는 공기나 물의 소용돌이
n. a whirlpool of air or water against the main current

**effrontery** [efrʌ́ntəri] 뻔뻔함, 몰염치
n. a behavior that is thought of as rude or impolite

**egalitarian** [igæ̀lətɛ́əriən] 정치, 경제, 사회 혹은 시민권에 있어서 평등한
adj. characterized by the belief that all peple should be equal in political, economic, social, and civil rights

**elegiac** [èlidʒáiək] 지난 일에 대해 슬픔을 표시하는, 애조를 띤
adj. expressing sorrow over past events

**elicit** [ilísit] 끌어내다, 알아내다
v. to do or say something to get a response or reaction

**elitism** [ilí:tizm] 우월하다는 인식 하에 특정한 자신들이 특혜를 받을 가치가 있다는 믿음, 엘리트주의
n. a belief that certain people deserve favor on the basis of their perceived superiority

**emaciate** [iméiʃièit] 마르거나 몸이 약해지다
v. to become thin or physically weak

**embroider** [embrɔ́idər] 수놓다
v. to stitch a design and put it on clothes or other types of fabrics

**energize** [énərdʒàiz] 활력을 불어 넣다
v. to fill with energy

**ensue** [ensúː] 뒤따라 일어나다
v. to occur immediately after another event

**entrancing** [entrǽnsiŋ] 매력적인, 놀랄 만한 호감을 주는
adj. charming and delightful enough to cause wonderment

**entry** [éntri] 입구, 입장
n. a way into a place; admittance

**equity** [ékwəti] 공평, 정당
n. the quality or state of being fair and just

**evacuate** [ivǽkjuèit] 비우다, 다른 곳으로 사람들을 후송시키다
v. to vacate a place or area; to send people out of a dangerous place

**exceptional** [iksépʃənl] 예외의, 예외적인, 특별한
adj. having qualities that are unusually rare and special

**excessive** [iksésiv] 과도한
adj. greater than is reasonable or necessary

**excitable** [iksáitəbl] 흥분하기 쉬운, 반응성의
adj. becoming easily anxious or nervous

**exclaim** [ikskléim] 큰소리로 갑작스럽게 외치다
v. to express loudly and suddenly

**excrete** [ikskríːt] 배설하다, 배출하다
v. to discharge from the body

**execrable** [éksikrəbl] 저주 받을 만한, 혐오할
adj. deserving of curses and damnation

**exhilarate** [igzílərèit] 유쾌하게 하다, 활기를 주다
v. to make happy or joyful; to enliven or animate

**explicate** [ékspləkèit] 명백하게 설명하다
v. to explain clearly

**exquisite** [ekskwízit] 훌륭한, 아름다운, 정교한
adj. characterized by excellence, beauty, and intricacy

**exude** [igzúːd] 발산시키다, 내뿜다
v. to discharge or emit

**factorable** [fǽktərəbl] ~의 약수를 결정할 수 있는
adj. capable of determining the factors of

**factual** [fǽktʃuəl] 사실의
adj. being true or authentic

**fascinating** [fǽsənèitiŋ] 매력적인, 매우 재미있는
adj. alluring and very interesting

**faultfinder** [fɔ́ːltfàindər] 트집을 잡아 비난하는 사람
n. one who scolds and criticizes

**feign** [fein] ~인 체 하다
v. to pretend or deceive

**felicitous** [filísətəs] 교묘한, 멋들어진
adj. clever or very skillful

**fictional** [fíkʃənl] 꾸며낸, 허구의
adj. having to do with things created through the imagination

**finicky** [fíniki] 몹시 까다로운
adj. being hard to please

**firm** [fəːrm] 굳은, 견고한; 회사, 상업 집단
adj. having a solid shape
n. an organization that markets or produces products or supplies assistance for which people pay

**flare** [flɛər] 환하게 불태우다, 비추다, 빛나다
v. to burn or blaze brightly

**flatten** [flǽtn] 평평하게 하다, 쓰러뜨리다
v. to make something level or flat; to knock down completely

**flint** [flint] 부싯돌
n. a piece of quartz which sparks when struck with steel

**flip** [flip] 재빨리 뒤집다, 젖히다
v. to turn over quickly

**florid** [flɔ́(ː)rid] 불그스름한, 혈색이 좋은
adj. having a ruddy complexion

**foil** [fɔil] 금속으로 된 얇은 박
n. a thin sheet of metal

**folly** [fáli] 어리석음, 어리석은 행동
n. a way of thinking, acting, or behavior that is considered foolish

**formality** [fɔːrmǽləti] 형식, 관습
n. a formal action that must be done as part of an official process or a social situation

**formidable** [fɔ́ːrmidəbl] 무거운, 경이감을 일으키는
adj. fearsome or intimidating; inspiring awe or wonder

**forsake** [fərséik] 저버리다
v. to abandon or desert

**fracture** [fræktʃər] 부러뜨리다, 골절시키다
v. to cause a slight crack or break

**fret** [fret] 초조해 하다, 마음을 졸이다
v. to be irritated, vexed, or agitated

**friction** [fríkʃən] 마찰, 알력
n. a force that makes it difficult for things to slide or move against something else

**frieze** [fri:z] 프리즈, 띠 모양의 장식
n. decoration high upon the walls of a room; consisting of a long strip of paper or panel of carving

# G

**gangly** [gǽŋgli] 사지가 길어 후리후리한, 껑충한
adj. tall and lanky with long limbs

**garment** [gɑ́ːrmənt] 의복
n. clothing

**gasification** [gæ̀səfikéiʃən] 기체의 형태로 전환하는 것 또는 과정, 기화
n. the process or act of converting into a gaseous form

**gaudy** [gɔ́ːdi] 겉만 그럴 듯한, 야한
adj. showy and tacky

**gauge** [geidʒ] 계량기, 계량기준, 척도
n. an instrument that measures and shows the amount of something; a standard dimension, quantity, or capacity

**glisten** [glísn] 빛나다
v. to be shiny

**glitch** [glitʃ] 가벼운 오류나 고장
n. a small error or malfunction

**glutton** [glʌ́tn] 대식가, 폭식가
n. one who consumes large amounts of food and drink

**goad** [goud] 선동하다; 자극, 격려
v. to urge or provoke someone
n. something that makes someone do something

**grain** [grein] 곡물, 조직, 결정
n. the seeds from cereal crops; the arrangement or a small piece of a substance

**grandstand** [grǽndstænd] 자랑하다, 관심을 모으려고 허세를 부리며 행동하다
v. to show off or act ostentatiously in order to impress

**grate** [greit] 갈다, 문지르다, 신경질 나게 하다
v. to shred into smaller pieces or rub against something and make an annoying sound; to irritate

**gravel** [grǽvəl] 자갈
n. a collect of very small stones

# H

**hack** [hæk] 마구잡이로 자르다
v. to cut or chop roughly and irregularly

**halt** [hɔːlt] 멈추다
v. to stop

**hapless** [hǽplis] 동정할 만한, 비참한, 불운한
adj. deserving pity; miserable and unfortunate

**heroic** [hiróuik] 매우 용감한, 당당한
adj. extremely brave and courageous

**herpetologist** [hə̀ːrpətálədʒist] 파충류학자
n. someone who studies reptiles and amphibians

**hieroglyph** [háiərəglìf] 상형문자
n. ancient writings that consist of pictorial symbols in the form of pictures

**hoax** [houks] 속이기
n. a type of trick

**homogeneous** [hòumədʒíːniəs] 동종의
adj. having parts of a group that are the same

**horn** [hɔːrn] 뿔, (악기) 호른, 경적
n. a type of bone that sticks out from the head of an animal; a musical instrument consisting of a tube; the object in a vehicle that makes a loud warning sound

**hypnotic** [hipnátik] 잠이 오게 하는, 최면하는
adj. tending to cause sleep; having the effect of causing a state of unconsciousness

# I

**idolatrize** [aidálətràiz] 우상을 숭배하다
v. to worship idols

**immobilize** [imóubəlàiz] 움직이지 못하게 하다
v. to stop someone or something from moving

**immure** [imjúər] 가두다, 감금하다
v. to confine or imprison

**impalpable** [impǽlpəbl] 촉감으로도 알 수가 없는, 무형의
adj. unable to perceive through the sense of touch

**imposter** [impástər] 사기꾼
n. someone who is pretending to be someone else in order to trick people

**imprecise** [ìmprisáis] 불분명한
adj. unclear or inexact

**improper** [imprápər] 부적절한
adj. being dishonest or doing things that are illegal

**impure** [impjúər] 더러운, 오염된
adj. having bad qualities, or being contaminated

**inadequate** [inǽdikwət] 부적절한, 불충분한
*adj.* being incapable of doing something; insufficient

**inanimate** [inǽnəmət] 활기 없는; 생명이 없는
*adj.* having no vitality; not alive

**inclination** [ìnklənéiʃən] 경향, 기질, 성향
*n.* an impression or sensation that makes someone want to do a particular thing

**indistinct** [ìndistíŋkt] 희미한, 흐릿한
*adj.* being unclear or difficult to see or recognize

**infer** [infə́ːr] 추론하다
*v.* to conclude or guess from facts

**infirm** [infə́ːrm] 약한, 견고하지 못한
*adj.* weak or ill

**inflexible** [infléksəbl] 확고한, 꿋꿋한
*adj.* being unable to change

**ingenuity** [ìndʒənjúːəti] 독창력, 정교
*n.* a talent for making new things; acuteness in devising

**ingest** [indʒést] 먹다, 입을 통해 섭취하다
*v.* to eat; to take in through the mouth

**inkling** [íŋkliŋ] 넌지시 비춤, 어렴풋이 알아차림
*n.* a slight hint or a vague notion

**insatiable** [inséiʃəbl] 만족할 줄 모르는, 탐욕스러운
*adj.* having a desire or greed that is unable to be satisfied

**insubstantial** [ìnsəbstǽnʃəl] 비현실적인, 미량의
*adj.* not seeming real; not very large in size or amount

**intelligence** [intélədʒns] 지능, 이해력
*n.* the ability to attain and use things that have been learned

**invidious** [invídiəs] 샘 나게 하는, 비위에 거슬리게 하는
*adj.* causing envy or resentment

**ire** [áiər] 화, 분노
*n.* a strong feeling of anger or rage

**irreducible** [ìridjúːsəbl] 줄일 수 없는
*adj.* unable to reduce to a smaller or simpler form

**irrelevant** [iréləvənt] 부적절한, 무관계한
*adj.* unimportant or unrelated to the topic or situation

# J

**jamb** [dʒæm] 문설주
*n.* a post that forms the upright sides of a window or door

**jeer** [dʒiər] 조롱하다
v. to speak in a way that makes fun of people

**jeopardize** [dʒépərdàiz] 위험에 빠트리다
v. to do something that may cause something to fail or be damaged

## K

**knack** [næk] 기교, 요령
n. ability and ease in performing a certain task

**knave** [neiv] 부정직한 사람
n. a dishonest or deceitful person

**knead** [niːd] 반죽하다
v. to mix or work by using one's hands to press, fold, and stretch something

## L

**labile** [léibil] 적응할 수 있는, 변화를 일으키기 쉬운
adj. adaptable and welcoming of change

**lachrymose** [lǽkrəmòus] 눈물이 날 것 같은, 눈물 나는
adj. prone to weeping

**lackluster** [lǽklʌ̀stər] 활기나 빛이 없는
adj. lacking of vitality or brilliance

**lambaste** [læmbéist] 치다, 엄하게 꾸짖다
v. to beat or reprimand harshly

**lampoon** [læmpúːn] 풍자문
n. a humorous way to criticize something

**lank** [læŋk] 길고 마른
adj. tall and lean

**largesse** [lɑːrdʒés] 너그럽고 아낌없이 주는 성격
n. generous and liberal nature in giving to others

**leverage** [lévəridʒ] 지레작용, 권력, 수단
n. the mechanical advantage of a lever; the power to control a situation or person

**lighthearted** [laithɑ́ːrtid] 근심이 없는, 마음 편한
adj. untroubled; free of worry or care

**linen** [línin] 아마포, 린넨
n. a type of fabric made from flax

**linoleum** [linóuliəm] 아마인 유 혼합을 굳혀서 만든 바닥 깔개
n. a floor covering made of a hardened linseed oil mixture

**liquefy** [líkwifài] 액화 시키다
v. to change from either solid or gas form to liquid form

**lissome** [lísəm] 유연한, 날씬한
adj. easy to bend or move; slim and limber

**literary** [lítərèri] 문학과 관련된, 문학의
adj. pertaining to literature

**locate** [loukéit] ~의 위치를 결정하다, 찾아내다
v. to determine or discover the position of

**lode** [loud] 광맥, 원천
n. an abundant bed of minerals found in rock formations

**longevity** [landʒévəti] 장기간, 장수
n. long continuance or duration; the fact of having a long life

**loutish** [láutiʃ] 세련되지 못하고 비열한
adj. boorish and contemptible in attitude or appearance

**magnanimity** [mæ̀gnəníməti] 매우 마음이 넓고 관대함
n. the quality of being very liberal and generous

**malaise** [mæléiz] 병이 나기 전에 몸이 불편한 것, 일반적으로 몸이 불편한 증상
n. the state of physical unease experienced before an illness; general sense of being ill at ease

**manuscript** [mǽnjuskrìpt] 필사본
n. a piece of writing that was written by hand

**mar** [mɑːr] 망쳐놓다, 훼손하다
v. to ruin or damage something

**margin** [mɑ́ːrdʒin] 여백, 한도, 가장자리
n. an area of empty space on paper; the border or edge

**mark** [mɑːrk] 표시
n. a sign that usually has a special meaning

**marvel** [mɑ́ːrvəl] 놀라운 일, 경이
n. an extraordinary event that has people in awe

**medley** [médli] 여러 원곡들을 모아 만든 혼성곡
n. a musical composition that is made up of songs from various sources

**meld** [meld] 혼합시키다, 결합시키다
v. to blend or merge

**mercurial** [məːrkjúəriəl] 경박한, 변덕스러운
adj. being volatile and erratic

**merit** [mérit] 장점, 공로
n. a quality that is praiseworthy; achievement or excellence

**mill** [mil] 제조공장, 제분소
n. a factory where a product is made or where grain is crushed and flour is produced

**misgiving** [misgívoŋ] 의심
n. a feeling that something is not right and the result will be bad

**misrepresent** [mìsreprizént] 부정한 의도로 잘못된 설명이나 정보를 전하다
v. to intentionally give misleading representations or information

**mite** [mait] 진드기, 매우 작은 양
n. a small parasitic insect that lives on plants and animals; a small amount

**montage** [mɑntɑ́ːʒ] 몽타주, 합성화
n. a composite picture

**mortar** [mɔ́ːrtər] 회 반죽
n. a mixture used to hold bricks together

**mortification** [mɔ̀ːrtəfikéiʃən] 굴욕
n. a strong emotion of embarrassment or humiliation

**mosaic** [mouzéiik] 모자이크
n. a work of art that consists of small pieces of glass, stone embedded in plaster

**motley** [mátli] 여러 가지 잡다한 색깔을 가진, 각양각색의
adj. having many colors or variety

**mourn** [mɔːrn] 슬퍼하다, 비탄하다
v. to be sad or grieve over

**mull** [mʌl] 문제에 대해 곰곰이 생각하다, 심사숙고하다
v. to ponder over a problem or question

**mumble** [mʌ́mbl] 중얼거리다
v. to speak in an unclear and quiet manner which makes it hard to comprehend

**mutate** [mjuːtéit] 돌연변이하다, 변화하다
v. to change as a result of a genetic flaw; to change or alter; to transform

# N

**nadir** [néidər] 밑바닥, 최하점, 천저
n. the lowest point in one's career or life

**naif (naive)** [nɑːíːf] [nɑːíːv] 순진한
adj. artless and unsophisticated; gullible

**narcissism** [nɑ́ːrsəsìzm] 자기도취, 자만
n. excessive love of or admiration of oneself; conceit

**naysay** [néisèi] 반대하다, 부인하다
v. to oppose or deny

**negligible** [néglidʒəbl] 무시해도 좋은, 대수롭지 않은
adj. being unimportant thus ignored

**negotiation** [nigòuʃiéiʃən] 협상
n. process of bargaining and conferring in order to reach a mutual agreement

**neologism** [niːάlədʒìzm] 신조어
n. the coining of new words or phrases

**noisome** [nɔ́isəm] 해로운, 불쾌한
adj. disgusting and loathsome

**nonconformist** [nὰnkənfɔ́ːrmist] 불순응주의자
n. someone who refuses to be obligated by common beliefs

**nonflammable** [nὰnflǽməbl] 불연성의
adj. incombustible, impossible to set on fire

**nonsensical** [nɑnsénsikəl] 터무니 없는, 부조리한
adj. lacking good sense; absurd

**novelty** [nάvəlti] 참신함, 신비로움
n. newness, quality of being fresh or new

**nurture** [nə́ːrtʃər] 양육하다, 먹이다
v. to nourish and feed

**obituary** [oubítʃuèri] 사망자의 명단
n. a notice of a deceased person which often includes a short biography

**oblique** [əblíːk] 모호한, 종잡을 수 없는, 기울어진
adj. obscure and evasive; not straightforward

**obsolete** [ὰbsəlíːt] 오래되어 더 이상 쓰지 않는
adj. old and no longer in use

**occlude** [əklúːd] 막다, 메우다
v. to close up or block the way

**onerous** [άnərəs] 성가신
adj. burdensome; troublesome or oppressive

**oppress** [əprés] 압박하다, 중압감을 주다
v. to handle people in an unfair manner often in a cruel way

**ore** [ɔːr] 광석, 금속
n. metal found in the earth

**organism** [ɔ́ːrgənìzm] 유기체
n. a particular form of life which has a body containing organs or other parts that work in agreement to one another to sustain life

**ornate** [ɔːrnéit] 화려하게 잘 꾸민
adj. having decorative patterns and shapes

**oscillation** [ὰsəléiʃən] 진동
n. the act of moving from one place to another

**overlook** [òuvərlúk] 간과하다
v. to miss or ignore

**overt** [óuvəːrt] 명백한, 공공연한
adj. obviously apparent; publicly observable

# P

**paean** [píːən] 찬가
n. a song of praise

**pall** [pɔːl] 지루하게 하다, 생기가 없게 하다
v. to make dull or lifeless

**panegyric** [pæ̀nədʒírik] 다듬어진 칭찬의 말, 찬사
n. an expression of elaborate praise

**panorama** [pæ̀nərǽmə] 전경, 파노라마
n. a widespread view of an area

**pariah** [pəráiə] 사회에서 버림받은 사람, 멸시되는 사람
n. one that is rejected or despised by society; a social outcast

**parochial** [pəróukiəl] 견해나 태도가 한정된, 편협한
adj. restricted or narrow in outlook or attitude

**parody** [pǽrədi] 풍자적 모방
n. a humorous imitation of a populpar work of art or person

**pathological** [pæ̀θəládʒikəl] 비정상적인, 정신적 혼란이나 행동에 문제가 있음을 입증하는
adj. abnormal; relating to mental disorders or behavioral problems

**pauper** [pɔ́ːpər] 극빈자
n. a very poor person

**pebble** [pébl] 조약돌
n. a tiny smooth stone

**peep** [piːp] 재빠르게 보다; 높고 날카로운 소리
v. to look quickly or secretly
n. a short, weak, and shrill sound

**peevish** [píːviʃ] 쉽게 화를 내는, 불평이 많은
adj. easy to annoy or vex; querulous

**pejorative** [pidʒɔ́ːrətiv] 가치를 떨어뜨리는, 경멸적인
adj. demeaning or belittling

**penalty** [pénəlti] 형벌
n. a punishment for breaking a rule or law

**personable** [pə́ːrsənəbl] 성격이나 용모가 매력적인
adj. engaging in personality or pleasing in appearance; attractive

**personnel** [pə̀ːrsənél] 인원, 직원
n. employees of a group, business, or organization

**pestle** [péstl] 공이, 절굿공이
n. a device used to pound or grind substances into powder

**piddling** [pídliŋ] 사소한, 하찮은, 얼마 되지 않는
adj. trivial and frivolous; paltry and trifling

**piety** [páiəti] 숭배, 신심
n. reverence and devotion to God

**pillar** [pílər] 기둥, 기둥모양의 것
n. a solid vertical structure used to support buildings

**plain** [plein] 평범한, 똑똑히 보이는
adj. common and not elaborate; being very clear and distinct

**plantation** [plæntéiʃən] 농원, 재배지
n. a large piece of farm land used to cultivate several different groups of trees and crops

**plastic** [plǽstik] 인공의, 부자연스러운, 가소성이 있는
adj. artificial or unnatural; flexible or adaptable

**plateau** [plætóu] 고원, 정체상태
n. a vast area of flat land that is higher than the surrounding area; a period of stability or little change

**plight** [plait] 나쁜 상태, 절망적인 상황
n. a bad or desperate situation; predicament

**posit** [pázit] 설치하다, 가정하다
v. to place in position; to assume the actuality of

**possess** [pəzés] 소유하다, 지니다
v. to have as an asset; to own

**pragmatic** [prægmǽtik] 실용적인
adj. practical, concerned with facts rather than abstract ideas

**predisposition** [prìːdispəzíʃən] 경향, 성질
n. a tendency or previous inclination

**preempt** [priémpt] 선취하다
v. to take ahead of others

**preface** [préfis] 서문, 머릿글
n. an introduction to a book which gives information on the work or author

**preference** [préfərəns] 어떤 것을 다른 것에 비해 더 좋아함
n. a predilection for something over another

**prefiguration** [priːfìgjəréiʃən] 예시하는 것, 전조
n. something that foreshadows

**preside** [prizáid] 권위 있는 자리에서 통할하다, 주재하다
v. to exercise control in a position of authority

**prissy** [prísi] 까다로운
adj. excessively proper and prim

**prologue** [próulɔːg] 프롤로그, 전조, 발단
n. an introduction or preface

**pronounce** [prənáuns] 발음하다, 선언하다
v. to use particular sounds to say a word; to formally state an official opinion

**proofread** [prúːfriːd] 교정하기 위해 읽어 보다, 교정하다
v. to check for and correct errors

**prophecy** [práfəsi] 예언
n. a foretelling or prediction

**prosecute** [prásəkjùːt] 기소하다
v. to begin or initiate legal action against

**protagonist** [proutǽgənist] 연극이나 이야기의 주인공
n. the leading figure in a drama or story

**protocol** [próutəkàl] 정확한 행동을 위한 일련의 규칙들, 예의
n. a set of rules for correct behavior

**providential** [prɑ̀vədénʃəl] 신의에 의해 행운이 일어난
adj. occurring as if by divine intervention

**puissance** [pjúːəsns] 힘, 세력, 권력
n. strength, might, or power

**punch** [pʌntʃ] 구멍뚫는 도구, 펀치, 주먹질
v. a tool for making a hole; a type of impact caused by the use of one's fist

**puzzle** [pʌzl] 난처하게 하다; 어려운 문제, 수수께끼
v. to confuse or mystify; to perplex
n. a problem or mystery that is difficult to solve

## Q

**quack** [kwæk] 의사인 척 행세하는 사람, 돌팔이 의사
n. an untrained person who pretends to be a doctor

**quaff** [kwɑːf] 벌컥벌컥 마시다
v. to drink with great relish

**quail** [kwéil] 겁내다, 움찔하다
v. to shrink back in fear or dread; to cower

**qualm** [kwɑːm] 불안, 메스꺼움
n. a sudden feeling of doubt or guilt; nausea

**quantify** [kwɑ́ntəfài] 양을 정하다, 나타내다
v. to determine or express the amount or number of

**quarantine** [kwɔ́ːrəntìːn] 격리시키다
v. to isolate for a period of time in order to prevent the spread of contagious disease

**quest** [kwest] 탐색, 탐구; 탐구하다, 추구하다
n. a search; an attempt to find something
v. to go in search of; to seek or pursue after

**queue** [kjuː] 변발, 줄
n. a single braid of hair; a line as of people waiting for something

# R

**raconteur** [ræ̀kɑntə́ːr] 좌담가
n. someone who can skillfully tell a story

**raffle** [ræfl] 추첨식 복권
n. a kind of lottery in which people buy chances to win a prize

**rambunctious** [ræmbʌ́ŋkʃəs] 떠들썩한, 흥청거리는
adj. noisy and lively; boisterous

**rankle** [rǽŋkl] 괴롭히다, 화나게 하다
v. to irritate or make resentful

**ration** [rǽʃən] (특히 군인을 위한) 고정된 식량 배급량
n. a fixed allotment of food especially for soldiers

**ream** [riːm] 다량, 종이 500장
n. a large amount of something; 500 pieces of paper

**rebuke** [ribjúːk] 비난하다, 질책하다
v. to speak harshly against something

**recite** [risáit] 낭송하다
v. to repeat text of a writing

**recognition** [rèkəgníʃən] 표창, 인식
n. the praise or identification of something

**recur** [rikə́ːr] 재발하다
v. to happen again

**reel** [riːl] 감는 틀
n. a device used to spin wire or film around a frame

**refugee** [rèfjudʒíː] 피난민, 망명자
v. one who flees to a foreign country in search of refuge as a result of war, persecution, or oppression

**regard** [rigɑ́ːrd] ~라고 여기다, 간주하다
v. to consider something in a particular way

**regret** [rigrét] 애도하다, 동정하다
v. to feel remorse or sorrow

**rehearsal** [rihə́ːrsəl] 시연, 총연습
n. a practice for a performance

**reiterate** [riːítərèit] 반복하여 말하다
v. to say again for emphasis

**relate** [riléit] 이야기하다, 말하다, 관련시키다
v. to tell; to show a relationship between two things

**relegate** [réləgèit] 좌천시킨다
v. to lower one's position

**reluctance** [rilʎktəns] 꺼려하는 행동이나 상태
n. the act or state of being unwilling

**repeal** [ripíːl] 폐지, 폐기
n. the act of revoking an official act

**repulse** [ripʎls] 격퇴하다, 퇴짜 놓다
v. to repel or drive back

**restrict** [ristríkt] 제한하다
v. to have a limit for something

**resuscitate** [risʎsətèit] 소생시키다
v. to revive from unconsciousness

**retract** [ritrǽkt] 취소하다, 철회하다
v. to withdraw or take back something said or done

**reveal** [rivíːl] 드러내다
v. to make aware or to show

**rigid** [rídʒid] 경직된, 엄격한
adj. not easy to change; strict

**rooted** [rúːtid] 뿌리박은, 정착한
adj. firmly fixed or established

# S

**sabbatical** [səbǽtikəl] 안식일 관련 휴가, 휴식
n. a leave or break from work relating to the Sabbath

**salutation** [sæ̀ljətéiʃən] 인사말
n. a greeting

**salvage** [sǽlvidʒ] 구조하다; 해난 구조
v. to save property from destruction
n. saving things from a disaster at sea

**sap** [sæp] 배수 설비하다, 약화시키다
v. to drain or weaken

**scholarly** [skálərli] 박식한, 학문적인
adj. having an intellectual manner

**scrappy** [skrǽpi] 싸우기 좋아하는, 공격적인
adj. willing to fight or argue; aggressive

**selective** [siléktiv] 선택적인
adj. characterized by careful choice; discriminating

**self-effacing** [sélfiféisiŋ] 겸손한, 주의를 끌기 싫어하는
adj. humble and modest; reluctant to draw attention to oneself

**shaft** [ʃæft] 길고 좁은 수직의 통로
n. a long narrow vertical passage

**shrill** [ʃril] 높고 날카로운 소리의
adj. having a high and unpleasant sound

**slide** [slaid] 미끄러지다, 활주하다
v. to move smoothly and quickly across a surface

**slope** [sloup] 경사, 비탈
n. an incline or slant

**solution** [səlúːʃən] 해답, 용액
n. an answer or conclusion to a problem; a liquid with another substance dissolved in it

**sonata** [sənáːtə] 소나타
n. a musical piece that consists of one musical instrument and a piano

**sonnet** [sánit] 소네트(14행시)
n. a rhyming poem that is made up of 14 lines with each line containing 14 syllables

**spectrum** [spéktrəm] 스펙트럼, 분광
n. a range of colors resulting from a light that is separated when passing through a prism

**stagnant** [stǽgnənt] 흐르지 않는, 움직임이 없는
adj. not flowing; motionless

**stamina** [stǽmənə] 육체적 혹은 도덕적 지구력이나 체력
n. physical or moral endurance and strength

**standardize** [stǽndərdàiz] 표준화 시키다.
v. to make features common, systematic, or standard

**stanza** [stǽnzə] (시의) 절, 연
n. a division of a poem

**stark** [staːrk] 완전한, 황량한
adj. absolute or complete; desolate

**stint** [stint] 절약하다; 제한, 할당된 시간
v. to be frugal or use sparingly
n. a period of time spent doing something

**stock** [stɑk] 재고품, 저장
n. surplus that is stored up for later use

**stockade** [stɑkéid] 방책, (미군의) 영창
n. a barrier made of wooden posts for defensive purposes; a military prison

**storyteller** [stɔ́ːritèlər] 만담가, 소설가
n. a person who tells or writes about an event usually to entertain

**strand** [strænd] 좌초시키다
v. to leave in a difficult or helpless position or an unfavorable place

**strict** [strikt] 엄격한
adj. rigid or exact; expecting discipline and severity

**stylus** [stáiləs] 철필, (레코드의) 바늘
n. the needle used to read a record on a record player

**subject** [sʌ́bdʒikt] 주제, 지배를 받는 백성
n. the topic of conversation, writing, etc. ; a person under control

**subpoena** [səbpíːnə] 소환장
n. a letter or document that requires a person to attend court

**subservience** [səbsə́ːrviəns] 복종
n. willingness to serve another's purposes

**subtle** [sʌtl] 구별하거나 이해하기 어려울 정도로 미묘한
adj. elusive or obscure; hard to pinpoint

**superfluous** [suːpə́ːrfluəs] 필요 이상의, 쓸데없는
adj. more than what is needed; extraneous

**supersede** [sùːpərsíːd] 대신하다
v. to take the place of or take over

**susceptibility** [səsèptəbíləti] 민감, 감수성
n. feelings or emotions that are easily affected

**suspend** [səspénd] 연기하다, 보류하다, 중지하다
v. to postpone or discontinue

**symphony** [símfəni] 교향곡, 조화
n. four separate movements or musical pieces played by an orchestra; harmony

# T

**tamper** [tǽmpər] 어리석게 혹은 서투르게 다루다
v. to foolishly play or tinker with

**tantalize** [tǽntəlàiz] 애타게 하다
v. to tease or torment by presenting something desirable but making it unattainable

**tapestry** [tǽpistri] 태피스트리, 벽걸이 융단
n. a thick piece of cloth that usually contains a picture woven or sewn in it and is often hung on walls

**taxing** [tǽksiŋ] 부담스러운, 성가신
adj. being very demanding or stressful

**tear** [tɛər] 잡아 뜯어 분리시키다
v. to pull apart or divide

**temper** [témpər] 기질, 화
n. a habitual state of mind or manner of feeling; a mood of anger

**temporize** [témpəràiz] 시간을 벌기 위해 미봉책을 쓰다.
v. to do something less important so as to give extra time to make a decision

**terror** [térər] 공포
n. a strong feeling of fear

**therapeutic** [θèrəpjúːtik] 치료학의
adj. relating to the treatment of disease

**tinge** [tindʒ] 색이나 맛을 띠게 하다
v. to infuse something with color, taste, or shade

**torpor** [tɔ́ːrpər] 기력과 에너지의 부족으로 인한 비활성, 무기력
n. inactivity due to lack of vigor and energy

**tout** [taut] 강매하다
v. to solicit in an aggressive manner

**transcend** [trænsénd] 초월하다
v. to rise above

**travesty** [trǽvəsti] 심하게 희화한 과장된 표현
n. a representation that is grossly exaggerated to the point of ridicule

**tribute** [tríbjuːt] 존경이나 찬사를 표함
n. declaration of esteem, respect, and admiration

**turbulent** [tə́ːrbjulənt] 사나운, 휘몰아치는
adj. having a lot of change, disorder, or violence; stormy

**turpitude** [tə́ːrpitjùːd] 비열함, 비도덕성, 사악
n. wickedness, vileness, or depravity

**typical** [típikəl] 전형적인, 상징적인
adj. normal and usual; symbolic

# U

**unconventional** [ʌ̀nkənvénʃənl] 관습에 얽매이지 않는, 자유로운
adj. not conforming to conventional standards or accepted rules

**understate** [ʌ̀ndərstéit] 줄잡아 말하다, (수효를) 적게 말하다
v. to indicate that something is less influential than it really is

**undeserved** [ʌ̀ndizə́ːrvd] 부당한, ~할 가치가 없는
adj. unfair or unjustifiable; unmerited

**unexceptionable** [ʌ̀niksépʃənəbl] 더 이상 나무랄데 없는
adj. beyond any reasonable objection

**unfettered** [ʌnfétərd] 통제되지 않은, 제한되지 않은
adj. being independent from rules or authority; unrestricted

**unimpeachable** [ʌnimpíːtʃəbl] 과실이 없는, 비난의 여지가 없는
adj. beyond doubt or reproach

**uninspired** [ʌninspáiərd] 독창성이 없는
adj. deficient in creativity

**unlikely** [ʌnláikli] 가망없는, 있을 법 하지도 않은
adj. not likely to be or happen

**unreflective** [ʌnrifléktiv] 무분별한
adj. irrational or unthinking

**unsophisticated** [ʌnsəfístəkèitid] 순박한, 정교하지 않은
adj. having very little experience and refinement

**unsubstantial** [ʌnsəbstǽnʃəl] 비현실적인, 내용이 빈약한
adj. scanty in amount or degree; without foundation

**unwieldy** [ʌnwíːldi] 다루기 힘든, 보기 흉한
adj. difficult to move or handle because of size, shape, or design; awkward

**unwitting** [ʌnwítiŋ] 우연의, 고의가 아닌, 알지 못하는
adj. not intended; not knowing

**utilize** [júːtəlàiz] 이용하다
v. to apply something to use

# V

**valediction** [vælədíkʃən] 작별 인사
n. a speech or phrase bidding farewell

**varnish** [váːrniʃ] 광택제
n. a translucent glossy coating that protects surfaces from air and moisture

**vendee** [vendíː] 매수인, 물건을 사는 사람
n. one who buys or purchases

**venerate** [vénərèit] 존경하다
v. to honor or respect with great reverence

**venom** [vénəm] 독
n. a poison that is found in animals such as snakes, bees, and scorpions

**ventilate** [véntəlèit] 환기하다
v. to enable new air to circulate

**verdict** [vɚ́ːrdikt] 평결, 판정
n. the outcome of a trial

**verse** [vəːrs] 시
n. a poem, stanza, or line

**vicissitude** [vɪsísətjùːd] 변화, 변천
n. a change, mutation, or alternation

**victimize** [víktimàiz] 피해자로 만들다, 사기치다
v. to make a victim of; to treat someone in a deliberately unfair way

**vitiate** [víʃièit] 손상시키다
v. to impair; to debase in moral status

**vitriolic** [vìtriálik] 신랄하고 거친 어조의
adj. bitter and harsh in tone

# W

**waffle** [wáfl] 모호한 말로 얼버무리다
v. to speak or write vaguely and evasively

**warmonger** [wɔ́ːrmʌ̀ŋgər] 주전론자
n. one who advocates war

**warrant** [wɔ́(ː)rənt] 정당화하다, 보증하다
v. to justify or show sufficient grounds for

**watchful** [wátʃfəl] 주의 깊은, 경계하는
adj. carefully observant or attentive

**watt** [wɑt] 전기단위 와트
n. calibration for electrical power

**wax** [wæks] 밀납, 왁스, 격노; 커지다
n. a substance that is used to make candles with; a protective layer of coating for certain surfaces; rage
v. to increase in size, number, or strength

**welter** [wéltər] 뒤죽박죽 상태
n. a confusing, jumbled mass; a muddle

**whet** [hwet] (칼 등을 갈아서) 날카롭게 하다
v. to make sharp

**whiff** [hwif] 한번 부는 바람
n. a brief gentle gust of air

**winnow** [wínou] 골라내다, 가려내다
v. to examine and then separate useful things from those that are not

**withdraw** [wiðdrɔ́ː] 빼내다, 철수시키다
v. to take out or extract

**woo** [wuː] 구애하다
v. to court or seek favor

**wordsmith** [wə́ːrdsmìθ] 문장가
n. a skilled or professional writer

**wordy** [wə́ːrdi] 말이 장황한
adj. using too many words; verbose

**worldly** [wə́ːrldli] 세상의, 속세적인
adj. being experienced in social activities, relating to the practical rather than the spiritual aspects of life

## Y

**yoke** [jouk] 결합시키다; 굴레, 속박
v. to join securely together
n. bondage

## Z

**zealot** [zélət] 열정가
n. one who is excessively enthusiastic; a fanatic

# SuperVoca
## Words Roots & Prefixes

# Words Roots and Prefixes  A

## a, an — not, without

abandon 184
abase 202
abash 202
abate 202, 263
abeyance 478
abrade 430
abrasion 450
abridge 368
abuse 403
achromatic 127, 217
acquiesce 430
albinism 170, 268

albino 170
alibi 217
align 248, 277
allay 292
alleviate 292, 404
aloof 45, 369
amorphous 369
anachronism 15
anaerobe 479
analgesia 185
anarchist 192, 479
anemic 479

anesthetic 139, 330
anodyne 444
anomalous 369
anomaly 439
anonymous 400
apathetic 170, 203, 260
aseptic 171
aside 158, 219
avoid 142

## ab — away from

abbreviate 216
abdicate 122, 233
aberrant 138
abet 138, 266
abhor 216
abide 216
abject 276

abjure 276, 448
abnegate 478
abode 330
aboveboard 44, 220
abrogate 112, 260, 478
abscond 14
absolve 478

absorb 44
absorbing 149
abstain 262
abstemious 60, 128, 142
abstract 60, 280
abstruse 108, 216

## ac, acr, acu — sharp, bitter

acerbic 138
acme 322

acrid 368
acrimonious 352

acute 262

## ad — to, toward

adamant 184
addict 122
addicted 122
address 478
adept 444
adhere 217
adjust 86, 276

admirable 322
admire 120
admonish 338, 343
adoration 297
adroitness 142
adulate 14, 175, 304
adulterate 14

adumbration 478
adventurous 39
adversary 478
advertent 44
advocate 74, 417

| aesthet | feeling |
|---|---|
| aesthete 60 | |

| ag, act | to do |
|---|---|
| aggrandize 262　　aggravate 262, 292　　aggrieve 263, 323
agitate 223, 276 | |

| agog | to lead |
|---|---|
| demagogue 434　　pedagogue 115 | |

| agon | to struggle |
|---|---|
| agonize 368　　antagonize 74　　protagonist 498 | |

| ali, alter | other |
|---|---|
| alibi 217　　alienable 184　　inalienable 184 | |

| alt | high |
|---|---|
| exalt 188 | |

| ambi | both, around |
|---|---|
| ambiguity 430　　ambiguous 341, 430　　unambiguous 224
ambivalent 170 | |

| ang, anx | to strangle, to hang |
|---|---|
| anger 189, 269　　disentangle 188, 213　　estrangement 269, 449
anxiety 340　　estrange 449 | |

| anim | breath, mind, life |
|---|---|
| animate 248　　inanimate 491　　unanimity 242, 456
animation 248 | |

| ante | before, in front of |
|---|---|
| anterior 292 | |

| anti | against, opposite |
|---|---|
| antibiotic 406 <br> antidote 185 | antipathy 90, 154, 362 <br> antithetical 324 | antipathy 90, 362 |

| apt, ept | fit |
|---|---|
| adept 444 | inept 142 |

| asper | to spray |
|---|---|
| asperity 414 | |

| astro, aster | star, outer space |
|---|---|
| astronomer 108 | astronomy 108 |

| aux, aug | to increase, to raise |
|---|---|
| augment 263 <br> augmentation 326 | augur 132, 219 <br> inaugurate 178 | inauguration 178 |

## Words Roots and Prefixes  B

| bar | pressure, first |
|---|---|
| barbaric 423 <br> barbarize 76, 432 | embarrass 174 <br> embarrassment 174, 203 |

| bas | bottom |
|---|---|
| abase 202 <br> base 25, 226 | baseboard 480 <br> baseness 480 | debase 173 <br> debasement 460 |

## bat — to beat

abate 202, 263 | debate 173 | exacerbate 175, 262

## be — thoroughly, to make

bedeck 480
befuddle 480
behavior 292
belabor 277
beleaguer 293, 312
belie 293

belief 225
belligerent 307
beloved 307
bequest 91
berate 34, 352
beseeching 442

besmirch 45
betray 480
browbeat 15, 308
misbehave 21, 440
obedient 131, 355

## belli, bell — beauty, war

belligerent 307

## bene — good, well

beneficial 322 | benevolence 458 | benevolent 298

## bi — two

abide 216
arbitrator 160
biased 480
dubious 174

exorbitant 449
flexibility 184, 299
indubitable 128
obituary 495

probity 40, 361, 456
rubicund 192, 334

## bio — life, living organisms

antibiotic 406 | symbiosis 332 | symbiotic 332

## bol, bl — to throw

blizzard 480
blurt 45, 102
bluster 46
bolster 308

crumble 16, 235
dabble 173
dabbler 173
embolden 202, 221, 384

hyperbole 419
parable 390
pebble 496
scribble 467

## Words Roots and Prefixes C

| caco | bad, wrong |
|---|---|
| cacophonous 357, 417 | cacophony 249 |

| capit | head |
|---|---|
| capitulation 415 | capitulate 54, 415 |

| car | wheel; to roll |
|---|---|
| cargo 347, 459<br>carouse 29 | carry 464 | cart 308 |

| carn | flesh |
|---|---|
| carnal 287 | |

| cata | down |
|---|---|
| catastrophe 36 | |

| cede, ceed, cess | to go, to yield |
|---|---|
| concede 205, 423<br>precede 145<br>precedent 145, 288<br>proceed 464 | accessible 108, 216<br>cessation 46<br>excessive 487<br>intercessor 95, 129 | unnecessary 69 |

| ceive, cept | to take |
|---|---|
| deceive 140, 434<br>deception 221<br>exceptional 487 | inception 412<br>perceive 80, 361 | susceptibility 502<br>unexceptionable 503 |

| cel | sky |
|---|---|
| celebrity 401 | |

| cens | to assess; tax |
|---|---|
| censor 436 | censure 440 |

## chrom — color

achromatic 127, 217     chromatic 481     monochromatic 463

## chron — time

anachronism 15     chronological 482     chronology 15
chronic 379

## cide, cis — to kill, to cut

accident 165     imprecise 490     precise 432
accidental 81     incision 85     precision 224
cistern 62     narcissism 494     vicissitude 345, 505
concise 132, 279, 380     precis 132

## circum — around

circumference 264     circumlocutory 441     circumspect 241, 353
circumlocution 20, 353     circumscribe 304, 353     circumvent 354

## clud, clus, claus — to close

recluse 126, 241

## co, con, col, cor — with, together

accolade 67, 232     coda 144, 249     collapse 308, 309
accommodate 478     coerce 446     collude 308, 372
beacon 172     coeval 482     colonnade 386
coagulant 259, 354     cogent 264, 356     combust 371
coagulate 172     colander 174     combustible 371
coalesce 186

comfort 323
comfortable 139
comity 415
command 339, 448
commencement 46
commend 339
commitment 170, 482
commodious 187, 339, 372
commonplace 339
commonsensical 145, 339
commotion 118, 340
comparable 340
compatible 116, 446
compendious 340
complacence 340
complain 109, 340
complaisance 446
complexity 341, 356
compliment 208, 341
comply 407, 482
compose 341
comprehend 36, 341
compress 342, 420
compression 342
compromise 342, 420
compunction 342
compunctious 354
concatenate 482
concavity 392
conceal 279, 416
concede 205, 423
concentrate 187, 279, 326
conciliate 114, 119, 279
conciliatory 279, 307, 396
concise 132, 279, 380
conclude 482
concord 157, 279, 343
concrete 482
concur 51, 280
condemn 280
condense 60, 280, 378
condescend 280
condign 482
condolence 482
condone 281
confession 323
confine 482
confirm 293, 323, 450
confirmation 323
conform 324
conformation 369
conformity 324
confront 354
confuse 324
confusion 234, 324
congeal 324
congenial 324
congruent 324
conjecture 133, 342
connect 482
connive 92
conniver 92, 433
connoisseur 482
consent 205
consequence 285
conservative 254
conserve 25
consolidate 433
conspicuous 299, 463
conspiratorial 92, 433
conspire 433
constancy 83, 194, 287
constant 482
constellation 233
constitute 233
constrain 301, 482
constrict 339, 372
consummate 265
contagion 372
contain 483
contemptible 94
contentment 17
continence 483
continuance 483
contract 295, 402
contraction 386
contradictory 98, 354
contrast 220, 483
contravene 402
contrite 354, 369
control 114
contumacious 131, 355
convalesce 242, 325
convenience 421, 355
converge 483
conversant 483
conversion 483
convert 355
convey 40, 483
convict 355
conviction 174
convince 264, 356
convivial 109, 242
convoluted 341, 356
convulsion 386, 402
cooperate 309, 372
copious 317, 415
cornucopia 483
coronation 270, 402
corporeal 227, 447
correspond 447
corrode 358, 483
corruptionist 257
coterie 483
decorum 164
discomfit 18, 462
discommode 18, 44, 312
discompose 18, 238
discontent 18
encomiast 310
encomium 436
excoriate 94, 251
inconsequential 16
inconsonant 279
inconspicuous 303, 376
incorrigible 123, 254
incorruptible 220
nonconformist 495
protocol 498
raconteur 499
rancor 204, 316
reconcile 452
reconciliation 452
recondite 241
reconnoiter 241
succor 228
unconformity 462
unconscious 468
unconventional 503

## contra, counter — against, opposite

**contra**dictory 98, 354
**contra**st 220, 483
**contra**vene 402
**counter** 483
**counter**feit 402
**counter**mand 403

## cor(d) — heart

ac**cord** 478
con**cord** 157, 279, 343
**core** 466
dis**cord** 206
in**corri**gible 123, 254
ran**cor** 204, 316

## corp(or) — body

**corpor**eal 31, 227, 447

## cosm — world

**cosm**opolitan 46, 393, 437

## cre, cret — to bear, to grow

ac**crete** 248
**cre**scendo 484
ex**crete** 487

## cred — to believe

**cred**ence 124
**cred**ulous 148, 403
dis**cred**it 29

## crit, cris — to discern

**crit**ical 442
**crit**icize 114

## cruc — cross

**cruc**ial 16

## cult — to take care

**cult**ivate 325
**cult**ivated 257

| cur, course | to run | |
|---|---|---|
| concur 51, 280<br>curate 484<br>curb 373<br>curmudgeon 415<br>cursory 205 | curt 16<br>curtail 17, 357, 392<br>discursive 30<br>excursive 63<br>mercurial 493 | precursor 409<br>precursory 409, 460<br>recur 499<br>course 150, 309, 483 |

| cycl | circle, wheel |
|---|---|
| encyclopedia 340 | |

## Words Roots and Prefixes

| de | from, down, away | |
|---|---|---|
| debacle 387<br>debase 173<br>debilitate 174<br>debunk 433, 470<br>decant 434<br>decanter 434<br>deceitful 196<br>deceive 140, 434<br>decelerate 434<br>deception 221<br>deceptive 221<br>decode 325<br>decorate 61<br>decorous 249, 347<br>decorum 164<br>decrepit 250, 454<br>defend 87, 156<br>defer 156<br>deferential 36<br>deferrable 156<br>defile 156<br>definitive 157<br>deflated 469<br>deflect 484<br>defuse 157, 326<br>defy 459<br>dehydrate 221 | deject 281<br>dejection 208, 281<br>delay 296<br>deliberate 178, 204, 295<br>deliberation 432<br>delirium 234<br>delusion 56, 325<br>demand 484<br>demean 404<br>demolish 434<br>demolition 109, 434<br>demur 416<br>demystify 484<br>denial 484<br>denounce 281, 338, 343<br>denunciation 484<br>deny 17<br>depart 14<br>dependence 484<br>deplete 416<br>deplore 329, 416, 452<br>deploy 187, 279<br>deportation 485<br>depose 187, 466<br>deprave 175<br>deprecate 435<br>depreciate 435 | deprivation 435, 469<br>deracinate 435<br>deride 459<br>derision 133, 177<br>derivative 460<br>descend 38<br>descendant 485<br>descent 485<br>desecrate 29<br>desire 177<br>destruction 109, 434<br>detach 77<br>detainment 485<br>detection 403<br>deter 92<br>determination 92<br>deterrent 140<br>detour 93, 394<br>detract 447<br>devalue 447<br>devastate 140<br>devote 160, 485<br>interdependent 332<br>self-denial 219<br>self-deprecating 435 |

| demo | people |
|---|---|

demotic 484

| dia | through, across, between |
|---|---|

diaphanous 205, 210
encyclopedia 340
incendiary 223, 276
mediate 95, 129
mediation 342
quotidian 393

| dict | to speak |
|---|---|

contradictory 98, 354
diction 485
dictionary 329
indict 80
interdict 91, 95, 410
predict 132, 273
prediction 132, 219
valediction 126, 504
verdict 504

| dign | worth |
|---|---|

condign 482
dignify 404

| dis, dys, dif | away, not, negative |
|---|---|

diffidence 157
disabuse 387
disaffected 17
disaggregate 186
disagreeable 485
disarm 485
disavow 17, 205
discern 18
discerner 262
discerning 18, 34
discharge 206
disclosure 206
discomfit 18, 462
discommode 18, 44, 312
discompose 18, 238
discontent 18
discord 206
discredit 29
discrepancy 485
discrete 30
discretion 437
discretionary 300
discriminate 30, 407
discriminating 460
discursive 30
disdain 30
disembodied 31
disembody 31
disengage 485
disentangle 188, 213
disgorge 309
disgruntle 31
disguise 31
disgust 31, 267
disinclination 139
disinfection 171
disingenuous 32
disintegrate 48, 184
disinter 404
disinterest 48
disjoint 485
dislike 209, 216
dismantle 48
dismiss 485
disordered 445
disparage 48
disparate 48, 340
dispassionate 22, 49
disperse 447
dispirit 447
dispose 161
disprove 49, 318
dispute 49, 118, 254
disquiet 485
disregard 49
disrespect 50, 327
disrupt 50, 226
dissect 485
dissemble 50
disseminate 50
dissent 51, 205, 280
dissimulate 92
dissipate 158
dissociate 154
dissolute 62, 190
dissolve 62, 433
dissonance 157
dissuade 54, 63
distillate 158

| | | |
|---|---|---|
| **dis**tinction 190<br>**dis**tort 63<br>**dis**tortion 63, 459<br>**dis**tract 63, 440<br>**dis**traught 341, 373 | **dis**tress 224, 404<br>**dis**tressed 368<br>**dis**turb 109<br>**dys**peptic 51<br>in**dif**ferent 127 | in**dis**tinct 491<br>pre**dis**position 497<br>un**dis**turbed 80 |

### duc, duct — to lead, to pull

| | | |
|---|---|---|
| aque**duct** 185<br>in**duc**ement 140, 421 | in**duct** 206<br>intro**duct**ory 392 | irre**duc**ible 491 |

### dol — sadness, pain

| | | |
|---|---|---|
| con**dol**ence 482 | **dol**eful 486 | **dol**orous 486 |

### don, dos, dot — to give

| | | |
|---|---|---|
| aban**don** 184 | con**done** 281 | **don**or 486 |

### doc, doct — to teach

| | |
|---|---|
| **doct**rine 486 | in**doct**rinate 115 |

### dur — to last

| | | |
|---|---|---|
| **dur**ation 357 | en**dure** 125, 436 | ob**dur**ate 131 |

## Words Roots and Prefixes

### e, ex, ecto — outside, external

| | | |
|---|---|---|
| **e**bullience 486<br>**e**bullient 455<br>**ec**centric 221<br>**ec**lipse 146, 296<br>**e**late 52, 344, 206<br>**e**lation 172, 206, 317<br>**e**licit 486<br>**e**litism 486 | **e**longate 373<br>**e**lucidate 19<br>**e**lude 436<br>**e**maciate 486<br>**e**mancipate 85, 188<br>**e**migrate 250, 394<br>**e**minence 250, 329<br>**e**minent 250 | **e**motion 141<br>**e**phemeral 436<br>**e**rect 125<br>**e**rode 358<br>**e**strange 449<br>**e**strangement 269, 449<br>**e**vacuate 487<br>**e**vade 286, 436, 460 |

evasive 314
evict 460
exacerbate 175, 262
exacting 100, 243
exaggerate 175, 419
exalt 188
examine 95
exceptional 487
excerpt 222
excessive 487
excitable 487
exclaim 487
excoriate 94, 251
excrete 487
exculpate 217, 252
excursive 63
excuse 103
execrable 487
execrate 125, 188
exemplary 19
exemplify 126, 232
exempt 64, 209
exhaust 161, 234
exhilarate 487
exhort 234
exhortation 97
exhortative 234, 273
exile 115
exonerate 255, 374, 450
exorbitant 449
exotic 128, 388
expansive 39
expedite 388, 417
expenditure 417
expense 117
experience 68, 178
explanation 296
explicate 487
exponent 74, 417
express 171, 228
expurgate 436
exquisite 487
extant 79
extenuate 405
extinct 79
extinguish 94, 406
extol 94, 251
extort 94, 446
extortionist 94
extract 110
extraneous 110, 444
extraordinary 110, 299
extravagant 111
extricate 449
extrinsic 111, 237, 328, 462
extrovert 207, 210
exude 487
exultant 32, 140, 276
inescapable 129
inevitable 142
overexpose 143
overexposure 143, 255
unexceptionable 503

## equi — equal

equipoise 20, 243
equity 487
equivalent 465
equivocate 32
equivocation 32, 54

## erg, urg — to work

energize 487
energy 346
urge 273

## err — to wander

aberrant 138
errant 309
erratic 338, 358
error 438

## esce — to begin

acquiesce 430
coalesce 186
convalesce 242, 325

## eu — well, good

eulogize 298, 310
eulogy 436
euphemism 163, 417
euphonious 417

| ev | time, age |
|---|---|
| coeval 482 | longevity 493 |

| exter, extra | outside of | |
|---|---|---|
| dexterous 77, 277<br>extract 110 | extraneous 110, 444<br>extraordinary 110, 299 | extravagant 111 |

## Words Roots and Prefixes

| fa, fess | to speak |
|---|---|
| affability 154 | confession 323 |

| fac, fic, fec, fect | to make, to do | |
|---|---|---|
| affect 34<br>artifact 171<br>disaffected 17<br>disinfection 171<br>effectiveness 253<br>facile 234, 414<br>facilitate 234, 344, 419<br>faction 252, 278 | factorable 487<br>factual 488<br>fecundity 252<br>fictional 488<br>gasification 489<br>infect 406<br>infection 406<br>munificent 348 | official 178<br>officious 163<br>ossification 37<br>ratification 98<br>satisfaction 100<br>significant 271, 331<br>soporific 272, 423<br>unaffected 117 |

| fan | to show |
|---|---|
| fantastic 389 | |

| fed, fid | to trust | |
|---|---|---|
| diffidence 157 | fidelity 405 | perfidious 83, 465 |

| fer | to carry | |
|---|---|---|
| circumference 264<br>defer 156<br>deferrable 156 | effervesce 159<br>infer 243, 491 | preference 497<br>proffer 85, 363 |

| fin | to end | |
|---|---|---|
| confine 482 | definitive 157 | infinite 161, 234 |

| flect, flex | to bend | |
|---|---|---|
| deflect 484<br>unreflective 331, 504 | flexibility 184, 299<br>flexible 37 | inflexible 491 |

| fort | strong | |
|---|---|---|
| effort 378 | fortify 20 | |

| fract, frag | to break | |
|---|---|---|
| fracture 91, 489 | refractory 22, 165 | fragile 176 |

| fug | to flee | |
|---|---|---|
| centrifuge 481 | subterfuge 227 | |

| fus | to pour | |
|---|---|---|
| confuse 324<br>confusion 234, 324<br>defuse 157 | effusive 265<br>infuse 54, 266<br>obfuscate 163, 238, 328 | profuse 192, 363<br>refuse 269, 298<br>suffuse 165 |

## Words Roots and Prefixes

| gen | race, birth, kind | |
|---|---|---|
| disingenuous 32<br>engender 266<br>general 19<br>generosity 203 | generous 190<br>genuine 71, 193, 359<br>homogeneous 127, 490<br>indigenous 128, 388 | indigent 37<br>ingenious 267<br>ingenuity 377, 491<br>oxygen 430 |

| ger, gest | to carry |
|---|---|
| exaggerate 175, 419  forgery 402 | ingest 491  swagger 182, 435 |

| gno | to know |
|---|---|
| ignore 48, 203 | |

| graph, gram | to write | | |
|---|---|---|---|
| cartographer 481  choreograph 371 | choreography 371  epigram 251 | lexicographer 329  petrography 115 | |

| greg | group, gather | |
|---|---|---|
| disaggregate 186 | gregarious 126, 369 | gregariousness 126, 241 |

| gress, grad | to step | |
|---|---|---|
| aggressive 478  digress 63, 265 | digressive 30  progress 69 | regressive 452  transgress 195 |

## Words Roots and Prefixes

| hap | to fall | |
|---|---|---|
| haphazard 72, 418 | hapless 490 | mishap 36 |

| hod, od | way |
|---|---|
| methodical 418 | |

| homo | same |
|---|---|
| homogeneous 127, 490 | |

| hum, hom | earth |
|---|---|

| humble 328 |
|---|

| hyper | over, above |
|---|---|

| hyperbole 175, 419 |
|---|

| hypo | beneath, under |
|---|---|

| hypothesis 450 |
|---|

## Words Roots and Prefixes

| ign | fire |
|---|---|

| ignite 132, 345 |
|---|

| il, in, im | into, not |
|---|---|

| illiterate 311 | impecunious 155, 378, 419 | improvidence 133, 392 |
|---|---|---|
| illuminate 328 | | improvisatorial 437 |
| illustrate 462 | impede 234, 376, 419 | imprudence 315 |
| imbibe 287 | impenetrable 251 | imprudent 437 |
| imitate 439 | imperative 161 | impugn 125, 437 |
| immaculate 118 | imperious 24, 328, 419 | impuissance 386 |
| immanent 111, 328 | impermeable 419 | impure 490 |
| immaterial 23, 328 | imperturbable 243, 420 | inability 39 |
| imminent 329 | impervious 196, 420 | inadequate 491 |
| immobilize 490 | impetuous 53, 295, 420 | inalienable 184 |
| immune 345 | implacable 420 | inane 189 |
| immunity 228, 345 | implant 66 | inanimate 491 |
| immure 490 | implode 309, 420 | inattentive 44 |
| immutable 345, 470 | imposter 490 | inaugurate 178 |
| impact 389 | imprecise 490 | inauguration 178 |
| impalpable 490 | impress 437 | inauspicious 377 |
| impartial 160 | impression 437 | incendiary 223, 276 |
| impassion 160 | impromptu 437 | incense 223, 376 |
| impassive 20, 173, 389 | improper 490 | incipient 236 |
| impeccable 123, 389 | improve 122 | incision 85 |

| | | |
|---|---|---|
| **in**cite 236, 256 | **in**finite 161, 234 | **in**stitute 112 |
| **in**clement 237 | **in**firm 491 | **in**struct 66 |
| **in**clination 491 | **in**flame 161 | **in**strumentalist 421 |
| **in**cogitant 237 | **in**flexible 491 | **in**subordinate 80, 411 |
| **in**consequential 16 | **in**formation 50, 241, 294 | **in**substantial 491 |
| **in**consonant 279 | **in**frequent 467 | **in**sular 46, 437 |
| **in**conspicuous 303, 376 | **in**fuse 54, 266 | **in**tangible 80, 361, 447 |
| **in**controvertible 49, 254 | **in**genious 267 | **in**temperate 110 |
| **in**corrigible 123, 254 | **in**genue 267 | **in**tensify 81, 130, 226, 334 |
| **in**corruptible 220 | **in**genuity 377, 491 | |
| **in**criminate 450 | **in**gest 491 | **in**tent 81 |
| **in**culpate 252, 255, 374 | **in**grain 462 | **in**tentional 81 |
| **in**cumbent 210 | **in**gratiate 462 | **in**timate 96, 372 |
| **in**defensible 255, 455 | **in**herent 237 | **in**timidate 96 |
| **in**dict 80 | **in**hibit 237 | **in**timidation 94 |
| **in**different 127 | **in**imical 218, 255 | **in**trepid 92, 112 |
| **in**digenous 128, 388 | **in**iquitous 283 | **in**tricacy 112 |
| **in**digent 37 | **in**iquity 283 | **in**trude 113 |
| **in**distinct 491 | **in**jure 82 | **in**trusive 75 |
| **in**doctrinate 115 | **in**kling 491 | **in**tuition 438 |
| **in**dolent 128, 148, 331 | **in**novate 450 | **in**ure 66, 303 |
| **in**domitable 128, 194, 326 | **in**novative 450 | **in**vective 29, 67, 341 |
| **in**dubitable 128 | **in**satiable 491 | **in**veigle 406 |
| **in**duce 421 | **in**sensible 34 | **in**vestigate 67, 361 |
| **in**ducement 140, 421 | **in**sight 34 | **in**veterate 67 |
| **in**duct 206 | **in**sipid 53, 440 | **in**vidious 491 |
| **in**dulge 60, 128 | **in**solent 53 | **in**vigorate 81, 86 |
| **in**eluctable 129 | **in**soluble 62 | **in**violable 81 |
| **in**ert 142 | **in**souciance 303 | **in**violate 362 |
| **in**escapable 129 | **in**souciant 53 | **in**vulnerable 82 |
| **in**evitable 142 | **in**spiration 237, 465 | un**im**peachable 504 |
| **in**fect 406 | **in**spire 54, 266 | un**in**itiated 78 |
| **in**fection 406 | **in**stigate 66 | un**in**spired 504 |
| **in**fer 243, 491 | **in**still 66 | |

## inter, intro — between

| | | |
|---|---|---|
| dis**inter** 404 | **inter**dict 91, 95, 410 | **intro**ductory 392 |
| dis**inter**est 48 | **inter**est 284, 406 | |
| **inter**cessor 95, 129 | **inter**preter 196 | |
| **inter**dependent 332 | **inter**rogate 95 | |

## Words Roots and Prefixes J

### jac, ject — to throw

abject 276
conjecture 133, 342
deject 281
dejection 208
object 28
objection 416
reject 285, 378
subject 265, 502

### jud — law

judicious 129, 155, 271
prejudiced 48

### jur — to swear

abjure 276, 448
perjure 187, 466
perjury 72

## Words Roots and Prefixes L

### lav, luv, lut, lot — to wash

dilute 326
dissolute 62, 190
irresoluteness 229
irresolution 92
lavish 82, 360, 400
resolute 54, 113, 195
solution 501

### leg, lect, lig — to gather, read, choose, or send; law

allege 478
allegiance 22
delegate 403
delegation 403
diligence 485
intelligence 491
intelligible 176
negligent 267
negligible 494
relegate 500
selective 501

### lev — light, not heavy

alleviate 292, 404
elevate 460
elevation 460
irrelevant 491
leverage 492
relevant 302

| liber, liver | free | |
|---|---|---|
| liberal 190 | liberality 190 | libertine 62, 190 |

| libr | balance | |
|---|---|---|
| calibrate 293 | | |

| lic | to permit | |
|---|---|---|
| elicit 486 | licentious 224 | |

| liter | letter | |
|---|---|---|
| alliterate 478 | literal 96, 162, 418 | obliterate 313 |
| illiterate 311 | literary 493 | |

| log | speech, word | |
|---|---|---|
| apologist 156 | epilogue 251 | neologism 218, 495 |
| apologize 369 | eulogize 298, 310 | prologue 498 |
| chronological 482 | logic 464 | syllogism 49, 318 |
| ecologist 189, 486 | | |

| logy | science, study | |
|---|---|---|
| anthology 90 | chronology 15 | eulogy 436 |

| loqu, locut | to speak | |
|---|---|---|
| grandiloquent 189 | circumlocution 20, 353 | circumlocutory 441 |
| loquacious 228, 438 | | |

| luc, lumin | light | |
|---|---|---|
| elucidate 19 | lucid 238 | translucent 179, 196 |
| illuminate 328 | luminary 250, 329 | |
| ineluctable 129 | pellucid 314 | |

| lud, lus | game, play | |
|---|---|---|
| allude 478<br>collude 309, 372 | elude 436<br>ludicrous 129, 155 | prelude 249 |

## Words Roots and Prefixes

| magn, maj | great |
|---|---|
| magnanimity 493 | |

| mal | bad | |
|---|---|---|
| maladroit 157, 284<br>malaise 493<br>malice 317 | malicious 298, 458<br>malign 298<br>malinger 298 | malingerer 286, 298<br>malodor 147, 312 |

| man | to stay | |
|---|---|---|
| dismantle 48<br>immanent 111, 328 | permanency 188 | permanent 358 |

| men, min | outstanding | |
|---|---|---|
| amenable 400<br>augmentation 326<br>ecumenical 17, 19<br>eminence 250, 329 | eminent 250<br>ignominious 450<br>imminent 329<br>menace 390 | prominent 158, 376 |

| meta | beyond, change |
|---|---|
| metaphor 162 | |

| min | little, less | |
|---|---|---|
| diminish 158, 326<br>diminution 326<br>ignominious 450 | mince 210<br>mineral 301 | minuscule 360<br>minute 360 |

## mir — wonder

admirable 322 | admire 120 | mirth 21, 293

## mis — bad, wrong

misanthrope 21, 327
misbehave 21, 440
mischievous 22, 172, 338
miscreant 35, 441
misdemeanor 35
misgiving 494
mishap 36
mislead 54
misrepresent 494

## mit, miss — to send

commitment 170, 482
dismiss 485
manumit 52, 195, 359
mitigate 97
permit 408
remiss 315, 331
submission 411
submissive 80
summit 349
unlimited 304, 353
vomit 309

## mob, mot, mov — to move

commotion 118, 340
emotion 141
immobilize 490
mobility 424
motility 214
motivate 97
move 124, 282, 306, 311
promote 376
remove 93, 313

## mono — one, alone

monochromatic 463 | monotone 365 | monotonous 451

## mony — state, condition

parsimony 271 | testimony 72

## morph — shape

amorphous 369

## mort — death

mortification 494

528 Supervoca words roots and Prefixs

| mut | to change |
|---|---|
| im**mut**able 345, 470 | **mut**ate 494 |

## Words Roots and Prefixes

| nai, nat | born | | |
|---|---|---|---|
| **nai**f (**nai**ve) 494<br>**nai**ve 253, 285 | **nat**ion 346 | **nat**ty 114, 395 |

| neg | to deny | | |
|---|---|---|---|
| ab**neg**ate 478 | **neg**ligent 267 | **neg**ligible 494 |

| nomin, nomen | name |
|---|---|
| ig**nomin**ious 450 | |

| non | not | | |
|---|---|---|---|
| **non**ymous 400<br>**non**flammable 371, 495 | **non**conformist 495<br>**non**descript 299 | **non**entity 285<br>**non**sensical 281, 495 |

| not(e) | known | | |
|---|---|---|---|
| **not**able 390<br>**not**e 371 | **not**ice 45 | **not**iceable 116 |

| nov | new | | |
|---|---|---|---|
| in**nov**ate 450<br>in**nov**ative 450 | **nov**elty 379, 495 | re**nov**ate 453 |

# Words Roots and Prefixes

| ob | in the way |
|---|---|
| obdurate 131<br>obfuscate 163, 238, 328<br>object 28<br>objection 416<br>obliterate 313<br>oblivion 313<br>obscure 36 | obscurity 401<br>obsequious 36, 424<br>obsess 36<br>obsolete 495<br>obstinate 22, 68<br>obstreperous 114, 469<br>obstruct 69 | obtuse 114<br>obtuseness 114<br>obviate 69 |

| oc, of, op | against |
|---|---|
| offend 163<br>offense 163, 417 | officious 163 | oppress 495 |

| ont, ent | being |
|---|---|
| nonentity 285 | |

| onym | name |
|---|---|
| anonymous 400 | |

| op | eye |
|---|---|
| myopia 211, 375 | synopsis 243 |

| oper | to work |
|---|---|
| cooperate 309, 372 | |

| or | mouth |
|---|---|
| adoration 297<br>adore 444 | oracle 451<br>orate 210 | oratory 210 |

| ord | to arrange | | |
|---|---|---|---|
| disordered 445<br>extraordinary 110, 299 | insubordinate 80, 411<br>order 161, 403 | orderly 15, 256, 385<br>subordinate 454 | |

## Words Roots and Prefixes

| pan | all | |
|---|---|---|
| deadpan 173, 389<br>expansive 39 | panegyric 496<br>panorama 496 | pantechnicon 69 |

| para | beside | |
|---|---|---|
| paradigmatic 439<br>paradox 439 | paragon 439<br>paramount 171, 439 | paranoia 390 |

| pass | to step |
|---|---|
| trespass 113, 150 | |

| path | feeling, disease, suffering | |
|---|---|---|
| antipathy 90, 362<br>apathetic 170, 203, 260 | pathological 496 | sympathetic 350 |

| ped, pod, pus | foot | |
|---|---|---|
| expedite 388, 417<br>impede 234, 376, 419 | impediment 93 | pedestrian 144 |

| pel, puls | to push |
|---|---|
| repel 422, 441 | repulse 500 |

| pend | to weigh, to hang | |
|---|---|---|
| compendious 340<br>dependence 484 | dependency 122<br>expenditure 417 | interdependent 332<br>suspend 502 |

## per — through, intensive

- asperity 414
- imperative 161
- impermeable 419
- imperturbable 243, 420
- impervious 420
- intemperate 110
- perceive 80, 361
- peremptory 375
- perfidious 83, 465
- perforate 164
- performance 358
- permanency 188
- permanent 358
- permit 408
- pernicious 408
- perplex 451
- perseverance 268
- persevere 268
- perspicacious 408
- persuade 22
- pertinacity 22
- pertinent 23, 302, 328
- perturb 23, 364
- pervade 23
- pervasive 23
- prosper 378
- prosperity 211
- prosperous 378

## peri — around

- peripatetic 465
- peripheral 80, 466
- periphery 466

## pet — to seek; small

- impetuous 53, 295, 420
- petty 116

## phon — sound

- cacophonous 357, 417
- cacophony 249
- euphonious 417
- symphony 421, 502

## pon, pos — to put, to place

- apostasy 384, 405
- apostate 384
- overexpose 143
- overexposure 143, 255
- ponder 315
- ponderous 53, 208
- pontificate 285, 348
- posit 497
- possess 497
- posture 117
- predisposition 497
- preponderance 145
- preponderant 242
- preposterous 145, 339
- repose 95, 422
- unprepossessing 108

## port — to carry

- deportation 485
- support 115
- rapport 206
- supportive 227

## pre, pro — before, forward, forth

appreciate 431
appreciation 86, 431
apprehension 479
comprehend 36, 341
misrepresent 494
precarious 144, 258
precede 145
precedent 145, 288
precipitate 145
precis 132
precise 432
precision 224
preclude 239
precursor 409
precursory 409, 460
predict 132, 273
prediction 132, 219
predilection 452
predisposition 497
preempt 497
preface 251, 497
preference 497
prefiguration 497
prejudiced 48
prelude 249
premeditate 331, 379
preponderance 145
preponderant 242
preposterous 145, 339
presage 374, 451
prescience 211, 375
preservative 146
preserve 146
preside 498
prestige 146, 202, 296
presumption 377
prevail 146
prevalent 146
prevaricate 146
prevarication 146
probation 361
proceed 464
procure 302, 362
profundity 234, 466
profuse 192, 363
progress 69
prohibit 363
prohibitive 103, 363
proliferate 376
prologue 498
prolong 55
promote 376
pronounce 498
prophecy 451, 498
prophetic 352
propitious 79
prosecute 498
protagonist 498
protest 348
protract 17, 392
protuberance 392
provisional 157
provisions 393
provoke 55, 393
represented 403
unprepossessing 108

## prim, prin — first

principal 454

## prob, prov — to test

approbation 431
approve 414, 431
disprove 49, 318
improve 122
improvidence 133, 392
probe 67, 361
probity 40, 361, 456
provident 392
providential 498
reprobate 21, 270, 440
reprove 441

## Words Roots and Prefixes

## quer, ques, quir, quis — to ask

inquisitive 466
quest 499
question 164

## Words Roots and Prefixes

### rap, rav — to seize

entrap 110, 273
rapacious 393
rapport 206
rapprochement 269

### re — back, again

disregard 49
disrespect 50, 327
irreducible 491
irrepressible 70, 463
irresoluteness 229
irresolution 92
react 142
reassure 212
rebuke 232, 499
recalcitrant 162, 225
recant 225
recidivism 240, 301
reciprocate 241
recite 499
recognition 499
reconcile 452
reconciliation 452
recondite 241
reconnoiter 241
recur 499
redolent 147
redoubtable 147
redundant 467
refined 165, 446
refractory 22, 165
refuse 269, 298
refute 412, 467
regard 147, 499
regressive 452
regret 499
rehabilitate 242, 434
rehabilitation 242, 325
rehearsal 500
reiterate 467, 500
reject 285, 378
rejoice 416, 452
rejuvenate 120
relapse 240, 301
relate 500
relative 421
release 111, 301
relegate 500
relevant 302
relief 228
relieve 302, 444
religion 377
relinquish 302, 362
reluctance 212, 500
reluctant 212
remember 131
remiss 315, 331
remonstrance 348
remonstrate 348
remonstrator 63
remorse 147, 164, 348
remove 93, 313
remunerate 349
remunerative 349
renew 453
renounce 408
renovate 453
repartee 99, 394
repatriate 250, 394
repeal 98, 500
repel 422, 441
repertoire 422
replete 422
repletion 422
repose 95, 422
reprehensible 440
represented 403
reprimand 441
reproach 453, 456
reprobate 21, 270, 440
reprove 441
repudiate 423
repugnance 441
repugnant 422, 441
repulse 500
rescind 24, 207
reserve 363
reserved 39
resilience 39
resist 54
resonant 453
respect 70
respiration 453
respire 453
respite 54, 223
resplendence 159, 206
resplendent 55
responsible 235
restive 70, 420
restored 141
restrain 70
restraint 224
restrict 500
resurgence 84
resurgent 84, 464
resuscitate 500
retain 85, 184, 363
retaliate 85
retard 65, 85
retort 99, 394
retract 500
reveal 500
revive 100
reward 302
rewarding 19, 302
unremarkable 379
unrepentant 342, 380

| reg, rect | rule; right, direct |
|---|---|
| directness 433 | rectify 257 | regimen 270 |
| erect 125, 395 | rectitude 195, 257, 283 | unidirectionally 241 |

| rid, ris | to laugh |
|---|---|
| deride 459 | derision 133, 177 |

| rog, rogat | to ask |
|---|---|
| interrogate 95 | |

## Words Roots and Prefixes

| sacr, secr | holy |
|---|---|
| desecrate 29 | |

| sci(o) | to know |
|---|---|
| prescience 211, 375 | unconscious 468 |

| sed, sid, sess | to follow |
|---|---|
| obsess 36 | sedentary 465 | supersede 502 |
| possess 497 | sedulous 128, 148 | unprepossessing 108 |
| preside 498 | subside 226 | |
| sedate 258 | subsidiary 227 | |

| sist, sta | to stand |
|---|---|
| assist 18, 44 | resist 54 | staff 181 |
| constancy 83, 194, 287 | resistance 415 | stagnant 501 |
| constant 482 | stability 144, 181, 307 | substantial 227, 469 |
| grandstand 489 | stabilize 304 | unsubstantial 504 |

| soci | to join; company | |
|---|---|---|
| associate 45 | dissociate 154 | society 356 |
| association 432 | sociable 109, 163, 242 | |

| solv, solut | to release | |
|---|---|---|
| absolve 478 | dissolute 62, 190 | resolute 54, 113, 195 |
| dissolve 62, 433 | irresoluteness 229 | solution 501 |
| solvent 62, 332 | irresolution 92 | |

| somn | sleep |
|---|---|
| somnolence 138, 349 | |

| soph | wisdom | |
|---|---|---|
| sophisticate 423 | sophistication 267 | unsophisticated 504 |

| spect | to look | |
|---|---|---|
| circumspect 241, 353 | prospect 301 | spectrum 501 |
| disrespect 50, 327 | respect 70 | |

| sper, spir | to breathe | |
|---|---|---|
| asperity 414 | inspiration 237, 465 | respiration 453 |
| aspirant 414 | inspire 54, 266 | respire 453 |
| conspiratorial 92, 433 | prosper 378 | spiritual 287 |
| conspire 433 | prosperity 211 | uninspired 504 |
| dispirit 447 | prosperous 378 | |

| stru, struct | to build | |
|---|---|---|
| destruction 109, 434 | instruct 66 | obstruct 69 |

## sub, suc, suf, sug — below, under, beneath

insubordinate 80, 411
insubstantial 491
subdue 128, 194, 326
subject 265, 502
subjugate 195
sublime 226
submerge 226, 385
submission 411
submissive 80
subordinate 454
subpoena 502
subservience 502
subside 226
subsidiary 227
subsidy 227
substantial 227, 469
subterfuge 227
subtle 502
subvert 227
succinct 228
succinctly 171, 228
succor 228
suffuse 165
unsubstantial 504

## sus — below

resuscitate 500
susceptibility 502
suspend 502
suspicion 390

## sue — to follow

ensue 487
issue 173

## super, supra — above

supercilious 424
superficial 295, 424
superfluous 212, 502
superior 424
supersede 502

## sur — over, above

surfeit 435, 469
surliness 154
surrender 166, 184
surreptitious 61, 455

## syl, sym, syn, sys — together, with

eleemosynary 268, 281
synopsis 243
syllogism 49, 318
asymmetrical 481
symbiosis 332
symbiotic 332
sympathetic 350
symphony 421, 502
symptom 145
systematic 72

# Words Roots and Prefixes T

| tail | to cut |
|---|---|
| curtail 17, 357, 392 | |

| tend, tens, tent | extend, stretch |
|---|---|

| | | |
|---|---|---|
| advertent 44 | intent 81 | potentate 84 |
| attendant 99 | latent 82 | stentorian 148, 252 |
| attentive 163 | ostentation 268 | tend 52, 455 |
| contented 31 | patent 84, 256 | tender 412 |
| discontent 18 | penitent 164 | tendinous 193 |
| inattentive 44 | penitential 380 | tension 180 |
| intensify 81, 130, 226, 334 | portentous 23 | |

| term | end, limit |
|---|---|
| determination 92 | terminate 412 | termination 412 |

| terr | to frighten |
|---|---|
| deterrent 140, 421 | terror 503 |

| tor, tort | to twist |
|---|---|

| | | |
|---|---|---|
| desultory 77 | extortionist 94 | torrid 149, 306 |
| distort 63 | retort 99, 394 | tortuous 223, 425 |
| distortion 63, 459 | torpid 455 | |
| extort 94, 446 | torpor 503 | |

| tract | to drag, draw |
|---|---|

| | | |
|---|---|---|
| abstract 60, 280 | detract 447 | retract 500 |
| attracted 36 | distract 63, 440 | tractable 182 |
| attractive 108 | extract 110 | |
| contract 295 | intractable 112, 446 | |
| contraction 386, 402 | protract 17, 392 | |

| trans | across, beyond, on other side |
|---|---|
| transcend 503<br>transgress 195 | transient 196, 197　　translucent 179, 196<br>translate 196　　　　transparent 196 |

| trud, trus | to thrust |
|---|---|
| intrude 113<br>intrusive 75 | trudge 55　　　　　　unobtrusive 365 |

| typ | impression, image |
|---|---|
| archetype 126, 232 | typical 369, 503　　　typo 425 |

## Words Roots and Prefixes U

| un | not |
|---|---|
| unaffected 117<br>unambiguous 224<br>unaware 264, 445<br>unconformity 462<br>unconscious 468<br>unconventional 503<br>uncouth 165, 259<br>unctuous 260, 332<br>undeserved 503<br>unexceptionable 503<br>unfavorable 45, 79<br>unfettered 504<br>unfit 166<br>unflappable 166<br>ungainly 273<br>unimpeachable 504 | unimportant 98　　　　　unsettle 207<br>uninitiated 78　　　　　unsophisticated 504<br>uninspired 504　　　　　unsound 56<br>unique 288　　　　　　unsteady 72, 250<br>unjustifiable 288　　　　unstoppable 463<br>unkempt 288, 433　　　unsubstantial 504<br>unlikely 504　　　　　　unsuitable 86<br>unlimited 304　　　　　untenable 87<br>unnecessary 69　　　　 untoward 102, 405<br>unobtrusive 365　　　　unwieldy 504<br>unprepossessing 108　　unwitting 504<br>unreflective 331, 504　　unwonted 119<br>unremarkable 379<br>unrepentant 342, 380<br>unruly 469<br>unscrupulousness 40 |

| uni | one, single |
|---|---|
| unanimity 242, 456<br>unidirectionally 241 | unique 288　　　　　　unity 48 |

| urb | city | | |
|---|---|---|---|
| urban 233 | urbane 197 | urbanity 90 | |

| us, ut | to use | | |
|---|---|---|---|
| abuse 403<br>usual 119 | usurp 87 | utilize 504 | |

## Words Roots and Prefixes

| vac, vag, void | empty | | |
|---|---|---|---|
| avoid 23, 142<br>evacuate 487<br>vaccinate 228 | vaccination 228, 345<br>vagrant 166 | vague 134, 260<br>void 412 | |

| val, vail | strong, worth | | |
|---|---|---|---|
| devalue 447<br>equivalent 465<br>prevail 146<br>prevalent 146 | valediction 126, 504<br>valiance 304<br>valiant 304 | valid 148<br>valuables 56<br>value 173, 435 | |

| ver | true | |
|---|---|---|
| veracious 310, 442<br>verdant 380 | verdict 504 | verify 433, 470 |

| verb | word | |
|---|---|---|
| verbose 279, 380 | verbosity 334 | |

| via, vey, voy | way | |
|---|---|---|
| convey 40, 483<br>obviate 69 | purvey 24 | trivial 68, 469 |

| vid, vis | to see | |
|---|---|---|
| improvidence 133, 392<br>invidious 491 | provident 392<br>providential 498 | visionary 56, 325<br>vivid 214 |

| voc, voke | to call | |
|---|---|---|
| advocate 74, 417<br>equivocate 32 | equivocation 32, 54<br>vociferous 244 | provoke 55, 393 |

| vita | life | |
|---|---|---|
| inevitable 142<br>vital 87 | vitality 103 | vitalize 370 |

| voc, voke | to call | |
|---|---|---|
| advocate 74, 417<br>equivocate 32 | equivocation 32, 54<br>vociferous 244 | provoke 55, 393 |

| vol | to fly ; will | |
|---|---|---|
| volatile 304 | volition 318 | |

| volv, volut | to roll | |
|---|---|---|
| convoluted 341, 356 | | |

| vor | to eat | |
|---|---|---|
| flavor 461<br>savor 100 | savory 100, 238, 368 | voracious 397 |

| ward | to watch | |
|---|---|---|
| aware 445<br>reward 302 | rewarding 19, 302<br>unaware 264, 445 | wary 26 |

www.goHackers.com

해커스 어학연구소

# SuperVoca
# Index

## A

abandon 184
abase 202
abash 202
abate 202 263
abbreviate 216
abdicate 122 233
aberrant 138
abet 138 266
abeyance 478
abhor 216
abide 216
abiding 216
abject 276
abjure 276 448
abnegate 478
abode 330
aboveboard 44
aboveboard action 44 220
abrade 430
abraded 430
abrasion 450
abridge 368
abrogate 112 260 478
abscond 14
absolve 478
absorb 44
absorbed 266
absorbing 149
abstain 262 358
abstemious 60 128 142
abstract 60 280
abstruse 108 216
abundant 400
abuse 403
accessible 108 216
accident 165
accidental 81
acclaim 478
acclimate 478
accolade 67 232
accommodate 478
accord 478
accost 445
accrete 248
accuracy 470
accused 80

acerbic 138
ache 185
achromatic 127 217
acme 322
acquiesce 430
acquisition 400
acrid 368
acrimonious 352
action 44
active 389
activity 360
actor 66 135
acute 262
adamant 184
addict 122
addicted 122
address 478
adept 444
adhere 217
adjust 86 276
admirable 322
admire 120
admonish 338 343
admonishment 61
adoration 297
adore 444
adorn 172
adroitness 142
adulate 14 175 304
adulterate 14
adumbration 478
adventurous 39
adversary 478
advertent 44
advocate 74 417
aerate 430
aesthete 60
affability 154
affect 34
affiliate 154
affinity 90 154
affirm 155 253 467
affliction 125
affluent 155 419
agenda 478
aggrandize 262
aggravate 262 292
aggressive 478

aggrieve 263 323
agitate 223 276
agonize 368
agreeable person 415
agreement 409
aid 102
aimless 300
alacritous 478
alacrity 170 212 285
albinism 170 268
albino 170
alchemy 478
alert 138 349
alibi 217 252
alienable 184
align 248
aligned 248 277
allay 292
allege 478
allegiance 22
alleviate 292 404
alliterate 478
allowance 116
allude 478
allure 93
aloft 306
aloof 45 369
altruist 14
amalgamate 48 184
amateurish 265
ambiguity 430
ambiguous 341 430
ambivalent 170
amble 217
ambrosial 217
ameliorate 122
amenable 400
amend 123 254
amenity 139
amicable 218 255 458
amorphous 369
amphibian 306
amplitude 179
amuse 202
amusement 202 369
anachronism 15
anaerobe 479
analgesia 185

544 **Supervoca Index**

analgesic 185
anarchist 192 479
ancestor 218
anchor 232 271
ancillary 171 439
anecdote 202 369
anemic 479
anesthetic 139 330
anger 189 269 278
animate 248
animation 248
anodyne 302 444
anomalous 369
anomaly 439
anonymous 400
answer 460
antagonize 74
anterior 292
anthology 90
antibiotic 406
antic 292
antidote 185
antipathy 90 154 362
anvil 479
anxiety 340
apathetic 170 203 260
apex 349
aphorism 139 218
apocalypse 352
apocalyptic 352
apologist 156
apologize 369
apophasis 479
apoplectic 370
apostasy 384 405
apostate 384
apothegm 66
appall 221 384
apparel 479
appeal 384
appearance 55
appease 113 384
applause 414 431
applicant 384
apposite 444
appreciate 431
appreciation 86 431
apprehension 479

approach 445
approbation 431
appropriate 166 431 467
approval 125 414 431
approximate 432
aqueduct 185
arbitrator 160
archaic 218
archaism 218
archetype 126 232
archive 233
arctic 149 306
ardent 248
arduous 414
argot 263
arid 218
arouse 300 385
arrange 385
arrest 370
arrhythmic 338
arrogance 131
art 60
artifact 171
artifacts 171
artisan 117
artless 90 101
artlessness 90 268
ascend 401
ascetic 195 219 333 449
aseptic 171
aside 158 219
askew 248 277
asperity 414
aspirant 414
assent 28
assert 28 277
assertive 338
asset 209
assiduity 28
assist 18 44
associate 45
association 432
assuage 60 161 310
assume 479
astound 479
astringent 479
astronomer 108
astronomy 108

asymmetrical 479
athletics 479
atrocious 171
atrocity 448
attach 479
attached 64
attachment 344
attendant 99
attentive 163
attenuate 74
attracted 36
attractive 108
audacious 249
augment 263
augmentation 326
augur 132 219
auspicious 23 45 123 267
austere 61 454
authentic 91
authenticity 91 222
authority 165 424
authorize 91 95
avarice 203
aversion 139 211
avid 127 219
avoid 23 142
avulse 479
aware 445
awkward 277
awl 144 458
awning 479
awry 15 256

babble 171 228
backdrop 479
backset 283
bad 171
badger 28
badinage 479
bait 277
bale 293
balk 306
balky 182
ballast 181 307
ballot 480
balm 307 463

balmy 237
banal 277 391
band 480
baneful 331 458
banish 29
bankrupt 332
banquet 386 480
barb 46 185
barbaric 423
barbarize 76 432
bare 352
barefaced 61 455
bark 370
barrenness 252
base 25 226
baseboard 480
baseness 480
bathetic 61 163
beacon 172
bedeck 480
bedlam 263
befuddle 480
behavior 292
belabor 277
beleaguer 293 312
belie 293
belief 225
belligerent 307
beloved 307
benediction 480
beneficial 322
benevolence 458
benevolent 298 458
bequest 91
berate 34 352
beseeching 442
besmirch 45
betray 482
beverage 84
biased 480
bigot 263
blame 309
blanch 185
bland 186 318
blandish 186
blandishment 186 459
blast 203
blatant 203 365

blazon 172
bleed 401
bleeding 35 401
blemish 123 389
blight 249
bliss 480
blizzard 480
blooming 480
blunder 480
blunt 15
blurb 45
blurt 45 102
blush 203
bluster 46
boast 56
bode 123
boding 123
boggle 480
bold 204
bolster 308
bombast 322 348
bonhomie 458
boor 445
bootless 385
border 264 480
bother 28
bottleneck 480
braggadocio 293
braggart 293
brake 434
branch 480
brash 204
brat 22 338
brattish 172
bravado 481
bravura 481
brazen 130 432
brazenness 157
breach 385
breezeway 481
brevity 139 218
bribe 220
brightness 252
bring to prominent 158
bristle 278
bromide 323
browbeat 15 308
bruit 483

bucolic 233
budge 124 483
buffer 389
buffoon 155
bully 15 96 308
bumptious 28 338
bungle 483
buoyant 226 385
burgeon 370
burlesque 238 371
burnish 401 407
busybody 75
buttress 108 402

cabal 432
cacophonous 357 417
cacophony 249
cadge 481
caisson 308
cajole 278
cajolery 135 278
calcify 481
calibrate 293
calibrated 293
callous 160 308 350
callow 308
calm 370
calmness 70
calumniate 323
camaraderie 481
cameo 39 481
camouflage 31 403
candid 278
candidate 401
candor 227 278 314
canopy 16
cantankerous 264
canvass 315 353
canyon 77
capitulate 54 415
capitulation 415
caprice 75 274
capricious 25 432
capture 481
careful 64 97
cargo 347 459

caricature 63 459
carnal 287
carouse 29
carp 109 340
carry 464
cart 308
cartographer 481
cast 116
castigate 61
castigation 61
casual 67
catalyst 75
catastrophe 36
categorical 75 191
catholic 91
caulk 109
caustic 46 185
cautionary 139
cautious 481
caveat 139
cavern 46 193
cavil 76 240
cavort 76 468
celebrity 401
cell 330
cement 91
censor 436
censure 440
centrifuge 481
cessation 46
chagrin 172
chain 346
chameleon 186
chaotic 445
charade 92
charge 481
charitable 204
charitableness 204 316
charlatan 140 434
chary 204
chasm 123 204
chauvinism 346
check 451
chef 386
chiaroscuro 220
chicanery 44 220 311
chisel 481
choke 395

choleric 302 371
chord 371
choreograph 371
choreography 371
chromatic 481
chronological 482
chronology 15
churl 259 409
churlish 223 445
cipher 76 294
circle 264
circuitous 433
circular 482
circumference 264
circumlocution 20 353
circumlocutory 441
circumscribe 353
circumscribed 304 353
circumspect 241 353
circumvent 354
cistern 62
citation 411
civilize 76 432
claim 179
clamor 343
clamp 342
clarify 163 204
clarion 484
clarity 32 358 430
cleft 123 204
clement 124
cliche 220 236
clinch 482
clique 96 252 278
clog 354
clot 172
cloth 297
cloture 482
clout 386
clumsy 16 444
coagulant 172 259 354
coagulate 172
coalesce 186
coarse 446
coax 186 459
coda 144 249
coerce 446
coercion 446

coeval 482
cogent 264 356
cognizant 264 445
colander 174 446
cold 372
collapse 308 420
collude 309 372
colonnade 386
colorful 461
combust 371
combustible 371
comfort 323
comfortable 139
comity 415
command 339 448
commencement 46
commend 339
commitment 170 482
commodious 187 339 372
commonplace 339
commonsensical 145 339
commotion 118 340
comparable 340
compatible 446
compendious 340
complacence 340
complain 109 340
complaisance 446
complexity 341 356
compliment 341
complimentary 208
comply 407 482
compose 341
composed 341
comprehend 36 341
compress 342
compression 342
compromise 342 420
compunction 342
compunctious 354
concatenate 482
concavity 392
conceal 279 416
concede 205 423
concentrate 187 279 326
conciliate 114 119 279
conciliatory 279 307 396
concise 132 279 380

conciseness 243
conclude 482
concord 157 279 343
concrete 482
concur 51 280
condemn 280
condense 280 378
condensed 60 280
condescend 280
condescending 280
condign 482
condolence 482
condone 281
confession 323
confine 482
confirm 293 323 450
conform 324
conformation 369
conformity 324
confront 354
confuse 324
confusion 234 324
congeal 324
congenial 324
congruent 324
conjecture 133 342
connect 482
connive 92
conniver 92 433
connoisseur 482
consent 205
consequence 285
conservative 254
conserve 25
consolidate 433
conspicuous 299 463
conspiratorial 92 433
conspire 433
constancy 83 194 287
constant 482
constellation 233
constitute 233
constrain 301 482
constrict 372
constricted 339 372
consummate 265
contagion 372
contain 483

contemptible 94
contenment 17
contented 31
continence 483
continuance 483
contract 295
contraction 386 402
contradictory 98 354
contrast 220 483
contravene 402
contrite 354 369
control 114
contumacious 131 355
convalesce 242 325
convenience 421
convention 355
conventional 355
converge 483
conversant 483
conversion 483
convert 355
convey 40 483
conviction 174 355
convince 264 356
convivial 109 242
convoluted 341 356
convulsion 386 402
cool 253
cooperate 309 372
copious 317 415
copy 255
coquette 207 386
core 466
cornucopia 485
coronation 270 402
corporeal 31 227 447
correspond 447
corrode 358 483
corruptionist 257
cosmopolitan 46 393 437
cosset 47 272
coterie 483
countenance 280 483
counter 483
counterfeit 402
countermand 403
country 29
courage 483

course 150 309 483
court 47
courtroom 483
coven 47
covenant 385
cover 16
covetous 393
coward 155
cowardice 37 76
cower 233
cozen 483
cramp 187
cramped 187
crass 484
craven 173
credence 124
credulous 148 403
creek 484
creep 124 272
crescendo 484
crest 140
crestfallen 32 140
crime 35
cringe 387
critical 442
criticize 114
crockery 484
cronyism 372
croon 373
crouch 484
crucial 16
crumb 484
crumble 16 235
crutch 62
crux 62
cryptic 76 294
cuisine 65
culpable 309
cultivate 325
cultivated 257
cunning 484
curate 484
curb 373
curmudgeon 415
cursory 205
curt 16
curtail 17 357 392
cut 222

# D

dabble 173
dabbler 173
daft 129 155
damaged 420
damp 181 342
dance 371
dandy 132 294
dank 343
dapper 288 433
dappled 281
daredevil 38 356
dastard 155 173
daunt 17
dauntless 17 150
dawdle 484
deadpan 173 389
deafening 415
dearth 205 213 391
debacle 387
debase 173
debasement 460
debate 173
debilitate 174
debrief 294
debunk 433
decadence 387
decant 434
decanter 434
deceitful 196
deceive 140 434
decelerate 434
deception 221
deceptive 221
decibel 484
declamation 484
decode 325
decorate 61
decorous 249 347
decorum 164
decrepit 250 454
dedicate 124
dedication 124 182
defend 87 156
defer 156
deferential 36
deferrable 156
defile 156
definitive 157
deflated 469
deflect 484
deft 157 284
defuse 157 326
defy 459
degree 202
dehydrate 221
deject 281
dejection 208 281
delay 296
delegate 403
delegation 403
deleterious 294
deliberate 178 204 295
deliberation 432
delicacy 297
delicate 295
delirium 234 324
deluge 325
delusion 56 325
demagogue 434
demand 484
demean 404
demolish 434
demolition 109 434
demotic 484
demur 416
demystify 484
denial 484
denigrate 343
denounce 281 338 343
denunciation 484
deny 17
depart 14
dependence 484
dependency 122
deplete 416
deplore 329 416 452
deploy 187 279
deportation 485
depose 187 466
deprave 175
deprecate 435
depreciate 435
depreciation 435
deprivation 435 469
depth 38
deracinate 435
derelict 356
deride 459
derision 133 177
derivative 409 460
descend 38 401
descendant 485
descent 485
desecrate 29
desert 218
desiccant 187
desiccate 29
desire 177
despicable 47
despise 47 485
despondent 24 47
destruction 109 434
desultory 77
detach 77
detainment 485
detection 403
deter 92
determination 92
deterrent 140 421
detour 93 394
detract 447
detrimental 485
devalue 447
devastate 140
devastated 140
devote 485
devoted 160
devout 77 316
dexterous 77 277 347
diaphanous 205 210
diatribe 403
diction 485
dictionary 329
didactic 250
diehard 124
difference 30
diffidence 157
dignify 404
digress 63 265
digressive 30
dilapidate 141
dilapidated 141

dilate 295
dilettante 295 424
diligence 485
dilute 326
diminish 158 326
diminution 326
din 343
dingy 387
diocesan 17
diocese 485
dire 357
directness 433
dirge 485
disabuse 387
disaffected 17
disaggregate 186
disagreeable 485
disarm 485
disavow 17 205
discern 18
discerner 262
discerning 18 34
discharge 206
disclosure 206
discomfit 18 462
discommode 18 44 312
discompose 18 238
discontent 18
discord 206
discredit 29
discrepancy 485
discrete 30
discretion 437
discretionary 300
discriminate 30 407
discriminating 460
discursive 30
disdain 30
disembodied 31
disembody 31
disengage 485
disentangle 188 213
disgorge 309
disgruntle 31
disgruntled 31
disguise 31
disgust 31 267
disinclination 139

disinfection 171
disingenuous 32
disintegrate 48 184
disinter 404
disinterest 48
disinterested 48
disjoint 485
dislike 209 216
dismantle 48
dismiss 485
disordered 445
disparage 48
disparate 48 340
dispassionate 22 49
disperse 447
dispirit 447
dispose favorably 161
disprove 49 318
dispute 49 118 254
disquiet 485
disregard 49
disrespect 50 327
disrupt 50 226
dissect 485
dissemble 50
disseminate 50
dissent 51 205 280
dissimulate 92
dissipate 158
dissociate 154
dissolute 62 190
dissolve 62 433
dissonance 157
dissuade 54 63 348
distillate 158
distinction 190
distort 63
distortion 63 459
distract 63
distracted 440
distraught 341 373
distress 224 404
distressed 368
disturb 109
ditch 77
ditty 326
diurnal 421
divergent 158 219

divestiture 400
divide 317
divulge 279 416
dizziness 396
doctrine 486
dodder 250
dogged 265
doggerel 265
doleful 486
dolorous 486
dolt 416
donor 486
doubt 124
doubtful 128
dour 63
douse 404
downplay 486
downpour 78
doyen 78
doze 486
drab 206
draconian 174
draconic 324
drain 174
drainage 354
drama 286
drawl 78
dread 387
drench 404
drift 334
drill 486
drivel 281
drizzle 325
droll 332 373
drone 451
droop 159
drudgery 19 302
dry 187
dubious 174
dulcet 357
dull 364
dune 357
dupe 388
duration 357
dutiful 119 486
dwindle 376 404
dyspeptic 51

eaglet 486
earshot 141
earsplitting 19
eat 64
eavesdrop 51
ebullience 486
ebullient 455
eccentric 221 355
eclipse 146 296
ecologist 189 486
ecumenical 17 19
eddy 486
edible 435
edifice 51 108
efface 158
effectiveness 253
effervesce 159
effete 159 297
efficacious 95 159
effort 378
effrontery 486
effulgent 159
effusive 265
egalitarian 486
elate 206
elated 52 344
elation 172 206 317
eleemosynary 268 281
elegiac 486
elevate 460
elevation 460
elicit 486
elitism 486
elliptical 296 313
elongate 373
elucidate 19 358
elude 436
emaciate 486
emancipate 85 188
embarrass 174
embarrassment 174 203
embed 404
embezzler 431
embolden 202 221 384
embrace 72 221
embroider 487

emigrate 250 394
eminence 250 329
eminent 250
emotion 141
empty 412
emulate 19
enact 207
enclose 239 436
encoded 325
encomiast 310
encomium 436
encourage 251
encouragement 138
encumber 93
encyclopedia 340
endorse 125
endow 448
endowment 448
endure 125 436
energetic 141
energize 487
energy 346
enervate 20 141 274
enfeeble 159
enfetter 160
enfranchise 160
engender 212 266
engrave 33 448
engross 266
engrossed 266
enhance 388
enigma 251
enlarge 282
enlighten 296
enmity 343 415
ennui 357
enormity 448
enormous 360
enrage 284
enrich 416
ensconce 207 418
enslave 52 359
ensue 487
ensuing 292
enter 150
enthusiasm 93 347
enthusiastic 357
entice 93

entrancing 487
entrap 110 273
entreat 448
entreaty 339 448
entry 487
enunciate 405
envelope 436
envious 78
enzyme 75
ephemeral 436
epicure 460
epigram 251
epilogue 251
equable 110
equipoise 20 243
equity 487
equivalent 465
equivocate 32
equivocation 32 54
erect 125 395
erode 358
errant 309
erratic 338 358
error 438
erudite 32 94 311
eschew 32
espouse 276 448
essence 110
esteem 79 339
estimable 94
estrange 449
estrangement 269 449
eulogize 298 310
eulogy 436
euphemism 163 417
euphonious 417
evacuate 487
evade 286 436 460
evanescent 188 216
evasive 314
evict 460
exacerbate 175 262
exacting 100 243
exaggerate 175
exaggerated 175 419
exalt 188
examine 95
exceptional 487

excerpt 222
excessive 487
excitable 487
exclaim 487
excoriate 94 251
excrete 487
exculpate 217 252
excursive 63
excuse 103
execrable 487
execrate 125 188
exemplary 19
exemplify 126 232
exempt 64 209
exhaust 161 234
exhilarate 487
exhort 234
exhortation 97
exhortative 234 273
exigent 156
exile 115
exonerate 255 374 450
exorbitant 449
exotic 128 388
expansive 39
expedite 388 417
expenditure 417
expense 117
experience 68 178
explanation 296
explicate 487
exponent 74 417
express succinctly 171 228
expurgate 436
exquisite 487
extant 79
extemporization 379
extenuate 405
extinct 79
extinguish 94 406
extol 94 251
extort 94 446
extortionist 94
extract 110
extraneous 110 444
extraordinary 110 299
extravagant 111
extricate 449

extrinsic 111 237 328 462
extrovert 207 210
exude 487
exultant 32 140

fabric 222
fabricate 91 222
facetious 222
facile 234 414
facilitate 234 344 419
faction 252 278
factorable 487
factual 488
fade 252
failing 235
faint 252
faith 384
faithful 396
fallacious 310 442
fallacy 387 464
falsehood 323
falter 310
familiar 34
fanatic 160
fantastic 389
farce 129 358
fascinating 488
fast 64
fastidious 64 205
fathom 32 94
fatigue 95 422
fatuous 111 271
faultfinder 488
favorable 79
fawn 79 258 375
fawning 79
faze 80
fazed 80
fear 233 326 390
feckless 235
fecundity 252
feign 488
felicitous 488
fence 127
fervid 20 425
fervor 64 203

fetid 282
fetter 111
fiasco 266 390
fictional 488
fidelity 405
fidget 175
figurative 96 418
filibuster 296
filigree 297
filly 52
finesse 52
finicky 488
firm 68 131 488
firmness 175
firsthand 380
fixed 166
flaccid 175
flagging 228 469
flannel 297
flare 488
flatten 488
flatter 14 175
flaunt 418
flavor 461
flaw 176
fleet 126
fleeting 126
flexibility 184 299
flexible 37
flinch 326
flint 488
flip 488
flirt 207
flirtatious 207 386
flit 282
flock 447
flooding 78
florid 488
flounder 418
flourish 418
flout 49
fluent 33 235
foible 235
foil 488
follow 349
follower 68
folly 488
foment 157 237 326

fondness 297
food 100 217 359
foot-dragging 388 417
footloose 344
forbear 207
forbid 358
forbidden 262 358
ford 188
forgery 402
forget 313
forgive 85
forgo 207
formality 488
formidable 488
forsake 488
forthcoming 329
forthright 20 353
fortify 20
fortunate 102 405
forward 452
foster 65 194
founder 306
fracture 91 489
fragile 176
fragrant 147
frail 176
frailty 176
fraud 176
fraudulent 176
frenetic 141
frenzy 141
fret 489
friable 16 235
friction 308 430 489
frieze 489
frigid 253
frivolity 282
frivolous 177 282
frivolousness 189
frog 306
frugal 33 115
frustrate 266
fulsome 208
fundament 147
fungi 189
furniture 69 242 318
furtive 20 278 424
fury 189

fuss 52 455
futile 95 159

 G

gainsay 155 253
gait 282
gall 310 311
galvanize 327
gangly 489
garble 19 358
gargantuan 344 360
garish 461
garment 101 327 489
gash 222
gasification 489
gauche 52 259
gaudy 489
gauge 489
general 19
generosity 203
generous 190
genial 51 264 344 360
geniality 63
genteel 223 445
gentle 304
gentleness 55
genuine 71 193 359
germ 149
gibberish 176
gibe 177
giddy 359
gist 62
give up 268
glaze 177 375
glee 374
glib 33 235 466
glisten 387 489
glitch 176 489
gloat 160
gloom 374
glossy 374
glut 65
glutton 65 143 489
goad 373 489
gobble 190 208
good will 352 406
gorge 142

gossamer 53
gouge 33 448
gourmet 65
graceful 208
graceful and light 208
grain 489
grand 209
grandeur 189
grandiloquent 189
grandstand 489
grate 489
gratify 177 263
gratuitous 177
gravel 489
gravity 177 282
greedy 78
green 178
greet 126
greeting 126
gregarious 126 369
gregariousness 126 241
grieve 235
grimace 142
grind 253
gripe 18
groove 374 468
grotesque 389
grouch 146 283
grove 405
grow 248
grudge 406
guidance 236 407
guile 90 253
guileless 347
guilt 323
gull 311
gulled 26
gullible 388
gush 33 259
gustation 461

 H

hack 490
hackneyed 220 236 287 323
halcyon 461
hale 159 297

halt 490
hamper 344
hamstring 253
hangdog 52 344
hankering 345
haphazard 72 418
hapless 490
harbinger 374 451
hardy 412
harebrained 359
harmful 83 408
harsh 208
hash 33
hasten 65 85
haunt 34 411
hauteur 79
havoc 449
headlong 178
health 270
hear 141
hearken 461
hearten 208 281
heat 134 426
hedge 127
hedonist 449
heed 461
heinous 254
heirloom 218
hem 327
heresy 98 461
heretic 462
heroic 490
herpetologist 186 490
hesitance 53
hesitate 310
hesitation 420
hidebound 254 450
hideous 254
hieroglyph 490
hike 283
histrionic 66
hive 389
hoard 36
hoax 176 490
hodgepodge 127 394
hole 164
homage 50 327
homeliness 301

homogeneous 127 490
honesty 50
honor 45 343
horn 490
hortatory 251
hovel 127
hue 127 217
humane 21 327
humble 328
humiliation 174
humility 300 328 419
humorous 120
husband 21
husbandry 21 158 362
husky 295
hymn 180 345
hyperbole 175 419
hypnotic 490
hypothesis 323 450

ichthyologist 236
ideas 257
identify 400
idolater 283
idolatrize 490
idolize 79
ignite 132 345
ignoble 161
ignominious 450
ignore 48 203
ill 123
illiterate 311
illuminate 328
illustrate 462
imaginative 144
imbibe 287
imitate 439
immaculate 118
immanent 111 328
immaterial 23 328
imminent 329
immobilize 490
immune 345
immunity 228 345
immure 490
immutable 345 470

impact 389
impalpable 490
impartial 160
impartiality 160
impassion 160
impassive 20 173 389
impeccable 123 389
impecunious 155 378 419
impede 234 376 419
impenetrable 251
imperative 161
imperious 24 328 419
impermeable 419
imperturbable 243 420
impervious 420
impervious to light 196
impetuous 53 295 420
implacable 420
implant 66
implode 309 420
important 330
imposter 490
imprecise 490
impress 437
impression 437
impromptu 437
improper 490
improve 122
improvidence 133 392
improvisatorial 437
imprudence 315
imprudent 437
impugn 412 437
impuissance 386
impure 490
inability to recover 39
inadequate 491
inalienable 184
inane 189
inanimate 491
inattentive 44
inaugurate 178
inauguration 178
inauspicious 377
incendiary 223 276
incense 223 376
inception 412
incipient 236

incision 85
incite 236 256
inclement 237
inclination 491
incogitant 237
inconsequential 16
inconsonant 279
inconspicuous 303 376
incontrovertible 49 254
incorrigible 123 254
incorruptible 220
incriminate 450
inculpate 255 374
incumbent 210
indefensible 255 455
indetection 403
indict 80
indifferent 127
indigenous 128 388
indigent 37
indistinct 491
indoctrinate 115
indolent 128 148 331
indomitable 128 194 326
indubitable 128
induce 421
inducement 140 421
induct 206
indulge 60 128
ineluctable 129
inept 142
inert 142
inescapable 129
inevitable 142
infect 406
infection 406
infer 243 491
infinite 161 234
infirm 491
inflame 161
inflexible 491
information 50 241 294
infrequent place 467
infuse 54 266
ingenious 267
ingenue 267
ingenuity 377 491
ingest 491

ingrain 462
ingrained 462
ingratiate 462
inherent 237
inhibit 237
inimical 218 255
inimitable 255
iniquitous 283
iniquity 283
injure 82
inkling 491
innovate 450
innovative 450
inquisitive 466
insatiable 491
insensible 34
insight 34
insipid 53 440
insolent 53
insoluble 62
insouciance 303
insouciant 53
inspiration 465
inspire 54 266
instigate 66
instill 66
institute 112
instruct 66
instrumentalist 421
insubordinate 80 411
insubstantial 491
insular 46 437
intangible 80 361 447
integral 80
intelligence 491
intelligible 176
intemperate 110
intensify 81 130 226 334
intent 81
intentional 81
intercessor 95 129
interdependent 332
interdict 91 95 410
interest 284 406
interpreter 196
interrogate 95
intimate 96 372
intimidate 96

intimidation 94
intractable 112 446
intransigent 430
intrepid 92 112
intricacy 112
introductory 392
intrude 113
intrusive 75
intuition 438
inure 66
inured 66 303
invective 29 67 232 341
inveigle 406
investigate 67 361
inveterate 67
invidious 491
invigorate 81 86
inviolable 81
inviolate 362
invulnerable 82
irascible 72 180 209
ire 491
iridescent 463
irk 284
irreducible 491
irrelevant 491
irrepressible 70 463
irresoluteness 229
irresolution 92
irritate 463
irritation 307 463
issue 173

jaded 143 255
jamb 491
jargon 263
jaundice 161
jaunty 182
jeer 492
jejune 284
jeopardize 492
jest 67 303
jingoism 346
jittery 113
jocund 256 284
jolt 311

jovial 67 284
judicious 129 155 271
juggernaut 463

keen 114
ken 297
kindle 94 406
kiss 422
knack 16 492
knave 492
knead 492

labile 492
labor 54 223
labyrinth 223 425
lacerate 224
lachrymose 492
lackluster 492
laconic 237
lambaste 492
lament 329
lamentable 116
lampoon 492
landfill 269 298
landmark 463
landslide 387
language 189
languid 346
languish 87
lank 492
lapse 438
larder 359 393
large 344
large amount 130
largesse 492
lassitude 113 248 333
lasting 196
latent 82
latitude 96
laud 34 352
laughter 21
lavish 82 360
law 24
lax 82

lazy 40
leaden 178
leader 156
length 368
leniency 21 346
lethal 83
lethargic 129
letters 447
leverage 492
lexicographer 329
liability 64 209
liberal 190
liberality 190
libertine 62 190
licentious 224
licentiousness 224
lien 179
lifeless 87
light 172
lighthearted 492
liken 407
limerick 329
linen 222 492
link 346
linoleum 492
lint 35
liquefy 324 492
liquid 62
lissome 97 273 493
listen 51
listless 68
listlessness 25 68
literal 96 162 418
literary 493
lithe 97 239
loathe 209
locate 493
lode 493
lofty 161 225 450
logic 464
longevity 493
longing 314 346
loose 82 101
loosely 64
loquacious 228 438
loud 19 415
loudness 252
loutish 493

loyalty 83 465
lubricant 450
lucid 238
ludicrous 129 155
lug 464
lugubrious 284
lull 214 311
luminary 250 329
lung 453
lurk 464
lush 35 410
lustrous 401 407
luxuriant 83 213

magnanimity 493
make compatible 116 446
maladroit 157 284
malaise 493
malice 317
malicious 298 458
malign 298
malinger 298
malingerer 286 298
malleable 312
malodor 147 312
manage 112
mandatory 407
mangy 249 347
mania 93 347
manifest 82 347 459
manipulate 77 347
manipulative 347
manumit 52 195 359
manuscript 233 493
mar 388 493
marble 212
margin 493
mark 493
martinet 21 346
marvel 493
massive 68
matriculation 179
mature 308
maudlin 35 97
maven 68
maverick 68 324

mawkish 97
meager 179
meagerness 179
meander 464
meaningful 189
measly 209
meat 435
mediate 95 129
mediation 342
mediocre 130
mediocrity 130
medley 493
meek 131 143
meet 86 166
meld 395 493
mellifluous 312
melody 249
membrane 330 375
menace 390
menacing 390
mend 299
mendacious 299
mentor 236 407
merchandise 359
mercurial 493
merit 493
metaphor 162
meteoric 83 126
methodical 418
meticulous 97
metrical 192
miff 113 384
mildness 414
milk 110
mill 493
mince 210
mineral 301
minuscule 360
minute 360
mirth 21 293
misanthrope 21 327
misbehave 21 440
mischievous 22 172 338
miscreant 35 441
misdemeanor 35
miser 36 411
misgiving 494
mishap 36

mislead 54
misleading 54
misrepresent 494
mite 494
mitigate 97
mnemonic 131
mob 191
mobility 424
mockery 238 371 459
moderate 130
moderation 449
modest 130 432
modesty 210
modicum 130
moisture 29 117 343
mollify 277 293 312
momentous 330
monochromatic 463
monotonous 451
montage 494
moral restraint 224
morale 447
moratorium 360
morbid 162 380
mordant 344 360
moribund 84 464
morose 67 256 284
mortar 494
mortification 494
mosaic 494
moth 438
moth-eaten 438
motility 214
motivate 97
motley 494
mottle 113 185
mottled 113
mourn 494
mouth 240
move 282 311
move ahead willingly 306
move swiftly 124 272
move unidirectionally 241
muffle 162
muffled 162 190 453
mulish 299
mull 494
mumble 494

mundane 110 299
munificent 348
mural 439
murmur 407
museum 171
music 312
mutate 494
myopia 211 375
myopic 18

nadir 322 494
naif (naive) 494
naive 253 285
narcissism 494
narrow 91
narrowness 156
nation 346
natty 114 395
naysay 494
nebulous 224
nefarious 162 244
negligent 267
negligible 494
negotiation 495 193 494
neologism 218 497
nepotism 421
nervousness 175
nettle 114
new and fresh 438
nibble 190 208
nicety 224
nitpick 114
nitpicker 114
noble 225 379
nocturnal 421
noisome 322 495
nomad 330
nonconformist 495
nondescript 299
nonentity 285
nonflammable 371 495
nonplus 451
nonsensical 281 495
nose 134
notable 390
note 371

notice 45
noticeable 116
novelty 379 495
noxious 98 180
nuance 190
nucleate 179
nudge 131 362
numb 303 330
nurture 495

obdurate 131
obedient 131 355
obey 162 225 459
obfuscate 163 238 328
obituary 495
object 28
objection 416
obligate 300
obligatory 300
oblige 312
oblique 495
obliterate 313
oblivion 313
obscure 36
obscurity 401
obsequious 36 424
observe 468
obsess 36
obsessed 36
obsolete 495
obstinate 22 68
obstreperous 114 469
obstruct 69
obtuse 114
obtuseness 114
obviate 69
occlude 495
occult 84 256 352
ode 143
odious 31 267 345
offbeat 61 163 221
offend 163 259
offense 163 417
offhand 331
official 178
officious 163

offish 163
ominous 267
onerous 495
opacity 179
opaque 205 210
opine 268 315
opportune 421
oppress 495
opulent 37
oracle 451
orate 210
oratory 210
order 161 403
orderly 15 256
orderly arrangement 385
ore 495
organism 495
original work 69
originality 70 339
ornate 495
orthodox 98
orthodoxy 98 461
oscillation 495
ossification 37
ossify 37
ostentation 268
ostracize 115
oust 210
outgoing 207 210
outmaneuver 238
overbearing 143
overexpose 143
overexposure 143 255
overindulge 65 143
overlap 30 423
overlook 496
overt 20 496
overture 144
oxygen 430
oxymoron 98 354 439

pacific 18 238
pacify 18
paean 496
pain 139 142
painstaking 408

palatable 100 238
palatial 127
pall 496
palliate 313
pallid 313
palmy 211
palpable 296 313
palter 278 314
paltry 271 331
pan 208
panache 300
panegyric 496
panorama 496
pantechnicon 69
parable 390
paradigmatic 439
paradox 439
paragon 439
paramount 171 439
paranoia 390
pariah 496
parity 465
parlance 465
parochial 496
parody 496
paroxysm 69
parrot 70
parry 164
parse 164
parsimonious 33 111 115 348 417
parsimony 271
partial 22 49
partisan 22
pastiche 69
patent 84 256
pathological 496
patron 115 448
patronize 115 280
pattern 316
paucity 239
paunchy 37 134
pauper 496
pebble 496
peccadillo 225
peck 422
pedagogue 115
pedantic 256

pedestrian 144
peep 498
peeve 144
peevish 496
pejorative 496
pellucid 314
penalty 496
penchant 211
penetrate 419
penitence 164
penitent 164
penitential 380
penurious 82 360
perceive 80 361
peremptory 375
perfidious 83 465
perforate 164
performance 358
perfunctory 465
peripatetic 465
peripheral 80 466
periphery 466
perjure 187 466
perjury 72
permanency 188
permanent 358
permit 408
pernicious 408
perplex 451
perseverance 268
persevere 268
persiflage 236 256
person 23
personable 496
personnel 71 497
perspicacious 408
persuade 22
pertinacity 22
pertinent 23 302 328
perturb 23 364
pervade 23
pervasive 23
pestle 33 253 497
petrography 115
petty 116
philanthropist 268 281
philistine 257
phlegmatic 300 385

picture 462
piddling 497
pierce 144 458
piety 499
pigment 170 268
pillar 386 497
pillar of society 356
pillory 314
pine 314
pinpoint 409
piquant 53 440
pith 98
pitiless 124
pittance 116
pity 116
placate 144 180 209
placebo 180
placid 211
plagiarism 257
plain 497
plan 77 391 410
planet 108
plangent 162 190
plant 435
plantation 497
plastic 497
plateau 497
platitude 277 391
plausible 99 191
play 422
playbill 116
pleasant 357
pledge 408
plethora 205 391
pliable 239
pliant 239
plight 497
plod 361
plot 391
pluck 37 76
plum 409
plumb 38
plummet 38
poem 90 143 329
poisoning 185
polarize 116 446
polemic 409
polish 300

polished 71 300
politeness 41
pollster 315 353
pompous 322 348
ponder 315
ponderous 53 208
pontificate 285
porcelain 177 375
pore 375
portentous 23
portrait 23
poseur 38 316
posit 497
possess 497
posture 117
potable 84
potentate 84
potter 117
pottery 213
pour 434
power 84 87
pragmatic 497
prairie 180
praise 180 345 431
prate 300
preach 391
preacher 391 410
preamble 392
precarious 144 258
precede 145
precedent 145 288
precipice 134
precipitate 145
precis 132
precise 432
precision 224
preclude 239
precursor 409
precursory 409 460
predict 132 273
prediction 132 219
predilection 452
predisposition 497
predominant 146
preempt 497
preen 132 191 294
preface 251 497
preference 497

prefiguration 497
prejudiced 48
prelude 249
premeditate 331
premeditated 331
preponderance 145
preponderant 242
preposterous 145 339
presage 374 451
prescience 211 375
preservative 146
preserve 146
preside 498
prestige 146 202 296
presumption 377
prevail 146
prevalent 146
prevaricate 146
prevarication 146
prey 301
primp 191
principal 454
prissy 498
pristine 239 272
probe 67 361
probity 40 361 456
proceed purposefully 464
proclivity 362
procrastinate 285
procure 302 362
prod 131 362
prodigal 362
prodigality 21 362
prodigious 409
profane 81 362
proffer 85 363
profligate 363
profundity 234 466
profuse 192 363
progress 69
prohibit 363
prohibitive 103 363
proliferate 376 404
prolix 376
prologue 498
prolong 55
prominent 376
promote 376

pronounce 498
proofread 498
propagate 451
propensity 452
propensity to dislike 452
prophecy 451 498
prophetic 352
propitiate 74 223 376
propitious 79 377
propriety 71 377
prosaic 267 377
proscribe 377 408
prosecute 498
proselytize 377
proselytizer 355
prospect 301
prosper 378
prosperity 211
prosperous 378
prostrate 125 392 470
protagonist 498
protest 348
protocol 498
protract 17 392
protuberance 392
provident 392
providential 498
provincial 393
provisional 157
provisions 393
provoke 55 393
prowl 301
prudence 38 356
prune 409
pry 466
prying 466
pucker 240
puckish 240
puissance 498
pulchritude 254 301
pulverize 317
punch 498
punctilious 315
pundit 268 315
punish 314
puny 364
purity 14 158
purlieu 467

purloin 467
purvey 24
pusillanimous 39 304
puzzle 498

quack 498
quaff 498
quail 498
qualified 75 191
qualify 191
qualm 498
quantify 498
quarantine 499
quarrel 211
quarry 212 414
quash 212 266
quell 66 132 287 442 463
quench 132 345
querulous 146 283 400
quest 499
question 164
queue 499
quibble 240
quibbler 76
quiescence 240
quotidian 393

rabble 191
rabble-rouser 434
rabid 191
raconteur 499
racy 411
raffish 164
raffle 499
rafter 315
rage 269
rambunctious 499
ramshackle 348
rancor 204 316
random 316
rankle 396 499
rant 269
rapacious 393
rapport 206

rapprochement 269 449
rapt 63 440
rarefy 378
rash 39 353
ratification 98
ratify 98
ration 499
rational 99
rationalization 99 191
react 142
realized 236
ream 499
reap 452
reasonable 438
reassure 212
rebel 192
rebuke 499
recalcitrant 162 225
recant 225
recidivism 240 301
reciprocate 241
recite 499
reckless 241
recluse 126 241
recognition 499
reconcile 452
reconciliation 452
recondite 241
reconnoiter 241
rectify 257
rectitude 195 257 283
recur 499
redolent 147
redoubtable 147
redundant 467
reel 499
refined 165 446
refractory 22 165
refugee 499
refuse 269 298
refute 467
regard 147 499
regimen 270
regressive 452
regret 499
regular 379
rehabilitate 242 434
rehabilitation 242 325

rehearsal 500
reign 270 402
reiterate 467 500
reject 285 378
rejoice 416 452
rejuvenate 120
relapse 240 301
relate 500
relative 421
release 111 301
relegate 500
relevant 302
relief 228
relieve 302 444
religion 377
relinquish 302 362
reluctance 212 500
reluctant 212
remember 131
remiss 315 331
remonstrance 348
remonstrator 63 348
remorse 147 164 348
remove 313
remove impediment 93
remunerate 349
remunerative 349
rend 299 316
renew 453
renounce 408
renovate 453
repartee 99 394
repatriate 250 394
repeal 98 500
repel 422 441
repertoire 422
replete 422
repletion 422
repose 95 422
reprehensible 440
represented 403
reprimand 441
reproach 453 456
reprobate 21 270 440
reprove 441
repudiate 423
repugnance 441
repugnant 422 441

repulse 500
rescind 24 207
reserve 363
reserved 39
resilience 39
resist 54
resistance 415
resolute 54 113 195
resonant 453
respect 70
respiration 453
respire 453
respite 54 223
resplendence 159 206
resplendent 55
responsible 235
restive 70 420
restored 141
restrain 70
restraint 224
restrict 500
resurgence 84
resurgent 84 464
resuscitate 500
retain 85 184 363
retaliate 85
retard 65 85
reticence 99
reticent 99 265 333
retinue 99
retort 99 394
retract 500
retrench 117 282
reveal 500
revere 70 444
reverent 283
revive 100
reward 302
rewarding work 19 302
ribald 24 133
rickety 242
rift 452
righteous 270
rigid 500
rigidity 441
rile 302 371
riot 394
rioter 394

river 188
riveting 364 426
rock 115
roil 258 270
roisterer 29
roof 315
rooted 500
roster 71 181
route 93 394
routine 103 117
rubicund 192 334
rude 409
rudiment 147
rue 147 348
ruffian 273
ruin 249
ruminate 331
ruminative 331
ruse 221
rustic 71 197 300

sabbatical 500
sabotage 227
saboteur 50 226
saccharine 138
safeguard 165
sagacious 270
sagacity 270
sage 271
saint 35 441
salient 303
salmon 236
salubrious 26 331 458
salutary 294
salutation 500
salvage 500
salve 260 332
sanctify 29
sanctimonious 77 316
sanction 377 410
sanguine 24 47
sap 500
satiate 100
satiated 100
satisfaction 100
satisfy 100 397

saturate 117
saturated 117
savor 100
savory 100 238 368
savvy 101
scan 192
scant 192 400
scanty 333
scarce 212
scatter 423
scattering 423
scene 274
scent 147 312
scheme 410
schism 242 456
scholarly 256 500
scintillate 271
scintillating 111 271
scorn 285 378
scrappy 501
scribble 467
scrupulous 40
scrutinize 468
sculpt 39
sculpture 39
scurrilous 71
scythe 452
seal 109
secondary 242
secrete 44
secure 258
sedate 258 270
sedentary 465
sedulous 128 148
see 297
seemly 24 133
selective 501
self-denial 219
self-deprecating 435
self-effacing 501
sensation 303
sensitivity 445
sentence 164
sentient 468
sentimental 35
sentinel 71
separate 395
sere 35 410

serendipity 378
serene 244 378
serenity 109 263 350 449
seriousness 405
sermon 391 410
servile 24
severity 97 174 313
shackle 85 188
shaft 501
sham 193
shape 312
shard 213
shift 232 271
shiftiness 361
shirk 286 298
shorten 373
shrill 501
shroud 433
shun 411
sidereal 148
signal 379
significant 271 331
silver 318
similarity 407
simpleton 270
sin 225
sincere 316
sincerity 32 38 316
sinew 193
sinewy 193
sing 373
sip 272 395
skeptic 87 148 403
skimp 271
skimpy 363
skirt 286
skit 286
slacken 119 180
slake 181
slate 401
sleep 423
slew 239
slide 418 501
slight 47 272
slippery 217
slipshod 286 408
slope 501
slothful 28

slouch 395
slovenly 114 286 395
slow 78
sluggard 40
slur 454
sly 101
smart 119
smell 282
smirk 40 286
smother 395
smug 40 160
smuggle 40
smugness 40 286
snarl 188 213 449
sneer 133
snobbish 165
snub 30 41 47
soak 181 342
sober 149 240
sobriety 226 349
sociable 109 163 242
society 356
solemn 303
solemn utterance 67 303
solicitous 303
solidify 317
solution 501
solvent 62 332
somber 332 373
somnolence 138 349
sonata 501
sonnet 501
soothe 396
sop 279 396
sophisticate 423
sophisticated 423
sophistication 267
soporific 272 423
sordid 379
sorrow 60 235
sound 468
soundness 348
sparse 317 415
Spartan 61 83 213
spat 211
spate 213
speak 45 46 194 285 407 465

specialist 173
specious 148
spectrum 501
speculate 133 342
speech 222 454
spelunker 46 193
spendthrift 133 392
spindly 176
sprited 276
spiritual 287
spleen 317
splendor 118
splint 424
spoilage 146
spontaneous 379
sporadic 379
spot 113 281
sprightly 76 468
spry 140
spurious 71 359
spurn 72 221
spurned 307
squabble 118
squalid 118
squall 118 340
squalor 118
squander 25
stability 144 181 307
stabilize 304
staff 181
stagnant 501
staid 182
stalemate 193
stalk 349
stalwart 194
stamina 501
stammer 194
stand erect 395
standard 138
standardize 503
stanza 501
star 148 233
stark 501
startle 214
stasis 214
stay aloft 306
steadfast 25
stealth 206 424

steep 134
steepness 134
stench 134
stentorian 148 252
sterile 149 380
stern 454
stickler 243 437
stiff 258
stifle 65 194
stimulant 272
stimulate 327
stingy 411
stint 501
stir 132 287
stirring 41
stock 501
stockade 501
stodgy 364
stoic 23 364
story 390
storyteller 502
stouthearted 39
straightforward 441
strand 502
strength 159 174 262
stress 292
striate 468
striated 374 468
strict 502
strict limitation 96
stridency 468
striking 393
strut 25 182
student 179
stultify 41
stultifying 41
stunt 325
stupid 408 416
sturdy 454
stylus 502
subdue 194
subdued 128 326
subject 265 502
subjugate 195
sublime 226
submerge 226 385
submission 411
submissive 80

subordinate 454
subpoena 502
subservience 502
subside 226
subsidiary 227
subsidy 227
substantial 227 469
subterfuge 227
subtle 502
subvert 227
success 390
succinct 228
succor 228
sudden 69
suffuse 165
sullen 317
sullenness 206 317
summary 222
summit 349
summon 411
sumptuous 226 349
sunder 317
supercilious 424
superficial 295 424
superfluous 212 502
superior 424
supersede 502
supine 425
supple 239 441
suppleness 258
supplicant 328 442
support 115 308
supportive 227
suppress 442
surfeit 435 469
surliness 154
surrender 166
surrendered 184
surreptitious 61 455
susceptibility 502
suspend 502
suspicion 390
suture 85
svelte 37 134
swagger 182 435
sway 195
sweltering 134
swift 272

swill 272 395
sybarite 195
sycophant 258
syllogism 49 318
symbiosis 332
symbiotic 332
sympathetic 350
symphony 421 502
symptom 145
synopsis 243
systematic 72

tacit 243
taciturn 228 438
tact 259
tactless 101 259
taint 156 239 272
talk 99
tame 411
tamper 502
tangy 186 318
tantalize 502
taper 425
tapestry 112 502
tarnish 318
tatty 119
taunt 55 393
taut 119
tautness 119
tawdry 101
taxing 502
teach 250
tear 316 503
tease 273
tedious 149
teeter 149
temerity 333 350
temper 503
tempestuous 461
temporize 503
tenable 56 255 288 455
tenacious 455
tenant 460
tend 52 455
tender 412
tendinous 193

tension 180
tepid 248 425
terminate 412
termination 412
terror 503
terseness 376
testator 91
testimonial 86 431
testimony 72
testy 72
tether 77 101
text 425
theatrical 149
therapeutic 503
thicken 259 354
thickness 74
thirst 181
thirsty 287
thought 237
threadbare 379
thrive 469
thriving 469
throne 122
thwart 102
ticklish 243
timorous 112 333 350
tinge 503
tinker 86 276
tint 165
tirade 442
tolerance 66 263 303
tonic 81 86
topsy-turvy 195
torpid 455
torpor 503
torrid 149 306
tortuous 223 425
totter 149
tourniquet 401
tout 503
toxic 102
tractable 182
tranquil 195
transcend 503
transgress 195
transient 196 197
translate 196
translucent 179 196

transparent 196
travesty 503
treacherous 396
treaty 257
tree 180 370 405
trenchant 135 260
trepidation 17 150 249
trespass 113 150
tribute 503
trickle 33 259
trite 287
trivial 68 469
troubled 373
troupe 135
truant 119
truculent 55 211
trudge 55
truncate 55
truth 146 299
tumult 240 350
tumultuous 378
turbulent 503
turgid 469
turncoat 287
turpitude 503
typical 369 503
typo 425

unaffected 117
unambiguous 224
unanimity 242 456
unaware 264 445
unconformity 462
unconscious 468
unconventional 503
uncouth 165 259
unctuous 260 332
understate 503
undeserved 503
undisturbed 80
uneasiness 212
unexceptionable 503
unfavorable 45 79
unfettered 504
unfit 166
unflappable 150 166

ungainly 273
unidirectionally 241
unimpeachable 504
unimportant point 98
uninitiated 78
uninspired 504
unique 145 288
unity 48
unjustifiable 288 455
unkempt 288 433
unlikely 504
unlimited 304 353
unnecessary 69
unobtrusive 365
unprepossessing 108
unreflective 331 504
unremarkable 379
unrepentant 342 380
unrequited 349
unruly 469
unscrupulousness 40
unsettle 207
unsophisticated 504
unsound 56
unstandardized 293
unsteady 72 250
unstoppable 463
unsubstantial 504
unsuitable 86
untenable 87
untoward 102 405
unwieldy 504
unwitting 504
unwonted 119
upbraid 453 456
uphold 260
upright 392 470
upset 150 166
urban 233
urbane 197
urbanity 90
urge 234 273
usual 119
usurp 87
utilize 504
utter 102

vaccinate 228
vaccination 228 345
vacillate 20 243
vacillating 318
vagary 273
vagrant 166
vague 134 260
valediction 126 504
valiance 304
valiant 304
valid 148
valuables 56
value 173 435
vanish 197
vapid 364 426
vapor 426
vaporization 426
variable 470
variegate 365
varnish 374 504
vary 365
vault 56
vaunt 56
veer 166
vehement 260
venal 456
vendee 504
vendor 24
veneer 318
venerate 47 504
veneration 53
venial 103 254
venom 98 102 504
ventilate 504
veracious 310 442
verbose 279 380
verbosity 334
verdant 380
verdict 504
verify 470
verse 265 504
vertigo 396
verve 25 68
veto 103 363
vex 119
vibrant 228

vicarious 380
vicissitude 345 505
victimize 505
vigilant 110 120 267 273 425
vignette 274
vigor 141 274
vigorous 250
vilify 304
vim 113 333
vindicate 412 437
virtuosity 130
virtuous 25
virulent 26
visionary 56 325
vital 87
vitality 87 103
vitalize 370
vitiate 505
vitriolic 505
vituperate 120
vituperative 322
vivacious 87 178
vivid 214
vociferous 244
void 412
volatile 304
volition 318
volubility 237
voluble 333
voluminous 333
voluptuary 333
voluptuous 333
vomit 309
voracious 397
votary 87
vulgarity 304
vulture 14

waffle 405 505
wait 464
walk 25 55 62 181 210 217 282 361
wall 439
wan 192 313 334
wander 334

wane 81 334
want 422
warehouse 359
warmonger 505
warrant 505
warranted 177
wary 26
waste away 418
watchful 71 507
water 185 221
watershed 103 117
watt 505
wave 140
waver 229
wax 505
waylaid 120
waylay 120
weakly 364
weary 214
weight 145
welcome 32
welter 385 505
wheedle 135 278
whet 15 505
whiff 203 505
whim 274
whimsical 75 274
wholesome 162 380
wholesomeness 387
wicked 244
wickedness 162 244
widely understood 241
width 425
wind 357
windbag 334
winnow 505
wise 251
witch 47
withdraw 505
wither 100 103 370
wizen 120
woo 505
word 216
wordsmith 505
wordy 16 506
worldly 285 506
worry 53
worth 385

write 467
wry 120

yield 238 455
yielded 265
yoke 506

zeal 124 182
zealot 64 506

초판 22쇄 발행 2025년 7월 7일
초판 1쇄 발행 2002년 12월 10일

| | |
|---|---|
| 지은이 | David Cho | 언어학 박사, 前 UCLA 교수 |
| 펴낸곳 | (주)해커스 어학연구소 |
| 펴낸이 | 해커스 어학연구소 출판팀 |

| | |
|---|---|
| 주소 | 서울특별시 서초구 강남대로61길 23 (주)해커스 어학연구소 |
| 고객센터 | 02-537-5000 |
| 교재 관련 문의 | publishing@hackers.com |

| | |
|---|---|
| ISBN | 978-89-951517-6-1 (13740) |
| Serial Number | 01-22-01 |

저작권자 ⓒ 2017, David Cho
이 책 및 음성파일의 모든 내용, 이미지, 디자인, 편집 형태에 대한 저작권은 저자에게 있습니다.
서면에 의한 저자와 출판사의 허락 없이 내용의 일부 혹은 전부를 인용, 발췌하거나 복제, 배포할 수 없습니다.